Quantity Food Purchasing

Quantity Food Purchasing

SECOND EDITION

LENDAL H. KOTSCHEVAR

JOHN WILEY & SONS, INC.

New York · London · Sydney · Toronto

Library of Congress Cataloging in Publication Data:

Kotschevar, Lendal Henry, 1908–
    Quantity food purchasing.

    Includes bibliographies.
    1. Food service. 2. Marketing (Home economics)
3. Food. I. Title.
TX943.K67 1975   641.3′1   74-17407
ISBN 0-471-50524-2

Printed in the United States of America

10-9 8 7 6 5 4 3 2

Preface to the First Edition

This book is written for those who are purchasing or will be purchasing food in quantity. Emphasis has been placed on the selection and specification requirements for the major foods purchased by food services. An attempt has been made to present purchase criteria as concisely as possible because of the wide variety of foods that must be covered.

It should be recognized that the types of foods being offered to institutions are changing rapidly. Technological advances promise to revolutionize the methods of quantity food production and the types of foods used. Grades and standards for these new products are, for the most part, lacking. Yet those who must purchase these foods will find much helpful criteria in this book, for an attempt has been made to remain basic regardless of the type of food purchased.

While this book stresses quantity food buying from the standpoint of the quantity food service buyer, salesmen, distributors, wholesalers and others who sell to food services will find much of value to assist them in meeting better the needs of their customers.

Seeley Lake, Montana, July, 1961 **Lendal H. Kotschevar**

Preface

A great deal has occurred in the field of purchasing since the first edition of this book. The market has changed, purchasing techniques have changed, and today a vast number of new foods have appeared, which have changed considerably our production and purchasing needs. Unfortunately, there are few quality standards to be used for purchasing these new foods and in establishing specifications for them. This challenges the buyer to tell purveyors exactly what he wants so that he can best meet the needs of the institution for which he buys. Inasmuch as possible, this textbook recognizes this problem and summarizes the current state of knowledge, which can be useful in obtaining the right product.

The field of procurement covers two areas: (1) fundamental principles and purchasing techniques and (2) product information needed to purchase in a special field. Although the first area generally applies to all purchasing, the second area covers products used by a specialized field. This textbook compromises by briefly covering the first area and emphasizing the second. The book is intended primarily as a reference manual, which a buyer can use to obtain the food items and supplies that he needs for a foodservice. It is assumed the buyer is knowledgeable about foods and their production in a food service, the legal background behind purchasing, and how to establish minimum and maximum stock levels, inventory control, record keeping and the flow of paper, for example, that must go on when purchasing is done. If an individual lacks adequate background about fundamental principles and purchasing techniques, the references in the bibliography will be helpful.

All books must have limitations and compromises. Occasionally, detailed information has been omitted on items and, if buyers need more complete information, they should consult the original sources. It is difficult sometimes to summarize highly technical, complex material, and one always runs the risk of being less than accurate and of omitting some detail that is extremely important in obtaining an adequate product.

I am grateful to the persons in the Dairy Products Division and the

Poultry and Egg Division of the USDA for reading chapters of the book that are within their field. They have been extremely helpful and generous in attempting to give up-to-date information, and I accepted most of their suggestions. I also thank Vern Olmstead and Jeremiah Wanderstock (now deceased), of Cornell University for reading and criticizing the chapter on meats. Many others of the USDA, Meat Purveyors Association, Canners Association, the Library of Congress, and the FDA of the Department of Health, Education and Welfare assisted greatly in obtaining information for use here. Without this kind of help, I could not have assembled all of the information required and have it as accurate as it must be. I am grateful to all of them.

Seeley Lake, Montana, 1975

Lendal H. Kotschevar

Table of Contents

Quantity Food Purchasing

1
Institutional Procurement

THE MARKET AND THE BUYER

The Complex Task of Procurement

Buying for an institutuon is a highly specialized job. Not just anyone can do it. The buyer must know not only a lot about the items he procures, but he must know thoroughly his market, buying procedures, market trends, and how the materials he purchases are produced, processed, and moved to market. Buying is not order giving. It involves planning, forecasting, organizing, controlling, and other management-level functions. The market in which the buyer functions is involved, frequently international in scope, and so complex that one can spend a lifetime studying only a small part of it. The buyer must know this market so that he can find the best sources of supply of merchandise at the most satisfactory prices for the necessary quality and quantity. There is a specific language of the market that the buyer must learn to communicate adequately. Buying also may be complicated because the buyer must buy not only for one unit but for many units, and he may have to purchase thousands of different materials. The market is dynamic and changes rapidly. Just keeping up with changes is a big job. A good buyer never stops learning; he constantly seeks to know more and to update his knowledge.

Adequate purchasing requires a knowledge of how commodities are grown, processed, stored, transported, marketed, and handled. Seasonal supply conditions and market time factors must be known so that goods are ordered on time. Product perishability and shelf-life must be considered so that waste and quality loss are minimized. After the goods arrive, adequate inspection, storage, and handling procedures must be instituted. Proper control and security are also needed.

1

Another big complex area of buying knowledge revolves around the legal factors that control the market, its practices and buying and selling functions. A failure to conduct business within these restraints may bring about serious loss to a company.

A buyer must also know how to organize his purchasing department and conduct the purchasing functions. The right personnel, system, and procedures must be used. Often, the proper use and control of the variety of forms and documents—bills of lading, invoices, traveling requisitions, purchase requisitions, purchase orders, inspection and receiving reports, inventories, market reports, and so forth—are a challenge. The buyer must also be able to develop a highly efficient procurement system that gets the right product at the right time with the least possible effort and cost. Concise and usable records must be kept and maintained to give needed information. If information is not used or is more costly to compile than its value, it should be eliminated. Today's buyer must know how to use IDP (integrated data processing), ADP (automated data processing), and EDP (electronic data processing) to reduce clerical detail and improve purchasing. Many operations use a computer for purchasing and tying together a wide number of operational procedures. The use of these new systems has considerably reduced detail and clerical work and allowed buyers to function more efficiently at the important management decision-making level.

Cost is always an important consideration in procurement, but it must not take precedence over other factors. A buyer must be able to analyze and compare costs of substitutes or alternative merchandise. He should realize that the cost AP (as purchased) is frequently not important. It is the cost of the food AS (as served) or the per-use cost of supplies and materials that is important. Hidden costs such as insurance, depreciation, deterioration, and interest should not be ignored.

A buyer must know how to establish maximum and minimum stock levels and maintain an adequate flow of goods to meet production requirements. Institutions should calculate the most economical quantity to order. This is not just a matter of obtaining the most economical amount based on costs of procuring and holding in inventory. Other factors such as storage facilities available, perishability, and risk also must be evaluated. Institutions frequently strive to achieve a 20 or more inventory turnover in dollar value a year for foods and a turnover of from 4 to 8 for alcoholic beverages.

The buyer is a part of the management team and must closely follow management policy, jealously guarding its interests. He should protect departmental interests but not at the sacrifice of the company's. Procurement is a management function delegated to the buyer. It is not a goal in itself but also a service of producing materials, supplies, and information so that the organization functions. Procurement must function closely with the operational, financial, management, and other departments of the firm. A waste of resources must not occur. Large sums are involved, and buying should function to promote the company's well-being. Planning and forecasting are an important part of a buyer's job, and he must constantly study and evaluate economic trends. The department is not established to speculate in commodities but should buy only amounts needed for a specific operating period. Nevertheless, buying must be attuned to cyclic and other changes inside and outside the firm and modified as conditions warrant.

A buyer needs to know a great deal about how his company functions. To purchase food, he must know a lot about food production and its service. The use of supplies and other materials should be understood as well as maintenance and operational requirements. If he does not know these things, the operational divisions he serves should guide him on their needs.

A buyer must possess special skills such as knowing how to search the market and evaluate offerings. He must be adept at negotiation. He deals not only with inanimate things but also with people, and he must be skillful in these dealings. He must develop a professional personality and character. A high code of ethics, a sense of fair play, open-mindedness, perseverance, and patience are needed.

A good buyer cannot learn everything from a book or in a formal class. Much knowledge must be gained through experience. He develops by learning everything he can about the market and procurement. By applying his knowledge in a practical situation, he learns to be a buyer.

There are two kinds of buyers: *industrial and ultimate*. The former purchases for manufacture or resale, whereas the latter purchases for his own use. It is much more difficult to buy to satisfy the needs of others than one's own needs. Utility factors such as performance in manufacture, cost reduction, quality improvement, and simplification of production procedures are important to the industrial buyer. Unnecessary factors that raise cost or reduce performance should be eliminated. An industrial buyer must purchase to best satisfy production need and get the best value for the company's money.

Value Analysis

The technique of precisely defining purchasing needs and securing materials that best satisfy them is called *value analysis*. After the buyer studies the performance of materials, he tabulates their essential, desirable, useful, and unnecessary characteristics. Then, he seeks to buy products having the greatest degree of essential and desirable factors. He may or may not include the useful ones, but he will certainly try to eliminate the unnecessary factors in the materials. Value is based on quality and price and is frequently indicated as $V = Q/P$. If P increases but Q does not, V is less. Contrarily if Q increases but P does not, V increases.

It is important in judging value that all factors affecting it be considered. One also should recognize that value can be affected by factors other than quality and price and, at times, these must be weighed in arriving at final value.

Value analysis requires that accurate performance records be kept of items as they go through production and that this information be studied and evaluated. Value analysis can be helpful in indicating whether new products should be used or whether some change should be made in present ones. The armed forces made distinct savings by eliminating bulk, weight, and waste in bones and fat when it changed from carcass and wholesale cuts to boneless, well-trimmed meat separated to meet specific cooking needs. Some institutions have found drip-dry bed or table linens a saving. Value analysis may show that installing a small laundry, rather than using a commercial laundry, can make a saving on flat laundry. It also may indicate whether it pays to purchase items prepared or to make them in the operation.

Value analysis and scientific research are developing fields in purchasing. Research can be the organized search for facts in any area influencing the purchasing function. It may cover new-product investigation, cost-price analysis, analysis of vendors' performances and their selection, future trends, purchasing systems, analysis of economic order quantities, and so forth. The investigation must be thorough and detailed and should give data upon which buyers make critical procurement decisions.

Both value analysis and purchasing research are used to keep up with technical advances, to improve efficiency in operating the purchasing department, and to study long-range purchasing plans. In large organizations value analysis and purchasing research may occupy the full time of one or more individuals. In a small facility they can be conducted on an informal basis by purchasing personnel using the same basic principles and techniques used in the larger operation.

The Market

The market is a place through which commodities move from producer to consumer, where an exchange of ownership takes place. It is distinguished not as much by physical factors as by the action occurring there. There are formal markets such as the Chicago Grain Exchange or the New York Fruit and Vegetable Auction, but a market can also exist over a telephone, in an

Fig. 1-1. Fruit buyers at an auction. This type of middleman is used to move large quantities of produce through marketing channels at low cost. Frequently these buyers represent or act for others. Courtesy USDA

exchange of telegrams, on the side of a road, in an office, or on a street corner. The important essential is that a transfer of ownership take place. In a market, buyers and sellers negotiate and agree on terms of sale. The amount of formality varies. Marketing activities may be conducted in a number of places during a long period of time. A buyer seldom sees or participates in all the activities. Marketing frequently involves creating a commodity or giving it time and place utility. Any factor concerned with the growing or production of a commodity, its harvest, processing, manufacture, storage, transportation, or distribution is marketing.

Marketing Functions

Functions that occur in a market are (1) exchange, (2) information, (3) physical supply, and (4) general business.

1. Exchange functions are buying, selling, merchandising, price setting, and other functions needed to transfer ownership. This may involve a search for a commodity on the market, a search for a buyer, evaluation and comparison of offerings, negotiation, specification or inspection, and receiving. The exchange function ceases when title of ownership changes.

2. A great deal of information must be available for a buyer to function in

a market. Newspaper market reports or marketing information, crop reports, and so forth published by the government provide data. A daily market report covering marketing events is available free from the United States Department of Agriculture (USDA). It covers commodities on the market, prices paid, railroad car movements, quantities sold, market conditions, and other information. The prices quoted are those paid to original large lot buyers, not smaller ones. Trade associations, vendors' catalogs, professional journals, and trade publications also give valued market information. Salesmen are good sources of information on market conditions, products, and trends.

Without grade information many markets would not function. Grading is the sorting of commodities into quality classes according to specified standards. Market confidence is built on these grades. They enable processors to standardize products and move them through the market. Financing through the use of trade acceptances, sight drafts, loans, contracts, and other financial dealings is facilitated. Legal problems are reduced. Personal inspection is not required and a sale is reached more quickly when grades exist. The market uses both federal and trade (wholesale) grades. Both usually are based on established market practices.

Advertising is a marketing information source. If it gives information of value and leads to rational purchases, it is of economic good. If it leads to unwise purchases it is not. Advertising may take many forms and occur in many mediums. Buyers shoould learn what these are.

Labeling is an information function. The National Canners Association has long favored descriptive labeling that is based on the use of single words or phrases of known definition in the trade to indicate quality factors. There is no attempt to rank products by quality. Some consumers are seeking further information on labels such as quality, ingredients, drained weight, nutrient values, and additives. They state that many package weights are misleading, giving net weight on canned products, for instance, instead of drained weight, and that many terms are not understood. Recent rulings by the Food and Drug Administration (FDA) require any marketing individual claiming nutrient values for a food to list all values. Other FDA regulations cover the labeling for natural and artificial flavors, govern the use of the word "imitation," establish standards of identity for mellorine and parevine (two frozen desserts), and prohibit their promotion as ice cream. Regulations affecting low-calorie foods and nutritional quality guidelines for frozen dinners also have been announced recently. Under growing consumer pressure further definition of information given by a label can be expected.[1]

[1]Further discussion of labeling will be found under information on the Pure Food Act and on textile labeling requirements later in this text.

Brands can be informative. They identify products and their quality in the consumer's mind. Branded products tend to be higher in quality than unbranded ones. Because the manufacturer or distributor has a reputation to uphold, a brand can assure a buyer of a consistent standard. Brands, however, are only what the manufacturer or distributor makes them and are unlike grades in this respect. A brand may be advertised as "of highest quality" and not have to conform to any standard except what the brand owner feels is highest quality. Branded products are usually higher in price and vary less in price than unbranded ones. Identical products have been known to carry different brands and sell for different prices. Nevertheless, brands may assure a buyer he is getting a product of the quality he wants. Many good buyers purchase by brand, by descriptive label, and by grade. Using all three together is recommended.

3. The physical supply functions usually revolve around transportation and storage. Improved shipping methods and refrigeration have broadened market offerings. Foods of high perishability now reach markets in better condition because of rapid rail, truck, or air-freight transport. Also, improved packaging, handling, and storage facilities have reduced loss and improved quality.

Without storage, the orderly flow of commodities would be disrupted, and high loss would occur. Staple and canned foods must be held for continuous supply to the market over the entire year. Bonded storage is provided for security and financing. Bonded storage, cold storage, and some other storage facilities operate under government supervision.

Improved storage for perishable foods is now available that not only controls temperature and humidity but introduces inert gas, special lighting, and other factors to give foods a longer shelf life. Huge low-temperature storage facilities exist today in which tremendous quantities of fruits, vegetables, meats, and other foods are held. Excellent cold storage facilities hold food at temperatures from 30 to 45°F for eggs, butter, meats, fruits, and vegetables,

"Cold storage" means holding over 30 days in such storage. The term "fresh" can be used to describe many foods held under this time. Some states limit the time foods can remain in cold storage; a common limit is 12 months. Identification of cold-storage foods is sometimes required. If they are removed, most states prohibit their return to cold storage.

4. General business functions of the market usually revolve around finance. Good finance procedures can facilitate buying and selling and reduce costs. There are many standard procedures. Credit, interest, insurance, taxes, and a host of other items come under finance.

It is important that buyers understand market costs so that they can evaluate marketing services. It costs money to carry goods on inventory;

Fig. 1-2. Studying the effects of differences in frozen temperatures in storage. Some frozen foods lose quality 15 to 20 times faster at 10 °F than at 0 °F. Courtesy USDA

waste, theft, space charges, insurance, interest, depreciation, and other factors also cost money. A purveyor who sells goods on the first of the month and waits for his money until the tenth of the next month has tied up his money for 40 days while the buyer uses it. This costs money. The cost of deliveries can vary from several dollars to five or six times this amount. A buyer who orders too frequently, orders in small lots, or fails to pay on time can be costly to service. Buyers should realize that they are the ones who eventually pay for marketing costs, and they must make every attempt possible to reduce them. Vendors cannot give good prices if they do not benefit from them. The buyer who thinks he gets something for nothing is ignorant.

Types of Markets

Different markets exist to perform different functions. A primary market is one in which price setting, quality standards, and other overall matters relating to one type of commodity occur. For instance, Liverpool, England, is the primary market in the world for grain; Chicago is this country's primary market for grain, but its prices and marketing patterns are frequently strongly influenced by the Liverpool market. New York is the primary market for sugar and coffee. Buyers learn to watch primary markets to learn in advance what might happen on their markets.

Fig. 1-3. Buyers bidding for cattle at a western auction market. These auctions have become much more important in the marketing of cattle, whereas the central stockyards have decreased in importance. Courtesy USDA

Many primary markets arose because they were located near producing areas with good transportation between them. Manufacturers and distributors also located in the area to be close to the major source of supply.

Secondary markets receive commodities from primary markets and distribute them to local ones. In recent years some secondary markets have become so large that they also function as primary markets. Chicago, once the primary market for meat, acts today only as a clearing house for many primary market activities. Most of its primary activities have been taken over by secondary markets such as Kansas City, Omaha, St. Paul, and Ogden, Utah. This change came about because it was possible to reduce transportation and other costs by centralizing slaughter and other primary marketing functions in these markets rather than in Chicago.

Market Trends

The dynamic nature of the food market can be seen in a visit to the formerly famous Water Street Market in Chicago. Once this fresh produce market was the largest and finest in the world. It not only served Chicago, it was a central destribution market for this country. Huge railroad yards were nearby where produce came from many production areas to await auction or sale and then reshipment.

Today the market is run-down; there are many empty stalls, and other businesses have moved into the vacant space. The huge auction house uses

Fig. 1-4. The large fresh produce center in Philadelphia, like the famous Water Street Market in Chicago, has gone steadily downhill as more and more produce is marketed through central warehouses owned by large retail outlets. Courtesy USDA

only a small part of its massive floor space, and the once teeming, active, raucuous auction room is now filled with a handful of tepid buyers.

This decline is the end of an era because direct buying has changed the old system. Buyers now operate out in the orchards or fields. They purchase and ship from there to urban centers in huge trucks. Shipments no longer go through Chicago. The trucks move to huge warehouses located on the outskirts of large urban centers. Here they are unloaded, and the lots are broken down and moved in smaller trucks into the urban area or elsewhere. Just one of these warehouses can now handle in a day more than the entire Water Street Market handles in several days. Because of the savings made in by-passing many middlemen and in reducing handling costs, chains that own these warehouses can put produce into their outlets at a lower cost than the Water Street broker can buy them.

The direct and mass buying of the chainstores for the retail market has also made other changes. Produce for them is packed in retail packages. Thus carrots may be pulled, topped, washed, and packed in single pound polyethylene bags. Shipment is no longer in 50- or 100-lb gunny sacks with repackaging elsewhere. Because of this trend, it is not unusual today for a large institution to have to buy 100 lb of carrots in single pound units because producers refuse to pack them differently. Since the institutional market represents only 25% and the retail buyer 75% of the volume, the wishes of the retail buyer usually predominate.

Some buyers for large institutions, governmental agencies, chains and so forth have followed the trend of purchasing directly or centrally and reducing the number of middlemen. Stouffers buys its meats in Chicago for all its operations and ships to each unit from there. McDonalds writes huge purchase contracts for its merchandise, obtaining price and other concessions, but delivery is from local suppliers to individual units. Such contracts must be made between companies that sell on a national basis and bring into play a highly professional buying agent and seller. Smaller operations may combine into buying groups or co-operatives to do the same thing, achieve a better buying volume, or be able to buy directly.

Many institutions still must purchase from wholesalers or brokers where the markup may be 25% of the sale price. Because of this, a buyer may see produce, chickens, meat, or other items advertised by retailers at prices lower than he can buy from his broker. This is possible because a chain may purchase a number of carloads of chickens and sell them at cost or below costs as leaders, whereas the small institution may purchase only several cases from a broker who similarly buys a small supply. A survey made by this author in 1969 indicated that 5% of institutions purchased some items in the supermarkets. In this survey it was also found that a purveyor would average 19 deliveries a month to an institution with the cost per delivery ranging from $2.50 to $12.50. In an attempt to increase volume and obtain larger orders many purveyors are attempting to diversify and offer more merchandise. Some may establish minimum order sizes or less frequent delivery.

Marketing Criticism

The institutional market has been criticized because so much of the dollar of its commodities goes to middlemen and other marketing costs. The following table shows the farmer's share in some commodities:

Commodity	Farmer's Share in Cents per Dollar Paid at Retail Level	
	Range	*Mean*
Unprocessed crops, such as beans, fruits, vegetables	18 to 46¢	35¢
Processed crops, such as flour, cereals, canned goods	19 to 71¢	49¢
Eggs		69¢
Bread	10 to 15¢	13¢
Poultry		60¢

Commodity prices are apt to fluctuate the most at the producer or farm level, next at the wholesale level, and least at the retail level because marketing margins are much less flexible than commodity prices. In a period of rising prices middlemen take less of the consumer's dollar; in a period of falling ones, they take more. As we have moved toward the use of more convenience foods, processors have taken more of the food dollar of institutions.

Producers, Middlemen, and Consumers

The market is distinguished by three types of individuals: 1) producers, 2) middlemen and 3) consumers. Producers create the items for the market. They may also act to give them form and substance. A producer can be a canner, meat packer, weaver, or potter. A cook is a producer. Similarly, a farmer, fisherman, or applegrower is a producer. A produce house that purchases bulk spinach, stems, washes, and packages it is a producer.

Middlemen act to bring commodities through marketing channels to consumers. They seldom change the form or substance of commodities, but create time and place utility in them. Because of their service and the risk they take, they add a charge to the commodity's price. The amount depends upon whether they take ownership and other costs incurred in

FARM VALUE OF WHEAT·RETAIL PRICE OF BREAD

1950
14¢ Retail Price
2½¢ Farm Value of Wheat

1966
22¢ Retail Price
3.2¢ Farm Value of Wheat

Fig. 1-5. In 1950 the farmer got 18% of the price of a loaf of bread, but as marketing costs took more and more in 1966 he got less than 15%. Courtesy USDA

rendering their service. Auctioneers, brokers, commission men, or middlemen taking goods on consignment do not take ownership and, therefore, have less costs. Their charge may be 5% or less. Wholesalers, jobbers, retailers, and others take ownership and store the commodity. Some may break it down into smaller lots and assemble other goods with it for delivery. They have risks, space, financing, insurance, and other costs. Wholesalers may mark up goods 25% and retailers mark up 35%.

Usually the fewer middlemen through which a commodity passes, the lower the charge. Often buyers fail to realize the costs carried by middlemen and the contribution made by them. They frequently cannot perform these same functions as economically or as well. In such cases, buyers are well advised to not try to compete with middlemen but to let them render a service that would in the end cost more if the buyer tried to do it himself.

A consumer is anyone using a commodity for himself (ultimate) or for manufacture or resale (industrial). An institution can be either.

Market Regulation

The institutional market is controlled by laws and regulations, plus voluntary regulations of associations and others active in the market. There is a great number of these laws and voluntary regulations. Only a few of the most important can be reviewed. Much information can be gained in addition to what is given here by referring to government publications and the materials listed in this book's references. There will also be further discussion of these regulations under specific topics later.

Nine main federal laws or jurisdictional bodies are important in regulating the institutional food market. Although at one time they were only applicable to interstate commerce, recent court rulings have made them effective *within* states as well. (If a state has a law that is more stringent than the federal law, the state law supersedes the federal.) These 9 laws follow:

1. The Pure Food, Drug, and Cosmetic Act of 1938 regulates many market activities. Under it, inspectors can enter any establishment at reasonable times to inspect the premises for sanitary and maintenance standards and to see if food is prepared, processed, and packaged in a sanitary manner. No product of a "diseased animal, contaminated, filthy, putrid, decomposed, or otherwise unfit food" can be used. Damage or inferiority cannot be concealed, and no substandard food can be added to increase bulk or weight or create an illusion of greater value than the food actually has. No valuable part of the food may be omitted. One food cannot be sold under the name of another.

Recent publicity has indicated that a lack of inspectors and funds makes it possible to inspect some plants only about every 7 years and that food which may not be "fit for human consumption" may be reaching the market.

Labels on packaged food must:

    a. bear the common name or names of the food,

    b. contain the name and address of the manufacturer, packer, or distributor,

    c. list the net contents by count, fluid, or avoirdupois measure,

    d. be sufficiently prominent to be easily comprehended,

    e. contain no foreign words to circumvent label requirements,

    f. bear the specific name and not collective name of ingredients if the product is not a commonly known food, except that group words such as *spice, flavoring,* and *coloring* may be used instead of the exact spice, flavoring, coloring, and so forth,

    g. bear in order of greatest to least proportion the names of ingredients if the food is not a common one; thus it would be illegal to list ingredients for corned beef hash as beef, potatoes, and onions if potatoes were in greater quantity than beef,

h. bear the exact definition of dietary properties if claims are made for
them,

i. bear the term "artificial if artificial coloring or flavoring is used or the
term "chemical preservative" if a chemical preservative is used.

Later amendments regulated the use of additives in food. Colorings,
preservatives, and other substances considered harmful are prohibited. A
manufacturer must bear the burden of proof that a compound is not injurious to health. Formerly, the government had to prove it harmful. The act is
administered by the FDA of the Department of HEW.

2. The Federal Meat Inspection Act was passed in 1906 and now has
been extended within states to any meat processor or individual in the
market who does enough business to be in interstate commerce. Not all
states have complied yet with the regulations of the act. This extension has
been bitterly opposed in some quarters, and delay in implementation has
occurred. The act provides for inspection by the USDA's Bureau of Animal Industry of establishments from which meat is shipped:

a. to detect and destroy diseased and unfit meat,

b. to require that preparation and handling of meat be done in a clean and
sanitary manner,

c. to require display of the federal shield to indicate inspection,

d. to prevent the use of harmful substances in meat foods,

e. to prevent false and deceptive labeling.

The provisions of the act also apply to poultry but not to fish. Some
consumers have sought extension of the regulations to fish but have failed
in their attempts.

3. The Agricultural Marketing Act provides for inspection and grading
of fresh and processed foods. Under its provisions the USDA instituted a
number of inspection divisions.[2] Cereal, dairy (including margarine), fresh
fruit and vegetable, poultry, egg, and meat divisions have been established.
A number of inspection agencies also have been set up, usually at shipping
points, destination markets, or other areas where commodities move
through marketing channels.

Each USDA division establishes the standards of quality for the foods it
inspects. Industry and other interested parties are consulted before a
standard is determined, and usually standards reflect present trade practices. Standards are frequently published as "tentative" and after a period

[2]See SRA-AMS, USDA, revised January 4, 1957, for a fuller explanation of inspection
procedures used by the various divisions.

Fig. 1-6. A federal acceptance seal indicating that a produce meets a buyer's quality standards. This stamp is used in acceptance inspection. Courtesy USDA

of testing may become "official." A standard can be tentative for many years.

In 1956 the provisions of the Agricultural Marketing Act were extended to cover fish and shellfish. The Fish and Wildlife Bureau in the Department of Interior was given the responsibility for establishing quality standards and regulations covering the inspection of marine foods.

USDA inspectors can examine a commodity and give it a grade. Or they can certify that it meets a trade grade or a buyer's quality as defined in his specifications. Items meeting federal grades can be certified as meeting them. Buyers can request a copy of a report certifying a grade for a food they buy. (See Figure 1-7.)

Food services frequently use a more precise statement of quality than that contained in a federal grade and can ask that foods be certified by government inspectors as meeting this more precise standard. If the product meets the buyer's standard, the inspector stamps the invoice, package, tapes, and seals to verify this fact. This is usually called "acceptance" inspection and is indicated by the use of the federal shield as shown in Figure 1-6. The purveyor usually pays the cost of this inspection.

Foods are certified for quality in different ways by the USDA. The processed fruit and vegetable division certifies quality in the following ways: (a) Processed food can be sent to its laboratories for inspection. This can result only in certification of the grade of the sample and not the lot from which it came. (b) Certification of a lot grade is possible if inspectors themselves withdraw representative samples from a lot and inspect them. (c) When an inspector is in the plant while food is being processed and he inspects the food, it can be certified for grade. If he or other inspectors are continuously in the plant, the inspection is called "continuous." (d) If an

F. P. I. 20   UNITED STATES DEPARTMENT OF AGRICULTURE

ORIGINAL   VIRGINIA DEPARTMENT OF AGRICULTURE AND IMMIGRATION

INSPECTION CERTIFICATE

N⁰   4377

This certificate is issued in compliance with the regulations of the Secretary of Agriculture governing the inspection of various products pursuant to the Act making appropriations for the United States Department of Agriculture, the Acts of Virginia Assembly, and is admissible as prima facie evidence in all courts of the United States and of Virginia. This certificate does not excuse failure to comply with any of the regulatory laws enforced by the United States Department of Agriculture, or by the Virginia Department of Agriculture and Immigration.

Inspection point **Winchester, Va.**   *Billing point* **Winchester, Va.**   *Date* **Oct. 4, 1945**

Applicant **Winchester Packing Co.**   *Address* **Winchester, Va.**

Shipper **Same**   *Address* **Same**

I, the undersigned, on the date above specified made personal inspection of samples of the lot of products herein described, and do hereby certify that the quality and/or condition, at the said time and on said date, pertaining to such products, as shown by said samples, were as stated below:

Car initial and number **FGEX 5 1 8 1 3**   *Kind of car* **Refrigerator**

Inspection begun **1:30 P. M. Oct. 4, 1945**   *Inspection completed* **6:15 P. M. Oct. 4, 1945**
                        (Hour, date)   (Hour, date)

Car equipment and condition at completion of inspection:

Products: **York Imperial APPLES - in tub type bushel baskets labeled "W Brand, Winchester Packing Co., Winchester, Va." and stamped "U. S. No. 1, 2¼ inches up, York." Loader's count 516 baskets.**

Loading: **Through load, end to end offset, 3x3 rows, 4 layers.**

Pack: **Tight. Ring faced. Paper pads under lids. Good amount of oiled paper distributed uniformly through baskets.**

Size: **Generally 2¼ to 3, mostly 2¼ to 2½ inches in diameter.**

Quality and condition: **Mostly well formed, some fairly well formed, clean, 15% to full red, mostly 25% to 50% good red color. Grade defects within tolerance. Generally hard. No decay.**

Grade: **As marked, U. S. No. 1, 2¼ inches up.**

Fee **$5.16**
Expenses
Total **5.16**   **L. F. Laney**
                                                Inspector.

U. S. GOVERNMENT PRINTING OFFICE 8—7194 A   PLEASE REFER TO THIS CERTIFICATE BY NUMBER

Fig. 1-7. Buyers may request quality certificates such as this one. Courtesy USDA

inspector is called into a plant just to inspect a specific lot as it is being processed, the inspection is called "intermittent."

The number of the inspection certificate may be used on bills of lading, invoices, and other papers to identify the grade of the lot. The use of a federal grade shield with a grade symbol inside indicates that a product meets the federal standard, and no certificate is required. The use of the shield and grade symbol is voluntary, however.

Meats and some other processed foods must be graded under continuous inspection. The federal grade shield may be used. Many other divisions certify quality by inspection samples as outlined previously in (b).

The federal courts have ruled that if a label uses a grade term and the food does not meet that standard, the food is misbranded. Thus if the word "choice" appears in wording on a canned fruit label, the fruit must be of that quality or better or be considered misbranded.

A federal inspector is usually concerned with three standards: (a) quality, (b) identity, (c) and fill. These three standards frequently are enforced by law.

a. Scores for various quality factors are established for grading a food. These factors are evaluated and a score assigned for each. The total score decides the grade. For instance, an item with a score of 85 or more may be called Grade A. Each food has specific factors evaluated such as marbling in meat, percent defects in dry prunes, color in a canned vegetable, or bacterial count in milk.

Fig. 1-8. Some of the tools used by a federal inspector who grades fresh produce. Such inspection may occur at shipping points or market terminals. Courtesy USDA

If a food fails to meet the minimum score, it must be labeled "Below Standard in Quality" with the reason stated. Such food is edible and can be used, but it may be excessively broken, contain excessive peel, or have some other defect.

b. The FDA establishes and promulgates standards of identity for foods. A standard of identity states what a food is.[3] Standards of identity, by describing exactly what a product is, prevent misrepresentation. Thus a mixture of water, pectin, acid, sugar, artificial coloring, strawberry flavoring, and grass seed cannot be called strawberry jam (although at one time it was) because the standards of identity for strawberry jam require that there be at least 45% strawberries in it. A few canned products must meet specific drained weights to meet standards of identity and also grade. Standards of identity require that if a word defined by the standards is used, the product must meet the definition of the standard. Thus "ice cream" means that the product has 8% or more milkfat, egg noodles must contain 5% or more egg solids, "brandy" means the product comes from grapes, and "wool" without any other qualifying term means the fiber comes from sheep. A product is called *misbranded* if it uses the identity name but does not meet the standard.

The standards of identity list the composition of *common* foods such as chili sauce, fruit cocktail, and succotash. If a product is called by its identity name, the mixture must meet the standard of identity for this food. Foods that are not listed as *common* foods must list on the label the ingredients in order of greatest to least proportion. Identity names must indicate precisely what a product is, and some are limited. For instance, "Roquefort" cannot be used for a blue cheese that does not come from Roquefort, France. A similar cheese made here must be labeled "American blue" or "domestic bleu." The words "semolina," "evaporated," "canned," and "peach" indicate a specific product or factor in food; the food must conform to the established meaning.

c. Standards of fill require that containers be properly filled. Slack or deceptive filling is prohibited. The standards vary for different commodities and different packaging. If a container does not meet a standard of fill, it must be labeled "Below Standard of Fill."

The use of a federal grade on a label of food of a specific grade is entirely voluntary. Standards of identity and fill, however, are not voluntary, and all commodities must comply with the provisions under these two standards. Seizure and destruction of the offending products is possible if the food is unwholesome, misbranded, or does not meet standards of identity,

---

[3]Identities for food are published in SRA No. 2, FDA, Department of HEW, Washington, D.C.

standards of fill, or a quality claimed for it. Prosecution may occur, and courts can order offenders to go out of business, pay fines, or go to jail, or they can combine any of these three penalties.

4. The Perishable Agricultural Commodities Act regulates fresh fruit and vegetable trade practices by licensing dealers and establishing fair-trade practices. Inspection of fruits, vegetables, or other items may be required. The USDA administrates the act.

5. The original framers of the Constitution considered the control of weights and measures so important that they provided for it. The Bureau of Standards in the Department of Commerce administers most laws dealing with weights and measures. Many state and local laws follow these regulations. For the most part, the Bureau of Standards has been more an advisory body than a regulatory one.

Three federal laws control weights and measures. (a) One law establishes the barrel at 7056 cu in. or 105 dry quarts or 9 more than 3 bushels. This barrel holds 2 98-lb sacks of flour. The cranberry barrel was fixed at 5826 cu in. or enough to hold about 100 lb of cranberries. (b) A Standard Container Act established sizes for 2-, 4-, and 12-qt climax baskets and the standard berry and till boxes at ½ pt, 1 pt, 1 qt, and multiples of a quart dry measure. No other sizes are permitted in these types. (c) A later act fixed the legal capacity of hampers and stave baskets at ⅛, ¼, ½, ⅝, ¾, 1, 1¼, 1½, and 2 bu. Splint baskets were limited to capacities of 4, 8, 12, 16, 24, and 32 qt dry measure. False bottoms and other deceptive practices are prohibited.

6. A United States Warehouse Act provides that agricultural and processed food products moving in interstate commerce can be certified for storage if inspected and graded according to federal standards. Bonded, cold, and other storage are covered by the act.

7. The Federal Trade Commission Act deals with advertising that might be injurious to an actual or potential trade competitor. Other trade practices come under the act. In 1938 the Wheeler-Lea Amendment provided penalties for misbranding, mislabeling, or misrepresenting a food item as to source, origin, or composition; giving false or misleading information; passing off a food for another; or presenting any disparaging information or misrepresentation regarding a competitor. Extravagant and false claims in advertising were also covered. Another amendment repealed features of the anti-trust laws so that milk and other foods could be controlled by boards or other groups without violating the law. This provision has enabled states to set up regulatory bodies to control the marketing of milk, fruits, vegetables, and other foods.

8. The Bureau of Public Health (HEW) has a great deal of responsibility for protecting public health in the areas of food production, marketing, and

Fig. 1-9. Visual aids such as these are used by federal inspectors and other individuals to judge possible shape, color, and other defects on fresh fruits. Courtesy USDA

consumption. Because of pollution from sewage in shellfish beds resulting in outbreaks of typhoid and diphtheria, the bureau must now certifiy areas from which shellfish come. It also supervises shellfish preparation and shipment, plus employees who work around foods, and so forth. It administers sanitary codes for restaurants and other food services.

9. The Bureau of Internal Revenue of the Treasury Department regulates the food market through administrative practices, tax collection, and by law. Through customs it exerts considerable influence on imports and exports in foods. It also controls alcoholic beverages through its Tobacco and Alcohol Division by imposing taxes, overseeing bottling, and checking for unfair competition, mislabeling, and misadvertising. Other laws cited previously also may influence the marketing of alcoholic beverages. Sanitary practices, mislabeling, and misbranding covered by the Pure Food, Drug, and Cosmetic Act or by the Federal Trade Commission apply also to

alcoholic beverages. Adulteration provisions in standards of identity prevent the use of rectified alcohol which, with colorings and flavorings, might be bottled and called "bourbon." Standards of identity also prevent the appropriation of names that mislead and make a buyer think he is getting one liquor when he is not.

The Buyer

An institutional buyer must weigh many factors. He must get the right kind and the right amount at the right time at the right price. The product must lead to good merchandising and a profit or at least satisfy budgetary constraints. Each product purchased must satisfy specific needs. Textiles must give satisfactory performance and appearance. Table top materials should please and provide a desirable atmosphere. Supplies must perform adequately and reduce labor requirements. Buyers should know what items must do and then select them for that purpose.

There is a time to enter and a time to stay out of the market. A buyer must find the balance between buying more to improve price against the added cost of carrying the commodity, the risk, and possible depreciation. Quantities available and food prices follow seasonal variations, and buyers should know when quality is highest and prices favorable. The price of corn eventually affects livestock prices and supply. Growing conditions such as frost, drought, or excessive demand are quickly reflected on the market. Most commodities are best in quality and lowest in price at their season peak. Awareness of social, political, and economic trends, and the effects of research and science will enable buyers to better evaluate market events.

Some items are relatively stable in price and follow general economic trends. For these, once the year's crop is in, a buyer can expect the price to vary little. Perishable items change more in price. Canned goods, flour, sugar, and fresh items such as apples, Irish potatoes, and winter cabbage that store well vary from 3 to 9% in price. Medium variability—10 to 15%—exists for items such as sweet potatoes, globe onions, garlic, and winter squash. High variability—16 to 25%—is found in lettuce, cantaloupe, peaches, spring cabbage, and so forth. If the market is well organized and a steady flow of the perishable products comes onto the market, prices tend to be stable as seen in bananas which, while highly perishable, are fairly steady in price. Improved market procedures with better storage and shipping are tending more and more to stabilize prices of perishable products.

The menu starts with buying, and buying starts with the menu. Buyers should keep the production department informed of market conditions, the quality, quantity, and cost of foods, and call attention to favorable buys or to items high in cost. Long-range buying needs to be tied closely to long-range menu planning. Menus, however, should not be dictated by market conditions. A menu planned on bargains is very apt to fail.

Low prices may not mean low final costs but could mean higher ones. High preparation losses or a high labor requirement may make a cheap item costly. The cost of labor in using an item should be known and should be included in the cost. Although a detergent may seem low in cost, another more expensive one might save enough labor to make it lower in cost in the long run. Or, the expensive one might do such a better job that the added cost is warranted. Buyers should know that the cost AP (as purchased) is not always significant; it is the (EP) edible portion or AS (as served) cost that counts. Value analysis applied to purchases can point to true costs and not just the price paid for an item.

Quality and value recognition are prime requisites for a buyer. Unless he knows what quality *is* and *recognizes* it, he is unable to make reliable price comparisons. When buyers cannot inspect goods before purchase, they must be able to establish specifications that do what personal inspection would do in securing the right product.

A buyer also must know how much is needed. Records should be maintained of quantities used so that they may serve to assist in quantity calculation. Forecasts of portions required should also be reliable and based on past records. To obtain adequate production without an excess, a buyer must have (1) a knowledge of the total portions needed with the portion size; (2) an accurate estimate of preparation, cooking, and portioning losses; (3) portion control, and (4) inventory control. Many tables in this text can be used to assist in calculating amounts required.

Buying Ethics

Buying requires a high standard of ethics. A buyer has considerable power in giving orders with value and prestige. Because of this, sellers may try to obtain orders by illegitimate means. A rigid, cold atmosphere in a buyer's office is not desirable, but too much of an informal atmosphere is not either. Cordial relationships should exist to promote effective negotiation and a free exchange of buying information. The point of compromise in relationships should be avoided. Acceptance of invitations to social functions or other favors from the seller may be unwise, although at other times a buyer may accept social courtesies without compromise. Buyers and sellers frequently develop bonds of respect and friendship that promote good buying. The important consideration is that a buyer in no way limit his freedom of action. Every buyer should establish for himself a high code of ethics. Codes of ethics are published by buyers' associations and professional groups. The following also could be helpful:

1. Be courteous at all times.
2. Establish regular hours for salesmen to call and adhere to this schedule. See out-of-town salesmen at once, if convenient. See everyone but devote only the time needed to promote purchasing business.
3. Be fair. There must be give and take in all purchase situations.
4. Keep a sense of humor.
5. Use a rational motives in buying. Evaluate all factors.
6. In dealing with competitors, do not play one against the other. Do not disclose another's prices, and do not pass information on.
7. Use the company's money as you would your own.
8. Do not discuss business affairs out of the office.
9. Set a high standard of conduct, and let others benefit by it.
10. Never compromise your freedom of action as a buyer.

Reciprocity is a procedure in which a company may purchase from someone because it is advantageous for the company to do so. For instance, if a seller is given orders, he may be able to influence sales for the company or in some other way contribute to the company's well-being.

Reciprocity restricts a buyer's freedom of action. He has only one source from which to buy. The problem of reciprocity should be covered by a management policy and, if reciprocity is to exist, should be decided by management. Reciprocity must not violate laws or regulations. Gaining an advantage because one purchases from a particular vendor may or may not be desirable. As in many cases of ethics and other considerations in procurement, it must depend upon the degree of freedom sacrificed and other factors involved in each individual case. If values and other considerations are the same as would be obtained in unrestricted purchasing, reciprocity may be condoned. As indicated previously, buying is not an end in itself, and the purchasing department's interests and those of other departments should not supersede those of the firm. If reciprocity does not violate ethical standards and is in the overall interest of the company, then the purchasing department should go along with it.

Legal Considerations[4]

A buyer should know how to conduct procurement matters so they proceed on a sound legal basis. To do this, he should know many of the common legal requirements of purchasing. If he does not, he should seek legal opinion on questionable matters to avoid misunderstandings, controversy, or perhaps litigation. Buyer-seller commitments are legally binding. If signed by a responsible individual in the company, an invoice, a purchase order, or a contract is a legal document. Some of the most common legal tenets relating to procurement revolve around the laws of agency, warranty, fraud, contracts, and title to goods.

Law of Agency. The buyer usually acts as an agent of his company. The seller may do the same for his. In either case, the power as agent is granted as a part of his job. How far agency extends has had to be interpreted by the courts. A salesman can take an order, agree on a price, a delivery date, and so forth, but there may be no contract until the order with its conditions is accepted by the main office of his company. Verbal promises of salesmen are frequently not binding; however, if someone in higher authority, such as a sales manager, verbally agrees to the conditions, they are binding. Middlemen at times have the status of an agent, but usually a company or individual acting as a selling agent cannot make binding agreements until the supplier accepts them. A company can limit the power of a buyer as its agent, and the seller should be advised of this. At times an agent's status can change. For instance, in the absence of the buyer, a chef or other responsible individual can place orders and conduct procurement matters for the company, whereas at other times this might not be possible.

Law of Warranty. A warranty is a guarantee that an item will perform in a specified manner. Courts have ruled warranties can be implied or expressed. All goods are sold with the implication that they are suitable for the purchase. If they are not and the seller knows it, he is guilty of a breach of warranty. It is therefore desirable for buyers to acquaint purveyors with how the items are to be used unless use is so commonly understood that this is not necessary. An expressed warranty, usually written, or a later warranty cancels a previous one. A salesman's statements are not guarantees, and his "trade-puffing" or over-praise of a product is not a guarantee. If, however, a salesman's claims are confirmed by a responsible person of his

---

[4]This discussion covers legal matters relating to procurement in an extremely limited manner. In general, the provisions stated here are true, but slight modification in practice may not make them so. If a buyer is not well versed in common legal practices in buying, he should consult references listed in the bibliography. The American Hotel-Motel Institute has an excellent correspondence course in business law that would be helpful to any buyer.

firm or the company indicates it is bound by his claims, there is a warranty. If in the past a salesman's claims have been accepted by his company, implying he has authority to make them, or, if there is fraud in his claims, there is warranty. If an item is sold "as is," no warranty exists. The buyer assumes full risk.

Buyers should examine written warranties carefully because many mean little. Many warranties are effective only when a notice is mailed to the guarantor indicating the date of purchase, purchaser, and so forth. Often the burden of proof of a warranty breach is on the buyer, and it may be difficult to prove. The amount of damages may also be difficult to prove. Frequently, under warranties, the goods can be returned, and the buyer is not obliged to pay for them. In many instances, if the seller cannot meet his warranty, the buyer can enter the market, get items that do meet it, and charge the excess cost to the seller. Most warranties have time limitations. Some cover only repair, defective parts, and so on.

In some cases, a warranty covers the value of the remaining use under the warranty. Thus a machine guaranteed for 5 years and used 2½ years before breakdown may leave the guarantor liable for only 50% of the machine since there was good use for 50% of the guaranteed life. Purveyors can be liable for damages because of a failure of a warranted item to perform properly, causing a loss to the buyer. Often under warranties the cost of replacing defective merchandise is chargeable to the purveyor. Buyers must report promptly any breach of warranty and, in most cases, cannot hold or continue to use the item. The courts have said that a seller cannot sell an item that he knows will not do the job intended without breaching warranty.

Law of Fraud. Any act or statement made before an agreement is reached that is intended to deceive a party in making an agreement is fraud. Fraud is a deliberate attempt to deceive. In fraud, one must prove deception, which may be difficult. If a seller leads a buyer to believe that the merchandise is as represented and knows it is not, there is fraud. If a buyer pays no attention to deceptive statements made by a seller but purchases regardless of them, there is no fraud. Inspection of the merchandise requires that the buyer use good judgment regarding quality, value, and other characteristics. If a buyer is not sufficiently experienced but relies upon false "facts" stated by the seller, there is fraud. A contract made on the basis of fraud is not valid. Prompt action must be taken by a buyer once fraud is discovered. If there is delay or if payment is made after fraud is discovered, the buyer may have no case.

"Trade-puffing" is not considered fraud, and buyers are put on their guard to use due caution in making agreements or purchases based on it.

The law is not set up to protect stupid buyers who do not exercise good judgment in performing their jobs.

Law of Contracts. An agreement becomes a contract when two individuals accept identical terms or conditions relative to a matter. Contracts of purchase are usually signed by both the seller and buyer, indicating an acceptance of the terms. A vendor's acceptance of a purchase order is only completed after he returns a signed acknowledgment copy to the buyer, but the purchase order must not be changed in any way from the others in the transaction. Purchase orders should include a promise to ship by a specified time since this implies acceptance of the order. If the purchase order is acknowledged but not accepted, there is no contract; if a shipping promise is included, the courts have ruled that this is acceptance. It also is recommended that purchase orders be signed under a statement, "We acknowledge and accept the above order and its conditions." Shipment of any part of an order implies acknowledgment and acceptance. Merely giving an order to a salesman does not make a contract. It must still be acknowledged by a responsible person in the seller's firm. Any change in *any way* in the terms of the original order voids a contract. A counter offer can be accepted and make a contract, providing it is not changed. Written and even verbal matters relating to an original order can be considered a part of a contract provided that they satisfy the basic requirements of a contract agreement.

A contract requires performance on the part of the two parties. If only one is bound, there is no contract. In a contract, a specific performance of one party imposes some obligation on the other. Usually, a buyer agrees to buy and pay a stated sum, and a seller agrees to sell and deliver merchandise or services under specific terms and conditions.

A failure to perform on a contract is a breach of contract subject to penalty. A contract may not be binding if the amount, price, time, or other important conditions are ambiguous or difficult to determine. A contract containing indefinite provisions can be cancelled by either party upon due notice.

Where quantity, time, price, or other considerations are decided by only one party, the contract is not binding because of a lack of consideration and mutuality. Approximate amounts should be given in contracts if actual figures are not known. Or a minimum to maximum quantity, price, or other condition might be named. Sometimes a variation by amount or percentage over or under is used.

Some prices may be assumed to be understood, and only if a price change occurs must the purveyor notify the buyer. If a price or quantity is subject to confirmation, acceptance of even a partial order by the buyer can be considered acceptance of quantity and price. An escalator clause is one in which the price or a condition can be changed if other conditions, events, or factors change.

Contracts are usually made for a specified time. Cancelation is sometimes possible previous to this by mutual agreement. Some contracts have a cancelation clause effective if certain conditions arise. Cancelation provisions set up conditions that protect either party from loss from such cancelation. If a buyer does not completely understand all the ramifications of a cancelation clause, he should seek legal advice. Cancelations can be made on the basis of default by either party, for the convenience of the buyer or seller, or by consent of both.

A failure to perform according to contract provisions is default, such as failing to meet a delivery date, delivering the wrong quantity or quality, or any other variation from agreed terms. If a buyer does not protest but accepts a violation, there is no default. And if a buyer allows continued violations, he cannot later claim default when one occurs. A party can give written notice that a violation is for once acceptable without agreeing to further violations. If a contract states that the parties are not in violation because of "acts of God" such as strikes, fires, earthquakes, and floods and such an event occurs, there is no default. In any case of failure to perform because of "acts of God," the other party should issue a formal notice that the contract is no longer valid because of a failure to perform.

If a contract is violated, the injured party can sue for damages. A buyer can go into the market, complete the seller's obligation, and charge the seller for the costs incurred over and above those that would have occurred if the contract had been honored. If a buyer cancels, the seller can recover if he is harmed. Mutual agreements to cancel should be in writing. A mutual agreement to change a condition of a contract cancels the contract unless affirmation of the entire contract's other provisions is made by both parties.

Agreements to purchase should specify clearly a delivery time. Purveyors must meet delivery schedules or be in default. The clause "time is of essence" gives a buyer the right to refuse orders not arriving at specified times. A contract is void if made in violation of a law or regulation. Thus a contract violating wage and hour laws is not valid. A contract also is not valid if based on fraud.

Sellers may give a conditional sale contract in some instances. This gives right of repossession more easily if the buyer fails to honor some provision of such a contract because title rests with the seller until the buyer completes all the contract terms.

Law of Title to Goods. Buying or selling involves a transfer of ownership or title. Time and place are important considerations in title transfer. Title can pass on a street corner if a buyer and seller complete all arrangements for transfer, including a consideration in which the buyer gives something of value to the seller for the goods. If there is no consideration, there is no title transfer. A buyer does not have to see the merchandise for title to pass. Title transfers to the buyer when a seller delivers merchandise FOB (free on board) a carrier for delivery to the buyer. Title does not transfer if delivery is in a conveyance owned by the seller. In this case, title does not pass until delivery is made, with the buyer inspecting the merchandise and signing an invoice or other acknowledgment of delivery. Goods delivered by an independent carrier found to be wanting may be returned to the seller, and it may be the seller's responsibility to come and get the merchandise. Often goods found wanting upon delivery are returned at seller's cost. Damages also may be assessed against the seller if the buyer can prove them.

Since title passes to the buyer when goods are delivered FOB on a carrier, the buyer must take responsibility for insurance and so forth. If the carrier in any way damages the goods or causes loss otherwise, the buyer takes action against the carrier. The buyer also must pay the seller for the merchandise and seek to recover his loss against the carrier. The courts have ruled that a seller cannot assume a carrier's responsibility, nor can a seller regain title to the merchandise after delivery to the carrier if he finds out that the buyer cannot pay for it because of bankruptcy or other circumstances.

If a seller retains merchandise that a buyer may have paid for and the seller becomes insolvent, the buyer only becomes a creditor and cannot claim his goods because they were never delivered. In this case the buyer becomes a creditor of the seller.

If a seller invalidates any provisions of the contract, the buyer does not have to assume title upon an FOB delivery to a carrier. A seller must take due precautions to see that goods are properly packed for shipment and are of the declared value for insurance and carrier liability purposes, he must follow the buyer's shipping instructions to be able to transfer title FOB the carrier. If he does not, the buyer does not have to assume title.

A seller who ships by independent carrier under terms FOB at the buyer's place of business or elsewhere as directed in the sale agreement must assume all responsibility for the goods until they are delivered and accepted. If the carrier fails in any respect, the seller now and not the buyer must take recourse against it. Tax liability and other considerations may vary depending upon where title transfer occurs. If title passes in Ohio, for instance, that state's tax laws apply and not Michigan's from where the goods may be shipped.

Buying Procedures

Procurement procedures must be based on an institution's individual needs and factors such as administrative and financial policies of the firm, storage available and nearness to supply, costs of holding inventory, perishability,

STEWARD'S MARKET QUOTATION LIST									
ON HAND	ARTICLE	WANTED	QUOTATIONS	ON HAND	ARTICLE	WANTED	QUOTATIONS	ON HAND
	BEEF				Pig's knuckles, fresh			
	Corned beef				Pig's knuckles, corned			
	Corned beef brisket				Pig, suckling			
	Corned beef rump				Pork, fresh loin			
	Corned beef hash				Pork, larding			
	Beef chipped				Pork, spare ribs			
	Beef breads				Pork, salt strip			
	Butts				Pork, tenderloin			
	Chuck				Sausages, country			
	Fillets				Sausages, frankfurter			
	Hip short				Sausages, meat			
	Hip full				Shoulders, fresh			
	Kidneys				Shoulders, smoked			
	Livers				Shoulders, corned			
	Loin, short				Tongues			
	Strip				Tongues, beef smoked			
	Shell strip				Tongues, fresh			
	Ribs beef				Tongues, lambs			
	Shins				Tripe			
	Suet, beef							
	Tails, ox				POULTRY			
					Chickens			
	VEAL				Chickens, roast			
	Breast				Chickens, broilers			
	Brains				Chickens, broilers			
	Feet				Chickens, supreme			
	Fore quarters				Cocks			
	Hind quarters				Capons			
	Head				Ducks			
	Kidneys				Ducklings			
	Legs				Fowl			
	Liver				Geese			
	Loins				Goslings			
	Racks				Guinea hens			
	Saddles				Guinea squabs			
	Shoulder							
	Sweet breads							

| MEATS | UNIT | Suppliers | |
		Smith Co.	Higgins Bros.
Pork loins 10/12#	6	(.45)	.46
Bacon hotel slice	50#	.45	(.43)
Boiled ham 8#	6	.62	(.61)
Corned beef brisket	50#	(.39)	.41
Calves liver	10	.55	.55
Hamburger	50#	(.35)	.38
Square chuck	150#	.39	(.38)
Round "good"	150#	.54	.54
Lamb 50–55# Aa	3	.42	(.41)

| FISH | UNIT | Suppliers | |
		City Market	Seafood, Inc.
Jack salmon dressed	50#	(.38)	.39
Filet sole	50#	.42	(.40)
Butterfly whiting	30#	(.30)	.31
Filet ocean pike	30#	(.36)	.37
Halibut—1 fish	35#	.40	(.38)
Shrimp—headless	20#	(.60)	.62

| PERISHABLES | UNIT | Suppliers | |
		Green Co.	Acme Co.
New cabbage 100# Bg.	3	($ .09)	$ .10
Carrots, bunches	10	.03	.03
Cauliflower 45/50# Ct.	3	(3.25)	3.35
Celery 72/92# Ct., pascal	3	(4.25)	4.30
Lettuce iceberg 24's Ct.	2	2.40	(2.20)
Mushrooms 4 qt. basket	3	(2.00)	2.10
Onions, Bermuda 50# Bg.	3	3.25	3.25
Lemons 360's	2	.40	(.35)

Fig. 1-10. Two examples of call sheets used by food services. These examples omit specification details frequently helpful in establishing buying requirements. An additional column immediately to the right of the item desired, where this information can be recorded, is recommended. Courtesy *Volume Feeding Management Magazine*

general market and economic conditions, production need, product, and type of market. Buying procedures can be classified as (1) informal, (2) semiformal, and (3) formal.

1. Informal (open) buying is frequently conducted through a salesman, over a telephone, or by other means. Negotiations are mostly oral. Buyers frequently work with specifications at hand listing type of product, amount needed, quality, quantity, and other essentials needed to inform vendors of the conditions of purchase. After price quotations and other essential information are received and the seller's reliability and service weighed with the price, the buyer makes a purchase decision. An experienced buyer knows that some vendors deliver a higher quality product than others, and a higher price can be paid. Other vendors may give more reliable service and be favored. Buyers should realize that orders must be of sufficient size to pay for delivery and handling. Where a small price differential exists, orders should be lumped together to make it more economical for a vendor to deliver. Informal buying is very common in institutions.

Comparative prices in informal buying should be obtained from more than one seller, but this may not always be possible. At times vendors may supply merchandise automatically based on a previous agreement to keep up an established inventory at the facility. In such cases management should check frequently to ascertain that quantities and qualities marked on delivery slips have been received.

A *call sheet,* also called a *price comparison* or *quotation and order* sheet, is used often in informal buying, especially where a number of sellers are nearby. Figure 1-10 shows several call sheets. The buyer lists what is needed on these and then calls various vendors to obtain prices and other information. It is frequently desirable to have an additional column briefly listing specification highlights of the items to be purchased. This produces fewer mistakes and brings about a better meeting of minds between buyer and seller.

When the buyer completes his calls, he studies the information and circles prices of the vendors from whom he wishes to purchase. A clerk or secretary can then place the orders. A copy of the call sheet can act as a receiving copy so that quantity, quality, and price can be compared upon delivery. A copy of this sheet after receiving can be sent to accounting to be used to check billings and so forth. If blind buying is desired—a method in which the receiver does not know the quantity nor quality of merchandise from receiving documents but must put these down after checking in the goods—the call sheet sent to the receiving unit can omit quantity and quality.

Informal buying procedures called *complete open* or *blank check* buying are used if a supplier must have complete freedom in obtaining merchandise. This may happen when shortages exist, and the seller may learn of merchandise availability and have to purchase immediately. Only reputable dealers should be trusted with this privilege.

In *cost-plus* buying, the seller is paid the purchase cost plus an approved markup for his services. Such buying is used when market conditions are unstable or when the price is not known and must be ascertained later. Cost-plus buying is becoming more and more common. Often a seller can give more favorable prices using it because he is assured of a specified volume for a period and does not have to contend with a buyer who may or may not give him business. Cost-plus can be used in formal buying.

2. The semiformal purchase method, called *negotiated* buying, is used if (a) time is restricted, (b) the number of sellers must be limited, (c) the amount is small, (d) the product is highly perishable, (e) it is not practical to allow competitive bidding, or (f) action must be fast. Negotiation allows the buyer to search the market among a restricted group of vendors and make a quick purchase.

Negotiation may be oral or written. Or inquiry may be written and a seller's response and acceptance may be oral or vice versa. Sometimes a procurement office requires at least three negotiated prices before an award can be made.

3. Bid buying is formal. Written notice of requirements is sent to vendors inviting them to submit prices on merchandise. As the degree of formality increases, more and more of the conditions of sale are specified in writing.

Bid invitations can be simple or elaborate. Sometimes a detailed statement is not needed between buyers and sellers well known to each other. Enough detail is needed, however, so that all parties understand the conditions and what is needed. Forms are frequently used. Bid requests usually contain (1) general conditions and (2) specifications.

1. General conditions cover provisions such as bid and performance bonds to be furnished by the seller, procedures for errors in bid, alternate or partial bids, discounts, terms of contract, samples, delivery, inspection and certification required for quality, packaging, billing instructions, and methods of payment. The bid may carry a requisition number, and this should be listed on all bills of lading and invoices associated with the bid. A specified date for the return of sealed bids may be given and the date for opening and award announced. Bid opening may be public or private. Bids are usually sent under certified mail, with date and hour of opening, bidder's name, and return address listed. Other bid conditions can be: Merchandise should be guaranteed for its normal shelf life, provided proper care and storage are given, or canned goods must be guaranteed against swells, flippers, and other defects for 12 months. Packaging must be

INVITATION, BID, AND AWARD

Issued by	Address	Date _____
Manager	1122 Supply Street	
Ever-ready Restaurant	Happy Haven, Maryland	

Sealed bids in duplicate will be received at the above office until _____ _____ , 19___ for the items and in the quantities indicated for delivery on the dates indicated. Quantities indicated are approximate and may be reduced on instruction of the buyer. Increases up to 20 percent will be binding at the discretion of the buyer.

All items to be officially identified by the U. S. Department of Agriculture for class and quality. Costs of such service to be borne by vendor.

Items	Supplies	Quantity	Unit	Unit Price	Amount
1.	Chicken, fresh chilled fryer, 2-1/2 - 3 lb, ready-to-cook - U.S. Grade A	500	lb		
	To be delivered_ _ _ _ _ _ _ _ _				
2.	Chicken, fresh chilled fowl, 3-1/2 - 4 lb, ready-to-cook, U.S. Grade B	100	lb		
	To be delivered_ _ _ _ _ _ _ _ _				
3.	Turkey, frozen, Young Tom 20 - 22 lb, ready-to-cook, U.S. Grade A	100	lb		
	To be delivered_ _ _ _ _ _ _ _ _				
4.	Ducks, frozen roaster duckling, 5 - 5-1/2 lb, ready-to-cook, U.S. Grade A	50	lb		
	To be delivered_ _ _ _ _ _ _ _ _				

Vendor_____

Fig. 1-11. A simple bid form that may be used for obtaining vendors' prices. Courtesy USDA

adequate to protect the product during shipment and shelf life, with the expected shelf life specified. How short weight or a failure to meet quality standards are to be adjusted is stated. Or a statement is included indicating that vendors failing to perform satisfactorily in bidding or in bid performance will be removed from a list of acceptable bidders.

2. Specifications are precise statements of qualities and other factors wanted in merchandise. They are more precise than federal standards. All merchandise purchased should be covered by specification.

Copying the specifications of others is not recommended. They should reflect precisely the production need of the particular institution. Each item also has its own individual specification requirements. Specifications should be brief and simple, giving only that information needed to assure proper definition. Using terms commonly accepted in the trade reduces word detail. Stating "U.S. Grade A," "sieve size 3," "IMPS No. 106," or "100 count" saves many words because these terms are understood in the market. It is better, however, to have specifications written in too much detail than for them to lack essentials. Items required by law or trade custom, such as standard of fill or wholesomeness, may be omitted from the specification, but some buyers like to remind sellers of the need to conform and include them. A specification should contain:

a. the trade or common name of the product,
b. the amount to be purchased by case, pound, carton, and so forth,
c. the trade, federal, or other grade or the brand desired,
d. container size and perhaps number of pieces in a shipping container,
e. the unit on which prices are to be quoted (by case of 24/2's, 12- to 14-lb hams, yard, dozen, gallon, and so on),
f. the specific factors needed to obtain the exact item.

The specific factors in f vary with different products, some of which might be:

Geographical area of production: Oregon Bluelake string beans, Florida limes, Hawaiian pineapple, Colombian coffee, Sea Island cotton, and Louisiana rice all might have desirable quality attributes.
Feed: Corn-fed or grass-fed steers, Smithfield or Iowa hams, milk-fed chickens, and Snake River trout have special flavors because of the feed.
Variety: Gravenstein apples are excellent for applesauce but too soft for baking. Telephone peas freeze well but do not can well. Marshall strawberries freeze better than other varieties.
Type: Long-cut or short-cut string beans, skinned or unskinned hams, fresh-chilled or frozen poultry, and so forth.
Style: Sticks, slices, or tidbits of pineapple; cream-style or whole-kernel corn may be desired to suit a production need.
Weave: Terry, huckaback, cut pile, or serge weaves make a lot of difference in a fabric.
Size: An 18-by-26-in. towel, a 4-sieve size bean, a 1000-lb steer, or a 25-to-28-lb watermelon may make a big difference in product satisfaction.
Count or portion size: Olives per gallon, a 4 oz veal cutlet not over or under ¼ oz, 83 count oranges, and a 5-oz baking potato are sized to meet specific needs.
Syrup density: Water, light, medium, heavy, or extra-heavy syrup pack.
Packing medium: Syrup, sugar, juice, or water; dry or wet pack for shrimp or corn; brine of dry pack for cured meats, and so forth.
Concentration or specific gravity: Used mostly for tomato products.
Percent mixture: Fat in ground meat, pork or cereal in sausage, various fruits in fruit cocktail, blend in Bourbon, type fibers in a fiber or yarn.
Container: Can, case, glass, keg, bag, fifth bottle.

Weight tolerance or fill: Struck full or *rounded full* on bushel baskets; fill equal to facing in cherries, tomatoes, and peaches; drained weight for canned products; pounds per case of eggs; maximum and minimum weight for meat cuts; count in container, and so on.

Age: Terms such as *yearling steers, tree-ripened, fryers,* and *very young.*

Cut: Side, quarter, or *primal cut, portioned* or *oven-ready* for meats; *bias* for fabric; sliced, diced, julienne, or short cut for canned items.

Cutting style: Chicago cut for cattle, Boston cut pork shoulder.

Type processing: Kiln cure for dishes; annealing for hardening glasses; rendered for lard, aging in meat, dry salt cure in meat.

Depth of fat permitted: ½ in. on rib roast, ¼ in. on cube steak.

Condition upon receipt: Hard frozen, fresh, or interior temperature 40°F.

Pure or imitation: Pure jam or jelly, imitation vanilla.

Type flavor or other: Sweetened or unsweetened, salt free.

Sex: Cow, steer, capon.

Manufacturers, processors, salesmen, trade associations, or governmental agencies can be of assistance in writing specifications. Although the task of writing them may seem formidable, if one to two are written occasionally, the accumulated group soon assumes sizable proportions.

If a commodity lacks established quality standards and purchase policies prohibit the use of a brand name, buyers may put enough detail into the specification to get an exact brand; for instance, specifying the chemical formula of a particular brand of baking powder restricts all others without naming a brand. Many buyers add "or equal" to avoid specifying a single brand; the buyer then determines what is or is not the equal. To eliminate unsatisfactory products, a board of judges may be established to evaluate samples and award on the basis of its judgment. Sometimes, the three top products after evaluation are named, and then a buyer selects one of these.

Forms for Buying. Procedures for buying must be designed to be as simple as possible and require a limited amount of forms and paperwork. Buying needs are usually stated on purchase orders or call sheets. Requisitions also may be used, but they frequently are used internally within the organization to withdraw supplies from inventories on hand. Individuals who can sign purchase orders or requisitions will be restricted, and policies for use of these forms should be followed. Procedures for using delivery and inspection forms, signing invoices, and so forth must also be established. The routing of forms and the number of copies prepared should be limited to only that necessary to facilitate purchasing, receipt, and record keeping. Many operations find that systems analysis and study can considerably simplify systems in purchasing. Converting to an EDP, ADP, or computer system may also simplify detail, change forms, and alter buying procedures. Continued scrutiny of any system is required if purchasing is to be done with maximum efficiency.

Inspection and Receiving

Unless adequate inspection and receiving procedures are employed, the best purchasing system may fail because it is at this point that determination must be made if the goods are those intended and if they meet the specification of the buyer. If such a check is not made, products varying considerably from those intended will be accepted. A failure to have adequate inspection may mean that higher costs, lower quality, and other undesirable factors occur. Poor inspection and receiving procedures can also lead to theft, fraud, and other undesirable practices. Adequate inspection and receiving procedures also are necessary for good inventory control.

Inspection is concerned with ascertaining the amount and quality of the goods upon delivery. They are compared with those listed on the receiving sheet or other information to be used to verify the correctness of the delivery. The results of the inspection should be recorded. If the goods meet requirements, they are accepted. Acceptance is indicated by signing an invoice or some other form, one copy of which is given to the delivery man indicating delivery has been made, the other copies go to accounting and so forth. In case of any discrepancy, the invoice or other document signed indicating delivery has been made should contain a notation of what the discrepancy is. If the goods do not meet inspection requirements, they are refused and no signature indicating delivery is given. At times a notation may be made on some documents indicating the reason for refusing the delivery. Upon acceptance of the merchandise, proper forms should be made out so that the accounting division and others in the company will be informed that the goods are on the premises and meet requirements except as noted. Partial orders with information as to when the full order will be completed should be noted on the receiving documents, if such information is available.

If the buyer and seller agree that inspection upon delivery is not required but that the seller agrees to accept inspection later by the buyer and abide by the results, the goods may be accepted and signed for without inspection. This sometimes is done to speed delivery and reduce delivery costs. The seller should agree under this arrangement that any discrepancies will receive prompt attention and correction.

If reference samples are held for inspection against goods delivered, comparison should be made at the time of delivery or soon after. If a question arises, federal inspection may be requested to end a dispute, the cost to be borne by the individual losing the dispute. Acceptance of goods should not mean that the buyer does not have recourse against the seller for latent defects, fraud, or gross mistakes amounting to fraud.

If goods are certified as to quality before delivery, the certification may be accepted and a quality evaluation eliminated upon delivery. Products that are subject to rapid deterioration should be inspected, however, even though a certificate of quality accompanies them.

Blind receiving is a procedure in which delivery slips are not marked as to quantity and often quality of the merchandise delivered. This may be written on some forms, but on those used for delivery the writing is on a black area so that it cannot be read. The individual doing the receiving is required to do his own count and quality evaluation and put this down on receiving data. Otherwise, if this information were on the receiving forms, he might automatically accept it when it could be in error. Often in blind receiving the price is also unreadable because the printing is on a dark area.

BIBLIOGRAPHY

Beckman, Theodore N., Harold H. Maynard, and William R. Davidson, *Principles of Marketing*, 6th ed., Ronald Press, New York. 1957.

Canada Department of Agriculture, *Buy by Grade*, Cat. No. A 73-1048, Ottawa, 1960.

Dukas, Peter, and D. Lundberg, *How to Operate A Restaurant*, Ahrens, New York, 1958.

Frooman, A. A., *Five Steps to Effective Institutional Food Buying*, A. A. Frooman Associates, Chicago, 1948.

Herrick, Arthur D., *Food Regulations and Compliance*, Revere Publishing, New York, 1944.

Reid, Margaret G., *Consumers and the Market*, 3rd ed., F. S. Crofts, New York, 1948.

Stewart, Jean L., *Foods: Production, Marketing and Consumption*, Prentice-Hall, New York, 1938.

Stokes, John S., *Foodservice in Industry and Institutions*, Brown & Co., Dubuque, Iowa, 1965.

U.S. Department of Agriculture, *Food Purchasing Guide for Group Feeding*, Agr. Handbook No. 284, Washington, D.C., 1965.

U.S. Department of Health, Education, and Welfare, Food and Drug Administration, Washington, D.C.:
Definitions and Standards under the Federal Food, Drug and Cosmetic Act, No. 2.
Food and Drug Administration—What It Is and Does, FDA Leaflet No. 1, 1958.

General Regulations for the Enforcement of the Federal Food, Drug and Cosmetic Act, Title 21, Part 1.

Read the Label, FDA Publication No. 3, 1958.

Requirements of the United States Food, Drug and Cosmetic Act, FDA Publication No. 2, revised.

U.S. Federal Supply Service, GSA, *Federal Specifications,* Washington, D.C., various dates.

West, B.B., I. Wood, and G. Shugart, *Food Service in Institutions,* 5th ed., Wiley, New York, 1970.

Wilson, Stephen, *Food and Drug Regulation,* American Council on Public Affairs, Washington, D.C., 1942.

Wood, Adeline, *Quantity Food Buying Guides,* Parts I and II, Ahrens, New York, 1957.

2
Fresh Fruits and Vegetables

Fresh fruits and vegetables are important as foods, both from an economical and a nutritional standpoint. Slightly over 300 lb a year per person are consumed. Of the total quantity produced, over 20% is used by the food service industry, or a little over a billion dollars a year.

The fresh-produce market is one of the most difficult markets in which to operate because (1) it is a highly dynamic market and changes occur very rapidly, (2) the product is highly perishable, and (3) there is a great variation in market practices, grading, and products.

1. The fact that supplies, demand, and other conditions are highly dynamic makes it necessary to follow the market closely. A heavy frost, drought, unfavorable weather, or other conditions may cause a sudden scarcity that results in high prices and lower quality. Favorable conditions suddenly may produce a market glut. Growers must estimate market needs a long time ahead and, at market time, they either must ship or let the crop rot. New varieties can be developed or new growing areas opened, and these may quickly take over the market. Changes in processing may cause a formerly plentiful item suddenly to become scarce. Fresh peas from Utah and winter spinach from Texas disappeared from the market in one year because freezing plants moved into these areas. The market also has been highly competitive, and this has caused some instability and rapid change.

The Perishable Agricultural Commodities Act aids in giving the market stability. It requires that all commission merchants, brokers, or dealers who handle fresh produce in wholesale or jobbing lots must be licensed and must observe fair business practices. Penalties are provided and licenses may be revoked. Quotas can be assigned to growers, and an orderly flow of produce to market can be established. Low-quality produce is kept from the market so that it will not depress prices of higher-quality items. Where considerable confusion formerly existed, market confidence has been

Fig. 2-1. Buyers at a fruit and vegetable auction. Courtesy USDA

built. The Act also has facilitated futures trading and has made it possible for buyers and sellers to deal apart from each other. Order has been promoted and growers have been encouraged to improve products and market procedures. A more stable market is the result.

2. The high perishability of fresh produce causes problems that do not exist in other markets. Fresh produce is still a living organism and can quickly lose quality if it is not handled properly. Elevated temperatures rapidly change sugar to starch or promote enzymatic reactions that cause a loss of flavor, appearance, or texture. Cool temperatures and good ventilation are needed at all times if quality is to be preserved.

Improved transportation and storage facilities are reducing quality losses and helping to stabilize the market. Automation in harvesting and packaging speeds handling. Better varieties have been developed to withstand the rigors of shipping and market handling. Vacuum cooling has improved quality. This is a process in which fresh produce is moved into huge chambers where, for about a half-hour, a low vacuum is maintained. This induces rapid surface evaporation that dissipates field heat quickly. The product is then shipped in refrigerated units without ice. Vacuum

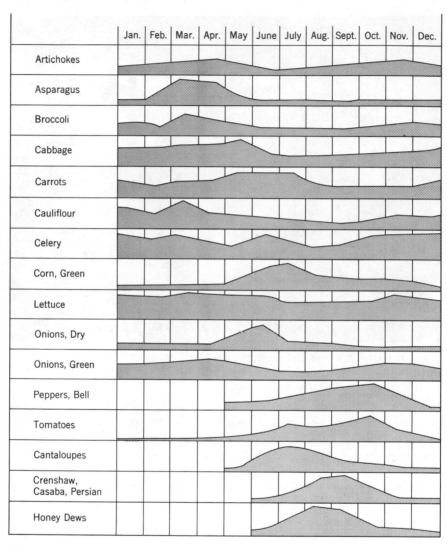

	Jan.	Feb.	Mar.	Apr.	May	June	July	Aug.	Sept.	Oct.	Nov.	Dec.
Artichokes												
Asparagus												
Broccoli												
Cabbage												
Carrots												
Cauliflour												
Celery												
Corn, Green												
Lettuce												
Onions, Dry												
Onions, Green												
Peppers, Bell												
Tomatoes												
Cantaloupes												
Crenshaw, Casaba, Persian												
Honey Dews												

Fig. 2-2. Main seasons are shown for some fruits and vegetables.

cooling has been more successful than icing or hydrocooling (water cooling). Although we have done a great deal to reduce losses, more must be done, since losses still are very high. Produce shipped in first-class condition can arrive in much worse condition.

Because of the high perishability of the produce, buyers of fruits and vegetables must know and recognize quality better than buyers in any other

Fig. 2-3a. A vacu-cooling chamber. Produce placed in this vacuum chamber loses its field heat rapidly because the rapid evaporation rate induced takes heat from the produce.

market. Reliance on a statement of grade is not enough. Personal inspection is needed. An item can be graded and then deteriorate considerably so that it is below grade when delivered. There is a difference on the market between the grade and the condition. An item graded "Fancy," can deteriorate in quality badly, and still be labeled "Fancy." Because of this, buyers should state that "the grade specified should be the condition of the item upon delivery." Otherwise apples that were graded U.S. Fancy when they went into storage but that came out of storage as a low utility grade could be delivered as U.S. Fancy. Recognizing this problem, many federal standards vary tolerances for grade between origin of shipment and enroute or at destination.

3. Wide dispersion has made it difficult to bring uniformity to the market. Transportation and storage conditions were not adequate when markets first formed, and items could not be shipped long distances. Thus each local market developed its own packaging, grading, and other procedures. As a result, grading terms are quite different on different markets.

Fig. 2-3b. A hydro-cooling operation that cools produce by putting finely chipped ice over it. Courtesy USDA

"Fancy" can mean first, second, or third grade, or a top grade can be indicated by "Extra Fancy," "Fancy," "Extra No. 1," "Grade AA," "Grade A," or "No. 1." Buyers must learn the proper grading terminology for the market.

Generally, buyers will find that U.S. No. 1 produce is of good average quality and represents about 50% of the crop. This grade is recommended for ordinary institutional purchases. U.S. No. 2 is usually the quality that is considered practical to sell under standard conditions. Grades may exist above U.S. No. 1, such as Extra Fancy or Fancy, but their quantity is limited. During off-seasons or under special conditions, buyers may be advised to purchase these higher grades. At a season's peak, adequate quality might be obtained in the No. 2 grade.

Grade standards on the produce market must be broad to cover the wide number of varieties of a particular item or to cover many conditions in different growing areas. In some cases, specific grade standards had to be developed for items marketed in different areas. Citrus fruits, for instance,

TABLE 2-1
Various Grades for Some Fresh Produce

Product	Consumer Grades		Wholesale Grades			
	1st Grade	2d Grade	1st Grade	2d Grade	3d Grade	4th Grade
Potatoes	U.S. Grade A Large U.S. Grade A Medium to Large U.S. Grade A Medium U.S. Grade A Small	U.S. Grade B Large U.S. Grade B Medium to Large U.S. Grade B Medium U.S. Grade B Small	U.S. Fancy	U.S. No. 1	U.S. Commercial	U.S. No. 2
Broccoli (Italian Sprouting)	U.S. Grade A	U.S. Grade B	U.S. Fancy	U.S. No. 1	U.S. No. 2	. . .
Brussels Sprouts	U.S. Grade A	U.S. Grade B	U.S. No. 1	U.S. No. 2	. . .	. . .
Carrots	U.S. Grade A	U.S. Grade B	(Topped carrots) U.S. Extra No. 1	U.S. No. 1	U.S. No. 2	. . .
Corn (Husked, on the cob)	U.S. Grade A	U.S. Grade B	(Green corn) U.S. Fancy	U.S. No. 1	U.S. No. 2	. . .
Cranberries	U.S. Grade A	. . .	. . .	. . .	. . .	. . .
Kale	U.S. Grade A	U.S. Grade B	U.S. No. 1	U.S. Commercial	. . .	. . .
Parsnips	U.S. Grade A	U.S. Grade B	U.S. No. 1	U.S. No. 2	. . .	. . .
Spinach Leaves	U.S. Grade A	U.S. Grade B	U.S. Extra No. 1	U.S. No. 1	U.S. Commercial	. . .
Tomatoes	U.S. Grade A	U.S. Grade B	U.S. No. 1	U.S. Combination	U.S. No. 2	U.S. No. 3
Turnips	U.S. Grade A	U.S. Grade B	(Topped turnips) U.S. No. 1	U.S. No. 2	. . .	. . .

TABLE 2-1 (cont'd)
Various Grades for Some Fresh Produce

	Consumer Grades		Wholesale Grades			
Product	1st Grade	2d Grade	1st Grade	2d Grade	3d Grade	4th Grade
Celery	U.S. Grade AA	U.S. Grade A (3d Grade— U.S. Grade B)	U.S. Extra No. 1	U.S. No. 1	U.S. No. 2	. . .
Apples	None	None	U.S. Extra Fancy	U.S. Fancy	U.S. No. 1 U.S. No. 1* Cookers U.S. No. 1† Early U.S. Hail Grade‡	U.S. Utility

*Same as U.S. No. 1 except for color.
†Same as U.S. No. 1 except for color, maturity, and size.
‡Same as U.S. No. 1 except for hail injury.

are graded differently, depending on whether they come from Florida, Texas, or California. The factors making up a grade may not always be the ones indicating the quality that an institution wants. Appearance may count heavily in determining grade, but this may not indicate inside quality. For instance, the redness of an apple is an important grade factor, but it may not indicate the quality of flesh inside. Buyers can also be confused by the fact that there are consumer and manufacturing grades in addition to wholesale grades.

Preparation losses can vary widely in fresh produce, and buyers may find it difficult to estimate the quantities needed. In this text, average preparation losses are noted but, in practice, they can vary widely. Table 2-17 gives the approximate quantities required for some fruits and vegetables. Buyers also may run into difficulty because federal grades are lacking for some items or the market does not use the federal grade but uses state, local, or trade grades. Where no grades exist, buyers may be forced to use commonly accepted market terms such as "good merchantable," "fair," or "ordinary to fair" in defining quality. The need to resort to these indefinite terms leaves much to be desired.

For brevity, only the most important quality factors are summarized in this chapter. Many tolerances, enumeration of specific quality factors for a particular variety, and similar details are omitted. Buyers who wish more information should consult federal grade or trade standards. They also should compile their own information as they learn. It is difficult to delineate quality by words; written descriptions are only guides. Actual experience is needed to give them meaning.

Although specific grades may be recommended for purchase in this chapter, at times qualities above or below the grades should be purchased. Buyers will have to decide this as the need arises. Illustrations are presented wherever possible so that buyers can identify items or consider quality factors affecting grade.

The produce buyer can also be confused by the wide variation in packaging in the market. More standardization is needed. Prices should be quoted by the pound rather than by the container. Listed here are some standard container weights, but wide variation on the market makes these weights somewhat academic. Loose packs should be watched for short weight and bruised items. "Struck full" means evenly leveled across the top; "bulging pack" means a tight fill rounded over the top level of the container. The fill of containers should always be specified as "equal to facing"; good tight facing assists in improving the appearance and in giving a tighter pack. Buyers should define open container weights in a specification for a particular product.

Packaging methods are also changing rapidly, making it difficult to know the quantity in a container. Automatic filling is changing packaging methods. Counts now may be controlled electronically or may be determined by filling a box and shaking it down—a process called *volume filling*. The count in volume filling can vary, but the labor saved is sufficient to make the process desirable. The huge volume of produce moving through supermarkets and the pressure of labor unions for lighter containers are increasing the demand for smaller units. Fiberboard, plastic bags, and other materials are replacing nailed or wire-bound wooden boxes.

Actual container counts and count terms differ. A count term may refer to the size of an item and not the number in a container. At one time the term indicated both, but as the container changed and, with it, the number in the container, the market tended to keep the term as a size indicator only. Frequently, the terms "176" for oranges, "300" for lemons, or "5 x 5" for tomatoes may not be indicative of the container count but only of a standard market size.

FRUIT

Apples (1972)

Although there are over 8000 varieties of apples, only about 30 have commercial importance. Many local apples come onto the market at peak season, but the Pacific Northwest, Appalachia, Great Lakes, Ozarks, New York, Missouri Valley, and California are the big commercial producers.

Selection Factors

Apples should be selected on the basis of (1) maturity, (2) intended use, (3) size, and (4) grade.

1. Apples are known as summer, fall, and winter varieties according to the time at which they are at their best quality. Summer apples are marketed in midsummer and last until early fall. They keep poorly. Fall and winter apples keep better. Winter varieties are available until the summer. To be best for use, apples should be selected at proper maturity, which is indicated by brown seeds, yellowing of the unblushed color, or the development of a blush color on red or blushed varieties and a slight softening of the flesh. Properly matured apples possess a rich, fruity apple aroma. The texture softens somewhat in turning from green to ripe; it can be too hard in immature apples and too soft in mealy, overripe ones. Large apples ripen more rapidly than smaller ones of the same variety.

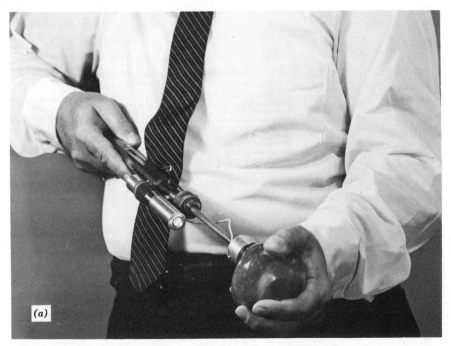

Fig. 2-4a. This device checks the maturity of an apple by directing sound waves into it. A reading is taken from a scale at the top of the instrument.

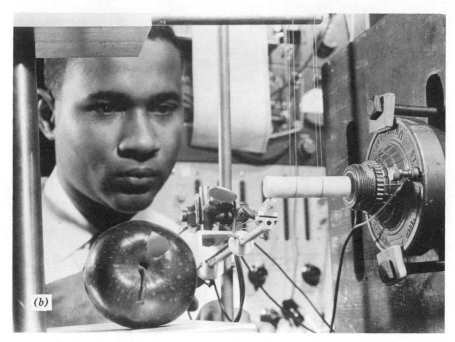

Fig. 2-4b. This device directs sound waves into the suspended core that are recorded on a graph. Both of these instruments are much more accurate in testing the maturity of an apple than the old method in which the thumbnail was used to pierce the apple. Courtesy USDA

Institutions should store apples at 36 to 38°F but warehouse storage will be at 31 to 32°F with relative humidity at 85 to 90%. Apples can absorb odors. Keep them away from potatoes, onions, oil, and other products. Apple odors can be absorbed by dairy products and other foods.

At an established time an apple variety starts to ripen. It is then at its best and should be selected for use. At the end of their storage life apples pass peak maturity rapdily, and they may appear at reduced prices when warehouses are emptied before quality declines to a point at which the apples are unmarketable. Overripe apples will yield easily to pressure and may show interior brown rot, decay, or wilt. Immature apples shrivel easily.

Flavor is usually lacking in immature or overripe apples. When an apple is overripe it loses acidity and flavor. Summer apples are juicy, crisp, sweet, and slightly acid with full flavor at ripeness, but they lose these qualities quickly. The fall varieties hold quality longer. Winter varieties hold them longest of all. Apple supplies are lowest in June through August.

Jonathan is bright red with deep yellow background; used raw is crisp and mildly tart; bakes up fast, holding red color, and has juicy, soft-textured, pleasant, tart flesh; holds shape in pie slices. Small to medium size and deep shiny red. September to January.

McIntosh is good for all purposes; aromatic, white, juicy, crisp flesh, good raw; bakes up soft, rather sweet-flavored, juicy, mild, holding characteristic aroma. Cooks smooth, but loses volume in pies. Highly red blushed. September to March.

Cortland has white flesh, high juice, is crisp; bakes well, holding shape. Flesh cooked is juicy, mildly tart, slightly firm, and dry. Not a prime pie apple. Deep solid red. September to February.

York Imperial is good raw, bakes well, giving a quite firm flesh, tart flavored, neither juicy nor really dry. Holds shape in slices for pies. Lopsided, pinkish blush. October to May.

Stayman has yellow flesh, juicy and crisp; bakes quite firm, tart flavored, and neither juicy nor dry; holds shape in pie slices with firm mellow flesh. Has deep white skin dots over red. Excellent keeper and all-purpose apple. December to May.

Roman Beauty lacks some crispness for use raw, but has excellent flavor, color, and acidity; top baker, cooking up fast, moderately tart, soft textured, and flavorful; in pies is medium dry, fairly tart, holding shape in slices. Red striped, white dots over red. November to May.

Fig. 2-5. Some common market apples. Note how the shape of the apple is an excellent means of identification.

TABLE 2-2
Marketing Data for Leading Apple Varieties

Variety*	Growing Areas	Marketing Season	Use Raw	Cooking Quality
Arkansas Black	Wash., Oreg., Ill., Me.	Nov. to May	Fair	Good for all
Baldwin	N.Y., N. Eng., Mich., Ohio	Nov. to Apr.	Fair	Good for all, esp. pies
Ben Davis	N.Y., N. Eng., Cumber-land-Shenandoah, Midwest, Colo.	Nov. to Apr.	Poor	Good for all
Cortland (3%)	N. Eng., N.Y., Pa., Ohio	Sept. to Feb.	Good	Good for all
Delicious (26%)	Northwest, Midwest, Cumberland-Shenandoah	Sept. to June	Excellent	Poor for all
Golden Delicious† (8%)	Northwest, Midwest, Appalachia	Oct. to Apr.	Excellent	Fair
Gravenstein‡	Calif., N. Eng., Appalachia	July to Sept.		All purpose except baking
Grimes Golden	Cumberland-Shenandoah, Midwest	Sept. to Dec.	Very good	Good for all
Jonathan (7%)	Midwest, Northwest, Appalachia	Sept. to Dec.	Excellent	Good
McIntosh (14%)	N. Eng., N.Y., Mich.	Oct. to May	Excellent	Good
Northern Spy (3%)	N.Y., N. Eng., Pa., Mich.	Nov. to May	Good	Excellent for all
Duchess (Olden-burg)	Mich., Ill. N.Y., N.J.	Aug. to Oct.	Poor	Good for all
R. I. Greening (2%)	N.Y., N. Eng., Mich.	Oct. to Feb.	Fair	Excellent for all
Roman Beauty (7%)	Northwest, Ohio, W. Va., Calif., N.J., Idaho	Oct. to Apr.	Good	Excellent, good baking
Stayman Wine-sap (5%)	Cumberland, Shenandoah, Ohio, Washington	Oct. to Apr.	Good	Good for all
Wagoner	Mich., N.Y.	Nov. to Jan.	Excellent	Good for all
Wealthy	N.J., Midwest, N.Y.	Aug. to Dec.	Good	Excellent for all
Winesap (6%)	Northwest Va., Ill.	Dec. to Aug.	Excellent	Excellent for pies
Winter Banana	Northwest	Sept. to Jan.	Good	Fair for all
Yellow Newton (3%)	Northwest, Calif., Va.	Nov. to May	Excellent	Good for all
Yellow Transparent	Ill., Pa., Del., W. Va.	July to Aug.	Poor	Good for pies and sauce
York Imperial (6%)	Northwest, Midwest, Appalachian area	Oct. to Mar.	Excellent	Fair

*These varieties form about 90% of the total apple crop. Percentages shown indicate the part of the crop the variety makes up.

†The Golden Delicious does not tarnish easily after peeling.

‡Other summer apples good for cooking when slightly immature but good eating raw when at exact ripeness are; Astrachan, Starr (good also for sauce and pies), Summer Rambo (all purpose), Williams Red (best raw), and Lodi (similar to Yellow Transparent).

2. Use different apple varieties for different needs. Delicious apples are excellent for use raw but perform poorly in cooking. Apples for use raw should be crisp and juicy, have moderate-to-low acidity, and have a high sweetness. A good baking apple such as Roman Beauty needs a soft, moist, firm texture with a sufficiently tough skin to hold shape when baked. It should have moderate acidity and good sweetness. Cooking apples should possess high to moderate acidity and have a good texture. For applesauce, a mealy, clear sauce with good tartness is sought. Apples with some firmness after cooking are needed for pies, although the summer apple for green apple pie has a very soft texture and loses shape easily. Some apples may be all-purpose—good for eating raw, for cooking, baking, or other purposes. Such an apple is the McIntosh, the Stayman Winesap, or the Roman Beauty.

3. An apple's size affects its usefulness. Sizes of apples on the market may vary from 56 to 252 per western apple box. Apples are sized by count per box or by diameter as measured not around the girth but from stem to

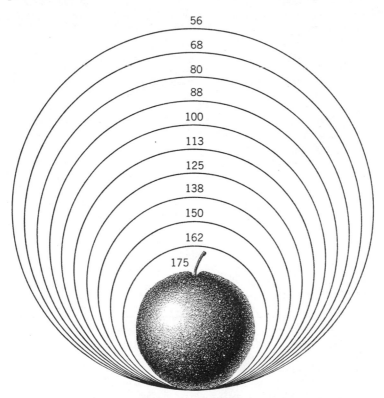

Fig. 2-6. Apple sizes and counts per western apple box.

blossom end transversely. Diameter sizes are usually used for apples packed in hampers and bushels; count is most often used in western boxes. All packages should show count or diameter. Approximately three medium-sized apples (113 count) equal a pound. This size is considered best for all-round use, giving good yield and, usually, the best flavor. Small apples may lack flavor and color and have a tight rubbery texture, whereas large apples may also lack flavor and be loose grained. The best baking size is 88's (3 in. diameter), but smaller sizes may be used for smaller portions. Normally, an eastern apple box contains 50 to 54 lb; a western box, 41 to 47 lb; and a bushel, 42 to 52 lb. The paring waste of a good grade should be approximately 24%, and a box weighing 40 lb should give 30 lb EP.

4. A specification should state the grade, and add that the grade "should be the condition upon delivery." Color is significant in assigning grade. Pacific Northwest apples must meet higher color standards than apples from other areas. Different varieties also must meet different color standards.

Watch for defects such as decay, internal browning, internal breakdown, scab, freezing injury, broken skins, and bruises. Russeting, sunburn, spray burn, limb rubs, hail or drought spots, scars, cracks, and insect, mechanical, or other damage are considered defects. Scald is seldom a problem today if the apples are warehoused properly. Watch for bruising, especially if the apples are loosely packed. Bulging packs control this, compartment packing also controls bruising although fewer apples can be put into a container when compartments are used. Most markets use either the State of Washington or federal grade standards. (See Table 2-4.)

Count per Western Box	Minimum Diameter Size*
175	1¼"
162	1½"
150	1¾"
138	2"
125	2¼"
113	2½"
100	2¾"
88	3"
80	3¼"
68	3½"
56	3¾"

*As measured not around girth but from stem to blossom end transversely.
Note: Federal standards call size 88 or less very large; 96 to 125, large; 138 to 163 medium; 175 to 200, small; and 216 to 252 very small.

TABLE 2-3

Color Requirements for Specified U.S. Grades of Apples by Variety

Variety	U.S. Extra Fancy	U.S. Fancy	U.S. No. 1
	Percent	Percent	Percent
Solid Red:			
Black Ben	66	40	25
Gano	66	40	25
Winesap	66	40	25
Other similar varieties[1]	66	40	25
Red Sport varieties[2]	66	40	25
Striped or partially red:			
Jonathan	66	33	25
McIntosh	50	33	25
Cortland	50	33	25
Other similar varieties[3]	50	33	25
Rome Beauty	50	33	15
Stayman	50	33	15
York Imperial	50	33	15
Baldwin	50	25	15
Ben Davis	50	25	15
Delicious	50	25	15
Mammoth Black Twig	50	25	15
Turley	50	25	15
Wagener	50	25	15
Wealthy	50	25	15
Willow Twig	50	25	15
Northern Spy	50	25	15
Other similar varieties[4]	50	25	15
Hubbardston	50	15	10
Stark	50	15	10
Other similar varieties	50	15	10
Red June	50	15	[5]
Red Gravenstein	50	15	[5]
Williams	50	15	[5]
Other similar varieties	50	15	[5]
Gravenstein	25	10	[8]
Duchess	25	10	[5]
Other similar varieties[6]	25	10	[5]
Red cheeked or blushed:			
Maiden Blush	[7]	[5]	[8]
Twenty Ounce	[7]	[5]	[8]
Winter Banana	[7]	[5]	[8]

TABLE 2-3 (cont'd)

Color Requirements for Specified U.S. Grades of Apples by Variety

Variety	U.S. Extra Fancy	U.S. Fancy	U.S. No. 1
	Percent	*Percent*	*Percent*
Other similar varieties	[7]	[5]	[8]
Green varieties	[9]	[9]	[9]
Yellow varieties	[9]	[9]	[9]
Golden Delicious	[10]	[10]	[9]

[1]Arkansas Black, Beacon, Detroit Red, Esopus Spitzenburg, King David, Lowry, Minjon.
[2]When Red Sport varieties are specified as such they shall meet the color requirements specified for Red Sport varieties.
[3]Haralson, Kendall, Macoun, Snow (Fameuse).
[4]Bonum, Early McIntosh, Limbertwig, Milton Nero, Paragon, Melba.
[5]Tinge of color.
[6]Red Astrachan, Smokehouse, Summer Rambo, Dudley.
[7]Blush Cheek.
[8]None.
[9]Characteristic ground color.
[10]75% or more of the surface of the apple shall show white or light green predominating over the green color.

TABLE 2-4

Federal and Washington Grades for Apples

Rank in Quality	Grade Name Washington	Federal	Grade Characteristics Washington	Federal
1st	Extra Fancy	U.S. Extra Fancy	Sound, clean, fully-matured smooth, well-formed, free from defects. All good mature fruit; good color, shape, and condition for variety; carefully packed.	Mature, not overripe, carefully hand picked, clean, well-formed, free from defects, amount of color specified for variety.
2nd	Fancy	U.S. Fancy	Clean, fully matured, and of good color for variety, free from defects, fairly well formed	Mature, not overripe, carefully hand picked, fairly well-formed, free from defects; amount of color specified for variety
3rd	Grade C	U.S. No. 1	Clean, fully matured fruit, fair color and fair shape; condition good, fairly free from defects.	Sames as U.S. Fancy except color may be lower than U.S. Fancy.

TABLE 2-4 (cont'd)
Federal and Washington Grades for Apples

Rank in Quality	Grade Name Washington	Federal	Grade Characteristics Washington	Federal
4th	None	U.S. No. 1 Early	None	Shall meet all requirements of U.S. No. 1 except for color. This grade is provided for Duchess, Gravenstein, Red June, Twenty Ounce, Wealthy, Williams, Yellow Transparent, and Lodi, or other varieties normally marketed during the summer months.
5th	None	U.S. No. 1 Cookers	None	Same as U.S. No. 1 except color; grade provided for apples which are mature but lack sufficient color to meet color standards of U.S. No. 1.
6th	None	U.S. Utility	None	Lack color, shape must not be seriously deformed, may have higher waste and labor preparation cost than saved by purchase of this lower grade.

Apricots (1928)

The main apricot varieties are the Blenheim, a large fruit with light flesh but slightly tart; the Moorparks, medium size with a light amber, sweet flesh; and the Royals, a small, sweet fruit with reddish amber flesh. June to July are the peak months, with some imports marketed in the winter. Only tree-ripened fruit is of highest quality and, since apricots are not a good shipper, local products should be used. A California lug holds about 24 lb. A buyer should learn his own market's packaging. Examine for overripe, decayed, or shriveled fruit; worms; skin cracks; or other blemishes. Select U.S. No. 1. Loss in pitting and peeling is 6%.

Fig. 2-7. Checking flesh characteristics of avocados at a USDA field laboratory.

Avocados

Florida, California (70% of the crop), and the Caribbean produce most of the avocado crop. The Fuerte and the Lula are the main varieties. The former has a thin, pliable skin, is green and pear-shaped, and is often called a Calavo since it is largely grown in California. Florida and Caribbean areas produce the Lula, a green or greenish-black and heavier avocado averaging 1½ lb. It is somewhat pear-shaped, with a smooth or slightly corrugated greenish, hard rind flecked with tiny yellow dots. It is graded (1957)[1] differently than Calavos. A Nabal avocado comes from Central America. It is more round than oval.

A high production peak occurs October to December; a lower one February to April. Supplies are light in the summer. California ships the year around, with peak months in the winter. Florida's peak season is also winter, with no supplies April through June.

Good quality fruit is fresh and bright appearing, with a flesh just begin-

[1]The use of data in parentheses in this text indicates the date of the federal standard for this product as of this printing.

ning to be soft and buttery. Ripeness is detected by placing the avocado in the palm and pressing to see if there is a slight yield. The fruit should be heavy for size and have a waxy shell. Soft, mushy, bruised, or decayed fruit, detected by the presence of dark sunken spots, should be rejected. If hard, an avocado can be ripened in 2 to 5 days by placing it in a warm place (70 to 80°F). Store at 50°F.

California ships in 13-lb flats sized per flat from 8 to 35; the best institutional size is 8 to 12 oz (16 to 28 per flat). Florida may ship 38-lb net boxes (wood or fiberboard). California grades are No. 1 and 2, and Florida's are No. 1, 2, and 3. There are no federal grades. California law prohibits marketing avocadoes with less than 8% oil. Purchase them firm, breaking,

Fig. 2-8. A banana tree with growing fruit (Cavandish variety). Courtesy USDA

or ready-to-eat. Fruit can generally be taken from the firm to breaking state in 4 to 5 days and the breaking to ready-to-eat stage in 1 to 2 days. The yields of flesh are Lula, 62%, and Fuerte, 76%.

Bananas

Bananas come mainly from Central America, usually the Gros Michel or Cavendish varieties. The Plaintain is a banana that is usually boiled or baked; it is reddish in color but is not commonly found on the market.

Tree-ripened bananas are insipid in flavor. Ripening in transit or storage is controlled by varying temperature and humidity. Ethylene gas can be used to remove greenness. Fast ripening is done in 3 to 4 days, medium ripening in 5 to 7 days, and slow ripening in 8 to 10 days. Properly ripened fruit has a bright, attractive, yellow color. The fruit should appear fresh, be firm and plump, and have good peel strength. *Full ripe* means no trace of green, with typical ripe-banana color, well flecked with light-brown to dark-brown specks of a size from pinpoints to spots ⅛ in. in diameter. They should be consumed in 24 hours. *Hard ripe* means a bright banana color with no trace of brown, firm texture, and some astringency in flavor; about 3 days are needed for ripening at room temperature. *Turning ripe* means pale banana color with a green tip, little flavor, and sharp astringency. These take 5 to 6 days at room temperature to ripen. Examine for size, fullness of fruit, and degree of maturity. Look for bruised fruit, fruit riper than specified, poorly colored skin, and mold. Chilling discolors the fruit. Store at about 50°F.

Bananas are sold cut from the stem or in bunches in 40-lb cartons. About three medium-sized bananas equal a pound. Grade refers to fullness of the fruit. There are no federal grades. Peeling loss averages 32%. Bananas are on the market in good supply throughout the year.

Berries

Today most institutions purchase frozen berries, except perhaps strawberries, raspberries, cranberries, and blueberries. Watch for deteriorated fresh fruit and purchase in quantities used in a few days. Store at around 40°F with good ventilation. Look for wet stains on the bottoms of boxes that indicate deteriorated fruit. Specify U.S. No. 1.

Strawberries (1965) are marketed from April to July in quantity, early Mexico, Florida, Louisiana, or Texas berries appear in February. Imports appear in off-season. Mature strawberries should be fully red, plump, firm, and free from dirt; bright and clean; and free from insect or other

Fig. 2-9. Two types of strawberries that show good quality. Note that the fruit is bright and clean, and it gives the appearance of firmness of texture and good fruit development.

Fig. 2-10. Mature cranberries. Courtesy USDA

damage. Dull fruit may be spoiled and have a poor flavor. Purchase U.S. No. 1 with hulls on. A quart weighs 1½ lb. Preparation waste is 8%.

Cranberries (1971) are marketed in 25- to 50-lb crates or 5-lb packages. Barrels are 100 lb. Maturity is indicated by color that can range from a bright red to almost black. Good quality berries bounce when dropped from 1½ to 2 ft onto a hard surface. Watch for worm damage, insect damage, rot, and frostbite. Purchase U.S. No. 1. Preparation waste is 4%.

Blueberries (1966) are on the market from May to September, with the peak in July. Many are frozen. Huckleberries are a different species from blueberries and are on the market during July and August. Blueberries are sized per two gill—*extra large,* 90 berries or less; *large,* 90 to 129; *medium,* 130 to 189; and *small,* 190 to 250.

Cherries (1971)

Dessert cherries—the sweet variety—may be used for eating-in-hand or for salads, desserts, or other preparations. The black varieties—Bing, Black Tartarian, Lambert, Republican, and Schmidt—are the best shippers. The Royal Anne is a cream-colored, sweet cherry with a red blush, but it ships poorly. The sweet cherry season is usually mid-June to mid-August.

Select cherries for firmness, size, a good color for variety, juiciness, and high flavor. Immature fruit has a bitter tang and lacks color. The fruit is

Fig. 2-11. A newly developed bluberry called the Colville (right) is compared with regular blueberries on the left. Both show good quality. Courtesy USDA

Fig. 2-12. Well-packed bing cherries. Note facing and that the specification should read "fill should be equal to facing" to assure that the cherries under are of the same size and quality. The information on the label and on the lug is highly desirable so that adequate buying information is given. Courtesy USDA

purchased in lugs or baskets, and quantities in these will vary according to size and type. California requires nonstandard containers to be labeled "irregular pack." Fill should be specified as equal to facing. Cherries should be picked with stems to prevent bruising. Examine for worms; soft, overripe, or shriveled cherries; and mechanical or insect damage. Sweet cherries split if rain strikes them when they are ripe. The cherries should be bright and fresh in appearance, full and plump, firm, juicy, sweet, and full-flavored. Watch for brown color, dull appearance, mold, and bruises. Specify U.S. No. 1.

Citrus Fruit

Oranges and grapefruit make up most of the citrus crop, but lemons, limes, and some hybrids are produced in good quantity. Florida, the Gulf States, California, and Arizona are the main growing areas. Some fruit is imported. Table 2-5 indicates main production seasons; at other times, quality is apt to be lower and prices higher.

Oranges

There are three main groups of oranges—the sweet, the mandarine or kid-glove type, and the Seville (sour or marmalade).

Sweet Oranges. The bulk of our orange crop is sweet oranges, a type characterized by a skin rather difficult to remove but with membranes that are easily removable. The Valencia (a summer orange) and the Navel (a winter orange) make up about 80% of the total sweet orange crop. The Navel is suited to the dry California climate. Florida grows a good quantity of Parson Brown, Hamlin, Pineapple, and Homosassa oranges in the winter and Valencias in the summer. California and Arizona (1957) oranges are bright in color and sweet and spicy in flavor. Because of their firmness and lighter juice content, they segment more easily. Florida oranges and tangelos (1973) are heavier in size and contain more juice than those from California. They are not as bright in color and are less sweet, but they carry a fuller flavor. The tangelo—a cross between a mandarin and a tangerine—and the Temple orange—a cross between the sweet orange and the tangerine—are produced in quantity in the winter, especially in Florida and Texas. Purchase oranges graded U.S. Fancy in No. 1

Mandarins. The mandarin or kid-glove orange is characterized by a skin that is easily removed, but the membranes are removed with difficulty. The skin is wrinkled and apt to be somewhat puffy. Most of these oranges have a coarse texture, a high juice content, and good sweetness, but they are less acid than the sweet orange. They have high aroma. The flavor is full and rich. To this group belong the Kings, a rather large, flat-shaped orange; the tangerines, with an orange-red peel; and the Satsumas, with a lighter yellow peel. Satsumas are much like tangerines, but usually they are not quite as juicy and have tougher membranes. They also come onto the market later than tangerines. Sometimes this orange is called the mandarin orange, but the term is usually applied to all kid-glove or loose-skinned varieties and not one specific variety.

Miscellaneous Oranges. Clementines and the Dancy tangerines are produced heavily in Florida and Texas. California produces less. The kumquat is a small fruit that looks like a tiny orange. It has smooth, tightly adhering skin and is usually eaten raw with the skin on. It makes excellent preserves.

Grapefruit (1950, 1969, and 1973)

The two main winter varieties of grapefruit are the Marsh and Duncan or

Florida Common. They may be either white or pink fleshed. Closely related to the Common are the Hall, Walters, McCarty, and Excelsior; in fact, they are frequently included with the Common. The Marsh is a seedless fruit

TABLE 2-5
Main Production Seasons for Citrus Fruits

Citrus Fruit	State	Variety	Main Marketing Months
Oranges (sweet)	Florida	Pineapple and Homosassa	December to March
		Hamlin and Parson Brown	October to December
		Temple (hybrid)	December to March
		Valencia	February to August
	California	Navel	November to June
	and Arizona	Valencia	March to January
	zona	Temples	November to February
	Texas	Valencia and Temples	February to June
		Navels	November to February
Oranges (mandarin or kid-glove)	Florida	Dancy	November through January
	Texas	Clementine	November to March
	California	Dancy mainly	November through January
Grapefruit*	Florida	*	October to June
	Texas	*	November to July
	California	*	March to August
	Arizona	*	December to July
Lemons	California	Lisbon and Eureka	All year, with June to September main peak in production
Limes	Florida	Tahiti (Persian)	All year, with June to September main peak in production
			(Mexican limes come onto market earlier and later than this)

*The Duncan or Florida Common grapefruit appears on the market early in October and bears heavily until January. The Marsh then appears in December and bears heavily in the late winter and spring. There are very few grapefruit on the market in August and September. The best grapefruit months are those from November to May.

Fig. 2-13. Note the difference in flesh and rind between the overmature (late bloom) grapefruit on the left and the properly mature grapefruit on the right. Note peaking of the late fruit. Courtesy USDA

outranking all others in quantities produced. The Thompson Pink is a pink Marsh. Pink-fleshed varieties can be detected by the slight pink blush on the rind.

Florida and Texas grapefruit are heavy, juicy, and full-flavored, with a thin skin and tender, delicate flesh. The Indian River (Florida) and Rio (Texas) regions produce high-quality fruit. California and Arizona have a bright, clear-colored fruit with a thicker skin, less juice, and less body and fullness of flavor. A tangelo is a cross between a tangerine and grapefruit. A pomelo is the fruit from which grapefruit has been derived.

Lemons (1964)

California and Arizona produce most of the lemons. Florida lemons are apt to be coarse and large and lack a good spicy, tart juice. Italian or other imports are apt to be more coarse than California lemons and lack some of their full, spicy flavor. The main lemon varieties are the Eureka and Lisbon. The Lisbon is a heavy producer, but the Eureka comes on the market at times when prices are higher and so is planted more. Purchase U.S. No. 1, which must have a 30% or more juice content.

Limes (1958)

Most limes come from Florida, off-lying Caribbean islands, and Mexico. There are two kinds: sour and sweet. The latter is not commerically important. Florida produces a large crop of sour Tahiti or Persian limes. The Mexican sour lime comes from warmer areas and has a longer season. U.S. No. 1 limes must have a 32% or more juice content.

Fig. 2-14. A cluster of sweet limes. Courtesy USDA

Quality Factors. Quality is best judged in citrus fruit by cutting and tasting. Select firm, well-formed fruit with fine-textured, thin skin, free from blemish, hard, dry, or broken rinds, bruises, scab, or other defects. Note shriveling or any traces of decay. Immature fruit has a high acid and low sugar flavor and lacks juice. Fruit is heaviest at the beginning and middle of the growing season. Rinds are thicker and the shape pointed in late season fruit. Size is smaller also as the season extends. California winter grapefruit is packed 27, 32, 36, 40, and 48 a carton and summer grapefruit (mid-May through mid-September) is packed 32, 36, 40, 48, and 64 a carton.

California and Arizona fruit has a brighter color than eastern fruit because of the bright sunshine and low humidity. A small mite tapping the oil cell causes the russeting or discoloration on the rind of Texas or Florida fruit. Although the blemish does not interfere with quality, it detracts from

TABLE 2-6
Important Characteristics of Orange Varieties

Variety	Size	Color	Shape	Rind	Seeds	Flesh	Flavor
Sweet orange varieties							
Hamlin	Med to small	Yellow-orange	Oval to round	Smooth, glossy	Few seeds	Medium juicy	Sweet and mild
Parson Brown	Medium	Rich yellow, orange	Oblongish round	Smooth, 1/8 to 3/16" thick	10 to 19	Medium fine	Juicy, sweet
Washington Navel	Large	Rich reddish orange to orange yellow	Round to tapering at base	Thin, 1/8 to 1/4" thick, smooth. Large oil cells.	None	Medium coarse	Medium juicy rich, sweet
Pineapple	Med to large	Deep orange with reddish tinge	Round	Smooth, glossy, 1/8" thick	Large, 8 to 15	Medium fine	Rich and juicy
Homosassa	Med to large	Deep orange	Round and oval	Smooth and glossy	15	Medium fine	Excellent, rich fragrant
Valencia	Large	Pale orange to yellow orange with tendency to show green	Slightly oval	Smooth or slight pebble thin, not tough	2 to 5	Good	Excellent, med juicy
Ruby Red	Medium	Deep orange; red at apex	Roundish thick	Medium smooth, thick	Many seeds		Rich, sweet almost spicy
Mandarin varieties							
Satsuma	Med to small	Pale to bright orange	Flat to oblate	Rough, large oil cells	Few	Coarse	Juicy, spicy
Dancy Tangerine	Medium	Deep orange	Oblate flat	Thin, glossy		Medium	Rich, juicy aromatic
King	Large	Light to deep orange	Roundish oblate	Very rough	Few	Coarse	Juicy, spicy
Temple	Medium	Deep orange	Oblate	Rough	Few	Moderate	Rich, aromatic, spicy

appearance. The quantity of russeting is a factor in differentiating *within* grade for Texas and Florida fruit.

Citrus fruit must be picked ripe; federal inspectors establish the picking time. Color does not necessarily indicate ripeness. The fruit is heaviest at peak maturity. The total solids and sugar-acid ratio of the juice are the best ripeness indicators. Citrus trees may bear flowers, green fruit, and ripe fruit at the same time. Fruit may ripen, turn a ripe color, and, if not picked, may turn green again and still be ripe. Grapefruit can ripen and be of good color on trees for 12 to 15 months. Some citrus varieties may never become ripe in color but may show some green. This "greening" is prevalent in the Valencia orange, especially Florida Valencias, and federal standards make allowance for more green color in this fruit. This greening may be removed in California fruit by sweating, a process in which ethylene gas or partially burnt kerosene fumes are introduced with warm humid air into storage chambers. Florida fruit does not respond well to sweating and frequently may have color rubbed on. If this is done, it must be labeled "color added." Greening is not always a defect. Limes command a better price and are of better quality when they are a deep green rather than a full ripe yellow. Some buyers select lemons showing some green, claiming that the lemons have higher acidity and better flavor.

TABLE 2-7
Purchase Characteristics of Some Common Grapefruit

Variety	Size*	Color	Rind Depth	Flesh	Flavor
Marsh	Medium 3½″	Light yellow	⅛″ thick	Greenish-gray, 11 to 13 sections, no seeds	Medium acidity and sweetness, faint bitterness
Hall	Large 4½″	Light yellow	³/₁₆″ thick	14 sections 32 seeds, high juice	Acidity, sweetness, and bitterness strong
Walters	Medium 3¾″	Pale yellow	¼″ thick	13 sections, 58 seeds	Acidity, sweetness, and bitterness strong
Duncan	Medium to small 3½″	Light yellow	¹/₁₆″ thick	Greenish-gray, 14 sections, many seeds	Acidity and sweetness medium with noticeable bitterness
Triumph	Small 3¼″	Light yellow	⅛″ thick	11 sections, 37 seeds, very juicy	Mild in acidity, sweetness, and bitterness; delicate flavor

*Inches refer to average diameter of fruit.

Selection Factors. Select fruit with thin skins. Puffy or spongy fruit with wrinkled, coarse rinds and pointed sharp necks lack juice and flavor, but wrinkling and coarseness of texture in kid-glove varieties should not be confused with lack of quality. Select fruit that is plump and firm, not soft and flabby, fine textured, with tiny oil sacs on the rind. Western citrus fruit has thicker skins than eastern. This factor is recognized in the federal grade standards.

Watch citrus for blue mold, white mold, or mechanical damage. Store at 37 to 39°F for oranges, 45 to 48°F for lemons, and 48 to 50°F for grapefruit. Relative humidity is best at 80 to 85%. Eastern citrus stores better than citrus from the western states.

Packaging. Today most citrus moves in fiberboard cartons. Some appears in bushel baskets, especially from Texas, and more mesh bags, plastic bags, and other containers are being used. Washing, packing, sorting, and handling are automated. Sorting for size, color, and shape can be

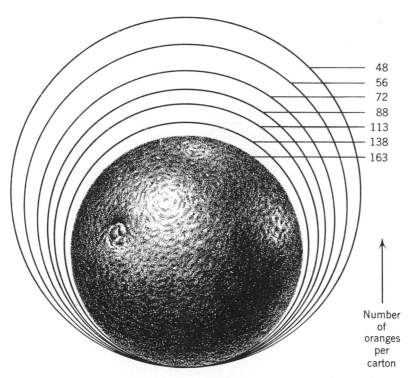

48
56
72
88
113
138
163

Number
of
oranges
per
carton

Fig. 2-15. California-Arizona sizes for oranges in standard 4/5-bu fiberboard cartons. Courtesy Sunkist Growers

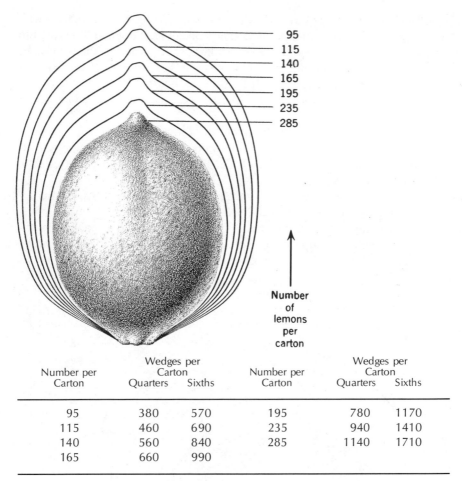

Number per Carton	Wedges per Carton		Number per Carton	Wedges per Carton	
	Quarters	Sixths		Quarters	Sixths
95	380	570	195	780	1170
115	460	690	235	940	1410
140	560	840	285	1140	1710
165	660	990			

Fig. 2-16. California-Arizona sizes for lemons in standard 4/5-bu fiberboard cartons. Courtesy Sunkist Growers

done electronically at the rate of 40 a second. Transistors count the fruit, and, when the required number is boxed, the box moves on and the next one is filled. A standard $^4/_5$-bu carton of California lemons or oranges has a net weight of about 38 lb and California grapefruit, 33 lb. The same container filled with Florida oranges has a net weight of 45 lb and filled with grapefruit, 40 lb. The Texas $^7/_{10}$-bu carton averages 35 lb when filled with grapefruit.

The federal government classifies oranges as *large,* 3⅜ in. or more diameter measured at right angles to a line from stem to blossom end, 326 grams or more each; *medium,* 3¼ in. to 2¾ in. diameter and 315 to 325 grams each; and *small,* 2½ in. diameter or less and 150 to 314 grams each. (See the preceding chart on sizing for Citrus Fruit.)

Sizing for Citrus Fruit

Florida
Oranges including Navels (⁴/₅ bu)

Size and Count	Pack	Rows	Layers	Diameter in Inches Minimum	Maximum
100's	4 x 4	5	5	3⁶/₁₆	
	or				
	5 x 5	4	5	3⁶/₁₆	3¹²/₁₆
125's	5 x 5	5	5	3³/₁₆	3⁹/₁₆
163's	7 x 6	5	5	2¹⁵/₁₆	3⁴/₁₆
200's	8 x 8	5	5	2¹¹/₁₆	3
252's	7 x 7	6	6	2⁸/₁₆	2¹²/₁₆
324's	9 x 9	6	6	2⁴/₁₆	2⁸/₁₆

except minimum count and size can be:

Size and Count	Minimum Diameter in Inches
96's	3⁶/₁₆
125's or 126's	3³/₁₆
150's	3
175's or 176's	2¹³/₁₆
216's	2¹⁰/₁₆
252's	2⁸/₁₆
288's or 294's	2⁶/₁₆
324's	2⁴/₁₆

The best buy for juice is the lowest price a pound or carton because similar varieties give about the same yield regardless of size, although some buyers state that 88 to 126 oranges, 36 to 48 grapefruit, and 195 to 235 lemons usually yield the lowest cost juice. If a half-orange is served, 48's or larger are needed, but 72's are used for two halves. A half 64 size grapefruit is a good serving. Extra large fruit is apt to lack flavor, have a coarse texture, and soft flesh. Very small fruit is usually insipid in flavor, high in acidity, and lacking in sweetness.

Grading. Federal grades for lemons are U.S. No. 1, 2, and 3. Limes are graded U.S. No. 1 and 2. Institutions usually find U.S. No. 1 citrus fruit adequate. Orange and grapefruit grades are U.S. Fancy and U.S. No. 1, 2, and 3. California and Arizona standards make allowance for slightly rougher rinds, and Texas fruit can have rougher rinds than Florida fruit. Rind thickness is a quality factor considered in western citrus. Florida and Texas provide for tolerances within grades for russetting. Their Fancy grades cannot have more than a tenth surface tarnish. Florida's grapefruit No. 1 Bright cannot have more than a fifth surface discoloration, Golden can have up to a third, and Bronze and Russet can have more than a third. Texas grapefruit or oranges graded No. 1 Bright may not have more than a tenth tarnish; Bronze will have greater than a tenth. Florida U.S. No. 1 oranges and tangelos cannot have more than a fifth discoloration in Bright, a third in Golden, and not more than a third in Bronze or Russet.

Temples and Tangelos ($^4/_5$ bu)

Size and Count	Pack	Rows	Layers	Minimum Diameter in Inches
54's	4 x 5	4	3	$3^6/_{16}$
66's	6 x 5	4	3	$3^2/_{16}$
80's	4 x 4	5	4	3
100's	5 x 5	5	4	$2^{12}/_{16}$
120's	5 x 5	6	4	$2^9/_{16}$
156's	7 x 6	6	4	$2^5/_{16}$

Murcott Honey Oranges ($^4/_5$ bu)

Size and Count	Pack	Rows	Layers	Minimum Diameter in Inches
100's	5 x 5	4	5	$2^{15}/_{16}$
120's	4 x 4	5	6	$2^{11}/_{16}$
150's	5 x 5	5	6	$2^8/_{16}$
176's	6 x 6	5	6	$2^6/_{16}$
210's	5 x 5	6	7	$2^4/_{16}$
246's	6 x 6	6	7	$2^2/_{16}$
294's	7 x 7	6	7	2

Oranges including Navels, Temples, and Tangelos ($^4/_5$ bu)

Size	Count	Pack	Rows	Layers	Minimum Diameter in Inches
100's	⎧48	3 x 3	4	4	$3^6/_{16}$
	or				
	⎩50	3 x 2	5	4	$3^6/_{16}$
125's	64	4 x 4	4	4	$3^3/_{16}$
163's	⎧80	5 x 5	4	4	$2^{15}/_{16}$
	or				
	⎩80	4 x 4	4	5	$2^{15}/_{16}$
200's	⎧100	5 x 5	4	5	$2^{11}/_{16}$
	or				
	⎩100	4 x 4	5	5	$2^{11}/_{16}$
252's	125	5 x 5	5	5	$2^8/_{16}$
324's	⎧163	7 x 6	5	5	$2^4/_{16}$
	or				
	⎩163	5 x 4	6	6	$2^4/_{16}$

except minimum count and size can be:

Size	Count	Pack	Rows	Layers	Minimum Diameter in Inches
96's	48	3 x 3	4	4	$3^6/_{16}$
125's or 126's	64	4 x 4	4	4	$3^3/_{16}$
150's	72	5 x 4	4	4	3
175's or 176's	88	4 x 3	5	5	$2^{13}/_{16}$
216's	112	4 x 5	5	5	$2^{10}/_{16}$
252's	125	5 x 5	5	5	$2^8/_{16}$
288's	150	6 x 6	5	5	$2^6/_{16}$
324's	162	6 x 7	5	5	$2^4/_{16}$

Grapefruit ($1^3/_5$ bu)

Pack Size	Diameter in Inches	
	Minimum	Maximum
36's	5	$5^9/_{16}$
45's or 46's	$4^{11}/_{16}$	$5^4/_{16}$
54's or 56's	$4^6/_{16}$	$4^{15}/_{16}$
64's	$4^3/_{16}$	$4^{12}/_{16}$
70's or 72's	$3^{15}/_{16}$	$4^8/_{16}$
80's	$3^{12}/_{16}$	$4^5/_{16}$
96's	$3^9/_{16}$	$4^2/_{16}$
112's	$3^7/_{16}$	4
125's or 126's	$3^5/_{16}$	$3^{14}/_{16}$

Tangerines

Pack	Diameter in Inches
100	$2^{15}/_{16}$
120	$2^{11}/_{16}$
150	$2^8/_{16}$
176	$2^6/_{16}$
210	$2^4/_{16}$
246	$2^2/_{16}$
294	2

Texas
Grapefruit ($1^2/_5$ bu)

Pack Size	Diameter in Inches	
	Minimum	Maximum
46's	$4^5/_{16}$	5
54's or 56's	$4^2/_{16}$	$4^{12}/_{16}$
64's	$3^{15}/_{16}$	$4^8/_{16}$
70's or 72's	$3^{13}/_{16}$	$4^5/_{16}$
80's	$3^{10}/_{16}$	$4^2/_{16}$
96's	$3^6/_{16}$	$3^{14}/_{16}$
112's or 113's	$3^2/_{16}$	$3^{10}/_{16}$
125's or 126's	3	$3^8/_{16}$

Oranges (1²/₅ and ⁷/₁₀ bu)

Size and Count in 1²/₅ Bushel	Count in ⁷/₁₀ Bushel	Diameter in Inches Minimum	Maximum
100's	48 or 50	3⁷/₁₆	3¹³/₁₆
125's	64	3³/₁₆	3⁹/₁₆
163's	80	2¹⁵/₁₆	3⁵/₁₆
200's	100	2¹¹/₁₆	3¹/₁₆
252's	125	2⁷/₁₆	2¹²/₁₆
288's	144	2⁴/₁₆	2⁹/₁₆
324's	162	2³/₁₆	2⁸/₁₆

(*Note:* California packs citrus fruit sizes very much on the same classifications as those used by Florida.)

Texas has only two russeting classifications: Bright and Bronze. The classifications for russeting in other citrus fruit may vary from these standards, but grapefruit in Florida and Texas follow those for oranges.

Florida has attempted to correlate fruit and juice quality. A U.S. Grade AA orange juice has a high solid, acid, and sugar content with 2½ gal of orange juice minimum yield per ⁴/₅-bu carton. A U.S. Grade A orange juice has a slightly lower solid, acid, and sugar content and a yield of 2¼ gal per ⁴/₅ bu. Florida has similar but slightly lower standards for juice yields for a carton of grapefruit. Lemons must have a juice content of not less than 32%. To meet federal standards limes must yield not less than 42%. The Perishable Commodities Act does not permit limes to be marketed if less than 1⅝ in. in diameter and, if between this and 1⅞ in. in diameter, they must posses a juice content of 48%. If over 1⅞ in. in diameter, they must contain 44% juice content. The 44% minimum juice content applies to Mexican limes. Under marketing agreements, oversupply is regulated, and growers receive prorated allowances for market shipment. Ripeness and other factors relating to quality are also covered by this act.

TABLE 2-8
Average Yields of Flesh and Juice from Citrus Fruits, by Percent of Total Weight

Type Fruit	Flesh (no membrane)	Juice Arizona	California	Florida
Lemons	64%	44%	44%	
Oranges	65%	48%	47%	54%
Grapefruit	47%	45%	42%	46%
Limes	57%			35%

Coconuts, Dates, and Figs

Few fresh coconuts, dates, and figs are purchased. Coconuts are on the market all year, with a peak from October through December and a sub-peak February to April. Packaging is in sacks containing 60 to 100 lb. Check for heaviness, size, and good shape; shake to hear milk inside. Coconuts that are dry inside are apt to be moldy. Examine for cracks, mold, or wet eyes. There are no federal grades. Waste in preparing is 47%. If cracked and placed in a 350°F oven for a short time, the meat comes easily from the shell.

Fresh dates are available, but most operations purchase dried products. Watch for a waxy, golden color, plumpness, and smooth skin. Dull color, dirt, or extraneous matter are defects.

Figs are usually California-grown, although there are occasionally imports. They are usually on the market June to October in 5-lb baskets. Overripe figs can be detected by a sour odor. Look for bruising, rot, and insect damage. Figs are quite perishable. For best quality, figs should be fully ripe. The Calmyrna fig is light green, soft, and sweet when ripe. Black Missions are stronger in flavor. Calmyrna figs are usually peeled for service. Peeling loss is 18%.

Fig. 2-17. Check the interior quality as well as the outside of figs. Courtesy USDA

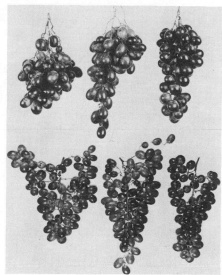

Fig. 2-18. The structure of the bunch is considered in grading grapes. Here bunches 1 through 6 are photographed hanging, with the same bunch underneath spread out on a flat surface. Bunches 1, 2, and 3 are straggly. Bunch 3 is just below the requirement for U.S. No. 1. Bunches 4 and 5 are not straggly but do not meet the standard of "fairly well filled" because of a lack of filling in the upper portions. Bunch 6 meets the minimum standard for "fairly well filled." Courtesy USDA

Grapes (1971)

We have American and European grapes for table use. The former are native to the United States and have loose skins separating easily from the pulp. For this reason, they may be called *slip-skin* grapes. The European grape has a pulp and skin not easily separated. American grapes are Concord, Catawba, Moore Early, Worden, Niagara, and Delaware produced in the midwest and on the eastern coast. The Muscadine is produced along the Gulf Coast and the Mississippi River. The European grapes used for table purposes are Emperor, Thompson Seedless (Sultanina), Flame Tokay, Red Malaga, Ribier, Almeria, White Malaga, Cardinal, Muscat, and Cornichon. California produces most of these. California grapes appear in the fall and are usually found in good supply until spring, although some are available the year around. Eastern grapes are marketed in the fall, and the season is short. Store grapes at 32 to 40°F.

Grapes near full maturity have the best quality. Early picking may rob a grape of flavor, sweetness, and best texture. Fully ripe grapes should have a cluster stem that is green and not brown. When shaken, few grapes fall from the bunch. Overshriveling of the stems indicates age. The seeds should be brown, not green, and should separate easily from the pulp in both types of grapes. The fruit should be plump and full and not in straggly bunches. Freezing damages grapes, and if they have a dull, dead color and the stem pulls out with meat or brush attached, freezing is indicated. A milky, opaque pulp and a flat flavor indicate freezing. Yields: American, pulp and juice, 57%; European, unstemmed, 89%. Purchase U.S. Extra Fancy or Fancy.

Mangos

Mangos are eaten fresh, as are cantaloupes. Green ones are used to make East Indian chutney. They may run from ¼ to 1 lb. Look for plump, fresh fruit, firm and clear in color. Taste before accepting because some mangos may have a turpentine flavor.

Melons

Most melons do not increase in sugar content after picking and should be picked ripe. Flavor sweetness, heavy aroma, color, and softening indicate maturity. Netting with some also indicates ripening. Tasting or plugging is one of the best ways to ascertain quality.

Cantaloupes

Cantaloupes or muskmelons (1968) appear in March as Mexican imports. Peak American production is from July to October, but late varieties can be obtained until November. Buy U.S. Fancy or No. 1. Softness at the blossom end can indicate ripeness. If the stem end scar is smooth and clean, it is called a *full slip;* if the stem is partially attached, it is called a *half slip*. If the stem did not come free but is cut or broken, the melon was green when picked. Early in the season, specify full slip and in warmest weather half slip. There are three stages of full slip: *full slip, hard ripe* showing a yellow-green color outside; *full slip, choice* with more yellow and a slight softening at the blossom end; and *full slip, full ripe,* completely yellow and at full ripeness. California and Arizona produce nearly 70% of the crop. Purchase U.S. No. 1 grade. Preparation waste to EP is 50%.

Packaging depends upon the producing area. The western jumbo crate often is used and holds 18, 23, 27, 36, and 46 cantaloupes. When full it holds net 83 lb. The standard crate holds 27, 36, and 45 melons. A bushel holds between 1½ to 2 dozen and weighs net 60 to 65 lb. Local supplies are marketed in a variety of containers. Purchase by the pound. Cantaloupes

Fig. 2-19. Cantaloupe picked at full-slip stage of maturity shows a stem pulled away from the melon, leaving a clean, cuplike hole. Courtesy USDA

average ¾ to 4 lb. The 45 count in the western jumbo crate weighs 1¼ to 1½ lb, and a half is a good portion. They have a 5 in. diameter.

The rich, salmon-colored flesh varieties are best. These are Hales Best, Bender, and Hearts of Gold. The Bender is produced in greatest quantity and is the best shipper. A heavy aroma, good netting, and a slightly yellowing are indicators of ripeness. Some of the other melons marketed are the Burrell Gem, Tip Top, Netted Gem, and Hackensack. These are mostly eastern melons. The largest quantity of Benders comes from Colorado.

Other Small Melons

The Honeydew melon (1967) is about 6 to 6½ lb in weight and about 6 in. in diameter, with a slightly oblong shape. It has a smooth, greenish-white rind that, at maturity, is a creamy yellow. The best melons show full or half slip. The flesh should be thick, greenish, fine grained, juicy, sweet, and mild in flavor. Softening at the blossom end plus odor may indicate ripeness. American production reaches a peak from July to October and imports usually appear from January to June. Specify U.S. No. 1. Waste is 59% to EP. Watch for decay as pink or black dots on the melon. A sour smell indicates overripeness and spoilage.

The Honey Ball is a slightly netted greenish-white or light yellow melon. Its flesh resembles the Honeydew.

The Persian melon is large running about 7 lb each. The rind is dark green and covered with fine netting. The flesh resembles that of a cantaloupe. The Persian does not slip. Eight to 15 melons are found in a standard crate and 12 to 15 in the jumbo crate. There is one grade, U.S. No. 1. Waste to EP is 50%.

TABLE 2-9
Sizes and Characteristics of Main Melon Varieties

Name	Size and Weight	Characteristics
Honeydew	6 in. diam.; 6 to 6½ lb each	Smooth, waxy, greenish-white rind; creamy white rind when ripe; does not slip; specify U.S. No. 1; sour smell indicates spoilage or overripeness; EP 50%
Honey Ball	Smaller than Honeydew	Similar to Honeydew
Persian	8 in. diam.; 7 lb	Dark green rind; fine netting; does not slip; specify U.S. No. 1; EP is 50%
Cranshaws (Crenshaws)	4 to 8 lb	Smooth rind, little netting and ribbing; specify full or half slip
Casaba	7 to 10 in. diam.; 5 to 8 lb	Rind is rough and deeply furrowed; keeps well until Thanksgiving or later; ripeness indicated by yellow color and blossom end softening
Santa Claus	6 to 8 in. diam.; 12 to 14 in. long	Rind is green with broad bands of slight netting; keeps well; on market until Christmas

Specify Cranshaws as full or half slip. They store well and appear on the market late. The smooth rind is mottled with a gold and green color and has little netting and very little ribbing. It averages 4 to 8 lb and has a sweet flesh, rich and mellow in flavor. The Casaba melon is a late variety with soft, creamy white, sweet, juicy flesh but little aroma. Ripeness is indicated by a yellowish rind and blossom-end softening. The Casaba is 6 to 10 lb with a diameter of 7 to 10 in. The rind appears rough, and it is deeply furrowed. It keeps well and may be on the market in late November.

The Santa Claus melon is another late melon and excellent keeper, and it may be on the market until Christmas. It is oblong, about 6 to 8 in. in diameter, and about 12 to 14 in. long. It has a green rind with broad bands of slight netting and a white or light yellowish-green sweet and juicy flesh.

When purchasing crated melons, require stamps on the crate that indicate crate size, number of melons, and the federal grade.

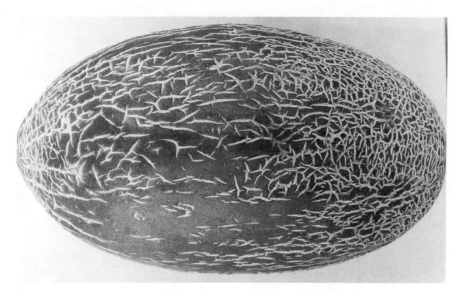

Fig. 2-20. The Santa Claus melon. The fruit is oblong, about 12 by 6 in., and weighs around 6 lb. Rind is green and gold, usually with a trace of netting. Flesh is a light green, with a Casaba flavor. It is a good keeper and may be obtained at times in midwinter. Courtesy USDA

Watermelons. (1954)

Watermelons are marketed from June to September; most come from the southern states. Red and yellow fleshed melons are grown, but the latter is a poor keeper and ships poorly. Melons should be mature. Ripeness is indicated by a firm, symmetrical shape; a fresh and attractive bloom giving a somewhat velvety appearance; and a good color that may vary from a deep, solid green to a gray, according to variety. The bottom should be yellowish in color and the seeds black, not white. A hollow sound on thumping can indicate ripeness. Immature melons have a hard, greenish, unripe appearance, with a white or pale green underside. Overmaturity is indicated by a dull, lifeless appearance and a soft or springy feel when pressure is applied. "White heart," not observable until cut, is a white streak running through the flesh and indicates a poor melon. The wilt-resistant Charleston Gray, which has a pale green rind with a grayish cast and dark green veins, is marketed most heavily. Other varieties are the Cannonball (also called Black Diamond, Black Diamond Yellow Belly, or Blackstone), Congo, and Garrison. Purchase 28-lb melons since these divide best into portions. Waste in preparation to EP is 54%.

SHAPES OF LONG TYPE MELONS

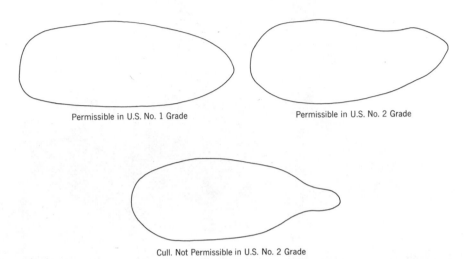

Permissible in U.S. No. 1 Grade   Permissible in U.S. No. 2 Grade

Cull. Not Permissible in U.S. No. 2 Grade

Fig. 2-21. Shapes of watermelons permitted within grades. Courtesy USDA

Fig. 2-22. The Charleston Gray watermelon is resistant to anthracnose fungus and therefore widely grown. Courtesy USDA

Fig. 2-23. Papayas are a tropical fruit commonly seen on some markets because improved transportation and marketing have reduced marketing hazards. Courtesy USDA

Nectarines and Papayas

The nectarine (1966) is not a cross between a peach and plum; it is a smooth-skinned peach that is either Cling or freestone. Its selection therefore should be based on quality factors listed below for peaches. Specify U.S. Fancy or Extra No. 1. Preparation waste to EP is 14%. Papayas or tree melons are spherical to oblong, with a large central cavity packed with seeds. They have a sweet yellowish orange flesh that mellows like cantaloupe flesh does. The average weight is between 1 to 2 lb. Growing areas are Hawaii and Florida; some come from Texas. They usually come in 10-lb flats. There are no federal grades. EP is 67%.

Peaches (1952)

Peaches are quite perishable. They store well at temperatures just above freezing for about 3 weeks. They should be picked just before maturity. The market peak is from July through September, with the yellow or creamy flesh varieties appearing late and the white early. Clings (a variety in which the flesh sticks to the pit) are not used as much as Freestones, which are a softer fruit and require less labor to prepare.

Fig. 2-24. A new technique of dipping ripe fruit such as these peaches into very hot water for a few seconds kills spoilage organisms. The peaches on the left, from the same orchard as those on the right, were not dipped, and the peaches on the right were treated in this manner. Courtesy USDA

Select for plumpness, maturity, freedom from blemishes, and firmness of flesh. Immature peaches have a pale yellow color, may show greenness, and have poor flavor, high acidity, and a hard rubbery flesh. Coloring does not always indicate maturity, but the disappearance of green and the appearance of yellowing with a full flush of pink, plus softening of the flesh, do.

Practices of packaging vary. The Los Angeles lug that holds net about 20 lb (32 to 96 peaches in two layers) is the most common pack. The bushel pack, net from 45 to 48 lb, is used by eastern and midwestern growers. The Carolinas and Georgia use six basket carriers. Approximately 3 to 4 peaches a pound is a common size. Waste in skinning and pitting is 24%.

Cut and examine for flavor and maturity; examine also for worms and decay. Gum exuding from the skin over a tiny mark indicates insect damage. Watch for mold or rot, growth cracks, and bruised fruit. Federal grades are U.S. Fancy, Extra No. 1, No. 1, and No. 2. Purchase may have to be in the higher grades to get acceptable fruit except at peak seasons.

TABLE 2-10
Some Purchasing Characteristics of Common Peaches

Variety	Flesh Color	Size and Shape	On Market	General Characteristics
Elberta	Yellow, red blush	Large, oval	August to September	Good shipper and keeper
Hale	Yellow, red blush	Large, round	August to September	Excellent flavor; excellent shipper and keeper
Halehaven	Yellow, high blush	Medium to large, round	August	Excellent flavor
Golden Jubilee	Yellow, slight blush	Large, oval	August	Juicy; good flavor; bruises easily
Hiley	White	Medium large	August	Excellent flavor; juicy
Cumberland*	White, high blush	Large, bell-shaped	July to August	Excellent flavor, high quality
Carman*	White	Medium to large	August	Good quality

*Semi-clingstone, may for this reason have limited use in institutions because of extra labor and higher waste.

Pears (1955)

Pears, like apples, should be purchased on the basis of size, use, maturity, and grade. Early varieties (Bartletts) come on in the summer and others in the fall and winter. (See Table 2-10.)

Pears are picked at a slightly immature stage since tree-ripened fruit is apt to be coarse and rough appearing. Full ripeness in storage is indicated by coloring specific to the variety and by softness of flesh. The Bartlett becomes yellow, with a red blush indicating ripeness; the d'Anjou turns greenish yellow; and the Bosc turns a yellow brown. Softness at the blossom end is an indication of approaching ripeness. Store at 30 to 32°F but ripen at 60 to 65°F for 3 to 5 days. To ripen, open polyethylene wraps and let air enter.

Pears are marketed in standard pear boxes sized from 70 to 245 a box; the best institutional sizes are 110 to 135 counts. Pears are also marketed in bushel baskets. Paring and coring wastes are 26%. Boxes should weight 45 to 46 lb and bushel baskets just slightly more.

Select pears that are clean, bright, and typically colored for variety. Avoid misshapen, soft, or wrinkled fruit. Watch for scars or damage, and

TABLE 2-11

Characteristics of Common Pear Varieties

Variety	Main Producing Regions	Maturity Season	Size	Color Ripe	Best Use	General Characteristics
d'Anjou	N.Y., Northwest and Southern states	Oct. through Apr.	Large	Creamy Yellow-green	Dessert Canning	Good keeper; good flavor.
Bartlett	N. Eng., N.Y., mid-Atlantic, Great Lakes and Midwest, Northwest and Calif.	Mid-July through mid-October	Large	Yellow, red blush	Dessert Canning	All purpose pear, soft and flavorful; medium keeping quality. Susceptible to blight.
Bosc	Northwest, Calif., N.Y.	Sept. to Jan.	Large	Yellow covered with brown russet	Dessert	Juicy, well-flavored; subject to blight. Good keeper.
Gorham	N. Eng., N.Y., Northwest, Calif.	Aug. to Nov.	Large	Yellow	Dessert Canning	Good all-purpose pear. Resistant to blight.
Hardy	Calif., mid-Atlantic; some in Midwest	July to Dec.	Medium	Green to yellow	Dessert	Good keeping quality.
Du Comice	Northwest and Southern states	Oct. to Mar.	Large	Light greenish-yellow	Dessert	Easily bruised, tender skin; soft flavorful flesh.
Winter Nelis	Northwest and N. Eng.	Oct. to Apr.	Small	Green-yellow with dark brown russet	Dessert	Excellent keeper; soft fine texture; juicy; good flavor.
Seckel	Midwest and Southern States	Oct. to Apr.	Medium	Yellow	Dessert Canning Pickling	Good flavor and quality; watch for grittiness.
Kieffer	N. Eng., N.Y., Mich.	Oct. to Dec.	Medium to large	Yellow	Cooking Canning	Not a good fresh item. Good keeper. Gritty.

Note: The term "blight" as used here means "scald" or "russeting."

insect or worm injury. Pears appearing late in the season may show scald or russeting similar to scald on apples. Some, such as the Kieffer, may be gritty and should be avoided. Summer varieties are highly perishable, but winter ones will hold a long time in proper storage. Winter pears are graded U.S. Extra No. 1, No. 1, and No. 2. Summer pears are graded U.S. No. 1 and No. 2. Purchase U.S. No. 1. Washington state grades Extra Fancy and Fancy are also commonly used. Yield EP is 78%.

Persimmons

The Oriental persimmon is of most commercial importance. It has a rounded apex ending in a black spot and is larger than the southern persimmon. The average is 3 to 4 a pound, and they are usually found in flats holding 11 to 13 lb net. Select those that are well-shaped, plump, smooth, soft, of good color, and have the stem cap attached. Reject those with broken skins. A slight wrinkling may indicate ripeness. There are no federal grades. The EP yield on the Oriental is 79% and on the southern persimmon, with seeds and calyx only removed, it is 82%.

Fig. 2-25. A persimmon and pomegranate are shown here. The persimmon is the pointed fruit in the foreground in the bowl. The cut pomegranate is on the right.

Pineapple (1953)

Fresh pineapple may appear any time, but peak supplies come in April and May. Florida's appear in February and Mexico's from March through June. Hawaii and the Philippines market the best pineapple.

Appearance and odor indicate maturity. Picking must be near maturity since sugar develops in the fruit only during the last 2 weeks before complete ripeness. It should have a distinct orange-yellow color with fully developed waxy, bright eyes or surface squares and a slight whiteness at the base. It should have a distinct pineapple aroma. Easily pulled spires may also indicate ripeness. Immature fruit appears small, is purplish-green in color, and has only partially developed, dull eyes. Plant-ripened fruit is superior in flavor but difficult to ship.

Pineapples should have dry bottoms, firm eyes, and be plump with well-trimmed bases. They should feel heavy for size. Mold first appears at the base and is indicated by a softness and a sour smell. Darkening under the skin can indicate rot. Specify *yellow-ripe,* which indicates firm fruit requiring 3 to 4 days holding to ripen. *Hard-ripe* fruit must be held longer.

Half crates with 9 to 21 pineapples averaging net 35 lb are usual on the market. The best institutional size is 18. Full crates are also found. On U.S. No. 1 fruit the length of the tops "shall not be less than 4 inches nor more than twice the length of the fruit." Crates should plainly state count. Yield EP in flesh is 52%.

Plums and Prunes (1969)

Plums are on the market from May through September with a peak from July to mid-September. Prunes appear in July and reach a peak in August, but they are found until October. The Oregon prune is slightly tart; the California or French or Imperial prune is sweeter. Market packages are crates with 4 to 6 tills with a net of 22 to 29 lb, the Los Angeles lugs holding 20 lb net, or bushel baskets or hampers holding 56 lb net. Plums and prunes may be classified according to color:

Purple or blue:	Italian or French prune; Damson plum.
Red:	Clayman, Climas, Hungarian, Santa Rosa, and Beauty (one of the earliest).
Yellow or green:	Yellow Egg, Beauty, Wickson, Kelsey, and Green Gage.

Mature plums and prunes of good quality are plump, firm, and full colored. Color may not indicate ripeness, but a softening at the tip end may, if the fruit is not bruised. Purchase U.S. Fancy or No. 1. Examine for insect damage; soft, overripe fruit; or rot. Yield after pitting and peeling is 85%.

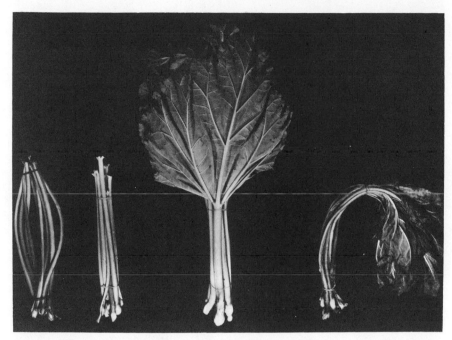

Fig. 2-26. Rhubarb that was wrapped immediately in polyethylene after harvesting is shown in the center; rhubarb that was not wrapped is shown on the two sides. Courtesy USDA

Pomegranates

The pomegranate, known since biblical times, grows on a bush or small tree and is about the size of an orange. It has a thin, leathery skin. Inside is a white pulp encasing seeds, surrounded by a red pulp, which is sweet in flavor, slightly acid, and rich in aroma. The juice is the base for grenadine. It appears from September through December, with a peak in October. Los Angeles lugs, 27 to 28 lb net, are a common pack. Select medium to large fruit, colored pink to bright red, with a thin and tough rind. Open to note plumpness of seeds, which should be tender. The flesh should have a rich, full flavor and good, red color. There are no federal grades. Red pulp yield with seeds is 64%; red pulp yield alone is 56%.

Rhubarb (1966)

Although botanically a vegetable, rhubarb is classified as a fruit because of its use. It may be field or hothouse grown. The latter is more slender, has an

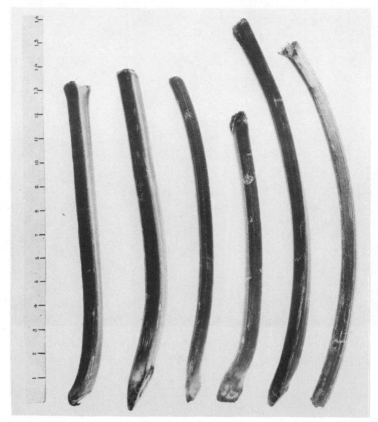

Fig. 2-27. The shapes of stalks of rhubarb permitted in U.S. Fancy and U.S. No. 1.

undeveloped leaf, and frequently is red in color because it grows early when the weather is cold. Cold retards the development of a green color. This red rhubarb, because of its color, is often called *strawberry* rhubarb. Hothouse rhubarb appears from January to mid-May and field rhubarb from April through the summer. Break or puncture it to note stringiness; select firm, fresh, crisp, and tender rhubarb, with good substantial stalks, not weak or shriveled ones. If leaves are still on note them, since size and openness indicate maturity. Michigan packs usually are 5 lb; Washington's are 20-lb lugs. Purchase U.S. Fancy or No. 1. Other grades are Michigan Extra Special Fancy, Extra Fancy, and Fancy, and Washington Extra Fancy and Fancy. U.S. Fancy must be 1 in. or more in diameter and not less than 10 in. long. Stalks without leaves yield EP about 86%.

VEGETABLES

Anise (1973)

Anise is a vegetable bulb that has a flavor resembling a combination of celery and anise seed. It should be marketed full length or cut to not less than 10-in. stalks. Some crates hold 2 to 4 dozen stalks (70 lb net); smaller wire-bound ones hold 2½ to 3 dozen stalks. Purchase by the pound. It is in best supply from October through December. Specify bulbs 2 in. or more in diameter. Purchase U.S. No. 1. Watch for split bulbs, decay, pithy branches, yellow or brown tops, wilt, disease, and insect or mechanical damage, Quality is indicated by fresh, clean, crisp, solid bulbs and stalks and characteristic color. Anise may be confused with sweet fennel, which is eaten in salads or as a boiled vegetable. It has no bulb.

Artichokes

The Jerusalem artichoke is a tuber resembling a potato and is used grated raw for salads, cooked, or pickled. The globe artichoke is the bud of a plant of the thistle family; two varieties are marketed—the Italian or long-head variety and the French or round-head variety. The globe artichoke is marketed in substantial quantities. The Jerusalem artichoke is found only in special markets.

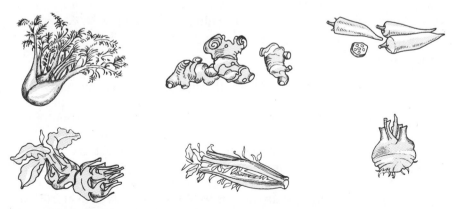

Fig. 2-28. (right to left, top) Anise, Jerusalem artichoke, and okra. (right to left, bottom) Kohlrabi, celery, and celery root. The last is a plant grown especially for its root and is not a part of the celery stalk grown as a green.

TABLE 2-12
Some Market Sizes of Fresh Asparagus

Base Diameter Size in 16's Inch	Number Spears a Pound	Market Grade Terms			
		Federal	New Jersey	California	Imperial Valley
14 or over	7 to 8	Very large	Colossal	Colossal	Mammoth
12 to 14	8 to 9	Very large	Jumbo	Jumbo	Giant
11 to 12	about 9	Large	Extra Select	Extra Select	Fancy Regal
8 to 11	9 to 10	Medium	Extra Fancy	Select	Regal
5 to 8	11 to 12	Small	Fancy	Extra Fancy	Fancy Standard
less than 5*	12 or more	Very small	Prime	Fancy	Standard

*Also called Pencil Grass on some markets.

Quality in the globe (1969) is indicated by compactness of leaves, plumpness, good symmetry, and heaviness for size. The color should be a bright, dark green. They brown with age or injury. Overmaturity is indicated by a dark pink or purple color and an open bud with a fuzzy center and petals spread. The sharp point at the tip becomes hard, thorny, and projecting. Globes are on the market from September to June, with a major peak from November to December and a subpeak from March to May. Size is not related to quality. Flats may contain 4 to 10 dozen. The best institutional size is 6 dozen a box or 3 to 4 a pound. Boxes holding about 40 lb net also are marketed holding 48 to 200 artichokes. Watch for worm holes or rot at the base. Purchase U.S. No. 1. Yield in pulp after cooking is 48%.

Asparagus (1966)

Asparagus appears from early March through June; California markets its second crop in October and November. Select it with about 2 in. of white, woody portion that draws moisture from wet moss on the bottom of the crate. This protects quality. Do not remove it from the crate until ready to use but store under refrigeration. It should have a bright green, fresh-appearing color and close, firm, compact tips that snap or break with ease at or slightly above the white, woody portion. Avoid too much white stem. Specify minimum length stalks of 7½ to 8½ in. and never over 10½ in. Wiry, tough asparagus has a dull, dried, shriveled look, with dark color and open tips. When young some varieties have purplish tips. Some bleached asparagus may be available.

Much western asparagus is placed in pramidal crates with two compartments, each of which hold six 2- to 2½-lb bunches. Others may market in 1, 2-, or 2½-lb bunches or be packed without bunching. Vacuum cooling gives a higher quality than other methods of cooling. The State of Washington's No. 1 grade is the equivalent of U.S. No. 1, and the Washington grades are used more commonly than the federal ones. Size is not a criterion of quality, but U.S. No. 1 asparagus should not be less than ½ in. in diameter at the base, with ²/₃ of the stalk green. Store at 32°F at 85 to 90% relative humdity. Use as soon as possible since it is quite perishable. Yield is 56% EP.

Beans

Lima beans (1938) may be purchased in the pod but are most often purchased fresh in a shelled form. Most institutions find frozen lima beans highly acceptable. There are three kinds: The Fordhook or butter bean, the

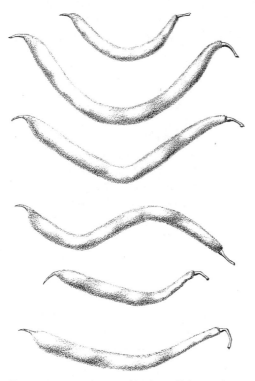

Fig. 2-29. Lower limits of fairly well-formed string beans permitted in U.S. No. 1 grade. Courtesy USDA

Potato or Baby, and the Fava (Faba or English or Windsor) broad bean. Pods are shipped in bushel baskets or hampers. Shelled beans should be plump, with tender skins of a light, whitish-green color. Watch for hard, tough skins and insect injury. Test for tenderness by puncturing the skin. Watch for souring, rot or mold. Purchase U.S. No. 1. Shelling loss is 61%. The peak crop appears from August to September and comes mainly from California.

Snap or common beans (1936) can be either green or wax (cream-colored). Most should not have strings at maturity. Select beans that have a fresh, bright appearance and a velvety touch. They should snap with a distinct, clean break without strings. The flesh texture should be fine and lack fiber in the walls. Look for evenness of maturity and shape, full size, and plump units with few tails. Open and inspect for immature, tender seeds. Length is not important to quality. Reject those having a dull, dead, or wilted appearance or those appearing tough, woody, or stringy. Purchase U.S. Fancy, but U.S. No. 1 can be acceptable at season peaks. State that condition on delivery shall meet the grade specified. Beans are marketed in bushel or hamper containers (30 lb net), in lugs, or in 16- to 24-qt splint basket. All packs should be tightly filled with solid; rounded tops. Trimming waste is 12%.

Beets (1955)

Beets are available all year. Winter beets may come from storage stocks or fresh from Texas or California. Beets may be marketed bunched, with 3 to 5 beets per bunch weighing around 1¼ lb. Crates (75 lb net) holding 5 dozen bunches, bushel basket, or hampers (40 lb net) are common. Late beets are usually marketed topped with not more than 2 in. of stem, although some early beets may be acceptable with 4-to-6-in. stems. Topped beets are usually marketed in 50-lb net bushel baskets or 50- or 100-lb bags. Specify winter beets with *short trim,* which is 2 in. or less of stem; some stem is desirable to prevent bleeding in cooking. Market sizes are:

Bunched		Topped	
Small	less than 2 in. diameter	Small	less than 2 in. diameter
Medium	2 to 3 in. diameter	Medium	2 to 3½ in. diameter
Large	3 in. diameter or more	Large	over 3½ in. diameter

Rough or ridged beets that have deep growth cracks are wasteful and may be tough and woody. A short neck covered with deep scars or the appearance of several circles or leaf scars around the top indicates age. Cut beets with a knife and, if one hears a grating sound or notes pronounced ridges inside, toughness is indicated. Soft, flabby, or shriveled beets lack quality. Note the freshness of leaves, although sometimes wilted leaves do not indicate lack of freshness. Purchase U.S. No. 1. AP to EP cooked is tops, 60%; part tops, 51%; and no tops, 24%. The tops may be cooked if their quality is good.

Broccoli

Broccoli is closely related to cauliflower, and a heading variety of broccoli may be sold as cauliflower. The commonly used Italian sprouting broccoli (1943) is green or slightly purple when young. Heaviest supplies appear from October to April, but some are on the market all year. Quality is indicated by a fresh, clean, deep-green color and compact buds. Wilted, flabby units with yellow leaves should be rejected. Opening of the buds or the development of yellow in them indicate overmaturity. Base trim should be even and excess leaves removed. Watch for cabbage worms and gray plant lice. Shake to see if the buds are firmly attached.

U.S. Fancy broccoli should be bunched in 2- or 2½-lb bunches and have stalks not less than 2¼ in. in diameter at the base and a length not more than 8½ in. nor less than 8 in. Watch for thick stalks and test by puncturing to see if tender. There are no diameter requirements for U.S. No. 1, but lengths should not be less than 5 in. and not more than 9 in. A compact head is required to meet this grade. Some eastern broccoli is marketed in 1½-lb bunches in crates holding 14, 18, or 28 bunches (42 lb net). Bushel baskets or hampers (25 lb net) may contain 14 bunches on the average. Yield from AP to AS is 60%.

Brussels Sprouts (1954)

Brussels sprouts are on the market from August through March, with a peak from October through January. They should be hard and compact, fresh and bright appearing with a good, cabbage-green color. Yellowed or wilted leaves indicate age. A smudgy, dirty appearance under the outer leaves may indicate plant lice. Watch for worm damage.

Western sprouts usually are marketed in 25-lb drums or in polyethylene bags. Eastern sprouts are usually sold in bushel (48 lb net) or half-bushel (24 lb net) baskets. Look for well-trimmed, solid, not burst heads. The base should be free from rot or damage. Uniform, even heads and fill equal to facing should be specified. Specify U.S. No. 1 with diameters not less than ¾ in. and length not more than 2 in.

Fig. 2-30. Well-trimmed and poorly trimme heads of Danish cabbage are illustrated her Courtesy USDA

Cabbage (1945)

Early cabbage appears on the market from December to May. It has a pointed and not too tightly packed head with a conical shape and comparatively smooth leaves. The color is soft green. The Domestic cabbage comes on about the end of the Early cabbage season. It has a flat top, is moderately green in color, and has a smooth, round head that is firm and tightly formed. The leaves are brittle and crisp. It is on the market until fall. Both Domestic and Early cabbage do not keep well.

The Danish cabbage is a late variety that keeps well in storage and ships well. It has a smooth, round, very hard, compact head. The color is almost white, and the leaves are tightly wrapped. Savoy cabbage is marketed from October through December. It has crinkled leaves, with heads loosely formed and usually flattened. The color is yellowish-green. Red cabbage has a pointed head and is purple-red in color. It is usually smaller than the white varieties. Chinese cabbage or celery has a long tapering head, with crinkly leaf ends on a solid core. It is about 4 in. thick and 18 to 20 in. long. It is used mostly for salads.

Fig. 2-31. The lower limit of reasonable solidity for U.S. No. 1 Domestic cabbage. To be U.S. No. 1 Grade, heads shall be at least fairly firm. Courtesy USDA

Cabbage is marketed in many containers. Purchase by the pound. A struck bushel will weigh around 40 lb net. Mesh sacks usually contain 50 lb. Head sizes may be specified as small, medium, or large. For Early cabbage this means, respecitvely, under 1½ lb, 1½ to 3 lb (best institutional size), and over 3 lb; for Domestic and Danish, respecitvely, under 2 lb, 2 to 5 lb

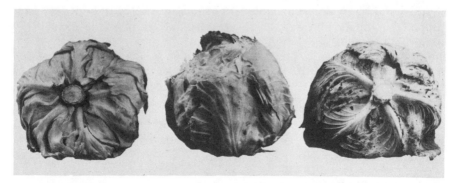

Fig. 2-32. The head on the left is overripe, as indicated by base leaves separating from the stem. The center head shows the seed stem breaking through the crown. Where this breaking does not occur, a bulge with excessive hardness may indicate that the seed stem is buried there. The head on the right shows bad worm injury. None of these heads are U.S. No. 1. Courtesy USDA

(best institutional size), and over 5 lb. Trimming in Early and Domestic cabbage is not as close as in the late varieties. A close trim must be given Danish to meet top grades.

Watch for worms, decay, yellowing of leaves, and broken or burst heads. Rub the stem end to see if it is dry. Look for crispness in leaves. The color should be typical, the head heavy for its size, and solid for the variety. Yellow or wilted leaves indicate age. Look for seed stems inside the head that can be detected by pressing on the head and feeling a hard, resistant core inside. Burst heads should be rejected. Note also broken sections around the stem base. Excessive softness indicates poor quality and high waste. Purchase U.S. No. 1. Waste in trimming and removing cores is 20% except for Chinese cabbage, which will be 38%.

Carrots (Bunched 1954, Topped 1965)

Today most institutions use fresh-grown and not storage carrots. Fresh-grown keep sufficiently long for institutional purposes but not for winter storage. The fresh-grown have a superior flavor and texture.

Like beets, carrots are marketed with tops, short-trim tops, or well-trimmed tops. Institutions should purchase fresh-grown carrots with tops cut back less than 1 in. Well-trimmed carrots should have stems not over 1 in. long, short-trim not over 4 in. long, and carrots with tops may have tops 12 to 20 in. long. "Snap top" means broken close to the carrot. "Clip top" means 2 to 3 in. of stem. Carrots should not be less than 3 in. in length and of the blunt-end type, not tapering since these have a high peeling waste. All carrots should be close to the same diameter, not less than ¾ in. nor more than 2 in. at the widest end. They are usually marketed in bunches if not topped, but topped may be in 25-, 50-, or 100-lb bags, or bushel baskets (50 lb net), or crates holding 55 to 60 lb.

California, Arizona, and Texas carrots, which are sweeter than many locally grown varieties, are light in color. Watch for flabby, wilted, soft, or shriveled carrots. Excessively thick masses of leaf stem at the top indicate large cores or hearts and toughness. A fresh appearance, smoothness, and good shape should be sought. The carrots should break with a crisp snap when bent. Loss in paring is: with tops, 41%; part tops, 28%; no tops, 20%. Purchase U.S. Extra No. 1 or 'U.S. No. 1.

Cauliflower (1968)

Cauliflower is on the market all year, but it peaks from October through December. Size has no relation to quality. Quality is indicated by white or creamy white, clean, heavy, firm, compact curd, with the jacket (outer leaves) fresh and green. The leaves should be trimmed within 1 to 2 in. from the curd. Spreading of the curd into a loose mass called *riciness, fuzzy, barber,* or *old man* indicates age. Brushing the hand over the top and getting a sensation of roughness indicates these qualities. Higher yields are usually obtained from larger heads. Good, fresh wrapper leaves may be used for chopped greens. Age is indicated by yellow leaves, but, if the head is white and firm, quality may still be good. Watch for plant lice, which appear as smudgy, dirty spots on the cauliflower. Spotted, speckled, or bruised curds should be rejected. Cauliflower is usually in western pony crates (net 42 lb) holding 12 to 15 heads. Purchase U.S. No. 1, which should not be less than 4 in. in diameter. Waste in trimming and preparation to EP is 65%.

Celery and Celeriac (1959)

Most celery marketed today is the green or Pascal type. It has crisp, juicy stalks and heavy strings or midribs. The white (blanched) or yellow (golden) celery is grown hilled or covered with dirt to bleach the stalk. It is tenderer and more delicately flavored but less in demand. Celery is on the market all year, with a peak from November through May.

In Pascal celery, select clean, brittle, 12-to-14 in. stalks with green leaves. that are well trimmed and have good thickness and solidity. The stalks should be fairly straight and not twisted, with good heart formation, solid and not spongy. Twist or press to note pithiness. Stalks 1 to 1¾ lb are best for institutional use; the outer whorl of branches should not be less than 6 in., which insures a good stalk. "Green" in a specification means that the outer branches should be green or a light-green color. Separate the branches and examine the heart for blackrot or formation of seed stems. Look for insect injury or insects. Bowing is a defect. To ascertain crispness, bend until the stalk snaps. Excessive stringiness is undesirable. Reject excessively dirty celery. Wilted or yellow leaves indicate age.

Celery is usually well trimmed or clipped, with the outer branches removed and sized. In the standard 16-in. crate (60 to 65 lb net) the lowest number of bunches is a dozen; sizes of 10 dozen or more are called *hearts*. The most suitable size is 2½ to 4 dozen. Many different containers are used, and buyers should ascertain market practices. Purchase by the pound, if possible. Specify U.S. Extra No. 1 or U.S. No. 1. The consumer U.S. Grade A is equal to U.S. No. 1, but the trimming provisions are more stringent in the former. Waste in untrimmed stalks AP is 25%.

Celery roots or knobs usually are celeriac, the turnip-rooted celery that forms a large bulb under the surface. It is seldom eaten raw but is used for soups and stews. It is 2½ to 4 in. in diameter and is a creamy white. It is marketed mostly in bushel baskets (45 to 50 lb net).

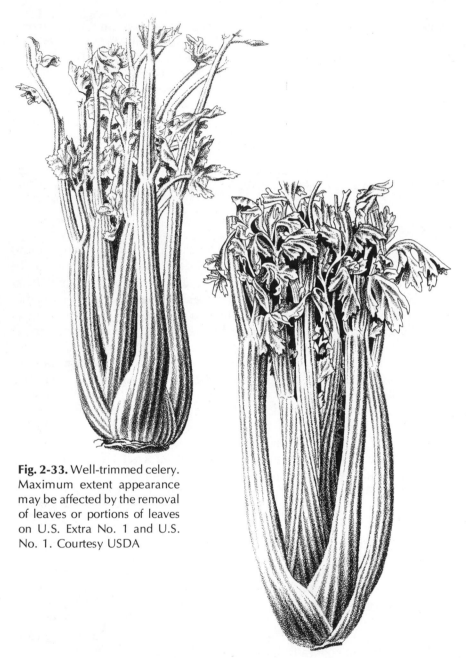

Fig. 2-33. Well-trimmed celery. Maximum extent appearance may be affected by the removal of leaves or portions of leaves on U.S. Extra No. 1 and U.S. No. 1. Courtesy USDA

Fig. 2-34. The lower limit of bowing and twisting allowed in U.S. Extra No. 1 celery. Courtesy USDA

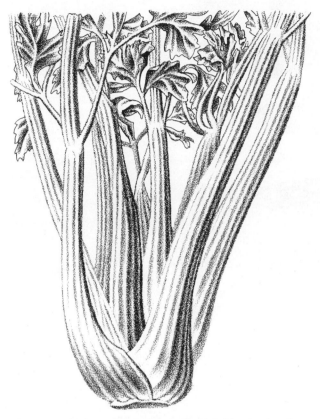

Fig. 2-35. The lower limit allowed in U.S. No. 1 celery in compactness. The condition shown here would be called fairly compact. Courtesy USDA

Corn (1954)

Fresh corn is on the market all year, but it may vary so much in quality that institutions are advised to purchase good quality frozen ears. Shipment is usually in 50-lb bags holding 5 dozen fresh ears. Specify U.S. No. 1 at the season's height and U.S. Fancy at other times. Note tassels or silks, which should be brown and not green. Look for fresh appearing husks that are not dry, and freedom from worm or other damage. Specify *sweet* corn to avoid getting field corn; the term ''roasting ears'' may mean immature field corn that is lacking in quality.

Cucumbers (1958)

There are two peaks in the cucumber market; the heaviest is from August to

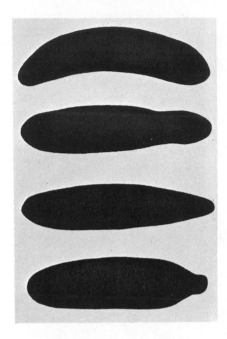

Fig. 2-36. Minimum cucumber shapes permitted in U.S. No. 1 Grade. Courtesy USDA

October, with another from April through June. Hothouse cucumbers are shipped off-season. Market containers vary, but the most common are the bushel basket or hamper or boxes containing about 2 dozen cucumbers (48 lb net). Fill should be equal to facing.

Quality is indicated by a fresh appearance, crispness, good shape, medium size, and dark-green color over at least $^2/_3$ the length, with a shiny, waxy appearance. Withered or shriveled cucumbers have a tough or rubbery flesh and a bitter flavor. Watch for good, even shape. Overmaturity is indicated by a dull-green or yellowish-green color, yellow underside, and a puffy, soft texture. Seeds should be tender in an almost translucent center that is firm, not jellylike. Decay shows as dark, sunken, irregular areas.

Grade and size are correlated. A U.S. Fancy and U.S. No. 1 cucumber must not be more than 2⅜ in. in diameter and not more than 6 in. in length. Hothouse cucumbers in this grade have no diameter restrictions but may not be less than 5 in. in length. Institutions should specify market type or slicing cucumbers to avoid obtaining pickling types in some markets. Specify U.S. No. 1 large and in off-season, U.S. Fancy.

Eggplant (1953)

A peak for eggplant occurs from August through September, with some

Fig. 2-37. Quality is indicated in eggplant by firm flesh, a soft sheen, and a well-filled, plump character. Courtesy USDA

supplies available all year. A mature eggplant of good quality has a diameter of 4 in. or more. The color is uniformly dark purple with a soft, silky sheen. The body is heavy, plump, and free from blemishes. Wilting, shriveling, softness, or flabbiness may result from extended holding or immaturity. Watch for worm injury. Eggplant is marketed in bushel baskets (33 lb net) or crates holding 16, 18, 24, 30, or 36 eggplant. The 24 or 30 size are best for institutions. Specify U.S. No. 1.

Garlic (1944)

Garlic may be pink or white. Creole garlic, a white, is strong in flavor. Tahiti, another white garlic, is milder and has large, good sized cloves measuring as a bulb about 2 to 3 in. in diameter. Italian garlic, which is pink, has a pungent flavor and many cloves, making it costly to prepare. Specify U.S. No. 1, which has a minimum diameter bulb of not less than 1½ in. Purchase by the pound. Preparation to EP is 12%.

Greens, Cooking

There are a number of plant leaves that are cooked. Immature leaves are tender but lack sufficient body to give good yield and eating quality. Look for fresh, tender leaves that are bright in color without yellowing, wilt, toughness, coarseness, stringiness, or insect or worm damage. Bruised, broken, or frozen leaves tarnish quickly. Slime and mold indicate severe deterioration. The stalks should be fresh and crisp and snap when bent. Watch for grit, dirt, sand, and extraneous matter. A bushel of dry greens weighs 18 to 20 lb net. Purchase by the pound.

Fig. 2-38. Some cooking greens:

Fig. 2-38a. Curled kale.

Fig. 2-38b. Stem lettuce.

Fig. 2-38c. Collards.

Beet greens are young beet tops marketed in hampers or bushel baskets. Federal beet standards can be used if tiny beets are desired on the greens. State that greens should be of high quality, not longer than 6½ in., with the beets not over ⅝ in. in diameter. Specify U.S. No. 1. Waste in preparation to EP is 44%. The peak season is spring.

Swiss chard is a beet grown for its leaves. The peak seasons are fall and winter. Pithiness or toughness is detected by twisting the stalk. It is shipped in crates, boxes, or bushels. There are no federal grades. Waste in trimming to EP is 30%.

Collards (1953) are greens closely associated with kale. They have curled leaves lightly folded at the heart. Peak quantities come in the fall; the best flavor occurs after a frost. (A type of broccoli is sometimes marketed as collards or turnip greens.) Specify U.S. No. 1. Waste to EP is 23%.

Dandelion greens (1955) are best in the spring. Specify U.S. No. 1. Waste to EP is 19%. They also can be used for salads.

Kale or borecole (1934) is related to the collard and cabbage. There are two types:(1) Scotch, green, Liberian, or blue kale, which has curly or krinkly leaves; and (2) spring, a smooth-leaved variety. Purchase washed

Fig. 2-38d. Sorrel. The last also can be used as a salad green. Courtesy USDA

as a whole plant, bunched and stripped. Bronzing or browning caused by cold weather during growing does not harm flavor but does harm appearance. If purchased by weight, be sure ice as packing is not sold for the price of kale. Well-packed kale weighs 20 to 25 lb net a bushel. Specify U.S. No. 1. Waste to EP is 30%.

Young, tender mustard green leaves also may be used as salad greens. There are several varieties, some of which are smooth, whereas others are curly. Color ranges from a light to dark green. Seed stems indicate age and toughness. Purchase U.S. No. 1. Preparation waste to EP is 30%.

Turnip greens are federally graded under mustard green standards (1953). If turnip greens are sold with roots, the maximum diameter of the root should be limited to 1½ in. Specify U.S. No. 1.

Spinach (1949) is on the market all year, but the production peak is from March to June. The Savoy variety usually is shipped because its crinkly leaves prevent packing and preserve quality, which the smooth-leaved varieties do not. Sprouts, buds, or crowns, may indicate poor quality and texture. Select U.S. No. 1 or U.S. Extra No. 1 when quality is undesirable in U.S. No. 1. The consumer U.S. Grade A equals U.S. Extra No. 1.

Greens, Salad

Plant leaves for salads should be selected on the basis of factors used for cooking greens. Good solidity or firmness of head is desirable. Raw

Fig. 2-39. Some of our most common salad greens:

Fig. 2-39a. Grand Rapids leaf lettuce,

Fig. 2-39b. Salad Bowl leaf lettuce,

Fig. 2-39c. Parsley leaf lettuce,

Fig. 2-39d. Butter or smooth-leaved lettuce,

spinach, cabbage, turnip greens, and others previously discussed may also be used for salads.

Chicory, endive, and escarole (1964) are often confused. A chicory root that is cooked is also on the market, adding to the confusion. Salad chicory

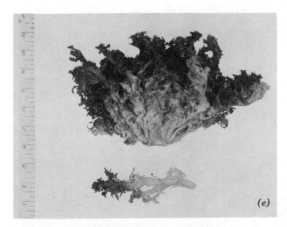

Fig. 2-39e. Curly-leaved endive, and

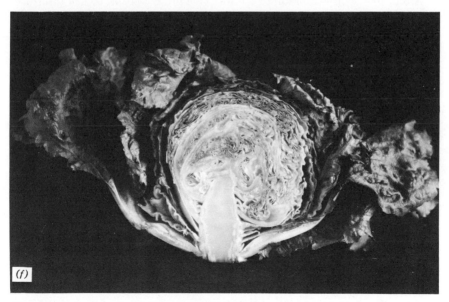

Fig. 2-39f. a cut head of Iceberg (crisp) lettuce showing good head solidity. Courtesy USDA

is a broad-leaved green with an upright, spreading growth. Endive may be called *curly chicory*. It is a flat, spreading plant with an almost white heart. The outer areas are green, but the spine or center is white. The leaves are narrow, finely divided, and curly. It may be 12 to 13 in. in diameter. Some varieties have broad ribs that are slightly rose-tinted and creamy white at the heart. It is marketed mostly from fall into spring. Escarole resembles endive or curly chicory but has a flat, spreading set of leaves with an almost white heart. The spine is white and the outer areas are green, but a deeper green than endive. The leaf is also broader. Escarole is available almost the year around, but its peak is in December about the same time as that of endives. French or Belgium chicory, endive, or Whitloof chicory is a slender, solid, small green-tipped white stalk on the market mostly in the winter. It is slightly bitter, like broad-leaved chicory. Its leaves are tightly folded around a core or heart to form a solid, elongated head.

Federal grades for chicory, endive, and escarole are the same. Use U.S. No. 1. No federal grades exist for French or Belgium endive. Crispness, freshness, cleanliness, and bright appearance are selection factors. Toughness or tenderness can be determined by breaking or twisting a leaf. Packs vary considerably. A bushel will weigh about 25 lb. Buy by the pound, if possible, or specify minimum container weights. Spread to see interiors. Select those free of rot and damage, and those that are fresh and bright appearing. Waste in trimming to EP is 25%.

Lettuce (1970) may be of several varieties. The most popular is Iceberg, which is crisp. Other varieties are Butterhead, Bibb, Cos or Romaine, leaf (bunching) or stem.

Eastern-grown Iceberg is usually pointed; western-grown lettuce is rounder, with a flatter head. In both, the outer leaves are pale, with the interior crisp, white, and tender. Peak production is from May through July. Local lettuce appears in the late spring, summer, and fall, but in the winter the big shippers are:

Salinas Valley, California (the biggest)	May through October
Imperial Valley, California	December through April
Other California shippers	Winter and spring
Salt River, Arizona	December through March
Yuma, Arizona	Fall through spring
Herford (Yvalde), Texas	September through October
Lower Rio Grande, Texas	December through February

Iceberg is an excellent shipper and good keeper. It is best vacuum-cooled and packed closely trimmed, 2 to 2½ dozen heads per fiberboard carton, not less than 40 lb. A carton can hold as many as 5 dozen heads.

The Boston (Butterhead) lettuce is a softer-headed variety, with leaves of fine, soft texture, oily to the touch, and very tender. It is greener than Iceberg lettuce, with a yellow-white inner leaf. Bibb or Limestone is a

Fig. 2-40. The three most common head types of lettuce used on the market: (left) Butter (soft or smooth-leaved), (front center) Iceberg (crisp), and (right) Cos lettuce or Romaine. Courtesy USDA

butterhead type lettuce. The small heads are cup shaped and about twice the size of a tulip. They have a deep, rich, green outer leaf that blends into white at the core. They are crisper than Butterhead.

Leaf or garden (bunched) lettuce (1964) is not headed but often comes cut in bunches, with the main stem attached or bunched in leaves. The leaf is curly or smooth, depending upon variety, and the color may be a pale green or a leaf touched with rusted red. It is not as durable as head lettuce and cannot be shipped far. It appears as U.S. Fancy hothouse lettuce in plentiful supply in the winter and available from local sources in the summer.

Stem lettuce is grown for its stems and not for its leaves. The stems are eaten raw or cooked.

Cos or Romaine (1960) is a cylindrical, elongated-headed lettuce with a coarse, stiff leaf and a slightly stronger but somewhat sweeter flavor than Iceberg. It is quite crisp and almost completely green. It is shipped in $^2/_3$

Fig. 2-41. Well-trimmed heads of Cos or Romaine. Courtesy USDA

crates from California and holds 2 dozen heads, or approximately a bushel. It is the green used in Caesar salad. Purchase U.S. No. 1.

Bibb and leaf lettuce from Michigan appear in 24-basket crates (10 lb net) or 12-qt basket crates holding half this. Many eastern crates hold 18 to 24 heads. Boston or Bibb is packed in 1 or 1½ bushel hampers or in crates holding 18 to 36 heads. A 4-dozen pack in a standard crate weighs 45 lb net. Iceberg in standard cartons can weigh from 40 to 50 lb. Specify minimum container weight. Purchase U.S. Fancy or No. 1 for headed lettuce and U.S. Fancy for greenhouse leaf lettuce. U.S. Fancy headed lettuce must be loaded with a core temperature of 35°F not over 6 hours from the time it was picked.

Look for rot, decay, tip burn, ragged leaves, or excess wrapper leaves and small heads. The color should be bright and fresh. It should be clean. Seeds stems developing in heads can be distinguished by pressing down and and feeling the hard core inside. Soft rot inside is difficult to detect. A distinct reddish tinge or rust on broken surfaces indicates age or excessive storage. The butt or stems should be small and light in color, either white or a light pink. Deep red indicates age and bitterness. Watch for aphis, freezing, and sunburn.

"Fairly well headed" applied to Romaine means that four or more inner leaves overlap each other at the top of the plant. "Well trimmed" applied to all lettuce means that there are no more than three wrapper leaves, none of which are excessively large or coarse. For lettuce cups, select less firm heads or use leaf lettuce. Endive (curly chicory) and escarole also make good salad underliners.

Watercress is a garnish as well as a salad green. It is available all year, but it is best in the spring through July. Select fresh, bright, green, crisp, and clean cress. Watch for worms and insects, yellowing of leaves, or wilting.

Fig. 2-42. Kohlrabi is a turnip-like bulb that grows above the ground. Courtesy USDA

A bunch usually weighs 3 to 5 oz. A large bunch may weigh 2½ lb. It is usually marketed in 10-dozen bunches to a box (30 lb net). Barrels may be shipped holding 25 to 30 dozen large bunches. There are no federal standards. Loss in preparation to EP is 8%.

Kohlrabi (Cabbage Turnip)

Kohlrabi means "delicate cabbage turnip"; it is a bulb or swollen stem growing above the ground. Specify bulbs 2 to 3 in. in diameter and reject those not meeting this size. The stem should be crisp and firm. Cut and note any stringiness or woodiness. Purchase by the pound or in bushels specifying a minimum weight. There are no U.S. grades. The peak is in June and July. Waste to EP after paring is 45%.

Leeks

Leeks resemble green onions but are larger. They also have flat leaves. They do not form enlarged bulbs at the root end but, like shallots, have a straight end with little or no rounded bulb development. Look for fresh green tops and medium-sized necks. The root end and top should be crisp and tender. A white color should appear up to 2 to 3 in. from the root. Root diameter should not be under ¾ in. If bruised, wilted, yellowed, or otherwise damaged, flabby, tough, or fibrous, the leeks will lack quality. Puncture with a thumbnail to ascertain tenderness. Watch for silt and grit. The market peak is from September through November, with some supplies available all year. There are usually 12 to 25 leeks to a bunch, and they are placed into bushel baskets or hampers holding 24 to 30 lb net. There are no federal grades. Loss to EP is 48%.

Mushrooms (1966)

Mushrooms are white or brown and are sold by the pound in 2-qt baskets. The caps should be firm and closed at the stem, with the veil joining the cap unbroken, leaving the gills unexposed. Stems should be closely trimmed

Fig. 2-43. Mushrooms are grown in heavily fertilized soil where there is a great deal of humus, good moisture, cool temperatures, and little light. Poor ventilation caused the higher and less desirable growth in the lower group compared with the upper group, which had proper growing conditions. Courtesy USDA

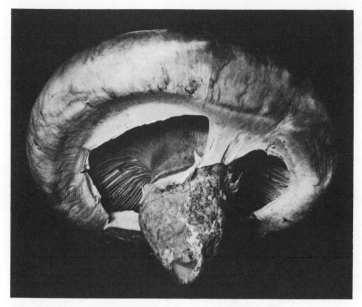

Fig. 2-44. This is a well-shaped mushroom, except that it has a broken veil. Courtesy USDA

and not over 1¼ in. in length. Cap diameter sizes are: Small, up to 1⅝ in.; and Large, 1⅝ in. or more. Watch for misshapen, dark mushrooms, bruising, mold, or other defects. The cut surface of stems should be clear and light, not dark or black, which indicates age. Peak season is from November through December, with a low point in August, but markets usually have them all year. Select U.S. No. 1, about 20 to 30 medium-sized mushrooms to a pound. Trim to EP, unpeeled, is 9%. Cook and freeze to hold for long periods.

Okra (Gumbo) (1928)

Green okra is more common on the market than white okra. There are long and short varieties. Peak harvest is from July through October. Select pods 2 to 3½ in. long. Look for tender, crisp pods with soft, white seeds. A woody pod with hardened seeds indicates overmaturity; dry, dull, or shriveled pods are apt to be tough. Misshapen pods, damage, or decay can be cause for rejection. Watch for dirty pods, foreign matter, disease, insects, or mechanical damage. About 35 3-in. pods make a pound. Containers vary in weight on the market. Specify U.S. No. 1. Loss to EP is 22%.

Fig. 2-45. Mature okra pods ready for harvest. Courtesy USDA

Onions

Green onions (1947) are young onions that lack bulb development in the top grades and sometimes in the lower grades. A scallion is a very young green onion. Green shallots (1946) are similar to young onions but grow in clusters as garlic does. Shallots are milder in flavor than onions. In all three, look for fresh, green tops and medium-sized necks. From 2 to 3 in. of the root should be clean, clear white, full, plump, and tender. Ascertain crispness and tenderness by twisting and puncturing with a thumbnail. Yellow, bruised, or wilted leaves indicate deterioration.

"Clipped tops" means all tops clipped back evenly; "trimmed" means some of the top cut away. Onions and shallots are sold 20 to 48 massed (10 to 12 onions per bunch) in a crate; 12 bunches should weigh 4 lb or over. U.S. No. 1 green onion standards state that the overall length of untrimmed bunches shall not be over 24 in. nor under 8 in. and no less than ¼ in. nor over 1 in. in diameter. The terms *"small," "medium,"* and *"large,"* respectively, indicate less than ½ in. in diameter, ½ to 1 in. in diameter, and over 1 in. in diameter. Green onions and shallots are available all year, but the peak is from May through August. Loss to EP is 65%.

Dry onions are our fifth largest vegetable crop. There are many varieties, each of which can be selected for a special production use. The early

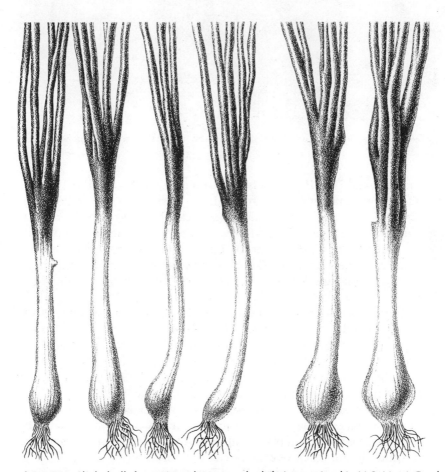

Fig. 2-46a. Slight bulb formation (shown on the left) is permitted in U.S. No. 1 Grades for green onions. Bulb formation called *not excessive* is permitted in U.S. No. 2 Grade (shown on the right). Desirable bulb formation is in the center. Courtesy USDA

Fig. 2-46b. Leeks, onions, chives, and shallots shown from left to right. Courtesy USDA

varieties are mild. The Bermuda is a flat, mild onion about 2½ to 2¾ in. in diameter, on the market from March to June. There are white, yellow, and red varieties. The mild Sweet Spanish (also called *Spanish* or *Valencia*) is large and sweet. It has a round-to-oval shape and comes in yellow and white varieties. The Early Grano or Barbosa is a yellow onion, mild in flavor and fairly new on the market. It has a pear shape and is fairly large. These mild onions are not good keepers, so stocks should be limited to several weeks' needs.

The Globe (Northern or Domestic) onion, somewhat pungent, is the most commercially important onion. The yellow variety is most common, but there are also red, white, and brown Globes. The white varieties are considered the mildest. They are excellent keepers and furnish a large part of the winter supply. They are also lower in cost. The Australian Brown, stronger than the Globe, and the Ebenezer (also pungent) are frequently on the markets. Creole (1943) onions are somewhat pungent. Yellow Creoles may turn pink on cooking, and this is cause for down-grading as a defect. The red variety is seen most often. All these more pungent onions are good keepers; but do not stock over a month's supply.

Onions are marketed all year. There are three peak periods: April and May, June and July, and August to March; the last period is dominated by Globes, which make up about 70% of the total market supply. Dry shallots

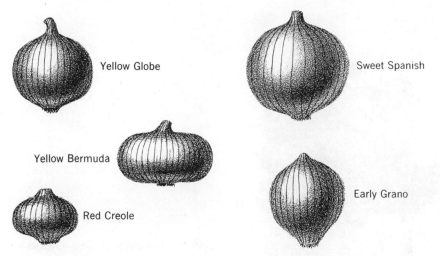

Fig. 2-47. Outlines of some of the most commercially important onions on the market. Optimum shape is shown.

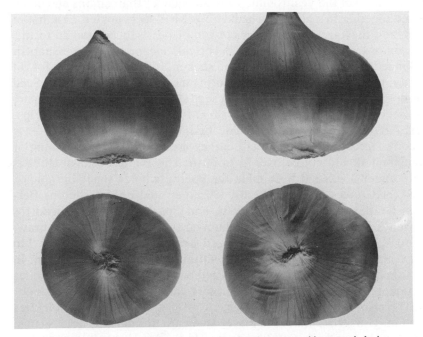

Fig. 2-48. The two views of the same onion on the top and bottom left show approximately the lower limit for shape in U.S. No. 1. The two views on the right, top and bottom, show a shape that put the onion into U.S. Commercial grade. Courtesy USDA

Fig. 2-49. Curly-leaved parsley. Courtesy W. Atlee Burpee Co.

are on the market the year round. They are smaller than onions and come bunched together in a cluster. The flavor of shallots is milder than that of onions, and they are preferred for cooked dishes, sauces, and so forth.

Dry onions and shallots should be bright, clean, hard, well-shaped, dry-skinned, and give a dry rattle when shaken. If they do not, look for rot or decay; look for interior decay by noting moist stems at the neck. Seed stems or coarse interiors resulting from seed stem growth cause high waste. These seed stem onions are called *seeders* in the trade. Watch for thrips, molds, fungus growths, and mechanical damage.

Specify size by diameter. Small onions are desirable for creaming or pickling and should not be over ½ to ¾ in. The White Portugal globe is usually under 1 in. and is suitable for boiling whole; small Bermudas, Globes, or Creoles also may be used. Large, mild onions such as Bermudas, Granex, Early Granos (1960), and Spanish are used sliced for sandwiches and salads, whereas medium sizes are suitable chopped raw. Bermudas, Granex, and Granos are sized small, 1 to 2¼ in.; medium, 2 to 3¼ in.; and large, 3 in. or more, with not more than 10% over 3½ in. In standard packs, other dry onions are sized brown, yellow, or red varieties 40% or more not less than 1½ in. and white varieties 30% or more 2 in. or over. U.S. No. 1 Boilers shall be from 1 to 1⅞ in. and U.S. No. 1 Picklers under 1 in. U.S. No. 2 onions in these same varieties must be not less than 1½ in. Creole standards (1943) state that U.S. No. 1's shall "not be less than 1¾ in. and No. 2's shall not be less than 1½ in." No. 2's are usually used for chopping. Onions are sold in 25-, 50-, or 100-lb mesh bags or plastic

Fig. 2-50. Minimum shapes permissible in U.S. No. 1 grade parsnips. Courtesy USDA

wraps. Some appear in 50-lb crates. A bushel holds 56 lb. Waste to EP is 10%.

Parsley (1930)

Curly-leaf parsley is purchased far more than the smooth-leaved type. U.S. No. 1 should be bright, green, fresh, free from dirt and yellowed leaves, and have a delicate, spicy fragrance. Watch for wilting, rot, or bruising. Dark green or browned parsley indicates age and a strong flavor. A bunch equals about 2 oz, and it usually comes 4 dozen bunches to a crate. A Hamburg parsley is a root vegetable, resembling a turnip.

Parsnips (1954)

Parsnips are sweetest and best when left in the ground until after a hard frost. Holding them for two weeks at low refrigerated temperatures also develops good sugar. Peaks are from October through January, but they are on the market throughout the year in small supply.

Select smooth, firm, small-to-medium-sized roots, with good, typical shape and a clear, creamy color. Softness or shriveling may indicate decay and flabbiness. Watch for pithy or fibrous roots. Large parsnips are apt to have woody cores. Reject those that are misshapen. The root should be straight. Four medium ones equal a pound. Select U.S. No. 1. They are marketed in bags or bushel baskets.

Peas (1942)

In institutions, frozen peas have largely replaced fresh peas, which take too much labor to be used. Fresh peas also rapidly lose quality. Peak production is from May through August. A bushel tub weighs 28 to 30 lb. net. Loss to EP is about 60%.

A Chinese pea, quite immature, is used as a pod. They are expensive and are bought frozen, not fresh, for institutional use. Southern black-eyed peas also are purchased fresh in the pod or shelled. Purchase on the same basis as listed for lima beans.

Green Peppers (1963)

The bell and the bullnose are two popular sweet green peppers; hot-type

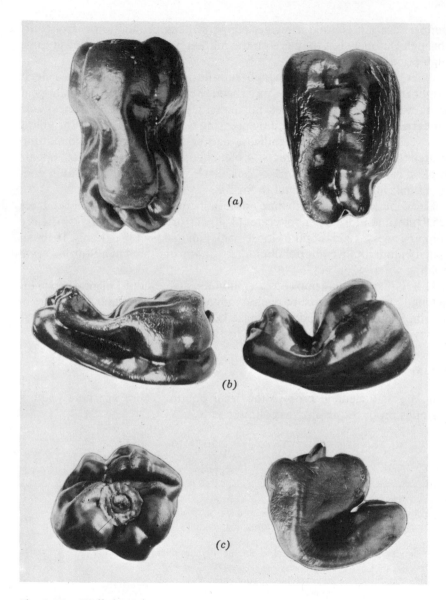

Fig. 2-51a. Well-shaped,

Fig. 2-51b. fairly well-shaped, and

Fig. 2-51c. badly misshapen peppers. The slight wrinkling noted in some may exist because the pepper is picked at an immature stage. Courtesy USDA

peppers are not classed as sweet peppers. Peak production is from July through October, but they are on the market all year, sometimes at quite high prices.

Select soft, pliable, good-shaped, thin-fleshed peppers that have a clear, bright green color and a soft, waxy sheen. Some bronze or red may appear as they mature, but this does not indicate a hot flavor. Crispness and tenderness may be determined by pressing with the thumbnail. Shriveling or excessive softness may indicate age or harvesting when immature. Watch for deformities or defects. A bleached, discolored area that appears sunken or resembles a water-soaked blister indicates decay. Watch container fill; fill should be equal to facing.

Local markets may sell in many different containers, but bushel baskets (25 lb net) and Florida pepper crates (34 lb net) are most often used in heavy shipping areas. Lack of fill or loose pack can make a bushel only 18 lb, so specify minimum weight per container. California ships in a Sturdee crate holding about 42 lb net.

U.S. Fancy peppers must have a minimum diameter of 3 in. and be 3½ in. in length; U.S. No. 1 must be a minimum of 2½ in. in diameter and 2½ in. in length. Shape affects grade. Purchase U.S. No. 1 at peak season and U.S. Fancy when supply is down. Loss to EP is 18%.

Potatoes (1972)

Our largest vegetable crop is the Irish potato. There are nine leading varieties produced mainly as follows:

Type	Description	Growing Area
Round White		
Katahdin	Large, short, medium thick; shallow eyes	East
Chippewa	Large, elliptical to oblong, medium thick; shallow eyes	Mainly N.Y.
Kennebec	Large, elliptical to oblong, medium thick; shallow eyes	East
Irish Cobbler	Medium to large, blunt ends; shallow to deep eyes	Midwest
Round Red		
Triumph	Medium to large, round, thick; medium deep eyes	Midwest
Red Pontiac	Large, oblong to round, smooth or at times netted; medium deep eyes	East and Midwest
Long White		
White Rose	Large, long, oval, flattened; numerous medium deep eyes	Largely California

Type	Description	Growing Area
Long Russet		
Russet Burbank	Large, long, oval, heavily netted, numerous shallow eyes	West
Aranac	Large, roundish oblong; medium deep eyes (a newly developed potato)	Midwest

The moisture and starch content of potatoes largely determines their best use. A moist, slightly waxy potato is suitable for boiling, hash browns, or potato salad, but a dry, mealy potato is desirable for deep-frying, mashing, or baking. Age or maturity, variety, and growing conditions affect the moisture and starch content of potatoes.

New potatoes (immature) have a high moisture and sugar content and a lower starch content, giving them a waxy, moist texture when cooked. Mature potatoes are drier and have a higher starch content. It is difficult to obtain good mashed or French-fried potatoes from a new potato. They are

Fig. 2-52. A USDA inspector checks potatoes for inside black rot. New electronic devices now can detect this defect with light waves. The defect results from holding potatoes too long at too low a temperature. Courtesy USDA

Fig. 2-53. Main potato varieties:

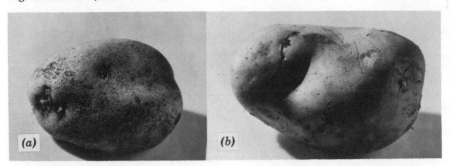

Fig. 2-53a. Superior,   **Fig. 2-53b.** Katahdin,

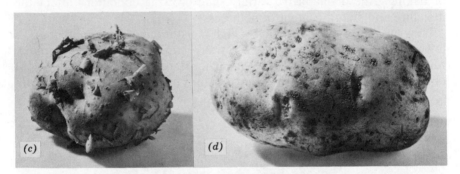

Fig. 2-53c. immature Cobbler,   **Fig. 2-53d.** Kenwick,

Fig. 2-53e. Russet,

Fig. 2-53f. mature Irish Cobbler, and

Fig. 2-53g. Chippewa. Courtesy USDA

overmoist when mashed and fail to color and crisp when deep-fried. They are good, however, for steaming or boiling. During the late spring the mature potato changes some starch to sugar, and at this time they lose some of their dry quality. Mature potatoes in storage around 35 to 40°F change starch to sugar and when withdrawn must remain at or above 50°F about 2 weeks to bring the starch-sugar ratio back to that desired.

Potatoes also vary in cooking properties according to variety. The mature Triumph and Irish Cobbler are moist, the Katahdin and Kennebec are moderately moist, and the White Rose and Russet Burbank are dry. The area and ground where the potato is grown also affects moisture and starch content. High-starch, mealy potatoes are produced in a light soil with good drainage, whereas potatoes grown in moist, mucky soil tend to be high in moisture; the latter may be called *river-bottom potatoes*. Western potatoes are high in starch and are mostly Russet Burbanks or White Rose. Some midwestern states produce fairly dry Burbanks, and the Aranac, developed for midwest growing, is a dry, mealy potato rapidly finding market acceptance. Maine and New York potatoes also are fairly dry. Most midwestern potatoes such as the Cobbler and Triumph are moist.

Specifications for potatoes can state the specific gravity to indicate the type of potato desired. A 1.08 specific gravity or more indicates a dry, mealy potato high in starch; 1.07 to 1.08, a moderately dry one, and below 1.07, a moist potato. Two ounces of salt in a pint of room-temperature water usually allows a 1.08 or higher potato to sink but floats those below this.

Fig. 2-54. Large, medium, and small potatoes. Courtesy USDA

TABLE 2-13
Sizes for Potatoes in Any Type Container

Size Designation	Minimum Diameter* or Weight		Maximum Diameter* or Weight	
	Inches	Ounces	Inches	Ounces
Size A†	1⅞	(‡)	(‡)	(‡)
Size B	1½	(‡)	2¼	(†)
Small	1¾	(‡)	2½	6
Medium	2¼	5	3¼	10
Large	3	10	4¼	16

*Diameter means the greatest dimension at right angles to the longitudinal axis, without regard to the position of the stem end.
†In addition to the minimum size specified, a lot of potatoes designated as Size A shall contain at least 40% of potatoes which are 2½ in. in diameter or larger or 6 oz in weight or larger.
‡No requirement.

TABLE 2-14
Sizes for Potatoes in 50-lb Cartons

Size Designation	Minimum Weight	Maximum Weight
	Ounces	Ounces
Under 50	15	
50	12	19
60	10	16
70	9	15
80	8	13
90	7	12
100	6	10
110	5	9
120	4	8
130	4	8
140	4	8
Over 140	4	8

Fresh potatoes are available all year, but mature potatoes may be in short supply in the summer when storage stocks run low and the new crop has not yet matured. Early (new) potatoes come on the market in January and last until fall. The mature crop appears in September and lasts until the next mature crop arrives. Store potatoes at 50°F. If potatoes are purchased in small lots, store them at room temperature and use them quickly. New potatoes do not keep well.

Potatoes are shipped in burlap polyethylene, or solid-paper sacks, 100 or 50 lb net. Baking potatoes of high quality may be shipped in fiberboard boxes holding 50 lb. These may be sized. Net contents as well as growing area, count, and variety should appear on the label. Less paring waste occurs if potatoes are separated roughly by sizes before machine peeling.

Wholesale federal standards are U.S. Fancy, No. 1, Commercial, and No. 2. U.S. No.1 is usually purchased. U.S. No. 1 potatoes must have a diameter "not less than 1⅞ in.; not more than 3% of the potatoes in any lot may fail to meet the specified minimum size, except that a tolerance of 5% shall be allowed for potatoes packed to meet a minimum size of 2¼ in. or more in diameter or 6 oz in weight. In addition, not more than 15% can fail to meet any specified maximum size." The minimum diameter size permitted in U.S. No. 2 potatoes is 1½ in., with some tolerances allowed. Buyers should distinguish between grade and condition. Grade indicates quality

Fig. 2-55. Defects affecting potato grades:

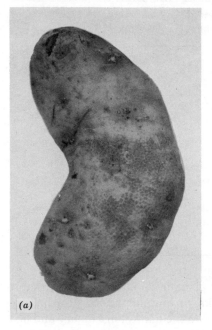

(a)

Fig. 2-55a. Lower limit of bent shape for long U.S. No. 1 type,

Fig. 2-55b. lower limit pinched shape for long type in U.S. No. 1,

when potatoes go into storage, whereas condition refers to quality at a specific time. Specify that the grade should be the condition upon delivery, as noted previously for apples.

Select good, firm, smooth-skinned potatoes. Potatoes with deeply set

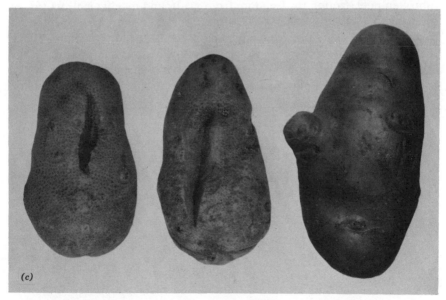

Fig. 2-55c. lower limit growth crack and knob or second growth for U.S. No. 1,

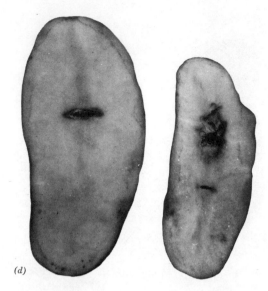

(d)

Fig. 2-55d. lower limit hollow heart for U.S. Nos. 1 and 2,

eyes have a higher paring waste and require more labor. New potatoes with a thin skin can be scraped. Mature potatoes should be dry and have unbroken peel. Watch for freedom from scab, and mechanical, worm, or other injury. Wilted, leathery, discolored potatoes should be rejected. A green coloring is sunburn, which gives a bitter flavor to the potato. Black heart is a disease developing in storage. Hollow heart is an open area in the interior that develops in large potatoes, probably because they grew too fast. Frozen potatoes may be detected by wetness or leakiness, or when

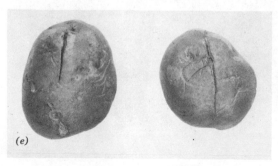

(e)

Fig. 2-55e. lower limit air crack and russet scab for U.S. No. 1. Courtesy USDA

they are cut across and show a black ring just within the outer surface. Shriveling may occur in potatoes lacking maturity or in mature potatoes as summer approaches. Heavy sprouting also may occur in the spring unless treated, or the potatoes are irradiated with Cobalt-60. Potatoes soften if in a sprouting condition or if held in a warm place; they will have a high paring waste. Sprouting potatoes have a high sugar content. Normal paring waste on old potatoes is 27% and on new ones, 20%.

Institutions use about 60% processed potatoes of the total used. These may be raw, frozen, or dried. Raw potatoes may be pared and cut into desired shapes and then treated with anti-oxidants to prevent tarnishing. They hold for 7 days at 32 to 40°F. Potatoes are available dried, cubed, and sliced, or in strips, dehydrated granules, and flakes. There are no government standards. Purchase by manufacturer reputation and after testing. Some come prepared so that an au gratin, escalloped, mashed, or other potato dish can be made just by adding hot water and giving some additional cooking treatment. The quality has been found to be high and the product satisfactory; therefore the use of the processed potato in institutions is constantly rising.

Fig. 2-56a. Processed potato puffs coming from the deep fryer.

Fig. 2-56b. Mashed potatoes are dried on a continuous roller drum, after which they will be processed into potato granules.

Federal standards (1954) for processed peeled potatoes are summarized as follows:

Grades: A (85)*, B (70).

Styles: Whole, whole and cut (less than 50% cut), cut and whole (less than 50% whole), sliced, diced, shoestring (French), cut pieces.

*The potatoes should be of good color, size, and shape; firm and solid; and practically free of peel, defects, and blemishes. Whole are 1½ in. or more in diameter, long varieties are 4¾ oz or more, and 60% of round types are 2⅛ or more in. in diameter. Whole and cut potatoes should have whole potatoes not less than 1½ in. in diameter; the whole potatoes in cut and whole should be of a similar size; 90% of the slices in sliced potatoes should not be greater than twice the size of the smallest slice. Strips should be at least 1 in. or more in length.

Frozen French-fried or blanched potatoes also have federal standards (1967). A summary follows:

Fig. 2-56c. Inspecting a preblanched potato strip for quality. The interior should be light, mealy, and dry and the outside crisp and lightly browned. Courtesy USDA

Grades: A (90)*, B (80).

Depth of color from frying: Extra light, light, medium light, medium, dark.

Styles: Straight cut, crinkle cut, strips (¼ x ¼ in., ⅜ x ⅜ in., ½ x ¼ in., ⅜ x ¾ in.), shoestrings (⅜ x ⅜ in. sq), slices, dices, rissole (whole or large cuts preblanched), miscellaneous shapes.

Lengths: Extra long, 80% more than 2 in. and 30% more than 3 in.; long, 70% 2 in. or more and 15% 3 in. or more; medium, 50% or more 2 in. or more; short, less than 50% 2 in. or longer.

*Product should have a good bright, characteristic color, and even size and shape. There should be few imperfections, blemishes, or defects. The texture should be such that external surfaces are moderately crisp. show no noticeable separation from the inner portion, and are not excessively oily. The interior portions should be well cooked, tender, and practically free from sogginess. Shoestring potatoes may be moderately crisp throughout. The potatoes should yield a highly palatable product when fried in 365°F oil of good quality for 1½ minutes or longer.

Potatoes, Sweet (1963)

The federal standards consider yams as sweet potatoes. Yams are more moist and have a deeper orange or reddish flesh and also tend to break up more easily. For that reason sweet potatoes are best for candied sweet potatoes or other purposes for which a distinct piece is desired. Some like the dry, mealier sweet potato for mashing. Yams and sweet potatoes must be mature before marketing. Select those that are clean, firm, and free from blemishes. Shape affects grade and waste. Damp potatoes may have rot in them. Potatoes that are shriveled, soft, and flabby are usually old, of poor

Fig. 2-57. Typical sizes and shapes of sweet potatoes. Courtesy USDA

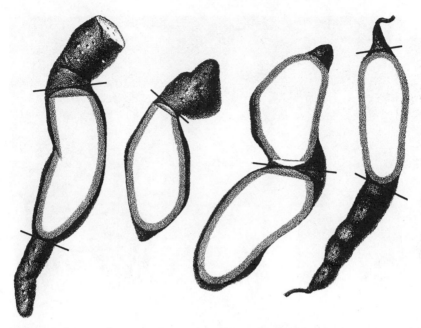

Fig. 2-58. Buyers of sweet potatoes should note shapes. These potatoes, termed fairly well shaped. show that there are one or more pieces of usable potatoes. Yield will be materially affected by the shape of the potatoes. Courtesy USDA

flavor, and wasteful. Cut to note coarse veining and stringiness inside. Purchase U.S. Extra No. 1 or No. 1. Machine paring loses 25%. Sweet potatoes are marketed all year but heaviest supplies are availablein the fall and winter. Imports from Puerto Rico and the Caribbean come in after the crop from our southern states.

Pumpkins

Good quality pumpkins are rich yellow in color and have no green rind. Select for heaviness for size. Loss to EP is 30%. No federal grades exist.

Radishes (1968)

The small, round, red radishes with a white tip or all-red radishes are most frequently seen on the market all year. Peak supplies come in spring and early summer. They should be well formed, smooth, firm, tender, crisp, and mild in flavor. The leaves should be fresh, bright, and green. Note

Fig. 2-59. Four varieties of radishes used in food services. The round, white-tipped variety shown alone is the most popular. Courtesy USDA and Burpee Co.

spongy or soft radishes indicating pithiness. Large radishes may be pithy. Diameter size may be specified as *small*, less than ¾ in.; *medium*, ¾ to 1 in.; *large*, 1 to 1¼ in.; and *very large*, over 1¼ in. Specify tops full-length or topped (tops clipped to not more than ⅜ in.). Many radishes are marketed

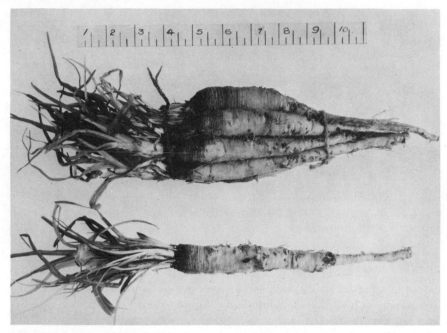

Fig. 2-60. Salsify or oyster plant. It is cooked and served mashed, buttered, or creamed. Courtesy USDA

topped and packed in polyethylene bags. Specify U.S. No. 1. Loss with tops to EP is 37%.

Rutabagas (see Turnips)

Salsify (Oyster Plant)

Salsify tastes somewhat like oysters, hence the name. Use quality factors for purchase previously named for parsnips. Like parsnips, they are sweeter and have better flavor after a heavy frost or after they are held under refrigeration for a time. There are no federal standards. It is on the market in the fall and winter. Waste to EP is 30%.

Squash

There are summer and winter varieties of squash. Purchase selection should be on the basis of production need because each variety performs differently in cooking.

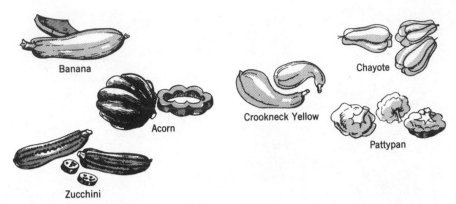

Fig. 2-61. Some varieties of squash. Banana and acorn squash keep better than the four summer varieties shown here.

Summer Squash (1945)

Summer squash is perishable and keeps poorly. Store at 32 to 40°F. They are usually soft-skinned and immature. Open to see if the seeds are tender and not hard because the squash is frequently cooked and eaten with the seeds. The pulp should be soft and moist after cooking and lack the

Fig. 2-62a. Acorn or Table Queen squash and

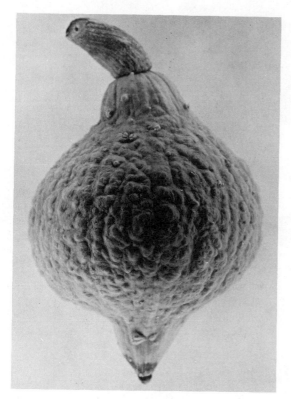

Fig. 2-62b. Golden Hubbard. Both are called winter squash. Courtesy USDA

mealiness found in winter varieties. Some hard-rind summer squash with yellowish flesh resembles winter squash more than the summer variety.

Select for freshness, heaviness for size, freedom from blemishes, and a rind sufficiently tender to be easily punctured, except in the hard-rind varieties. A bushel holds about 48 lb net; small lugs, 20 to 30 lb net; and cartons, 40 lb net. Purchase by the pound. Preparation waste varies but if the squash is washed, trimmed, and used with the rind on, it is 10%. Summer squash is on the market all year, especially common varieties such as zucchini, but the peak is in summer and early fall.

Winter Squash (1944)

Winter squash usually has a hard rind, yellowish-orange flesh, and hard, white seeds. They are usually fair-to-good keepers. Some may have smooth rinds, others rough. The rind may be various colors, depending upon type. The squash should be firm, with a thick, hard, nearly un-

Fig. 2-63. Varieties of summer squash:

Fig. 2-63a. zucchini,

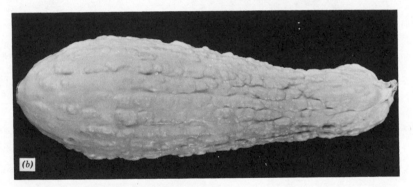

Fig. 2-63b. straightneck, and

Fig. 2-63c. cymbling (scallop or pattypan). Courtesy USDA

blemished rind. It should be heavy for size. Examine for rot or mold and press to feel firmness and condition. Split to examine for interior condition. Purchase by the pound. A bushel weighs around 50 lb net. Specify U.S. No. 1 for summer and winter squash. Preparation wastes for winter to EP are: Acorn, 26%; Boston Marrow, 12%; Butternut, 48%; Hubbard, 34%.

Tomatoes (1961)

Fresh tomatoes' season peak is late summer and early fall. Good supplies come from California, Florida, Texas, Mexico, and hothouses in the winter. Although vine-ripened tomatoes are of superior quality, growing

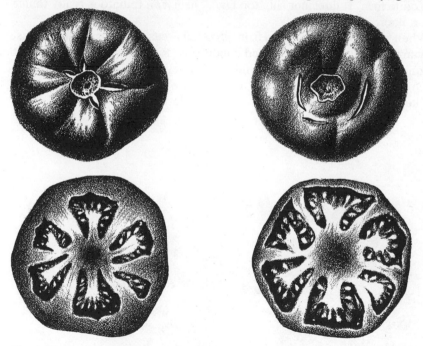

Fig. 2-64. Limits of growth cracks and puffiness allowed in U.S. No. 1 Grade for tomatoes. The left tomato at the top shows maximum aggregate length of radial growth cracks permitted on 2½-in. tomatoes. The tomato at the right top shows concentric growth cracks affecting appearance to the same extent as maximum aggregate length of radial growth cracks permitted in U.S. No. 1 Grade. These limitations apply in all stages of maturity. The lower limit allowed in puffiness is shown in the bottom tomatoes. The proportion of open space permitted is dependent upon wall thickness. Tomatoes with thicker walls may have proportionately greater amounts of open space. Tomatoes with thinner walls must have proportionately lesser amounts. Courtesy USDA

areas far from markets pick before ripeness. A variety that is firm and never quite softens is grown to reduce shipping loss.

Tomatoes may be picked at one of several points in their development. *Immature green* tomatoes show no red or yellow color. They have immature seeds and a skin that can be rubbed off. Their quality is usually quite low on ripening, and many are harvested this way. *Mature green* tomatoes have some gloss but no red color. Seeds are sufficiently hard to resist cutting with a knife, the skin is waxy and will not rub off, and a bit of white appears on the blossom end. *Turning* tomatoes show a trace of red color or yellow. This is also called the "breaker" stage. They give fair quality on ripening. A *pink* tomato has more than 50% of the surface light red, but it is still quite firm. It does not ship too far. A *firm ripe* tomato is ready to use and a poor shipper.

When tomatoes are received from growing areas at storage warehouses, they are put under well-controlled conditions. Ripening rooms are kept at around 65°F and 88% relative humidity. Ethylene gas may be used to assist ripening. At desired ripeness, the tomatoes are repacked and moved to the market. Different varieties show different coloring so buyers should select

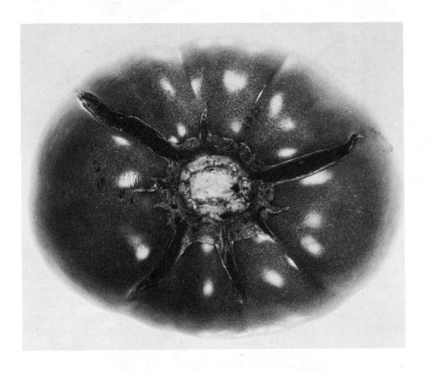

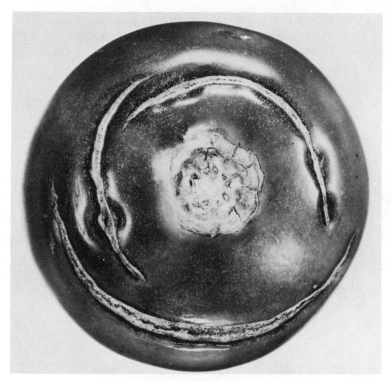

Fig. 2-65. Heavy growth cracks considerably reduce the grade of the tomato. Courtesy USDA

on the basis of variety, if possible, as well as color. As noted, vine-ripened fruit has a better color, has a much thinner, more tender skin and a superior flavor.

Small, medium, large, and very large tomatoes are, respectively, under 3 oz, 2 to 6 oz, 6 to 10 oz, and over 10 oz. Greenhouse tomatoes are termed small, medium, and large, respectively, when under 3 oz, 3 to 8 oz, and over 8 oz. Lugs holding three layers weigh about 30 to 32 lb net. Packing is frequently arranged; it is called *place pack*. Wrapping is individual unless double wrap is specified, in which case two tomatoes are wrapped in a wrapper. Packing varies in the standard California lug:

Straight pack   All layers have the same number of tomatoes except, if a diagonal pack is used, a variation of not more than one tomato is permitted in different layers. (A *straight square–offset* or *straight square–diagonal* pack has a straight pack on top and diagonal in the other layers.

Extra row pack	The lower layers do not contain more than one additional row one way of the lug; for instance, a 5 × 5 pack may have lower layers of 5 × 6 but not 6 × 6 or 5 × 7.
Bridge pack	A part of an additional layer is packed in the lug, and the lower layers do not contain more than an additional row from the top layer.
Double wrap pack	One tomato to a wrapper on the top layer and not more than two in a wrapper in the lower layers.
Double wrap bridge pack	Not more than one tomato per wrapper in the top layer and not more than two per wrapper in the lower ones, with an additional layer packed in the lug.
Irregular pack	No designated arrangement.

The trade frequently uses pack size terms to refer to a tomato size rather than the way the tomatoes are packed. Table 2-15 indicates size according to the standard pack term.

TABLE 2-15

Placements in Los Angeles Lug		Diameter in Inches*	
Row	Column	Minimum	Maximum
4 ×	4	$3^5/_{16}$	$3^{15}/_{16}$
4 ×	5	3	$3^{10}/_{16}$
5 ×	5	$2^{14}/_{16}$	$3^6/_{16}$
5 ×	6	$2^{11}/_{16}$	$3^3/_{16}$
6 ×	6	$2^8/_{16}$	$2^{14}/_{16}$
6 ×	7	$2^4/_{16}$	$2^{10}/_{16}$
7 ×	7	2	$2^6/_{16}$
7 ×	8	$1^{14}/_{16}$	$2^4/_{16}$

*A 10% tolerance is allowed.

Tomato crates, wire-bound or nailed, contain about 60 lb of tomatoes; standard fiberboard cartons, 40 to 50 lb; small, wire-bound crates 38 lb; field boxes, 60 lb; bushel baskets or hampers, 53 lb; a half bushel container, 27 lb; 12-qt climax baskets, 18 to 20 lb; 16-qt splint baskets or 16-qt

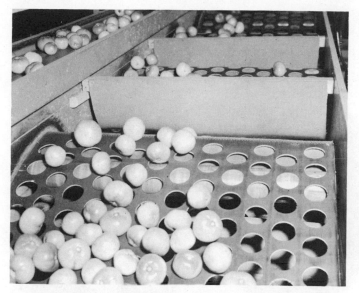

Fig. 2-66. Mechanically grading tomatoes for size. Note that the tomatoes at this point of marketing are immature. They will ripened later. Courtesy USDA

hampers, 27 lb; ⅝-bushel hamper, 33 to 34 lb; 8-qt splint basket or fiberboard box, 12 lb; and 4-basket crate, 22 lb. Tomatoes do not ship too well in the larger containers. Hothouse tomatoes are usually marketed in baskets holding around 10 lb.

Select for flavor, firmness, internal characteristics, color, and size. Quality is indicated by maturity without the tomato being overly ripe or soft, plus good shape. It must be fairly smooth and free from decay, freezing injury, and damage caused by dirt, bruises, cuts, sunscald, sunburn, puffiness, catfaces, growth cracks, scars, disease, insects, hail, or mechanical or other means. Watch for worm damage, decay, mold, or wateriness. Purchase U.S. No. 1 or a lower grade if quality is high. Greenhouse tomatoes should be U.S. Fancy or U.S. No. 1 depending upon quality. Removing skins, hard cores, stem ends, and trimming gives a loss of 12%.

Turnips and Rutabagas (1955)

Federal grade standards for turnips and rutabagas are the same, and quality factors for their selection are also. Turnips may be white or white with a

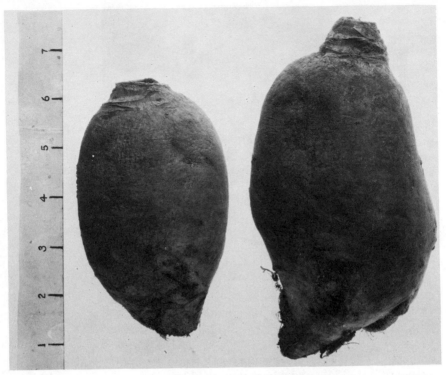

Fig. 2-67. Permitted and nonpermitted shapes in rutabagas for U.S. No. 1. USDA

light purple top. Best sizes are those listed as desirable in beets. They may be sold in bunches with tops not less than 3 to a bunch, and a bunch should weigh a pound. Rutabagas may be called *Swedish turnips*. They are yellow in color, are larger than turnips, have a longer shape, and may be almost oval. They have a denser flesh. Rutabagas and turnips may be marketed trimmed (4-in. top remaining) or topped (not more than ¾-in. top).

Store in a cool, well-ventilated area for only a short time since older turnips and rutabagas become strong in flavor. They may be waxed and show a high gloss. They may come in 50-lb bags or in bushel baskets (55 lb net). U.S. No. 1 standards state that turnips and rutabagas shall have a minimum diameter of 1¾ in. Specify that turnips over 2½ in. in diameter will be rejected. Rutabagas may be larger. Tops should be fresh and green. Watch for rough skins, puffiness, and leaf scars on top. Cut and examine for woodiness and crispness. Medium sizes are usually best quality. Spongy, wrinkled, or shriveled items should be rejected.

TABLE 2-16
Federal Standards for Fresh Fruits and Vegetables at the Wholesale Level*

Fruits
  Apples

  Apricots
  Avocados, Florida
  Cantaloupes
  Cherries, Sweet
  Cranberries
  Dewberries and Blackberries
  Grapes, American Bunch
  Grapes, European, Sawdust Pack
  Grapes, Table
  Grapefruit (California and Arizona)
  Grapefruit (Florida)

  Grapefruit (Texas)

  Honey Dew and Honey Ball Melon
  Lemons
  Limes (Persian) Tahiti
  Nectarines
  Oranges (California and Arizona)
  Oranges and Tangelos (Florida)

  Oranges (Texas)

  Peaches
  Pears, Summer and Fall
  Pears, Winter
  Pineapples
  Plums and Prunes
  Rhubarb
  Strawberries and Raspberries
  Tangerines

  Watermelon

Vegetables
  Artichokes, Globe
  Asparagus

  Beans, Lima
  Beans, Snap
  Beets
  Beet Greens

Extra Fancy, Fancy, No. 1, No. 1 Cookers,
  No. 1 Early, Utility
No. 1, No. 2
No. 1, Combination
No. 1, Commercial
No. 1, Commercial
Grade A (Consumer grade)
No. 1, No. 2

Fancy, Extra No. 1, No. 1
Fancy, No. 1
Fancy No. 1, No. 2, Combination, No. 3
Fancy No. 1, No. 1 Bright, No. 1 Golden,
  No. 1 Bronze, No. 1 Russet, No. 2, No. 2
  Bright, No. 2 Russet, No. 3
Fancy, No. 1, No. 1 Bright, No. 1 Bronze,
  Combination No. 2, No. 2 Russet, No. 3
No. 1, Commercial, No. 2
No. 1, Combination, No. 2
No. 1, Combination, No. 2
Fancy, Extra No. 1, No. 1, No. 2
Fancy, No. 1, Combination, No. 2
Fancy, No. 1 Bright, No. 1, No. 1 Golden,
  No. 1 Bronze, No. 1 Russet, No. 2 Bright,
  No. 2, No. 2 Russet, No. 5
Fancy, No. 1, No. 1 Bright, No. 1 Bronze,
  Combination No. 2, No. 2 Russet, No. 3
No. 1, No. 2
No. 1, Combination, No. 2
Extra No. 1, No. 1, Combination, No. 2
Fancy, No. 1, No. 2
Fancy, No. 1, Combination, No. 2
No. 1, No. 2
No. 1, No. 2
Fancy, No. 1, No. 1 Bronze, No. 1 Russet,
  No. 2, No. 2 Russet, No. 3
No. 1, Commercial, No. 2

No. 1, No. 2
No. 1, No. 2 (Washington No. 1, Washington
  No. 2 are more used in the markets)
No. 1, Combination No. 2
Fancy, No. 1, Combination, No. 2
No. 1, No. 2
No. 1

TABLE 2-16 (cont'd)
Federal Standards for Fresh Fruits and Vegetables at the Wholesale Level*

Broccoli, Italian Sprouting	Fancy, No. 1, No. 2
Brussels Sprouts	No. 1, No. 2
Cabbage	No. 1, Commercial
Carrots, bunched	No. 1, Commercial
Carrots, topped	Extra No. 1, No. 1, No. 2
Carrots, short-trimmed tops	No. 1, Commercial
Cauliflower	No. 1
Celery	Extra No. 1, No. 1, No. 2
Collard or Broccoli Greens	No. 1
Corn, Green	Fancy, No. 1, No. 2
Cucumbers	No. 1, No. 1 large, No. 2
Cucumbers, Greenhouse	Fancy, No. 1, No. 2
Dandelion Greens	No. 1
Eggplant	Fancy, No. 1, No. 2
Endive, Escarole, Chicory	No. 1
Garlic	No. 1
Kale	No. 1, Commercial
Lettuce	No. 1, No. 2
Lettuce, Greenhouse Leaf	Fancy, No. 1
Mushrooms	No. 1
Mustard Greens and Turnip Greens	No. 1
Okra	No. 1
Onions, Bermuda, Granex	No. 1, No. 2, Commercial
Onions, Creole	No. 1, No. 2, Combination
Onions, Northern Grown	No. 1, No. 1 Boilers, No. 1 Picklers, Commercial No. 2
Onions, Green	No. 1, No. 2
Parsley	No. 1
Parsnips	No. 1, No. 2
Peas, Fresh	Fancy, No. 1
Peppers, Sweet	No. 1, No. 2
Potatoes	Fancy, Extra No. 1, No. 1, No. 2, Commercial
Potatoes, Sweet	Extra No. 1, No. 1, Commercial, No. 2
Radishes	No. 1, Commercial
Romaine	No. 1
Rutabagas or Turnips	No. 1, No. 2
Shallots, Bunched	No. 1, No. 2
Spinach, Fresh	Extra No. 1, No. 1, Commercial
Squash, Fall and Winter type	No. 1, No. 2
Squash, Summer	No. 1, No. 2
Tomatoes, Fresh	No. 1, Combination, No. 2
Tomatoes, Greenhouse	Fancy, No. 1, No. 2

*Prefix U.S. before all grades.

TABLE 2-17
Quantities to Order of Fresh Produce†

Produce Item	Unit of Purchase	Wt per Unit	EP Yield %	Portion AS	Portions per Purchase Unit	Units per 100 Portions
		Vegetables				
Asparagus	lb	1.00	49	4 med spears, or 3	3.83	29¾
Asparagus	crate	28.00	49	cut spears	73.17	1⅓
Beans, lima, green, pod	lb	1.00	40	3 oz	2.13	47
Beans, lima, green, pod	bu	32.00	40	3 oz	68.27	1½
Beans, lima, green, shelled	lb	1.00	102	3 oz	5.44	18½
Beans, snap, green, or wax	lb	1.00	84	3 oz	4.48	22½
Beans, snap, green, or wax	bu	30.00	84	3 oz	134.40	¾
Beet greens, untrimmed	lb	1.00	44	3 oz	2.35	42¾
Beet greens, untrimmed	bu	20.00	44	3 oz	46.93	2¼
Beets, with tops	lb	1.00	43	3 oz	2.29	43¾
Beets, no tops	sack	50.00	76	3 oz	202.67	½
Blackeyed peas, shelled	lb	1.00	93	3 oz	4.96	20¼
Broccoli	lb	1.00	62	3 oz	3.31	30¼
Broccoli	crate	40.00	62	3 oz	132.27	¾
Brussels Sprouts	lb	1.00	77	3 oz	4.11	24½
Cabbage, cooked	sack	50.00	79	3 oz	213.33	½
Cabbage, for slaw	sack	50.00	79	2 oz	316.00	⅓
Carrots, no tops	sack	50.00	75	3 oz	200.00	½
Cauliflower	lb	1.00	45	3 oz	6.56	15¼
Cauliflower	crate	37.00	44	3 oz	86.83	1¼
Cauliflower	crate	50.00	44	3 oz	117.33	⅚
Celery, cooked	lb	1.00	70	3 oz	3.73	27
Celery, raw	lb	1.00	75	2 oz	6.00	16¾
Celery, raw	crate	60.00	75	3 oz	240.00	⁴/₁₀
Celery hearts, 24	box	30.00	95	2 oz (raw)	228.00	½
Chard, untrimmed	lb	1.00	56	3 oz	3.00	33
Collards	bu	20.00	81	3 oz	86.40	1¼
Corn, 60 ears	sack	40.00		1 ear	60.00	1⅔
Cucumber, raw	bu	48.00	95	3 oz	243.20	⁴/₁₀
Eggplant	bu	33.00	75	4 oz	100.00	1
Endive, Escarole, Chicory	lb	1.00	75	1 oz	12.00	8⅓
Endive, Escarole, Chicory	bu	25.00	75	1 oz	300.00	⅓
Kale, untrimmed	bu	18.00	81	3 oz	77.76	1⅓
Lettuce, head	lb	1.00	74	2 oz	6.00	17
Lettuce, head	carton	2 doz	74	⅛ head	144.00	13 heads
Romaine	lb	1.00	64	2 oz	5.12	20
Mushrooms	lb	1.00	67	1 oz	10.72	9½
Mushrooms	basket	9.00	67	3 oz	32.16	3¼
Mustard greens	bu	20.00	59	3 oz	62.93	1¾

TABLE 2-17 (cont'd)
Quantities to Order of Fresh Produce†

Produce Item	Unit of Purchase	Wt per Unit	EP Yield %	Portion AS	Portions per Purchase Unit	Units per 100 Portions
		Vegetables				
Okra	bu	30.00	96	3 oz	153.60	¾
Onions, green, raw	lb	1.00	60	3 oz	3.20	31¼
Onions, mature	sack	50.00	76	3 oz	202.67	½
Parsley	lb	1.00		1 sprig	8 c	2
Parsley	crate	19.00		1 sprig	9 gal	¹/₁₀
Parsnips	bu	50.00	84	3 oz	224.00	½
Peas, shelled	lb	1.00	96	3 oz	5.12	19¾
Peas, in pod	lb	1.00	36	3 oz	1.92	52¼
Peppers, green, raw	lb	1.00	82	1 oz	13.12	7¾
Peppers, green, raw	bu	25.00	82	1 oz	328.00	¹/₃
Peppers, green	carton	30.00	82	½ pepper	300.00	¹/₃
Potatoes, pared	sack	100.00	76	4 oz	360.00	.3
Potatoes, stripped and french fried	sack	100.00	54	2 oz	416.00	¼
Potatoes, jacket	sack	100.00	100	1 med	300.00	¹/₃
Pumpkin, mashed	lb	1.00	63	4 oz	2.52	39¾
Radishes, no tops	lb	1.00	90	1 oz or 4	12.00	8¹/₃
Rutabagas	bu	56.00	77	4 oz	3.08	32½
Spinach, untrimmed	bu	20.00	67	3 oz	71.47	1½
Squash, summer	bu	35.00	83	3 oz	154.93	¾
Squash, acorn	lb	1.00		½ squash	2.00	50
Squash, Hubbard	lb	1.00	58	4 oz	2.30	45
Sweet potatoes	bu	50.00	81	4 oz	162.00	²/₃
Tomatoes, medium	lb	1.00	91	2 slices	7.50	13½
Tomatoes, medium	lb	1.00	91	wedge	12.00	8¹/₃
Tomatoes, medium	lug	32.00	91	wedge	384.00	¼ +
Tomatoes, medium	bu	53.00	91	3 slices	265.00	⁴/₁₀
Turnip greens	bu	20.00	48	3 oz	146.00	¾
Turnips, no tops	bu	50.00	73	3 oz	190.00	½ +
Watercress	bunch	1.00	92	½ c	27.77	4
		Fruit				
Apples, 113's	box	40.00		1 apple	120.00	−1
Apples, 113's, raw	lb	1.00		2 oz	6.08	16½
Apples, 113's, cooked	lb	1.00	70	3 oz	4.00	25
Apples, 113's, pie*	lb	1.00	70	2.12 lb/pie	2.83	36
Apricots	lug	24.00		2 med	144.00	¾
Avocados	lug	12.00	75	2 oz	72.00	1½
Avocados, ⁴/₅ bu	box	36.00	75	2 oz	216.00	½
Bananas, medium	box	25.00		1	75.00	1½
Bananas, medium	lb	1.00	68	3 oz	3.63	27¾

TABLE 2-17 (cont'd)
Quantities to Order of Fresh Produce†

Produce Item	Unit of Purchase	Wt per Unit	EP Yield %	Portions per Portion AS	Portions per Purchase Unit	Units per 100 Portions
Blackberries	qt	1.42	95	3 oz	7.18	14
Blackberries	qt	1.42	95	garnish	21.53	4¾
Blackberries, 34 qt	crate	34.00	95	qt/pie	6.00	½
Cantaloupe	lb	1.00	50	3 oz	2.67	37½
Cantaloupe, 36's	crate	80.00		½	64.00	1½
Cherries, pitted	lb	1.00	89	3 oz	4.75	21¼
Cherries, pie	lug	16.00	89	1.6 lb/pie	60.00	1²/₃
Cranberries, sauce	lb	1.00	182	2 oz	14.56	7
Cranberries, raw	lb	1.00	96	1 oz	15.36	6¾
Cranberries, cooked	box	25.00	239	2 oz	478.00	⅕
Figs	box	6.00		3 med	24.00	4¼
Grapefruit, juice	lb	1.00	44	4 oz	1.61	62¼
Grapefruit, 64's	carton	38.00	47	4 oz	64.56	1½
Grapefruit, 64's	carton	38.00		½	64.00	1½
Grapefruit, segments	gal	8.44	100	4 oz	32.75	3
Grapes	lug	24.00	94	4 oz	90.24	1.1
Honeydew melon	melon	4.00	60	⅛ wedge	8.00	12½
Honeydew melon	melon	4.00	60	3 oz	12.80	8
Lemons, 4/lb, juice	lb	1.00	43	2 oz	3.16	31¾
Lemons, 4/lb, wedge	carton	36.00		1	864.00	−⅛
Lemons, 4/lb, slice	carton	36.00		1	1152.00	−¹/₁₀
Limes, 4/5 bu, juice	carton	40.00	48	2 oz	140.80	¾
Limes, wedge	carton	40.00		¼	1080.00	¹/₁₀
Mangoes	lug	24.00	67	3 oz	85.76	1¼
Oranges, Cal.	carton	38.00	70	4 oz	106.40	1
Oranges, Fla.	carton	42.50	70	4 oz	120.00	−1
Oranges, Fla., juice	carton	42.50	50	4 oz	78.00	1½
Oranges, segments	gal	8.56	100	4 oz	32.00	3
Peaches, sliced	bu	48.0	76	3 oz	194.56	½
Peaches	lug	20.00	76	3 oz	80.00	1¼
Peaches	lb	1.00	76	2 lb/pie	3.00	33⅓
Pears	bu	46.00	78	3 oz	191.36	½
Pineapple, 18's	crate	35.00	75	⅙	108.00	1
Pineapple, 18's	crate	35.00	52	3 oz	97.07	1
Pineapple chunks	gal	8.76	100	3 oz	21.00	5
Plums, pitted	lb	1.00	94	3 oz	5.01	20
Plums	lb	1.00		2 med	4.50	22
Plums, 4-basket	crate	28.00	94	1 oz	22.87	4½
Raspberries, 24 qt	crate	35.00	97	3 oz	140.37	−1
Raspberries, 24 qt	crate	35.00	97	.7 qt/pie	200.00	½
Rhubarb, trimmed	lb	1.00	103	3 oz	5.49	18¼

TABLE 2-17 (cont'd)
Quantities to Order of Fresh Produce†

Produce Item	Unit of Purchase	Wt per Unit	EP Yield %	Portions per Portion AS	Portions per Purchase Unit	Units per 100 Portions
		Vegetables				
Rhubarb, trimmed	lb	1.00		1.5 lb/pie	4.00	25
Strawberries, 24 qt	crate	35.00	87	3 oz	162.40	.7
Tangerines	box	45.00		1 med	180.00	.6
Watermelon	lb	1.00	74	3 oz	3.95	25½
Watermelon, flesh	lb	1.00	36	3 oz	2.45	41
Watermelon, 1/16	25	25.00		wedge	16.00	6¼

†*Source:* USDA, Agricultural Handbook 284

TABLE 2-18
Equivalents of Canned and Frozen to Fresh

Produce Item	Fresh Lb	To No. 10 Cans	Frozen Lb	Fruit-Sugar Ratio
	Vegetables			
Asparagus	8–9	1		
Asparagus, crate		3 to 4	15	
Beans, lima	5	1		
Beans, lima, bu	32	6	29	
Beans, snap	4 to 5	1		
Beans, snap, bu	30	6 to 8	24	
Broccoli, crate	40		23	
Carrots, no tops	8	1		
Carrots, no tops	50	6	23	
Corn, cob, kernel	17–18	1		
Corn, cob, kernel, bu			8	
Okra	1½	1		
Peas, green	3 to 6	1		
Peas, green, shelled, bu		6 to 8	27	
Pumpkin or winter squash	17½	1		
Pumpkin or winter squash, bu			32	
Spinach, etc., cooked	8	1		
Spinach, etc., cooked, bu		2 to 3	10½	
Sweet potatoes	2 to 3	1		
Sweet potatoes, bu		7		
Tomatoes	2½ to 3½	1		
Tomato catsup	19	1		
Tomato paste	40½	1		
Tomato sauce	21	1		

TABLE 2-18 (cont'd)
Equivalents of Canned and Frozen to Fresh

Produce Item	Fresh Lb	To No. 10 Cans	Frozen Lb	Fruit-Sugar Ratio
		Fruit		
Apples	10	1		
Apples, bu		4 to 5	26–31	5 to 1
Berries, except Strawberries	5	1		
Berries, except Strawberries, crate	34	7	34	4 to 1
Cherries, sour	7	1		
Cherries, sour, bu		8	53	4 to 1
Peaches	2 to 3	1		
Peaches, bu	46	6 to 7	41 to 44	4 to 1
Pears	2 to 3	1		
Pears, bu	46	5 to 6		
Plums	1½ to 2½	1		
Plums, bu		9 to 10		
Strawberries	1½ to 3	1		
Strawberries, crate	35	6	42	3 to 1

Source: USDA, Agricultural Handbook 284

TABLE 2-19

Vegetable	Pre-storage Care	Refrigerator Temperature	Storage Time	Preparation
Globe Artichokes		32–40°F	8–15 days maximum 30	Wash and trim about 1″ off top. Trim stem to 1″ from base. Pull off loose bottom leaves. Snip each leaf with scissors. Prepare ahead but hold in refrigerator.
Asparagus	Very Perishable	35–40°F	7–10 days	Flavor declines above 32°. Keep butts of stalks moist to prevent toughening. When ready to use, break off stalk where it snaps easily. Wash. Keep refrigerated till cooking time.
Snap Beans		40–45°F		
Beets		32–35°F		
Broccoli	Very Perishable	32–35°F	7–10 days	Wash well. Trim ends of stem. Make lengthwise gashes up to flowerets if stem is over 1″ diameter. Prepare ahead of cooking time but keep refrigerated. DO NOT soak in water.
Cabbage	Remove all loose and wilted leaves	32–40°F well-vented area	3–6 weeks	Wash head. Cut into wedges and remove core. Prepare ahead by putting in plastic bags or cover with clean damp towel. Keep refrigerated. DO NOT soak in water.
Carrots and Parsnips	Remove tops. Store in slat crates	32–50°F	4–5 months topped 10–14 days bunched 3 weeks packaged	Wash carrots. Remove skin with vegetable peeler. Prepare ahead of time. Put in plastic bags or covered with clean damp towels in refrigerator.
Cauliflower	Jacketed heads and not cello wrapped can be sprinkled with water	32–40°F	3 weeks, heads 10–14 days, flowerets	Wash head. Remove any discoloration and outer green leaves. Leave head whole or separate into flowerets. Prepare ahead of cooking time but keep in refrigerator.

Vegetable	Storage Notes	Temperature	Storage Time	Preparation
Celery	Remove wilted branches. DO NOT break stalk apart	32–35°F	2–3 weeks	Trim off root and wash branches. Prepare ahead of time but keep in plastic bags or covered with clean damp towels in refrigerator.
Corn	Very Perishable Remove husk and silk	32–35°F	DO NOT STORE	Ready for cooking.
Cucumbers		45–50°F		
Lettuce and Greens		32–40°F	2 weeks	Remove wilted or coarse leaves. Hit core of lettuce on side of sink to loosen. Remove core and let heavy stream of water run into head. Turn upside down and drain. *Leafy Greens:* Cut off root and wash leaves in cold water. Drain in colander. Can be prepared before serving if kept in plastic bags or large pan covered with damp cloth in refrigerator. Avoid putting small individual tossed salads in refrigerator because of dehydration.
Dry Onions	Dry storage 80–85°F well-vented area	32–40°F	Several weeks	Remove outer dry skin. Can be prepared ahead of time. Keep in cool area, covered with damp clean towel.
Green Onions		32–40°F	2 weeks	Wash. Cut off root; cut tops within 4" of bulb. Wash tops and use for garnish. Remove outer skin of bulb if discolored. Prepare ahead of time by keeping in plastic bag in refrigerator.
Sweet Peppers		45–50°F	8–10 days	Will injure if temperature goes below 45°. Wash. Remove stem and seeds. Prepare ahead of time and cover with damp clean towel in refrigerator.
Potatoes	Dry, dark and vented	50–65°F	Several weeks	Wash and remove skin with peeler unless preparing for baking. Should be prepared near cooking time. Soaking potatoes in water to keep them from turning dark means a loss of important nutrients.

TABLE 2-19 (cont'd)

Vegetable	Pre-storage Care	Refrigerator Temperature	Storage Time	Preparation
Summer Squash		50–55°F	2 weeks	Wash and cut into serving pieces. Prepare and cover with damp clean towel. Keep refrigerated till ready to use.
Winter Squash	Dry storage	50–55°F 70–75% humidity	2–3 months	Wash well. Can be baked whole or cut into sections. Remove seeds after cooking.
Tomatoes		50–55°F pinks & ripes 60–70°F mature greens	8–12 days	Wash. Remove core and blemishes. Scald if removing skin. Keep in refrigerator till ready to use.
Turnips and Rutabagas		32–35°F		

A high relative humidity 85–90% and low temperatures are needed to retard the aging process within the vegetables and lessen dehydration. The amount of produce stored in the box affects the level. When the refrigerator is filled, a high relative humidity is maintained. When the inventory is reduced, over a 48-hour period, the relative humidity is lowered. Keep fresh vegetables dry rather than wet to delay the growth of decay producing organisms.

Chart adapted from Western Growers Association, 3091 Wilshire Blvd., Los Angeles, California 90005

BIBLIOGRAPHY

Hill, R. G., *A Fruit and Vegetable Buying Guide,* Home and Garden Bulletin No. 41, USDA, Washington, D.C., April 1955.

Household Finance Corporation, *Better Buymanship, No. 3, Fresh Fruits and Vegetables,* Chicago, 1941.

United Fresh Fruit and Vegetable Association, *Fruit and Vegetable Pointers,* 777 14th St., N.W., Washington, D.C.

U.S. Department of Agriculture, Agricultural Marketing Service, Washington, D.C.:

Potatoes for Consumer Education, AIB No. 178, 1957.

Regulations Governing the Inspection and Certification of Fresh Fruits and Vegetables, SRA-AMS 93, 1957.

Standardization and Inspection of Fresh Fruits and Vegetables, Misc. Pub. 604, 1946.

U.S. Standards for Fresh Fruits and Vegetables, Fresh Fruit and Vegetable Division, dated variously.

3
Processed Fruits and Vegetables

Processing has enabled man to carry over his food supplies from years or seasons of plenty to time of scarcity; it has also enabled him to reduce the amount of work he must do when he wants to use the food. This latter factor is becoming increasingly important as we incorporate more and more labor in our food, using preservation as a means to incorporate labor, not to carry the food over to times of scarcity.

Methods of processing have been changing rapidly in the past few years. Frozen foods have increased appreciably, but many expect that dried foods will become increasingly important in the future. Our knowledge of how to partially process foods and then hold them chilled is leading to another important development that gives foods some extended shelf life and a rather freshly cooked quality. No doubt as technology in the processed food area increases, we will see different methods and a swing from some of the traditional methods of preservation to more novel and sophisticated procedures.

FOOD PRESERVATION

For many years man has delayed food spoilage by various methods of processing. To do this he usually must prevent bacteria, molds, yeasts, and other deteriorative agents from attacking food.

Since man's early history, drying, salting, pickling, smoking or curing, and sweetening commonly have been used to preserve food, but within the last century freezing, canning, and some sophisticated preservation methods have been emphasized. Food is frequently preserved not by one method but by a combination of methods. Common table salt, plus nitrities, nitrates, and smoke preserve meat. Salt and lactic acid developed in fermentation preserve sauerkraut. Acid and sugar preserve dried fruits even though they have a 20 to 25% moisture content. Spices, acid, and some benzoate of soda preserve catsup. Some foods may contain natural preservatives. For instance, cranberries contain a high amount of acid and benzoic acid which are both preservatives.

Drying denies bacteria, molds, and other agents the moisture needed to develop. Sun-drying, one of the oldest preservation methods, is used to dry fruit, vegetables, and other foods. Sulfur dioxide fumes, obtained by using sodium sulfite or by burning sulfur under fruit as it lies in racks in the sun, may be used to aid the sun. Both preserve color and retard oxidation that causes browning. Some foods are preserved if they contain 5% or less moisture, such as dry milk, eggs, tomato flakes, and potato granules. Others such as flour keep well if they contain 13% moisture or less. Dried fruit (as noted) keeps well if it has a 20 to 25% moisture content. Freeze-dry food has up to a 2% moisture content. If moisture is too high in some foods, they will not keep. Dried foods have a lighter shipping weight, require less stable packaging, and need less expensive storage than some other foods.

Tunnel-drying is a method of drying foods using fast-moving drafts of warm, moisture-hungry air. At times, warm, dry inert gases are introduced to avoid oxidation that may give a straw-like flavor. Products that whip to a foam, such as eggs or milk, can be dried effectively as foams. Spray-drying, a method in which a slightly concentrated liquid, such as milk, is sprayed into a chamber where the moisture is extracted from the fine mist as the solids drop to the floor, is used frequently. Drum-drying uses a drum heated inside with steam, the drum rotating into and out of a liquid. The liquid dries on the drum part out of the liquid. It is then scraped off before the drum

Fig. 3-1. Instant dry sweet potatoes are made by a drying method that reduces bulk from 7½ lb of fresh potatoes to 1 lb of the dried product. Courtesy USDA

enters into the liquid to pick up more solids. Drum-drying can be done inside a vacuum so oxidation and other undesirable reactions are better controlled. Vacuum-drying uses a vacuum chamber to induce rapid drying. Continuous vacuum drying is used for potatoes, onions, and so forth. Freeze-drying is a method by which food is frozen and then put into a vacuum so that the ice sublimates or turns into a vapor without becoming a liquid. It is used for drying shrimp, meats, coffee, fruit, vegetables, and other foods. Although it is a more expensive method of drying than some others, it produces such a high-quality product that the cost is worthwhile.

Foods spoil with difficulty if they contain 10% or more salt. Salt pickles keep well with a 16% salt content. Dill and other similar pickles with 10% salt and around 0.6 to 0.8% lactic acid keep fairly well under refrigeration. Since food with above 2% salt lacks palatability, we try to reduce the amount of salt and combine its retarding action with other substances such as acid and smoke. Salt preserves because it draws moisture from a spoilage agent so that the agent cannot grow.

Pickling, which develops acid, has been used for many years to preserve foods. At a pH lower than 4.5 or 4, many spoilage agents are ineffective. Therefore we add vinegar or let fermentation and other actions form acid to pickle the item. Sauerkraut is preserved at a 2½% salt and a 1.8% lactic acid content. Salad dressings, tomato catsup, and other quite acid foods keep well because spoilage agents cannot exist in such a low pH. This is important to remember in reducing food poisoning possibilities. A food such as mayonnaise may be quite safe, but once it is mixed with other foods so that the pH is higher, harmful agents can invade and reproduce. Botulinum, a bacteria that produces a toxin so violent that a millionth of a gram can kill a man, cannot exist at a pH of 4.5 or lower.

Smoke preserves because it contains creosote and other products antagonistic to spoilage agents. Common table salt, nitrites, nitrates, and other compounds are used to assist smoke in preserving food. Some spices also have an antagonistic effect against spoilage agents and, when used in food, act to preserve. There are many other chemicals that preserve food, but they must be approved for use both in kind and amount. For instance, benzoate of soda or benzoic acid is allowed up to $1/10$ of 1% of total weight. Sulfur dioxide or sodium sulfite cannot exceed 200 to 300 parts per million (ppm) in dried fruit. Calcium or sodium propionate, a preservative used in bread, cannot exceed .32 parts for each 100 parts by weight of flour.

Some foods can be destroyed by chemical reactions, such as oxidation of fat which develops rancidity. Substances such as BHA (butylated hydroxyanisole), propyl gallate, and citric acid in propylene glycol may be added to fats or oils to reduce such deterioration. These types of substances also must be approved in kind and amount.

There has been criticism of the government and industry for allowing the addition of some substances to preserve food or retain quality. For instance, the use of nitrites is under attack because some data show it can combine in the body to make nitrosoamines that may be carcinogenic (cause cancer). Stilbesterol, used at one time to desex male chickens and make them into capons, was removed from the approved list because it too was suspect of being a carcinogen.

Undoubtedly, there is a need to exercise great caution in allowing substances to be used to preserve foods or retain desirable qualities. If evidence is sufficient to show that a substance not over a given amount is not harmful but can be of benefit, however, there should be no reason for its restriction.

A food high in sugar will not spoil. In ancient times food was preserved in honey. A jam or jelly keeps if the sugar content is 55%. Candied fruits and other foods have a higher sugar content than this. Frequently, sugar plus other preservation agents are used together.

Yeast attacks carbohydrates (sugars, starches, and so forth) and converts them into alcohol. When a product such as wine contains 14% alcohol, fermentation stops because yeast cannot function in this much alcohol. Wine 12 to 14% in alcohol content keeps for a long time. Acids and some other substances in wine also aid in preserving it. If wine is allowed to stand exposed to air, vinegar bacteria begin to turn the alcohol into an acid. A liqueur or spirit high in alcohol arrests all actions that would cause deterioration. Some alcoholic products are heated to preserve them and then placed into sealed containers. Filters so fine that they take out all yeasts, bacteria, and other spoilage agents now are used to avoid such heat treatment. This is why a canned beer or ale can be called *draft*. Draft beer is beer that has not been heat treated and for this reason is somewhat perishable. However, if these filters are used, the same thing is accomplished without heat and so the term ''draft'' as meaning ''unheated'' can be used.

We can refrigerate a food and delay the action of spoilage agents. Growth is extremely slow below 45°F and practically stops at 32°F; in fact' bacteria, trichinae, and other undesirable organisms gradually die off in frozen storage, but this is no guarantee that a frozen food will not contain them if the food was originally contaminated when it went into frozen storage. Freezing stops the action of spoilage and many deteriorative agents, especially if the temperature is 0°F or lower.

Slow freezing can destroy quality because it encourages expansion of the moisture in the cell to a point where the cell ruptures or large, sharp crystals pierce the cell and cause it to collapse. This can be noted when we allow ice cream to freeze slowly in a tray. Fast freezing such as in a blast tunnel at low temperatures, contact freezing, or freezing by immersion in liquid nitrogen, freon, and so forth develops small crystals that do less harm. In fact, tomatoes, avocados, bananas, and so on can be frozen in liquid nitrogen with extreme rapidity so that little harm to the cellular structure occurs. These products, if carefully thawed, are much like fresh ones. A tomato after being frozen this way and thawed, for instance, can be sliced and used in salads. A frozen dessert such as sherbet can slowly develop a coarse crystalline structure if it is stored where a temperature fluctuation occurs. Meat and other flesh products develop a heavy drip loss when frozen slowly or when they are allowed to remain where temperatures vary. Similarly, frozen vegetables and fruits lose quality quickly if they are not frozen rapidly or if temperatures vary.

Heat above 140°F destroys most spoilage agents but, to be sure, foods are heated to much higher temperatures to preserve them. Pasteurization is a heat treatment used to destroy organisms that can harm an individual. It also preserves if the item is refrigerated and not allowed to come in contact with air or anything that might introduce organisms. Milk is pasteurized by heating it 30 minutes at 143°F or 15 seconds at 161°F. If it is to be used for making cheese, it must be reinoculated with lactic acid producing bacteria because pasteurization destroys them, and they must be present to produce a good clabber. Eggs are pasteurized by heating them at around 138°F for a period of time, a temperature that is below their coagulation point.

Foods may be heated in sealed plastic wraps and then refrigerated. In a number of instances, this gives them a shelf life of up to 60 days. Chilled foods on the market have frequently been treated this way. The AGS system of preparing foods in pouches for later use uses this method but exhausts air from the package before heating so that undesirable oxidation is not so apt to occur.

If raw or cooked food is put into a sealed container so that it cannot come in contact with a contaminant and this container is then heated so that all spoilage agents are destroyed, the food keeps a long time. A method of doing this commercially was discovered by a Frenchman named Appert in 1809. This was the beginning of canning (Appertizing).

Today, there are more canned foods than any other type of preserved food. Food placed into sealed metal cans is loaded into a retort, the retort is sealed tightly, and steam at high pressure is introduced to cook the food if it is raw and make it sterile. As long as the seal is not broken, the food should remain unspoiled, although for practical purposes a year is considered as long as any canned food should be held. Some high-acid foods such as plums, tomatoes, and sauerkraut, should be kept for shorter periods of time, if possible. A new method called *flash-18* is presently used to can thick foods such as macaroni and cheese, Spanish rice, and hash and cream-style corn. This method avoids having to hold the food at elevated temperatures in the retort for long periods of time, which harms flavor and texture. In the flash-18 method, the food is cooked in large stock pots in a room under 18 psi (pounds per square inch). At this pressure water boils at 253°F, a temperature extremely effective in destroying organisms. This gives an assured thermal kill. The food is put into sterile cans, a sterile lid is put on it, and the can is sealed. It is then allowed to cool inside the can before being removed to an outside chamber. The men in this room work with sterile gloves and in clean, sterile clothing, When they leave the room they must enter a decompression chamber so that the 18 psi pressure can be brought slowly to normal. This avoids giving them the "bends," a condition in which gas forms in the bloodstream and causes death.

Many new and novel methods of preserving food are being introduced. Investigations are presently being conducted to ascertain if osmotic drying

Fig. 3-2. Dehydro-freezing is a process in which foods are partially dehydrated and then frozen. The extraction of some of the water reduces the chance for rupturing of the cells upon freezing. The fresh apples on the right would make the amount of canned apples shown in the center and the amount dehydro-frozen ones shown on the left. Courtesy USDA

is practical. This is a method in which a strong salt solution or other substance attracts moisture in the cells of meat, vegetables, or fruit and pulls it out. Dry steam also is being considered. Superheated steam is terrifically moisture-hungry, and if exposed to food not only cooks it but pulls much of the moisture from it. Dehydro-freezing is a method in which an item is partially dehydrated and then frozen. Removing a part of the moisture from the cell reduces cell damage in freezing. It has been used successfully on many fruits and vegetables. Irradiation from a substance such as Cobalt-60 has been under investigation. At one time the U.S. Army authorized irradiated bacon for use in the armed services, but because of a high destruction of some vitamins, difficulty in destroying some *Salmonella* and *Streptococci,* and problems in controlling enzymatic reactions, this product was taken off the approved list. Considerable research still is going on, and perhaps in the future irradiation will assume more prominence. Surface irradiation has been successful in helping to reduce spoilage in fresh fruits and vegetables. Mature potatoes given low dosages of irradiation do not sprout. Cereals can be quickly rid of insect infestation and the eggs destroyed with irradiation.

Other advances are being made. Dried or freeze-dried fruits and vegetables are compressed into extremely small packs to eliminate shipping bulk, and to reduce packaging, storage space, and transportation weight. Volume reductions range from 75% for green peas, corn, and some meats to 94% for green beans. Because of these reductions, the cost of these dried, compressed products is about equal to frozen or canned products. Undoubtedly, irradiation, novel drying methods, compression, and other sophisticated methods of preservation will be used more and more, bringing new foods of better quality on the market.

CANNING

Today's cannery is usually highly mechanized. Little or no handwork occurs in preparing, washing, sizing, grading, peeling, shelling, trimming, loading into cans, or other manipulations. Canneries also are located close to raw materials now, and some products may be processed right in the field in which they are harvested.

After selection and preparation, food is usually blanched in boiling water or by steam to fix color, improve flavor, destroy enzymes and bacteria, soften tissues, or remove gases and dirt. Blanched asparagus is more pliable and goes into cans better after this treatment. Bulky spinach and other greens are compacted so that they can be packed into cans. Some fruits have a more uniform color and do not turn brown if blanched. After

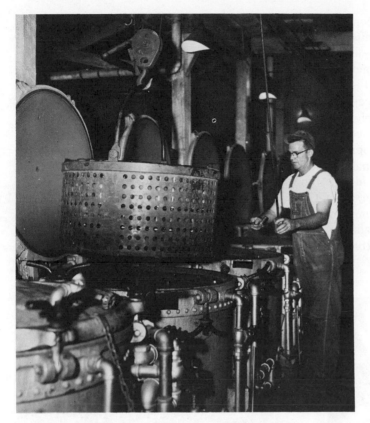

Fig. 3-3. Sealed cans of food are lowered into a retort where they will be subjected to steam under pressure so that the food is sterilized and will be preserved. Courtesy USDA

blanching, the foods are ready to be put into cans; only a few are completely cooked at this point. They are put into the can either with or without a packing liquid. The cans then are closed and exhausted either by heating or by using a mechanical vacuum, and they are machine sealed. Steam processing then occurs. After processing, the cans are rapidly cooled.

Canners code the can tops with letters and numbers so that the product inside can be identified and the date of canning can be ascertained. The federal government keeps a record of all can coding so that it can trace foods to the canner, if necessary.

Crimped, double-seam cans have considerably simplified the making of cans. The development of enamels to prevent foods from reacting with can metals has been another big advancement. An enamel or lacquer can be applied in a uniform film over metal sheets and then baked at high temperatures, leaving an insoluble, inert, resinous film that resists attack from foods on the metal of the can. The Sanitary, also known as the Standard or "R-," enamel is used for cans in which highly colored fruits, berries, or beets are processed. It prevents metal salts from joining with the acid and anthocyanin pigments (red), which would develop a brownish purple color. C-enamel is used for canning products with considerable sulfur in them. It retards development of ferrous sulfide in corn, fish, meat, and other products. Additional enamels are used to resist the specific action of alcohol, fats, meat, acid, and other products.

Most canners do not market their own products but sell them to brokers who put on their own labels with their own brand designations. For instance, the California Packing Corporation packs a tremendous amount of food for other brokers. If it markets its own product, the brand name will be designated as "Del Monte," a well-known label. But if it sells the canned

Fig. 3-4. An example of a good descriptive label. Note the words used that have a precise meaning as to age, quality, and so forth. Because the product is colored with an artificial green coloring, it must be labeled "Below Standard in Quality," but the food is high in other quality factors. Courtesy Green Giant Co.

Fig. 3-5. An example of a good label. Some information is not required by law but tells the buyer much about the product. The "1.06" refers to the specific gravity of the tomato puree. The use of the word "fancy" indicates that the seller claims his product meets U.S. Fancy quality but makes no claim that it has been federally graded. Under court rulings, this product, if shipped in interstate commerce, may be considered misbranded if it does not meet standards for U.S. Fancy quality. Courtesy Frank M. Wilson Co.

goods to others, it may put their labels on. Thus a buyer may find he is offered two identical items that bear different labels.

The Pure Food and Drug Division's provisions must be observed in labeling. The label must list the product's name, the canner's or distributor's name and address, the net can contents, and the ingredients if the product is not a common food. If the product is below standard in quality or fill, the label must state this. If it is below standard in quality, the reason must be given. The packing medium must be listed along with the style pack, variety, and the use of artificial or imitation flavors or colors, if they are used. Pictures on labels must be representative of the product inside. Many words may not be used because they may confuse or misinform.

Many labels use descriptive terms to indicate quality, kind, and so forth. Some use the words "very young," "young," or "mature" to indicate age. Terms such as amounts, number of servings, number of pieces in the can, can size, and others may be used; they mean specific things and buyers should know what these terms mean.

Standards of Quality

The USDA has established quality standards for most processed fruits and vegetables. The use of a grade on a label is entirely voluntary on the part of the canner or distributor. The federal grades are:

Fruits	Vegetables
U.S. Grade A or Fancy	U.S. Grade A or Fancy
U.S. Grade B or Choice	U.S. Grade B or Extra-Standard*
U.S. Grade C or Standard	U.S. Grade C or Standard

*California may grade tomatoes "Choice" since they are defined as a fruit.

Fig. 3-6a. Frozen food packed under continuous inspection and graded by federal graders, and

Fig. 3-6b. canned goods similarly packed. Courtesy USDA

"U.S." before a grade or the use of a federal shield with the grade in it indicates that the product has been graded by a federal inspector. Courts have ruled that if a term that indicates a grade or quality in federal grading is used in any way, even in explanatory matter, the product must meet this grade.

Establishing Grades

Federal grades are established by scoring specific factors and adding these to get a total score; 90 or above is usually Grade A or Fancy, 80 to 89 is Grade B or Choice or Extra-Standard, 70 to 79 is Grade C or Standard, and below 70 is Substandard. Substandard does not mean that the food is unwholesome; it merely means that some quality defects lower the grade below Standard. The product may be considerably broken up or off-color, or it may have a great number of defects. Where form or appearance may not be important, Substandard food is sometimes used.

Often fruit or vegetables juices have only two grades: Fancy or Grade A running from 85 to 100 in score, and Grade B or Extra-Standard (Choice) from 70 to 84. Sometimes there is no Grade B, but a Grade C or Standard runs from 70 to 84. Buyers will find that foods carry only the number of grades needed to move them on the market.

A product can have a high score and still not make a grade. For instance, the total score for pears may be 80, which would make them Grade B or Choice, but because the pears failed to score 16 or more for color, they must be graded Grade C or Standard. This is called a *limiting rule* and means that unless the product scores a specific number of points or more in

Fig. 3-7. Three grades of canned tomatoes. The front tray contains U.S. Grade A or Fancy tomatoes. These are whole, practically uniform; good, red, typical color; practically free from defects; normal tomato flavor and odor. The back tray contains U.S. Grade B or Extra-Standard tomatoes. They are mostly whole; reasonably good, red, typical color; reasonably free from defects; normal tomato flavor and odor. The tray at the right contains U.S. Grade C or Standard tomatoes. These are mostly pieces; fairly good, red, typical color; fairly free from defects; normal tomato flavor and odor. Courtesy USDA

a particular factor, it cannot be graded that high. Thus in order to Grade B, pears must score 16 or more, and if they grade 14 or 15 or less, they cannot be graded B regardless of whether the total score is 80 or higher. A *partially limiting rule* is one which allows freedom in imposing or not imposing the rule. Thus the grader may decide that the other factors in a product score so high that he will not invoke the limiting rule. (See footnotes in Figure 3-9.)

Factors usually scored for fruits and vegetables are color, absence of defects, and character. The last covers tenderness, texture, and maturity. Uniformity and symmetry may be scored under defects. Flavor is usually not scored but is considered a characteristic "under the masthead," which means that good flavor and odor must be present.

The level of the score is an important consideration in buying. Two lots of pears scoring respectively 89 and 90 points may be similar in quality but separated by grade and, consequently, price. Some packers or distributors consistently sell products that score at the bottom of the grade, whereas others market those with higher scores. Scores of products can be obtained by requesting a grade certificate. For certain needs some factors making up a grade may not be important: for example, uniformity of size and symmetry for pears or peaches that are to be cut up. If the score is low for these two factors, it is not too important.

The grading of processed fruits and vegetables has been undergoing changes in the past few years. These changes are being introduced as new

Score Sheet for Canned Fruit Cocktail.

Three standards are indicated: Grades A, B and Substandard (SStd).

Size and kind of container_____
Container mark or identification_____
Label_____
Net weight (ounces)_____
Vacuum (inches)_____
Drained weight (ounces):
( ) Meets fill of container_____
( ) Fails fill of container_____
Brix measurement_____
Sirup designation (extra heavy, heavy, etc.)_____
Proportions of fruit ingredients:

Peach:	__ oz ___ % ( ) Meets ( ) Fails_____
Pear:	__ oz ___ % ( ) Meets ( ) Fails_____
Pineapple: __ oz ___ % ( ) Meets ( ) Fails_____
Grape:	__ oz ___ % ( ) Meets ( ) Fails_____
Cherry:	__ oz ___ % ( ) Meets ( ) Fails_____
Total	__ oz 100 %

Count:
Pineapple ( ) Sectors ( ) Diced_____
Cherry halves_____

Factors	Score points		
Clearness of liquid media_____	20	(A) (B) (SStd)	17–20 14–16 ¹0–13
Color_____	20	(A) (B) (SStd)	17–20 ²14–16 ¹0–13
Uniformity of size_____	20	(A) (B) (SStd)	17–20 ²14–16 ¹0–13
Absence of defects_____	20	(A) (B) (SStd)	17–20 ¹14–16 ¹0–13
Character _____	20	(A) (B) (SStd)	17–20 ¹14–16 ¹0–13
Total score_____	100		

Normal flavor and odor_____
Grade_____

¹ Indicates limiting rule.
² Indicates partial limiting rule.

Fig. 3-8. Courtesy USDA

Score Sheet for Canned Asparagus.

Note three standards are indicated, A, C and Substandard.

Number, size, and kind of container_____
Label_____
Container mark or identification_____
Net weight (ounces)_____
Vacuum (inches)_____
Drained weight (ounces)_____
Type_____
Style_____
Size or sizes (Spears, tips, and points)_____
Length of cut_____
Heads (cut) (percent, by count)_____

Factors	Score points		
Liquor _____	10	(A) (C) (SStd)	9–10 7–8 ¹0–6
Color _____	20	(A) (C) (SStd)	17–20 14–16 ¹0–13
Defects_____	30	(A) (C) (SStd)	25–30 ¹21–24 ¹0–20
Character _____	40	(A) (C) (SStd)	34–40 ¹28–33 ¹0–27
Total score_____	100	_____	

Flavor (A, C, or SStd)_____
Grade_____

¹ Indicates limiting rule.

standards are published or revisions made. They are based, however, on the methods used in the past.

There is a growing tendency to indicate the number of samples that must be tested to establish a grade and also the sample size that must be tested. The sample size usually depends upon the size of the container. It also is becoming more and more common to indicate the number of severe, major, and minor defects a sample can have and what the average number of severe, major and minor defects can be to make a grade. For instance, for leafy greens to grade U.S. A, the average defects among samples tested cannot be over 0.75 for severe defects and not over 4.5 per sample for major defects. It is becoming more and more common to precisely define defects and not leave them up to the judgment of the grader. The use of a statistical approach in obtaining drained weights and quality factors is also occuring. Additionally, in the past only drained weights were considered in evaluating products. Fill had to conform more or less to general standards. But in the newer standards being published there is an increasing tendency, especially in canned fruits, to establish standards of fill for the specific item. The following indicates how these recommended fill weight values are compiled for canned Clingstone peaches:

| Size Can | Sliced—Fill Weight Values in Ounces | | | | | | |
	$\overline{X}_{min}$	$LWI_{\overline{x}}$	$LRl_{\overline{x}}$	LWL	LWL	$\overline{R}$	R_{max}
8 Z tall	5.4	5.0	4.8	4.4	4.0	1.0	2.1
No. 300	9.7	9.2	8.9	8.5	7.9	1.4	3.0
No. 303 glass	10.7	10.1	9.8	9.4	8.7	1.5	3.2
No. 303	10.7	10.1	9.8	9.4	8.7	1.5	3.2
No. 2	13.1	12.4	12.1	11.6	10.9	1.7	3.7
No. 2½	19.0	18.2	17.8	17.2	16.3	2.1	4.4
No. 2½ glass	18.5	17.7	17.3	16.7	15.8	2.1	4.4
No. 10	72.0	70.6	69.8	68.8	67.2	3.7	7.9

$\overline{X}_{min}$ means minimum lot average fill; $LWI_{\overline{x}}$ means lower warning limit for subgroup averages; $LRL_{\overline{x}}$ means the lower reject limit for subgroup averages; LWL means the lower warning limit for individual fill weight measurements; LRL means lower reject limit for individual fill weight measurements; $\overline{R}$ means a specified average range value over or under the established standard that is permitted; and R_{max} means a specified maximum range for a subgroup in this factor.

The following score sheet indicates how a sheet must now be set up to allow for the scoring of an item such as leafy greens for which defects are classified as minimum, major, and severe. Note that in some cases there are no minor, major, or severe defects, and the area for these is blanked out. Note also that the total for each class is obtained and that the sample average for minimum, major, and severe defects must be detailed. This score sheet compared with Figures 3-9 and 3-10 shows the departure that is being made in the new grading standards.

No., Size, and Kind of Container

Label

Container or Identification		1			2			3		
Container or Identification	Cans/Glass									
Container or Identification	Cases									
Net weight (ounces)										
Vacuum (inches)										
Drained weight (ounces)										
Sample unit number		1			2			3		
Quality factors		Min.	Maj.	Severe	Min.	Maj.	Severe	Min.	Maj.	Severe
Color										
Character										
Damage										
Harmless Extraneous Material	PLANT									
Harmless Extraneous Material	Green, fine									
Harmless Extraneous Material	Green, coarse									
Harmless Extraneous Material	Other									
Harmless Extraneous Material	Seed head									
Harmless Extraneous Material	Root crown									
Harmless Extraneous Material	Root stub									
	Other Than Plant									
Total (each class)										
Cumulative total (all classes)										
Flavor and Odor	Good									
Flavor and Odor	Objectionable									

Sample average: Min. Maj. Se-vere

Usually top, middle, and lower grades meet the following descriptions:

U.S. Grade A or Fancy products are highest quality. Fancy vegetables must have clear liquor; a typical, uniform color; normal flavor; appropriate size; and be tender, succulent, well formed, and free from blemishes and extraneous water. Fruits must have typical color without blemish, greenness, or tarnishing. Color must be uniform. Shape and symmetry must be good. Crushed, broken, split, or other damaged items must fall within established tolerances. Similarly, defects such as stems of fruit, caps in berries, peel, and evidences of poor workmanship, as in coring pears or pitting peaches, must be within narrow tolerance limits. The term "practically free" is usually used to indicate quality levels in this grade.

TABLE 3-1

	Score Range from Maximum to Minimum			
Factors	A	B	C	(Substandard)
Peas				
Clearness of liquor	9–10	7–8	5–6	0–4
Uniformity of color	14–15	11–13	8–10	0–7
Absence of defects	27–30	23–36	19–22	0–18
Maturity	40–45	34–39	28–33	0–27
Total score range	90–100	75–89	60–74	below 60
Pears				
Color	18–20	16–17	14–15	0–13
Uniformity of size and symmetry	18–20	16–17	14–15	0–13
Absence of defects	27–30	24–26	21–23	0–20
Character	27–30	24–26	21–23	0–20
Total score range	90–100	80–89	70–79	0–69

U.S. Grade B (Extra-Standard or Choice) products are not usually as tender or succulent, well trimmed, or fine flavored as the higher grade. Vegetables may have two or three but not all of these defects: lack of symmetry or form, lack of uniformity of color, lack of the deepness of color of a Fancy product, slight blemishes or spots, larger or smaller pieces than in Fancy, or pieces not as uniform. Fruits, similarly, may lack the color, shape, symmetry, or character of Fancy. "Reasonably free" is a term frequently used to describe quality in this grade.

Score Sheet for Frozen Broccoli.

Size and kind of container
Container mark of identification
Label
New weight (ounces)
Style
Count (of stalks)

Factors		Score points	
Color	20	(A)	18–20
		(B)	¹16–17
		(SStd.)	¹0–15
Uniformity of size	20	(A)	9–10
		(B)	8
		(SStd.)	²0–7
Absence of defects	20	(A)	31–35
		(B)	¹28–30
		(SStd.)	¹0–27
Character	40	(A)	32–35
		(B)	¹28–31
	———	(SStd.)	¹0–27
Total score	100		

Flavor and odor
Grade

¹Indicates limiting rule.
²Indicates partial limiting rule.

Score Sheet for Frozen Strawberries.

Number, size, and kind of container
Label: Style or pack: Fruit-sugar ratio (if shown)

Container mark or identification	Containers or sample Cases

Net weight (ounces)
Style
Size or sizes (whole)
Under ⅝" (percent by count)

Factors		Score points	
Color	40	(A)	36–40
		(B)	¹32–35
		(C)	¹28–31
		(SStd)	¹0–27
Defects	40	(A)	36–40
		(B)	¹32–35
		(C)	¹28–31
		(SStd)	¹0–27
Character	20	(A)	18–20
		(B)	¹16–17
		(C)	¹14–15
	———	(SStd)	¹0–13
Total score	100		

Flavor and odor
Grade

¹Indicates limiting rule.

Fig. 3-9. Courtesy USDA

U.S. Grade C or Standard products are good, edible food, wholesome in every respect, but they may lack tenderness, have fewer whole pieces or less uniform pieces, or lack uniformity of color. More blemishes, or broken or mashed items may be found. Greenness or paleness of color also may be more evident. Several but not all of the following defects may be present: off-color, excessive spots, blemishes, hard portions or other defects detracting from appearance or quality, lack of uniformity of size or symmetry, insufficient trim, coring, or peeling. Frequently, the term "fairly free" describes characteristics within this grade.

U.S. Substandard (SStd) products lack the required quality of C Grade. Noticeable variation in grade factors may be present. At times the term

**Score Sheet for Chilled or Canned
Orange Juice.**

Size and kind of container
Container mark (packages)
   or
Identification (cases)
Label (including ingredient statement, if any)
Liquid measure (fluid ounces)
Style
Brix (degrees)
Acid (grams/100 ml.: calculated as anhydrous
   citric acid)
Brix-acid ratio (   )
Recoverable oil (% by volume)

Degree of coagulation $\left\{\begin{array}{l}(\ \ )\ \text{None}\\(\ \ )\ \text{Slight}\\(\ \ )\ \text{Serious}\end{array}\right.$

Factors		Score points	
Color	40	(A)	36–40
		(B)	¹32–35
		(SStd)	¹0–31
Defects	20	(A)	18–20
		(B)	¹16–17
		(SStd)	¹0–15
Flavor	40	(A)	36–40
		(B)	¹32–35
	——	(SStd)	¹0–31
Total score	100		

Grade

¹Indicates limiting rule.

Fig. 3-10. Courtesy USDA

"U.S. Grade D" may be used to refer to a fruit U.S. Grade C except that it is packed in water. An item U.S. Grade E is Substandard, lower than C, and is also packed in water.

Water, solid, or heavy packs are not necessarily substandard but may be any grade. Even Grade A fruit is packed in water. *Solid pack* means that no water is added. *Heavy pack* means that only a small quantity is added. The term "pie pack" may be used to indicate solid or heavy packs, but most frequently the term means a U.S. Grade E item. There would be less confusion if buyers would use the first four grades, A, B, C, or SStd, and indicate whether the pack was water (about 30 to 35% to product), heavy, or solid pack.

Standards of Identity

Most canned foods must conform to the Food and Drug Administration's standards of identity which require that foods bearing a specific name be a specific item and that terms used to describe foods indicate exact properties. Thus if a label says grapefruit, the product must be mature *Citrus paradisi* and not another variety. If the label says "cubed," the size and shape must meet specific definitions. FDA also requires that many labels for foods *list ingredients in order of greatest to least quantity*. Names cannot be used to infer a ratio of foods that does not exist. Thus to say "Chicken and Noodles" is not permitted if noodles are in greater quantity than chicken. It must be "Noodles and Chicken." An exception is that the term "Pork and Beans" can be used when beans are in greater quantity than pork because this is a traditional name that was used before the standards came into effect.

Standards of Fill

Some canned items must be filled to $3/16$ in. from the container top. Others must be filled to 90% of the water capacity. Still others must be filled as "full as practical" without impairment to quality or breaking or crushing of the ingredients. If the standard of fill is not met, the label must state prominently "Below Standard in Fill" or "Slack Fill." The National Canner's Association recommends the following fill from the top if it does not impair products:

No. 10 and No. 3 cylinder cans	$27/32$ in.
No. 2½ cans	$20/32$ in.
No. 2 cans	$19/32$ in.

Drained Weight

Drained weight usually is not a factor influencing grade, but government quality standards usually state a recommended drained weight for a product.

Drained weight refers to the weight remaining after the liquid has been allowed to drain for 2 minutes on a screen.[1] It is important to know this because it is directly related to how many portions will be obtained per unit. Servings vary according to the amount of fruit or vegetable in a can to packing medium. "Net weight of can contents" is both the weight of the product and the liquid in the can and not drained weight. Buyers should specify the minimum drained weight acceptable. Compiling information on yields can be helpful in indicating actual portions obtained. (See Table 3-2.)

Density of a product may be specified instead of drained weight for products such as cream-style corn or apple butter. A casual density test is to stir the product and then place a small amount in a mounded mass on a smooth, flat surface. After 2 minutes the spread and amount of separation of free liquid is noted. Some buyers use a blotter and put samples of equally measured product on it. They then note the moisture ring formed in 2 minutes on the underside. Flow tests also can be made on a consistometer.

Specify *heavy* tomato catsup as 33% solids with a specific gravity of 1.15 or more, and *light* as 25% solids with a specific gravity of 1.11 to 1.14. Usually, catsup has not less than 25% solids, tomato paste not less than 24%, and tomato puree not less than 25%.

Count and Size

To obtain proper size portions and control costs, specify can counts or size. This text indicates many sizes. Watch sizing or counts. It may be better to give two 64-count slices of pineapple rather than one large 28-count slice per No. 10.

To ascertain the number of cans to use in place of another can of different

---

[1]To determine the drained weight, the contents are emptied on a circular mesh screen, set on a frame with the vertical side higher than the level of the product on the screen. The can contents are distributed over the screen to form a layer of uniform depth, accomplished usually by tilting the open container so as to distribute the contents evenly over the screen, which has been previously weighed. Fruits in halves are turned pitside down during the draining to permit complete drainage, but this is done in such a way as not to express additional liquid. Two minutes from the time drainage begins, weigh the screen and the drained item. The weight, less the screen weight, is the total drained weight. Four types of circular screens are used to determine drained weights: (1) 8-in. screen with 8 meshes to the inch for all goods packed in No. 2½ cans or smaller, except tomatoes; (2) 8-in. screen with 2 meshes to the inch for tomatoes in No. 2 cans or smaller; (3) 12-in. screen with 8 meshes to the inch for all foods packed in No. 3 cylinder, No. 10, or 1 gal cans, except tomatoes; and (4) 12-in. screen with 2 meshes to the inch for tomatoes in No. 10 cans. The bottom of the sieve or screen is woven-wire cloth, which complies with the specifications for Sieves, published March 1, 1940, in LC 584 of the U.S. Department of Commerce, National Bureau of Standards.

size or the number of cans to use in place of other cases of different size, use Table 3-2. To obtain the total net yield (packing medium and product) in a case, multiply the number of cans per case times the ounces (volume) per can. Thus, in a case of No. 300 cans, 36 per case, there are 486 oz (36 × 13½ oz). A case of 6/10s of similar product contains 662 oz (6 × 103.7 oz). To ascertain the number of 300 cases needed to equal a case of 6/10s, divide the 300 case yield into the 6/10s case yield (622 ÷ 486), which will indicate that 1.3 cases of No. 300 cans, 36 per case, would equal a case of 6/10s. Thus buyers who need to calculate yields among various can sizes can do so by using the proper data as listed in Table 3-3.

Syrup Density

A label must state the type of packing medium. But the packing medium is not a grade factor, although very frequently higher-grade fruit has a heavier syrup. The heavier the syrup, the less chance fruit has of breaking up. Packing mediums on fruit may be water, juice, slightly sweetened juice, light syrup, medium syrup, heavy syrup, or extra-heavy syrup.

A syrup's density will differ for different fruits. Density can be tested by using a Brix hydrometer or a polarscope. A light syrup on peaches is between 14 and 19° Brix; whereas a light syrup on cherries is 16 to 20° Brix.

Apricots *packed* in a 55, 40, or 25° Brix syrup will come out of the can at 25, 21, and 16° Brix, respectively. Thus the fruit absorbs some of the sugar. Syrup density at packing is called *put in;* the density on use is called the *cut out*. Cut outs should not be tested until 15 or more days after packing. Normally, for every degree Brix, a fruit has 1% sugar, a fact helpful in dietary planning. The amount of nonsucrose sugars that can be combined with sucrose in syrups is controlled by the government.

Deterioration

Cans are very durable, but occasionally a can is dropped, a seam springs, or a top fails to seal and spoilage occurs. Some high-acid foods can eat through the metal and develop leakage. Any distended can or one containing food that does not appear, feel, or smell right should be discarded. Most spoiled food can be detected by its distasteful odor, soft and sloughy texture, and deteriorated appearance. Never taste suspect food.

Leaking cans that lose some of their contents are called *leakers*. A *swell* is any distended can. A *puffer* is a swell caused by meat spoilage. A *hydrogen swell* is caused by acid reacting with can metals, freeing hydrogen gas. The food is not harmful, but the best practice is to throw it out and take no chances. A swell caused by nonbacterial causes is called a

TABLE 3-2
Sizes and Quantities of Fruit in Some Can Sizes

Fruit	Can Size	Amount or Number in Can*	Size Serving or Number per Serving	Servings per Can
Apples, heavy	No. 10	7 lb 8 oz		Makes 6 pies
Applesauce	No. 10	6 lb 11 oz	½ c	25
Apricot, halves	No. 10	75–85	3 to 4 halves	23–25
Apricot, halves	No. 2½	20/23	3 to 4 halves	6–7
Apricots, whole	No. 10	50	2	25
Apricots, whole	No. 2½	12/16	2	6–8
Blackberries	No. 2	1 lb 4 oz	½ c	5
Blackberries	No. 10	6 lb 10 oz	½ c	25
Blackberries, heavy	No. 10	6 lb 7 oz		Makes 4–5 pies
Cherries, RSP	No. 10	6 lb 14 oz		Makes 5 pies
Cherries, sweet	No. 10	240/260	½ c (8 to 10)	30
Cherries, sweet	No. 2½	65/70	½ c (8 to 10)	7 to 8
Figs, kadota	No. 10	110/120	3	30–40
Figs, kadota	No. 2½	28/32	3	10
Fruit cocktail	No. 10	6 lb 14 oz	½ c	25
Fruit cocktail	No. 2½	1 lb 14 oz	½ c	7
Fruits, salad	No. 10	6 lb 14 oz	½ c	25
Fruits, salad	No. 2½	1 lb 14 oz	½ c	7
Grapefruit	No. 3 cyl	3 lb 2 oz	½ c	11
Grapefruit, broken	No. 10	6 lb 9 oz	½ c	25
Peaches, halves	No. 10	35/40	2	17½–20
Peaches, halves	No. 2½	10/12	2	5–6
Peaches, sliced	No. 10	6 lb 14 oz	½ c	25
Peaches, sliced	No. 2½	1 lb 14 oz	½ c	7
Peaches, solid	No. 10	6 lb 10 oz		Makes 4–5 pies
Pear, halves	No. 10	40/50	2	20–25
Pear, halves	No. 2½	10/14	2	5–7
Pineapple, slice	No. 10	57/64	2	29–32
Pineapple, slice	No. 2½	14/16	2	7–8
Pineapple, crushed solid pack	No. 10	6 lb 14 oz	½ c	25
Pineapple, crushed	No. 2½	1 lb 13 oz	½ c	7
Pineapple, broken or half slice	No. 10	6 lb 11 oz	½ c	25
Pineapple, broken or half slice	No. 2½	1 lb 13 oz	½ c	7
Pineapple chunks	No. 2	48/55 (2½c)	½ c	5
Pineapple chunks	No. 2½	72/80 (3½ c)	½ c	7
Pineapple chunks	No. 10	232/290 (12–13 c)	½ c	25
Pineapple tidbits	No. 10	6 lb 11 oz (512/960)	½ c	25
Pineapple spears	No. 2	16 spears	3	5

TABLE 3-2
Sizes and Quantities of Fruit in Some Can Sizes

Fruit	Can Size	Amount or Number in Can*	Size Serving or Number per Serving	Servings per Can
Plums, pruple	No. 10	65/90	3	22–30
Plums, gage or egg	No. 10	45/55	2–3	22
Prunes, dried	No. 10	140/170	3–4	50
Prunes, heavy pack, dried	No. 10	210/280	3–4	80

*Numbers given here are good averages for institutional use. Data based on experience in use.

TABLE 3-3
Some Common Can Sizes Used for Food Facilities

Can Name	Dimensions, in. Diameter	Height	Canner's Designation	Volume, oz	Approxi- mate Cups	Number per Case
2Z	2⅛	2¼	202 × 204*			
	2⅛	2⅞	202 × 214	4¾‡	½‡	12,24, 48
6Z	2⅛	3½	202 × 308	5¾	⅔	24, 48
8Z tall†	2¹¹⁄₁₆	3¼	211 × 304	8.3	1	24, 36, 48, 72
No. 1 picnic	2¹¹⁄₁₆	4	211 × 400	10½	1¼	24, 48
No. 211 cylinder	2¹¹⁄₁₆	4⅞	211 × 414	12	1½	24, 36, 48
No. 300	3	4⁷⁄₁₆	300 × 407	13½	1¾	24, 36, 48
No. 1 tall	3¹⁄₁₆	4¹¹⁄₁₆	301 × 411	15	2	24, 48
No. 303	3³⁄₁₆	4⅜	303 × 406	15.6	2	12, 24, 36
No. 303 cylinder	3³⁄₁₆	5⁹⁄₁₆	303 × 509	19	2⅓	
No. ½ flat	3⁷⁄₁₆	2¹⁄₁₆	307 × 201			48
No. 2	3⁷⁄₁₆	4⁹⁄₁₆	307 × 409	19.9	2½	12, 24
No. 2 cylinder	3⁷⁄₁₆	5¾	307 × 512	23	3	24
No. 2½	4¹⁄₁₆	4¹¹⁄₁₆	401 × 411	28.5	3½	12, 24
No. 3	4¼	4⅞	404 × 414	33.6	4	12, 24
No. 3 cylinder	4¼	7	404 × 700	46	5¾	12
No. 5	5⅛	5⅝	502 × 510	56	7	12
No. 10	6³⁄₁₆	7	603 × 700	103.7	12¾	6
Gallon	6³⁄₁₆	8¾	603 × 812	130	16	4, 6

*Diameter is represented by first number and height by second; the first digit in each three-digit group indicates inches and the second and third digits, sixteenths of an inch. Thus 303 by 406 is a can 3³⁄₁₆ in. in diameter and 4⅜ in. in height.
†Also called No. 55 or the 8-oz can.
‡One fluid ounce equals ¹⁄₁₆ pint and one cup equals ½ pint. Net weight of contents not given since foods vary in density and thus in net weight contained in cans.

flipper or *springer*. Overfilling, storage at high altitudes, heat, can denting, or other reasons can develop a flipper or springer.

Some bacteria (called *anaerobes*) can grow without air, and even though a can is sound, spoilage occurs because the bacteria are inside after processing. Some bacteria such as *Clostridium Botulinum* can exist in spore form, which is bacteria enclosed in hard, case-like shells that protect them from high temperatures. Later the bacteria break out of the spore and develop. Botulinum are anaerobes that form a toxin that is so powerful a cupful could destroy all the people on the earth. Botulinum can reproduce in foods over a pH of 4.5 such as beets, string beans, cream soup, tuna, peas, and other nonacid foods but not in tomatoes, fruit juices, and so forth. Antitoxins have been developed to counteract the poison, and not all individuals eating food containing the toxin will die if the antitoxin is administered quickly. Foods containing the toxin may not be readily detected. Boiling foods containing botulinum for 10 minutes destroys the toxin. This is why we advise in quantity food preparation to subject most canned foods to some heating.

Thermophilic (heat-loving) bacteria withstand high processing temperature and can be in foods after processing. Some may never be a problem unless the food is held at elevated temperatures (100°F or more), in which case they can grow and cause spoilage. A spoilage caused by some thermophiles is called a *flat sour*. This produces an acid but no gas, and the cans do not swell. The spoilage can be detected by the high-acid odor, the disintegration of the food, and a sloughy, soft texture. Color changes also may be evident. Some thermophiles grow under anaerobic conditions, developing a gas that distends the can. The food has an odor best described as "cheesy." Some other anaerobic thermophiles form hydrogen sulfide, a gas soluble in the can's liquid contents; therefore no swelling occurs. A strong, unpleasant, nauseating odor and blackness from the formation of iron sulfide can indicate such spoilage.

Discoloration may be caused by metals reacting with food, by the effect of high or prolonged heat, or by bacterial action. Corn can become blue-gray from copper sulfide formation; peas turn black when contaminated with copper. Blackening of hominy is caused by a failure to remove all the lye used in processing. Copper increases the darkening of canned milk products. Iron darkens fruits. At high temperatures the sulfur in foods breaks down, and a black deposit can form in the can's headspace. This black material also can become detached and adhere to some of the food, as seen at times in canned corn where the C-enamel has failed to protect the can lining from attack. Pears may turn pink if subjected to too high a heat in processing.

FROZEN FRUITS AND VEGETABLES

The shorter the time between harvest and freezing and the faster the freezing process, the higher the quality of the frozen item. Preliminary preparation of fruits and vegetables for freezing is the same as for canning, but a blanching in hot water or steam occurs in vegetables to destroy enzymes and frequently to fix color. Blanching also makes food more pliable for packing or wilts it down so that it is reduced in bulk. Fruit may be treated with an antioxidant such as sulfur dioxide fumes or ascorbic acid to avoid browning on the surface. Vegetables have about 1% salt added, and are usually frozen without liquid. Sugar is added to fruit to preserve flavor, color, and, to a certain extent, the texture. A syrup can be used in place of sugar. A "4:1" or a "5:1" on a label indicates the fruit-sugar ratio.

Frozen fruit is packed in 10- or 12-oz and 1-, 6-, 6½-, 25-, and 30-lb units. If the quantity used is large, it may come in larger tins, containers, or even barrels. Vegetables come in 10- or 12-oz, 1-, 2-, 2½-, 3-, and 5-lb packs, but potatoes, peas, corn, and some others may come in larger packs.

Most of the commonly used frozen fruits and vegetables have federal grade standards; these are the same as canned standards, with sums of scores of quality factors deciding the final grade. Grade terms also are identical with those of canned goods for first, second, third, and substandard grades. Most packers pack only one or two grades.

Frozen fruit is graded after thawing and vegetables after cooking. Good flavor and odor are requirements and are not part of the total score. Sometimes a percentage based on number of defects is compiled and used to establish a score of a factor. The following gives maximum scores for frozen raspberries, blueberries, and peas:

	Raspberries	Blueberries	Peas
Color	40	20	20
Absence of defects	40	40	40
Character	20	40	40
Total score	100	100	100

Temperatures in storage and transportation should be −10°F to properly retain quality. As noted previously, fluctuating temperatures are harmful to quality. Thawing and refreezing is quite harmful, and products that receive such treatment may drop in grade; therefore it is wise to state in specifications that the "condition upon delivery should be the grade specified."

PROCESSED JUICES

Processed juices on the market are fresh chilled, canned single strength, canned concentrated, frozen (usually concentrated), and dehydrated. Frozen juices outrank all others in quantities used.

Chilled Juices

Chilled juices, sweetened or unsweetened, are available in highly populated urban centers, especially those close to heavy citrus growing areas. Some chilled juices may not be heat treated but may merely be prepared from fresh fruit or concentrated juices and then marketed. Heat, refrigeration, and the acidity of the juice makes it possible to hold many of these

Fig. 3-11. Chilled orange juice under processing. The USDA inspector will withdraw representative samples and examine these not only visually and by taste, but he also will ascertain the acidity, Brix, the acid-Brix ratio, percent oils, and so forth. Courtesy USDA

juices for longer periods without deterioration. Juices preserved with chemical preservatives do not qualify as chilled juices.

Watch for coagulation and material separation. Good flavor and odor should be present without noticeable traces of oil from the fruit. Color should be good for the product. In orange juice, the color should be a bright yellow or yellow orange. Dull, dark, murky juice should be rejected. Watch for seed or portions of fruit, rind, cells, pulp, or other extraneous material. Excessive sediment should be cause for rejection. Brix readings for density vary according to the quality, the amount of sweetener, and whether the juice is made from single or concentrated-strength products. Such readings will vary from 11 to 12.5°. The Brix-acid ratio also is a quality factor and may vary according to product from 11:1 to 17:1 in high-quality juices. Federal standards for quality exist for orange juice only; minimum scores for Grades A and B are 85 and 70.

Canned Juices

Federal grades exist for canned apple, grape, grapefruit, blended grapefruit and orange, lemon, orange, pineapple, tangerine, and tomato juices. Some sauerkraut, carrot, blended vegetable, or blended fruit juices, and some tropical fruit juices are marketed. Federal grades are U.S. Grade A (Fancy) and U.S. Grade C (Standard); U.S. Grade D is Substandard. Minimum scores for Grades A and C are 85 and 70, respectively.

A canned juice should have a bright, sparkling typical color for the product, not dull, dark, or excessively cloudy. The juice should be practically free from sediment or other residue, particles of pulp, seeds, specks, or other extraneous matter. The consistency should be typical for the product.

Tomato juice should have some viscosity whereas others should not. Flavor should be pleasant and that of well-ripened, mature fruit, with aroma typical of the fruit. Because of processing, the flavor may differ from that of fresh juice, but there should be no flavor of fermentation, excess oil from peel, or any other off-flavors.

Brix and acid limits have been established for juices with federal standards. Some juices must meet a Brix-acid ratio. A U.S. Grade A grapefruit juice must have a Brix-acid ratio of 7:1 when the Brix reading is 10.5° or more.

Buyers should watch for coagulation in the juices or a tendency to separate. Juices may or may not be sweetened. If a blend is purchased, specify the ratio of juices. Fill of container should be 90% of the total water capacity.

TABLE 3-4
Brix and Acid Values for U.S. Grade A Fruit Juices

Juice	Brix Minimum		Anhydrous Acid per 100 ml, in grams	Type Acid
	Sweetened	Unsweetened		
Canned single strength				
Apple		11.5	0.25 to 0.70	malic
Grape	16.0	14.0	0.45 to 1.40	tartaric
Grapefruit	11.5	9.0	0.85 to 2.00	citric
Grapefruit*	11.5	10.0		citric
Grapefruit and orange	11.5	10.0	0.80 to 1.70	citric
Grapefruit and orange*	12.5	11.0		citric
Lemon		8.0	5.00 to 7.00	citric
Orange, Calif. and Ariz.	10.5	10.5	0.70 to 1.40	citric
Orange, other	10.5	10.5	0.60 to 1.40	citric
Pineapple	12.0	10.5	1.35	citric
Tangerine		10.5	0.65 to 1.35	citric
Canned concentrated				
Grapefruit		10.5†		citric
Orange		11.5†		citric

*Reconstituted type.
†Calculated after rehydration to normal concentration.

Canned Concentrated Juices

Federal standards exist for canned concentrated grapefruit, orange, and tomato juice. Minimum scores for the two grades U.S. Grade A (Fancy) and U.S. Grade C (Standard) are 70 and 85, respectively. The juices are graded after being brought to normal strength. Quality factors, Brix, and acid values after reconstitution should be similar to those listed for canned juices. Juices concentrated for manufacturing should not be accepted.

Frozen Juices

Most frozen juices are concentrated, therefore a water-juice ratio of 3:1 is required to bring them to normal strength, but the ratio can vary from 2:1 to

18:1. These juices may be blends of single fruits or of different fruits and may be sweetened or unsweetened. Evaluate quality after reconstitution using factors previously cited for fresh juice. The flavor should be more that of fresh than canned juice.

Federal standards exist for grape, grapefruit, grapefruit and orange, lemon, lime, and orange juices, with grades of U.S. Grade A (Fancy) and U.S. Grade B (Choice) with minimum scores of 85 and 70, respectively. Case packs may vary from units of 6 oz to a gallon in size. Some juices may be frozen in heavy-weight polyethylene bags. Lemon or lime juices may come sufficiently sweetened to be used for the making of ades.

Dehydrated Juices

Dehydrated grapefruit, orange, tomato, and other juices are marketed. Federal standards exist for the grapefruit and the orange juice as U.S. Grade A (Fancy) and U.S. Grade B (Choice), with respective minimum scores of 85 and 70. Evaluate after rehydration using factors considered for other juices. The moisture content should not be more than 3% when purchased. The juices may be sweetened or unsweetened.

FRUIT SPREADS

The standards of identity of the federal government state that jellies, jams, preserves, and marmalades must not be less than 65% solids and must contain not less than 45 parts fruit or fruit juice and 55% sugar. Fruit butter must not contain less than 43% soluble solids and must be a "smooth, semisolid paste made from not less than 5 parts by weight of fruit and 2 parts by weight of sweetener." Nonsucrose sweeteners may not be more than 25% in relation to sucrose. Pectin or acid can be added only in amounts needed to make a desirable jel. One fruit or combinations of two to five may be used in jellies and jams. Special jellies such as mint, honey, or wine can vary somewhat from these standards; for instance, wine jelly may be made from 11% apple pectin, 56% sugar, and 33% wine. "Pure" means only fruit and sugar are in the product; "imitation" must be used on the label when artificial color, flavor, or other nonnatural components are used.

Jams and preserves have fruit suspended in the jel. A jam usually has fruit that is mashed or broken, whereas a preserve has whole or large pieces suspended in the jel. Marmalades are clear jellies in which slices or cut pieces of fruit or peel are suspended. A great deal of orange marmalade is made from the bitter, sour Seville orange. Mixed citrus marmalades are on the market as are items such as gingerroot, carrot, and mixed fruit. A jelly is a clear product made only from fruit juice and sugar. Fruit butters are semisolid pastes of cooked, strained fruit pulp. Spices may be added. They should be smooth, heavy enough to spread, and have good flavor.

Federal grades for fruit spreads are U.S. Grade A (Fancy) or U.S. Grade B (Choice), except for apple butter and cranberry sauce, which have grades of U.S. Grade A (Fancy) and U.S. Grade C (Standard). The minimum score for Grade A in both is 85; the minimum score for either the B or C grade is 70.

No. 10 cans of fruit spread are usually used in food services. Jars may be 1, 2, 4, 5, and 8½ lb, approximately 11 lb, and a gallon. The 30-gal wooden tub is used when large quantities are required. Many facilities use the individual packs becuase of the control of the portion and sanitary features. These may come about a tablespoon each in cases of 100 a box, 12 boxes a case.

DRIED AND LOW-MOISTURE FRUIT

We process in this country over a billion pounds of dried or low-moisture fruits. Most fruits should be fully ripe for this processing. Prunes and figs are allowed to drop to the ground from ripeness and are gathered and then dried. This gives high sugar and maximum flavor. Pears are picked just before ripening and are ripened in storage. Apples may be picked at good maturity and held. If processed at proper maturity, quality should be good.

Because of the high maturity at which most fruits are dried, there is a chance of damage or defects, and good inspection should be given. The

Fig. 3-12. Trays of peaches spread for drying. Courtesy USDA

character of many fruits is considerably changed by drying, and damage caused by insects, molds, or decay may be hidden. Modern methods of cleaning and processing have improved quality; thus sanitation and defects are of less concern than they were in the past.

Container sizes vary. Food services usually use 25- or 30-lb cases or 4-lb packs, 6 to the case. If the quantity used is small, purchase 1-lb packages. Dates come in 60-, 10-, 5-, and 1-lb packs. The 5- or 10-lb pack is best for a food facility. If fruits in the slab are chopped or not readily observable, check carefully for defects. Low-moisture items come in No. 10 cans, 6 per case usually.

Moths, weevils, and other insects attack dried fruits; to avoid this, storage may have to be in a refrigerated area. Normal storage is 40 to 50°F. If the product is sealed in a can, such as vacuum-dried fruits, no storage other than normal needs to be provided. All dried products can darken and lose flavor if held too long. Purchase about a month's supply.

TABLE 3-5
Sizes for Dried Fruit, in Inches

	Figs					
Sizes	Adriatic or Kadota	Calimyrna	Mission	Apricots	Peaches	Pears
No. 1 Jumbo	1⁸/₁₆ up	1⁹/₁₆ up	1⁵/₁₆ up	1⅜ up	2 up	1⅞ up
No. 2 Extra Fancy	1⁵/₁₆–1⁸/₁₆	1⁶/₁₆–1⁹/₁₆	1³/₁₆–1⁵/₁₆	1¼–1⅜	1¾–2	1¾–1⅞
No. 3 Fancy	1³/₁₆–1⁵/₁₆	1³/₁₆–1⁶/₁₆	1¹/₁₆–1³/₁₆	1⅛–1¼	1½–1¾	1½–1¾
No. 4 Extra Choice	1¹/₁₆–1³/₁₆	1¹/₁₆–1³/₁₆	¹⁵/₁₆–1¹/₁₆	1–1⅛	1⅜–1½	1⅜–1½
No. 5 Choice	¹⁵/₁₆–1¹/₁₆	¹⁵/₁₆–1¹/₁₆	¹³/₁₆–¹⁵/₁₆	¹³/₁₆–1	1⅛–1⅜	1⅛–1⅜
No. 6 Standard	under ¹⁵/₁₆	under ¹⁵/₁₆	under ¹³/₁₆	under ¹³/₁₆	under 1⅛	under 1⅛

Note: Figs and pears are measured by width of stem to calyx end, and apricots and peaches are measured by diameters. The number of size is the same for pears, but the size terms are jumbo, extra large, large, medium, small, and extra small, respectively.

As in many other foods, the quality factors for dried foods are empirical and cannot be reduced to writing. Color, uniformity of size and shape, absence of defects, and character (texture, tenderness, and maturity) indicate quality. Flavor and odor are important.

Federal standards for quality exist for dried fruits of market importance and for some low-moisture fruits. Certificates of grade may be obtained. Trade terms of "good," "reasonably good," and "fairly good" refer to U.S. Grades A (Fancy), B (Choice), or C (Standard), respectively. Grading is done by counting defects and assigning a percentage factor. These

Work Sheet for Scoring Processed Raisins.

Size and kind of packages and/or cases_____
Markings_____
Label or brand_____
Net weight_____
Type_____
Size or sizes_____
Moisture content_____

Flavor	A	B	C
Defects		Maximum	
Pieces of stem:			
Thompson Seedless_____	1 per 96 oz____	2 per 96 oz____	4 per 96 oz____
Other types_____ _____	1 per 32 oz____	2 per 32 oz____	3 per 32 oz____
		Maximum (per 16 ounces)	
Capstems:[1]			
Thompson Seedless_____	15	25	35
Muscat_____	10	15	20
Sultana_____	25	45	65
Seeds in Muscat Seeded only[1]_____	12	15	20
Loose capstems: Muscat, uncapstemmed___	20	20	20
		Maximum (by weight) (percent)	
Undeveloped:			
Thompson Seedless "Small size"_____	1	2	2
All other raisins_____	1	2	2
Damaged:			
Thompson Seedless and Sultana_____	2	3	5
Muscat_____	3	4	5
Sugared (all raisin types)_____	5	10	15
		Maximum (by count) (percent)	
Moldy (all raisin types)_____	2	3	4
Shattered (or loose) individual berries and small clusters of 2 or 3 berries each.	Practically free.	Reasonably free	_____
Damaged by fermentation (all raisin types). Affecting appearance or edibility.	Not affected____	No more than slightly affected.	Not materially affected.
Grit, sand, or silt (all raisin types). Affecting appearance or edibility.	None of any consequence.	None of any consequence.	Not more than a trace.

Color	Maximum by weight (percent)	
Thompson Seedless:		
Sulfur bleached and golden:		
Well-bleached (Extra Fancy)_____	½	
Reasonably well-bleached (Fancy)_____ _____	3	
Fairly well-bleached (Extra Choice)_____	6	Definitely dark berries.
Sulfur bleached: Bleached (Choice)_____	15	
Golden: Bleached (Choice)_____	20	
Muscat: Soda dipped unseeded, and seeded: _____ Grade A__	10	
Grade B__	15	Dark reddish brown berries.
Grade C__	20	

Grade_____

[1] Not applicable to layer (or cluster) or uncapstemmed muscat raisins.

Fig. 3-13. Courtesy USDA

factors are added to obtain a total score. Federal standards use size as a grade factor for apples, prunes, and raisins. Trade grades are based almost completely on size. The California Dried Fruit Association certifies trade quality for fruit shipped from California. Trade grades are listed in Table 3-5. Dried fruits packaged for retail are sized differently than the grades listed here.

Work Sheet for Scoring Dried Prunes.

Size and kind of container_____

Container mark or identification_____

Label or brand_____

Varietal type_____

Size: Count per pound (Average)____ _____ Uniformity_____

    ( ) Extra large.   ( ) Large.

    ( ) Medium.   ( ) Small.

Moisture content_____percent; Uniformity_____

Varietal characteristics: ( ) Similar. ( ) Dissimilar.

Defects and summary of allowances[1]	Grade A maximum	Grade B maximum	Grade C maximum	Substandard maximum
Total of all defects, including off-color.	10 percent___	15 percent___	_____	No limit except as indicated below.
Total of all defects, including off-color and poor texture.	_____	_____	20 percent___	
Poor texture, end cracks, skin or flesh damage, fermentation, scars, heat damage, insect injury, other means. mold, dirt, foreign material, insect infestation, decay.	But no more than 6 percent.	But no more than 8 percent.	_____	
End cracks,[2] skin or flesh damage, fermentation, scars, heat damage, insect injury, other means, mold, dirt, foreign material, insect infestation, decay.	_____	_____	10 percent[2]__	
Skin or flesh damage, fermentation, scars, heat damage, insect injury, other means, mold, dirt, foreign material, insect infestation, decay.	_____	_____	But no more than 8 percent.	
Mold, dirt, foreign material, insect infestation, decay.	3 percent____	4 percent____	5 percent____	5 percent.
Decay _____	But no more than 1 percent.	But no more than 1 percent.	But no more than 1 percent.	But no more than 1 percent.

Total _____

U. S. Grade (including all factors)_____

[1] Percentages of defects are "by weight."

[2] Except that each 1 percent of end cracks to, and including 8 percent, by weight, shall be considered as ½ percent damaged by end cracks; and any additional end cracks shall be calculated as true percentage, by weight.

Fig. 3-14. Courtesy USDA

Look for uniformity of color and a lack of discoloration or off-colors. Highest grades have light colors, bright and typical for the product. Check

ORIGINAL   INSPECTION No. 1267

Dried Fruit Association of California
APPLICATION FOR INSPECTION

Shipper __FLEETWOOD PACKING CO., INC.__   __SAN JOSE, CALIFORNIA__

*For Steamer*__SEATTLE__   __JOHNSON__   *Line*

_____*Car No.*_____   *Route*_____

NUMBER OF PACKAGES	STYLE OF PACKAGE	VARIETY AND GRADE	CROP	SHIPPING MARK
450	48/15 Oz. Cartons	Select Natural Thompson Seedless Raisins	1959	1267 Norway
500	30# Cases	40/50 Santa Clara Prunes	1959	
800	24/1# Cartons	Fancy Blenheim Apricots	1959	

CONTRACT REQUIREMENTS
(State fully all conditions of sale necessary to enable Inspector to properly pass on shipment.)

__FLEETWOOD PACKING COMPANY, INC.__
Shipper

OFFICIAL CERTIFICATE OF INSPECTION

THIS IS TO CERTIFY, that on the 1 ST *day of* __MARCH_____, *19* 60, *an official inspector of this Association, carefully examined and tested the above described goods prepared for shipment to*_____ NORWAY _____, *and that the same are of good merchantable quality, equal to or better than the average of the season, in good condition and of the grade and character described in the above application of shipper.*

*IN WITNESS WHEREOF, this Association by its*_____
Secretary duly authorized has this 7 TH *day of* __MARCH___, *19* 60, *issued this certificate in its corporate name and under its official seal.*

DRIED FRUIT ASSOCIATION OF CALIFORNIA.

*By*_____
Secretary

F 2A

Fig. 3-15. A trade inspection certificate for dried fruit. Courtesy Dried Fruit Association of California

for end cracks, lack of ripeness, flesh damage, scars, molds, dirt, extraneous matter, decay, fermentation, and other defects. Insect infestation or damage is common. Reject excessively sugared fruit. Check each season to ascertain which size is most plentiful and lowest in price because this varies from season to season.

In checking dried apples, note that the units are fairly large and are not screenings; look for core, bruises, or skin defects. The apples may have bitter pit or corky tissue. Slab apricots are the product of mature, well-ripened fruits, which, in drying, have become flattened and misshapen so that they lack normal contour. Whole, pitted, dried apricots are available on the market. Natural and steamed apricot kernels may be purchased. Black figs should have a typical, natural black or dark reddish-brown color and be reasonably free of serious scar damage. White figs should be fairly free of blemishes and defects and be of uniformly light color. Bleached Calimyrnas are lightened with hydrogen peroxide. Tray-dried Kadota figs are bleached with sulfur and dried in layers. Their color should be white to light amber. Dried peaches are either freestone or cling. Varigrade peaches are those that contain mixed varieties and slabs and may be variable in color, appearance, and size but should be reasonably free from dark, off-color pieces. Pears that show dingy brown or red discoloration are downgraded.

When purchasing low-moisture fruits, look for quality factors similar to those cited for dried fruits. A wide variety are available, and each year the market offerings change. Apples may be available as applesauce, flakes, pieces, pie pieces, slices, granules, or diced. Apricots may come as halves, nuggets, slices, or granules. Slices or halves of figs may be processed. A fruit mix that can be returned to a satisfactory fruit cocktail mix exists. Prunes are available in many forms, as well as plum granules. Many different forms of peaches and pears are available. Even a low-moisture fruit cake mix is on the market. Dessert mixtures such as apple and cherry, apple and blueberry, or apple and raspberry can be obtained. At times low-moisture banana slices may be available. When purchasing, note the types available.

Within recent years a wide number of fruit crystals have come onto the market for use in making beverages or for serving as fruit juices. Orange crystals or powder fortified with ascorbic acid may be obtained. Others available may be apple, cranberry, grape, lemon, lime, pineapple, prune, or fruit mixtures. These are marketed sweetened or unsweetened. Beverage mixtures of different types are found. Normally, for judging quality of new products on the market, reconstitute and judge as a fresh product or a product similar to that for which quality standards exist.

DRIED VEGETABLES

Federal standards of quality exist for dried beans, lentils, and peas. They are U.S. No. 1, 2, and 3. There are many of these items on the market such as red, kidney, Mexican (chili), pinto, marrow, old-fashioned yellow-eye, navy, great northern, or lima. Limas are sized baby (small), medium, and large. Trade sizes for white beans are small and large. Hulled split peas are either green or yellow. Dried, black-eyed peas are marketed.

Examine for extraneous matter such as sticks, stones, and dirt. The product should be full, plump, well dried, and mature. Look for weevil damage. Indications of shriveling, broken pieces, split seeds, and damaged or crushed units lower quality. Cook to ascertain texture, flavor, and color. Beans, lentils, and peas may be purchased in 1-, 5-, 10-, 15-, 20-, 25-, 50-, and 100-lb lots.

Many dried, nonseed type vegetables also are on the market, and the quantity used and variety available is increasing each year. Many are vacuum-dried to avoid a straw-like flavor; others may be dried with warm, inert gases such as nitrogen to accomplish the same thing.

Low-moisture and freeze-dried vegetables are becoming more and more common. A few federal quality standards have been compiled. Quality evaluations can be made on the basis of rehydrating and then cooking. The moisture content of dried vegetables should be below 5%. Dehydrated potato granules, flakes, slices, or diced units are available. Some potato granules have dried milk added and may be fortified with ascorbic acid. Other dried potatoes may come in mixtures so that, with the addition of water, items such as escalloped, au gratin, or duchess potatoes can be obtained. Many other dried products such as chopped parsley; chives; minced garlic or garlic powder; chopped, sliced, or toasted onion slices;

Fig. 3-16. The dehydrated onions shown in the center are the equivalent of the fresh onions shown on the left. The volume after reconstitution is shown on the right. Courtesy USDA

chow mein vegetables; mixed vegetables; green peas or beans; carrots; bell peppers (green or red); tomato flakes; cabbage; celery; carrots; and mushrooms are available.

Look for good color and defects such as blemishes, peel, broken or damaged units, and extraneous material. The aroma after cooking should be natural and typical, with no moldy, musty, or other objectionable off-odor. Look for weevil and other damage.

Most low-moisture items are packed in No. 10 cans, 6 per case. To evaluate, compare with a cooked fresh product. If the item is used as a seasoning, the quality may not have to be as high as when the item is used in place of a fresh, frozen, or canned item.

SPECIFICATIONS

A specification for a processed food should follow the form suggested in Chapter 1. A specification should list the name, the amount wanted, the federal or trade grade or brand, the packaging, the price basis, such as a case or pound, and miscellaneous factors needed to get the right item such as styles, drained weight, fruit-sugar ratio, and enamel lining for the can.

Changing market conditions may cause items to change, but in the material that follows most factors required in a specification for a processed food will be listed. The various grades are listed, and the one usually used by institutions is indicated by an asterisk; for example; Grade A (90)*. This asterisk also refers to the quality standard listed after this summary for this grade. The quality standards for the other grades are not listed.

In setting up a specification, the buyer can use these summaries to see if all factors have been listed. Frequently, besides grade, the size or count, packing medium, style, recommended drained weight, and so forth must be listed, and the summary will list most of these. Recommended net can contents for canned items are given in Tables 3-6 and 3-9. Packaging for frozen or dried items has been mentioned previously. The sizes of cans for canned fruits, vegetables, and other products also has been discussed. The date in parentheses after the name of a product indicates the date of the federal standard from which most of the information in the summary is taken.

Certificates for grade requested by buyers of processed fruits and vegetables should not be older than 3 months and for some highly perishable products might have to be even more recent.

Some examples of specifications for some processed items follow:

a. Peaches, yellow cling, halves, canned

b. (List quantity wanted for purchase)
c. U.S. Grade 3 (Choice)
d. Packed in 6/10s, count per No. 10, 30 to 35 halves
e. Quote price by dozen cans
f. In heavy syrup, 19 to 24° Brix, minimum drained weight 66 oz per No. 10. Certificate of grade required.

a. Corn, cream style
b. (List quantity wanted for purchase)
c. U.S. Grade B (Extra-Standard) or Green Giant Brand
d. Packed in No. 2 cans, 24/case
e. Quote price by dozen cans
f. C-enamel lined cans; Minnesota grown. If not Green Giant, federal certification of grade required.

a. Asparagus, frozen
b. (List quantity wanted for purchase)
c. U.S. Grade B (Extra-Standard)
d. Packed in 2½-lb carton; 12 cartons/case
e. Quote price per case
f. Spears (stalks), large, all green; deliver at 10°F interior case temperature or lower.

a. Strawberries, frozen, whole
b. (List quantity wanted for purchase)
c. U.S. Grade B (Choice)
d. 30-lb can
e. Quote price per lb
f. Sugar-fruit ratio 1:4; Marshall variety only acceptable.

a. Tomato juice, canned
b. (List quantity wanted for purchase)
c. U.S. Grade A (Fancy)
d. 46-oz cans, 12/case
e. Quote price per dozen cans
f. Certificate of quality required; cans shall be R-enamel lined.

a. Jam, apricot and pineapple, Type II
b. (List quantity desired in this order)
c. U.S. Grade A (Fancy)
d. No. 10 can, 6/case; net can contents not less than 8.5 lb
e. Quote per 6/10 case
f. Ratio of apricots to pineapple 3:1; shall be pure fruit.

a. Raisins, Thompson seedless
b. (List quantity desired in this order)
c. U.S. Grade B (Choice)
d. 25-lb carton, polyethylene lined
e. Quote per lb
f. Soda and oil dipped, Extra Fancy color, size Select.

a. Prunes, Italian (tart)
b. (List quantity desired in this order)
c. Trade grade, Extra-large size
d. 25-lb carton, polyethylene wrapped
e. Quote per lb
f. Size 30/40; moisture content not over 25%.

Canned Fruits

Apples (1953)

> *Grades:* A (85)*, C (70).

> *Type:* Acceptable varieties are Northern Spy, Baldwin, Greening, R. Beauty, York Imperial, Grimes Golden, Arkansas Black, Newtown, Jonathan.

> *Styles:* Sliced.

> *Recommended minimum drained weight:* Solid pack: No. 10, 96 oz; No. 2½, 26 oz; No. 2, 18 oz; No. 303, 14 oz.

*Bright, uniform color, white, creamy or yellowish depending upon variety, not gray, pinkish, or brown. Uniform size 1¼ in. in length, thickness variance not greater than ¼ in. Tender, crisp, and crunchy without mushiness, damaged or broken slices. Whole or practically whole slices. Watch for excessive hardness or softness, excessive carpel tissue, peel, seeds or other defects. Cook to ascertain quality for specific use. (Quartered or whole baked apples are also on the market.)

Applesauce (1970)

> *Grades:* A (90)*, B (80).

> *Type:* Some acceptable varieties are Baldwin, Northern Spy, 20 Ounce, Gravenstein, Newtown, Transparent, Starr.

*Clear, bright not slightly pink, gray, brown, or dull. Consistency—stir and empty some on dry flat surface; should form moderately mounded mass that at end of 2 minutes has no more than slight separation of free liquor. Good finish, not pasty, "salvy," lumpy; no hard particles but can be granular. Watch flavor and odor carefully; taste for excessive tartness, blandness, cooked or scorched flavor. Watch for peel, carpel, seeds, specks, and other extraneous matter.

Apricots (1971)

Grades: A (90), B (80)*, C (70).

Styles: Halves, slices, whole, mixed pieces. May be peeled or unpeeled, pitted or unpitted; A Grade C and Substandard solid pack is marketed.

Syrup density: Extra heavy 25–40°, heavy 21–24°, light 18–20° Brix and water.

Recommended minimum drained weight in oz:

| | Whole | | | | Halves, Slices, Pieces, | |
| | Peeled | | Unpeeled | | | |
Container Size	(1)*	(2)†	(1)*	(2)†	and so forth	Solid Pack
No. 10	60.4	62.0	60.0	61.5	62.0	92.0
No. 2½	15.7	16.1	15.1	15.5	16.7	25.5
No. 2	9.8	10.1	10.5	10.7	11.5	
No. 303	8.9	9.1	8.5	8.7	9.5	

*In extra heavy or heavy syrup.
†In any other liquid medium.

*Reasonably bright, typical color, green areas or pale color should not be excessive and little browning evident. Even size and symmetry with no abnormal shape. Worm holes, insect damage, dark bruises, or brown spots considered serious defects. Watch for excessive freckling, loose pits, stems, skin, and so forth. Reject overripe, mushy, or hard and underripe fruit. Flavor should not be tart or astringent.

Berries (various dates)

Grades: A (90), B (80)*, C (70).

Syrup density:	Extra heavy	Heavy	Light
Most berries	24–35°	19–24°	14–19° Brix
Red raspberries	28° up	22–28°	14–22° Brix
Black raspberries	27° up	20–27°	14–20° Brix
Blackberries	25–35°	20–25°	15–20° Brix

Recommended minimum drained weight:	No. 10	No. 2½	No. 2	No. 303
Red or purple raspberries	53 oz.	14¼ oz	10 oz	8 oz
Red or purple raspberries, solid pack	60 oz	14½ oz	10¼ oz	8¼ oz
Black raspberries	55 oz	14¼ oz	10 oz	8 oz
Blackberries	62–66 oz*		11–12 oz*	8½–9¼ oz*
Blueberries or Huckleberries	55 oz		10 oz	7½ oz

Apricot Sizes

Number in Can

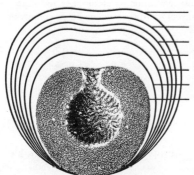

13 or less in No. 2, 18 or less No. 2½, 67 or less No. 10
13 to 15 No. 2, 18 to 20 No. 2½, 67 to 75 No. 10
15 to 17 No. 2, 20 to 23 No. 2½, 75 to 85 No. 10
16 to 18 No. 2, 23 to 36 No. 2½, 85 to 96 No. 10
18 to 23 No. 2, 26 to 33 No. 2½, 96 to 122 No. 10
23 to 27 No. 2, 33 to 39 No. 2½, 122 to 144 No. 10
27 up No. 2, 39 up No. 2½, 144 up No. 10

Cherry Sizes

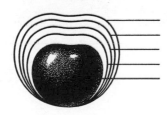

35 to 40 No. 2, 50 to 60 No. 2½, 210 to 235 No. 10
36 to 39 No. 2, 65 to 70 No. 2½, 240 to 260 No. 10
54 to 64 No. 2, 80 to 90 No. 2½, 290 to 335 No. 10
64 to 75 No. 2, 90 to 103 No. 2½, 335 to 390 No. 10
90 to 95 No. 2, 130 to 135 No. 2½, 480 to 540 No. 10

In between sizes of cherries not shown:

40 to 45 No. 2, 60 to 65 No. 2½, 225 to 240 No. 10
48 to 55 No. 2, 70 to 80 No. 2½, 260 to 290 No. 10
75 to 90 No. 2, 105 to 130 No. 2½, 390 to 480 No. 10

Fig. 3-17. Apricot and cherry sizes in canned foods.

| Other berries | 55–60 oz* | 9½–10 oz* | 7¾–8½ oz* |
| Other berries, solid pack | 70 oz |

*Heaviest drained weight is for water or light syrup, and lowest is for extra heavy syrup pack.

*Reasonably bright and typical color of well-ripened berries, uniform size and limited number small berries. Reasonalby free of undeveloped berries, cap stems, crushed, broken, mashed, or otherwise damaged fruit. Tender texture. Watch for insects, worms, or other extraneous matter. Since these fruits are fragile, it may be desirable to specify packs for table use to be extra heavy or heavy syrup packs to preserve shape.

Cherries, Red Sour, Pitted (1972)

Grades: A (90)*, C (80).

Recommended minimum drained weight: Syrup pack: No. 10, 70.2 oz; No. 2, 12.7 oz; No. 303, 10.2 oz. Water pack: No. 10, 72 oz; No. 2, 13½ oz; No. 303, 11 oz.

*Bright, typical color with little or no prominent brownish or mottled areas. Reasonably free from extraneous material, pits, mutilated or damaged cherries, and cherries blemished by scab, hail, discoloration, scar tissue. Tender, soft, yet retaining plumpness and shape. Fullness of flavor with tartness. Watch for bird or insect injuries. Most packs are heavy or solid packs.

Cherries, Sweet (1973)

Grades: A (90), B (80)*, C (70).

Styles: Pitted or unpitted.

Types: Royal Anne is a light-colored cherry; others are usually dark such as Bings, Tartarians, and Lamberts.

Syrup density: Extra heavy 25–35°, heavy 20–25°, light 16–29° Brix.

Recommended minimum drained weight in oz:

	Extra Heavy Syrup	Heavy Syrup	Other Packs
No. 10	64.5	66.5	70.0
No. 2½	17.5	18.0	18.5
No. 2	12.0	12.5	12.7
No. 303	9.7	10.0	10.2

*Reasonably good color typical of mature cherries, bright not dull. Royal Annes should have no purplish cast or excessive discoloration of the skin. Reasonably absent from such defects as extraneous material, portions of cherry stems, pits, growth, or other circular cracks, broken, mashed, or otherwise damaged cherries. Good shape and reasonably free from undersize cherries, all reasonably uniform in shape. Full fleshed, tender, no trace of astringency: good flavor. Not less than 5% are less than $^9/_{16}$ in. in diameter.

Figs, Kadota or Other (1973)

Grades: A (90), B (80)*, C (70).

Styles: Whole, whole and split, split and whole, split or broken.

Syrup density: Extra heavy 26–35°, heavy 21–26°, light 16–21° Brix.

Recommended minimum drained weight: No. 10, 63 oz; No. 2½, 18 oz; No. 2, 12½ oz; No. 303, 10 oz. (For over 71 figs per No. 10, drained weight should be 66 oz or more).

*Reasonably bright uniform color. In Kadota figs light greenish-yellow color. Reasonably uniform in size and symmetry. Reasonably free from scab, scars, bruises, discoloration, or other abnormalities. Watch for worm holes, insect damage, or other injury. Split or broken figs should conform to style specified; whole and split have less than 50% split or broken and split and whole have over 50% split or broken. Tender, ripe, flesh, full of lush flavor.

Fruit Cocktail (1973)

Grades: A (85)*, B (70).

Syrup density: Extra heavy 22–35°, heavy 18–22°, light 14–18° Brix.

Recommended minimum drained weight: Federal standards of identity require that drained weight shall be 65% or more of the fill of the container. No. 10, 71.15 oz; No. 2½, 19¹/₃ oz; No. 2, 13¹/₃ oz for Grade A.

Ratio of fruit in mixture: Peaches, diced, 30 to 50%; pears, diced, 25 to 45%; grapes, whole, seedless, 6 to 20%; pineapple, diced or wedge, 6 to 16%; cherries, approximate halves, 2 to 6%. Ratios should be based on drained weight.

*Liquid should be clear, bright in color, with no slight trace of pink or dullness. Small quantity of flocculent pieces of fruit may be present. Fruit should be bright and typical of variety. Diced units should be cleanly cut and even and not more than ¾ in. in greatest dimension. Sectors of pineapple shall be from ⅜ to ¾ in. on outside arc, from ⁵/₁₆ to ½ in. thick and from ¾ to 1 in. long. Reasonably free from harmless extraneous material, peels, pits, cap stems, broken or crushed grapes, uneven or broken cherry halves. Texture and tenderness should be firm, with little disintegration.

Fruit for Salad (1973)

Grades: A (85)*, B (70).

Syrup density: Same as for fruit cocktail above.

Recommended minimum drained weight in oz: No. 10, 64½; No. 2½, 18; No. 2, 12½.

Ratio of fruit in mixture: Peeled peaches, quartered or sliced, 23–46%; peeled or unpeeled apricots, halves or quarters, 15–30%; pears, peeled, quartered or sliced, 19–38%; pineapple wedges, 8–16%; cherries, 3–8%; grapes, 6–12%.

*Reasonably good color, free from artificial dye stain. Pieces uniform, not broken, crushed, or otherwise damaged. Look for defects similar to those described for individual fruit.

Gooseberries (no federal standard)

Grades: Specify Fancy, Choice*, or Standard.

Recommended minimum drained weight: No. 10, water pack, 70 oz, solid pack 80 oz.

*Berries reasonably whole with few split, excessively small, or immature berries, stems and blossoms. Reasonably uniform color of pale whitish green and uniform size. Tender, free from defects, such as scars, scab, insect or worm injury, insects or worms, or other extraneous matter.

Grapefruit Sections (1971)

   Grades: A (90), B (80)*, C (70).

   Syrup density: Recommended 16° Brix cut out.

   Drained weight is a part of grade

	No. 3 Cylinder	No. 2	No. 303
Grade A	29.05–30.65	11.55–12.15	9.50–10.00
Grade B and Broken	27.45–28.25	10.90–11.20	8.95–9.20

*Shall be not less than 50% by weight of drained fruit in whole or almost whole segments. Color reasonably uniform, bright, slightly variable but not off-color. Reasonably free from extraneous material, seeds, membrane, dry cells, "ricey" cells, or fibrous material. Use the broken grade, which confroms to Grade B except for wholeness of segments where segments need not be whole. Watch for scorched, caramelized, bitter or flat taste. Soft, tender flesh.

Orange and Grapefruit Sections

   Grades, drained weight, and syrup density as above for grapefruit sections. Quality factors are similar to those for grapefruit sections, except color of orange should be typical of that for oranges. Orange sections to grapefruit sections based on drained weight shall be 37½ to 60% in Grade A and in Grade B and Broken, 32½ to 60%.

Grapes (1973)

   Grades: A (85)*, B (70).

   Type: Thompson Seedless.

   Syrup density: Extra heavy 22° up, heavy 18–22°, light 14–18° Brix.

   Recommended minimum drained weight: No. 10, 62 oz; No. 2½, 17 oz; No. 2, 12 oz.

*Color should be typical for variety. Grapes should have reasonably uniform color, size, firmness, tenderness, and be intact with few broken or crushed grapes. Bruised grapes, stems, leaves, or other defects should be limited.

Peaches, Clingstone (1973)

   Grades: A (90), B (80)*, C (70), D (60). (Also, Grade C Solid Pack.)

   Styles: Halves, slices, diced, whole, mixed pieces, units, or salad pieces.

   Syrup Density: Extra heavy 24–35°, heavy 19–24°, light 14–19°.

   Recommended minimum drained weight in oz:

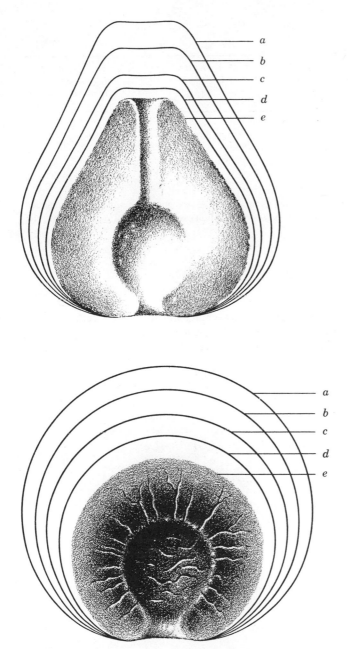

Fig. 3-18. Pear and peach sizes in canned foods.

Container Size	Sliced *	†	‡	Diced	Halves *	†	‡	Quarters *	†	‡	Heavy	Solid
No. 10	64.5	66.5	68.5	70.0	63.0	65.0	67.0				76.0	92.0
No. 2½	17.4	17.8	18.2	18.5	17.0	17.4	17.8				20.0	25.5
No. 2	12.0	12.3	12.6	12.7	12.1	12.4	12.7	12.1	12.4	12.7		

*In extra heavy syrup.
†In heavy syrup.
‡In other packing mediums.
Note: Halves in No. 10s, 24 count or more are 1½ oz heavier and in No. 2½, 7 or more are .6 oz heavier.

*Quality factors are much the same as for freestones except clings will show less raggedness, a better trim around the seed, and a more solid flesh. The syrup also will be somewhat syrupy.

Pears

Grades: A (90), B (80)*, C (70).

Types: Bartlett or Kieffer.

Styles: Halves, quarters, slices, diced, whole, mixed pieces, units, or salad pieces. Halves, quarters, or whole may be peeled or unpeeled.

Syrup density: Extra heavy 22–35°, heavy 18–22°, light 14–22° Brix.

Recommended minimum drained weight in oz:

Container	Quarters or Smaller	Halves	Diced
No. 10, less than 26 count	65.5	62.7	67.0
No. 10, more than 25 count	65.5	64.1	67.0
No. 2½, less than 9 count	17.2	16.4	19.0
No. 2½, more than 8 count	17.2	16.9	19.0
No. 2, less than 8 count	11.8	16.0	13.0
No. 2, more than 7 count	11.8	16.5	13.0

*Reasonably good color, clear white or creamy white, not pink, tarnished, or touched with brown. Not dead or chalky white. Reasonably uniform for style of pack. Few ragged, crushed, damaged, or broken pieces. Few halves split. Note workmanship in coring and trimming. Few pieces of extraneous matter, such as peels, seeds, stems, and other blemishes. Juice clear. Watch for grainy, tough, hard, or mushy fruit.

Pineapple (1957)

Grades: A (90), B (80)*, C (70).

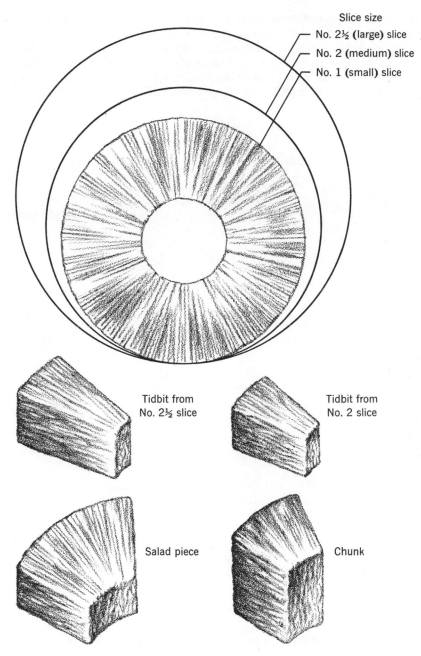

Fig. 3-19. Pineapple sizes in canned pineapple.

Styles: Whole slices, half slices, broken slices (arc or slice pieces not uniform), tidbits (small—length of arc ⅜ to ¾ in., length or radius ¹¹/₁₆ to 1¼ in., thickness ⁵/₁₆ to ½ in.; large—length of arc ¾ to 2 in., length of radius ¹¹/₁₆ to 1¾ in., thickness ⁵/₁₆ to ½ in.), chunks (⁹/₁₆ in. wide, 1½ in. long, and ½ in. thick), cubes or diced (not more than ⁹/₁₆ in. on any side), spears or fingers (not less than 2½ in. long), crushed (finely shredded or cut—can be called coarse, medium or crisp or fine cut).

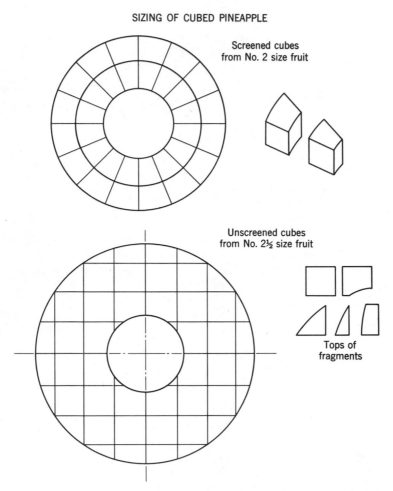

SIZING OF CUBED PINEAPPLE

Screened cubes
from No. 2 size fruit

Unscreened cubes
from No. 2½ size fruit

Tops of
fragments

Fig. 3-20. Cubed pineapple may be either screened or unscreened, and cube shapes will vary according to the type cutting used.

Syrup density: Extra heavy 22–35°, heavy 18–22°, light 14–18°.

Recommended minimum drained weight: Canned crushed pineapple other than heavy or solid pack less than 63% of net weight of contents must be labeled "Below Standard in Quality" followed by either "Good Food—Not High Grade" or "Contains Excess Liquid." Heavy pack must be 73 to 78%, and solid must be 78% or more. Drained weights for packs other than crushed are:

	No. 10 Can	No. 2½ Can	No. 2 Can
Slices	61½ oz	18¼ oz	12¾ oz
Half or broken slices	62½ oz	18 oz	12½ oz
Chunks	63¾ oz	18¼ oz	12¾ oz
Cubes	71¼ oz	18¼ oz	12¾ oz
Spears		18¼ oz	12¾ oz
Tidbits	65¾ oz	18¼ oz	12¾ oz

*Relatively few blemishes, such as deep fruit eyes, bruised portions. Not more than 0.4 oz core per lb of fruit. Reasonably uniform size and shape; little mashed or crushed pieces except in crushed; little raggedness of pieces. Reasonably good yellow color; not more than slightly dull; not too deep or too light; some shading and white radiant streaks allowed, providing it does not seriously affect appearance. Tender but not soft; fairly free from porosity. Good, rich, mellow pineapple flavor with some tartness; not bland. Not too tart (not over 1.35 grams anhydrous citric acid per 100 ml of fruit).

Approximate Sizes of Slices

Slice Size	Number of Slices per No. 10 Can	Slice Size	Diameter, in inches
No. 2½	28	No. 2½	3½ (overall)
			1¼ (center)
No. 2	50	No. 2	2⅞ (overall)
1⅛ (center) No. 1	64	No. 1	$2^{9}/_{16}$ (overall)
			⅞ (center)

Plums or Prunes (1972)

  Grades: A (90), B (80)*, C (70).

  Types: Prunes or purple-type plums, Green Gage, Yellow Egg, and so forth.

  Styles: Half or whole, peeled or unpeeled, pitted and unpitted.

  Syrup density: Purple types: extra heavy 26–35°, heavy 21–26°, light 16–21° Brix.

Other types: extra heavy 24–35°, heavy 19–24°, light 16–19° Brix.

Recommended minimum drained weight in oz:

Can Size	Purple Types		Green, Yellow Types	
	Halved, Unpeeled	Whole, Unpeeled	Whole, Peeled	Whole, Unpeeled
No. 2	12.0		11.5	10.9
No. 2		10.5 (under 17)**		
No. 2		11.0 (over 17)**		
No. 2½	17.0		16.7	16.3
No. 2½		15.5 (under 16)**		
No. 2½		16.0 (17 to 22)**		
No. 2½		16.5 (over 23)**		
No. 10	63.0		62.4	60.8
No. 10		60.0 (under 70)**		
No. 10		62.0 (over 70)**		

*Reasonably uniform color for variety, little variation or off-color, browning, or greenness. Look for loose pits, stems, leaves, burn, scars, worm holes, scab, and so forth. Reasonably uniform in size, few crushed or broken fruit. Reasonably uniform texture, plump, fleshy, firm yet tender. Few shriveled or abnormal fruit. Fruit should be well matured, holding shape. Skin should be tender and not tough. Juice should be clear and not murky, dull, or filled with excessively flocculent material.

**The numbers in parentheses are counts per can.

Prunes, Dried

Grades: A (90), B (80)*, C (70).

Types: Sweet—French (Robe), Imperial, Sugar; Tart—Italian (Oregon).

Syrup density: Extra heavy 30° up, heavy 24–30°, light 18–24° Brix.

Recommended minimum drained weight in oz: No. 10, 70; No. 2½, 19; No. 2, 13; heavy packs—No. 10, 110; No. 2½, 29.

*Typical black, blue-black, or reddish-brown color, depending upon variety. Reasonably uniform color, with only small amount of dull chocolate or brown color or abnormal flesh darkening. Reasonably uniform size, with largest prune not larger than twice the weight of the smallest. Buyers should state size desired by number of dried prunes per pound as 20/30, 30/40, 40/50, as given in dried fruit. Reasonably free of growth cracks, splits, breaks, insect injury, skin damage, scab, loose pits, stems, or other matter. Tough or firm areas caused by thrips damage should be noted. Watch also for evidence of mildew damage, leaf chafing, or limb rubs. Reasonably good tender, plump, fleshy texture. Skin reasonably tender. No caramelization, cooked or scorched flavor in prunes.

TABLE 3-6

Trade Association Recommendations for Minimum Net Weight of Contents for Canned Fruit

Fruit	Grade	Size Can No. 10	No. 2½	No. 2
Apples				
Slices		90 oz	26 oz	18 oz
Solid pack		96 oz		
Sauce		107 oz	29 oz	20 oz
Apricots, peaches, and plums	A	110 oz	30 oz	21 oz
	B	108 oz	30 oz	20 oz
	C	106 oz	29 oz	20 oz
	D		28 oz	
Pie		104 oz		
Water		103 oz	28 oz	
Solid		106 oz		
Berries	A	108 oz	30 oz	20 oz
	B	106 oz	29 oz	20 oz
	C	105 oz	29 oz	20 oz
Water		103 oz	28 oz	19 oz
Cherries, RSP	A	110 oz		20 oz
	C	105 oz		
Water		103 oz		
Cherries, sweet, unpitted	A	110 oz	30 oz	21 oz
	B	108 oz	30 oz	20 oz
	C	106 oz	29 oz	20 oz
Water		104 oz	28 oz	20 oz
Cherries, sweet, pitted	A	110 oz	30 oz	21 oz
	B	107 oz	29 oz	20 oz
	C	105 oz	29 oz	20 oz
Water		103 oz	28 oz	19 oz
Cranberries		117 oz		22 oz

Fruit	Grade	Size Can No. 10	No. 2½	No. 2
Figs				
Water	A	112 oz	30 oz	21 oz
	B	112 oz	30 oz	20 oz
	C	108 oz	29 oz	20 oz
		105 oz	29 oz	20 oz
Fruit cocktail and Fruits for salad	A	110 oz	30 oz	21 oz
	B	108 oz	20 oz	20 oz
Grapes (Same as sweet, unpitted cherries)				
Gooseberries		105 oz		20 oz
Peaches (See Apricots)				
Pears	A	108 oz	30 oz	20 oz
	B	106 oz	29 oz	20 oz
	C	105 oz	29 oz	20 oz
Water		104 oz	28 oz	
Pineapple				
Whole, slices, and chunks	A	108 oz	30 oz	20 oz
Broken slices	A	107 oz	29 oz	20 oz
Crushed	A	109 oz	30 oz	20½ oz
Water		106 oz	29 oz	20 oz
Crushed		107 oz		
(B and C grades are slightly lighter than those listed for grade A)				
Plums (See Apricots)				
Prunes, dried	A	110 oz	30 oz	20 oz
	B	108 oz	30 oz	20 oz
	C	106 oz	30 oz	20 oz

Canned Vegetables

Asparagus (1973)

   Grades: A (85)*, C (70).

   Types: Green, green tipped, green tipped and white, and white.

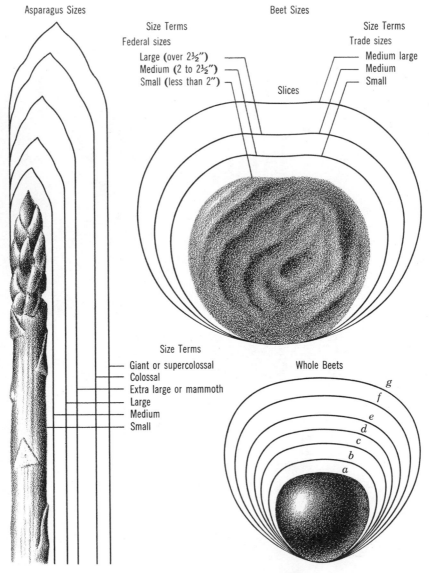

Fig. 3-21. Asparagus and beet sizes in canned vegetables.

Styles: Spears or stalks (more than 3¾ in. in length), tips (2¾ to 3¾ in. in length), points (2¾ in. or less in length), cut spears (15% may be 1¼ in. or less, but 20% must be 1¼ in. or over), cuts or bottom cuts (tips removed), mixed.

Recommended minimum drained weight in oz:

| | Spears, Tips, and Points | | | | Cut Spears or Bottom Cuts | |
| Can | Small to Large | | Extra Large Up | | | |
Size	*	†	*	†	*	†
No. 10					64.5	60.2
No. 5	43.0	39.0	41.0	38.0	42.0	38.0
No. 2½	19.0	17.2	18.0	16.7	18.5	16.9
No. 2	13.0	11.8	12.3	11.3	12.7	11.7
No. 303	10.7	9.5	10.1	9.2	9.7	9.2

*White or green tipped and white.
†Green or green tipped.

*The liquor should be fairly clear with some cloudiness but not excessive cloudiness. Some accumulation of sediment that is slightly gray or brown, but not seriously objectionable, may be present. Over 25% of the total height of the column of liquid is considered excessive. Color should be good for type 90% or more uniformity. Watch for grit, silt, poorly cut or misshapen pieces. Well-developed, without seedy appearance. Compact heads, tender without toughness or strings. Few soft or mushy pieces, stringy or frayed edges, poor cuts, not smooth or at right angles, or small pieces permitted. Watch for sloughy texture, noticeable bitter or undesirable flavor.

Beans, dried (1947)

Grades: A (85)*, C (70).

Types: White, Lima, Red, Black-eye (also called Black-eye Peas).

Styles: Tomato sauce, tomato sauce with pork or meat, brine, sweetened (contains molasses), and sweetened with pork or meat.

*Smooth, even color. No hard, coarse, grainy or lumpy beans, or excessive water, with not more than a slight separation of liquid except in brine pack, which may have a noticeable separation. Presence of one piece of extraneous material allowed for each 20 oz of net weight; few beans with loose skins or broken or mashed or damaged beans. Even, soft texture. (See also Kidney beans.)

Number Whole Beets per Can

Legend	No. 2	No. 2½	No. 10	Legend	No. 2	No. 2½	No. 10
a	60 to 75	80 to 105	300 to 375	e	15 to 24	22 to 34	75 to 124
b	50 to 60	70 to 85	250 to 300	f	10 to 14	15 to 21	50 to 74
c	35 to 49	50 to 70	175 to 250	g	6 to 9	8 to 14	35 to 49
d	25 to 34	35 to 54	125 to 175				

| Grade A Head Development | Grade C Head Development | Substandard Head Development |

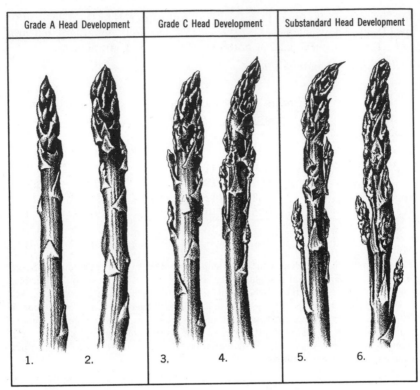

1.   2.   3.   4.   5.   6.

Fig. 3-22. The asparagus on the left shows head development in canned asparagus qualifying for U.S. Grade A. The center asparagus heads will grade C. The ones to the right will be Substandard Grade. Courtesy USDA

Beans, Snap (1972)

Grades: A (90), B (80)*, C (70).

Types: Green or wax; Blue Lake, Oregon recommended for green and Kentucky Wonder for wax.

Styles: Whole, whole vertical, sliced lengthwise (French), cut, short cut, mixed.

Sieve sizes: See Figure 3-23 and Table 3-7.

Recommended minimum drained weight in oz:

Can Size	Whole	Whole Vertical	Cuts, Less than 1½ in.	Cuts, Longer than 1½ in.	Mixed, Long and Short Cuts	Sliced Lengthwise or French
No. 10	57.5		63.0	60.0	63.0	59.0
No. 2½	15.8	16.8	16.2	16.0	16.2	16.0

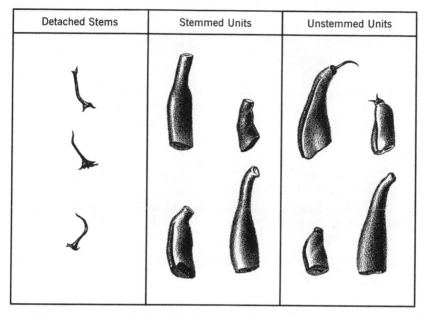

Detached Stems	Stemmed Units	Unstemmed Units

Fig. 3-23. Some defects buyers should watch for in purchasing canned beans. Note in accompanying text methods of measuring lengths. Courtesy USDA

Can Size	Whole	Whole Vertical	Cuts, Less than 1½ in.	Cuts, Longer than 1½ in.	Mixed, Long and Short Cuts	Sliced Lengthwise or French
No. 2	10.5	11.9	11.2	11.0	11.2	11.0
No. 303	8.5	9.5	9.2	8.7	9.2	8.7

*Liquid should be reasonably clear, slightly cloudy, with a small amount of sediment. The color should be reasonably uniform and typical for variety. Watch for blemishes, leaves, stems, and other extraneous matter, ragged cut or split units, small pieces of pods less than ½ in. long, broken, crushed or damaged pods, free seeds, and other defects. There should be few tough strings. Beans should be plump, tender. Note in measuring beans that a straight line is used from end to end and not along length of bean.

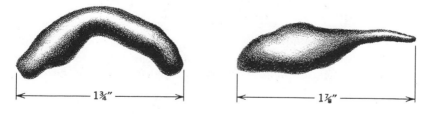

Beans, Kidney

   Grades: A (90), B (80)*, C (70).

   Styles: May vary; usually plain pack.

*Quality factors are similar to those for dried beans. Beans should have (as dried beans) good consistency, with smooth sauce, neither grainy nor lumpy, and a product that forms a molded mass when placed on a flat surface, with not more than slight separation of liquid.

Beans, Lima (1960).

   Grades: Grade A (90), B (80)*, C (70).

   Types: Thin-seeded (Henderson, Bush, Thorogreen), Thick-seeded (Fordhook or Baby Potato, Evergreen).

   Sizes: See Figure 3-25.

   Recommended minimum drained weight: No. 303, 11 oz; No. 2, 13½ oz; No. 10, 72 oz.

*Color may be green or white, reasonably uniform, good typical color, not mixed. Liquor reasonably clear. Sieves No. 1, 2, and 3 should not have a viscous liquid, but sieve size No. 4 may have a somewhat viscous liquid. Look for extraneous matter, broken beans, loose cotyledons and skins, sprouted, or otherwise blemished beans. Reasonably young and tender, not tough or starchy.

Fig. 3-24. USDA inspector matches canned lima beans to color of the color dictionary to ascertain how the samples compare with federal standards. Courtesy USDA

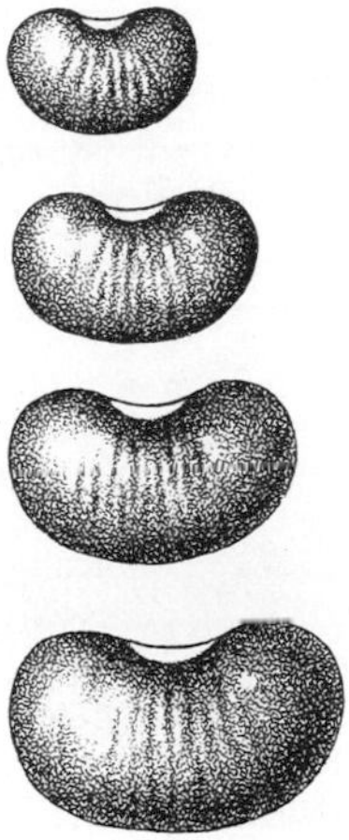

	Commercial Sizes			Federal Sizes	
Sieve	Inches*	Trade Name	Inches*	Size Name
No. 1	$\frac{5}{16}$ or less	Tiny		
No. 2	$\frac{5}{16}$ to $\frac{6}{16}$	Small	$\frac{28}{64}$ or less	Midget
No. 3	$\frac{6}{16}$ to $\frac{8}{16}$	Medium	$\frac{28}{64}$ to $\frac{30}{64}$ $\frac{30}{64}$ to $\frac{34}{64}$ $\frac{34}{64}$ to $\frac{38}{64}$	Tiny Small Medium
No. 4	$\frac{8}{16}$ or larger	Large	Larger than $\frac{38}{64}$	Large

*Greatest width through center at right angles to the longitudinal axis.

Fig. 3-25. Lima bean sizes.

TABLE 3-7
Sizes of Canned Green and Wax Beans*

| Thickness in 64th's Inch | Sieve Number | Round Type† Size Name | | Flat Type† | |
		Whole	Short Cut or Cut	Sieve Number	Size Name
Less than 14½	1	Tiny	Small	2	Small
14½ to 18½	2	Small	Small	3	Medium
18½ to 21	3	Medium	Small	4	Medium large
21 to 24	4	Medium large	Medium	5	Large
24 to 27	5	Large	Large	6	Extra large
27 or more	6	Extra large	Extra large	6	Extra large

*Sieve sizes and size names are based on federal standards.
†Round-type beans have a width not greater than 1½ times the bean thickness, and flat-type beans have a width greater than 1½ times the bean thickness.

Beets (1955)

Grades: A (85)*, C (70).

Styles: Sliced (not more than ⅜ in. thick), whole, quarters (cut into even quarters), diced (evenly cut cubes), julienne (shoestring or French), cut.

Recommended minimum drained weight:

Can Size	Whole Sizes 1–3*	Sizes 4–6*	Sliced Small	Medium and Large	Diced	Quar- tered	Juli- enne
No. 10	69 oz	68 oz	69 oz	68 oz	72 oz	70 oz	68 oz
No. 2	12½ oz	12¼ oz	12½ oz	12 oz	12¾ oz	12½ oz	11½ oz

*Size is measured by obtaining the smallest diameter through the center transverse to the longitudinal axis of the beet.

*Uniform, bright, deep red color, not off, brown, oxidized, or light pink. Practically uniform in size; evenly cut for cut styles. No woodiness, coarse texture, or excessive softness, poor trimming, peel, or black spots. Not too many first cuts (slabs), frayed edges, deep knife marks, or other injury. Grade A whole beets shall not be over 2¼ in. in diameter; quartered beets shall come from beets of a similar size; sliced beets should have slices not over ⅜ in. thick, with diameters not more than 3½ in.; diced beets should be in ⅜-in. cubes or less; julienne not wider than $3/16$ in. and relatively few below 1½ in. in length; cut individual units should not be less than ¼ oz and not more than 2 oz in weight. See Figure 3-21 and Table 3-8. Grade A must be practically uniform in style and shape, whereas Grade C can vary somewhat in these factors.

TABLE 3-8
Sizes of Canned Whole and Sliced Beets

	Trade Sizes		
Size Name	No. 2 Can	No. 2½ Can	No. 10 Can
Midget or Petite	35 or over	55 and over	175 and over
Tiny or Very Small	25 to 34	35 to 54	125 to 174
Baby or Small	15 to 24	22 to 34	74 to 124
Ruby or Medium	10 to 14	15 to 21	50 to 74
Large	6 to 9	8 to 14	35 to 49

		Federal Sizes		
Sized Name and Number		No. 2 Can	No. 2½ Can	No. 10 Can
Tiny	1	44 and over	70 and over	250 and over

Federal Sizes

Sized Name and Number		No. 2 Can	No. 2½ Can	No. 10 Can
	2	31 to 43	50 to 69	175 to 249
Small	3	22 to 30	35 to 49	125 to 174
	4	13 to 21	20 to 34	75 to 124
Medium	5	9 to 12	15 to 19	50 to 74
	6	Less than 9	Less than 15	Less than 50

Carrots (1959)

Grades: A (85)*, C (70).

Styles: Whole slices, quartered, diced, julienne (shoestring or French), cut.

Sizes: Diameter of whole carrots is measured through the center transverse to the longitudinal axis of the carrot, using the largest diameter. Whole carrots are not more than 1¾ in. in diameter; quartered carrots are from carrots not larger than 2½ in. in diameter; sliced carrots are not more than ⅜ in. thick with diameters not more than 2½ in.; diced carrots should be ½-in. cubes or less; julienne should be ³/₁₆ in. wide and very few less than ½ in. long; cut units should not be less than ¼ oz and the weight of the largest unit not more than four times the weight of the second smallest unit.

Recommended minimum drained weight:

Can Sizes	Whole		Sliced				
	Up to 1¼" Diameter	Over 1½" Diameter	To 1½" Diameter	Over 1½" Diameter	Diced	Quar-tered	Juli-enne
No. 10	60 oz	68 oz	69 oz	68 oz	72 oz	70 oz	68 oz
No. 2	12½ oz	12¼ oz	12½ oz	12 oz	12¾ oz	12½ oz	11½ oz

*Orange-yellow color, bright and typical, with little or no green. Practically uniform in size and shape. Tender, not mushy or soft. Coarse texture, pronounced fiber, and caramelized taste or odor are cause for rejection.

Chili Sauce (1953)

Grades: A (85)*, C (70).

*Color bright, with tomato red predominant. Heavy bodied, so when emptied on a flat surface it forms moderately mounded mass showing only slight separation of free liquid at mass edges. Finely divided and mixed mass, tender, reasonably firm and crisp ingredients. Practically free from such defects as peel or other items. Good flavor and odor. No scorched flavor.

Corn, Cream Style (1953)

Grades: A (90), B (80)*, C (70).

Types: White or golden (yellow).

*Reasonably uniform color, typical of tender sweet corn of the variety packed. Reasonably good, creamy consistency, with not more than a moderate appearance of curdling, with flow just sufficient to level off to a nearly uniform depth or may be moderately stiff and mounded with some slight separation of liquid after standing 2 minutes on a dry, flat surface. Reasonable absence of silk, cob, husk, off-colored kernels, and other extraneous material. Tender kernels taken in the middle to late cream stage. Good characteristic flavor and odor typical of reasonably tender, canned sweet corn.

Corn, Whole Kernel or Whole Grain (1952)

Grades: A (90), B (80)*, C (70).

Types: White or golden yellow).

Packs: Brine or vacuum; pack is vacuum when 20% or less of net weight of contents is liquid.

Recommended minimum drained weight:
No. 10 (Grade A) 70 oz, (Grades B and C) 72 oz.
No. 2 (Grade A) 12¾ oz, (Grades B and C) 13¼ oz.

*Reasonably uniform color, typical of tender sweet corn. Reasonably smooth cut surface, uniform and of even depth, with little adhering cob tissue. Reasonably free from defects, such as cob, husk, discolored kernels, silk, and other extraneous material. Reasonably tender from kernels in the cream stage of maturity. Firm, not pasty. Few dented kernels. Watch for musty, scorched, salty, or mealy tasting corn.

Hominy (1958)

Grades: A (85)*, C (70).

Types: White and golden (yellow).

Styles: Whole, grits, and grits in jel (grits, jellied pack).

Recommended minimum drained weight:	No. 2	No. 2½	No. 10
Whole	12 oz	18 oz	72 oz
Grits	14¼ oz	21¼ oz	76 oz

(Grits, jellied pack, are in a mass and have no drained weight)

*White or yellow clear color for type, reasonably free from defects. Whole kernels should have few or no broken pieces, damaged or mutilated parts. Reasonably firm, with little evident softness or mushiness. Tender. Flavor characteristic of sweet, well-processed hominy.

Mustard or Leafy Greens (1971)

Specify Fancy, with applicable factors outlined for spinach. Minimum drained weight for a No. 10 can is 58.4 oz.

Mushrooms (1962)

Grades: A (90)*, B (80).

Styles: Buttons, whole, sliced whole, sliced buttons, random sliced whole, sliced buttons, stems and pieces.

Size of diameter: No. 0 (midget), No. 1 (tiny) ½ to ⅝ in., No. 2 (small) ⅝ to ⅞ in., No. 3 (medium) ⅞ to 1⅛ in., No. 4 (large) 1⅛ to 1⅝ in., No. 5 (extra large) over 1⅝ in.

Recommended minimum drained weight: Under 11-oz can must drain out 56% of net can contents; 11 to 25 oz, 59%; over 25 oz, 62%.

*Color may be white (creamy) or brown; practically uniform, bright and typical color. Practically uniform in size and shape; whole mushrooms not smaller than ⅛ in. Sliced whole should be sliced lengthways, while sliced buttons should be sliced crosswise the width of the caps. Stems and pieces may be irregular in size and shape. Practically free from defects. Mushrooms should be intact, tender, and free from fibrous or rubbery units, with at least 95% with closed veils.

Okra (1957)

Grades: A (85)*, C (70).

Style: Cut, whole, and whole salad (pods ½ to 1 in. long).

Recommended minimum drained weight:	Whole and Whole Salad	Cut
No. 2	12 oz	12¾ oz
No. 2½	17¾ oz	18¾ oz
No. 10	60 oz	60 oz

*Liquor clear and bright, with thin, gelatinous consistency. Uniformly light green color. Uniform size, with pods not over 3½ in. in length for whole. Cut means transverse slices from pods, pieces intact, not shattered or broken. Whole pods should be intact, not shattered or broken to an extent detracting from appearance or use. Tender okra, seeds small and in earlier stages of development. Typical characteristic okra flavor.

Onions, Whole (1957)

Grade: A (85)*, C (70).

Size: Tiny, small, and medium. In a No. 10 can there will be 200 or more tiny onions, 100 to 199 small onions, and 80 to 99 medium onions.

Recommended minimum drained weight: No. 10 (tiny) 64 oz, (small) 63 oz, (medium) 60 oz.

*Reasonably bright, characteristic color. May be touched with slight greenish area on surface. Uniform size and shape. Well trimmed, with few blemishes, mechanical damage, or other defects. Should retain shape; reasonably firm and tender, not soft or spongy.

Peas (1955)

Grades: A (90), B (80)*, C (70).

Types: Early (Alaska or other smooth skin varieties), Sweet or Sugar (wrinkled varieties).

Sizes: See Figure 3-26.

Recommended minimum drained weight: None established. On refilling original container with peas, the level of peas, 15 seconds after the peas are returned to the can, should completely fill the container.

*Color reasonably bright and uniform, typical of mature canned peas. Reasonably free from defects, such as spotted, discolored peas, harmless extraneous material, pea plant, leaves, pods, stems, thistle buds, nightshade berries, and so forth. Relatively few pieces r broken or crushed peas, skins, cotyledons, and so forth. Shall be reasonably tender, and in a brine flotation test the maximum number of peas of all sizes for Grade B which will sink in 10 seconds should be: sweet varieties 15% in 13% brine salt solution, 4% in 15% solution; early varieties 30% in 13½% brine solution and 8% in 15% solution. Watch for mealy taste showing maturity. Flavor should be pleasant and sweet.

Canned Peas and Carrots (1970)

Grades: A (90)*, B (80).

Style and Mixture: Peas, sweet type, not less than 50% by drained weight; carrots, not less than 25% by drained weight either sliced, diced, double-diced, or strips.

Recommended minimum drained weight in oz:

| | If style carrot is: | |
	Sliced or strips	Diced or double-diced
No. 10	70.0	71.0
No. 2 (vacuum)	9.5	9.5
No. 303	10.6	10.8

*Flavor and odor shall be good; peas and carrots shall have good, natural color; product shall not be mushy nor broken up and uniform in size and shape; shall be practically free from harmless extraneous vegetable material and be tender, free from stringy or coarse fibers.

Federal and Commercial Sizes		
Sieve	Inches*	Size Name
6	$\frac{13}{32}$ to $\frac{14}{32}$	Large
5	$\frac{12}{32}$ to $\frac{13}{32}$	Medium large
4	$\frac{11}{32}$ to $\frac{12}{32}$	Medium
3	$\frac{10}{32}$ to $\frac{11}{32}$	Medium small
2	$\frac{9}{32}$ to $\frac{10}{32}$	Small
1	$\frac{9}{32}$ or less	Tiny

*In diameter; $\frac{14}{32}''$ or larger peas are called No. 7 sieve size.

Fig. 3-26. Pea sizes.

Peas, Black-eye (See also Dried Beans.)

Grades: A (85)*, B (70).

Styles: May be with or without unshelled immature pods (snaps) or pieces of pod.

Recommended minimum drained weight in oz: No. 2, 13½; No. 10, 72.

*Typical color of fresh black-eye peas, practically free from loose or pieces of loose skins, loose or pieces of loose cotyledons, and other extraneous material, broken, mashed, or damaged peas. Texture should be tender of peas fairly early in stages of maturity. Flavor should be good.

Pimientos (1967)

Grades: A (90)*, B (80).

Styles: Whole, halves, whole and pieces, pieces, slices, diced, chopped.

Recommended minimum drained weight in oz:

Can Size	Whole	Whole and Pieces	Pieces	Diced	Sliced
4 Z	3.2	3.2	3.2	3.2	3.2
No. 300	10.0	10.2	10.2	10.2	10.2
No. 303	11.0	11.2	11.2	11.2	11.0
No. 2	13.2	13.5	14.0	14.0	13.2
No. 2½	20.2	20.5	20.5	20.5	20.2
No. 10	70.7	72.7	74.0	74.0	71.7

*Color red or reddish yellow according to variety, but uniform and clear. Bright, with relatively few blemishes, spots or off-coloring. Practically uniform in size and shape. Practically free from grit, sand or silt, seeds, undeveloped seeds, core stem, peel, trimmed units, or other blemishes. Firm fleshed and tender, with no apparent disintegration. To meet grade, the product must meet established standards for size, shape, and color.

TABLE 3-9

Trade Association Recommendations for Minimum Net Weight of Contents for Canned Vegetables

Vegetable	Can Size			Vegetable	Can Size		
	No. 10	No. 2½	No. 2		No. 10	No. 2½	No. 2
Asparagus, tips				Succotash	108 oz		20 oz
and spears			19 oz	Tomatoes	102 oz	28 oz	19 oz
Asparagus, cuts	103 oz	28 oz	19 oz	Tomato catsup			
Beans, dried	110 oz	31 oz	21 oz	Specific gravity			
Beans, snap type	101 oz	28 oz	19 oz	1.11	111 oz	30 oz	21 oz
Beans, lima	105 oz		20 oz	1.15	115 oz	32 oz	22 oz
Beets	104 oz	28 oz	20 oz	Tomato paste			
Carrots	105 oz	28 oz	20 oz	Specific gravity			
Corn	106 oz		20 oz	1.11	111 oz	30 oz	
Mushrooms	103 oz	28 oz		1.14	114 oz	31 oz	
Okra	99 oz	27 oz	19 oz	Tomato puree			
Pimientos	106 oz	28 oz	20 oz	Specific gravity			
Sauerkraut	99 oz	27 oz	19 oz	1.035	104 oz	28 oz	19 oz
Spinach	98 oz	27 oz	18 oz	1.05	105 oz	29 oz	20 oz
Squash	106 oz	29 oz	20 oz				

Spinach (1971)

Grades : A*, B; there is a tendency to base grades more on defects and product failures than total scores as has been common in the past, and these grades for spinach without scores is an indication of this trend.

Styles: Cut leaf, chopped, whole leaf.

Recommended minimum drained weight in oz: No. 10, 58.4; No. 2½, 18.6; No. 2, 12.6; No. 303, 10.2.

*Should have good flavor and odor, be attractive in appearance and eating quality, and meet high standards for color, character, stem material, damage, and harmless extraneous material.

Succotash (1967)

Grades: A, B*, C; no scores for grades established.

Ingredient proportions: Proportions by weight shall be within the ranges of corn, 50 to 87½%, snap beans, 25 to 50%; fresh lima beans, 12½ to 30%; dry (soaked) lima beans, 12½ to 30%; and tomatoes, 10 to 30%. Corn can be kernel or cream style.

*The individual vegetables making up the succotash shall meet standards established for them in their grades.

Tomatoes (1964)

Grades: A (90), B (80)*, C (70).

Packs: Whole (95% or more whole to be Grade A), Solid pack (no added liquid), tomatoes with juice, tomatoes with puree.

Recommended minimum drained weight in oz: Drained weight is a part of grade as follows:

Can Size	Grade A 66%*	Grade B 58%**	Grade C 50%**	Whole
No. 10	72.2 to 76.6	63.5 to 67.9	59.1 to 54.7	54.7 to 67.9
No. 2½	19.6 to 20.8	17.3 to 18.5	14.9 to 16.1	14.9 to 18.5
No. 2	13.5 to 14.4	11.9 to 12.7	10.3 to 11.1	10.3 to 12.7

**Must be this drained weight or more to make the grade.

*Color should vary from uniform, good red, typical color for Grade A to fairly good red, typical color for Grade C. Defects should be practically free, reasonably free, and fairly free for Grades A, B, and C tomatoes, respecitvely. Wholeness is a grade factor. Grade A should have 80% of the tomatoes whole or almost whole. Grade B should have 70% whole or almost whole. Grade C can have less than 70%. About 0.026% calcium chloride may be added to give more firmness.

Turnip Greens (See Mustard and Leafy Greens)

Fig. 3-27. This consistometer measures the flowing quality of catsup and other thick products. Standards have been established that limit the amount of flow within a given time period for certain heavy liquid products. Courtesy USDA

Tomato Catsup (1953)

Grades: A (85)*, B (85)*, C (70). Grades A and B are similar except that the former contains not less than 33% total solids and the latter 29%. Grade C has not less than 25% solids and has lower quality factors than the others.

*Color from well-ripened red tomatoes. Consistency such that not more than a slight separation of free liquid shows when the catsup is stirred and poured onto a tray, flowing not more than 9 centimeters in 30 seconds at 20°C in the Bostwick consistometer. Watch for defects such as dark specks or scale-like particles, seeds, core material, and so forth. Flavor should be distinct and good. The flavor and odor should be free from scorching or other objectionable flavors.

Tomato Paste (1970)

Grades: A (90)*, C (80).

Concentrations: Extra heavy, 39.3% or more salt-free solids; heavy, 32–39.3%; medium, 28–32%; light, 24–28%. Normally, heavy has a 1.14 specific gravity, medium 1.11, and light 1.09.

Textures: Fine or coarse.

*Color should be red, varying somewhat in degree from Grades A to C. Grade A should be practically free from defects, whereas Grade C should be fairly free. Both should possess a typical, pleasant tomato flavor, free from scorched, bitter, green tomato flavors or other objectionable flavors and odors.

Tomato Puree (Pulp) (1970)

Grades: A (90)*, C (80).

*Extra heavy puree is 15 to 24% natural tomato solids; heavy puree, 11.3 to 15%; medium, 10.2 to 11.3%; and light, 8.0 to 10.2%; 12% solids has an approximate specific gravity of 1.05 and 8.00% a specific gravity of 1.03. The puree should possess a good ripe to fairly good ripe, red color, be practically or reasonably free from defects, depending on grade. Watch for off-color, predominantly yellowish red; scorched, bitter, salty, or green tomato flavor should be cause for rejection. Watch for excessive presence of dark specks and scale-like particles from seeds, tomato peel, or core; poor consistency tending to thinness should lead to rejection.

Tomato Sauce (1960)

Grades: A (85)*, C (70).

*Concentrated liquid from tomatoes to which salt, spices, sweeteners, vinegar, onion, garlic, or other vegetable flavoring ingredients are added to make tomato sauce. The color should be typical of well-ripened tomatoes, with some variation for Grade C. On a tray, the consistency of Grade A should show not more than 14 centimeters flow in 30 seconds at 20°C in the Bostwick consistometer. The sauce should also possess a sufficient fluidity to give some flow. There should be no noticeable separation of free liquid. Dark specks, scale-like particles, seeds, tomato peel, core material, or other extraneous matter should be checked. Flavor should be pleasant, with no scorched taste.

Tomatoes and Okra (1957)

Grades: A (85)*, C (70).

Recommended minimum drained weight: None.

*Mixture shall be at least 50% tomatoes and 12½ to 50% okra; the mixture must be called "Okra and Tomatoes" if the quantity of okra exceeds that of tomatoes, and the proportion in this case must be at least 50% okra nad 12½ to 50% tomatoes. Check for flavor and odor, color typical of reasonably ripe tomatoes and young tender okra. The product should be reasonably free of dirt, silt, sand a and harmless extraneous material. Watch for damaged pods with good wholeness of tomato and tenderness and texture of okra.

Frozen Fruits[1]

Apples (1954)

  Grades: A (85)*, C (70).

  Styles: Sliced.

  Sugar-fruit ratio recommended: 1:7.

  Usual packaging: 25- to 30-lb tins.

*Uniform brightness in internal and external parts. Color characteristic for variety. Uniform, practically whole slices (¾ slice or more is considered a whole slice), 1¼ in. or longer in length, and thickness that does not vary more than ¼ in. Reasonably free from harmless extraneous matter, carpel tissue, peel, seeds, stems, damage, and other defects. Texture should be firm, tender, and crisp. Watch for discoloration and mushy apples.

Apricots (1963)

  Grades: A (90), B (75)*, C (60).

  Styles: Half or whole. Either pitted or unpitted may be obtained in whole.

  Sugar-fruit ratio recommended: 1:5.

  Usual packaging: 8- or 10-lb packs or 25- or 30-lb tins.

*Reasonably uniform, bright typical color of mature apricots, with little green, tarnishing, or browning. Some pale areas may be evident around stem end. Only a few misshapen ones. The weight of the largest apricot should not exceed the smallest by more than 75% and no half should be less than ²/₅ oz. Reasonably free from blemishes, such as stem pits and worm holes. Uniform, tender texture, thick and fleshy fruit only slightly ragged. Usual drained weight, 64%.

Berries (except Blueberries, Raspberries, and Strawberries) (1967)

  Grades: A (85)*, B (70).

  Specify type berry: Blackberries, loganberries, dewberries, youngberries, and so forth.

  Sugar-fruit ratio recommended: 1:4.

  Usual packaging: 25- or 30-lb tin.

*Color typical for variety, with little variation in intensity or luster of well-ripened berries. Defects such as leaves, stems, caps, undeveloped berries, blemishes, extraneous matter, insect or pathological damage, and other injuries should be limited. Few unripe berries. Juice should be practically free from detached seed cells. There should be little crushing of ripe, plump, tender fruit. Watch for not more than 4 sepal-like bracts per pound and not more than 1 leaf or the approximate equivalent of 1 full cap per 4 lb. Not more than 5% of the berries may be damaged. Usual drained weight, depending upon variety, 50 to 65%.

[1]Score or judge thawed, not frozen.

Blueberries (1955)

Grades: A (90), B (80)*, C (70).

Types: Wild or cultivated.

Sugar-fruit ratio: 1:4. (Sometimes local supplies are frozen without sugar.)

Usual packaging: 20-, 25-, 30-lb tins or packs.

*Reasonably uniform in color, possessing a red-purple color, with few green berries. Few berries in clusters. No dull or off-color. Reasonably few defects, such as cap stems, undeveloped berries. May be lacking in firmness and fleshy texture, but only reasonably so. Berries should be reasonably whole, with little crushing, splitting, or broken berries evident.

Cherries, Red, Sour, Pitted (RSP) (1964)

Grades: A (90)*, C (80).

Sugar-fruit ratio recommended: 1:4 or 1:5.

Usual packaging: 30-lb tins.

*Good flavor and odor; reasonably red color of well-matured cherries without market discoloration from oxidation, improper processing, or undercoloring in fruit. Few pits, pieces of pits, damaged or mutilated or blemished berries. Usual drained weight, 55%.

Cherries, Sweet (1958)

Grades: A (85)*, C (70).

Usual-fruit ratio recommended: 1:7.

Usual packinging: 25- or 30-lb tins.

Types: Light (Royal Anne or Napoleon), Dark (Bing, Schmidt, Black Republican, Lambert, Tartarian).

Styles: Pitted and unpitted.

*Practically uniform typical color. Minimum weight of single, unpitted cherry should average about $1/10$ oz, and the variation in size of diameter of largest over smallest should be not more than ¼ in. Cherries should be 90% or more free from pits or pieces of pits, unseparable doubles, bruised, checked, cracked, or damaged cherries. Watch for oxidation and browning. Cherries should be thick fleshed, firm, and well ripened. There should be few split or crushed cherries. Usual drained weight is 56%.

Cranberries (1971)

Grades: A (90), B (80)*, C (70).

*The cranberries should possess a good color, be practically free from defects such as harmless extraneous plant material, sunscald, blemishes, fine stem, possess a good character, and normal flavor and odor. They should have similar varietal characteristics and have no grit or silt present that affects appearance or edibility. Not more than 5% should be less than $13/32$s of an inch in diameter.

Grapefruit (1951)

Grades: A (90), B (80)*, Broken (70). (Broken is same grade as B in all other respects except for wholeness of pieces.)

*At least 50% whole but not more than 75% whole or almost whole segments. (Above 75% whole is a requirement of Grade A.) Reasonably good clear color, not dull. Reasonably good characteristics, with fairly firm, plump flesh, with but few ricey segments. Color bright, with only a small amount of color variability.

Melon Balls (1962)

Grades: A (90)*, B (80).

Types: Cantaloupe, honey dew, mixed (at least 50% cantaloupe and 33$^1/_3$% honey dew), other types (such as cantaloupe and honey dews mixed with other type melon balls).

*The balls should have a good flavor, odor, and color, be practically uniform in size and shape, free from defects, and have good character. The ripening should be uniform and from reasonably well-ripened melons. The balls should be almost spherical units with few misshapen units. The texture should be good and firm and not sloughy.

Peaches (1961)

Grades: A (90), B (80)*, C (70).

Types: Yellow clings, and yellow, white, and red freestones.

Sugar-fruit ratio recommended: 1:4.

Usual packaging: In containers not less than 6½ lb net; usually 25- or 30-lb tins.

Styles: Half, slices, quarters, diced, and mixed.

*Reasonably unifrom, bright, typical color, which is yellow-orange or creamy white, depending on type. Size and symmetry uniform, with few mishapen pieces. Watch for split, broken, crushed, or otherwise mutilated sections. There should be limited raggedness. No half should weigh less than $^3/_5$ oz and no quarter less than $^3/_{10}$ oz. Slices should be reasonably full, with few broken ones. Reasonably free from defects, with limited slight browning from oxidation. Uniform tender texture, which may be slightly soft to slightly firm. Usual drained weight, 64%.

Pineapple (1949)

Grades: A (90), B (80)*, C (70).

Variety: Hawaiian or Philippine are best varieties.

Sugar: Specify syrup density 20 or 25° Brix, which is fairly heavy.

Usual packaging: 25-lb containers.

Styles: Whole slices, half slices (2 pieces should approximately equal 1 whole slice), broken slices (should be approximately the same thickness and diameter), chunks (must not exceed 1½ in. in any dimension), crushed (may be shredded or crushed), tidbits, or wedges.

*Reasonably uniform in yellowish color, no gray cast or dull color. Reasonably uniform shape and symmetry, with little crushed or broken fruit or raggedness, unless crushed. Reasonably uniform ripeness, compact structure, and porosity. Taste for fullness of flavor.

Plums (1956)

Grades: A (85)*, B (70).

Varieties: Red (Satsuma or Santa Rosa), Yellow-green (Yellow Egg, Jefferson, and Reine Claude), Purple or Blue (Prunes, Damson plum).

Styles: Halved or whole. Whole may be pitted or unpitted.

Sugar-fruit ratio recommended: 1:5.

Usual packaging: 25-lb containers.

*Reasonably uniform, bright, typical color, with reasonable freedom from browning. Reasonably uniform in size and symmetry, with the weight of the largest unit not more than twice the weight of the smallest one. Reasonably free from defects, harmless extraneous matter, crushed and broken units, pits, and other materials. Reasonably good texture of plump, well-ripened, tender fruit. Usual drained weight, 65%.

Raspberries (1948)

Grades: A (85)*, B (70).

Varieties: Red or Black; latter may sometimes be called *black caps.*

Sugar-fruit ratio recommended: 1:4.

Usual packaging: 25- or 30-lb tins.

*Practically uniform, typical color, with marked intensity and luster of wellripened berries, with no darkening from overmaturity or oxidation. Practically free from harmless extraneous material, sepal-like bracts, caps, stems, undeveloped, hard, or damaged berries. Mature, well-developed, fleshy, tender character. The liquor should be practically free from detached seed cells. Usual drained weight, 50%.

Rhubarb (1945)

Grades: A (85)*, B (70).

Varieties: Crimson or Green; Crimson may be called *red, strawberry,* or *hothouse.*

Sugar-fruit ratio recommended: 1:3 or 1:4.

Usual packaging: Containers 25- or 30-lb net.

*Judge after thawing for color, glossy, bright, typical clear, not dull or gray. Practically free from defects, extraneous material, leaves, root ends, growth cracks, and other defects. Reasonably good tenderness and texture means that not more than 5% of the units may be tough, spongy, or stringy. Cook and judge for color, flavor, tenderness, and texture; use 5 oz water to 12 oz rhubarb and sugar. Sweeten if rhubarb is unsugared in freezing. Judge after 6 minutes of boiling.

Strawberries (1958)

Grades: A (90), B (80)*, C (70).

Styles: Whole or sliced; sliced means 2 or more slices per strawberry.

Sugar-fruit ratio recommended: 1:4.

Usual packaging: 6½-lb, 8-lb, 10-lb, 15-lb, 20-lb, and 30-lb containers.

*Color reasonably uniform, characteristic pink to red, not materially affected by dull, gray, or reddish brown. Specify Marshall variety, which, when sliced, will not show a white core but all solid red meat. Good color should appear on $4/5$ of the berry. Reasonably free from grit, sand, caps, stems, and damage. Firm, plump, tender, soft berries, with only a reasonable amount of crushing or mushiness. Strawberries may be specified in sizes as:

Small	Diameter* less than ⅝ in.
Medium	Diameter* ⅝ to 1¼ in.
Large	Diameter* over 1¼ in.

*Diameter measured at right angles to a straight line running from stem to apex. (To meet U.S. Grade A, whole berries may not contain more than 5% by count of strawberries that fall into small classification.) Usual drained weight, 51%.

Frozen Vegetables[2]

Asparagus (1970)

Grades: A (85)*, B (70).

Styles: Spears or stalks (head and adjoining portion of shoot 3 in. or more in length), tips (head and adjoining portion of shoot less than 3 in. in length), cut spears or cuts and tips (head and portions of the shoot cut transversely into units 2 in. or less but not less than ½ in.), center cuts or cuts (portions of shoots that are cut transversely into units 2 in. or less, but not less than ½ in.).

[2]Do not judge frozen. Cook and judge.

Sizes: Small (No. 1) less than ⅜ in., medium (No. 2) ⅜ to ⅝ in., large (No. 3) ⅝ in., extra large (No. 4), ⅞ in. or larger.

Color: All green, green, green-white.

*Asparagus should possess good characteristic color, typical of well-developed and tender asparagus, with all green, or green having little or no white color evident. Uniformity of size and length should be good. Defects such as grit, silt, loose material, shattered heads, misshapen units, poorly cut units, or otherwise damaged, discolored, or broken units should be noted. Heads should be compact and well developed, not shriveled. The entire product should be tender and the texture good, with few tough fibers.

Beans, Snap, Green or Wax (1954)

Grades: A (90), B (80)*, C (70).

Styles: Whole (pods not less than 2¾ in. in length or transversely cut pods not less than 2¾ in. in length); julienne—French, shoestring, or sliced lengthwise (cut into thin strips lengthwise); cut (pods transversely into pieces ¾ to 2¾ in. in length; short cut (¾- to 1¼-in. transverse cuts); mixed (any mixture of above).

Types: Round or flat; the former has a width not greater than 1½ times the thickness, and the latter a width greater than 1½ times the thickness.

*Reasonably good, uniform color, bright and typical of young and tender beans. Reasonable amount only of extraneous matter, small pieces, or other blemishes. Stems, free beans, damaged pods, and other defects should be noted. Reasonably good maturity but not late maturity. Units should not be materially affected by sloughing; tender, with reasonably good plumpness and fleshy structure. Determine flavor and odor after boiling 15 minutes.

Beans, Lima (1957)

Grades: A (90), B (80)*, C (70).

Types: Thin-seeded (Henderson Bush, Thorogreen), thick-seeded (Baby Potato, Baby Fordhook, and Evergreen).

*Reasonably good color for type; possessing a typical color and a uniform color in the thin-seeded types of 65% green and 35% white, and in the thick-seeded varieties, 60% green and 40% white, with white defined as lighter in color than the typical pale green of fresh, frozen lima beans. Reasonably free from defects, such as free pieces of flesh, skins, shriveled or hard beans, sprouted beans, and extraneous matter. Check flavor and odor after cooking 18 minutes in boiling salted water.

Broccoli (1962)

Grades: A (90)*, B (80).

Styles: Spears or stalks (not less than 3 in. and not more than 6 in. in length), short spears or florets (not less than 1 in. nor more 3 in.), cuts (spears or stalks cut into ¾- to 2-in. pieces containing not less than 25% head material and not more than

25% leaf material), chopped (units less than ¾ in. in size containing not less than 25% head material and not more than 25% leaf material), pieces (units not in excess of 2 in. in length which may or may not contain head or leaf material).

*Good, bright green color of young tender broccoli; no yellowing of head material. Uniform size; free from grit, silt, sand, harmless extraneous vegetable material, such as weeds or grass. Reasonably free from loose leaves, detached fragments, and showing good workmanship in trimming. Few broken or damaged pieces. Well-developed bud clusters, compact and well closed, not showing more than slight elongation. Tender and free from tough fiber. Cook to ascertain characteristics.

Brussels Sprouts (1951)

 Grades: A (90), B (80)*, C (70).

*Reasonably good color, with more than 5% but not more than 25% yellowish and the remainder yellow-green or more green in color. Reasonably free from grit, silt, harmless extraneous material, loose leaves, and loose small pieces. Look for poorly trimmed cuts and damaged pieces. Shou'd be well developed, compact, well formed, and reasonably firm. Only 10% allowed in loose structured, spongy, or soft heads. Cook for flavor, texture, and color evaluation.

Fig. 3-28. Leaves, leaf spurs, and small shoots are neatly trimmed on the frozen broccoli on the left. This illustrates a well-trimmed unit. The center spear has a slightly ragged appearance from short, small leaf spurs and small side shoots. The ragged appearance of the sample on the right is caused by large, coarse leaf spurs. This sample illustrates a poorly trimmed unit. Courtesy USDA

Fig. 3-29. Degrees of "well-developed" stalks, of which at least 80% are required in Grade A or Fancy frozen broccoli, in addition to other requirements of color, uniformity of size, defects, and tenderness. The practically compact heads, buds closed and no elongation of individual bud stems illustrate near top quality for well-developed frozen broccoli. Courtesy USDA

Carrots, Diced (1962)

Grades: A (85)*, B (70).

*Bright, typical orange-yellow color, with only slight evidence of any green. Uniform size of cubes from ¼ to ½ in. Practically free from damaged, unpeeled units or otherwise blemished units. Cook to ascertain flavor. Carrots should have tender texture, not fibrous or tough. Flavor should be sweet and characteristic of sweet, young carrots.

Cauliflower (1951)

Grades: A (85)*, B (70).

*White to light cream color, which may be slightly variable, with a slight green color or blue color on the branching parts and a greenish yellow to light green or modified green on the bracts. Reasonably free from poorly trimmed clusters and small clusters, damaged clusters, from pieces and detached fragments, and other defects. Reasonably free from "ricey" or fuzzy units. Cook for flavor, texture, and color evaluation.

Corn on the Cob (1970)

Grades: A (90)*, B (80).

Types: Yellow or golden; white.

Styles: Trimmed or natural.

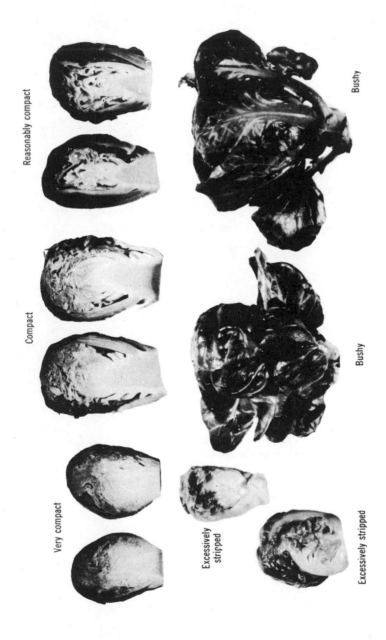

Fig. 3-30. Degree of compactness, stripping, and bushiness considered in grading frozen brussels sprouts. Courtesy USDA

Lengths: Regular, 3½ in. or more; short, 3½ in. or less. Ears must be uniform in size.

*Bright, uniform, typical color of young and tender corn. Good flavor and odor must be present. Practically free from loose material, poorly trimmed ears, damaged kernels, or other defects. Tender kernels that are in the milk or early cream stage of maturity. Evenly filled cobs; with no worm damage or excessive trimming. Free of silk, husks, and other extraneous material.

Corn, Whole Kernel or Whole Grain (1952)

Grades: A (90), B (80)*, C (70).

Types: Yellow or golden; white.

*Reasonably good yellow color or creamy white of tender young corn. Reasonably bright and free from "off-variety" kernels. Reasonably free from defects, such as damaged kernels, cob, husk, silk, ragged or crushed kernels, extraneous vegetable matter, and loose skins. Check flavor and odor after cooking. Kernels should be reasonably tender and in the cream stage.

Greens (other than Spinach) (1952)

Grades: A (85)*, B (70).

Types: Beet, Collards, Dandelion, Endive, Kale, Mustard, Swiss chard, Turnip.

Styles: Whole leave, sliced leaves, cut or chopped.

*Sound, succulent, clean leaves from fresh leafy greens, washed, trimmed, sorted, blanched, and frozen. Practically a uniform color, bright for variety. Reasonably free from grit, sand, and silt, damaged or yellow or brown leaves, extraneous matter. Reasonably tender, without coarse or tough leaves or stems.

Mixed Vegetables (1954)

Grades: A (90), B (80)*, C (70).

*Mixture should be composed of snap beans, green or wax varieties, cut into transverse pieces ½ to 1½ in. in length, diced carrots in ⅜- to ½-in. cubes, sweet, whole kernel corn, and peas of the early or sweet type. If the mixture consists of three vegetables, no vegetable can be in excess of 40%. If of four vegetables, none may be less than 8% nor more than 35%, and if of five vegetables, none may be less than 8% nor more than 30%. Color should be bright and good for each vegetable. Practically free from defects or extraneous material. All units should be tender, full, and plump for variety and type.

Okra (1969)

Grades: A (90)*, B (80).

Styles: Whole, cut; in latter pods are cut transversely into pieces; specify that pieces shall not be less than ½ in. in length for cut. Size is measured from stem end to end of tip.

*Practically uniform bright, young, and tender okra. Practically free from extraneous vegetable matter, sand, silt, grit, poorly trimmed units, small pieces of ¼ in. or less, damaged units, misshapen units, and blemishes. Few broken or crushed pieces. Seeds tender and white, not developed toward maturity. Desirable length in pods (whole) is 3½ in.

Onion Rings, Breaded (1959)

Grades: A (85)*, B (70).

*May be deep fried or uncooked. When cooked should be free of rancid or bitter flavor, or any caramelized or oily flavors. Color should be golden brown. Color of uncooked should be creamy white. Should not possess excess breading in either type. Both should be reasonably free from broken or imperfect rings, blemishes, extraneous matter, black specks, or other deformities or defects.

Peas (1959)

Grades: A (90), B (80)*, C (70).

Types: Early or sweet. (Best freezing variety, Telephone pea.)

*Reasonably uniform, typical green color. Few spotted or off-color brown, gray, creamy, or yellow-white peas. Reasonably free from harmless extraneous vegetable material and other defects; few crushed or broken peas; few peas without skins; few loose skins. Tenderness and maturity of young, tender peas. Not more than 12% after removing skins should sink within 10 seconds in a 15% salt brine solution.

Peas and Carrots (1955)

Grades: A (90), B (80)*, C (70).

Proportions: Peas, not less than 50% by weight of early or sweet type; carrots not less than 25% by weight of diced carrots predominantly ¼- to ⅜-in. cubes.

*Reasonably good color, bright and typical of reasonably young, tender peas and carrots. Reasonably uniform color. Reasonably free from leaves, stems, pods, thistle buds, night-shade berries, or damaged units. Few broken, mashed, loose cotyledons, loose skins, spotted or off-colored units. From reasonably mature, plump, full-fleshed peas or carrots.

Peas, Black-eyed or Field (1961)

Grades: A (90)*, B (80).

*Good typical color of reasonably young field peas or black-eye peas. Reasonably free from extraneous vegetable matter, such as loose skins, pieces of skins, loose cotyledons, broken units, or otherwise damaged units. Tender and in a reasonably young stage of maturity.

Peppers, Sweet (1959)

Grades: A (85)*, B (70).

Types: Green, red, or mixed red and green.

Styles: Whole stemmed or whole unstemmed (shall be 2½ in. in length and 2½ in. in diameter as measured at widest part), halves from whole peppers, sliced (at least 1¼ in. in length), and diced (½ in. square approximately).

*Good characteristic bright color for type. When appearance of the product is seriously affected by a mixture of red and green, it shall be considered mixed. Practically free from grit, sand, silt, excessive trimming, and damaged units. Cut styles should be fairly free from seeds and extraneous matter. Uniform in size and shape. Reasonably full fleshed, firm, full, and plump.

Spinach (1964)

Grades: A (85)*, B (70).

Styles: Whole leaf, cut, chopped, cut leaf (sliced).

*Practically uniform, bright, characteristic green color; practically free from grit, sand, or silt, seed heads, grass and weeds, crowns of root stubs, and other blemishes or defects. Watch for brown or yellow leaves, stems, coarse or tough stems or leaves, or insect injury. The leaves should not be ragged or torn.

Squash, Summer (1953)

Grades: A (85)*, B (70).

Styles: Sliced (transverse cuts), cut (in pieces).

*Fresh, sound, immature product from summer squash varieties. Color should be bright and typical of young, tender squash. Practically free from sand, grit, and silt, poorly cut units, damaged units, discolored, scarred, or other defects. Fleshy, full, plump units. Texture should be tender not tough. The seeds should be soft and undeveloped, as in immature young summer squash.

Squash, Winter (Cooked) (1953)

Grades: A (85)*, B (70).

*The squash, after warming and mixing on a flat, dry surface, should form a well-rounded mass, which, after 2 minutes, has only a slight separation of liquor at the edges. The color should be practically uniform, bright and typical, free from discoloration from oxidation or other causes. The texture should be even and may be granular, but not lumpy, pasty, and the particles should not be hard. Practically free from sand, grit, and silt, pieces of seed, fiber, and dark or off-colored particles.

Succotash (1959)

 Grades: A (90), B (80)*, C (70).

Recommended proportions by weight:	Not more than	Not less than
Corn, white or golden	75%	50%
Lima beans, fresh not dried	50%	25%
Soybeans, vegetable	50%	25%
Green or wax beans	50%	25%

The lima beans may be thin- or thick-seeded varieties. Green or wax snap beans may be cut or short-cut style.

*Colors of vegetables should be bright and typical of young, tender products. Practically free from pieces of pod, leaves, stems, pieces of cob, husk, silk, damaged units, or other defects. Tender, young, immature, full, plump vegetables.

Sweet Potatoes (1962)

 Grades: A (90)*, B (80).

 Styles: Whole peeled, baked unpeeled, stuffed in peel or preformed shell, halved peeled, sliced, French-cut or strips, diced, cut or chunks, mashed or souffle, mixed or combination.

*The product should have a good color, odor, and flavor typical of good quality sweet potatoes. The units should be practically uniform in size and shape and be practically free from defects, possess a good character, and be practically free from blemishes, specks, and so forth. The product may or may not be cooked and may be seasoned with seasonings, sweeteners, antioxidants, edible oils, or other additives permissible under the Federal Food, Drug, and Cosmetic Act. If in a high-density syrup, the cooked potatoes may be called *candied sweet potatoes.* If in baked or stuffed form, edible fat and other seasonings may be added, and the product may be returned to its shell or preformed shell.

Fruit Spreads[3]

Apple Butter (1957)

 Grades: A (85)*, C (70).

*Uniform, polished, dark-chocolate brown color, which may possess a reddish shade. Practically free from defects, with not more than a slight amount of black specks, particles of seed, stem, peel, calyx, or other particles. Stir and place on a flat surface so a prominently mounded mass is formed, but one not so stiff that it cannot be spread readily. At the end of 2 minutes there should be no more than a slight separation of free liquor. The texture should be fine-grained, evenly divided, and smooth. Flavor should be free from any traces of bitter, scorched, caramelized, molasses-like, or noticeable brown sugar flavor.

[3]Type I fruit spread is prepared from a single fruit and Type II from 2 or more fruits.

Cranberry Sauce (1951)

  Grades: A (85)*, C (70).

  Styles: Whole, jellied or strained.

*Product should possess a dark red color, typical of canned red cranberries. The jel should be tender and in whole style, uniformly spread throughout. Reject stiff or rubbery jellied products. There may be some slight separation of liquor evident. In whole, look for defective crown stems. Both styles should possess good flavor and odor.

Fruit Jelly (1948)

  Grades: A (85)*, B (70).

  Types: Type I made from a single fruit; Type II made from 2 up to 5 fruits.

*Bright, typical color for fruit variety, sparkling luster, not more than slightly cloudy, and free from any dullness. Tender to slightly firm, retaining compact shape, with little or no syneresis (weeping). Not tough or rubbery. Distinct and normal flavor characteristic of the fruit ingredient or ingredients. Free from any caramelized or objectionable flavor. In jellies of 2 or more fruits, the weight of each fruit used must not be less than 20% of the total used. If the jelly is made of 2 to 5 fruit juices, the name "jelly" is preceded or followed by the words "mixed fruit" or by the names of the fruits used.

Fruit Preserves or Jams (1956)

  Grades: A (85)*, B (70).

*Color bright, practically uniform throughout, and characteristic of the variety or varieties of fruits used; free from dullness. Fruit particles should be dispersed uniformly throughout the jellied product. The jel should be tender, not stiff or rubbery. There may be a small tendency to flow, and preserves will be somewhat less viscous than jams. Wholeness of fruit should be evident in preserves, and wholeness should be specified if desired. In jams or preserves made from 2 to 5 fruits, the weight of each fruit must be not less than 20% of the total. If the jam or fruit is a mixture of 2 or more fruits, the name "jam" or "preserve" is preceded or followed by the words "mixed fruit" or by the names of the fruits used.

Orange Marmalade (1951)

  Grades: A (85)*, B (70).

  Varieties: Sweet—made from Navel or Valencia oranges or other sweet oranges; bitter—made from Seville or sour oranges; sweet and bitter—made from equal proportions of sweet and sour oranges.

  Styles: Slices or thin strips, chopped or small pieces either irregular or diced.

Types: Type I is a clear jellied product with peel suspended in the translucent semisolid mass; whole type II is a peel suspended in a cloudy opaque jel.

*Color uniform, bright and sparkling. Little or no dullness. Practically free from green-colored peel. Firm but tender. Jel possesses a very slight tendency to flow. Jel should contain a substantial amount of peel evenly distributed but not an excessive amount. The peel should be tender and if sliced into strips, the strips should be $1/32$ to $1/16$ in. wide. In chopped types, the peel should be reasonably uniform in size. Practically free from harmless extraneous material, seeds or parts of seeds, blemished peel, specks, and other particles. Flavor and odor characteristic of the type orange used. The flavor should be neither excessively tart nor excessively sweet and should be free from caramelized flavor or other objectionable flavor or odors.

Dried Fruits[4]

Apples, Dry (1955)

  Grades: A, B*, C.

  Styles: Slices or rings (circular portions of cored apples), wedges (sectors cut longitudinally and radially from cored apples), pie pieces (irregular sectors), cuts (irregular shapes).

  Size: Size is a grade requirement.

	Grade A	Grade B	Grade C
Pie pieces			
Approximate thickness	$1/16$ to ¼ in.	$1/16$ to ¼ in.	$1/16$ to $5/16$
Length, 1 in. or more (minimum)	85 percent	60 percent	40 percent
Pass through $5/16$-in. square			
(maximum)	2 percent	6 percent	10 percent
Slices (or rings)			
Approximate thickness (maximum)	¼ in.	¼ in.	$5/16$ in.
Whole and practically whole rings			
(minimum)	75 percent	60 percent	40 percent
Length, 1¼ in. or more (minimum)	75 percent	60 percent	40 percent
Wedges			
Variation in thickness (maximum)	¼ in.	¼ in.	$5/16$ in.
Length, 1¼ in. or more (minimum)	90 percent	75 percent	50 percent

*Not more than 24% moisture. Normal flavor and odor; reasonably uniform in size and shape. Reasonably free from defects. Good, clear, bright color. Watch for discoloration, blemishes, seeds, stems, peel or other defects. Cook and note flavor, odor, texture and color.

[4]Cook for best quality evaluation.

Apples, Low Moisture or Dehydrated (1955)

> *Grades:* A (85)*, B (70).

> *Styles:* Flakes (parallel cut, irregularly shaped pieces around $^3/_{16}$ in. or less thick and ¾ in. or more long), wedges (fairly thick sectors not over ⅝ in. thick), small pieces or nuggets (about the size of unpopped corn or smaller), fine cut (pass through ⅜-in. square opening).

*Moisture content 2½% or less. Product should possess normal flavor and odor, good texture and color, be reasonably uniform in size, and practically free from defects. Watch for discoloration, seeds, stems, blemishes, and other defects.

Apricots, Dry (1967)

> *Grades:* A, B*, C.

> *Types:* Loose or slab.

*Reasonably uniform, bright, typical color characteristic of well-matured apricots, but some may possess a pale yellow area around the stem, not more than 25% of the outside surface. Defects of immaturity, pits or pieces of pits, damage from discoloration, hail, sunburn, scab, disease, insects, mold, decay, dirt, foreign material, and others should be watched. Inspect for insect infestation. For loose type, B Grade, not more than 15% can be in slabs. Apricots may be sulfured to prevent discoloration. Moisture should not be more than 26% for sizes No. 1 and No. 3 and slabs, and not more than 25% for larger sizes. (A slab is a fruit that has lost its normal contour.)

Apricots, Low Moisture or Dehydrated (1959)

> *Grades:* A (85)*, B (70).

> *Styles:* Nugget (foam-like, evenly sized pieces that will pass through a ⅝-in. square hole), pieces (irregular pieces that will pass through a ⅝-in. square hole, diced (cube-shaped units), slices (predominantly parallel-cut strips of irregular shape and thickness).

*Moisture limits are: nuggets 3½%, pieces 3½%, diced 5%, sliced 5%. Should be made from clean, sound, ripe apricots. May be sulfured to preserve color. Flavor and odor should be good, with no objectionable flavors or odors, scorched flavors; and so forth. Should be practically free from defects and seriously damaged units. Look for such defects as those listed above for dry apricots.

Currants (1965)

> *Grades:* A*, B.

> *Varieties:* Black Corinth or White Corinth.

Types: I Zante (domestic) unseeded or seeded; II, other than Zante, such as Amalias, Patras, Vostizza.

*Not more than 18% moisture. Good typical color, flavor from well-matured berries. Watch for defects, such as stems, grit, sand or dirt or foreign material, cap stems, sugared currants, damaged berries, poor development, mold, decay, and seeds in unseeded. Stem in raisins and currants means portion of main stem. Cap stem means small body stems not more than ⅛ in. in length.

Dates (1955)

Grades: A (90), B (80)*, C (70) for fresh; B (80)*, C (70) for dry.

Styles: Whole—pitted or unpitted, pieces (cut or sliced pitted dates), macerated (ground, chopped, mashed or broken pitted dates), slab (whole or pieces in slab not loose form).

*Good color, free from defects. Watch discoloration, checking, deformities, puffiness, mashed or broken dates. Severe checking, in which flesh becomes dark, crusty, and dry, may occur. Side spot damage is a dark area in the flesh, which may indicate mold. Best grades of dates are light in color, turning darker as the grade lowers. Watch for pits, stems, caps, and extraneous matter. Dry dates are only to be purchased by those operations using large quantities of dates for large quantity processing. If dates are to be broken up or chopped, purchase macerated or slab dates.

Figs (1967)

Grades: A, B*, C.

Color types: White to dark brown (Adriatic, Calimyrna, Kadota), Black (Mission).

Styles: I—whole, loose, pulled, or flattened—may be slightly split; layer or slab usually in staggered arrangement. II—sliced (cut into slices ¼ in. thick).

*Even, clear, uniform color of well-matured figs. Reasonably uniform in size. Watch for mold, decay, scars, blemishes, sunburn, mechanical injury, damaged, broken, or crushed fruit. Look for visible sugaring. Cook to ascertain flavor and odor. Size is not a factor of grade.

Peaches, Dry (1967)

Grades: A, B*, C.

Varieties: Freestone (Muir, Lovell, Elberta, and others), Clingstone (Midsummer, Phillips, and others).

*Not more than 15% can be slabs. Use factors discussed above for dried apricots for judging quality. Size is not a part of federal grade.

TABLE 3-10
Yields of Dried Fruit

One Pound Dried Fruit	Cooked Yield	Portion	Number Portions per Pound
Apples	4 lb 8 oz	½ c	17
Apricots	2 lb 15 oz	4 halves	10
Figs	2 lb 7 oz	3 figs	10
Peaches	2 lb 10 oz	3 halves	11
Pears	2 lb 10 oz	2 halves	14
Prunes	2 lb 3 oz	5 prunes	12
Raisins	3 lb 4 oz	⅓ c	17

Peaches, Low-moisture or Dehydrated (1959)

Grades: A (85)*, B (70).

Styles: Same as for low-moisture apricots above.

*Moisture content: nugget 3%, pieces 3%, diced 5%, sliced 5%. Use factors discussed above for low-moisture apricots for judging quality.

Pears, Dry (1967)

Grades: A, B*, C.

*Moisture content not over 26%. Use factors discussed above for judging quality of dried apples. Size is not a factor of federal grade.

Prunes (1965)

Grades: A, B*.

Size and Type: Type I—French or Robe (sweet); sizes per pound, 30/40, 40/50, 50/60, 60/70, 70/80, 80/90, 90/100, 100/120, 120 and over. Type II—Italian (tart); sizes per pound, 25/35, 35/45, 30/40, 40/50, 50/60, 60/70, 70/80, 90/100. Type III—Imperial or Sugar (sweet); sizes per pound, 15/20, 18/24, 20/30, 30/40, 40/50, 50/60, 60/70. Type IV—mixtures of the above.

Trade nomenclature for size: Extra large, average 43 per lb. Large, average 53 per lb. Medium, average 67 per lb. Small or Breakfast, average 85 per lb.

*Moisture content: 60 or less per pound, 25%; 61 or more per pound, 64%. Look for good color, black or blue-black. Tough, dry, rubbery prunes should be rejected. Watch for end cracks, skin or flesh damage. Smell for fermentation; and examine for scars, insect infestation or injury, heat damage, mold, dirt, foreign material, decay. Low-moisture prunes have federal standards and are available as nuggets, pieces, or whole pitted prunes. Grades are A and B.

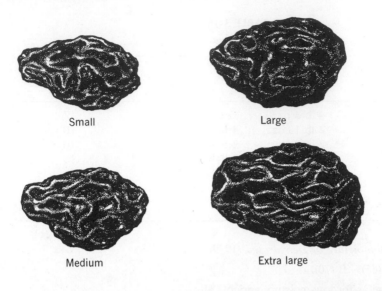

Small   Large

Medium   Extra large

Fig. 3-31. Grapes spread out to dry into raisins. Note the chance for incorporation of foreign items from the soil. Courtesy USDA

Raisins (1968)

Grades: A, B*, C for Thompson Seedless; A*, B for Muscat and Sultana.

Types: Type I—Thompson Seedless, unbleached or natural, sulfur-bleached or golden seedless, soda dipped; Type II—Muscat, seeded, unseeded cap stemmed (loose), unseeded uncap stemmed (loose), layer or cluster; Type III—Sultana; Type IV—Mixed (any mixture of above).

Size: Size is not a factor for grade in any except Type II, Muscat layer or cluster. Buyers may specify size as follows for raisins in diameter sizes:

Thompson Seedless: Small or midget, 20/64 to 22/64 in., select-22/64 to 24/64 in.
Muscat, seeded: Small or midget, $^{11}/_{32}$ in.; select-$^{17}/_{32}$ in.
Muscat, unseeded: 1 crown, smaller than ⅜ in.; 2 crown, ⅜ in.; 3 crown, $^{17}/_{32}$ in.;
4 crown, $^{21}/_{32}$ in. (Three crown is the smallest that cluster Muscat raisins can be and meet grade B.)
Sultana: No size classifications.

(Mixed may mean a mixture not meeting any specific size.)

*Moisture content may vary 18 to 23%, depending on type of raisin. Look for stems and cap stems. A stem is a portion of the main stem, and a cap stem is a small woody stem not more than ⅛ in. attached to the raisin. Watch for poorly developed, damaged, sugared, moldy, fermented, or decayed berries. Inspect for insect infestation. Examine for dirt, foreign material, decay, grit, sand or silt, shattered or damaged berries.

Color is not a factor for grade, but the best quality is indicated by the lighter, more uniform grades for type. Thompson Seedless may be specified as Extra Fancy (well-bleached color); Fancy (reasonably well-bleached color, predominantly yellow or golden to greenish yellow or light amber); Choice (bleached or yellowish green to dark amber or dark greenish amber); Standard (definitely dark or dark amber in color). Higher tolerances for darkness of color are allowed for the golden type as against the sulfur-bleached type. Soda-dipped raisins are used by bakers for decorating the tops of bakery products. The soda causes the raisin to swell or puff and the skin to check. These raisins may be oil dipped to give them a higher gloss.

TABLE 3-11
Yields in Prunes

Size Prune	Pits per Pound	Size Portion	Number Portions per Pound Dried Prunes
Extra large	2½ oz	4 prunes (3 oz)	11
Large	2½ oz	5 prunes (3¼ oz)	10½
Medium	2¾ oz	6 prunes (3 oz)	11
Small	3⅝ oz	7 prunes (2⅘ oz)	12

Approximate Sizes in Raisins

Thompson Seedless	Muscat, Seeded	Muscat, Unseeded
Small or midget	Small or midget	2-crown (1-crown any size smaller)
Select	Select	3-crown
		4-crown

TABLE 3-12
In Cooking
Increase by Weight in Some Dried Vegetables

Dried Vegetable	Increase in Cooking
Beans, all types	2½ times
Peas, split	2½ times
Peas, black-eyed	2²/₃ times
Cabbage, low-moisture	5¹/₃ times
Carrots, low-moisture	6 times
Celery, low-moisture	7 times
Onions, low-moisture	4½ times
Potatoes, diced, low-moisture	4½ times
Tomatoes, low-moisture	4½ times

TABLE 3-13
Cooking Chart for Vacuum-Dry, Low-Moisture Fruits

Vaccuum-Dry Low-Moisture Fruit	Pounds of Fruit	Water		Minutes Cooking Time	Sugar*		Approximate Yield Cooked
		lb	Qt		lb	Cup	
Apple sauce nuggets —small cut (sauce)	1	10	5	15	½	1	1¼ gal
Apple pie slices (stewed)	1	9¼	4⅝	20	½	1	1 gal
Apricot slices (stewed)	1	5	2½	15–20	½	1	2¾ qt
Peach slices (stewed)	1	5	2½	15–20	½	1	2¾ qt
Whole pitted prunes (stewed)	1	4	2	†	½	1	2½ qt
Fruit mix—large cut (stewed)	1	6	3	10–15	½	1	3⅓ qt
Fruit cocktail mix (stewed)	1	5½	2¾	5	½	1	3¼ qt

*Sugar may be varied to taste. Add sugar during the last 5 minutes of cooking for all fruits except prunes and figs. Add sugar to prunes and figs at the beginning of cooking. *DO NOT OVERCOOK.*
†Bring to boil, only.

Fig. 3-32. These apple puffs are being released from retorts above under pressure. The pressure inside the small apple particle puffs the item up so that it is light and fluffy. It then dries as it falls down the shoot. This is the same way that many puffed cereals are "shot from guns." Courtesy USDA

BIBLIOGRAPHY

American Can Co., *Canned Food Manual,* Davis, Delaney, and Harris, publishers, New York, 1943.

American Hospital Association, *Manual of Specifications for Canned Fruits and Vegetables,* Chicago, 1947.

U.S. Department of Agriculture, Agricultural Marketing Service, Washington, D.C.:

Outline of Suggested Specifications for Purchasing Processed Fruits and Vegetables; Misc. Pub. No. 565, 1945.

Questions and Answers on Government Inspection of Processed Fruits and Vegetables, Misc. Pub. No. 598, 1946.

U.S. Standards for Processed Fruits and Vegetables, various dates.

4
Dairy Products and Margarine

MILK AND CREAM

Because dairy products are so important as food, are highly perishable, and can be easily adulterated, contaminated, or develop undesirable characteristics, buyers should purchase only the highest quality products and see that they conform to established codes and standards that have been developed to assure quality and wholesomeness. Most state and local regulations for milk products are based on the Public Health Service's *Grade A Pasteurized* Milk Ordinance. Standards for manufactured dairy products have been developed by the Dairy Division of the USDA, which also seek to assure that products meet high standards. Products manufactured from milk also are controlled, and only milk that meets certain standards can be used in them. For the most part the standards cited in this chapter agree with these federal standards but may be at times stated as a range because many states do not follow completely the federal standards.

Specifications for the purchase of milk and its products should conform to local and state codes or regulations and refer to the federal code if criteria have to be established for them that do not exist. Buyers should require that all dairy products be produced and handled in accordance with the best sanitary practices and that manufacturing and processing plants shall meet the highest standards of sanitation. All milk products should come from milk that has been pasteurized. Purchase by brand may be recommended in many instances.

Fresh Fluid Milks and Creams

Fluid milk is fresh, clean cow's milk free from objectionable odors and flavors. It should be produced under local, state, or federal code provisions. It should contain "not less than 8¼% non-fat milk solids and not less than 3¼% milk fat," but some states allow 8% and 3%, respectively. It should contain no added water, preservatives, neutralizers, or other foreign substances, except perhaps 400 U.S.P. units of vitamin D per quart may be added. Local or state codes may allow fortification with additional milk solids. Whole milk should have a specific gravity at 60°F of 1.028. Quality in milk or cream and their products is based on flavor, odor, and frequently the quantity of solids present. Bacterial counts may be a part of grade.

Milk is pasteurized by heating it at 145°F for 30 minutes or 161°F for 15 seconds. Other products higher in milkfat are heated to 150°F for 30 minutes or 166°F for 25 seconds. Milk to be pasteurized should be cooled immediately after milking to 50°F and be held below this point until pasteurization. This raw milk can have a bacterial count up to 300,000 per ml for Grade A milk. It must be cooled to below 45°F and not go above that temperature after this. After pasteurization, it should not have over a 20,000 bacterial count and a 10 coliform count per ml, but this can vary in different states. Some local and state codes do not permit any coliform or have different counts for Grade A milk. Certified raw or pasteurized milk cannot have higher than a 10,000 count per ml and no coliform. Cultured milks must conform in temperature and coliform counts to regular milk but not in bacterial counts.

Milk is homogenized by forcing it under pressures around 2500 psi or more through tiny orifices to divide fat globules so finely they remain in permanent suspension.

Skim or nonfat milk is like regular milk except the milkfat content is ½ to 3¼%, depending upon state requirements. Low-fat milk may have a milkfat content from ½ to 3¼% also. Fortified milk and its products have had substances added, usually to increase their nutritional value. These might be vitamins A or C or added milk solids. These added substances must be approved. Flavored milk is regular milk to which a sweetener and/or flavoring is added. If the milkfat or milk solid content is changed from regular milk, some codes require that this be labeled *milk drink* or some other term indicating that it does not meet the standards of regular milk. Eggnog-flavored milk is milk containing 3¼% milkfat, ½% egg solids, and some sweetener and flavoring. Eggnog is a milk product containing 3½% to 8% milkfat, ½ to 1% egg yolk solids, and some sweetener and flavoring. A ½% stabilizer may be added to these 2 eggnog products. A low-sodium (dialyzed) milk may be obtained for low-sodium and other special diets. It is expensive.

Cream is made by centrifuging milk so that its heavier nonfat fluid is thrown to outer areas and the lighter cream to the center where it is drawn off. It must contain not less than 16 to 18% milkfat and should not have a bacterial count after pasteurization over 60,000 per ml and not more than 20 coliform per ml. Half-and-half is not cream but equal parts of whole 3¼% milkfat and cream of 18% milkfat, which makes it about 10½% milkfat; some states allow it to be only 10%. Soured or cultured half-and-half is available and must have a similar milkfat content and more than 0.2% acidity expressed as lactic acid. Table (light or coffee) cream usually runs from 16 to 22% milkfat but can go as high as 30%. Sour cream must have a similar milkfat content and more than 0.2% acidity expressed as lactic acid. Whipping cream is 30 to 36% milkfat, light is 30 to 34% usually, and heavy is over this but it varies. Whipping cream is usually ripened 3 days before being marketed.

Buttermilk is a fluid left after making butter, but most buttermilk today is made from whole, lowfat, or skim milk and soured by bacterial cultures. It contains 8 to 9% milk solids and a milkfat content consistent with the product from which it is made. *L. acidophilus* or *L. bulgaricus* are 2 bacteria used to make buttermilks thought to have some therapeutic value. Good buttermilk should have a titratable acidity between 0.70 and 0.85%. Yogurt is a cultured, spoonable, whole or nonfat milk with a slightly higher milk solid content than regular milk. It may be flavored.

Milk is purchased in half pints, pints, quarts, half gallons, and either 5- or 6-gallon dispenser units. Bulk milk may be available in cans or other packaging for kitchen use. Cream and half-and-half are usually purchased either in pints or quarts but can be obtained in larger packages for heavy use. Some individual packs of half-and-half or coffee cream are available for institutional use.

Dry milk solids may be reconstituted into milk, but some codes require that the reconstituted item be labeled "imitation." If it contains fat other than milkfat, it is called a filled milk. Most of these reconstituted products must conform in bacterial count and so forth to the standards applied to regular milk. Some can be fortified.

Dry or liquid diet foods made from milk products are on the market. They usually are high in milk solids and highly fortified with vitamins, minerals, proteins such as soy, and other substances, especially if used as dietary supplements. Some dry or liquid milk products are used today for reducing diets and come variously flavored and heavily fortified. Baby formulas also are on the market either as dry or liquid products. Check labels to ascertain what is in the product.

Artificial dairy products usually contain no milk or other dairy products. Some that resemble half-and-half, coffee, or whipping cream are used widely in food services. The dry products of this type contain sugar, emulsifiers such as polysorbate 60, sorbitan, monostearate, or a glyceride;

Fig. 4-1. Dairly-like toppings like this are commonly used today instead of whipping cream in institutions. They are more stable and are less expensive. If properly fortified with nutrients, they also can be as nutritious as the true dairy product. Courtesy USDA

gums are used for thickeners such as carrageenan or guar gum; sodium caseinate for body and foaming ability and perhaps artificial flavor and color. Some are fortified with vitamins and other substances. Institutions usually use the liquid types rather than the dry; the liquid types are the same as the dry except that they contain water. Some liquids used to imitate whipped cream are forced from their containers and are aerated by nitrous oxide and chloropentofluoroethane. A whipped frozen product resembling whipped cream is on the market.

The labels for imitation or artificial dairy products should be checked to ascertain their contents. For instance, many contain sodium caseinate, sodium silicoaluminate, and so forth not allowed on low-sodium diets. Others may contain saturated fats such as coconut oil and should not be used on low-saturated fat diets. In many instances, the natural product may be preferable from the standpoint of nutrition or other reasons. If in doubt about products in these items, write the manufacturer to find out what is meant in the list of ingredients by such things as "vegetable fat" or "emulsifier."

Concentrated Fluid Milks

Evaporated or condensed milks should be made from milk meeting high standards. Evaporated milk is 7.9% milkfat and 18.0% nonfat milk solids. It may be homogenized and fortified with vitamin D to yield 25 U.S.P. units per fluid ounce. It is manufactured by extracting moisture by boiling milk at 130 to 140°F under vacuum. Purchase may be in cases of 48/6-oz, 6/10- or 48/14½-oz cans. If water in the amount of 2.2 times the evaporated milk is added, the equivalent of whole milk is obtained. Thus a 14½-oz can makes a quart of whole milk equivalent. Lactose (milk sugar) crystallizes easily in such milk and so food services often turn cases every 6 months to retard crystal development. Sweetened condensed milk usually contains not less than 19.5% nonfat milk solids, 8.5% milkfat, and enough sugar to prevent spoilage (usually 45%, which is the equivalent of 19 to 20 lb per 100 lb of fresh milk). Condensed milks may be sold in bulk and need not be sterilized in cans as evaporated milk must be.

Dried Milks

Milk solids with only 2 to 5% moisture in tight seals keep a long time without deterioration. Whole dried milk contains not less than 26% milkfat and a maximum of 4 to 5% moisture. Nonfat dried milk usually contains not more than 1½% fat and not over 5% moisture. Watch for staleness, oxidation, tallowiness, caramelization, or other off-flavors. Whole milk can become rancid. Specify that the dried milk shall come from pasteurized milk.

Spray-dried milk is usually the highest quality. Roller-dried milk processed under vacuum also is of good quality. Milk is spray-dried by first removing a half to three-fourths of the moisture and then spraying this concentrate as a fine spray into a drying chamber; drum-dried (roller-dried) milk is obtained by rotating a steam-heated drum or roller in a vat of milk and removing the dried solids as the unit comes out of the milk and dries on the surface.

Federal grades for dry whole milk are U.S. Premium, U.S. Extra and U.S. Standard. Institutions should select either of the first two. Premium grade should have a sweet flavor, with not more than a slight cooked flavor and odor, white or light cream natural color, and be free from lumps that fail to break under slight pressure. It should be practically free from brown and black scorched particles. It should not have over a 30,000 bacterial plate count and not more than 90 coliform per gram and a 26% or more milkfat content. Federal grades for nonfat dry milk are U.S. Extra and U.S. Standard. Extra is preferred for food service use unless the milk is to be

Fig. 4-2. The lower portion of a spray dryer for milk. About a half to three-fourths of the moisture is extracted in condensers and the remaining moisture is extracted in this cone-shaped dryer. Forced under a pressure of 7000 psi through small holes in a special nozzle, the milk enters the top as a fine spray. Filtered, heated air removes the moisture, and the milk particles fall to the bottom where they are drawn off through suction pipes. Courtesy USDA

used for manufacturing, bakery production, and so forth. Bacterial counts for Extra should not be over 50,000 per gram and for Standard not more than 100,000 per gram. The flavor of Extra should be sweet, with not more than a slight, cooked, feed and flat, chalky flavor and odor and have the other factors indicated above for whole dry milk, except for milkfat.

Dry buttermilk grades are U.S. Extra and U.S. Standard. Extra is usually specified. It should have a good flavor and odor, free from nonbuttermilk flavors and odors. The color should be cream to light brown, and it should be free from lumps failing to break under slight pressure and practically free from black or brown scorched particles. The acidity should not be less than 0.1% nor more than 0.18% expressed as lactic acid, moisture not over 4%, and milkfat not more than 4½%. Bacterial limits are 50,000 per gram.

Malted milk is a dried milk product with about 3½% moisture, 7½% milkfat, and the dried solids of a fluid mixture of 40 to 45% nonfat milk and

55 to 60% malt extract. Each pound of malted milk contains the solids of 2.2 lb of fluid whole milk; total milk solids are usually 29%. Double malted milk contains twice as much malt as does regular malted milk.

If the quantity of dried milk used is large, purchase in 50- or 100-lb bags or 200-lb drums. Specify high-heat-treated milk for milk used for yeast products since regular pasteurized milk has thermophilic bacteria in it that can interfere with yeast development. If lesser quantities are used, purchase the milk packed in 6/10 cases, 10-lb bags, and so forth. Purchase by the pound. Instant milk goes into solution much easier than does regular dry milk and, if the milk is reliquefied rather than being used dry, this is a much easier product to use.

Store dry milk in a dry, cool, well-ventilated place. If it becomes higher than 5% in moisture, it will stale, discolor, lump, and so on. Keep dry milk away from products from which they might absorb objectionable odors. The Dairy Division Laboratory, AMS, USDA, 1819 West Pershing Road, Chicago, 60609 can be helpful in problems relating to dry milk and other dairy products.

FROZEN DESSERTS

Before freezing, frozen desserts should be pasteurized at 155°F for 30 minutes or 175°F for 25 seconds. The increase in volume from freezing and whipping, called *overrun,* should be from 80 to 100% for ice cream, around 40% for sherbets, and 25% for ices. Ice cream by weight should be 8 to 12% nonfat milk solids and 14 to 18% sugar (corn sugar can be 25 to 30% of the total sweetener). A ½% of stabilizer such as agar agar, gelatin, or a mixture of monoglyceride and gelatin can be used. The minimum acidity of fruit sherbet and water ice is 0.35%. The government standards for frozen desserts in addition to this are as follows:

	Ice Cream				
	Vanilla and Light Flavors	Bulky Flavors	Ice Milk	Fruit Sherbet	Water Ice
Minimum % milk fat	10	8	2	1	0
Minimum % total milk solids	20	16	11	2	0
Minimum lb wt per gal	4.5	4.5	4.5	6	6
Minimum lb total food solids per gal	1.6	1.6	1.3		

Note: Some states may vary in the above percentage requirements.

A 10% milkfat mix often is used for bulky flavors such as chocolate, nut, strawberry, and so forth. These flavors are added usually in the amount of 2% of the mix, which reduces the milkfat content. Because of this, standards allow bulky flavors to be only 8% milkfat rather than 10%. Surplus government butter and dry milk make excellent ice cream and other frozen desserts, but the institution must have a pasteurizer, homogenizer, freezing and hardening equipment to make a satisfactory product. Fluid dairy products after pasteurization should not have a bacterial count of more than 50,000 per ml and not more than 10 coliform per ml, and dry dairy ingredients and frozen dessert (plain) should not have similar counts per gram of product.

Quiescently frozen dairy products are those frozen without mixing. The swell from freezing therefore cannot be over 10%. Frozen confections of this type can contain ½% of stabilizer and must contain not less than 17% by weight of total food solids. Frozen dairy confections of this type must contain not less than 13% by weight of milk solids, not less than 33% of food solids, and not more than ½% of stabilizer. Not more than $\frac{1}{5}$% by weight of emulsifier is allowed. Mellorine-type products are those containing fats other than milkfat but otherwise resemble frozen desserts. They are sold under trade names such as Mellorine, Lo-Rine, and Sherbine.

Philadelphia ice cream is plain milk, cream, sweetener, flavor, and stabilizer. French ice cream is Philadelphia ice cream but contains 1.4% by weight or 1.12% of egg solids if a bulky flavor. It can be flavored with ground vanilla bean. Lowfat frozen dessert may be from 5 to 10% milkfat usually. Store frozen desserts at below 0°F and have them at 10 to 15°F for dishing.

There are no grades for frozen desserts, but they may be scored as follows: flavor, 35 points; texture, 20 points; body, 20 points; appearance, 15 points; and packaging, 10 points. A metallic, old cream, rancid, bitter, stale, or cooked flavor lowers the score. Proper acidity and sweetness plus other off-flavors may lower the score. Excess or insufficient flavoring or inferior flavoring are evaluated. Body and texture may be considered together and both can affect flavor. Check the amount of overrun. The frozen structure, smoothness, and aftertaste in the mouth make up body plus the fineness, creaminess, and firmness of grain. A slightly open grain for lightness is sought. Texture defects can be fluffiness, weakness, crumbliness, wateriness, iciness, sogginess, and gumminess. Poor ingredient quality or inferior freezing gives poor body and texture. Appearance may be partly based on naturalness, proper amount, and evenness of color. Grain can affect appearance. The product should have a bright, smooth sheen called *bloom*. Products with low milk solids have the most brilliance. Allow the dessert to melt. Note the consistency and taste it.

CHEESE

There are many kinds of cheeses available and buyers should know the quality factors for those they purchase. To know quality, one must know how cheese is made, aged, and stored.

Manufacture

Whole, partially defatted, or nonfat milk may be used for cheese, depending upon type. Cow's milk usually is used and must be of approved quality. Annatto, which gives a yellowish-range color, or other colorings must be approved for use by the FDA. The addition of annatto need not be noted on the label. Cheese is made from pasteurized milk unless cured over 60 days; curing over 60 days destroys harmful bacteria. The quantity of milkfat and moisture in many cheeses is controlled by federal standards.

A clabbered curd from milk is usually the base of cheese. This is obtained by coagulating milk with rennet, by lactic acid producing bacteria, or other substances. Bacteria called *starters,* usually lactic acid type, are used to

Fig. 4-3. When milk is at the proper acidity and temperature, the rennet is added. This sets the milk into a soft curd. After the curd forms, workers on opposite sides of the vat cut the curd into small particles with fine wire knives. Courtesy USDA

increase milk acidity so that the milk forms a more solid curd when rennet is added. Different bacteria are also used to product different cheeses. For instance, *Penicillium roqueforti* produce the mold in blue-type cheeses; *Propioni-bacterium shermanii* give the sharp flavor and large eyes to Swiss, and *Penicillium camemberti* are used to give the rich flavor and soft texture to Camembert. About 10 lb of cheese are obtained from 100 lb of whole milk.

Foreign and Domestic Cheeses

American cheese producers have been able to imitate well many foreign cheeses. They can use very similar products and techniques plus introduce conditions that parallel very well European aging conditions. Some caves near St. Paul have almost identical environmental aging conditions to those in Roquefort, France. Generally, however, foreign cheeses are superior in flavor, and are drier and smoother in texture because of better manufacture, longer aging, and the use of milks other than cow's. Even the best American blue cheese made from cow's milk cannot duplicate true Roquefort flavor made from ewe's milk. The famous Cheshire cheddar of England can have few imitators because its flavor is influenced by the unique character of Cheshire soil.

Some names of foreign cheeses cannot be used here; for instance, the name Roquefort for a blue cheese is prohibited from use by a treaty with France. Some names of foreign cheeses can be used if in front of the name of the cheese the word "domestic" or "American" is used, such as "domestic Swiss" or "American Brie."

American cheeses are usually factory-made under highly scientific and controlled conditions. Although more and more European cheese is factory-produced, many are still farm-made—the English call these *farmhouse* cheese, and their character varies much as wine of the same kind is different when produced by different vineyards.

We have developed some of our own typical cheeses, although most we manufacture have been copied from foreign counterparts. Brick originated in this country, and took its name from its shape. It is a semihard, smooth cheese resembling Muenster somewhat in texture, but it is filled with tiny, sweet holes. Its flavor is between that of Limburger and cheddar, mildly sharp but mellow. Like Limburger, it ripens from the outside in but never becomes as soft as Camembert or Brie. It slices well. Another American cheese is Liederkrantz, developed by the Borden Company. It is a Limburger-like cheese with a soft, creamy texture. Monterey Jack is a California cheese that imitates some of the Italian cheeses.

Classification of Cheese

Cheese can be classified as soft, semihard, and hard. The degree of cooking and other factors influence the degree of hardness.

Ripening is another way of classifying cheese. Some such as cream or cottage cheese are not ripened. Others are ripened by adding bacteria or mold and ripen from the *inside out* as do Roquefort or Swiss. Others are treated with bacteria or mold and ripen from the *outside in* such as Camembert, Brie, and Limburger. If ripened from the inside out, the cheese usually keeps well, especially dry, hard ones such as the Granas. Those ripened from the outside in start as firm cheese but soften during ripening. If carefutly controlled, the cheese is ready to eat in about 4 to 5 weeks. Underaging is indicated by too much firmness and a powdery, thickly coated whiteness on the rind. Most properly aged cheeses of this kind have a softness throughout evidenced by yielding gently to pressure in the center. Some such as Camembert should be so soft and so tacky that they almost flow. In a short time, these cheeses start to become firm again, which indicates overaging. Overage also is indicated by a heavy, rusty crust, a strong ammoniacal odor, or the loss of the rich subtle flavor. Most cheese ripened from the inside out develop a heavy rind that is eaten with the cheese. Stock only several weeks supply of the cheeses ripened from the outside in.

The Cheddar Process

American, our most popular cheese, is made by the cheddar process, which is a method of pressing moisture from strips of fresh curd by putting other strips on top of them. Many other cheeses are made by this method.

Whole or partially defatted cow's milk is used for American cheddar. It is pasteurized usually and cooled to around 86 to 88°F, and a lactic acid starter is added. If the cheese is colored, the color is added at this time. Rennet is added in the amount of 3 oz per 1000 lb of milk; about 30 minutes later the milk is a firm, glossy clabber. It is then cut into cubes with curd knives or wires—the instrument used for Swiss cheese is called a *Swiss harp* because of the formation of its wires. Whey now flows from these cubes.

Next the temperature is raised; this is called *cooking*. The higher the cooking temperature, the firmer and harder the cheese. Cheddar cheese is cooked to below 100°F, but Swiss may go as high as 110°F, giving a firmer cheese. After good stirring, the curd is piled against the side of the trough to drain, a process called *ditching*. During ditching, further whey is lost. The

Fig. 4-4. The ditched cheese is cut into blocks and turned for the first time. This turning and resting are known as cheddaring. Courtesy USDA

cubes now form a solid, rubbery mass that is cut into about 8-in.-wide strips, piled about 3 to 4 deep, and left to drain. They are frequently alternated to give equal pressure to all strips, a process called *cheddaring*. The acidity is now about 0.45 to 0.60% expressed as lactic acid, and moisture is around 50%.

Next the curd is cubed (a process called *milling*), salted, and piled into hoops. For some cheeses, special molds or bacteria are added at this time, if they have not been added before. The hoop cloths are tightened, the product pressed for several hours and placed into coolers for several days to dry. The cheese then is dipped into paraffin and moved into curing which is a process that changes the texture from a resilient, rubbery mass to one that is softer, more flexible, and waxy. The flavor is sharper, more pungent and biting, and smoother. For some cheese, temperature, humidity, and salting are used to control aging. For instance, Swiss may be brine-dipped or salt-rubbed to slow down curing actions. If aging is too rapid, the cheese can burst. This is called a *failure*. The man in charge of curing must have as much skill as a brewmaster in a brewery.

Fig. 4-5. Here the 8-in. strips are piled to cheddar. Courtesy USDA

When well ripened, a plug drawn from good cheddar will be solid, compact, translucent, and have a close grain with few small openings caused by gas or yeast development—unless it is a cheese such as Swiss. Holes in cheese are called *sweet* or *Swiss* holes. Flecks of white are evidence of good ripening. By exerting proper control a cheese with no rind can be made. Such cheese is wrapped and sealed in special wrapping materials.

The term "current" for American cheddar means under 30 days cure; "medium," 30 to 180 days ; and "cured or aged," over 180 days. "Current" for Swiss is under 90 days cure; "medium," 90 days to 6 months; and "aged or cured," over 6 months. Forced cure is curing at 45 to 55°F and 80% humidity. This forced curing ages cheese as much in 90 days as 8 to 10 months regular cure at 38 to 40°F, or a regular cure for 12 to 18 months at 32 to 34°F and 70% humidity, but it results in a greater number of failures.

American Cheddar Cheeses

Table 4-3 lists market sizes for some American cheddars. Many are colored a yellow-orange. Federal grades are AA, A, B, and C. Cheddar must contain not more than 39% moisture and have 50% or more milkfat based on dry weight. On a moist basis the fat must be 31% or more. Grade is established on the basis of body, texture, flavor, aroma, color, general finish, and appearance.

Many areas produce excellent cheddars such as upper New York, Wisconsin, and Oregon's Tillamook County. Variations on cheddar cheese are found. A pineapple cheddar originated in Connecticut; it is a highly cooked cheese hung in a net that gives it a pineapple shape and name. Oil is rubbed on the surface during curing. This gives it a bright, yellow, glossy exterior. Curing is 4 to 6 months.

TABLE 4-1
Origin, Characteristics, and Mode of Serving Commonly Used Cheeses

Cheese	Characteristics	Mode of Serving	Place of Origin
American	Hard; smooth; light yellow to orange; mild. Made of cow's milk (whole). Cheddar type.	As such; in sandwiches; in cooked foods.	United States
Apple	Hard; sharp flavor; apple-shaped. Made of cow's milk (whole). Smoked.	As such.	Italy
Asiago	Hard; granular texture; piquant flavor (sharp in old cheese). Made of cow's milk (whole).	As such; as seasoning (grated) when old.	Italy
Blue	Semihard; white with blue mold; flavor similar to Roquefort. Made of cow's milk (whole).	As such (dessert); on crackers; in cooked foods; in salads.	France and Italy
Brick	Semihard; smooth; flavor between Limburger and Cheddar. Made of cow's milk (whole).	As such; in sandwiches; with salads.	United States
Brie	Soft; flavor resembles Camembert. Made of cow's milk (whole).	As such (dessert).	Paris, France
Caciocavallo	Hard; sharp flavor; ten-pin shape. Made of cow's milk (whole or partly defatted). Smoked.	As such; as seasoning (grated).	Southern Italy
Camembert	Soft; full flavor, often ammoniacal. Made of cow's milk (whole).	As such (dessert).	Camembert, France
Cheddar	Hard; smooth, light yellow to orange; mild. Made of cow's milk (whole or partly defatted).	As such; in sandwiches; in cooked foods.	Cheddar, England
Cottage	Soft; white; mildly sour flavor. Unripened; usually made of cow's milk (defatted). Cream may be added to finished product.	As such; in salads; in cooked foods.	Uncertain
Cream	Soft; smooth; buttery; mild, slightly sour flavor. Unripened; made of cream and cow's milk (whole).	As such; in sandwiches; with salads; on crackers.	Uncertain
Edam	Hard; rubbery; Cheddar flavor, but nut-like; "cannon-ball" shape. Made of cow's milk (partly defatted).	As such; on crackers.	Northern Holland
Gammelost	Hard; golden brown; strong flavor; pungent. Made of cow's milk (defatted, soured).	As such.	Norway

Cheese	Description	Uses	Origin
Gorgonzola	Semihard; marbled with blue mold; spicy flavor. Made of cow's milk (whole).	As such (dessert); with salads.	Gorgonzola, Italy
Gouda	Semihard; flavor like Edam. Made of partly defatted milk.	As such; on crackers.	Southern Holland
Gruyere	Hard with gas holes; nut-like, salty flavor. Made of cow's milk (usually partly defatted).	As such (dessert).	Gruyere, Switzerland
Jack	Semihard; smooth; mild; made of cow's milk (whole).	As such; in sandwiches.	United States
Limburger	Soft; full flavor; highly aromatic. Made of cow's milk (whole or partly defatted).	In sandwiches; on crackers.	Limburg, Belgium
Muenster	Semihard; flavor between brick and Limburger. Usually made of a mixture of cow's and goat's milk (whole).	As such; in sandwiches.	Muenster, Germany
Neufchatel	Soft; creamy; white; mild flavor. Unripened. Made of cow's milk (whole).	As such; in sandwiches; on crackers; in salads.	Seine Inferieure, France
Parmesan	Hard; granular texture; sharp flavor. Made of cow's milk (partly defatted).	As such; as seasoning.	Parma and Lodi, Italy
Port du Salut (Oka)	Semihard; rubbery texture; flavor between Limburger and Cheddar. Made of whole, slightly acid cow's milk.	As such (dessert).	Trappist Monasteries, France and Canada
Primost	Soft; light brown; mild flavor. Unripened, made from whey.	As such.	Norway
Provolone	Hard; sharp flavor; usually pear-shaped. Made of cow's milk (whole). Smoked.	As such.	Italy
Roquefort	Semihard; white with blue mold; sweet, piquant flavor. Made of sheep's milk (whole).	As such (dessert); on crackers; with salads.	Roquefort, France
Sapsago	Hard; green color; flavored with clover leaves; small; cone-shaped. Made of cow's milk (defatted and soured), buttermilk, and whey.	As such; as seasoning (grated).	Glarus, Switzerland
Stilton	Semihard; white with blue mold; spicy flavor. Made of cow's milk (whole with added cream).	As such (dessert); in cooked foods; with salads.	Stilton, England
Swiss	Hard with gas holes; nut-like, sweet flavor. Made of cow's milk (partly defatted).	As such; in sandwiches; with salads.	Emme Valley, Switzerland

Courtesy National Dairy Council

TABLE 4-2

Classification of Cheese on the Basis of Hardness or Softness

Hard		Semihard			Soft		
Bacteria Ripened 12–16 months	Bacteria Ripened 3–12 months	Bacteria Ripened 2–3 months	Bacteria Ripened 1–8 months	Mold Ripened 2–12 months	Bacteria Ripened 1–2 months	Mold Ripened 2–5 months	Unripened
Cheshire	American	Appetitost	Bel Paese	Bleu	Hand	Brie	Cottage
Parmesan	Apple	Nokkelost	Brick	Blue	Limburger	Camembert	Cream
Reggiano	Asiago	Kumminost	Fontina	Gorgonzola		Livarot	Neufchatel
Romano	Cheddar		Gammelost	Roquefort		Pont l'Eveque	Primost
Sardo	Edam		Gouda	Stilton			Ricotta
	Gjetost		Jack				
	Gruyere		Muenster				
	Provolone		Port du Salut				
	Sapsago						
	Sbrinz						
	Swiss						

Courtesy National Dairy Council

TABLE 4-3
Common Market Sizes of Cheddar Cheese

Market Name	Shape	Number in Box	Weight of Each Piece
Cheddar	Cylindrical	1 (13½ to 14 in. diam.)	70 to 75 lb
Twin or flats	Cylindrical	1 or 2*	30 to 33 lb
Daisy	Cylindrical	1 to 3†	19 to 21 lb
Longhorn	Cylindrical	4	11½ to 13 lb
Picnic	Cylindrical	Varies	1 to 2 lb
Square	Rectangular	Varies	10 lb
Print	Rectangular	Varies	10 lb

*Two flats in a box are called *twins*.
†Called *single, double,* or *triple daisies,* depending upon number in box.

Fig. 4-6. Milling the curd. Courtesy USDA

TABLE 4-4

Quality Factors in U.S. Grade A Cheddar Cheese

Quality Factor	All Cures	Fresh or Current	Medium Cured	Cured or Aged
			Type Cures*	
Flavor	Free from undesirable flavors and odors but may have slight regional or seasonal feed flavors.	Practically no flavor development.	Mild characteristic cheese flavor; may have some slight acid flavor.	Well-developed characteristic cheese flavor; may be slightly acid.
Body and Texture	Practically solid, compact and close, although it may have a few mechanical openings, but these are not large and connecting; may not have more than 2 sweet or Swiss holes per trier sample; should be free from yeast holes and other gas holes; is translucent.	Firm, smooth, and curdy or may be partially broken down if the cheese is over 3 weeks old.	Reasonably firm, smooth and waxy; may be slightly curdy or not entirely broken down or slightly short, mealy or weak.	Reasonably firm, smooth and waxy; may be slightly short or mealy, or slightly weak and pasty.
Color	May be uncolored or medium colored† and slightly seamy.	Same as given for all cures.	Same as given for all cures.	May have tiny white specks in addition to color factors listed for current make.

*Current, under 30 days cure; medium, 30 to 150 days; cured or aged, over 150 days.

†In the South and other areas a deeper-colored cheddar is preferred, and graders may allow additional coloring, even to yellow orange, in cheese evaluated for that area.

English Daisy is also a highly cooked cheddar and is so hard it is usually grated. Some American cheddars have sage or other flavorings added. Colby, Washed Curd, and Stirred Curd resemble cheddar but are made by a method slightly different from cheddaring. They contain more moisture that in these three is 40%, 42%, and 42%, respectively. Curing is about 30 days at 38 to 40°F. They lack the texture and flavor of aged cheddars and should be purchased in smaller quantities since they do not keep well. Federal grades for Colby are AA, A, and B.

Well-ripened cheddar, ground free of lumps and pressed into a loaf or packed into jars, is called *club* or *cold-pack* cheese. It can be pasteurized. About 10% butter is blended into it, which makes it spread well. Milled club is unpasteurized. Flavorings, wines, and so forth are added to clubs.

Monterey Jack (Jack or Monterey) resembles brick in texture and color (a light creamy white) but is slightly more compact. Small holes should be evident, like apertures between layers of rock, and the surface should be slightly dull, not glazed. A bright, attractive appearance should be evident. The texture should be reasonably firm with numerous small mechanical openings evenly distributed throughout the product. It should pull from the mass, tearing rather than crumbling. Poorer grades have large, splotchy

Fig. 4-7. From the press the young Swiss cheese goes into a brine tank to float for several days. This treatment adds salt to the cheese and also controls undesirable curing reactions. During the curing process some dry salt may be rubbed into the cheese to control undesirable reactions. Courtesy USDA

X-ray

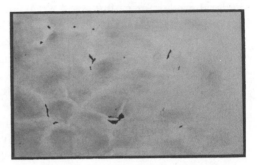

X-ray

Exterior

Exterior

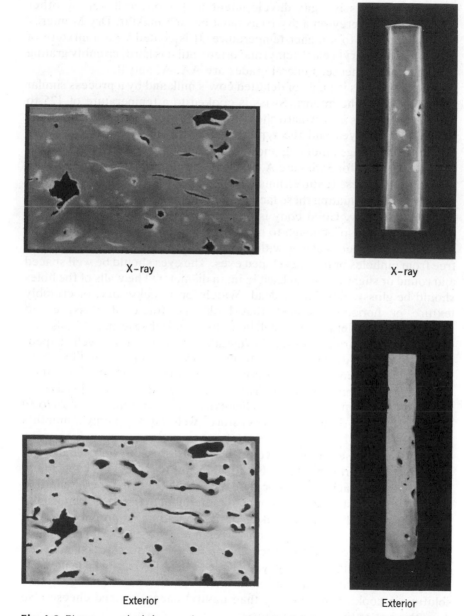

X-ray

X-ray

Exterior

Exterior

Fig. 4-8. Pictures on the left page show a good grade of cheese with fine holes. Pictures on the right page show excessive development of holes during curing. The holes result from gas, which forms during the curing process. These holes are called *sweet* or *Swiss* holes.

holes from excessive gas development and a bitter flavor or other off-flavors. Monterey on a dry basis must be 50% milkfat. Dry Monterey has been cooked to a higher temperature. It is coated with a mixture of pepper, oil and baryta earth (clay) and dried until it is hard, crumbly grating like dry Italian cheese. Federal grades are AA, A, and B.

American Swiss is made of defatted cow's milk and by a process similar to that used for the import. Swiss is cooked to a temperature of 125 to 130°F, which gives a fairly hard cheese. Bacteria are added to produce a gas to develop the eyes and the typical flavor. Curing is difficult. Excess humidity encourages molding and too low humidity causes rind checks.

Federal grades for Swiss are A, B, C, and D, determined on the basis of flavor, body, eyes, texture, finish, appearance, salt, and color. Age is considered in evaluating these factors. The flavor should be characteristic and full and nutty. Good body is one that is firm, smooth, and flexible, resisting bite but soft enough to mold between the fingers like solidifying wax. Picks and checks can be within an inch of the surface, but it should be free from pinholes or overdeveloped eyes. The eyes should be well spaced and round or slightly oval, at least ½ in. in diameter. The walls of the holes should be glossy, not dull or dead. Watch for a sticky, dry, or crumbly texture or horizontal cracks that look like fractured glass, called *glassiness*. "Nizzlers" have small holes like brick cheese and "blinds" no eyes at all. Both are causes for downgrading. Good Swiss is well shaped, with a clean, sound, dry rind, free from mold unless it is the rindless type. Salting should be correct and uniform. The color of young Swiss is creamy, increasing in whiteness with age. Swiss can be purchased in blocks, drums, or rounds. Blocks usually have smaller eyes. A small round is from 20 to 30 lb and a large one 50 to 60 lb. Swiss stores well, but keep only a month's supply on hand.

Processed cheese was first developed by a Mr. Borden, who founded the company now bearing his name. He noted in northern New York that many failures were sold at low prices or were fed as feed to pigs. Experimentation indicated that pasteurization stopped bacterial action and, if emulsifiers were added and the cheese packaged, a smooth, edible product was obtained that aged no more. Today only a relatively few cheese failures make up the total cheese used for processed cheese, and the process is now so well perfected that almost any type of cheese and flavor can be produced. Because of its processing and emulsifiers, processed cheese goes into solution in cooking more easily than natural cheeses. Aged cheese also does this better than unaged cheese.

Foreign Cheeses

The white or yellow cheese from Cheddar, England is imitated probably

Fig. 4-9. A good quality Swiss cheese that has cured for 3 months. Eyes start to form 2 to 3 weeks after the cheese goes into the curing room. As the curing progresses, the eyes grow in size. Note shiny eyes, large in size, indicating quality. Excessive eye development is undesirable. Courtesy USDA

more than any other cheese in the world. Farmhouse cheddars from Somerset have a world-wide reputation for excellence after aging for 6 months or more. Cheshire is a great cheddar with a hard texture that is loose, flaky, and crumbly. Its color can be pale yellow, red (carrot), or sometimes blue from mold development. Lancashire cheddar is a white, yellowish cheese, slightly sharp and spreadable when young, the flavor mellowing with age. Leicester is another local cheddar with a rich, zesty flavor and a flaky, creamy texture good for cooking, for sauces and rarebits. Caerphilly is a village near Cardiff, Wales, but the cheddar of this name comes largely from Worcester and Somerset. It is creamy in color, with a rather grainy texture and a buttermilk-like taste. White Wensleydale is a factory cheddar having a crumbly texture and a concentrated milk flavor that can grow in the mouth. A farmhouse Blue Wensleydale has blue mold inside but otherwise resembles the white brother. A Single Gloucester cheddar is half the size of a Double Gloucester and has a rather bland, insipid taste compared to a Double, which has a mild, slightly ripe flavor. Both are orange in color. Derby is better known as Derby Sage because it is flavored with that spice. It also is given a bright green marble effect by adding chopped spinach to it. It is mild in flavor and has a tendency to flake, although it is rather a soft, creamy product. It is best after aging about 6 months. The Stilton from Stilton, England, is a famous bleu ranking with Roquefort and Gorgonzola. It has a rather red, crinkled rind and a delightful spicy, more biting flavor than Roquefort. It has creamy white flesh streaked plentifully with blue mold. It is made largely in the summer, and aging should be not less than 6 months. Whole cow's milk is used fortified with cream. It comes largely in rounds.

France has probably more different cheeses than any other country. Roquefort, called the *cheese of kings,* is a world-known bleu made from ewe's milk. It is cave-ripened for 3 months or more at 45 to 48°F and 75% relative humidity. Aging over 6 months does little to improve quality. It comes in 5- or 10-lb rounds but can be purchased in 3-oz, 1¼-oz, and ¾-oz packs. All Roquefort will have on the label a red seal with the word *Roquefort* over a ewe in the center and the words *Garanti Veritable* under. There are a number of other French bleus, some of the most common are Septmosell and Gex.

Camembert is a Normandy cheese made from whole cow's milk. It is cured from the outside in and is a soft cheese with a rich, piquant flavor, slightly astringent or ammoniacal but pleasantly so. Its color is creamy yellow and the texture should be soft and tacky. It is cooked to a low temperature. It comes in a small 4-in.-diameter round in a wooden box labeled *Syndicat des Fabricants du veritable Camembert.* Brie comes from near the Champagne area, with the finest coming from Meaux or the Ile de France area. It is a larger round than Camembert with a firm crust and a firmer body. It has a rich, mellow flavor somewhat like Camembert. Reblonchon has a firmer flesh than Camembert with a deeper yellow or orangish skin. It is mild in flavor and should be consumed rather young since it gets bitter with age. Livarot is a soft cow's milk cheese from Normandy resembling Camembert. It has a reddish crust that is not eaten. The disc is slightly larger than Camembert's. The body is soft, yellow, with a flavor somewhat more pungent than Camembert. It is enclosed in 5 reed bands. It can easily overripen and should not be held too long. Epoisse comes from Burgundy and is eaten fresh in the summer or as lightly ripened cheese in early winter. In France it may be flavored with black pepper or fennel or put into white wine or brandy. It is soft and creamy and comes in a cylinder shape with an orange-crusted ring. Other French cheeses resembling Camembert are Coulommiers and Melun. Most of these cheeses are rather high in salt.

Port du Salut (Oka or Trappist) was developed by Norman Trappist monks, but it now is made in other countries, among them Canada. It is made from whole, slightly acid cow's milk into a creamy, somewhat rubbery cheese with a mild Limburger flavor. The color is yellowish or creamy. Color and flavor increase with age. St. Paulin also was first made in a Norman monastery and resembles Port Salut. It is made from whole cow's milk into a rich yellow-colored, firm-to-touch cheese with a mildly ripe taste. It dries out rapidly. Muenster now is largely produced in Muenster, Germany, but originally came from Alsace, France. It is a semihard cheese made from a mixture of whole cow's and goat's milk. It has a flavor between brick and Limburger and is cured by the outside-in process. It also may be called *beer* cheese. It has different sizes but resembles brick cheese in texture and color. Sometimes caraway seeds are added to it. When quite soft, it becomes very creamy and delicate. Gerome resembles Muenster but may be milder in flavor.

Cantal is one of the besk-known cheddar-like French cheeses produced in Auvergne. It is a hard, yellow cow's milk cheese made in a form called *fourmes de Cantal,* which may have given rise to the words *fromage* (French) and *formaggio* (Italian) for cheese. It keeps well but is best as a winter cheese. Softer cheeses are the Tome de Savoie (*tome* is local Savoy for cheese). It has a waxy consistency and a soft, mild flavor. It is ripened in dried grape skins and pips, giving it a woody aroma and a pebblish appearance. Another Savoy cheese is St. Marcelin, which is a soft, cream cheese that comes in small rounds made from a mixture of goat and cow's milk. It has a mild flavor with a slightly salty undertaste.

A number of French cheeses come from goat's milk. One resembling Camembert, called St. Maure, is shaped like a small Swiss roll and comes from a town of that name in Touraine. It has a soft, pungent flavor and a soft texture and, like other cheeses of this type, does not keep well. Poitou produces a mild, tangy, creamy goat cheese called La Mothe St. Heray. It is distinguished by its shape of a flattened pyramid. Banon is a pungent goat cheese that is treated with herbs and grapes and then wrapped in chestnut or vine leaves and ripened for 2 months. Chevre also comes from Touraine and has a white, crumbly texture and a mild flavor that is unmistakably goaty. Valancy comes from the Indre area, southeast of Tours. It is full flavored and creamy. Its shape is that of a small pyramid that becomes slate gray from a dusting of ashes. Crotin de Chavignol is a goat cheese that has a slightly acrid aftertaste. It comes from the Sancere wine area in a small mold weighing 2 oz.

Italy is famous for its cheeses, many of which flavor typical Italian dishes. The hard cheeses are cooked to a high temperature and then dried. They are used in grated form. They are called Grana cheese, which is another name for Parmesan-type cheese, also called Parmigiano cheese. They come in large, black 50-lb cylinders and keep well. Age is related to cost. The oldest is Stravecchione, Stravecchio is next, and Vecchio is about 3 years old and the youngest. They should be a deep yellow color, craggy and lightly pitted with a rich, tart, and somewhat sharp, mellow flavor. Imports to this country must be aged 14 months or more. Romano is another hard, granular, yellow-white cheese with a piquant flavor. Cow's milk makes a milder Romano than the milk from sheep or goat. A Sardo Romano is made from cow's milk. Asiago and Reggioano are two other Grana types. Both have rather sharp flavors. Caciocavallo is a hard, sharp-flavored cheese made from whole or partly defatted cow's milk. It has a 10-pin shape and weighs from 3 to 6 lb. It is smoked to give it a special flavor.

A cheese somewhat like Camembert is Taleggio produced in Lombardy. After ripening it is soft and runny with a pleasant piquancy underlining a somewhat bland flavor. It can be overaged and, if it smells ammoniacal, its quality is gone. It comes in a round disc with a rough, pink-tinged crust. A cheese somewhat like Port du Salut in appearance, texture, and color is Bel Paese, a soft, mild, popular cheese. It has a high fat content and is a good cooking cheese sometimes substituted for Mozzarella, but it is stronger in flavor and less stringy. Mozzarella originated in the Naples-Salerno region and was made from buffalo milk but is now made from cow's milk. It is used in pizza and is a cheese that is pulled or worked to develop its stringy quality. It is not aged and keeps poorly. It is mild in flavor, creamy white in color, and can be purchased shredded. Some keep it under refrigeration in water. Scarmorze is a small, hard, sweetish cheese made from buffalo milk. (Domestic Scarmorze is made from cow's milk.) It is high in moisture, sweet and mild in flavor, and sold when less than 10 days old. It too can be used for pizza. Ricotta is a cheese resembling cottage cheese but slightly drier and stronger in flavor. It comes from ewe's milk. It keeps poorly. It is used to make gnocchi, tortni, croquettes, or for stuffing ravioli or cannelloni. Pecorino is a hard, pungent ewe's milk cheese. It is frequently eaten fresh and is used for famous Italian dishes such as *Spaghetti a la Matriicana*. Sardo is made of ewe's milk and is somewhat like Pecorino. It too is used for certain dishes such as *pesto sauce*. It comes from southern Italy in pear, sausage, or other shapes. It is made from cow's or buffalo's milk. The color is creamy and the rind thin, shiny, and yellowish. It may be corded. There are two types: *dolce* (mild) and *piccante* (strong).

Provolone is a cheddar-like cheese but smoother in texture. After milling, the curd is dipped into 160°F whey and pulled like taffy. It is then salted, formed into a bottle-like shape, and smoked. It should have not more than 45% moisture and at least 45% milkfat on a dry basis. Fontina is a rich, firm buttery cheese made in the Val d'Aosta in Piedmont from ewe's milk. It is yellow and has tiny eyes somewhat like Gruyère. The rind is pale brown. Fontina for summer use is given a light smoke to help preserve it. It is essential to some Italian dishes such as white Piedmont truffles or the famous Torinse *fonduta* (fondue).

Gorgonzola from Gorgonzola northeast of Milan, Lombardy, is a famous bleu cheese made from cow's milk. It is creamy in color and equal to Roquefort and Stilton in flavor. The mold is grayish and the color cream. Gorgonzola keeps in refrigerated storage and can become quite strong if held long. Imports are made quite salty to hold quality. Dolcelatte is a mild and creamy Italian bleu cheese also made in Lombardy.

Switzerland produces many excellent cheeses. The most famous is Emmentaler (Swiss) made in the Emmental valley near Bern. It has large, shiny eyes and is creamy in color. Imports are usually slightly more acid, drier, and fuller and stronger in flavor than domestics. Gruyère produced near Fribourg is made from cow's milk and is much like Swiss but has finer holes. Emmentaler and Gruyère are used interchangeably. Both are used in Swiss fondue. Other countries making cheeses somewhat like Swiss are Denmark (Samsoe), France with three: Appenzell, Conte, and Sbrinz, and Lapland with a reindeer milk cheese slightly softer than Swiss.

An interesting hard cheese from Glarus, Switzerland, is Sapsago, made from defatted and soured cow's milk, buttermilk, and whey. It is cone-shaped and green in color because it is colored and flavored with fresh clover leaves. It is usually grated and used as a seasoning. A fine, soft cheese from the Joux (Vaud) valley is creamy like Brie and has a mild, ripe flavor typical of these Camembert-like cheeses. It has a hard, wrinkled, honey-colored rind. It is usually made in the autumn.

Holland makes several cheeses resembling cheddar even to using annatto to give a yellowish-orange color. They have lower fat contents than our American cheddar and are somewhat smoother in texture. Edam is a small, round, reddish-colored cheese popular for its mild, sweet flavor and fine, compact grain. It is given a medium cure so it is somewhat rubbery. It should have not more than a 45% moisture content and should be 40% or more in milkfat on a dry basis. It is always factory-made. Gouda is another similar cheese but higher in fat content and therefore preferable for cooking. The round is often slightly larger than Edam, and it may be colored with saffron. The flavor is somewhat like Edam but more nut-like. Leyden is a flat, cylindrical, creamy colored cheese spiced with cumin seed. It is yellowish and quite firm. It is a good "beer" cheese served with pumpernickel or rye bread and pickled cucumbers. It is identified by crossed keys stamped in black on the rind.

Denmark is most famous for its bleu, which is made from homogenized cow's milk. It is very white and heavily streaked with greenish-blue mold. It has less salt than Roquefort and a pleasing, sharp flavor typical of this type of cheese. Connoisseurs claim the flavor does not equal Stilton, Roquefort, or Gorgonzola. Samsoe comes from a Danish island of that name in the Kattegat. It is smooth and full-flavored somewhat like Port Salut and Bel Paese and resembles them in texture and color, but it is slightly firmer. In this respect, it resembles Swiss or Gruyère without the large eyes. It improves with age and keeps well.

Scandinavia has some interesting cheeses. One is Gjetost (Myost)—*Gjet* means goat—which is made by stirring whey from cow's or goat's milk or both while heating it to evaporate moisture to bring it to the consistency of thick milk. Cream may be added. It then is poured into wooden troughs and stirred until cool. Stirring prevents the formation of lactose sugar crystals. It is a fudge-like, sweet-sour flavored cheese that does not taste like a typical cheese. Primost is a similar cheese. Both are coffee brown in color and sweet in flavor. Both are creamy in texture and somewhat hard. Gammelost is a hard Norwegian cheese made from skimmed sour milk. It too is golden brown in color. The flavor is strong, developed by mold that develops on the outside while curing in wet straw. It is related to Camembert in that it ripens from the outside in. Its flavor is somewhat like Limburger. It comes in 8-oz units. Noekkelost is a semihard cheese similar to Leyden but flavored with cloves and cumin instead of just cumin. The amount of milkfat in Noekkelost decides its price which, in descending order, is *helfet* (whole fat), *halvet* (half fat), and *mager* (meager fat).

Germany has many cheeses, but one of the most famous is Limburger, which is ripened at least 30 days—best cure is 55 to 70 days—after the outside is smeared with *Brevibacterium linens*. It is cooked to a low temperature. When well ripened, it is soft and pasty and has ammoniacal odor that is somewhat sweet and pleasing but strong. It is made from partially defatted milk. Curing changes it from a white to a reddish, creamy yellow. Curing is at 60 to 65°F, with relative humidity 95%. It is available in 6-oz, 8-oz, 1-lb, and 2-lb bricks. Holstein is made from sour skim milk or skim milk to which buttermilk has been added. It is like brick or Muenster. It comes in 12- to 14-lb bricks.

Soft or Curd Cheeses

Lactic acid bacteria, rather than rennet, may be used to develop acidity to set the curd for a number of soft cheeses, although sometimes rennet may be used with the bacteria. Most of these soft cheeses are not cured.

The acid, crumbly, delicately flavored soft Greek Fetta is used in many Greek and Arabic dishes. Austria markets a yellowish curd soft cheese that has a smoky flavor. It has been widely imitated. The Hungarians are famous for their soft Liptauer (Liptai) curd cheese, which is mixed with butter and various seasonings such as paprika, mustard, chives, caraway, salt, pepper, capers, or garlic. In Hungary the curd is served alone and the butter and seasonings are served on the side so that one makes one's own mixture.

Cottage or Farmer's cheese is the soft, uncured curd from pasteurized milk or reconstituted, concentrated dried milk. Low-fat products are available. If it contain 4% or more milkfat, the product can be called *creamed*. Its moisture content should not be more than 80%. It is cooked to only 90°F and, after cutting of the curd and draining of the whey, it is heated lightly for about 15 minutes after which it is washed, and salt is added in the amount of about 1% by weight. Curd size is regulated by the size of the knife used.

A pot cottage cheese is an uncreamed, freshly made mass with large curds about the size of popped corn. Baker's cottage cheese is an uncreamed product with small curds. Many dried baker's mixtures using dried cottage cheese and so forth to use in filling bakery goods, making cheese cakes, and so on also are available. A flake-type curd cheese also is available. Dry curd cottage cheese is specified for making salads and other products and should have about a 70% or more moisture content. If too dry, the curd is harsh, with a sawdust-like texture.

The coliform count of cottage cheese should be under 50 per gram and the combined yeast and mold estimate not over 100 per gram. Calcium chloride (0.02%) can be added in some states to give a firmer curd. Gelatin in a few others may be added in the amount of ½% but should not be added to hold more moisture.

Cottage cheese is usually packed in 5-, 10-, and 25-lb containers. Defects consist of off-color, excess acid, and off-flavor (yeasty, fruity, feed, mold, and so forth). Excess moisture, hard curd, or excessively dry, grainy, or gritty cheese will lack required quality standards. Look for broken, messy curd. The flavor should be sweet, slightly acid, and mild.

Cream cheese has a smooth, fine texture, creamy and mild to taste. It should have not less than a 33% milkfat content, and the water-free solids should not be less than 65% milkfat. Sweet cream cheese should be acid free. Sour cream cheese may have a mild acidity. Neufchatel is a French cheese resembling cream cheese but has a higher moisture and lower fat content (20%). It may, like cream cheese, be flavored with pimientos, olives, or other ingredients and be used as a spread.

Fig. 4-10. A USDA inspector checks a sample of butter as it comes from the churn. Courtesy USDA

BUTTER AND MARGARINE

Butter

Federal standards require that butter contain not less than 80% milkfat. It may contain salt and coloring. Unsalted butter is on the market. Butter is usually about 80.3% milkfat, 0.9% milk solids or curd, 2.0% salt, and 16.3% moisture. Cream for butter must be pasteurized at not less than 165°F for 30 minutes or more or 185°F for 15 seconds. About 100 lb of milkfat produces 120 to 125 lb of butter.

After pasteurization, cream can be made more acid (about 0.18% expressed as lactic acid for best flavor) by adding bacteria, or it can be reduced in acidity. Annatto can be used as a coloring, and the label need not state its use. After the cream is churned to produce butter and buttermilk, the buttermilk is drained away. The butter is then washed, salted, and worked. Working is important to give a waxy, compact, tenuous body. Overworking gives a loose, sticky body that is somewhat greasy.

Butter is graded Grade AA (93 score), Grade A (92 score), Grade B (90 score), and Grade C (89 score). To score flavor, body, salt, color, and

Fig. 4-11. A trier (the round-shaped chisel-like instrument in the right hand) is inserted into butter or cheese and a plug drawn for examination for quality. Odor, flavor, color, and other factors are checked, and a grade assigned. Courtesy USDA

packaging a grader inserts a trier into a block of butter and brings out a long cylindrical plug to examine. Maximum scores for these factors are 45, 30, 20, 10, and 5 in the trade, but the government uses a different scoring system to arrive at the grades listed here. (See Table 4-5.)

Aroma is a part of flavor, and body is partly appearance and partly texture. The federal standards for butter state that the "U.S. grade of butter is determined on the basis of classifying first the flavor characteristics and then characteristics in body, color and salt. Flavor is the basic quality factor . . . and is determined organoleptically by taste and smell."

Commercial circles may use terms different from those used in government grading. For instance, a *shakes* grades 94 or more, *specials* 93, *extras* 92, and *firsts* 91 to 90. Firsts may be divided into *high, medium,* and *low firsts.* Carload lots of butter manufactured in one plant scoring 90 or higher may move on the market as *standard* grade.

The federal grader first assigns a grade for flavor and then scores other factors. Table 4-5 shows that a butter assigned a flavor of AA grade can lose a ½ point on body and still be AA grade, but if it loses another ½ point on color, it drops to 92 score or A grade.

Butter is sold in ¼-lb or 1-lb prints, cubes (64 lb), or sometimes in bulk or other lot sizes. Pats come in 5-lb cartons usually from 72 to 90 pats per lb. Sometimes these are on paper or plastic chips.

TABLE 4-5

Example No.	Flavor Classifica- tion	Disratings Body	Color	Salt	Total Dis- ratings	Permitted Total Dis- ratings	Disratings in Excess of Total Permitted	U.S. Grade or U.S. Score
1	AA	½	0	0	½	½	0	AA or 93
2	AA	½	½	0	1	½	½	A or 92
3	AA	0	1	0	1	½	½	A or 92
4	AA	½	1	0	1½	½	1	B or 90
5	A	½	0	0	½	½	0	A or 92
6	A	0	½	½	1	½	½	B or 90
7	A	0	1	0	1	½	½	B or 90
8	A	1	½	0	1½	½	1	C or 89
9	B	½	0	0	½	½	0	B or 90
10	B	½	½	0	1	½	½	C or 89
11	B	1	0	0	1	½	½	C or 89
12	C	½	½	0	1	1	0	C or 89
13	C	0	1	0	1	1	0	C or 89

Courtesy Dairy Division, USDA

Margarine

Federal standards of identity state that margarine is a "food, plastic in form, which consists of one or more of the various approved vegetable or animal fats mixed with cream." Optional ingredients are vitamins A and D, butter, salt, flavoring, emulsifiers, artificial color, and preservatives. Labels must state their presence and for some the quantities used. In some cases, quantities allowed are controlled. Most margarines contain 15,000 I.U. of vitamin A per pound. Finely ground soy beans may replace up to 10% of the moisture. The product must be labeled margarine or oleomargarine. Coloring is almost universally permitted today in all states. Some states require that margarine sold in individual pats be triangular in shape and not square and that a sign in the dining area state that margarine is served. The number of pats per pound is the same as for butter. Margarine can be purchased in ¼-lb, 1-lb, or 64-lb cubes. It also is sold in bulk or barrels. Many special margarines are made for food service use such as those for rolled-in doughs or puff pastes. Margarine must not be less than 80% fat.

At one time much margarine was processed from olein (beef) fats, but now soy oil exceeds all other fats used. Some cottonseed, corn, and other vegetable fats are used. Some margarines are blends of animal and vegeta-

Fig. 4-12. Various grade stamps used to indicate the grade of butter or cheese.

Fig. 4-13. Cheese comes in many shapes and has many uses. Courtesy USDA

ble fats. Unsaturated margarines are made from safflower oil or other oils of this type. Hydrogenated corn oil (hardened) or cottonseed oil are saturated, and even though the oil itself is not highly saturated, after hydrogenation it is.

The margarine must be sound, clean, and fit for food. A good specification might read: "Good grade product, sweet, fresh, clean, with firm and uniform body, not sticky or mottled. The color should be a delicate straw yellow, and coloring should not cover inferior merchandise. The products should contain not less than 1% milk solids and 9000 I.U. of vitamin A per lb. It should contain 80% or more of approved fats and not more than 15% moisture and 4% salt." State also packaging and whether it is to come in pats, pats with chips, pound prints, 5-lb prints, 30-lb cubes, barrels, and so forth.

Evaluate margarine using butter standards. The color should be uniform and the body and texture that of good butter. Flavor should be pleasing, clean, sweet, and free from taint or foreign odor. Off-flavors or odors can be detected if the margarine is warmed slightly. When heated, margarine melts with little foam and browning, but if lecithin is present as an emulsifier, the margarine will foam and brown like butter. The keeping quality of margarine is slightly better than that of butter, and it is less likely to absorb flavors. Store margarine and butter under refrigeration where they will not absorb odors.

TABLE 4-6
Amount to Purchase of Dairy Products

Dairy Product as Purchased	Unit of Purchase	Weight per Unit	Portion	Portions per Purchase Unit	Number Units per 100 Portions
Cheddar cheese	lb	1.00 lb	4 oz	4.00	25
Cheddar cheese	lb	1.00 lb	2 oz	8.00	12½
Cheddar cheese	lb	1.00 lb	1 oz	16.00	6¼
Cheddar cheese	Longhorn	11 to 13 lb	2 oz	88 to 104	1¼
Cheddar cheese	Daisies	20 to 25 lb	2 oz	160 to 200	½ to ¾
Cheddar cheese	Flats	32 to 37 lb	2 oz	256 to 296	under ½
Cheddar cheese	Cheddars	70 to 78 lb	2 oz	560 to 624	under ½
Cheddar cheese	Block	20 to 40 lb	2 oz	160 to 320	½ to ¾
Cottage cheese	lb	1.00 lb	2 or 4 oz	4 or 8	25 or 12½
Cream cheese	lb	1.00 lb	1 oz	16.00	6¼
Processed	lb	1.00 lb	1 or 2 oz	8 or 16	6¼ to 12½
Half-and-half	Pt	1.07 lb	1½ T	21.33	4¾
Half-and-half	Qt	2.14 lb	1½ T	42.67	2½

TABLE 4-6 (cont'd)
Amount to Purchase of Dairy Products

Dairy Product as Purchased	Unit of Purchase	Weight per Unit	Portion	Portions per Purchase Unit	Number Units per 100 Portions
Light cream	Pt	1.06 lb	1½ T	21.33	4¾
Light cream	Qt	2.13 lb	1½ T	42.67	2½
Sour cream	Pt	1.06 lb	1 T	32.00	3⅛
Sour cream	Qt	2.13 lb	1 T	64.00	1½
Whipping cream	Qt	2.10 lb	1¼ T	51.20	2
Brick ice cream	Qt	1.25 lb	½ c (slice)	8.00	12½
Bulk ice cream	Gal	4.50 lb	No. 12 scoop	22 to 26	4
			No. 16 scoop	31 to 35	3
			No. 20 scoop	38 to 42	2½
			No. 24 scoop	47 to 51	2
Ice cream cups	3 oz	.19 lb	1 c	1	100
	5 oz	.31 lb	1 c	1	100
Sherbet	Gal	6.00 lb	No. 12 scoop	25.00	4
			No. 16 scoop	35.00	3
			No. 20 scoop	42.00	2½
			No. 24 scoop	50.00	2
Fluid milk	Qt	2.15 lb	1 c	4.00	25
	Gal	8.60 lb	1 c	16.00	6¼
	5 Gal	43.00 lb	1 c	80.00	1¼
Condensed milk	14-oz can	.88 lb			
Evaporated milk	14½-oz can	.91 lb			
Dry nonfat, instant	lb*	1.00 lb	1 c fluid	17.06	6
Dry nonfat, regular	lb†	1.00 lb	1 c fluid	17.06	6
Dry whole, regular	lb†	1.00 lb	1 c fluid	14.22	7

*By measure 6½ c.
†By measure 3¼ c.
Adapted from Agriculture Handbook 284, USDA.

BIBLIOGRAPHY

American Dry Milk Institute, *The Grading of Dry Milk and Sanitary and Quality Standards,* Bulletin 913, Chicago, 1947.

Kraft Foods, *The World of Cheese,* Chicago, April 1954.

Kosikowski, Frank V., *Cheese and Fermented Milk Foods,* Edwards Bros, Ann Arbor, Michigan, 1966.

National Dairy Council, *A Newer Knowledge of Cheese,* Chicago, 1954.

Nelson, John and Malcomb Trout, *Judging Dairy Products,* 4th ed., Olsen Publishing Co., Milwaukee, Wis., 1964.

Sammis, J. J., *Cheese Making,* 10th ed., The Cheesemaker Book Co., Madison, Wis., 1942.

Sanders, G. B., *Cheese Varieties and Descriptions,* Agr. Handbook No. 54, USDA, Washington, D. C., 1953.

U.S. Department of Agriculture, Washington, D.C.:

The Grade A Pasteurized Milk Ordinance, 1973.

Standards for Dry Whole Milk, Dry Buttermilk, Instant Non-fat Dry Milk, Spray Process Dry Milk and Roller Process Dry Milk, various dates.

Standards for Monterey, Swiss, Colby and Cheddar Cheeses, various dates.

Standards for Frozen Desserts, 1968.

Standards for Butter, 1960.

Federal and State Standards for the Composition of Milk Products, Agr. Handbook No. 51, May 1971.

U.S. Department of Health, Education, and Welfare, *Standards of Identity for Dairy Products,* Washington, D.C., various dates.

5
Beverages, Cereals, Fats, and Oils

BEVERAGES

Coffee

Coffee is the berry of an evergreen shrub grown in tropical or semitropical climates. South and Central America grow the Arabica variety, which originated near the Red Sea; Africa and other producing areas may grow the Robusta, Liberacia, or Stenophylla varieties. Climate and soil are important to coffee quality. Plateaus or mountain areas 2000 ft or higher above sea level produce the best coffee. The coffee grown at lower levels produces a soft, large, flabby bean that has a grassy, pungent, undesirable cup flavor. A small amount of low-grown coffee may be used in blending to give some desirable astringency and bitterness, and it may be called *rio* from the Spanish word for "river."

Some shade on the coffee bush is desirable, so shade trees are frequently found in coffee plantations. In some areas clouds or fog provide this shade. In a wet harvest the beans become overmature, causing them to become too soft and to lack cup quality. Too hot or too dry weather causes the cherries, or fruit, to dry on the bushes. The resultant seeds, or beans, are hard, flinty, and gnarled; some may be immature, shriveled, and blighted. Good shape indicates possible good quality while misshapen beans can indicate a lack of desirable mellow, delicate flavor of top quality.

After picking, the flesh is removed by either fermentation or washing. Washed coffee has a better flavor than fermented. The beans are then dried and hulled. The green beans are bagged and are now ready for the market. The bean is now hard, semitranslucent, and bluish-green to tan, with a shape varying from a small round bean to an extra-long flat bean.

Most coffee is a blend of different beans. American coffee usually

Fig. 5-1. Good shade must be provided the coffee bush. In Arabia the fogs off the Red Sea act as a shade much of the day. Here tall trees provide it. Courtesy the Coffee Brewing Institute

contains a large amount of Santos coffee from Brazil, which produces about 60% of the world's coffee crop. Bourbon Santos usually are high in quality, mild in flavor, and slightly acid. "Old Crop" Santos are mildest in flavor and acidity. Not all Santos make good coffee—the Victoria, for instance, has a poor reputation. Venezuela is noted for its Marcaibo coffee, which is mild, rich, and flavorful but does not hold up well as an urn coffee. Colombian coffees are sought for the best blends. The Excelsos, or Bogotas, which includes Medellins, Armenias, Sevillas, Manizales, and Giradots have great body and a full, aromatic flavor.

Mexican Coatepecs have excellent flavor and good body. They make good urn coffee and some blends may contain 20% of these beans. Oaxacas from Mexico lack as high a quality but have good flavor and life and are good in blends. Rios from Mexico are somewhat harsh and pungent but may be used in blends. Jamaica produces the high-quality Blue Mountain coffee popular in England. Puerto Rico's coffee is prized by the Spanish,

Fig. 5-2. The coffee flower and the green cherries. Courtesy the Coffee Brewing Institute

who take almost all of its annual crop. Java produces a coffee much like the Santos. Arabia near the Red Sea is considered the birthplace of coffee. The great Mochas are grown there. They have a mild, rich-flavored bean with good vitality and holding quality in institutional blends. Sumatra produces the sweet, delicate Ankola and Mandhelling coffees, well known for their quality. Until recently the Robustas and Libericas from Africa were known as strong, harsh, acid, pungent coffees with a somewhat neutral flavor, but improved care of the plantations and processing has changed this. They are now used extensively in many good blends.

Not all nationalities like the same coffee. Arabs like a coffee that has a strong, acid, astringent flavor and a heavy body. Many Europeans want a similar coffee with less astringency and acid but with heavy fullness of flavor. For the most part, Americans desire a mild, rich, full-flavored coffee with limited astringency and acidity. A coffee termed "soft" is said by tasters to possess a fine flavor readily extracted from the bean and means the opposite of "harsh" or "rio." If the term "strictly soft, fine cup" appears in a description, a top-quality coffee is indicated.

Coffee should be judged on the basis of its appearance, quality, and character. *Appearance* deals with the size, shape, color, uniformity of size, and defects of the beans. Extraneous matter, defects such as shriveled beans, broken beans, lack of plumpness, and unevenness of size and roast should be noted. The beans should be brittle and crisp.

Quality indicates the taste and odor as determined in cup-testing and may be described by a taster as "desirable" or "undesirable." "Richness,"

Fig. 5-3. Removing pulp residue and washing. Courtesy the Coffee Brewing Institute

"excellence," "fineness," "smoothness," "mellowness," "goodness," "heaviness in body," and "good body" are all terms that can describe good quality. Undesirable qualities are described as "winy," "bitter," "fermented," "medicated," and "poorly processed" or "poorly handled." Age deterioration gives a "woody" flavor, and specifications should state that beans should come from current (that year's) crop. Coffee may absorb flavors and should not be stored with oils, paints, chemicals, hides, leather, or other items.

Character is taste and aroma or flavor, which can be described as "acid," "sweet," "neutral," or "bitter." Some acidity is desirable, as is some sweetness. Ankolas and Mandhelings from Sumatra are prized for their sweet character but Brazil rios, with as much sweetness, are undesirable because other characteristics are not in balance. All coffees must be somewhat bitter or astringent but not objectionably so. A neutral coffee is not acid, bitter, or sweet. A coffee described as "thin" is neutral and lacks quality.

The New York Coffee and Sugar Exchange has established standards for coffee. Grades are based on defects per pound: No. 1 Grade allows up to 9 defects; No. 2, 10 to 21; No. 3, 22 to 45; No. 4, 46 to 90, and so on. The Food and Drug Administration prohibits the sale of coffee under names of origination that do not belong to them and does not allow the importation below No. 8 Grade or artificially colored (sweated) coffee.

Fig. 5-4. Careful sorting of the split green beans improves grade. Courtesy the Coffee Brewing Institute

Green coffee has almost no flavor; roasting develops it. In roasting the bean becomes chestnut, dark brown, or almost black depending on the degree of roast. A light roast means a light brown or pale chestnut color; medium roast is coffee roasted until dark brown; a heavy, dark, or high-roast coffee is dark chocolate or darker in color. Heavy roasts, sometimes called *French* or *Italian,* are preferred by some nationalities and are used for *café expresso.*

Roasting temperatures range from 385 to 500°F. The beans swell about 50% in size and lose about 15% in weight, mostly moisture. The caramelization of carbohydrates and the formation of volatile esters, furfuryl derivatives, and other aromatic substances develop flavor. The cell walls rupture, which makes the flavor and color more easily extracted in hot water. Coffee contains from 0.75 to 2% caffein, a mild stimulant. Decaffeinated coffee is about 97% caffein-free. Roasting may end with a "dry" or "water" finish ("dry finish" means no water is used). The steam developed by adding water to the hot beans in finishing produces a more uniformly colored and better-appearing bean. But finishing by using over a gallon of water to 100 lb of coffee is undesirable. Glazing may be done to improve appearance, protect flavors from oxidation, and assist in clarification, but most authorities doubt it does nothing more than add 5 to 10% in weight and improve appearance. The glaze is usually a mixture of eggs, starch, gelatin, and sugar.

Coffee is adulterated with parched wheat, peas, beans, or chicory. Chicory is used to add color and give a more bitter flavor. If used, the label must state this. Some locales, such as New Orleans, like chicory in the coffee. If chicory is present, ground coffee sticks together when pressed firmly in the hand. Or, it quickly colors a clear glass of water brownish red and sinks rapidly to the bottom of the glass. Or, real coffee tends to float longer and does not stain the cold water. If a solution turns blue when iodine is added, the presence of starch is indicated, which is in chicory but not coffee. Artificially colored coffee is detected by cutting through the bean and noting localization of color on the bean's surface.

Coffee grinds are important to coffee quality. The right grind should be

Fig. 5-5. An expert coffee taster samples blends. The coffee is not swallowed. Only the taste and aroma are sampled. The coffee is then spit out. Courtesy the Coffee Brewing Institute

selected for the equipment and brewing method used. Steel cut is a coarse grind passing through a $^6/_{64}$-in. screen; medium grind allows about 50% to pass through screens having 16 meshes to the inch, while fine grind will all pass through a screen with 24 meshes to the inch. Urn coffee should be either coarse or medium grind. Rapid extraction methods, such as silex or drip, requires fine grinds. Turkish coffee and *café expresso* are made from very fine grinds. Ground coffee should have a distinctly pleasant aroma and little chaff or extraneous matter.

Coffee flavors are quite volatile and rapidly lost, especially in ground coffee at room or higher temperatures. The flavor also rapidly deteriorates from oxidation or other reasons. Roasted beans hold their flavor longer than ground, so many institutions buy roasted beans and grind them fresh for immediate use. Quality is easier to distinguish in bean than in ground coffee.

Coffee holds quality well when frozen. Vacuum coffee loses only a slight bit after canning. A swelled can may indicate the release of carbon dioxide by the ground coffee inside; there is no deterioration indicated by this. Some coffee packed in airtight polyethylene wraps holds its flavor better than coffee packed in paper bags. Ground coffee held at room temperature loses 20% of its freshness in 24 hours; at the end of 20 days 50% of the flavor is lost. After 5 days a high-quality coffee at room temperature becomes only *fair* in flavor and at the end of 8 days *poor*.

Purchase ground coffee in the package size needed for brewing to reduce errors in measurement. Buy only a several days' supply and use old stocks first. A pound of coffee makes from 2 to 2½ gal of coffee or approximately 40 to 50 6-oz cups. The cost differential between the higher and lower grades is usually not great.

Pure soluble coffee is the dry, powdered, water-soluble solids extracted from coffee percolated under vacuum. Some carbohydrate may be added. Quality has improved tremendously over the last 10 years, and a freeze-dry instant type can be used frequently. To the critical taster, however, the lack of adequate aroma and a slight taste difference tips the scales in favor of the regular product.

The following could be used for a specification for a good institutional coffee after adding the degree of roast, type grind, packaging, and so forth:

20% Santos, grading 3's or 4's,[1], Bourbon, medium to good bean shape, strictly soft, solid bean, good greenish color and good cup quality.

40% Colombian of usual good cup quality; may be Excelsos of the following growths: Medellin, Armenia, Sevilla, Manizales, Giradot.

40% high-grown washed Central American coffee from Salvador, Costa Rica, Guatemala or Genuine Coatepecs of Mexico.

[1]This is a New York Coffee and Sugar Exchange grade.

Fig. 5-6. The young tea bushes in the nursery are being tended before transplanting to the main garden. Courtesy the Tea Council of U.S.A.

Tea

Tea comes from a tropical evergreen bush or tree that grows wild from 15 to 30 ft, but under cultivation may be pruned so women can easily reach the leaves. An acre produces up to 1000 lb of finished tea a year. Plucking occurs every 7 to 10 days from a year to 8 or 9 months depending on seasons. The terminal bud and the next two leaves are the standard pluck. Delicacy of flavor and body start with the terminal bud. Pungency and heavier flavor come with leaf progression. Tea is of best quality if grown at 6000 feet or above sea level.

After plucking, tea is withered and rolled. Green tea is immediately fired to dry it after rolling; oolong tea stands to oxidize a short time, and black tea stands for several hours. This longer standing, called fermenting, oxidizes tannins, develops flavors, and causes the tea to be darker after firing. Withering makes the leaves flaccid and removes some moisture so they can be rolled without breaking. Rolling is done by machine and ruptures the tiny cell walls, which releases flavor and enzymes so fermentation is facilitated. To ferment, tea is spread on glass, cement, or wooden tables. Firing at 210 to 235°F stops fermentation and removes all but about

Fig. 5-7. Two leaves and a bud, the standard pluck. Courtesy the Tea Council of U.S.A.

5% of the moisture. Basket-fired tea is carefully lifted and dropped by women as they hold the tea over hot, dry air; it is more expensive because of this. Hand-rolling instead of machine-rolling also increases price but improves quality.

Over 90% of our tea comes from India, Ceylon, Indonesia, and Africa. China supplies only a small amount of green and oolong tea. Japan and Taiwan export some good green and oolong teas. Transcaucasia in the Union of Soviet Socialist Republics produces some good tea.

Leaf size heavily influences the grade of tea. Quality depends on (1) locality and elevations of growth, (2) soil, especially mineral content, (3) climate, and (4) processing. Leaves may be broken or cut to reduce size, which improves quality. Much tea in tea bags is broken to give more rapid extraction and therefore a better tea. Stems or large leaves indicate lower quality. Black-tea grades are listed in Table 5-1. Green-tea grades in order of quality are frequently Gunpowder, Young Hyson, Hyson, and Imperial, but other terms are also used.

Blends are used for tea bags to give better flavor. Some brands of tea may also be blends. A blend may contain from 5 to 30 different teas. Jasmine flowers, orange peel, cloves, or other flavorings may be added to specialty

Fig. 5-8. The first stage of manufacture is known as withering. The leaves are spread evenly and thinly on specially prepared racks and allowed to remain there until they turn into a flaccid condition. Courtesy the Tea Council of U.S.A.

teas. Many teas are not blended and are purchased for their special flavor. Green tea has more tannin than the other teas and therefore is slightly more bitter. It has a delicate, greenish-yellow, pale liquor and a rather fruity flavor. Oolong tea is darker, less bitter, still fruity, and possesses a softer flavor. Black tea's brew is copper-colored with a soft, mild, subtle flavor lacking in heaviness but slightly acid. Some describe the flavor of a desirable black tea as "brisk." Tea grown in low, tropical elevations has a lush growth and lacks flavor but has good color and body. In a wet season, even high-grown tea can be thin and uninteresting—a defect called *weathery*.

Some of the better known growing areas are:

India
  ASSAM—Ideal for blends with good appearance and strong, pungent, and good flavor; early season growth has a fine, golden-tippy appearance and brings high prices.
  DARJEELING—High elevation gives a fine quality and distinctive, delicate flavor sometimes described as "blackcurrant" or "muscatel" because of its fruity, distinctive, soft flavor; used in special blends.

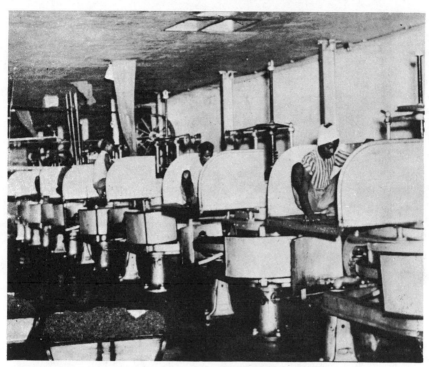

Fig. 5-9. The rolling machines process the withered green leaves, which are twisted or rolled. This breaks open the cells, which contain the stimulating flavored juice of the tea. Courtesy the Tea Council of U.S.A.

Fig. 5-10. After withering and rolling, the leaves are spread out in a cool, humid place to absorb oxygen from the air, a process known as fermentation. Courtesy the Tea Council of U.S.A.

TABLE 5-1
Black Tea Grades

Trade Size Term	Trade Abbreviation for Grade	Description of Grade
Leaf grades*		
Orange Peko	O.P.	Thin, long, wiry leaves that sometimes contain tip leaf. Tea liquor is light or pale.
Pekoe	P.E.K.	The leaves are shorter and not so wiry and the liquors have more color.
Souchong	SOU.	A bold and open leaf; makes a pale liquor.
Broken-leaf grades†		
Broken Orange Pekoe	B.O.P.	Best grade generally; much smaller than leaf grades; contains tip; tea liquor has good color and strength.
Broken Pekoe	B.P.	Slightly larger than B.O.P., with less color. Used as a filler in blends.
Broken Pekoe Souchong	B.P.S.	A little larger and bolder than B.P., giving a lighter color; also used as a filler in blends.
Fannings	E.N.G.S.	One of the top grades today because of tea bag use; smaller than B.O.P.; gives a good flavored brew with good color; more quickly made because of finer size.
Dust	D.	Smallest grade; useful for quick brewing of a good strong cup of tea; used in blends with larger sizes.

*About 10% of the crop.

†About 90% of the crop.

DOOARS—Smooth, mellow, full-bodied with good color; popular as a flavor binder in blends. Fall teas—also true of Assams and Darjeelings—have a good, distinct flavor and strength called "autumnal," which is not considered undesirable.

CACHAR—Lower-quality Indian tea; useful as a filler; plainer and thinner in flavor.

SOUTHERN INDIA—High-grown Travancore and Nilgiri Hills teas are best. Others good in blends to give a moderate flavor, bright-colored liquor. Not as pungent as North India teas, with more of a Ceylon character (and may be used for them at times).

Pakistan

Sylhet is the main producing area; the teas are similar to Cachars.

Ceylon

High-grown teas are bright, aromatic in flavor, and sought for blending; seasonal variations vary quality. High-growns have a full, rich liquor and aromatic flavor and good blending quality; distinct flavor is indicated by some areas, such as Nuwara Eilya, Dimbula, and Uva. Low-grown tea has a black leaf that gives a highly colored brew, but it lacks flavor and is used as a blend filler.

Indonesia

Main areas are Java and Sumatra, with few distinct growing areas. Quality varies little because of even seasons. Their good appearance, color, and flavor make them desirable for blending. High elevation Pengelengens have distinctive flavor, giving a brew equal in quality to good Indian or Ceylon teas.

Fig. 5-11a. The process of firing heats the fermented and damp leaves to a high temperature, imparting the familiar black appearance of tea to the fermented leaves. Courtesy the Tea Council of U.S.A.

Fig. 5-11b. The finished tea leaves are sorted according to their sizes and quality. Courtesy the Tea Council U.S.A.

Africa

Myasaland, Kenya, Uganda, Tanganyika, Mozambique, and the Belgian Congo produce some very good teas that are sought on the world markets. They have grown rapidly in importance in the last 20 years.

Until 1972 a tea board consisting of six industry members and one government individual established tea standards in purity and quality for the United States. Because of much improvement in the production of teas in the world, the tea board was abolished in 1972.

Cocoa

The *theobroma cacao* tree is indigenous to Central and South America, but plantations are found also in Africa and the West Indies. The fruit is a pod 4 to 7 in. in length. It has a hard, thick, leathery rind containing 25 to 75 seeds in 5 rows imbedded in a soft white or pinkish pulp. From 150 to 200 lb of clean cacao beans are produced per acre. Quality depends on variety, climate, soil, and processing. Some are mild while others are more aromatic or vary in pungency, acidity, bitterness, or fragrance. Blends are common to bring about desirable flavor characteristics.

The picked pods are cut open and fermented, after which the beans are removed and cleaned. Fermenting reduces bitterness. Roasting is done next to develop flavor. Then the dried beans are cracked into small pieces, or nibs, and the chaff is removed. The nibs are ground or milled into chocolate liquor, which is from 45 to 50% cacao butter. If hydraulic

Fig. 5-12. A cacao pod is broken open, revealing the seeds from which chocolate is manufactured after drying, fermenting, roasting, and processing. Courtesy USDA

pressure removes some of this fat, the product can be ground into a powder called *cocoa*. Government standards of identity require that breakfast cocoa contain not less than 22% cacao butter. Some cocoas may contain as much as 35% cacao butter. Low-fat cocoas may have only 10 to 12% cacao butter for use in baking. Added fat can bring their quality up to that of the cocoas close to those containing more natural fat.

Breakfast cocoas should be mild and rich in flavor. Color depends on the degree of roast and bean. Treating beans with an alkali breaks down some fiber or cellulose, giving a product that is richer in appearance, smoother in flavor, and more soluble in liquids. This process is called the *Dutch process* because it was discovered by a Dutch cocoa manufacturer, C. J. Van Houten.

Bitter chocolate is straight cacao liquor. It can be sold sweetened or combined with milk. Sweetness varies, and the products may be called either sweet or semisweet depending on the amount of sugar they contain. Milk chocolates also vary in the quantity of milk they contain. Some products used in bake shops or for other cooking purposes will contain added cacao butter and perhaps an emulsifier such as lecithin.

CEREALS

Cereal products are widely consumed by man. Wheat and rice far outstrip others in amounts used. Purchase specifications should be written with care for cereal products so correct items are obtained for the production need. The type and quality purchased materially affects the quality of food made from them.

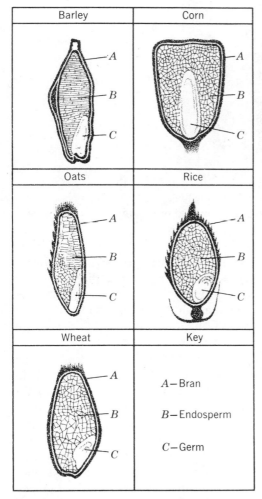

Fig. 5-13. The structure of various grains. The interior of the grain contains the endosperm from which farina, semolina, hominy, and other products are derived, depending on the grain.

Wheat

Different wheat flours must be used to achieve desirable results in baking and cooking. Yeast breads must be made from "hard," or "spring," wheat flours. Such flours have a strong protein that withstands the rigorous

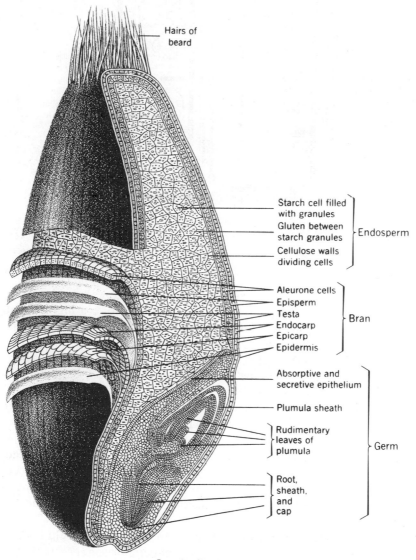

Hairs of beard

Starch cell filled with granules
Gluten between starch granules
Cellulose walls dividing cells

}Endosperm

Aleurone cells
Episperm
Testa
Endocarp
Epicarp
Epidermis

}Bran

Absorptive and secretive epithelium

Plumula sheath

Rudimentary leaves of plumula

Root, sheath, and cap

}Germ

Longitudinal Section of a Grain of Wheat

Fig. 5-14.

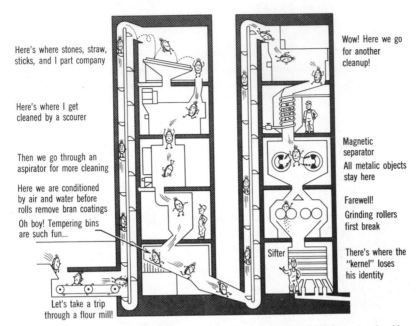

Here's where stones, straw, sticks, and I part company

Here's where I get cleaned by a scourer

Then we go through an aspirator for more cleaning

Here we are conditioned by air and water before rolls remove bran coatings

Oh boy! Tempering bins are such fun...

Let's take a trip through a flour mill!

Wow! Here we go for another cleanup!

Magnetic separator
All metalic objects stay here

Farewell!
Grinding rollers first break

There's where the "kernel" loses his identity

Sifter

Fig. 5-15. In the first step in milling, the wheat is cleaned. Next it is cracked by passing it between steel rollers running in opposite directions at high speed. This is called *the first break*. The broken grain is then sifted or bolted to separate the fine flour particles

fermenting and handling procedures given yeast breads. Macaroni, spaghetti, some dumplings, and other pastes also require a high-protein flour. They are usually made from durum flours, which comes from a spring wheat. Biscuits, muffins, pies, and other pastries are best made from a "soft," or "winter," wheat that has a less strong protein. Delicate cakes and other bakery goods must be made from an even more delicate soft-wheat flour.

Hard wheat grows in the northern United States and Canada and is sown in the spring. Soft wheat is produced in Kansas, Nebraska, Washington, and so on. It is sown in the winter and harvested in early summer. This wheat is sometimes called *red wheat* because of the color of the seed. Hard-wheat flour is yellowish; it feels grainy or rough when rubbed between the fingers and will not hold its shape when pressed firmly in the palm after the hand is opened. Soft wheat holds this shape; it also feels smoother and is whiter in color.

A good wheat flour specification indicates that the flour should contain approximately 13% moisture, less than ½% mineral or ash, about 1% fat, and about 75% starch. Cake flours have about 7 to 8% protein, and hard (bread) flours may have 11% or more. The quantity of starch varies in-

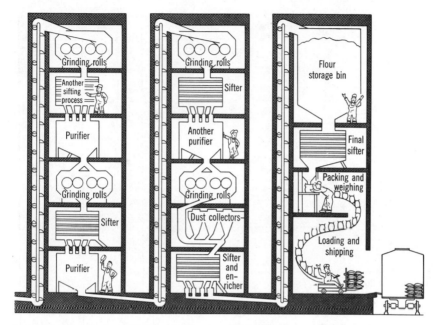

Grinding rolls

Another sifting process

Purifier

Grinding rolls

Sifter

Purifier

Grinding rolls

Sifter

Another purifier

Grinding rolls

Dust collectors

Sifter and enricher

Flour storage bin

Final sifter

Packing and weighing

Loading and shipping

from the kernel. A purifier is used to remove some bran. The kernel portions pass through successive breaks or rollings and boltings. Not all the bran can be removed and the clears or last breaks of flour may be tinted by it. Courtesy Wheat Flour Institute

versely with the protein. Flours should be enriched with thiamin, riboflavin, niacin, and iron. (Most cereal products are specified "enriched" except, perhaps, oats.)

A gray, dull color indicates a poor flour. This lack of vivacity in appearance is seen if an ounce of flour is patted onto a flat surface, dipped quickly into water, and placed into a moderate oven for about 30 to 45 seconds. Good hard-wheat flour absorbs about 65% of its weight in water and still forms a pliable, nonsticky ball. Good pastry flour absorbs less moisture. A "strong" hard flour means it has a strong gluten and builds a strong structure in products. A strong soft flour indicates one that can carry high ratios of fat, eggs and sugar and give good quality products. Bakers frequently take bread flour and work it for 5 min or more into a stiff dough, let it rest 15 min, and then carefully wash out the starch—leaving a yellow ball of gluten. They may bake this to see how the gluten swells and reacts to heat. A good gluten ball indicates a good flour.

To make flour, cleaned wheat is cracked between rollers and then sifted. As many as 9 rollings and siftings may occur. Each rolling and sifting is called a *break* or *stream*. The best flour, called *patents*, comes in the early streams. These early streams are higher in protein and lower in ash than the

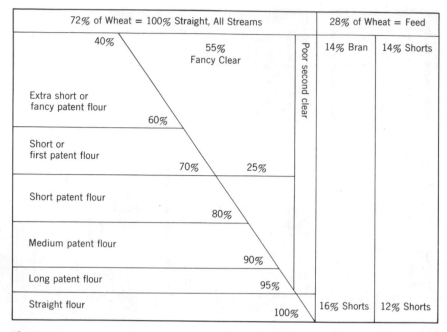

Fig. 5-16.

clears, which come off in the later streams. When all flour is extracted, bran and some wheat remains. This is called *red dog,* which is used as an animal feed.

About 72% of the wheat kernel is used in making flour, and this entire 72% is called *straight* or *100%* flour. Only 40 to 60% of straight flour is used for the best patents. Fancy or extra-short patents come from the first breaks. Medium (baker's or standard) patents are about 90% straight flour.

Fig. 5-17. Three gluten balls before baking made from equal amounts of (from left to right) bread (hard), pastry (soft), and cake (soft) flour. Note the difference in the amounts of gluten in each, the condition of the gluten indicating strength, and the ability to form a solid, firm structure.

"Long" or "family" patents are about 95% straight flour. A fancy patent (60% straight flour) leaves a fancy clear flour (35%). A "filled" flour contains more clears than straight flour normally would. Whole wheat, or graham, flour is straight flour with some bran. "Light" whole-wheat flour contains less bran. Unbolted whole-wheat flour contains the wheat germ in addition to a good deal of bran. It keeps poorly.

Flour can be aged 8 to 10 weeks to condition and bleach it. If chemicals are used for bleaching, the label must so indicate. Unaged flour lacks pliable qualities in doughs, and products from it are apt to be "bucky" and hump in baking. It is often called *green* flour.

Flour is sold by the barrel, which is two 98-lb sacks or 196 lb. Fourths or eighths of a barrel may be 48 or 49 and 24 or 24½ lb respectively. Some specialty flours, such as cake flours, are sold in 100-lb sacks. Buyers should note whether prices are for 100 or 98 lb. Market prices are usually stable, and it is unwise to purchase more than a several months' supply. A contract for a year's supply may be written and taken in lots that last a month or so. Large users may have flour delivered to them in bulk. Store sacks off the floor, crisscrossed for good ventilation. Flour can absorb odors. Store in a dry, cool area. Mice, insects, and flooding are dangers to stored flour.

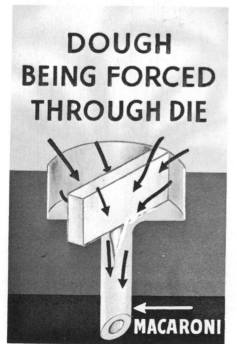

Fig. 5-18. How the hole is made in macaroni. The macaroni dough, when pushed against the die, is split by the wings and then pressed together around the lower end of the pin to form a solid tube. As it comes from the bottom of the die, the macaroni is cut to proper length.

Macaroni Products

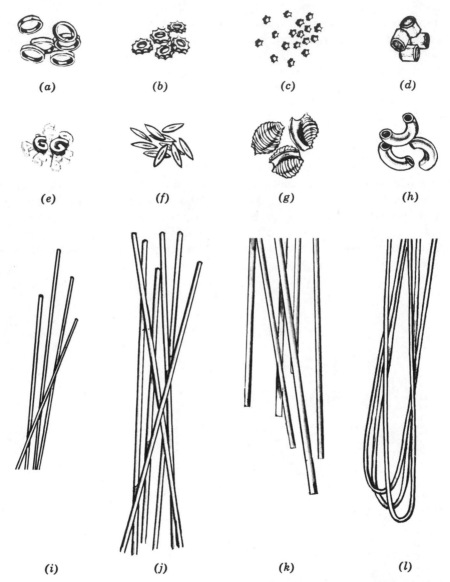

Fig. 5-19A. Forms of macaroni pasta. *(a)* Spaghetti rings, *(b)* stars, *(c)* pastina, *(d)* salad macaroni, *(e)* alphabets, *(f)* rosemarias, *(g)* shells (also made in larger sizes), *(h)* elbow macaroni, *(i)* 5-minute spaghetti, *(j)* vermicelli (thinner than spaghetti and smaller), *(k)* Manchu (thin ribbons used for chow mein and fried noodles), *(l)* spaghettini (thinner than vermicelli usually).

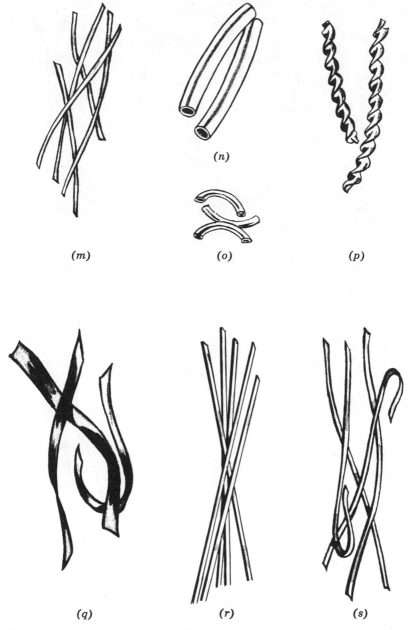

Fig. 5-19B. *(m)* Chinese mein noodles (no egg), *(n)* cut macaroni, *(o)* quick-cooking spaghetti, *(p)* twisted egg noodles, *(q)* vegetable noodles (used for fetuccine), *(r)* long Chinese noodles, *(s)* fine noodles. Courtesy Golden Grain Macaroni Company

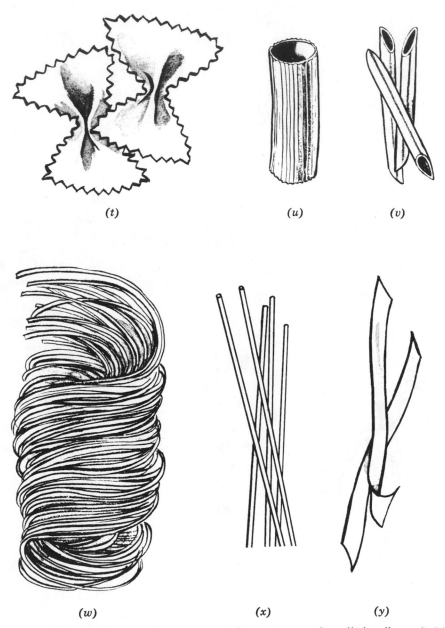

Fig. 5-19C. *(t)* bow-tie noodles, *(u)* rigatoni (larger sizes may be called *stuff-a-roni*), *(v)* mostaccoli, *(w)* coil pasta, usually spaghetti, vermicelli, or capellini (the latter is the thinnest pasta made and also is called *fedeo*), *(x)* spaghetti, *(y)* medium noodles. Courtesy Golden Grain Macaroni Company

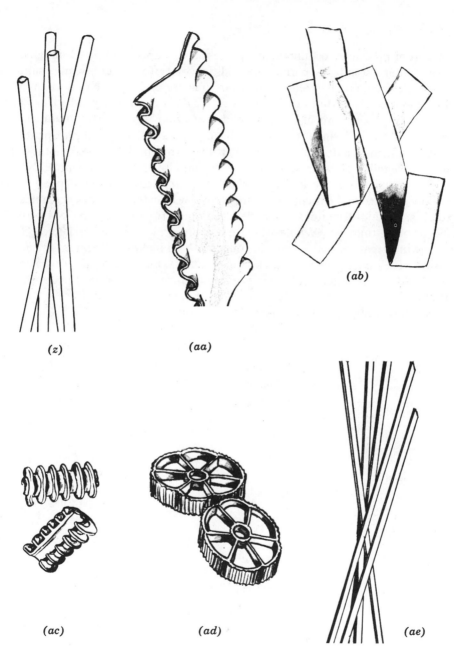

Fig. 5-19D. (z) long macaroni, (aa) lasagna, (ab) wide noodles, (ac) space noodles (usually contain egg), (ad) spaghetti wheels, (ae) egg tagliarini. Courtesy Golden Grain Macaroni Company

Macaroni Products

Macaroni products, or alimentary pastes, are shaped and dried doughs. Government standards permit the addition of ½ to 2% egg white, salt, onions, celery, and bay leaf, in addition to water and flour. No more than 13% moisture is permitted. If the term "egg" is used, the product must contain 5½% or more of dry-egg solids based on weight. Maximum salt should be 1 to 2% since it weakens these products. Disodium phosphate may be added as a dough conditioner. If the term "milk" is used, not less than 3.8% milk solids must be present. Protein must be 13% or more. No yellow coloring can be added, and egg products cannot be wrapped in yellow paper to make them appear more yellow than they are. If vegetables (e.g., spinach or tomatoes) are added, their quantity must not be less than 2% or more than 5%. Whole-wheat macaroni products are marketed.

The inner part of the kernel from durum wheat makes the best macaroni pastes. This inner-durum wheat kernel is called *semolina* and gives a paste that holds shape after cooking, has some texture, and does not collapse. Pastes from poor farina, the inner part of nondurum wheat, are a dull gray-white and cook up to a soft, flabby product.

TABLE 5-2
Classification of Macaroni Products

		Sizes	
Type	Name	Trade	Federal Standards
Solid round rods	Vermicelli	¹/₃₂″ diameter	not more than 0.06″ in diameter
	Spaghettini	¹/₁₆″ diameter	
	Spaghetti	³/₃₂″ diameter	0.06–0.11″ in diameter
Hollow tubes, plain	Foratini or Maccaroncelli	³/₃₂″ diameter	
	Forati or perc-catelli	⅛″ diameter	
	Mezzarrelli or Mezzani	⁵/₃₂″ diameter	
	Macaroni or Mezzani	¼″ diameter	0.11–0.27″ in diameter
	Zitoni	½″ diameter	
Hollow tubes, corrugated	Mezzani regati	¼″ diameter	
	Zitoni rigati	½″ diameter	

TABLE 5-2
Classification of Macaroni Products

Type	Name	Sizes	
		Trade	Federal Standards
Noodles, flat ribbons	Broad	¼" wide, 0.030" thick	
	Medium	⅛" wide, 0.033" thick	
	Fine	¹/₁₆" wide, 0.035" thick	
Sheets, scalloped	Lasagne (the widest) Reginette and Margherite		
Elbows, hollow, small, smooth	Tuchetti	⅛ to ⁵/₃₂" diameter	
Elbows, hollow, large, smooth	Ditali lisci	¼ to ⁷/₁₆" diameter	
Elbows, hollow, cor-rugated, very large	Rigatoni	⁹/₁₆" diameter	
Elbows, hollow, hexagonal	Bonballati	⅜" diameter	
Bunches, curled	Vermicelli rella (morella) Spaghetti rella		
Fancy small pastes	Alfabeto Puntette Stelletta Crowns, and so forth		

Quality in macaroni products is indicated by a good yellow color and a hard, brittle, or flinty quality. The product should be semitranslucent and break squarely across with a clean, glassy fracture. Rod types should be springy and make a good arc before snapping. Poor products break unevenly. A reddish cast indicates red durum or soybean flour. The dry finished product should be reasonably free from broken, misshapen, or checked pieces. Cook to ascertain texture, taste, odor, and appearance.

Purchase in 10-lb, 15-lb, 20-lb, or 40-lb containers and not in 300-lb barrels unless use is heavy. Some buyers may purchase in 100-lb bags. Stock about a month's supply. Broken products may be purchased for economy reasons. About 8 lb gives 100 portions; a pound cooked yields about 2½ qt.

Crackers

A flour paste containing salt, shortening, leavening, malt, and a small bit of sugar formed into a shape and baked makes crackers. Regular size should be $^3/_{16}$ to ¼ in. thick and 2 in. square, running from 120 to 190 per lb; if 2 × 1$^1/_3$ in., crackers will run 180 to 235 per lb. Oyster crackers should be round or nearly so, approximately square or hexagonal in shape, ½ to ⅝ in. in diameter, and about $^7/_{16}$ in. thick, with a count of 575 to 700 per lb. No crackers should contain over 5% moisture and have less than 10% fat by weight. Salted crackers should have a pound of salt topping per 100 lb of crackers. Graham crackers should contain not less than 30% whole-wheat flour and be about $^5/_{16}$ in. thick and 1½ to 2½ in. square, running 50 to 95 crackers per lb. The fat content should not be less than 10% and moisture not more than 6%. Raisin-filled sweet crackers should run 30 to 45 per lb and contain not less than 40%, by weight, of seedless raisins. They should have not less than 5% total fat, should contain not more than 11% moisture, and be reasonably crisp.

Rice

There are two kinds of rice: (1) pearl, the small, round kernel that cooks into a somewhat sticky product, and (2) long-grain, which cooks into a separate, whole-grain product. Brown rice is unpolished rice with some bran left on it. It has a richer flavor than polished rice but does not keep as well. Undermilled rice has less bran on it than brown rice. Converted polished rice is steamed, nutrients are added, and the product is redried. Instant rice is precooked and dried; it is usually fortified. Converted and instant rice are less subject to insect infestation than those with bran or even regular polished rice. Purchase rice in 100-lb bags if use is large. Trade grades are Extra Fancy, Fancy, Extra Choice, Choice, Medium, and Sample Grade. Federal grades are U.S. No. 1, No. 2, No. 3, No. 4, No. 5, and Sample Grade. Grades are decided by cleanliness, wholeness, freedom from foreign matter, and mixture of varieties. Do not mix varieties because they cook up in different times. Brown rice has four trade grades: Extra Fancy, Fancy, Choice, and Sample Grade. U.S. No. 1, 2, 3, and 4 are similar grades. Rice purchased by institutions should usually be Fancy or Extra Choice (U.S. No. 2 or 3). It takes 6 to 8 lb to give 100 portions.

TABLE 5-3
Common Rice Varieties

Long Grain	Medium Grain	Short Grain	Pearl (Round)
Rexoro, Edith, Fortuna, Lady Wright, Blue Bonnet, Nira	Blue Rose, Early Prolific	Calrose, Magnolia, Zenith	American Pearl, California Pearl

Corn

Hominy comes from the inner portion of corn. It is made by soaking corn in lye to soften the outer bran for removal; after this it is dried. Pearled hominy, coarser than cornmeal, is used for cornflakes and other corn products. Pearly hominy, or coarse hominy (samp), is cooked in milk or water and served as a vegetable. Table grits, or granulated hominy, are finer than pearled hominy and come as coarse, medium, and fine in size. They are used for breakfast grits. Cream or pearl cornmeal is finer than grits. Hominy flakes are made from thinly pressed paste; it cooks rapidly. Hominy should have a good characteristic color, have a natural ground taste and odor, and be free from rancid, bitter, nasty, or other undesirable tastes or odors.

Cornmeal is made from degermed endosperm of corn but contains more of the kernel than hominy. It may be purchased either white or yellow and either coarse or fine. Stone-grinding, or old-process, cornmeal has the bran and germ remaining. It can also be called *old-fashioned* or *water-ground*. Corn flour is finely ground and sifted cornmeal. Bolted cornmeals are high in bran.

Cornstarch is the pure, unmodified, pulverized siftings from corn. It should be uniformly white and free from any foreign taste or odor with no lumps or hard or gritty particles. It is used to thicken sauces, puddings, pie fillings, and the like.

Waxy maize starch and modified starches are special-type starches used in berry pies and for thickening products that must be frozen since they do not break down under freezing. They have greater clarity, softness, and pliability in thickened mixtures. They make mixtures as thick when hot as when cold. Instant starches are precooked and dried. They thicken without cooking and are used in instant-pudding mixes, meringue stabilizers, cream-puff fillings, marshmallow toppings, and so on. About $14\frac{1}{3}$ oz of cornstarch are required to give the same thickening power to a gallon of liquid as $10\frac{1}{4}$ oz of waxy maize or converted (modified) starch.

Oats

After removing the outer husk, the kernel or endosperm of oats, called the *groat*, remains. Scotch or regular, a long-time cooking breakfast oatmeal, is made by steaming the groat, cutting it into small pieces, and then pressing them flat between rollers; it is then dried. Extra steam treatment, plus finer division, makes quick-cooking oatmeal. Oatmeal should have a bright, uniform, creamy color with a natural flavor of oats. It should be free from rancid, bitter, musty, or other undesirable flavors or odors. Stone-ground oatmeal is called *old-fashioned,* stone, or *buhr* ground. Old-fashioned may also indicate the long-cooking type. Some breakfast oats are "steel cut," which means they are cut into small pieces somewhat like cracked wheat.

Barley, Rye, Buckwheat, and Soy

Barley is used more to make malt than as a cereal. Malt comes from sprouted barley; sprouting changes starch to maltose, a sugar, that has a malty flavor. Pearled barley is used in soups and is the inner part of the barley kernel. It should be clean and sound and not possess rancid, musty, sour, or other undesirable tastes or odors. It comes in first and second grades. First grade should have no bran showing at the crease of the barley endosperm and should be light in color, uniform in size, and have few broken pieces. Barley may be white or brown, the brown having bran on it. Sizes may be large, medium, or small.

Rye is used mainly as a flour in food preparation. Because it lacks gluten, wheat flour must be used with it. Three types of rye flour are avaialble: light, medium, and dark, the amount of bran in the flour deciding the color. Pumpernickel flour is coarsely ground, whole-rye flour.

Buckwheat is a plant and not a grass, but because its seed can be ground to a meal or flour it is classified as a grain. Lighter buckwheat flour has most of the bran removed, and some can be almost as white as wheat flour. The darker flours have more bran and stronger flavors. Wheat flour is used with buckwheat to give the needed protein.

Soy is not a true cereal, but because it can be ground into a meal or flour it is classed with cereals. It has a high protein content and may be used with foods to increase their dietary value. Soy gives a yellowish cast to bread, which detracts somewhat from its desirability. It can be used in piecrusts for flavor enhancement and tenderization. Soy meal is used in some breakfast cereals.

Breakfast Cereals

There are breakfast cereals that must be cooked and others that are ready-to-eat. New instant-types of those that must be cooked are on the market. All these need is hot water added to them. They immediately thicken into a product that appears much the same as the regular cooked products.

Cracked wheat, farina (the inner portion of the wheat kernel), and malted wheat require cooking. Quick-cooking types should cook in 5 min after coming to a boil. Some cracked wheat may be rolled or flaked. Cornmeal and oatmeal are also used for cooked breakfast cereals. Finely ground meals require about 7 lb of cereal to give 100 portions, while the coarser-ground ones will take 1 or 2 lb more for the same amount.

A number of prepared breakfast cereals are on the market. Shredded wheat is made from a paste that is formed in a shredding machine into biscuits and then baked. Baking should be even and the color golden brown. Large biscuits are from ½ to 1 oz each. There are 28 to 70 to the ounce of small ones. The biscuits should be crisp, porous, and friable with no hard particles except, perhaps, at the seam edge. Some biscuits may be circular in shape.

Wheat flakes are made from soft wheat from a heavy paste that is flaked and toasted. Toasting should be even and the color a golden brown. Malted wheat flakes are flavored with malt. Bran flakes are made similar to wheat flakes but contain 25 to 40% bran. If they contain raisins, they should be seedless, pliable, meaty, well developed, of good color, and reasonably uniform in size. Bran cereal is a paste that is extruded and then cut into small lengths and toasted.

Puffed wheat is wheat that is cooked in a steam chamber and then suddenly shot into air so the pressure inside forces the kernel to expand as it travels through the air; it is then toasted. Malted cereals are often baked in loaves and then ground. Puffed rice is made in the same manner as puffed wheat, a method sometimes called *gun-puffing*. Puffing should give an expansion about 8 times the size of the original grain. The finished product should be sound and clean and have a good color, a light, porous texture, and a good flavor.

Cornflakes are made from a paste of pearly hominy flavored with malt, sugar, salt, and other seasonings. It is flakes and then toasted.

Miscellaneous Cereal Products

A number of starches from plants are classified as cereals. Tapioca comes from the root of the cassava plant, which is ground and the starch extracted. A dough is then made from it. Pearl tapioca is made by passing the dough through sieves, the pellet size depending on the size sieve. Flakes are made by spreading the dough thinly on a surface and baking it. It cooks more quickly than pearl tapioca. Finely ground flakes are called *minute* tapioca.

Sago is a product of the pith palm similar to tapioca in appearance and use. Arrowroot is the root of the arrow plant. It is a very fine starch that makes a fine-quality pudding, sauce, or gravy. Cookies and other pastries made from it are considered high-quality items because of the tender, delicate quality given by the arrowroot. Arrowroot is considered easy to digest. Potato starch is used to thicken sauces and the like. It can also be used in making breads, crackers, and other items.

Bakery Products

The purchase of prepared bakery products, either frozen or fresh, has increased remarkably in the last several decades, raising the need for new specifications. Since few grades or other purchase criteria exist for them, many institutions have been at a disadvantage in defining the products they want. However, a start has been made to compile such standards, and these are increasing rapidly.

This section presents some of this new information, which institutions can use in setting up their own specifications. Certainly, much more needs to be done. Buyers should do much more research and investigation to see what information can be put into specifications that would improve the purchasing of bakery products. Help from purveyors and federal and state agencies should not be overlooked in the search for information.

Bread and rolls should be specified as having crusts of uniform color and thickness. Shapes should be even, with a gently rounded top. There may be a slight break or shred on the side of loaves, but not a significant one. Crust color should be golden brown. The interior crumb should be clear white or slightly creamy. A grayish cast denotes inferior flour or poor processing. The crumb should have a soft sheen and, when a slice is held up to the light, it should be semitranslucent. The texture of the grain should be soft and velvety, with no large holes; its consistency should be soft and delicate, not crumbly or doughy.

Ingredients allowed in bread are flour, shortening, water, milk or buttermilk, sugar, salt, and yeast. The type flour and proportions vary according to the bread. If made from dry milk or buttermilk, the ratio of milk solids by weight to flour should be 8.2 parts solids to every 100 parts flour. This gives a bread of the same milk content as if liquid milk were used. Whole-wheat bread should be from all whole-wheat flour and not whole-wheat and refined-wheat flour unless specified. Raisin breads or breads containing fruit or nuts should be specified as having not less than 50 parts for each 100 parts flour.

Calcium or sodium propionate, used to give softness and keeping qualities, should not be more than 0.32 parts for each 100 parts flour when used in white bread and 0.38 parts for each 100 parts flour for whole wheat, rye, or other breads. It is best to omit propionates for sandwich bread to reduce bread moistness and the tendency to soak from moist fillings. In fact, if the quality of bread continues to drop as it has, institutions may be advised to bake their own until the baking industry realizes that adding every substance and using every technique possible to increase the moisture in the bread—which propionates do—is producing a product the public is turning against. It should also be realized that bread is an important part of the diet of many people, and when they do not consume what they should they are not getting an adequate diet. Responsible buyers can do much to awaken the industry to the need for an improved product and the need to have a greater awareness of the responsibility of food manufacturers to see that their products meet nutritional needs

Bread should come wrapped unless hard-crusted. Standard loaf slices are ⅜ in. thick, but may be varied up to ⅝ in. if desired; 4½ × 4½ in. sandwich slices are from ¼ to ½ in. thick. Buyers should specify the number of slices per pound to obtain proper thickness of slice and good portion control. Hard-crusted breads may be called *hearth-type, Vienna, French,* or *Italian.* Braided products are also available. Sourdoughs are those that have a small portion of overfermented bread dough added to a normal dough. Sourdough is used in making some rye and hard-crusted breads. Vary the size, the variety, and merchandise bread. It is essential in many diets and a wonderful, low-cost food.

Sweet dough contains eggs, high quantities of sugar and fat, and is used to make cinnamon rolls, butterhorns (snails), Danish pastries, and other products. Danish, or rolled in, products have butter or vegetable shortenings alternated with dough to make them flaky. Salt-rising bread is an overfermented bread with a cheesy flavor resulting from adding yeast to milk, salt, and cornmeal. Cheese bread should be specified as having 20 parts cheese to 100 parts flour. Boston brown bread is steamed and is a mixture of rye and wheat flour, cornmeal, molasses, milk, and salt; it is usually canned. Matzo is unleavened bread made from whole flour and water resembling a cracker but thinner; it is used by the Jewish people during Passover. Zwieback is a toasted, sweetened bread. Both matzo and zwieback are crumbled and used in food preparations.

Cakes can be specified as made with common ingredients of water, sugar, flour, whole eggs, butter or vegetable shortening, monoglycerides and diglycerides, corn syrup, nonfat dry or fresh whole milk, leavening, salt, starch, and vanilla. Frostings may be fondant, foam, or otherwise specified. The size of the cake should be specified, such as 25 × 11¾ in., (7½-lb minimum wt); 11⅜ × 15¾ in. (4-lb minimum wt); pound-pan cakes 8⁵/₁₆ × 4¼ × 4 in., from 12 to 13½ oz; round or square-tier cakes will vary according to size and number of tiers. Added ingredients can be bananas for fresh banana cake; fresh oranges for fresh orange cake; chocolate or cocoa for chocolate types; and spices, flavorings, and nuts as needed. All colors and flavorings should meet U.S. certification requirements. The pack should be specified as "one unit per package, 4 per case" for 11⅜ × 15¾ in. single-layer cakes or 12 per case for pound cakes, and so on. Cakes should be frozen upon delivery and unsliced. Portioning on top of frostings can be indicated.

Cake mixes can be specified by type. Type 1 is with dried eggs, while Type 2 must have fresh eggs added. Institutional packs are usually 5-lb and 50-lb bags. Some other mixes may move in 24/22-oz packs per case and in 6/10 cans. Doughnut mixes, cake and raised types, are available in 5-lb and 50-lb bags. Various types of pancake and waffle mixes will come in 5, 10, and 50-lb bags. Frozen waffles, square shape, are often purchased 20 per sheet, 4 sheets per case, or packed 96 to the case weighing 8½ lb net. Turnovers and some other products will usually come a gross to the case. In many of these, specify polylined cartons and a 60- or 90-day shelf life, depending on the product. Frozen Danish rolls, 3 in. in diameter, weighing 1 oz each, will come packed 240 to the case.

Pies should come individually boxed, 6 to the case. Normally, they arc 10 in. in diameter, but some 9-in. pies are on the market. Ascertain which, because this should make a difference in price. Cream pies may be chocolate, vanilla, banana, lemon, strawberry, or other flavors. Boston cream pies, 10 in., usually are either vanilla or lemon cream. Other pies, such as mincemeat, custard, pumpkin, and variety pies are on the market. Specify freshness by indicating time between baking and delivery. Frozen fruit pies will usually come unbaked, but creams and others are baked and need only thawing to be ready-to-serve. As with most other bakery products of this kind, check quality and then buy by brand and purveyor. Establish standards as indicated in some of the criteria listed in Table 5-4. List ingredients, method of processing, and makeup.

Bake bakery products from mixes to judge quality. Evaluate taste and odor, thickness and color of the crust, texture and color of the crumb, grain (should be moist, even, and smooth), and volume. Specifications should limit moisture content of the dry mix and indicate the cooked volume the product must reach. Some factors a specification might indicate for specific products are listed as follows:

Item	Maximum Moisture %	Volume Increase*
Buttercakes	5	2.5 times
Angel cakes	5	3½ in. height††
Cornbreads	9	2.2 times
Plain muffins	6	2.4 times
Biscuits	10	2.4 times
Pancake, waffle, or buckwheat cakes	10	‡
Bread and rolls		3.75 times
Sweet rolls		3.33 times
Cake doughnuts	8½	2.6 times

*Leave baked product in the pan and fill with rapeseed to level full. Measure volume of the seed. Remove the product and fill the empty pan with rapeseed. Measure it. Subtract the volume of the seed when the product was in the pan from the volume when the pan was empty. Divide this by the weight of the product to get specific volume.

†In a 7⅜ × 9⅜ in. tube pan, top and bottom diameters respectively, add 625 grams (1 lb 6 oz) of batter; height should be not less than 3 ½ in. after baking.

‡After baking the height in the center should not be less than ¼ in. or more than ⅜ in. using 1.6-oz batter and allowing it to flow naturally on a hot griddle.

Specifications for crisp cookies should state that they be uniformly baked and have an even, golden-crust color or color suitable to type. The finished cookie should be tender and crisp without any burned or scorched flavor. Broken cookies should not be over 5% of the total. Use the following factors to establish specifications:

Type Cookie	Size	Count/lb	Fat % (not less than)	Moisture % (not more than)
Vanilla wafer	Disc shape ⅜ in. thick, 1½ to 2½ in. diam.	50 to 120	12	9
Gingersnaps	1³/₁₆ to 2¹/₃ in. diam.	50 to 70	7½	7

Type Cookie	Size	Count/lb	Fat % (not less than)	Moisture % (not more than)
Shortbread		40 to 65		5
Macaroons*		20 to 35	12	5
Fig bars†	1½ in. wide, ½ in. thick, 1½ to 4 in. long	14 to 40	4½	18
Vanilla-cake type			17	
Chocolate-cake type‡			17	

*Should contain 35 lb of macaroon coconut for every 100 lb soft flour.
†Should contain 50% by weight ground, clean, sound figs.
‡Should contain 17½ lb of cocoa or 1½ lb chocolate liquor per 100 lb soft flour.

About a 6 months' supply of bakery mix is enough to stock because extended storage causes a loss of volume and flavor in the baked product. Specify that mixes be prepared from high-quality, clean, wholesome ingredients. Check competing products for odor, taste, texture, thickness, and the like. Mixes should be prepared by the single-step method for the most part and should contain dry eggs so fresh eggs are not required. Brand purchase is recommended once qualities of the various brands are ascertained.

FATS AND OILS

There is no single all-purpose fat or oil. Manufacturers process oils or fats to meet specific needs in cooking and baking, and buyers should select the right one to suit the particular production need.

Types of Shortenings

A fat, or shortening, is a solid triglyceride that melts when warm. It rises in temperature when heat is applied until it begins to smoke, breaking down into water, various hydrocarbons and acids. Fats have shortening power, that is, they make many bakery items tender. They can be creamed to incorporate air. Because they are good heat conductors and impart a crisp texture, nutty flavor, and golden-brown color to foods, they are used for frying.

Vegetable shortenings are derived from nuts, seeds, or grains. Animal

TABLE 5-4

Recommended Purchase Factors for Baked or Frozen Fruit Pies

Pie	Type Fruit	% Fruit in Filling by Weight	% Filling to Total Pie Weight	Other Allowed Ingredients
Apple	Dried or canned Jonathan, Spy, McIntosh (see canned apples section in Chapter 3)	40	67	Water, enriched flour, starch, sugar, vegetable shortening, modified food starch, lemon juice, dextrose, nonfat dry milk, salt, cinnamon, citric acid, leavening, ascorbic acid, and orange oil
Apple/Rhubarb	Apples as above and strawberry rhubarb	25 apples 25 rhubarb	67	Water, enriched flour, sugar, starch, vegetable shortening, modified food starch, corn syrup, dextrose, nonfat dry milk, salt, lemon juice, leavening, citric acid, ascorbic acid, U.S. certified food color
Blueberry	U.S. Grade A cultivated Genus Vaccinium blueberries	47	66	Water, enriched flour, vegetable shortening, sugar, modified starch, corn syrup, dextrose, nonfat dry milk, salt, lemon juice, vegetable gum, corn syrup solids, leavening, blueberry and raspberry extracts with other natural flavors, citric acid, cinnamon
Cherry	Montmorency RSP cherries	60%*	66	Enriched flour, sugar, vegetable shortening, water, modified food starch, dextrose, nonfat dry milk, salt, lemon juice, citric acid, leavening, cinnamon, U.S. certified food color
Peach	U.S. Grade A firm peaches of the Rio Oso variety	46 sliced and 4 pure peach puree	66	Enriched flour, water, sugar, vegetable shortening, corn syrup, modified food starch, dextrose, nonfat dry milk, salt, lemon juice, dried apricots, citric acid, leavening, ascorbic acid, and U.S. certified food color

*Shall be guaranteed to be substantially above the 25% cherries required by law.

shortenings come largely from pork, lard, and beef suet. Vegetable and animal shortenings can be blended together to produce different kinds of shortenings. They can also be treated or modified so they have specific characteristics.

Lard

Lard is fat rendered from fresh, clean, sound, fatty tissues of hogs in good health at the time of slaughter. Leaf lard comes from the fat surrounding the kidney and abdominal walls and is of the highest quality. Lard may not be processed from bones, heads, ears, and other similar meats or tissues. If it comes from sources other than fatty tissues, it must be labeled "rendered pork *fat*," not lard.

Moisture-rendering by using large steam kettles produces "kettle-rendered" lard, usually considered of highest quality. There are three types of kettle-rendered lard: drip, dry, and neutral. Drip-rendering introduces steam around the fat in the kettle and allows the fat to drip down and run free from the tissues. This subjects the lard to a minimum of heat. Dry-rendering is the drawing off of fat as it accumulates in the kettle, the kettle being heated by steam from the outside. If the kettle is heated by water instead of steam and the same method is used as in dry-rendering, the lard is called *neutral*. This product is often used for oleomargarine and medicinal purposes. "Prime steam" lard is rendered in a closed tank in direct steam, but because the product is exposed to heat for a longer period of time, it is not as high in quality as kettle-rendered lard. Natural lard is derived from slowly heated back fat and leaf lard. It is very white in color and lacks a definite flavor.

Hydrogenation can make lard more firm and improve its plasticity as well as raise its melting point. Lard is used widely in the making of bread, crackers, and piecrusts. It has a lower smoking temperature than vegetable oil and is seldom used for frying purposes unless specially treated.

Lard is evaluated according to color, texture, and flavor. Color is best observed when the lard is melted. It should have a light, golden color and not be turbid. Smell and taste it while melted. Cold lard should be snow-white, firm, and moderately resistant to pressure of the finger. It should have no graininess. Lard may have strong flavors resulting from too high a temperature in rendering or too long a rendering period. Rancidity develops easily in lard unless approved antioxidants are added. A good-quality lard should not contain more than ½% free fatty acids.

Beef Suet

Beef fat, or suet, is marketed as oleo or oleo stearin. It is used in the making of crackers and some other bakery goods, but is most frequently blended with other shortenings to give it greater plasticity and other required characteristics. Suet from the abdominal cavity is of highest quality, and trimmed fats from the carcass are next. Fats accumulated in meat-cutting and rendered are called *shop fat* and are of lowest quality.

Vegetable Shortenings

Vegetable shortenings are made from oils that are hydrogenated, a process in which hydrogen is attached to a free bond in the oil molecule. To do this, the oil is heated and hydrogen gas is bubbled through it under pressure. Nickel as a powder is added to act as a catalyst for the reaction. Upon cooling, this hydrogenated oil becomes a solid. Cottonseed and corn oil are common hydrogenated shortenings.

Shortenings and sometimes oils may have antioxidants added to them, such as butylated-hydroxy-anisole (BHA), citric acid, and other substances. Shortenings used for pastries and cakes will contain monoglycerides or diglycerides. This gives them greater spread or emulsifying power in batters and doughs. Solid frying fats may contain stabilizers, such as silicones and other substances, to help them withstand high frying temperatures and breakdown in use. Fats can be treated so they develop either a waxy texture desirable for use in piecrust and puff paste or a pliable, soft texture that allows them to incorporate large quantities of air, a characteristic desirable in shortenings used for cakes, cookies, and sweet doughs. Labels will always state the substances added. These must be approved by the federal government. A Ⓤ indicates the shortening (or oil) meets Kosher (Jewish religious) requirements.

Types of Oils

Cold extraction gives a higher-quality oil than heating. This can be done by crushing and using centrifugal expellers or hydraulic presses. Some oils are extracted in solvents, and then the solvent is distilled from the oil and reused. Oils as well as shortenings may be decolored or deodorized.

Olive Oil

About 14 to 40% of the ripe olive is oil. Quality depends on the pressing, growing conditions, and soil. If pits are removed before pressing, a higher-quality oil results. Pressing must come immediately after crushing. The first oil is the highest quality and is called *virgin* or *sublime*. Refined oils come from later pressings, and some may result from heat extraction. Refined oils and oils from the third and fourth pressings are not recommended for food use.

California and Arizona produce significant quantities of olive oil. The Lucca district of Italy (near Florence and Pisa) produces the world's finest oil, but adulteration is so common and so many areas other than Lucca claim their oil comes from there that it is difficult to obtain the true oil. Purchase only reliable brands. The Olive Oil Association of America has developed standards and recommends labeling to indicate origin, extent of adulteration with other oils, quality, and other factors of interest to buyers. The Food and Drug Administration prohibits adulteration and the use of the name "olive oil" if other oils are added to olive oil. It also inspects all imports to determine purity.

A good olive oil should have a light-greenish to yellow color. The flavor and odor should be pleasing; typical of olive oil; free from strong, green-olive odors and flavors; and free from musty, moldy, butyric, zapateria, rancid, or other off-odors or flavors. Taste before purchase. Maximum free fatty acids are 3%. U.S. Grade A olive oil cannot have more than 1.4% free fatty acids, Grade B not more than 2½%, and Grade C 3%. Purchase Grade A with a score of not less than 90. To meet standards of identity, the iodine number of olive oil must be between 79 and 90 Hanus and have a refractive index of 1.4668 to 1.4830 at 25°C.

Cottonseed Oil

The average oil content of the cottonseed is 18 to 25%. Conditions of soil, season, fertilizer, variety, and methods of extraction affect quality. After hulling and crushing, the oil is hydraulically expelled. Good oil is slightly amber in color, clear, and has a fresh, sweet odor. Dark color indicates low quality and poor refining methods. A high fatty acid content indicates an oil of low quality. The United States produces large quantities of this oil, but imports some from India, China, Egypt, and South America.

Corn Oil

Corn or maize contains between 3 to 6½% oil and comes as a by-product from the manufacture of syrup, starch, cornmeal, or hominy. When fresh, good oil has a distinctive cornmeal flavor and a light amber, clear color. It is used for salads and frying. It has a high smoking temperature. Oils for salads should be *winterized* to remove heavy oil molecules that cause the oil to solidify when chilled. Their removal is usually accomplished by centrifuging. Unwinterized oils may be cloudy at room temperature.

Soybean Oil

Soybeans contain from 11 to 25% fat. The condition of the soil, seasonal and climatic conditions, and processing affect quality. After crushing, the seeds are cooked to remove the oil. Unless treated soy oil *reverts,* which is a condition brought about by the loss of oxygen from the molecule. The oil should be a clear, yellowish color. It has a high smoking temperature and is excellent for deep-frying or frying. A reverted oil has a beany or fishy flavor.

Peanut Oil

From 38 to 50% of the peanut may be oil. The oil is extracted by hydraulic or expeller process. After refining, the oil has a nutty, pleasing flavor and should be amber in color, like corn oil. Some may be darker than cotton-seed or corn oil and still be of good quality. It is a good frying or deep-frying oil.

Unsaturated Oils

The use of unsaturated oils for dietary reasons has increased considerably in the last 10 years. While an unsaturated oil will have as many calories as any other, it is said to be more desirable for those with cardiac or arteriosclerosis problems. Oils from the sesame seed, rapeseed, sunflower seed and safflower seed are more unsaturated than oils from corn, cottonseed, and peanuts, although these are not as saturated as butter, lard, suet, and other animal fats. Coconut oil is quite saturated. It is used frequently in the manufacture of margarines, but may also be a fat listed as an ingredient in other foods. Cacao butter is another quite saturated fat. It is used largely in confections and in some bakery products. Unless sold for special dietary purposes, foods may not contain mineral oil. The Food and Drug Administration has interpreted the use of mineral oil as an adulterant and a nonfood unless used for medical purposes.

Handling of Fats and Oils

Oils and fats can deteriorate by discoloring or developing rancid flavors. Light, air, and moisture can cause deterioration. Air should be excluded by sealing in airtight containers. Light should also be reduced. High-storage temperatures assist in breaking down fats and oils. Storage should not be above 70°F and in a dry place. Thin surfaces of oil or fat deteriorate rapidly; and an oilcan that is left to stand and then refilled with oil may rapidly develop an off-flavor. Wash all containers well before using again.

6
Miscellaneous Groceries

The number of miscellaneous items used by food services has grown tremendously. Many of these new items are used to reduce labor or do highly specialized things in food production. Instead of one emulsifier, we may use several—at one time we used none at all. We will use several different starches instead of the old reliable cornstarch, and instead of one salad dressing we may use a wide number. At one time about 4% of the total food cost was for miscellaneous groceries, but now it is closer to 6%. If the cost is not significant, the contribution many of these items make may be. Although only a small quantity may be used, the flavor contribution or effect it has on the food may be considerable. It usually pays to purchase the best. Few quality standards exist for many of these items and so the buyer must know his products and also his production need to purchase them satisfactorily.

PICKLED PRODUCTS

Olives

Fresh olives may be processed into ripe, green, Sicilian-style green or salt-cured, oil-coated olives.

Ripe Olives

The Mission olive originated in California from olive seeds brought there by missionaries. It is largely used today for ripe, black olives. It is firm in texture, rich in oil, and can become riper than other varieties and still give a good olive. It is small, seldom running over extra-large in size. Larger ripe olives must come from varieties of olives used for green olives. These green

TABLE 6-1
Characteristics of Leading California Olives*

Variety	Shape	Characteristics
Mission	Smallest variety; oval in shape.	Originated in California. Rich in oil; has mellow, firm flesh when ripe. Cures well.
Manzanillo	Round, cherry shaped; moderate size.	Spanish variety maturing earlier than the Mission and used where frosts endanger late-maturing olives.
Sevillano	Oblong shape, very large.	Spanish variety rivaling Manzanillo in production. Requires mild cure because of tendency to shrivel from salt osmosis. Cures into a desirable Queen or Green olive.
Ascolano	Resembles Sevillano in size and shape.	Italian olive; also tends to shrivel in processing. Highly popular for Queen or Green olives.
Barouni		Coarse, woody, and difficult to cure; it is frequently used for Sicilian green olives.

*Ranked in order of greatest to least quantity produced in this country.

varieties cannot be ripened as much, which gives a less desirable product. Mission ripe olives are almost black whereas the others are brownish-black.

The Missions also produce the green-ripe olive which is like the black ripe olive except for its green color. It must be ripened on the tree to an almost pink stage and therefore is slightly softer than the black-ripe. This olive is green because during processing it is never allowed to come in contact with the air, the factor that causes olives to turn black. Both black and green ripe olives are packed in enamel-lined cans, covered with salt brine, and heat-treated to preserve them. This cannot be done with green olives.

Green Olives

We import large quantities of green olives from Spain and Italy. Sevillano, Manzanillo, Ascolana, and Mission olives are preferred in that order for making green olives. Green olives also are called *Queen* or *Spanish* olives. Barouni olives give a poor texture. Green olives are firmer in texture and

TABLE 6-2

Single Sizes			Allowances
Designation(s)	Illustration	Approximate Count (per pound)	Average Count (per pound of drained olives)
Small (or) Select (or) Standard(s)		135	128 to 140 inclusive
Medium		113	106 to 121 inclusive
Large		98	91 to 105 inclusive
Extra Large		82	76 to 88 inclusive
Mammoth		70	65 to 75 inclusive
Giant		53 to 60 inclusive	53 to 60 inclusive
Jumbo		46 to 50 inclusive	46 to 50 inclusive
Colossal		36 to 40 inclusive	36 to 40 inclusive
Super Colossal		Not to exceed 32	32 or less
Special Super Colossal		28 or less	28 or less

TABLE 6-3
Trade Designations of Blended Sizes in Ripe Olives

Blended Sizes		Average Count (per pound of drained olives)
Designation	Composition of Blend	
Family	Medium, Large, and Extra Large and no more than 15%, by count, of Standard(s).	91 to 105 inclusive
King	Giant, Jumbo, and the smaller half of Colossal and no more than 15%, by count, of Mammoth.	45 to 53 inclusive
Royal	Large half of Colossal; and Super Colossal or Special Super Colossal.	Not to exceed 34
Other blends	Two or three adjacent sizes, as in Table I, and no more than 15%, by count, of smaller size(s).	Not applicable

more bitter in flavor than the ripe ones. Immediately after harvest both green and ripe olives are soaked in lye to remove a bitter glucoside. Green olives are soaked a shorter time and so are slightly more bitter. The lye is then removed by washing, and fermentation follows. Ripe olives are then exposed to air for 2 to 3 days, which causes them to darken.

Pattern or place packing of green olives is called *stick packing* and is more expensive than thrown or jumble packing. After curing, salt brine is poured over the olives and they are sealed from the air. Government standards state that the acidity of green olives shall not be more than 4.00 pH and have a salt content not less than 6%. Sicilian green olives are not lye soaked and are more bitter than regular green olives. They also may be spiced.

Salt-cured, oil-coated olives are also Greek, Greek-style, or oil-cured. These receive a moderate lye soak and after fermentation are not left in brine but are dipped in oil and packed without brine with only salt on them. The salt draws moisture from them, causing them to shrivel.

Olive Quality

Uniformity of size and color, flavor, texture, and defects decide the grade of olives. Ripe olives showing light meat under the skin are graded higher than those showing dark meat. Excessive bitterness is cause for downgrad-

TABLE 6-4

Size No.	Trade Term	Federal Count per Pound	Spanish Equivalent per Kilo	Approximate Size of Olive
00	Peewee	181/220	400/420	
0	Midget	141/180	380/320	
1	Small	128/140	280/300	
2	Medium	106/127	240/200	
3	Large	91/105	200/220	
4	Extra Large	76/90	180/200	
5	Mammoth	65/75	140/160	
6	Giant	53/64	120/140	
7	Jumbo	42/52	100/120	
8	Colossal	33/41	70/80	
9	Super Colossal	32 or under	60/70	

ing. If lye is not completely removed, olives may taste soapy. A musty or moldy flavor develops when the processing is too long. This flavor also develops if ripe olives are stored too long before processing. Butyric or zapateric odor and taste indicate decomposition.

Pickles

Cucumbers are the most common item pickled, but green tomatoes, man-

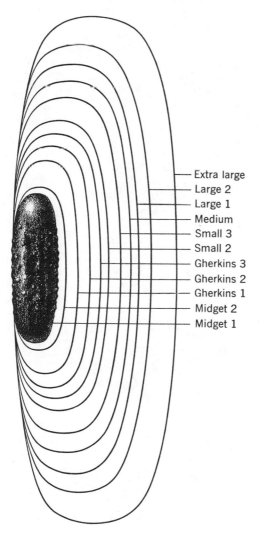

Extra large
Large 2
Large 1
Medium
Small 3
Small 2
Gherkins 3
Gherkins 2
Gherkins 1
Midget 2
Midget 1

Fig. 6-1. Standard pickle sizes. Courtesy USDA

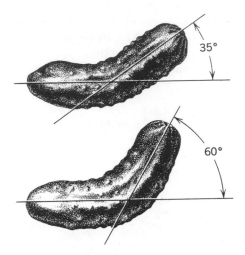

A curved pickle has an angle of 35° to 60° while a nubbin has an angle greater than 60° as shown. The angle is formed by intersecting lines projected from either end approximately parallel to the sides.

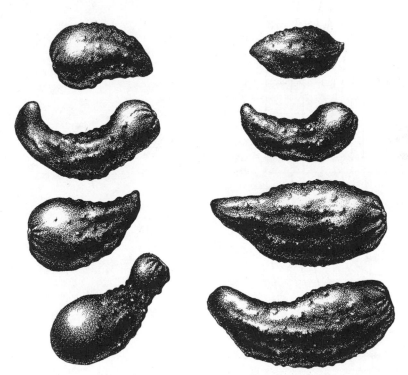

Nubbins or badly misshaped pickles   Slightly misshaped pickles

Fig. 6-2. Standards for curved, slightly misshapen, and badly misshapen pickles. Courtesy USDA

goes, onions, cauliflower, cabbage, beans, green and ripe (red sweet) peppers, carrots, watermelon rind, peaches, pears, walnuts, corn, and other fruits and vegetables may be pickled. The process may be a natural cure or with hot vinegar, salt, sugar, and spices. Heat treatment also may be used to further preserve both products.

Cucumbers for pickles are picked immature and sent to salting stations for inspection, washing, and grading for size. They are then fermented in a salt brine until sufficient lactic acid is formed to stop the pickling action. Natural or genuine pickles are cured in a brine containing approximately 5% salt for about 4 weeks. Dill, dill emulsion, and vinegar may be added. Calcium chloride or alum is used to obtain crispness. In pickling, the outside color changes to a dark green olive and the flesh to a light creamy white. This flesh is slightly translucent. Adding turmeric removes the dead white color and makes it a light, whitish yellow. The green areas and flavor are not affected by the turmeric. Mushy or soft pickles develop if temperatures are too high. "Floaters" are pickles having hollow areas developed in pickling either because of too rapid fermentation or undesirable bacterial action. Black, ropy, or slimy pickles are usually the result of undesirable bacterial actions. Natural-cure pickles keep for about 6 months providing they are kept in a cool place. If heat treated, some quality is lost.

Pickles can be made from salt stocks. These are cucumbers that are immediately placed in a salt brine from 7 to 10% salt. They do not ferment in this but keep until needed for processing. Salt-stock pickles lack the flavor and texture of the genuine-cure, but they do keep much better.

Green tomatoes and other items may be pickled the same as cucumbers either by the genuine or salt-stock method and they are available over the entire year.

Ripe Olives (1971)

Grades: A (90), B (80)*, C (70).

Type: Ripe, green-ripe.

Styles: Whole, whole pitted, halved, sliced, chopped or minced, broken, pitted.

Recommended minimum drained weight: No. 10—Mammoth size or smaller 66 oz; Giant or larger 64 oz, blends of large sizes 64 oz, blends of small sizes 66 oz, halves 50 oz, chopped or minced 100 oz, sliced 50 oz, broken pitted 55 oz.

*Color for ripe should be almost black or blackish brown. Color should be uniform or nearly so between olives. Normal color for green-ripe is yellow green, green yellow or other greenish casts and some mottling may be evident. Should be uniform in size. Whole olives should not vary in standard counts more than $3/16$ in. in diameter. Cutting on cut styles shall be even with little or no raggedness evident. Fairly free from defects such as blemishes, wrinkles, mutilated olives, pits or pit fragments, stems, injuries or damaged units. Free from harmless extraneous material. The flesh should be reasonably firm.

Green Olives (1967)

  Grades: A (90), B (80)*, C (70).

  Styles: Unpitted; pitted without stuffing; pitted stuffed with pimiento, onion, almond, celery; sliced; chopped or minced; broken pitted or salad.

  Packs: Thrown or jumble, place or stick packed.

  Recommended drained weight:

Container size	½ pt	pt	qt	gallon
Drained weight	4½ to 5½ oz	9½ to 11 oz	19 to 22 oz	86 to 88 oz

  Flavorings added: Plain, spiced with dill, anise, garlic, pepper. (Buyers should ascertain flavoring in olives called Bordelaise, French, Kosher or Italian. Cuban usually means tomato paste has been added.)

*Reasonably uniform typical color, which is yellow-green to green color typical of variety. If olives are stuffed, the stuffing shall possess a good characteristic color for the stuffing used. Packing brine shall be clear and not cloudy. There should be few broken pieces. Workmanship should be reasonably good. Texture should be reasonably uniform, reasonably good with a moderately firm and crisp flesh only slightly tough, which must be characteristic of variety. Reasonably free from slip skins, extraneous material, pits or pit fragments and other defects.

  Note: Sicilian-style green olives have only one grade, No. 1. These are olives of similar varietal characteristics, which are green or straw in color, clean, firm, and fairly well formed; are free from damage caused by discoloration, shriveling, hail, wind, frost or other means; and possess the normal flavor of Sicilian-style olives.

Certain terms are used in the trade to indicate kinds of pickles. *Kosher* indicates natural or processed dills with garlic, onions, and peppers (the last two are optional) added. If natural dills contain onions, garlic, and red peppers, they are *Polish* or *Hungarian* dills. *Pasteurized* pickles are heat treated. *Sweet* dills and *mild* sweet pickles are less sweet than sweet pickles. *Iceberg* dills are quartered. If cut into smaller sizes, they are called *dill sticks. Sour* pickes have added vinegar. Spices may or may not be added. A *chow-chow* is either a sour or sweet pickle mixture seasoned with prepared mustard. Peppers used in pickle mixtures are the sweet type, but if the label uses the term "hot," red pepper capiscums have been added. *Chutney* is a tart, sweet Indian relish made from mangoes, green ginger, mustard seed, raisins, East Indian tamarind, chili peppers, black pepper, butter, and spices. *American chutney* is made from vinegar, green tomatoes, orange marmalade, raisins, lemon peel, dates, lime juice, onion, flour, and spices. *Mixed chutney* may be American chutney or contain pickles, cauliflower, and other vegetables imitating real chutney. *Bread and butter* or *country-style* pickles are thin cucumber slices cured in strong salt stock and then packed in heavily vinegared and spiced, sweet syrup

TABLE 6-5
Proportions of Ingredients in Pickle Mixtures

Type Ingredient	Cut Piece Mixtures*	Chopped (Minced) Relishes
Percent by Weight of Drained Weight of Product		
Cucumbers	60 to 80	
Cucumbers, chopped		60 to 100
Cauliflower, pieces	10 to 30	
Cauliflower, chopped		10 to 30†
Onions, whole (maxium diam. 1¼ in.)	5 to 12	
Onions, sliced or cut	5 to 12	
Onions, chopped		5 to 12†
Green tomatoes, whole or pieces	10 (maximum)	
Green tomatoes, chopped		10 (maximum)†
Sweet type peppers	†	†
Cabbage	†	†
Olives	†	†
Tomato paste in hamburger relish		Required
Mustard or prepared mustard	Required in mustard or chow-chow	Required in mustard relish; in hamburger relish†

*Such as sour mixed, sweet mixed, sour mustard or chow-chow, or sweet mustard or chow-chow.
†Optional.

containing celery seed. Capers are pickled buds from the caper shrub growing in southern Europe. The buds are dried and shipped. Processors then put them into a sweetened solution of 6 to 7% vinegar. *Fresh-pack* pickles are differentiated from genuine (natural) and salt-cure pickles as being prepared from uncured, unfermented cucumbers and are packed in a vinegar solution. Sufficient heat treatment is given them to preserve them in hermetically sealed containers.

Quality

Top quality pickles should be uniform in shape, almost cylindrical, with well-rounded ends, smooth and uniform color, and few defects that are obvious or objectionable. Curved or misshapen pickles lower the grade.

Fig. 6-3. Minimum shapes recommended for Grade A dills. Courtesy USDA

TABLE 6-6
Flavor Pack Requirements for Grade A Pickles

Type Pickle	Acid,* grams per 100 ml	Packing Density Salometer	Brix (Minimum)	Braumé (Minimum)
		Cured Type		
Dills, natural or processed	0.6	10 to 19°		
Sour, sour mixed, sour relish	1.7 to 2.7	10 to 19°		
Sweet, sweet mixed, sweet relish	1.7 to 2.7	3 gm/100 ml	32.64°	18.0°
Mild sweet, mild sweet mixed, mild sweet relish	1.0		20.0°	12.0°
Sour mustard or sour chow-chow	1.7 to 2.7†	3 gm/100 gm		
Sweet mustard or sweet chow-chow	1.7 to 2.7†	3 gm/100 bm	28.0°	15.5°

TABLE 6-6 (cont'd)
Flavor Pack Requirements for Grade A Pickles

Type Pickle	Acid,* grams per 100 ml	Packing Density Salometer	Brix (Minimum)	Braumé (Minimum)
		Fresh-pack Type		
Dills	0.5 to 1.1	1.75 to 4.75 gm per 100 ml		
Sweetened dills or sweetened dill relish	0.5 to 1.1	1.75 to 4.75 gm per 100 ml	7.2°	4.0°
Sweet and mild sweet	0.8 to 1.65	1.25 to 2.75 gm per 100 ml	18.0°	10.0°

*Calculated in dills as lactic acid and in others as acetic.
†Grams per 100 grams.

TABLE 6-7
Whole Pickle Sizes

Size Term	Count per gallon	Diameters
Midget	270 or more	¾ in. or less
Small gherkin	135 to 269	Up to ¹⁵/₁₆ in.
Large gherkin	65 to 134	Up to 1¹/₁₆ in.
Small	40 to 64	Over 1¹/₁₆ to 1⅜ in.
Medium	26 to 39	Over 1⅜ to 1½ in.
Large	18 to 25	Over 1½ to 1¾ in.
Extra large	12 to 17	Over 1¾ to 2⅛ in.

Sweet pickles should have a more firm texture and break with a cleaner snap than others because the sugar strengthens the pickle. Pickles should not be soft, slippery, or contain hollow, spongy centers. The interior flesh should be uniform in color and translucent. There should be no white or opaque flesh or badly shriveled pickles outside tolerance allowances. Flavor characteristics for grades are well defined. See Table 6-6 for some of these flavor requirements. Taste pickles for quality.

Federal grades are U.S. A and B. Styles in cured pickles are dills (natural or processed), sour, sweet and mild sweet, sour mixed, sweet mixed, mild sweet mixed, sour mustard or sour chow-chow, sweet mustard or sweet chow-chow, sour pickle relish, and sweet pickle or mild sweet pickle relish. Fresh-pack styles are dills, sweetened dills, sweetened dill relish, sweet and mild sweet, sweet relish and mild sweet relish, and dietetic. The last may be prepared in any style with or without the addition of sweeteners, salt, or other approved ingredients.

TABLE 6-8
Sizes and Counts per Gallon of Pickles

Size Term	Size Number	Approximate Count per Gallon	Length in Inches
Midgets	1 Midget	445/545	1½ or less
Midgets	2 Midget	330/444	1½ to 2
Gherkins	1 Gherkin	225/329	2 to 2¼
Gherkins	2 Gherkin	135/224	2 to 2½
Gherkins	3 Gherkin	100/134	2½ to 2¾
Small	1 Small	80/99	2¾ to 3
Small	2 Small	66/79	3 to 3¼
Small	3 Small	52/65	3¼ to 3½
Medium		40/51	3½ to 4
Large	1 Large	26/39	4 to 4¼
Large	2 Large	22/25	4¼ to 4¾
Extra Large		16/21	4¾ to 5¼

Note: A special type of gherkin, called the *Burr Gherkin,* is a West Indian fruit, not a true cucumber. It is used for small, sweet cucumber pickles. It is pale green and covered with prickly spines. Some of the smallest midgets and gherkins are made from this product.

Sizing

The smallest pickles bring the highest prices, but size is not related to quality. Size affects grade only when it varies to affect uniformity. Whole pickles are sized: 2¾ in. or less with no length variation more than ¾ in., 2¾ to 4 in. with no more variation in length than ¾ in., and over 4 in. with no greater variation than 1½ in. Parts of pickles less than whole must conform to size requirements as indicated in the grade summary that follows:

Cucumber Pickles (1966)

Grades: A (85)*, B (70).

Recommended minimum drained weight: Cured, sweet 92%; cured, other than sweet 88%; fresh-pack, sweet 85%; fresh-pack, other than sweet 80%. Fill of cured must be 55% or more and fresh-pack 57% or more of container volume.

Packaging

Pickles usually are purchased in gallon or barrel lots. A case is 4 gallons. No. 10 cans or 3¼-qt packs are also common, packed 6 per case.

*The pickles should be free from objectionable flavors, possess the characteristic normal flavor of the pickle type, and should meet standards for acidity, sugar, and salt content. Color should be typical, practically uniform, and practically free from bleached areas. Uniformity in size within reasonable limits is a requirement. Check for damaged units, blemishes, improper processing soft units, nubbins, curved or misshapen units. Check workmanship on cut styles. There should be no extraneous matter and few stems or other material.

Sauerkraut

Finely shredded or cut cabbage fermented in a small amount of water containing 2½ lb of salt per 100 lb of cabbage produces sauerkraut. Fermentation must be carefully controlled. To retain quality, the kraut is put into enamel-lined cans and given heat treatment. If untreated with heat, it keeps in a cool place for 4 to 6 months. (See specifications in Chapter 3 for sauerkraut).

SPICES

About 0.6% of the food dollar goes for spices. About 60% of a spice's value is aroma. The amount of essential oil or flavoring in one varies from ½ to 4%. These volatile aromas are lost rapidly and only a month's supply should be on hand. They also lose flavor rapidly in open or paper containers or in storage areas where heat or moisture is high.

Select spices on the basis of strength and flavor. Watch for imitations or weak or poorly flavored products. Purchase from reliable spice dealers. Packaging is 1 oz, 4 oz, 1 lb, 6 lb, and 10 lb. There are no federal standards for quality but standards of identity exist. Fresh, good quality spice should possess a soft, earthy freshness of color and not be dull. The aroma should be fresh and pungent. Check quality of grind, wholeness, extraneous material, and broken, shriveled, or damaged units.

Allspice

Allspice is the nearly ripe, dried berry of an evergreen tree growing mainly in Jamaica, Mexico, Guatemala, Honduras, Brazil, and the Leeward Islands. It has the flavor of a blend of cinnamon, nutmeg, and cloves. A small quantity gives a strong flavor. It usually is purchased ground.

Anise

The anise seed is greenish brown and small and oval in shape like caraway. It has a licorice flavor. Most comes from Spain and Mexico. Star anise from China is used as a food flavoring and is similar in flavor to true anise. It is a somewhat larger, round seed.

Basil

Sweet basil, grown commercially in the north Mediterranean, is a member of the mint family. The leaves are a greenish brown when dry. The flavor is sweet and warm with a pungent overtone.

Bay Leaf

Sweet bay, an evergreen laurel growing in Turkey, Greece, Yugoslavia, and Portugal, produces bay leaf. The leaves are a yellow-olive green about 3 in. in length. The flavor is distinctively pungent. Purchase whole or crushed.

Caraway

Caraway is related to parsley and produces a brown, hard seed about $3/16$ in. long, curved, and tapered at the ends. The flavor is pleasant, slightly sharp, with a sweet undertone. The best comes from Holland.

Cardamon

Cardamon is a member of the ginger family producing a creamy white, irregularly round seed about $3/32$ in. long. The flavor is aromatic and pungent. Most comes from Guatemala, but India and Ceylon also ship.

Cassia

Cassia buds have a pungent cinnamon flavor. They are ripe or immature fruit of the cassia plant that grows in the tropics.

Cayenne

An orange-red to bright, deep red small capiscum when ground produces cayenne. It has a hot, pungent flavor. Most comes from Louisiana.

Celery Seed

A plant related to parsley grown in France and India produces celery seed, which is a small, round pellet, light brown or tan in color. The taste is similar to that of celery. Celery salt is ground seed and salt.

Chervil

Chervil leaves have the flavor of mild parsley and come from a plant belonging to that family.

Chili Powder

Ground cumin is the main ingredient of a blend of spices making up chili powder. Other spices frequently are chili pepper, red pepper, ground oregano, ground garlic powder, ground cloves, ground allspice, and ground dried onion. It may not be hot, and different brands have different flavors.

Cinnamon

The bark of the Cassia tree produces the cinnamon used in this country. It is dark brown in color and the flavor is sweet, slightly pungent, milder, but similar to the flavor of cloves. It comes ground and in rolled sticks. Ceylon cinnamon tree bark is true cinnamon but is not used much in this country. Its flavor is milder and the color lighter than Cassia bark. Most countries use this true cinnamon.

Cloves

"Clou" in French means nail, the shape of the dried, unopened bud of the evergreen tree producing cloves. It comes from the islands of Zanzibar and Madagascar. The flavor is strong, pungent, and sweet.

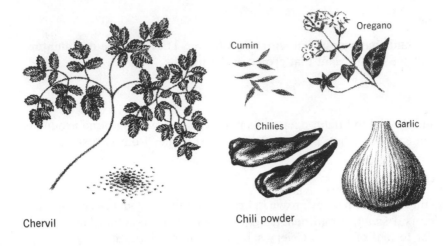

Chervil

Cumin

Oregano

Chilies

Garlic

Chili powder

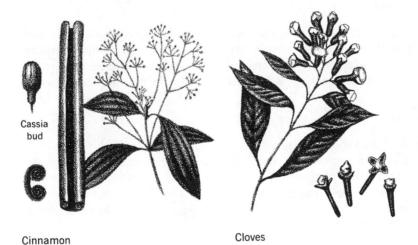

Cassia
bud

Cinnamon

Cloves

Fig. 6-4. Spices come from many parts of a plant. Chervil leaves come from a member of the mint family. Chili powder is a combination of leaves, seeds, roots, and peppers, with cumin seeds the main ingredient. Cinnamon may come from bark or from the cassia bud. Cloves are the bud of a plant.

Coriander

Coriander seeds are small with a color ranging from white through orange to a yellowish brown and a shape that shows alternating straight and wavy edges. The flavor is pleasant, mild, distinctive, and aromatic, somewhat like lavender or a blend of "lemon peel with sage." It comes whole or ground. It is related to the parsley family and is produced mostly in Yugoslavia or Morocco.

Cumin (Comino or Cummin) Seed

Cumin is another member of the parsley family grown in Iran and Morocco. The seed is yellow-brown, oval and thin, about ⅛ to ¼ in. long. The flavor is strong, pungent, and somewhat sweet.

Curry powder

The main spices in curry are fenugreek, cayenne, turmeric, coriander, and cumin. Select one that has a sweet, mild flavor, not harsh, and one that gives foods a bright, deep-yellow color, not a dirty tan.

Dill

Most dill comes from India or Europe. It belongs to the parsley family, having a seed small, ovular, crescent-shaped, hard, brownish with a mellow, sweet tang faintly reminiscent of caraway. Some describe the flavor as "weedy." It comes ground or whole.

Fennel

Fennel seed from another parsley relative is long and oval with a yellowish-brown color. It has an agreeable odor and an aromatic, sweet taste resembling anise. It comes ground or whole. Most comes from India or Rumania.

Fenugreek (Foenugreek)

Fenugreek is small, with an irregular, oval shape, from a plant of the pea family grown in India, France, Lebanon, and Argentina. The seed is yellowish-brown with a distinctive, pleasant, slightly bitter flavor like burnt sugar. It comes whole or ground.

Garlic Powder

Ground dehydrated garlic is used for garlic powder. Garlic salt is a combination of powder and salt, mostly salt.

Ginger

A root or rhizome of a tropical tuberous plant with a aromatic, sweet, spicy, pungent flavor makes ginger. Ground ginger is a light buff. Whole, dried ginger may be peeled or unpeeled. Fresh green ginger also is on the market. A candied ginger and also one in syrup is available.

Mace and Nutmeg

Mace is the skin of a seed from the nutmeg tree, a tropical evergreen producing peach-like fruit. Mace is the lacy network around the nutmeg seed. It is milder and less pungent than nutmeg. Nutmeg is a round ball up to 1 in. in diameter and is usually coarsely ground. The flavor is sweet, with a warm, spicy undertone.

Marjoram

Marjoram leaves from a mint plant come from France, Chile, or Peru. They are gray-green with a distinctly aromatic flavor and a slightly bitter undertone. It comes whole or ground.

Mint

Dried, domestically grown mint is usually used either whole or crushed. It has a strong, sweet, tangy, cool flavor.

Mixed Pickling Spice

A number of mixed spices such as bay leaf, cinnamon, cloves, cardamon, and peppers make up pickling spice.

Mustard

Most mustard seed is domestically grown. There is a black and brown seed. Both are hot, sharp, pungent, with a slightly sweet overtone. It is ground and also comes as seeds. Prepared mustard is a paste made from turmeric mostly and a small amount of mustard. Hot mustard is largely ground mustard seed in a slightly sweetened vinegar. It is quite hot.

Onion Powder

Ground dried onions are onion powder. Onion salt is salt and onion powder, and like most salts is mostly salt.

Oregano (Oreganum, Mexican Oregano or Sage, Origan)

Oregano is the leaves from a mint plant. They are dried and are light green in color. The flavor is strong and aromatic, with an assertive, pleasantly bitter undertone resembling that of marjoram and bay leaf. It comes crushed or ground.

Paprika

A red capiscum, mild in flavor, produces ground paprika. That from Hungary is darker in color than Spanish paprika and also has less flavor and is cheaper. Some California-grown paprika resembles Hungarian. Paprika has a mild, pleasant, delicately sweet flavor.

Parsley

Parsley leaves are dried and have a sweet, aromatic, delicate flavor with just a soft bit of spice. The same flavor comes from fresh leaves.

Pepper

Red pepper is not as hot as cayenne but is redder. It comes from California, Louisiana, the Carolinas, and Turkey, mostly in ground or crushed form. It also is called *pepperoni rosso, pizza pepper, coarse crushed red pepper,* and *red pepper, crushed.* It comes ground, chopped, or whole. Whole chili peppers are red pepper capiscums. Some pickled or dried green peppers also are hot. True pepper, the black and white varieties, comes from a small, dark brown, dry berry, and is not related to the capsicum family. The plant is a climbing vine. Most imports come from India, Indonesia, and British Malaya. Ground pepper shows both the light and dark portions of the berry. White pepper is the inner part of the berry and black pepper is usually the outer portion with a bit of the interior. White pepper should have no trace of outer shell in it. It is hotter but somewhat milder in flavor than black pepper. Black pepper has a more penetrating odor and a more pungent taste. Black pepper comes either ground or in the whole berry, whereas white pepper is largely found only ground, although some whole, white interior kernels may be obtainable. Some institutions grind their own pepper.

Poppy Seeds

Holland produces the best poppy seed. They are round, tiny, and may be tan or darker in color.

Poultry Seasoning

A ground blend of sage, thyme, marjoram, and savory may be poultry seasoning with sometimes rosemary and other spices added.

Pumpkin Pie Spice

A blend of cinnamon, cloves, ginger and nutmeg or mace makes up pumpkin pie spice. Most operators prefer their own blends.

Rosemary

An evergreen shrub of the parsley family growing in France, Spain, and Portugal produces rosemary. It is a curved and crescent-shaped leaf resembling a pine needle. The flavor is fresh, distinctive, and sweet. Some seeds may be over 1 in. in length.

Saffron

A crocus-like flower grown in Spain produces saffron, one of our most expensive spices. Only the 3 stigmas are used, and it takes 225,000 stigmas, 75,000 blossoms, to make a pound. It has a pleasantly bitter, mildly distinctive flavor and gives a rich, yellow or orange color to foods.

Sage

Dried leaf or ground sage comes from an herb of the mint family. Dalmatia produces most of the world's crop. It has a mild, delicate flavor, somewhat astringent and bitter. Domestic sage and others of the world lack the flavor of the Dalmatian product. It also comes rubbed or crushed.

Savory

Summer savory is the dried leaf of a mint plant coming largely from Spain and France. The leaves are small, brown-green in color, and have a distinctively warm, aromatic, slightly resinous flavor. It comes whole or ground.

Sesame

An annual grown in Nicaragua, Salvador, Egypt, and Brazil produces sesame or benne (bene) seed. Texas seed is used mostly for sesame seed oil. The seed has a rich, toasted nut flavor and is available hulled or unhulled. It is seldom ground.

Tarragon

The leaves and flowering tops of an herb grown in Europe and this country produce tarragon. It has a delicate flavor resembling anise. It is used largely whole or crushed. It seasons tarragon vinegar.

Thyme

A mint grown in France, Spain, and the United States that is a brownish-green with a distinctively warm, aromatic, and pungent flavor resembling that of sage is called *thyme*. It comes both as a leaf or is ground.

Turmeric

Turmeric is a root or rhizome of a plant related to the ginger family growing in India, Haiti, Jamaica, and Peru. The flavor is distinctive, differing from ginger in that it is mild, sweet, and highly aromatic. It is available either whole or ground. The color is a bright yellow.

FLAVORINGS

Flavorings are esters or essential oils extracted from roots, bark, fruit, sap, leaves, or other portions of a plant and dissolved in a solvent such as water or alcohol or as an emulsion in an oil. Some come in dry form. Vanilla beans may be added whole to give flavor and then be removed, or they may be added as a ground product as they are in French ice cream. Imitation flavorings are artificial and must be labeled "imitation." In the trade, "artificial" indicates flavors similar to but not quite like the natural product, whereas "imitation" is a synthetic product. Some flavorings are best natural, but others such as banana, walnut, maple, raspberry, cherry, pineapple, or strawberry are better as synthetics.

Vanilla

Pure vanilla is a bean from an orchid native to Mexico but now grown elsewhere. The bean usually contains about 2% vanilla. Madagascar gives the beans a hot water soak before drying; Mexican beans are sun dried only. A new method of curing the chopped fresh bean in a curing tank before drying produces a high-grade vanilla. South American, Java, and Tahiti vanilla usually are not as high in quality as Mexican or Madagascar vanilla. Federal standards for "single-fold" vanilla is the extract from 13.35 oz of vanilla beans plus an ounce of vanillin per gallon of extract; therefore 100 cc must contain the soluble matter of not less than 10 grams of vanilla beans. To test for flavor and aroma, add a teaspoon to 8 oz of room-temperature milk and smell and taste. Concentrates may be used in some cases in food services.

Imitation vanilla is made from vanillin, a colorless crystalline compound with a sharp, pleasant flavor and aroma similar to pure vanilla. It is obtained from wood from a coniferous tree or heavy oil of cloves. The latter, called *eugenol,* can be changed chemically into vanillin. Coumarin, once used in imitation vanilla, cannot be used.

Lemon Extract

Extracted volatile oils of lemon in alcohol is lemon extract. The pure flavor should contain not less than 5% oil of lemon and not less than 80% ethyl alcohol. Natural lemon esters contain 90% terpenes and 4 to 6% each of aldehyde and alcohol esters. Imitation extract is made from oily terpenic aldehyde. It is relatively unstable and must either be made into an emulsion or have stabilizers added to it.

Other Flavorings

Pure extracts of mint, cloves, cinnamon, tonka, spearmint, peppermint, anise, wintergreen, almond, and orange are made usually with a ratio of natural oil to solvent of 5 or 8:100. Some natural fruit flavorings are made. Imitations are usually essences rather than flavors.

Storage

Store flavorings in a cool place, but many should not be stored in a refrigerator since cold shocks flavor and may precipitate the natural essence out of the solvent. Keep flavorings away from sunlight. Purchase only a 3 months' supply.

CONDIMENTS

A condiment is "an agent used to give relish to foods and to gratify taste." A blend of spices, flavoring ingredients from cereals or other foods, vinegar, tomato, or others may make up a condiment.

Tomato catsup is a common condiment. It is the strained tomato pulp to which vinegar, sugar, and spices have been added. Chile sauce also contains tomato pulp, but seeds are allowed to pass through the pulpers. Vinegar, sugar, and spices complete the condiment. Tomato catsup and chili sauce standards are discussed under canned vegetables.

Worcestershire sauce is basically soy sauce and vinegar seasoned by items such as East India tamarinds, capiscums, cloves, garlic, onions, anchovies, black pepper, mushrooms, lemons or limes. After aging 2 months, the product is bottled and marketed. Chop suey sauce or soy sauce was made by boiling soy beans with equal quantities of roasted wheat or barley. The mash was fermented and the sauce drained off, but this product no longer can be sold in this country. The present sauces are hydrolyzed proteins from soy beans, wheat, corn, yeast, and other products.

One type of pepper sauce is the original New Orleans variety made by filling a bottle with whole red pepper or chili pods and pouring vinegar over them. Another type is tabasco or hot sauce made by concentrating an extraction from the long-podded tabasco peppers.

Mustard sauces are made by grinding ripe mustard seeds and moistening them with vinegar. Prepared mustard, largely turmeric, must be of the best quality, prepared in accordance with the finest commercial practices under strict sanitary conditions, and it should be free from preservatives and impurities. USDA inspection and grading certificates may be specified, with the product complying with Federal Specifications EE-M-821b. It comes in 24 8-oz jars per case; in gallon jars, 4 per case; or in 50-gallon barrels.

Condiments keep well, but unopened products should be used soon. Unopened tomato products may show some darkening at the end of 3½ months of storage, especially if held at somewhat elevated temperatures.

SUGARS AND SYRUPS

Sugars

Cane and beet sugar are the same thing; both are almost pure sucrose. White granulated sugar is sized from coarse to very fine. If finer than coating sugar, it is ground and "X" denotes its fineness. Coarse or sanding sugars are used to coat candied fruits and so forth. Common granulated sugar is moderately coarse. Berry (fruit or breakfast) sugar is finer and may be used in the bakeshop for products needing a sugar that goes rapidly into solution. It also is used for breakfast. Extra fine sugar is used at the bar and in the bakeshop. Coating sugar is the finest of crystallized sugars. Some bakers use a transformed sugar, which is crystal clusters that incorporate more air into the batter in creaming. XX sugar is standard powdered sugar. Four X (XXXX) is confectioner's sugar commonly used for icing. Six X also is used for this purpose. The finest sugar is 10X. Fondant icing sugar makes a smooth, creamy mixture. It is actually a dehydrated fondant. Prepared icings may be purchased in gallon jars or 6/10 cans or smaller containers. A wide variety of different sugar products are available today and buyers should ascertain what the market offers by checking with bakery supply houses.

Brown sugar's color decides its grade. This color is imparted by molasses, ash or minerals, and other impurities not found in granulated sugar. Brown sugar is about 85 to 92% pure sucrose, 4% moisture, and the remainder invert sugars. Grades run from 1 to 15; the lowest number indicates the lightest color. Trade grades also are called *light, medium,* and *dark.*

Corn sugar can be used in many food products, but the quantity is limited by federal standards of identity for products in which they are used. The ratio allowed usually is stated as a percent to sucrose. Corn sugar comes from cornstarch inverted by enzymatic action. It is sweeter than sucrose and less expensive.

Maple sugar is crystallized from the concentrated sap of maple. Maple concrete can be purchased and water added to make maple syrup.

Syrups

Molasses is graded A (Fancy), B (Choice), C (Standard), and Substandard. Food services usually use the first 2 grades only. Grade A may contain not less than 79% total solids, not less than 63½% sucrose or other sugars, and not more than 5% ash. The color should be light. Grade B should contain not less than 79% total solids, 61½% sugar, and not more than 7% ash. Color should be medium. Cloudiness, sediment, or extraneous matter lower grade. Poor molasses is excessively dark, bitter, and harsh in flavor. Taste and use to judge quality.

Grade AA (Fancy) maple syrup shall be light amber; A, medium amber; B, dark amber. The highest grades are clear and brilliant; any opaqueness lowers grade. The flavor shall be characteristic of maple for all grades and

Fig. 6-5. In the early spring of the year when the sap begins to flow in the maple, some of the flow is collected and then boiled down to make maple sugar or syrup. Courtesy USDA

shall be ''clean, free from fermentation and free from damage caused by scorching or other objectionable flavors.'' It is about 35% moisture and nearly 65% sugar. A gallon of maple syrup and other syrups should weigh 11 lb or more. Much of the typical flavor comes from ash and impurities.

Sorghum from the sorghum plant is similar to sugar cane syrup but has more of a distinctive flavor and may be slightly bitter and acid. It is high in iron which with other impurities give it its dark amber color. It is not as sweet as cane syrup. It will contain 30% moisture and about 2½% ash. It is used largely in manufacturing.

Corn syrup is called *glucose, dextrose, confectioner's glucose,* or *unmixed glucose* and is made by changing cornstarch into sugar by enzymes. It is sweeter than cane syrup. It will contain 5% ash, 30% dextrin, 35% glucose, 20% maltose, and 15% moisture. Some retail products have a higher glucose, ash, and moisture content than this.

A blend of granulated and maple sugar syrup should contain not less than 25% of the latter. Individual packs are available in 1-, 2-, and more than 2-oz packages.

Maltose usually is purchased as a syrup, although it can be a sugar. It is used in the bake shop for yeast breads. Its amber color and distinctive flavor limit the quantity that can be used. It has 20% moisture and about 65% maltose or malt sugar. The remainder is invert sugar.

Honey should be pleasantly sweet and slightly acid. The color and flavor is decided by the flowers from which the nectar is taken. Fireweed, orange, or clover honey are considered of best flavor. Honey should not be over 25% moisture, ½% ash, and 8% sucrose. Extracted honey is centrifuged from the comb. It should be free of crystallization and comb. Grades are A, B, and C. Grade B is usually satisfactory for cooking and A for table use. The flavor should be good, free from smoke, scorching, fermentation, or objectionable flavors, and reasonably free from defects. Colors may be "water white," "extra white," "white," "extra light amber," "light amber," or "dark amber." Federal grades for comb honey are U.S. Fancy, No. 1, and No. 2. Purchase it as comb section, section frame, wrapped cut-comb honey, and chunk (bulk-comb) honey. Individual portion packs of clear honey are frequently used in institutions. Clear honey is available in pint, quart, or gallon sizes.

NUTS

Specify that nuts shall come from the current year's crop, and buy only limited quantities since they can become rancid and easily infested with insects. They should be sweet and full flavored. Inspect on delivery. Purchase broken grades if they are to be chopped or broken.

Shelled almonds are graded U.S. Fancy, Extra No. 1, No. 1, Select Sheller Run, and Standard Sheller Run. Either Extra No. 1 or No. 1 is suitable for food service use. Kernels should be whole, clean, well dried, free from decay, rancidity, insect injury, foreign matter, doubles, splits, and broken kernels. "Mixed" means 1% bitter almond varieties may be included. Whole almonds with broken pieces are graded U.S. No. 1 Whole and Broken or U.S. No. 1 Pieces. Pieces should not be less than ⅛ in. in diameter. Shelled almonds also may be purchased skinned, whole, sliced, or pieces. There are no federal grades for these. Whole sizes are per ounce: 16 to 18, 18 to 20, 20 to 22, 22 to 24, 23 to 25, 24 to 26, 26 to 28, 27 to 30, 30 to 34, 36 to 40, 40 to 50, and 50 or smaller.

Shelled filberts are not graded. Quality factors applicable to other shelled nuts should be used for specifications. Check for freshness, rancidity, damage, flavor, and so forth.

Shelled, Virginia-type peanuts are graded (1969) U.S. Extra Large Virginia, Medium Virginia, No. 1 Virginia, Virginia Splits, and No. 2 Virginia.

A split is a separated half. Sheller Runner-type shelled peanuts are graded (1956) U.S. No. 1 Runner, Runner Splits, and No. 2 Runner. Watch for defects such as noted for other nuts. Sizing is ⅝ in., running about 512 per lb; ⁹/₃₂ in., 640 to the lb; ¹⁵/₆₄ in., 800 per lb. In the ⅝ in. size, not more than 10% by weight can be splits; in the others, not more than 25% by weight can be.

Peanut butter is ground, roasted peanut kernels which may or may not be emulsified or stabilized and seasoned. Grinds may be specified fine (fine, smooth texture), medium (grainy texture), and coarse or chunky (coarse texture or tiny chunks combined with fine). Colors of roast may be light or heavy. Grades (1972) are U.S. Grade A or B. Off-grade may be called C or *Standard*. Use Grade A. This grade should have a good, bright, typical color for the roast, be free of inorganic residue, fairly free from particles of brown to black seed coat, and scorched or discolored peanut tissue. The flavor and odor should be that of freshly roasted peanuts free from staleness, rancidity, or objectionable flavor or odor of any kind. Color is an important factor in evaluating quality.

Shelled pecans are graded (1969) U.S. No. 1 and Commercial for halves and pieces. Halves should be well dried, clean, free from pieces of shell and center wall, foreign material, chipped halves, broken kernels, particles and dust, noticeable shriveling, rancidity, mold, decay, and insect injury, and from damage caused by leanness, hollowness, discoloration, or other means. Commercial grade may have some chipped halves, and there is not as high a requirement for uniformity of size and color. Sizes of halves may be:

Trade Size	Number per Pound	Trade Size	Number per Pound
Mammoth	200–250	Medium	551–650
Junior Mammoth	251–300	Topper	551–750
Jumbo	301–350	Large amber*	400 or less
Extra Large	351–450		
Large	451–550	Regular amber*	more than 400

*Used only for Commercial Grade.

Pecan pieces have the same quality factors as halves except there are no restrictions on the proportion of broken halves that may be included. Piece size shall not be less than ⅛ in. in diameter.

Grades (1959) for shelled English walnuts are U.S. No. 1 and Commercial. No. 1 kernels shall be well dried, clean, free from shell, foreign matter, insect injury, decay, rancidity, and damage caused by shriveling, mold,

Fig. 6-6. English walnuts about to fall. Courtesy USDA

discoloration of the meat, or other means. Specify colors as extra light, light, light amber, or amber. Allow only 15% ¾, ½ kernels, or pieces.

Prepared coconut should be sweet and fresh. It is the shredded sweetened product of the coconut tree. Stabilizers and hydroscopic agents may be added, such as sorbitol and propylene glycol. Shreds come in long, medium, and short form. An extremely short shred, called *grated,* is used for dipping. Do not purchase more than a 1 or 2 month supply since it dries out easily.

CHOCOLATE PRODUCTS

Chocolate (bitter chocolate, cooking chocolate, chocolate coating, baking chocolate, or bitter chocolate coating) must contain 50 to 58% cacao fat and optional ingredients such as ground spices, vanilla, butter, milk fat, and malt cereal, but food services usually use plain chocolate with perhaps ½% by weight of an emulsifier such as lecithin or mono or diglyceride. Sweet

Fig. 6-7. A cocoa pod full of seeds from which chocolate and cocoa are taken. Courtesy USDA

chocolate is the solid or semiplastic food prepared from finely ground chocolate liquor, with or without the addition of cacao fat, sweetened by an approved sweetening agent. It can contain optional ingredients and must contain 15% by weight of chocolate liquor or more. If semisweet (bittersweet) the content must not be less than 35%. Milk chocolate must contain not less than $3^2/_3\%$ by weight of milk fat, not less than 12% milk solids, and not less than 10% by weight of chocolate liquor. It is sweet. Skim milk chocolate is similar except that it contains less than $3^2/_3\%$ milk fat and over 12% milk solids. Buttermitk chocolate is usually sweetened. It has the same milk fat and milk solid content requirement as skim milk chocolate.

VINEGAR

Vinegar is a dilute solution of acetic acid, the flavor coming from the products from which it is made. Apple vinegar must come from fermented apple juice or cider. Vinegar also can be made by fermenting wood chips. Specify strength by grain or percent acid. Regular pickling or table vinegar is 50 grain and contains 5% acetic acid. Purchase in gallons, 4 gallons to the case, or in barrels. White and amber vinegars are available. Color does not affect quality. Keep on hand only about a month's supply.

YEAST

Compressed yeast is usually purchased in pound bricks and stored in a refrigerated area. It molds and deteriorates if held too long. It should be creamy white or light tan, with a slight grayness evident. The product should be moist, not slimy, and should crumble easily. The odor should be that of fresh yeast. Stale or old yeast becomes slimy, brown in color, and has a strong flavor. Compressed yeast may be frozen, but it loses strength slowly in frozen storage. Thaw under refrigerated conditions. Dry, active yeast is as efficient as fresh, compressed yeast and is much more stable. Cans should be dated to indicate time of processing. It requires only ordinary storage.

BIBLIOGRAPHY

American Spice Trade Association, *Spices, What They Are and Where They Come From,* New York, 1956.

U.S. Standards for Comb and Extract Honey, April 1951; for Maple Syrup, February 1940; for Olives and Pickles, dated variously; for Nuts and Peanut Butter, dated variously; for Refiners and Sugar Cane Syrup, January 1952 and April 1951.

7
Poultry and Eggs

POULTRY

Considerable change has occurred in the growing and marketing of poultry, its acceptance in the market, and the various poultry products offered in the past 15 years. Poultry production is now a big business, no longer coming from barnyards; growing is·done in huge production centers where tremendous quantities are produced throughout the year. The breeding, care, feeding, and other production factors have become much more scientific and controlled. The time required to bring birds up to market weight has been considerably reduced and market controls on quality, wholesomeness, and product definition have vastly improved.

Compared with other high protein meats, poultry is relatively inexpensive. Poultry prices are usually stable throughout the year, which allows food services to establish good plans for its use. Of the total slaughter, 9% of the broilers, 18% of the mature chickens, 95% of the ducks, and 78% of the turkeys are marketed frozen. Fresh or chilled chicken or turkey broilers are available the year round. Turkey production retains a seasonality, with most turkeys being marketed in the August-November period.

Poultry consumption has increased rapidly. From 1962 to 1972 broiler-fryers went from 25.7 lb to 38.8 lb per capita consumption a year, a 51% increase, and turkeys rose from 7.0 to 9.1 lb (30%) during that same time. Production of broilers from 1962 to 1972 increased 66%, from 6907 million to 11,478 million pounds. A part of this increase is the result of the increasing variety of poultry products available, their ease of use, and also the relatively stable supply and price.

Because the market has changed so rapidly, buyers today must know much more than they used to about how to select the right products for their production need, especially in purchasing cooked, prepared items that are in an almost ready-to-serve state.

Fig. 7-1. Young broiler chickens are being produced in 10,000 lots on this North Carolina poultry raising farm. Their production is highly scientific and controlled to produce quality birds in the shortest possible time. Courtesy USDA

Purchase Factors

Institutions purchase raw poultry as ready-to-cook carcasses or parts. Some poultry is purchased that must meet religious dietary laws, and this will be in a form different from usual marketed products, the differences being recognized in federal and trade standards.

Poultry marketed in this country must conform to the regulations of the U.S. Department of Agriculture and the Food and Drug Administration. If a state has statutes that are equal to or better than the federal provisions, they apply, but, if not, the federal provisions must apply. In most states, inspection is a joint responsibility of the state and federal government.

Inspection

Poultry is inspected for wholesomeness before and after slaughter. Post mortem inspection is made on an individual basis and, until the bird and all its parts are inspected, they are not separated. A part may be condemned and separated from the carcass if the remainder is fit for human consumption. Birds may be held for further inspection, condemned, or passed. Condemned products must be destroyed for human food purposes. Approved products bear the "Inspected for Wholesomeness" legend of the

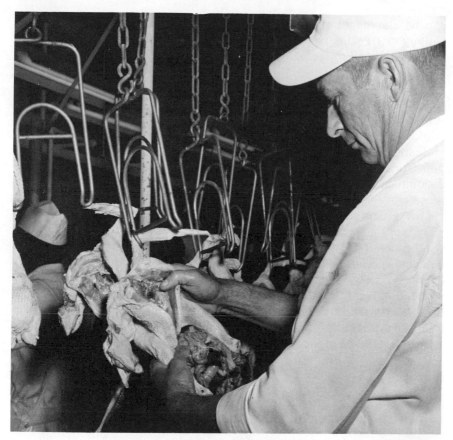

Fig. 7-2. A USDA inspector examines the interior of a bird to see if it meets standards of wholesomeness and can be stamped with the circle stamp "Inspected and Passed for Wholesomeness." Courtesy USDA

USDA, which also may include a number that identifies the establishment where the product was produced. Certificates of inspection are issued upon request.

Slaughter and Processing

After killing, poultry is bled, then scalded and defeathered. Defeathering is usually done by machine. The bird then is eviscerated and inspected for wholesomeness. Unless it is to be frozen or cooked, it must be chilled immediately to an internal temperature of 40°F, with subsequent storage at 36°F if kept in the plant over 24 hours. Chilling and freezing descriptions can be eliminated in specifications by stating that "all procedures for chilling or freezing of poultry shall conform to paragraph 381.66 of the *USDA Poultry Products Inspection Regulations.*"

Grading

Various grades exist for poultry. Some institutional buyers will use consumer grades which are U.S. Grades A, B, and C. Factors establishing the grade are (1) conformation, (2) fleshing, (3) fat coverage, (4) freedom from pinfeathers and vestigial feathers (hair and down), and (5) degree of freedom from defects such as tears, cuts, bruises, blemishes, freezer burn, and disjointed or broken bones. Table 7-1 summarizes the quality factors for these grades.

U.S. Procurement grades are used by very large buyers. U.S. Procurement No. I must be 90% or more U.S. Grade A except (1) fat covering and conformation may be of B quality, (2) trimming of skin and flesh to remove defects is permitted to the extent that not more than a third of the flesh is exposed on any part and the meat yield of any part is not appreciably affected, (3) discoloration of the skin and flesh may be for B quality birds, (4) one or both drumsticks may be removed if the part is severed at the joint, (5) the back may be trimmed in an area not wider than the base of the tail and extending to the area between the hip joints, (6) the wings or parts

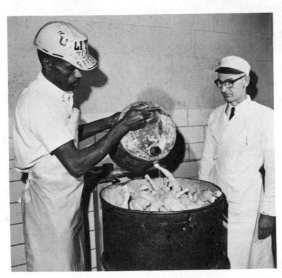

Fig. 7-3. Condemned chickens must be destroyed for use as human food. This photo shows denaturing of the carcasses of condemned birds. Courtesy USDA

of wings may be removed if severed at the joint, and (b) the balance of the carcasses meet the same requirements except they may have only moderate covering of flesh. U.S. Procurement No. II birds may have less flesh covering and more major defects. For instance, the trim of the flesh must not exceed 10% of the meat, and portions of a carcass weighing not less than 50% of a whole carcass may be included.

Buyers also may occasionally find local markets using commercial or trade grades such as *Extra* (90% or more are U.S. Grade A and the remainder B), *Standard* (90% or more are U.S. Grade B and the remainder C), and *No Grade* which may be market run birds that are usually of low quality but wholesome.

Processed Poultry Standards

Ready-to-cook rolls, roasts, bars, or logs called *poultry roasts* to be U.S. Grade A must come from raw, deboned U.S. Grade A young poultry after all tendons, cartilage, large blood vessels, blood clots, and discolorations are trimmed away, and pinfeathers, bruises, hair, and excess fat are removed. The outer surface should have 75% or more covered with skin either attached to the meat or used as a wrap. The skin should not be over 15% of the total net weight. The wrap of the skin and fat should not overlap. The product must appear neat, attractive, and be practically free from seepage. Fabrication should be such that the item does not break into more than 3 pieces when sliced warm after cooking. Seasonings or flavor enhancers should be uniformly distributed.

Grade A boneless poultry breasts and thighs should meet the U.S. Grade A quality requirements as specified for ready-to-cook parts. The bone or bones should be removed in a neat manner without undue mutilation of the flesh. When the grade is specified, many factors are also. For instance, when U.S. Grade A is specified, the skin and fat cannot exceed natural proportions in a product, and all cartilage and so forth as indicated for poultry roasts must be largely removed.

Kinds and Classes

Specifications should identify poultry by class and kind. Kinds of poultry are chickens, turkeys, ducks, geese, guineas, and pigeons. Rock Cornish game hens are a class of chicken. Pea-fowl, swans, quail, wild ducks or geese, pheasants, chukkars, snipes, and others are classed as game birds. A class is a division within a kind and reflects physical characteristics as influenced largely by age and sex. (See Table 7-2).

Styles

The state in which the poultry is to be delivered needs definition in a

TABLE 7-1

Summary of Specifications for Standards of Quality for Individual Carcasses of Ready-To-Cook Poultry and Parts Therefrom
(Minimum Requirements and Maximum Defects Permitted)

September 1, 1965

Factor	A Quality	B Quality	C Quality
CONFORMATION:	Normal	Moderate deformities	Abnormal
Breastbone	Slight curve or dent	Moderately dented, curved or crooked	Seriously curved or crooked
Back	Normal (except slight curve)	Moderately crooked	Seriously crooked
Legs and Wings	Normal	Moderately misshapen	Misshapen
FLESHING:	Well fleshed, moderately long, deep and rounded breast	Moderately fleshed, considering kind, class and part	Poorly fleshed
FAT COVERING:	Well covered—especially between heavy feather tracts on breast and considering kind, class and part	Sufficient fat on breast and legs to prevent distinct appearance of flesh through the skin	Lacking in fat covering over all parts of carcass
PINFEATHERS:			
Nonprotruding pins and hair	Free	Few scattered	Scattering
Protruding pins	Free	Free	Free
EXPOSED FLESH:[1]			
Carcass Weight	*Breast and Legs[2]* *Elsewhere[2]* *Part*	*Breast and Legs[2]* *Elsewhere[2]* *Part*	

Minimum	Maximum	A Quality — Breast and legs	A Quality — Elsewhere	B Quality — Breast and legs	B Quality — Elsewhere	C Quality
None	1½ lbs.	None	None *(Slight trim on edge)*	¾"	1½"	*(Moderate amount of the flesh normally covered)* No Limit
Over 1½ lbs.	6 lbs.	None	None	1½"	3"	
Over 6 lbs.	16 lbs.	None	None	2"	4"	
Over 16 lbs.	None	None	None	3"	5"	
DISCOLORATIONS:[3]						
None	1½ lbs.	½"	¼"	1"	2"	½" — No Limit[4]
Over 1½ lbs.	6 lbs.	1"	¼"	2"	3"	1" — Limit[4]
Over 6 lbs.	16 lbs.	1½"	½"	2½"	4"	1½"
Over 16 lbs.	None	2"	½"	3"	5"	1½"

Factor	A Quality	B Quality	C Quality
Disjointed bones	1	2 disjointed and no broken or	No limit
Broken bones	None	1 disjointed and 1 non-protruding broken	No limit
Missing parts	Wing tips and tail[5]	Wing tips, 2nd wing joint and tail	Wing tips, wings and tail
FREEZING DEFECTS: (When consumer packaged)	Slight darkening over the back and drumsticks. Few small ⅛" pockmarks for poultry weighing 6 lbs. or less and ¼" pockmarks for poultry weighing more than 6 lbs. Occasional small areas showing layer of clear or pinkish ice.	Moderate dried areas not in excess of ½" in diameter. May lack brightness. Moderate areas showing layer of clear, pinkish or reddish colored ice.	Numerous pockmarks and large dried areas.

[1]Total aggregate area of flesh exposed by all cuts and tears and missing skin.

[2]A carcass meeting the requirements of A quality for fleshing may be trimmed to remove skin and flesh defects, provided that no more than one-third of the flesh is exposed on any part and the meat yield is not appreciably affected.

[3]Flesh bruises and discoloration such as "blue back" are not permitted on breast and legs of A quality birds. Not more than one-half of total aggregate area of discolorations may be due to flesh bruises or "blue back" (when permitted), and skin bruises in any combination.

[4]No limit on size and number of areas of discoloration and flesh bruises if such areas do not render any part of the carcass unfit for food.

[5]In geese, the parts of the wing beyond the second joint may be removed, if removed at the joint and both wings are so treated.

From USDA Poultry Grading Manual, Agr. Handbook No. 31.

TABLE 7-2
Classes of Poultry*

Chickens

Rock Cornish game hen or Cornish game hen
 A Rock Cornish game hen or Cornish game hen is a young immature chicken (usually 5 to 7 weeks of age) weighing not more than 2 pounds ready-to-cook weight, which was prepared from a Cornish chicken or the progeny of a Cornish chicken crossed with another breed of chicken.

Broiler or fryer
 A broiler or fryer is a young chicken (usually 9 to 12 weeks of age), of either sex, that is tender-meated with soft, pliable, smooth-textured skin and flexible breastbone cartilage.

Roaster
 A roaster is a young chicken (usually 3 to 5 months of age), of either sex, that is tender-meated with soft, pliable, smooth-textured skin and breastbone cartilage that may be somewhat less flexible than that of a broiler or fryer.

Capon
 A capon is a surgically unsexed male chicken (usually under 8 months of age) that is tender-meated with soft, pliable, smooth-textured skin.

Stag
 A stag is a male chicken (usually under 10 months of age) with coarse skin, somewhat toughened and darkened flesh, and considerable hardening of the breastbone cartilage. Stags show a condition of fleshing and a degree of maturity intermediate between that of a roaster and a cock or old rooster.

Hen or stewing chicken or fowl
 A hen or stewing chicken or fowl is a mature female chicken (usually more than 10 months old) with meat less tender than that of a roaster, and nonflexible breastbone tip.

Cock or old rooster
 A cock or old rooster is a male chicken with coarse skin, toughened and darkened meat, and hardened breastbone.

Turkeys

Fryer-roaster turkey
 A fryer-roaster turkey is a young immature turkey (usually under 16 weeks of age), of either sex, that is tender-meated with soft, pliable, smooth-textured skin, and flexible breastbone cartilage.

Young hen turkey
 A young hen turkey is a young female turkey (usually 5 to 7 months of age) that is tender-meated with soft, pliable, smooth-textured skin, and breastbone cartilage that is somewhat less flexible than in a fryer-roaster turkey.

Young tom turkey
 A young tom turkey is a young male turkey (usually 5 to 7 months of age) that is tender-meated with soft, pliable, smooth-textured skin, and breastbone cartilage that is somewhat less flexible than in a fryer-roaster turkey.

Yearling hen turkey
> A yearling hen turkey is a fully matured female turkey (usually under 15 months of age) that is reasonably tender-meated and with reasonably smooth-textured skin.

Yearling tom turkey
> A yearling tom turkey is a fully matured male turkey (usually under 15 months of age) that is reasonably tender-meated and with reasonably smooth-textured skin.

Mature turkey or old turkey (hen or tom)
> A mature or old turkey is an old turkey of either sex (usually in excess of 15 months of age) with coarse skin and toughened flesh.

> For labeling purposes, the designation of sex within the class name is optional and the three classes of young turkeys may be grouped and designated as "young turkeys."

Ducks

Broiler duckling or fryer duckling
> A broiler duckling or fryer duckling is a young duck (usually under 8 weeks of age), of either sex, that is tender-meated and has a soft bill and soft windpipe.

Roaster duckling
> A roaster duckling is a young duck (usually under 16 weeks of age), of either sex, that is tender-meated and has a bill that is not completely hardened and a windpipe that is easily dented.

Mature duck or old duck
> A mature duck or an old duck is a duck (usually over 6 months of age), of either sex, with toughened flesh, hardened bill, and hardened windpipe.

Geese

Young goose
> A young goose may be of either sex, is tender-meated, and has a windpipe that is easily dented.

Mature goose or old goose
> A mature goose or old goose may be of either sex and has toughened flesh and hardened windpipe.

Guineas

Young guinea
> A young guinea may be of either sex and is tender-meated and has a flexible breastbone cartilage.

Mature guinea or old guinea
> A mature guinea or an old guinea may be of either sex and has toughened flesh and a hardened breastbone.

Pigeons

Squab
> A squab is a young, immature pigeon of either sex, and is extra tender-meated.

Pigeon
> A pigeon is a mature pigeon of either sex, with coarse skin and toughened flesh.

---

*Table prepared from USDA's "Regulations Governing the Grading and Inspection of Poultry,"
July 1, 1971.

Fig. 7-4. Official USDA stamps for ready-to-cook poultry. All poultry bearing federal grades must be inspected for wholesomeness. Grade stamps and inspection stamps may be on the individual bird or on packaging. Federal-state grading means that the program is jointly administered by both. Note tags may be on wings, on the wrapper, and so forth. Courtesy USDA

specification. Whole, ready-to-cook style means the carcass exterior is singed and pinfeathers and vestigial feathers are removed. The head, shanks at the hock joint, crop, windpipe, esophagus, entrails, gall bladder, lungs, and mature sex organs and immature testicals plus the oil gland must be removed. The giblets, consisting of the heart, liver, and gizzard, are adequately cleaned, drained, and wrapped in nonabsorbent paper and may be placed in the body cavity along with neck or may be bulk packed.

Parts must be from ready-to-cook birds proportional to the carcass or as selected parts. Parts for chicken are defined by the USDA as follows, but processors may cut them differently as long as the labeling appropriately reflects the contents of the container of such poultry:

(1) ''Breasts'' shall be separated from the back at the shoulder joint and by a cut running backward and downward from that point along the junction of the vertebral and sternal ribs. The ribs may be removed from the breasts, and the breasts may be cut along the breast-bone to make two approximately equal halves; or the wishbone portion, as described in subparagraph (3) of this paragraph, may be removed before cutting the

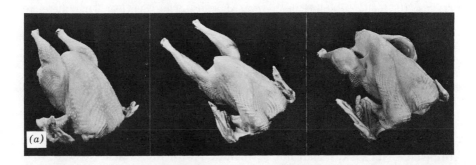

Fig. 7-5a. Young hen turkey carcasses: (left to right) A Quality, B Quality, and C Quality—the C Quality carcass shows better conformation than the B Quality bird but because of the excessive tears on the leg, it has been graded down.
Fig. 7-5b. Young tom turkey carcasses: (left to right) A Quality, B Quality, and C Quality. Courtesy USDA

Fig. 7-6. This high-grade bird is graded down because of the slight tear. It may therefore be put into U.S. Procurement Grade I. Courtesy USDA

remainder along the breastbone to make three parts. Pieces cut in this manner may be substituted for lighter or heavier pieces for exact weight-making purposes and the package may contain two or more of such parts without affecting the appropriateness of the labeling as e.g., "chicken breasts." Neck skin shall not be included with the breasts, except that "turkey breasts" may include neck skin up to the whisker.

(2) "Breasts with ribs" shall be separated from the back at the junction of the vertebral ribs and back. Breasts with ribs may be cut along the breastbone to make two approximately equal halves; or the wishbone portion may be removed before cutting the remainder along the breastbone to make three parts. Pieces cut in this manner may be substituted for lighter or heavier pieces for exact weight-making purposes and the package may contain two or more of such parts without affecting the appropriateness of the labeling as "breasts with ribs." Neck skin shall not be included, except that "turkey breasts with ribs" may include neck skin up to the whisker.

(3) "Wishbones" (Pulley Bones), with covering muscle and skin tissue, shall be severed from the breast approximately halfway between the end of

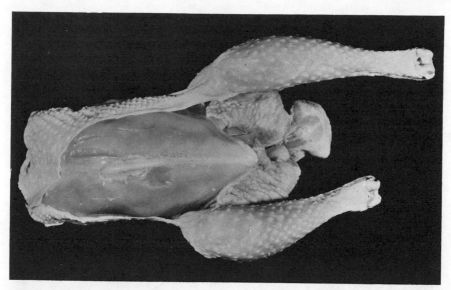

Fig. 7-7. This bird meets the requirements for U.S. Procurement Grade II, which has a lower yield of meat than Procurement Grade I. Note skin tears can be major and wings are missing. Procurement grades are used by quantity buyers such as schools, hospitals, restaurants, and others who are primarily concerned with meat yield for use in casseroles, and so forth. Courtesy USDA

the wishbone (hypocledium) and front point of the breastbone (cranial process of the sternal crest) to a point where the wishbone joins the shoulder. Neck skin shall not be included with the wishbone.

(4) "Drumsticks" shall be separated from the thigh by a cut through the knee joint and the hock joint (tarsal joint).

(5) "Thighs" shall be disjointed at the hip joint and may include the pelvic meat, but shall not include the pelvic bones. Back skin shall not be included.

(6) "(Kind) legs" shall be the poultry product which includes the thigh and the drumstick, i.e., the whole leg, and may include the pelvic meat, but shall not include the pelvic bones. Back skin shall not be included.

(7) "Wings" shall include the entire wing with all muscle and skin tissue intact, except that the wingtip may be removed.

(8) "Backs" shall include the pelvic bones and all the vertebrae posterior to the shoulder joint. The meat shall not be peeled from the pelvic bones. The vertebral ribs and/or scapula may be removed or included without affecting the appropriateness of the name. Skin shall be substantially intact.

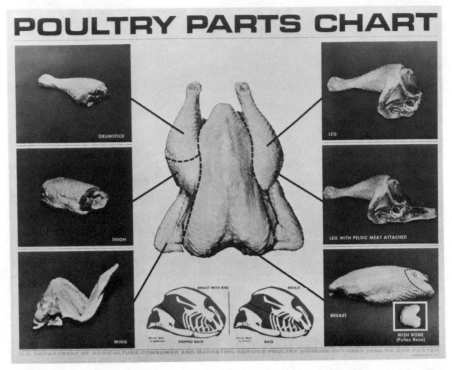

Fig. 7-8. The major parts of a chicken are shown here. Note in the bottom center that the dotted line shows the difference between a breast with ribs and a breast without ribs. Courtesy USDA

(9) "Stripped backs" shall include the vertebrae from the shoulder joint to the tail, and include the pelvic bones. The meat may be stripped off of the pelvic bones.

(10) "Necks," with or without neck skin, shall be separated from the carcass at the shoulder joint.

(11) "Halves" are prepared by making a full-length back and breast split of an eviscerated poultry carcass so as to produce approximately equal right and left sides. Specify removal of the breastbone.

(12) "Quarters" consist of the entire eviscerated poultry carcass, which has been cut into four equal parts, but excluding the neck.

(13) "Breast quarter" consists of half a breast with the wing and a portion of the back attached.

(14) "Breast quarter without wing" consists of a front quarter of a poultry carcass, from which the wing has been removed.

(15) "Leg quarter" consists of a poultry thigh and drumstick, with a portion of the back attached.

(16) "Thigh with back portion" consists of a poultry thigh with back portion attached.

(17) "Legs with pelvic bone" consists of a poultry leg with adhering meat and skin and pelvic bone.

(18) "Wing drummette" consists of the humerus of a poultry wing with adhering skin and meat attached.

(19) "Wing portion" consists of a poultry wing except that the drummette has been removed.

(20) "Cut-up Poultry" is any cut-up or disjointed portion of poultry or any edible part thereof, as described in this section.

(21) "Giblets" consist of approximately equal numbers of hearts, gizzards, and livers, as determined on a count basis.

Many facilities today purchase poultry products processed beyond the ready-to-cook or parts stage. Most of these need only be heated thoroughly to be ready for service. Buyers frequently will find that specifications and standards for these are lacking, and they may have to establish their own. The federal government has established some purchase standards for these, and buyers may find these helpful in developing specifications, although often the government minimum for quantity of meat is not adequate to meet the needs of the institution so that this may have to be increased.

Federal regulations require that if a label uses the following terms the ratio of light and dark meat must be as follows unless the product contains less than 10% deboned meat or is processed so light and dark meat cannot be identified:

Label Terminology	% Light	% Dark	Lable Terminology	%Light	%Dark
Natural proportions	50 to 65	50 to 35	Dark and light meat	35 to 49	65 to 51
Light or white meat	100	0	Mostly white meat	66 up	35 or less
Dark meat	0	100	Mostly dark meat	34 or less	66 up
Light and dark meat	51 to 65	49 to 35			

Furthermore, natural proportions of skin for chicken shall be 20% raw and 25% cooked and for turkey 15% raw and 20% cooked. The term "chicken meat" means boned white and dark meat; "chicken" means other edible

TABLE 7-3

Class of Substance	Substance	Purpose	Products	Amount
Antifoaming agent	Methyl polysilicone	To retard foaming	Soups	10 ppm.
			Rendered fats	10 ppm.
			Curing pickle	50 ppm.
Antioxidants and oxygen interceptors.	BHA (Butylated hydroxyanisole)	To retard rancidity	Various	0.01 percent based on fat content. (0.02 percent in combination with any other antioxidant listed in this table based on fat content.)
	BHT (Butylated hydroxytoluene)	do	do	Do.
	Propyl gallate	do	do	Do.
	Tocopherols	do	do	0.03 percent based on fat content. (0.02 percent in combination with any other antioxidant listed in this Table based on fat content.)
Binders and extenders	Algin	To extend and stabilize product.	do	Sufficient for purpose.
	Carrageenan	do	do	Do.
	Carboxymethyl cellulose (cellulose gum).	do	do	Do.
	Gums, vegetable	do	do	Do.
	Methyl cellulose	To extend and to stabilize product (also carrier).	do	0.15 percent.
	Isolated soy protein	To bind and extend product.	do	Sufficient for purpose.
	Sodium caseinate	do	do	Do.
	Whey (dried)	do	do	Do.
Chilling media	Salt (NaCl)	To aid in chilling	Raw poultry products	700 lbs. to 10,000 gals. of water.*
Coloring agents (natural)	Annatto, Carotene	To color products	Various	Sufficient for purpose.
Coloring agents (artificial)	Coal tar dyes (FD&C certified), Titanium dioxide.	To color products to whiten products.	Salads and spreads	0.5 percent.

			Various	
Cooling and retort water treatment agents.	Calcium chloride	To prevent staining on exterior of canned goods.	do	Sufficient for purpose.
	Citric acid	do	do	Do.
	Dioctyl sodium sulfosuccinate	do	do	0.05 percent.
	Disodium-calcium ethylene-diamine-tetra-acetate.	do	do	Sufficient for purpose.
	Disodium ethylenediamine-tetraacetate.	do	do	Do.
	Disodium phosphate	do	do	Do.
	Ethylenediamine-tetraacetic acid	do	do	Do.
Cooling and retort water treatment agents—Con.	Isopropanol	do	do	0.002 percent.
	Potassium pyrophosphate	do	do	Sufficient for purpose.
	Propylene glycol	do	do	Do.
	Sodium bicarbonate	do	do	Do.
	Sodium carbonate	do	do	Do.
	Sodium dodecylbenzene sulfonate	do	do	0.05 percent.
	Sodium gluconate	do	do	Sufficient for purpose.
	Sodium hexameta-phosphate	do	do	Do.
	Sodium laurylsulfate	do	do	0.05 percent.
	Sodium metasilicate	do	do	Sufficient for purpose.
	Sodium n-alkylbenzene sulfonate (alkyl group predominantly C and C and not less than 95 percent C to C).	do	do	0.05 percent.
	Sodium nitrite (The sodium nitrite must be decharacterized with 0.05 percent powdered charcoal. Bulk decharacterized sodium	To inhibit corrosion on exterior of canned goods.	do	600 parts per million.

TABLE 7-3 (cont'd)

Class of Substance	Substance	Purpose	Products	Amount
	nitrite when in cook room shall be held in locked metal bin or container conspicuously labeled "Decharacterized sodium nitrite—To be used by authorized personnel only.").			
	Sodium pyrophosphate	To prevent staining on canned goods.	do	0.05 percent.
	Sodium tripolyphosphate	do	do	Do.
	Zinc oxide	do	do	0.01 percent.
	Zinc sulfate	do	do	Do.
Curing agents	Ascorbic acid	To accelerate color fixing and to preserve color in storage.	Various	75 ozs. to 100 gals. pickle at 10% pump level; ¾ oz. to 100 lbs. of poultry product; 10% solution to surfaces of the product prior to packaging (the use of such solution shall not result in the addition of a significant amount of moisture to the product).
	Erythorbic acid	do	do	Do.
	Sodium ascorbate	do	do	87.5 ozs. to 100 gals. pickle at 10% pump level; ⅞ oz. to 100 lbs. of poultry product; 10% solution to surfaces of the product prior to packaging (the use of such solution shall not result in the addition of a significant amount of moisture to the product).
	Sodium erythorbate	do	do	Do.

Additive	Function	Products	Amount
Citric acid or sodium citrate	Accelerate color fixing	Cured products	May be used in cured products to replace up to 50% of the ascorbic acid or sodium ascorbate that is used.
Sodium or potassium nitrate	Source of nitrite	do	7 lbs. to 100 gals. pickle; 3½ ozs. to 100 lbs. of poultry product (dry cure); 2¾ ozs. to 100 lbs. of chopped poultry meat.
Sodium or potassium nitrite (supplies of sodium nitrite and potassium nitrite and mixtures containing them must be kept securely under the care of a responsible employee of the establishment. The specific nitrite content of such supplies must be known and clearly marked accordingly).	To fix color	do	2 lbs. to 100 gals. pickle at 10% pump level; 1 oz. to 100 lbs. of poultry product (dry cure); ¼ oz. 100 lbs. chopped poultry meat. The use of nitrites, nitrates, or combination shall not result in more than 200 p.p.m. sodium nitrite in finished product.
Emulsifying agents			
Acetylated monoglycerides	To emulsify product	Various	Sufficient for purpose.
Diacetyl tartaric acid esters of mono- and diglycerides	do	Rendered poultry fat or a combination of such fat with vegetable fat.	Do.
Glycerol-lacto stearate, oleate or palmitate.	do	do	Do.
Lecithin	To emulsify product (also as antioxidant).	Various	Do.
Mono- and diglycerides (glycerol palmitate, etc.).	To emulsify product	do	Do.
Polysorbate 80 (polyoxyethylene (20) sorbitan monooleate).	do	do	1 percent when used alone. If used with polysorbate 60, the combined total shall not exceed 1 percent.

TABLE 7-3 (cont'd)

Class of Substance	Substance	Purpose	Products	Amount
	Propylene glycol mono- and diesters of fats and fatty acids.	do	Rendered poultry fat or a combination of such fat with vegetable fat.	Sufficient for purpose.
	Polysorbate 60 (polyoxyethylene (20) sorbitan monostearate).	do	do	1 percent when used alone. If used with polysorbate 80, the combined total shall not exceed 1 percent.
Flavoring agents; protectors and developers.	Approved artificial smoke flavorings.†	To flavor product	Various	Sufficient for purpose.
	Approved smoke flavoring[2]	do	do	Do.
	Autolyzed yeast extract	do	do	Do.
	Citric acid	To protect flavor	do	Do.
	Corn syrup solids	To flavor product	do	Do.
	Disodium inosinate	do	do	Do.
	Disodium guanylate	do	do	Do.
	Hydrolyzed plant protein	do	do	Do.
	Malt syrup	do	do	Do.
	Milk protein hydrolysate	do	do	Do.
	Monosodium glutamate	do	do	Do.
	Sodium sulfoacetate derivative of mono and di-glycerides.	do	do	0.5 percent.
	Sugars approved (sucrose and dextrose).	do	do	Sufficient for purpose.
Gases	Carbon dioxide solid (dry ice)	To cool product or facilitate chopping or packaging.	Various	Do.
	Carbon dioxide liquid	Contact freezing	do	Do.
	Nitrogen	To exclude oxygen from sealed containers.	do	Do.
	Nitrogen liquid	Contact freezing	do	Do.

Class	Substance	Purpose	Products	Amount
Miscellaneous	Sodium bicarbonate	To neutralize excess acidity; cleaning vegetables.	Rendered fat, soups, curing pickle.	Do.
	Calcium propionate	To retard mold growth	Fresh pie dough	0.3 percent of calcium propionate or sodium propionate alone, or in combination, based on weight of the flour used.
Phosphates	Sodium propionate	do	do	Do.
	Disodium phosphate	To decrease the amount of cooked out juices and protect flavor.	Various	0.5 percent in product.
	Monosodium phosphate	do	do	Do.
	Sodium hexametaphosphate	do	do	Do.
	Sodium tripolyphosphate	do	do	Do.
	Sodium pyrophosphate	do	do	Do.
	Sodium acid pyrophosphate	do	do	Do.
Synergists (used in combination with antioxidants).	Citric acid	To increase effectiveness of antioxidants.	Poultry fats	0.01 percent alone or in combination with antioxidants in poultry fats.
	Malic acid	do	do	Do.
	Monoisopropyl citrate	do	do	0.01 percent poultry fats.
	Phosphoric acid	do	do	0.0 percent.
	Monoglyceride citrate	do	do	0.02 percent.

*Special labeling requirements are prescribed in 381.120 for raw poultry products chilled in a medium with more than 70 lbs. of salt to 10,000 gals. of water.
†These are proprietary products, and a list thereof can be obtained from the Laboratory Serivces Division, Animal and Plant Health Inspection Service, U.S. Department of Agriculture, Washington, D.C. 20250.
Courtesy USDA.

parts such as skin and fat in natural proportions plus the meat. If skin, giblets, or fat are in a product and the label states that the product is "chicken meat," the label must list each ingredient. The same rules apply to the labeling of other poultry. A list of substances that can be added to poultry products is given in Table 7-3. Any substances injected into poultry to increase flavor, tenderness, and so forth, or in which poultry is marinated, may not increase the weight as a prepared product more than 3%. Substances must be FDA approved and noted on the label, such as "injected for flavored basting." Table 7-4 indicates some other federal requirements for poultry products. Liquids may be broth or extractives or others.

Boneless turkey breasts and breast rolls cannot have more than 14% skin on a raw basis; boneless turkey thighs or thigh rolls cannot have more than 8%. Boneless turkey or turkey rolls cannot have more than 15%. Boneless chicken breast or chicken breast rolls cannot have more than 18% on a raw basis or 20% on a cooked basis, and boneless chicken or chicken rolls cannot have more than 20% on a raw basis or 25% on a cooked basis.

Specifications for processed poultry products should be varied to meet the individual food service's needs. Raw parts or other products must be specified for size. Assorted chicken portions come from 1 to 5 oz; raw chicken or other poultry parts, 2 to 3 per lb; frozen turkey chunks and pieces or ground turkey rolls 10 lb each unless specified differently; frozen deboned turkey either in parts or whole will vary; turkey rolls are usually around 10 lb each; turkey wings, 2 joint, in bulk pack or turkey drumsticks usually run from 16 to 20 oz each. Specify also type of packing, type of wrap, and so forth.

Cooked products will be of a wide range such as either chicken or turkey a la king; chicken or turkey and dumplings or noodles, dumplings or noodles with chicken or turkey, turkey or chicken pie filling, chicken or turkey chop suey or chow mein, cooked poultry rolls with a ratio of white to dark meat 60/40 or all light or dark meat, hunter-style chicken, char-broiled chicken, smoked turkey, etc.

One of the problems is to set up specifications that will control the quantity of vegetables, poultry meat, gravy, sauce, and so on. Most items in sauce or gravy are marketed with from 15 to 25% cooked meat with vegetables around 15 to 25% of the product weight and gravy or sauce running 55 to 60%. The remainder will be seasonings and so forth.

Unless a specification specifically limits products most manufacturers meet the federal standards. A turkey pie or pie filling with only 14% deboned, cooked meat is often lacking in sufficient turkey to meet the individual food service's standards and thus a specification might have to state, to get a desirable product, that the pie or pie filling contain 20% meat,

8% carrots, 4% peas, and 3% onions, with the remainder sauce. If milk is an added product in this, the minimum milk solid content might be specified as being somewhere around 3½%, with minimum milkfat about 5%, or the minimum or maximum of milk fat and other fat around 7%.

To control proportions another specification might state that poultry meat in a stew must be 25% or more on a cooked, deboned basis in natural proportions and that to 100% meat, carrots should not be more or less than 30%, onions 50%, celery 10%, potatoes 60%, and peas 20%. This allows 170% vegetables to meat or 42½% vegetables of the total weight of the product. The remaining 22½% can be gravy or other specified ingredients.

Many institutions allow a 20:80 ratio of breading or batter to cooked breaded or batter-fried products, but federal standards usually allow a 30:70 ratio. To limit fillers, a specification might state "egg noodles shall not be over 50% on a cooked basis and a garnish of cooked frozen peas and pimentos and gravy 25% with 20% cooked, deboned meat are required." Many facilities allow 5% moisture on cooked rolls, roasts, and so forth. Some specifications may state that the skin in poultry mixtures be ground through a $^1/_{16}$-in. plate. Others do not allow neck meat or giblets to be in the product.

Table 7-4 summarizes some of the USDA minimum meat requirements for processed poultry products.

TABLE 7-4
Minimum Percent Cooked Deboned Meat in Some Prepared Poultry

Product Name	Minimum %	Product Name	Minimum %
(Kind)* ravioli	2	Gravy with (kind)	15
(Kind) soup	2	(Kind) Tetrazzini	15
(Kind) chop suey	2	(Kind) chili with beans	17
(Kind) chow mein with noodles	4	(Kind) cacciatore	20†
(Kind) tamales	6	Creamed (kind)	20
(Kind) with noodles	15**	(Kind) fricassee	20†
(Kind) with dumplings	15**	(Kind) a la king	20
(Kind) stew	12	(Kind) croquettes	25
(Kind) salad	25	Sliced (kind) with gravy	
(Kind) hash	30	and dressing	25
Noodles with (kind)	6**	Sliced (kind) with gravy	35
Dumplings with (kind)	6‡	(Kind) fricassee of wings	
Minced (kind) barbecue	40	with bones	40

*In place of kind add the name of the poultry.
†With bones 40%.
‡With bones 30%.
**Or rice or some other similar macaroni or starch product.

If a product contains less than 2% poultry meat it need not be inspected and passed for wholesomeness unless the buyer requires it in his specifications. Some other standards that might be seen in institutional specifications for poultry products would be the following and would vary from those given in Tables 7-4 and 7-5.

Chicken and dumplings	25% cooked, deboned chicken meat in natural proportions; 50% egg noodles or dumplings or rice on a cooked basis; liquid to be only chicken broth and milk, 5% garnish of peas and pimientos allowed.
Chicken fricassee	45% cooked, deboned chicken, 5% peas, and 50% sauce.
Frozen turkey, sliced in gravy	Turkey in natural proportions in $3/16$-in.-thick slices not smaller than 2 in. in diameter or square; at least 50% turkey.

TABLE 7-5
Definitions of Some Prepared Poultry Products

Product and Label Terms	Definition
Boned (kind)*, solid pack	Deboned seasoned meat, skin and fat in natural proportions, no gelatin, stabilizers or similar solidfying or emulsifying agents; 5% liquid may be added; 95% poultry on cooked basis.
Boned (kind)	Same as solid pack but may have 10% liquid added and be only 90% poultry meat on a cooked basis.
Boned (kind), with broth, gelatin added	Same as the above but can contain gelatin, stabilizers, or similar solidifying or emulsifying agents not in excess of a total of ½% of total ingredients, 20% liquid and 80% meat.
Bones (kind) with natural juices	Same as solid pack, but no liquid can be added during or after preparation.
Shredded (kind)	Deboned (kind), solid pack reduced to a shredded state.
Strained or chopped (kind)†	Not less than 43% cooked, deboned meat and not more than 57% liquid; meat in natural proportions.
High meat dinner†	Not less than 18¾% cooked deboned meat.
(Kind) roll	Binding agents not in excess of 3% for cooked rolls and 2% for raw.

TABLE 7-5 (cont'd)
Definitions of Some Prepared Poultry Products

Product and Label Terms	Definition
(Kind) roll, binder or gelatin added	Binding agents can be in excess of 3 or 2%.
(Kind) roll with broth	Liquid is in excess of 2% but is not in excess of the amount normally cooked out during preparation.
(Kind) roll with natural juices	Liquid is in excess of 2% but no liquid other than natural juices exuding from the product in normal cooking included.
(Kind) roll, with broth	Liquid added in cooking but not greater in the product than that would result in normal cooking; is in excess of 2%.
Burgers or patties	100% poultry with skin and fat in natural proportions; if the product contains binders, the word "patties" must be used.
A la Kiev	Meat stuffed with butter, seasoned and wrapped in sufficient skin to cover the product. It may be dipped into batter of breaded, fried, and frozen.
Steak or fillet	Boneless slice or strip of poultry.
Baked or roasted	Ready-to-cook poultry dry heat cooked.
Barbecued	Ready-to-cook poultry dry heat cooked while being basted with a barbecue or other seasoned sauce.
Barbecued, moist heat cooked	Ready-to-cook poultry cooked in moist heat with a barbecue sauce.
Breaded	Coated with a batter or breading not in excess of 30% of the total product weight.
(Kind) pies	Deboned cooked meat must be 14% of total weight or 1⅛ oz, whichever is greater; or 25% or 2 oz raw deboned weight, whichever is greater.
(Kind) dinners	18% or 2 oz whichever is greater; a minimum of 45% (5 oz/dinner) whichever is greater of cooked poultry including bone and breading may be used in lieu of the minimum. The cooked poultry including bone and breading shall contain not more than 30% breading.

*In kind, the type poultry is added.
†Label must indicate the product is for geriatric or infant feeding if prepared for such purposes.

Skinless, cooked chicken or turkey weiners, clear or red, should be specified as having meat, skin, and giblets in natural proportions. Binding agents should be limited to 3½% fiber 0.09%, ash 3.6%, fat 25%, and moisture 59.25%. The protein content should not be less than 12½%. Allowed ingredients are chicken or turkey, water, soy protein concentrate, salt, flavoring, corn syrup, sodium phosphate, monosodium glutamate, dextrose, sodium erythorbate, sodium nitrite, and sodium nitrate. Bologna from chicken or turkey may be specified similarly.

The federal government controls many phases in the processing of poultry products through sanitation and other regulations and has control over some cooking procedures and subsequent handling such as chilling and freezing. Canning methods also are prescribed. Noncured, cooked products in processing must reach an internal temperature of 160°F. Cured products must reach an internal temperature of 155°F. Establishments also may wish to include additional directions, however. Some specify that fresh fowl before cooking be chilled 12 hours but not over 24 hours and that frozen fowl be thawed at 40°F and cooked immediately after thawing. Some require the carcass, minus giblets, be simmered in an open kettle until the meat is completely cooked and tender. Clean, potable water must be used without seasonings or other additives. Some require that salt be iodized. After cooking, the carcass must be drained thoroughly and cooled to 40°F as rapidly as possible and promptly deboned, keeping large pieces intact. Tolerances for bone, bone splinters, feathers, viscera, and cartilage should be zero. Size of the dice or chunk may be specified or the quantity of fine meat to other pieces limited.

Roasted fowl may be specified as coming from U.S. Grade B or better birds and be dry-oven roasted. Shaping of products may be specified. Ingredients used in breadings or batters may be specified as for breading: "wheat and rye flour, cornmeal, salt, pepper, nonfat milk, dextrose, potato starch, monosodium glutamate, whole egg powder, cracker crumbs, and seasoning." The type shortening in which an item is fried may be specified.

It also is strongly recommended that specifications require that immediately before a prepared product is frozen a bacteriological count be taken and the product be limited to the following bacterial counts per cc or gram:

1. Total plate count   10,000
2. Staphylococcus   negative
   a. coagulase positive negative
3. Coliform   less than 10
   a. fecal coliform negative
   b. Salmonella   negative

Core temperatures of frozen items upon delivery should be 0°F or less.

Type Poultry

At one time specific market terms were used to indicate the state of refrigeration of poultry. These terms are used much less today, but buyers may still encounter them. A "fresh killed" bird was killed and cooled immediately and not held longer than 3 days under refrigeration and was delivered iced using 20 lb of ice per 80 lb of poultry. "Storage" birds were those held longer than 3 days but not over 30 days under refrigeration. "Hard-chilled" poultry was held in frozen storage not longer than 60 days, and "frozen storage" over 60 days but not longer than 100 days usually. Today the only terms that may be commonly used are "fresh frozen" poultry, indicating fresh poultry recently frozen by rapid freezing methods, and "fresh killed."

Size

A 2½- to 3-lb broiler including neck and giblets (about 5 oz) gives 4 good portions about 9 to 11 oz, raw weight. A 1½-lb fryer makes 2 liberal portions when split. A 3- to 3½-lb duckling after baking cuts into 4 portions. Ducks should not be carved but served with the skin and bones since the portion appears more adequate. It takes from 12 to 16 oz of goose, raw weight, to give a good portion and about 8 to 12 oz of turkey. Turkeys over 18 lb yield more meat per pound than those under 18 lb. The skeleton size is almost the same for a 30-lb bird as for a 15-lb one, and therefore the yield on

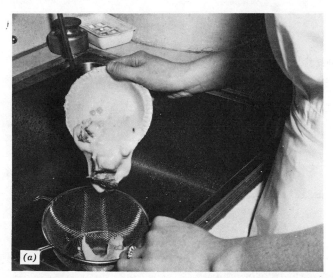

Fig. 7-9a. An inspector empties poultry pie filling into a container before washing it to ascertain the amount of poultry meat, vegetables, and other ingredients.

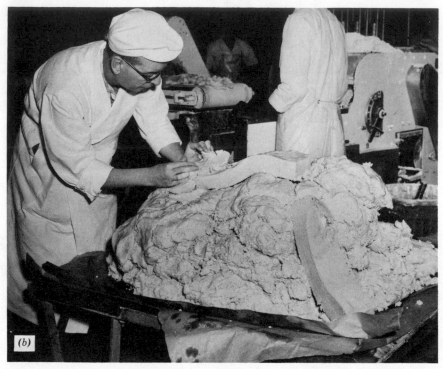

Fig. 7-9b. Another inspector checks pastry dough to be used in these pies. Courtesy USDA

the former is considerably greater, plus the price is less per pound. The following indicates some yields obtained in roasting turkeys:

Ready-to-Cook Weight	Final Roasted Weight	Edible Meat Yield
28.8 lb	73.6%	58.0%
13.5 lb	69.9%	48.8%
6.6 lb	62.2%	45.5%

A 21½-lb ready-to-cook turkey in a test yielded about 3½ lb of dark meat slices, 4 lb of white meat slices, plus giblets, wings, and picked meat for a total yield of cooked meat of around 12½ lb.

Fowl or hens of laying breeds over 4½ lb usually are wasteful because of

Fig. 7-10. This duckling has been cut into 4 portions for service, a recommended method of portioning this product. Courtesy USDA

excessive abdominal fat. A 5-lb roasting chicken yields 48.8% roasted weight and 29.3% edible meat. About ½ to ¾ lb of chicken, bone in, is a portion. This does not include giblets or neck, which should be deducted from the ready-to-cook weight.

Proper sizing is important to good portion control. Specify geese, ducks, and turkeys by individual weight. Chickens, squabs, and some other smaller birds may be specified by individual weight or by the dozen with a minimum or maximum weight limit allowed per bird. Packaging for poultry such as chickens may be 12 to 24 per box. Most turkeys, ducks, and geese are individually wrapped and, depending upon size, come packed 2, 4, or 6 to the box. Containers should plainly show net weight, kind, class, style, grade, and certification of inspection. Table 7-6 summarizes some portion information for poultry.

Breeds

The yield and the flavor of the meat is affected by breed. Most broiler-fryers come from a cross of a Rock Cornish game hen and a white Plymouth

Fig. 7-11. Peking ducks are raised in large numbers for the market on Long Island.

Fig. 7-12. A White Chinese gander, a goose coming into popularity because of its rapid growth to maturity and its white, delicate bloom, which gives it a good market appearance. Courtesy USDA

Rock. Roasting chickens are young chickens with tender meat usually coming from heavy breeds raised for their meat rather than for egg-laying. At certain times, fowl from egg-laying breeds are on the market. They are usually culls from flocks because they have lost their laying potential and are marketed at low prices. These usually must be cooked with moist heat.

Broad breasts, plump short legs, and compact structure is desirable for a high meat yield. Most turkeys are the broad-breasted Beltsville breed. The most usual duck on the market is the Peking, a white duck, sometimes called the *Long Island duckling* because so many are produced there. The Toulouse goose is a gray bird weighing from 20 to 26 lb alive at maturity. It has a dark skin after plucking and so the white Emden with a better bloom and lighter skin, although not as heavy, is usually found on the market. Homer or Carneaux pigeons are most commonly raised for their meat. They are usually sold as squabs or very young pigeons.

RABBITS

Although rabbits are not poultry, their inspection, grading, and handling are very similar to poultry. Inspection and grading by federal authorities are offered on a voluntary basis. Fryers are young domestic rabbits weighing not less than 1½ lb up to 3½ lb ready-to-cook weight and usually less than 12 weeks old. A roaster is a mature or old domestic rabbit of any weight, usually over 4 lb and usually 8 months old. Grades are U.S. Grade A, B, or C. Top grade rabbits have short, thick, well-rounded, and full-fleshed bodies with a broad back, broad hips, and broad, deep-fleshed shoulders. The muscle texture should be firm and tender. Strips of fat should appear over the loins, shoulders, and back, and there is a fair amount in the interior. Many of the characteristics indicating quality in poultry can be used to indicate quality in rabbits.

EGGS

Food facilities purchase eggs as shell eggs, liquid, frozen, or dried. Whole eggs, whites, yolks, and blends are available in the liquid, frozen, or dried form. Buyers should know which to select to obtain the right product for the production need. The total weight of an egg is made up of approximately 58% albumen or white, 31% yolk, and 11% shell.

TABLE 7-6
Portions for Poultry per lb AP

Item	Portions/lb	Portion Size	lbs/100 Portions	Additional Yield Information
Frying chicken				
Whole, 11/box, 66 lb	2.18	2 oz*	16.7	Fryers 2¼ to 3¼ lb
Breast half with ribs; 6.4 oz ea	2.50	½ breast; 3.1 oz*	40.0	lb AP = .53 lb*
Breast, no ribs, 5.9 oz ea	2.71	½ breast; 3.2 oz*	36.9	lb AP = .55 lb*
Breast with back, 6.9 oz ea	2.32	½ breast; 3.0 oz*	43.0	lb AP = .44 lb*
Legs, 7 oz ea	2.30	leg; 3.1 oz*	44.0	lb AP = .44 lb*
Drumsticks, 3.3 oz ea	4.85	drumstick; 1.4 oz*	21.0	lb AP = .42 lb*
Thighs, 3.7 oz ea	4.32	thigh, 1.7 oz*	23.0	lb AP = .45 lb*
Thighs with backs, 7.3 oz ea	2.20	thigh, 2.9 oz*	45.7	lb AP = .40 lb*
Back pieces, 5.2 oz ea	3.08	back piece; 1.3 oz*	32.5	lb AP = .25 lb*
Lower back pieces, 5.5 oz ea	2.91	back piece; 1.4 oz*	34.4	lb AP = .24 lb*
Rib back pieces, 4.3 oz ea	3.72	back piece; 1.5 oz*	26.9	lb AP = .34 lb*
Wings, 3 oz ea	2.67	2 wings; 2 oz*	37.5	lb AP = .32 lb*
Whole, no giblets or neck	3.04	2 oz*	32.9	lb AP = .39 lb*
Whole, giblets and neck	3.25	2 oz*	30.8	lb AP = .41 lb*
Breast with ribs	4.25	2 oz*	32.9	lb AP = .53 lb*
Breast, no ribs	4.40	2 oz*	23.5	lb AP = .55 lb*
Drumsticks	3.32	2 oz*	30.2	lb AP = .42 lb*
Thighs	3.59	2 oz*	27.9	lb AP = .45 lb*
Back, whole	1.97	2 oz*	50.8	lb AP = .25 lb*
Necks	3.02	2 oz*	33.2	lb AP = .38 lb*
Wings	2.60	2 oz*	38.5	lb AP = .32 lb*
Gizzards	4.10	2 oz*	24.4	lb AP = .51 lb*
Heart	4.00	2 oz*	25.0	lb AP = .50 lb*
Liver	5.20	2 oz*	19.3	lb AP = .65 lb*
Boned, canned	7.11†	¼ c, 2 oz*	14.1	lb AP = .90 lb*
Boned, canned, solid pack	7.11†	¼ c, 2 oz*	14.1	lb AP = .95 lb*
Boned, canned, with broth	7.11†	¼ c, 2 oz*	14.1	lb AP = .80 lb*
Shredded	7.11†	¼ c, 2 oz*	14.1	lb AP = .80 lb*
Chicken a la king	2.37†	¾ c, 1⅓ oz*	42.2	lb AP = .20 lb*
Chicken barbecue	3.56†	½ c, 1¾ oz*	28.1	lb AP = .40 lb*
Chicken hash	2.67†	⅔ c, 1¾ oz*	37.5	lb AP = .30 lb*

TABLE 7-6 (cont'd)
Portions for Poultry per lb AP

Item	Portions/ lb	Portion Size	lbs/100 Portions	Additional Yield Information
Chicken, noodles				
or dumplings	1.78†	1 c, 1¹/₃ oz*	56.2	lb AP = .15 lb*
Chicken with gravy	2.67†	²/₃ c, 2 oz*	37.5	lb AP = .35 lb*
Creamed chicken	2.37†	¾ c, 1¹/₃ oz*	42.2	lb AP = .20 lb*
Sliced chicken				
with gravy	2.67†	²/₃ c, 2 oz*	37.5	lb AP = .35 lb*
Turkey				
Whole, neck and giblets	3.80	2 oz*	26.4	lb AP = .48 lb*
Whole, no neck or giblets	3.78	2 oz*	26.5	lb AP = .47 lb*
Whole, no neck, giblets				
or skin	3.24	2 oz*	30.90	lh AP = .40 lb*
Breast quarter	4.08	2 oz*	24.60	lb AP = .51 lb*
Breast quarter,				
no skin	3.60	2 oz*	27.80	lb AP = .45 lb*
Leg quarter	3.84	2 oz*	26.10	lb AP = .48 lb*
Leg quarter, no skin	3.44	2 oz*	29.10	lb AP = .43 lb*
Breast only	4.66	2 oz*	21.50	lb AP = .58 lb*
Breast only, no skin	4.06	2 oz*	24.70	lb AP = .51 lb*
Drumstick	3.70	2 oz*	27.10	lb AP = .46 lb*
Drumstick, no skin	3.28	2 oz*	30.50	lb AP = .41 lb*
Thigh	4.21	2 oz⁺	23.80	lb AP = .53 lb*
Thigh, no skin	3.89	2 oz*	25.80	lb AP = .49 lb*
Backs	2.97	2 oz*	33.70	lb AP = .37 lb*
Backs, no skin	2.46	2 oz*	40.70	lb AP = .31 lb*
Necks	3.66	2 oz*	27.40	lb AP = .46 lb*
Wings	2.97	2 oz*	33.70	lb AP = .37 lb*
Gizzards	3.94	2 oz*	25.40	lb AP = .49 lb*
Hearts	4.55	2 oz*	22.00	lb AP = .35 lb*
Livers	5.62	2 oz*	17.80	lb AP = .70 lb*
Cooked turkey	7.36	2 oz*	13.60	lb AP = .92 lb*
Turkey roll or				
roast, raw	5.63	2 oz*	17.80	lb AP = .70 lb*
Turkey roll or				
roast, cooked	7.36	2 oz*	13.60	lb AP = .92 lb*
Turkey salad	2.67	²/₃ c, 1 ½ oz*	37.50	lb AP = .25 lb*

*Cooked, deboned meat.
†Also applies to canned turkey.

Shell Eggs

Quality in shell eggs depends upon interior and exterior factors. The condition of the yolk and white and the size and condition of the air cell indicate interior quality. The shell soundness, cleanliness, shape, and texture are judged for exterior quality. Flavor is not evaluated, but certain quality characteristics may indicate flavor. Few eggs today are hand candled, but most are now graded by mass scanning or flash checked to ascertain quality factors. Light showing through the egg will show yolk position, the size of the air cell, any blood or meat spots, or other defects. To assure high-quality eggs, graders may break random samples of eggs from their shell and visually note the condition of the white and yolk. They also may check it with a micrometer that reads the height of the white at the yolk. This test is known as the "Haugh Unit Breakout Test."

A high-quality egg has a large amount of thick white and a firm yolk.

(a)

Fig. 7-13a. Today's large scale commercial handling of shell eggs is a highly mechanized and controlled process. Hens are bred for laying and are fed scientifically balanced rations. Prompt gathering of the eggs is important.

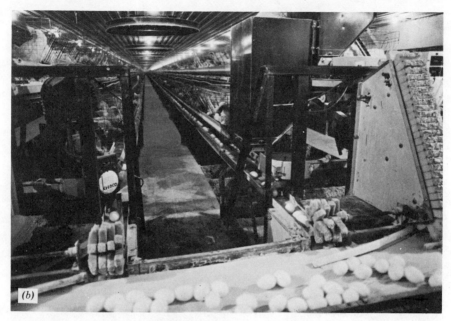

Fig. 7-13b. An even more modern method of gathering eggs using an automatic belt, which delivers the eggs directly to the washing area. Courtesy USDA

When broken out, the egg covers a small area and the white and yolk stand high. A newly laid egg may have a cloudy or milky white appearance which disappears as the egg ages. This change in cloudiness to clarity occurs as carbon dioxide is lost. Fresh eggs that are sprayed with oil also may show a cloudy or milky white even after considerable storage.

The yolk of a good egg should be in the center held in place by 2 twisted, rope-like strands of albumen called *chalazae*. The membrane wall enclosing the yolk is strong and the air cell is small. An egg with a sound shell when clicked together with another gives a bell-like tone, whereas a slightly cracked one gives a flat tone. Cleanliness of shell is a grade factor.

An egg loses carbon dioxide and moisture in aging. As this happens, the air cell increases in size. The white becomes thin and watery and the yolk flattens out so that the egg covers a wide area when broken out. The membrane enclosing the yolk weakens, and the yolk may break when the egg is shelled.

An egg is at highest quality when newly laid. It deteriorates rapidly after laying, if not given proper care, particularly if the temperature is above 45°F. An egg at room temperature quickly loses quality. If properly kept

Fig. 7-14. Eggs are graded for quality both on interior and exterior factors. Eggs of AA and A quality have shells which are practically normal. B quality eggs as shown here may have slightly abnormal shells with defects such as small ridges or rough spots.

under refrigeration, eggs retain quality for several weeks. Of course, even under refrigeration they slowly lose carbon dioxide and water. Most eggs on the market today are fresh, and only a few storage eggs are marketed to institutions.

The marketing of eggs has undergone considerable change. Egg markets have become much less important as direct marketing has increased. This has eliminated many middlemen. Producers now frequently grade and pack

TABLE 7-7
Summary of United States Standards for Quality of Individual Shell Eggs
Specifications for Each Quality Factor

Quality Factor	AA Quality	A Quality	B Quality
Shell	Clean. Unbroken. Practically normal.	Clean. Unbroken. Practically normal.	Clean to slightly stained. Unbroken. May be slightly abnormal.
Air Cell	⅛ in. or less in depth. Practically regular.	3/16 in. or less in depth. Practically regular.	⅜ in. or less In depth. May be free or bubbly.
White	Clear. Firm.	Clear. May be reasonably firm.	Clear. May be slightly weak.
Yolk	Outline slightly defined. Practically free from defects.	Outline may be fairly well defined. Practically free from defects.	Outline may be well defined. May be slightly enlarged and flattened. May show definite but not serious defects.

*If they are small (aggregating not more than ⅛ in. in diameter).

their own eggs or send them to large egg terminals where this is done. As a result of these changes, the market has tended to move more to consumer grades of eggs and less to the procurement and wholesale market grades.

Egg Standards

Federal consumer grades are U.S. Grade AA (or Fresh Fancy), U.S. Grade A, and U.S. Grade B. There is no longer a U.S. Grade C consumer grade.

Since 1972 only egg processors can utilize checks, dirties, leakers, and other restricted eggs. Institutions cannot purchase or use them.

Under the USDA voluntary grading program, the grade must be shown within the shield. The egg size is found on the carton and occasionally is included within the shield. The date of grading and federal plant number in which the grading occurred may be shown. Buyers should specify that not

TABLE 7-8
Consumer Grade Requirements for Egg Quality at Origin and Destination

Grade	Quality Required*		Quality Required†	
	At Origin	At Destination	At Origin	At Destination
Grade AA or Fresh Fancy Quality	85% AA	80% AA	75% AA, 15% A, 10% B	70% AA, 20% A, 10% B
Grade A	85% A	80% A	75% A, 25% B	70% A, 30% B
Grade B	85% B	80% B	75% B	70% B

*In lots of 2 or more cases.
†In individual case or carton in a lot.
Note: The remaining eggs must be either Grade A or B, depending upon the grade classification of the eggs. It is illegal today to use eggs in food services below Grade B. The tolerances indicated in federal standards for Grade C, Check, Dirties, Leakers, or Loss eggs pertain only to egg processors who still can use such eggs.

TABLE 7-9
Procurement Grade Requirements for Egg Quality at Origin and Destination

Grade	A Quality or Better*		Maximum Tolerance Permitted†	
	Origin	Destination	Origin	Destination
I	85%	80%	Up to 15% B, not over 5% C, Dirty, Leaker, or Loss	Up to 20% B, not over 5% C, Dirty, Check, Leaker, or Loss
II	65%	60%	Up to 35% B, not over 10% C, Dirty, Check, or Loss	Up to 40% B, not over 10% C, Dirty, Check, Leaker, or Loss

*Individual cases may not exceed 10% less A quality eggs than permitted for the lot average.
†These tolerances apply only to eggs moving to processors; eggs below Grade B cannot be used by food services; within each tolerance for qualities below B, the grades may contain no more than 3% Checks and a combined total of 0.30% Dirties, Leakers, and Loss. Loss other than meat and blood spots shall not exceed 0.15% at origin and 0.20% at destination.

TABLE 7-10
Weight Classes for Consumer Grades of Shell Eggs

Size or Weight Class	Min. Net Wt. per Doz.	Min. Net Wt. per Case*	Min. Wt. for Individual Eggs at Rate per Doz.
Jumbo†	30 oz	56 lb	29 oz
Extra large	27 oz	50½ lb	26 oz
Large	24 oz	45 lb	23 oz
Medium	21 oz	39½ lb	20 oz
Small	18 oz	34 lb	17 oz
Peewee†	15 oz	28 lb	

*A case is 30 dozen.
†Jumbo and Peewee size are usually not on the institutional market; food services usually use large-size eggs.
Note: A lot average tolerance of 3.3% for individual eggs in the next lower weight class is permitted as long as no individual case in the lot exceeds 5%.

more than 3 days shall elapse between grading and egg delivery and that eggs shall be kept in storage until that time not above 45°F. Certificates of grading can be obtained. Different standards for quality apply to eggs graded at their place of origin and those graded at their destination.

Purchase Factors

Shell eggs are usually purchased by food services by the case of 30 dozen eggs. A lot in wholesale terms means 2 or more cases. Half cases are sometimes marketed. Table 7-10 indicates the market sizes of eggs and the accepted weight per case. If buyers know the standard weight of the case in which eggs are delivered, the case can be weighed, the weight of the case deducted to determine the weight of the eggs in that case.

There are many chances for error in grading eggs. Eggs graded AA can rapidly lose quality and become grade A unless properly handled. Thus buyers should purchase eggs from a reliable dealer and handle them properly after they are delivered. Limit egg purchases to what is required for about a week's needs.

Food services usually use large eggs, and recipes are usually standarized on this size, if count is used. The weight classes for consumer grades appear in Table 7-10. Note that the weight difference is about 15%. If the price difference between sizes is greater than this, it might pay to change sizes, but it may bring about problems within the institution in translating yields from shell eggs of different size.

Fig. 7-15. The Haugh Unit Break Test is used to check the quality of a random sample of eggs. The micrometer shown here is used to measure the height of the thick egg white immediately adjacent to the yolk. Courtesy USDA

Buyers also should know that quality and size are not related. Small eggs can be as high in quality as large ones. The shell color does not affect cooking performance or nutritive value, but some areas of the country prefer brown eggs because they have traditionally appeared there, whereas others prefer white eggs for the same reason. Table 7-11 indicates some quantities of eggs required in quantity work.

Processed Eggs

High-quality whole eggs are frozen for use by institutions for breakfast

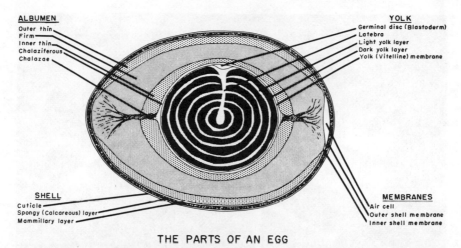

ALBUMEN
Outer thin
Firm
Inner thin
Chalaziferous
Chalazae

YOLK
Germinal disc (Blastoderm)
Latebra
Light yolk layer
Dark yolk layer
Yolk (Vitelline) membrane

SHELL
Cuticle
Spongy (Calcareous) layer
Mammillary layer

MEMBRANES
Air cell
Outer shell membrane
Inner shell membrane

THE PARTS OF AN EGG

Fig. 7-16. The parts of an egg. The yolk is anchored in the white by the two chalazae cords. As the egg ages, the firm white decreases and turns either into a thin outer or inner portion; the air cell increases in size, the chalazae weaken, allowing the yolk to lose its central position. The yolk membrane also becomes weakened so that the yolk may break when shelled. Courtesy USDA

TABLE 7-11
Equivalent Quantities of Processed Eggs for 100 Portions

Type Egg	Unit of Purchase	Wt per Unit	Portion AS	Portions per Unit	100 Portion Requirement
Frozen, whole	lb	1.00 lb	1 egg = 3 T, 12 eggs = 2¼ c	10 eggs	10 lb or 20 c (1¼ gal)
Frozen, white	Can	30.00 lb	1 egg	300 eggs	10 lb
Frozen, yolks	lb	1.00 lb	1 yolk = 1⅓ T, 12 yolks = 1 c	24 yolks	
Frozen, whites	lb	1.00 lb	1 white = 2 T, 8 whites = 1 c	16 whites	
Dried, whole	lb	1.00 lb	½ oz (2½ T) + 2½ T water = 1 egg	32 eggs	
Dried, whole	13 oz	.81 lb		26 eggs	
Dried, whole	No. 10 can	3.00 lb		96 eggs	
Dried, whole	25-lb pack	25.00 lb		800 eggs	
Dried, yolks	lb	1.00 lb	1 yolk = 2 T + 2 t water	54 yolks	
Dried, yolks	3-lb	3.00 lb	1½ c + ½ c water = 12 yolks	162 yolks	
Dried, whites	lb	1.00 lb	1 white = 2 t + 2 T water		
Dried, whites	lb	3.00 lb	½ c + 1½ c water = 12 whites		

Note: All equivalents are based on large eggs, 24 oz average per dozen.

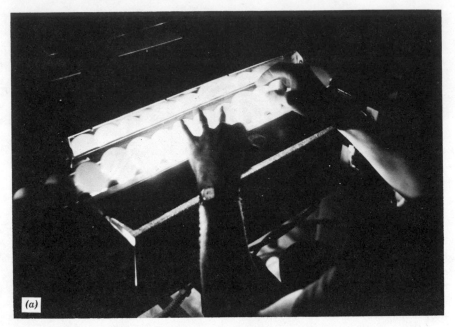

Fig. 7-17a. Eggs on a moving belt being scanned by an expert grader.

purposes such as omelets, French toast, and scrambled eggs. They are low in bacterial count because they come from high-quality eggs and are processed with considerable care. They also will be pasteurized below coagulation temperatures to eliminate pathogens. A specification for frozen breakfast eggs should read: "The eggs shall come from high quality, clean, edible eggs, free of shells and be reasonably free from blood clots or other defects. There shall be no off-flavors or off-odors. No storage, check, dirty, or leaker eggs can be used. They should be in natural proportions of yolks and whites. They should be pasteurized and free from Salmonella, Staphylococcus, and Coliform of any type."

Other frozen eggs of lower quality are used by bakeries to save on the cost of shelling eggs and for convenience.

Frozen eggs for bakery use are available as mixed whole eggs, whites, yolks, salt whole egg (2% salt or more), fortified whole egg, and blends such as 24 to 38% egg solids plus yolks with 2 to 12% nonegg solids (mostly sugar), sugar yolk (2% or more sugar), and salt yolk (2 to 12% salt). Freezing eggs alone gives a toughened product upon thawing, but if some electrolyte is added or a substance such as sugar or glycerine is added, this toughening does not occur. Sugared yolks are well liked by many bakers for

Fig. 7-17b. Candling eggs by a "mass scanning" method is much faster than using a moving belt in (a) or candling by hand. Candlers must be highly skilled to meet their job requirements. Courtesy USDA

cakes and other products. Homogenization improves the quality of frozen eggs.

A 30-lb can of frozen whole eggs is equivalent to approximately 23 dozen, 60 dozen yolks, or 35 dozen whites. There are about 9 to 10 large eggs to the pound, 14 to 16 whites, and 24 to 26 yolks per pound.

Dried eggs should not have more than 3 to 5% moisture and may be obtained by spray drying, albumen flake drying, or foam drying. As in dry milks, spray drying usually produces the best product. Freeze-dried eggs also are on the market. Dried eggs can deteriorate rapidly. Development of off-colors and off-flavors is reduced by fermenting or using enzymatic action to eliminate the glucose in egg whites. Whole eggs and yolks retain storage stability longer when acidulated during processing. They are brought back to a natural pH after processing. Gas-packed eggs keep better than those that are air packed. Store dried eggs in a cool place, preferably in refrigerators. After opening, seal tightly for storage and refrigerate. Whole eggs, whites, and yolks are available as dried products. A number of

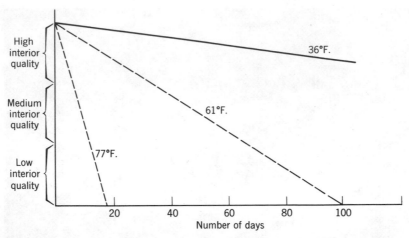

Fig. 7-18. Egg quality loss is rapid when the eggs are held at high temperature. Courtesy *Poultry Processing and Marketing Magazine*

preparations such as meringue powders and icings high in dried egg whites are on the market.

All liquid, frozen, or dried egg products come under mandatory inspection regulations of the federal government. They also must be pasteurized. Whole eggs must be pasteurized for 3½ minutes at 140°F.

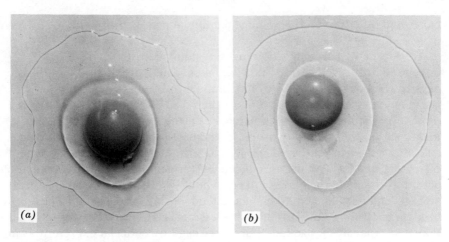

Fig. 7-19a. U.S. Grade AA (or Fresh Fancy) egg,
Fig. 7-19b. U.S. Grade A egg, and

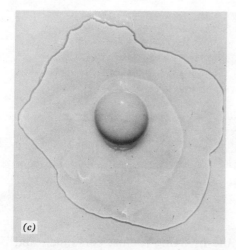

Fig. 7-19c. U.S. Grade B egg. Note the difference in the thicker and thinner portions of whites.

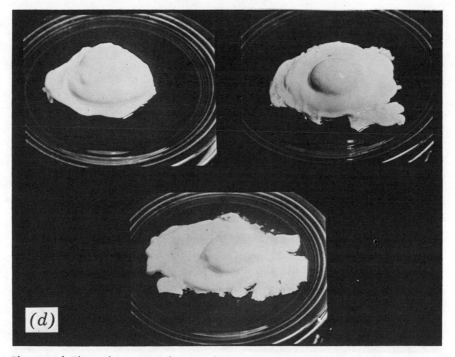

Fig. 7-19d. These three eggs after poaching. Courtesy USDA

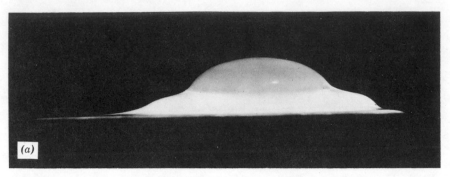

Fig. 7-20a. A side profile of a U.S. Grade AA egg after frying it.

The handling of processed eggs, the breaking rooms, personnel, and other factors that could affect quality or sanitation also are controlled. Processing methods are defined. Any additives in processed eggs must be approved by the FDA. The official inspection mark indicates the eggs were processed under federal-state inspection. Lots numbers must be placed in

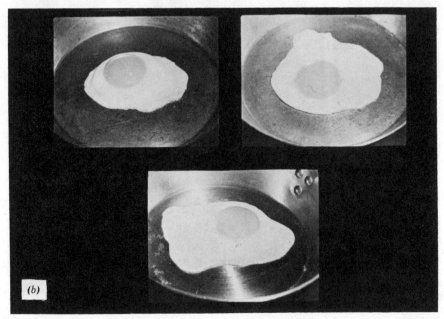

Fig. 7-20b. A U.S. Grade AA egg (top left), a U.S. Grade A egg (top right), and a U.S. Grade B egg (lower center) after frying. Courtesy USDA

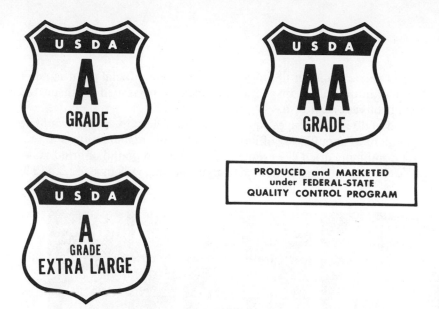

Fig. 7-21. Grade stamps used for eggs. The stamp at the upper left is most frequently seen today. The stamp at the upper right is used when eggs are graded under a joint federal-state quality control program. It is permissible to place the egg size in the grade shield, but this is being done less and less today. Courtesy USDA

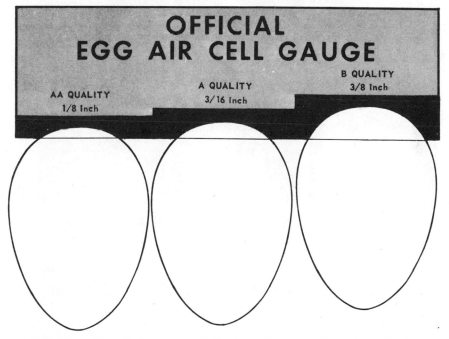

Fig. 7-22. An egg grade depends partially upon the depth of the air cell in the top interior of the egg. The relative depths of the air cell to meet grade requirements is shown here. Courtesy USDA

the federal shield stamp or upon the container. The official plant number must appear in the shield. Inspection certificates are issued for inspected products if buyers request it.

A pound of dried whole eggs equals about 32 large eggs, which would be the equivalent of about 3½ lb of large eggs. Follow manufacturers' directions for combining dried egg products. Normally, a pound of dried yolks plus 2¼ c (18 oz) water are combined to give a normal yolk mixture, and 3 lb

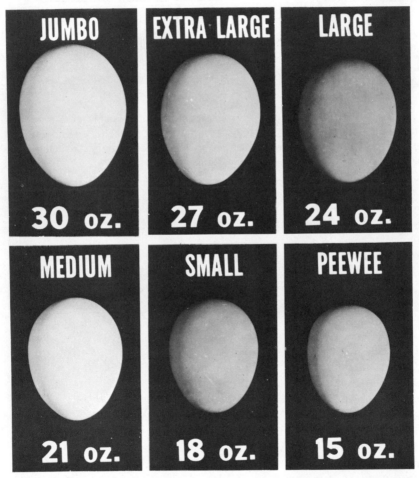

Fig. 7-23. The 6 official egg sizes. Institutions usually purchase large eggs and seldom, if ever, will find Jumbo or Peewee sizes available to them on the market. The ounces indicate the minimum weight per dozen for each of these weight classes. Courtesy USDA

Fig. 7-24. An example of a stamp used by the USDA to indicate that the purchase requirements of a buyer have been met under acceptance buying.

of dried whites and 7 lb of whites for the same for whites. Usually, a pound of dried whites plus water equals 67 large fresh egg whites, and a pound of dry yolks equals about 54 large fresh yolks.

ACCEPTANCE BUYING OF POULTRY AND EGGS

Many facilities today use the USDA's Acceptance Service for poultry and egg purchases. Federal graders will examine products before delivery and certify that purchases are "accepted" as meeting the requirements of the buyer or, if the product does not meet the specifications, he will reject it. The cost of the service usually is paid for by the purveyor. The basis of an acceptance is the buyer's specification which he gives to the federal grader and also to the purveyor. If the products meet the standards established in the specification, the federal grader applies an acceptance stamp to each container, stating "USDA Inspected for Contract Compliance." The grader then seals the container to prevent tampering or opening prior to delivery and prepares a poultry products grading certificate stating that all contract requirements for the product have been met. This certificate includes the date that inspection was made and other pertinent information. (See Fig. 7-25.) On request government graders will assist in drawing up specifications. A buyer needing assistance should contact his closest poultry or egg grading branch office. Other institutions may find manufacturers or purveyors of products helpful.

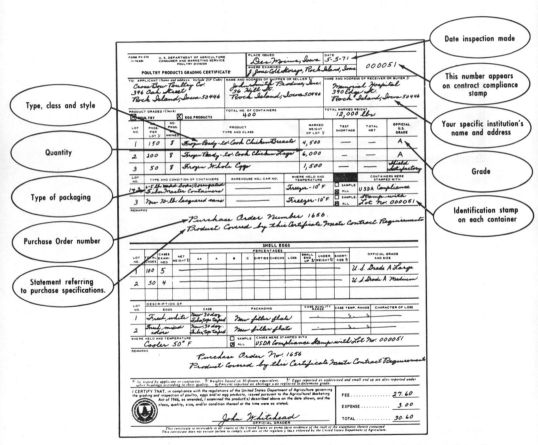

Fig. 7-25. USDA's form PY-210 completed by one of its graders. It indicates that all contract requirements have been met by the purveyor as outlined in the buyer's specification. This certificate is attached to the invoice accompanying the delivery to the buyer. Courtesy USDA

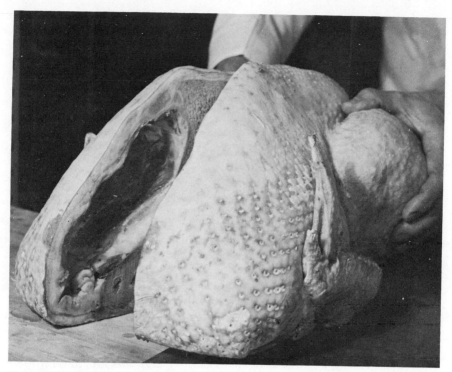

Fig. 7-26. This turkey carcass shows the effects of freezer burn. At first, white areas appear as pock marks. These gradually grow larger and larger until an entire surface area is covered. Once this type of dehydration occurs, little can be done to correct the loss of flavor, texture, and moistness that results from such deterioration. Courtesy USDA

BIBLIOGRAPHY

Eggs

Handy, Elizabeth, "Eggs, Nature's Prepackaged Masterpiece of Nutrition," *Agriculture Yearbook 1969,* USDA, pp. 139-145, Washington, D.C.

USDA, *Egg Grading Manual,* Agr. Handbook No. 75, Government Printing Office, Washington, D.C., 1969.

USDA, *USDA's Acceptance Service for Poultry and Eggs,* Marketing Bulletin No. 46, Government Printing Office, Washington, D.C., 1971.

USDA, "New Law Affects Egg and Egg Product Users" (News release), Consumer and Marketing Service, Washington, D.C., August 6, 1971.

USDA, *Regulations Governing the Inspection of Eggs and Egg Products,* 7CFR, Part 59, Agricultural Marketing Service, Poultry Division, Washington, D.C., July 1, 1972.

USDA, *Regulations Governing the Grading of Shell Eggs and U.S. Standards, Grades and Weight Classes for Shell Eggs,* 7CFR, Part 56, Agricultural Marketing Service, Poultry Division, Washington, D.C., July 1, 1971.

U.S. Government, "Egg Products Inspection Act," Public Law 91-597, 91st Congress, H. R. 19888, Washington, D.C., December 29, 1970.

Poultry

Crosby, Violet B. and Ashley R. Gulich, "Poultry: A Tasty, Anytime Delight That's Popular Dozens of Ways," *Agriculture Yearbook 1969,* USDA, pp. 117–126, Washington, D.C.

USDA, *Poultry Grading Manual,* Agr. Handbook No. 31, Government Printing Office, Washington, D.C., 1971.

USDA, *Poultry Products Inspection Regulations,* Volume 37, No. 95, Part II of *Federal Register,* Washington, D.C., May 16, 1972.

USDA, *Regulations Governing the Grading and Inspection of Poultry and Edible Products Thereof and U.S. Classes, Standards and Grades with Respect Thereto,* 7CFR, Part 70, Washington, D.C., July 1, 1971.

USDA, *Regulations Governing the Grading and Inspection of Domestic Rabbits and Edible Products Thereof and the U.S. Specifications for Classes, Standards and Grades with Respect Thereto,* 7CFS, Part 54, Washington, D.C., July, 1, 1972.

8
Fish and Shellfish

Wide variety and economy can be gained by featuring fish[1] on a menu. It is popular, and the cost is usually less than that of meat or poultry. The average consumption of fish per capita per year has been increasing. California generally leads in tonnage of fish caught, with Massachusetts and the North Pacific area following in that order. Tuna, salmon, shrimp, and oysters lead in value of catch.

PURCHASE FACTORS

Buyers need to know what is available and when on their markets. Price is important and also quality factors desirable in fish. Menu selection must be based on use, and buyers need to know which fish suit various preparation methods. Amounts to purchase also may be challenging.

Availability

Fresh fish is available for short periods of time, and varieties offered will usually be restricted to local catches. High perishability limits shipment. Fish in off-seasons is more costly and perhaps lower in quality. The peak catch is from June through October with the highest landings in August and the lowest in February. During low periods of fresh supplies, frozen, canned, and cured stocks are purchased. In some instances, some fresh fish may come onto the market in liberal supply during the low periods, and it is wise to feature it on the menu. Fresh-water fish is important in local areas, but the total tonnage caught is not significant compared with the quantities of salt-water fish docked.

[1]The term "fish" used from here to Fresh Water and Sea Fish includes shellfish and all other marine life used as flesh food. The context or the word "shellfish" will indicate other use.

411

Markets

The main fish markets in this country are located in the main catch areas: Boston, New York, Gulf (New Orleans), Seattle, and Chicago. Other markets are Baltimore, Norfolk, Savannah, Gulf ports, San Francisco and Portland, Oregon. Trade practices vary considerably among them.

The Boston market reflects trading practices of the New England Fish Exchange, whereas the New York market, moving more fish to consumers than any other, has practices growing out of the Fulton Fish and Peck Slip markets. The shrimp ports and New Orleans have influenced the Gulf market, and Seattle's practices reflect those of the Pacific Coast, including Alaska. Chicago, an inland market, reflects practices common to the four, but because it also is a large fresh-water fish market, it has developed practices of its own.

Much confusion exists among markets in terminology and marketing practices. Fish identities are not always the same. Buyers should learn the names on their own markets. Most fresh fish are sold without a label and, because of close similarity, substitutions are possible, some dishonest. Accepted practices on some markets allow substitutions, and buyers should learn these. Normally, buyers should hold sellers closely to firm specifications and not accept substitutions or other changes without negotiation.

Quality Standards

In 1956 the Agricultural Marketing Act was extended to include some processed fish. Control was under the Bureau of Commercial Fisheries, U.S. Fish and Wildlife Service, Department of the Interior. Under the act quality standards are developed. Fish covered by the act must come from wholesome material of good odor and taste and be processed under sanitary conditions. Fish may be inspected and certified by continuous inspection, intermittent at-plant inspection, specific lot inspection, and, without certification, inspected from unofficially drawn samples. These inspections are explained in Chapter 3.

Inspection for wholesomeness of fresh fish products is not required as it is for meat and poultry. All items graded, however, must meet standards that would eliminate unwholesome products. In addition, the sanitary provisions of the Pure Food, Drug and Cosmetic Act and other regulations assist in assuring a wholesome product. In some markets—Boston, for instance—state inspectors can inspect catches as they come in or are unloaded. The U.S. Public Health Service must certify that the beds from which shellfish are taken are approved. An approval number indicates this and must be put on original packages.

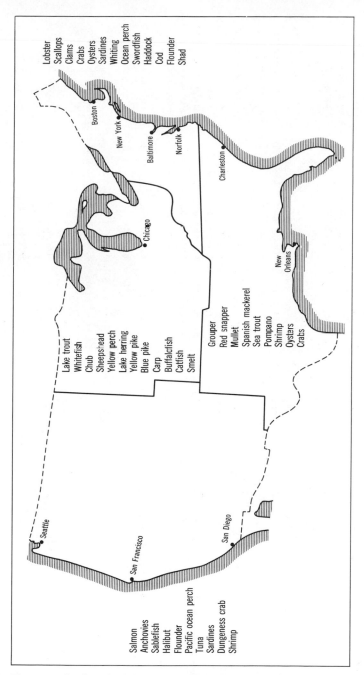

Fig. 8-1. The five primary fish markets—Boston, New York, New Orleans, Chicago, and Seattle—are shown, along with the heaviest production of fish by species. Other important markets are shown, some of which may dock larger tonnages of fish during a year than some of the primary markets.

TABLE 8-1
A Buyer's Guide for the Purchase of Fish*

Common Name	Other Common Names	Normal Size in Pounds	Main Production Area	Season	Yield from Round Form	Fat or Lean	Common Market Forms
Barracuda		5–10	California	June	51% to fillet	L	Round, dressed, steaks, fillet
Bluefish		1–7	Mid-Atlantic	All year	52% to fillet	L	Round, drawn, fillet
Bass	Sea, striped, black-fish, black sea-bass, common, rockfish	2–600 depending on type	Atlantic and Pacific	Depends on type	around 40% to fillet for all types	L	All forms
Butterfish	Harvestfish	¼–1¼	Mid-Atlantic	June–Oct.	51% to fillet	F	Round, drawn, fillet
Catfish or Bull-heads		1–10	Rivers, lakes	All year	19% to fillet	L	Round, dressed
Chub		2–5 oz	Great Lakes	All yeal	33% to fillet	F	Dressed, smoked
Cod, Atlantic		1½–10	New England	All year	31% to fillet	L	All forms
Cod, Pacific		1½–10	Pacific Coast	All year	31% to fillet	L	All forms
Croaker, Atlantic	Hardhead	½–2	South Atlantic	June–Oct.	39% dressed	L	Round, dressed, fillet
Cusk		1½–10	Atlantic	All year	58% to fillet	L	Drawn, dressed
Drum (red)	Channel bass, red-fish	2–25	South Atlantic, Gulf	Winter	36% to fillet	L	Round, drawn
Drum (black)	Oyster cracker, oyster drum, sea drum	1–40	Atlantic, Gulf	Winter	38% to fillet	L	Round, drawn
Flounder (sole)	Atlantic:		Atlantic				Dressed, fillet
	Blackback (winter)	¾–2		Late winter	41% to fillet	L	
	Fluke (summer)	2–12		Summer	42% to fillet	L	
	Dab (seadab)	¾–2½		Apr.–May	36% to fillet	L	
	Gray	¾–4		Apr.–June	40% to fillet	L	
	Lemon	¾–4		June	41% to fillet	L	
	Southern	2–12		All year	54% to fillet	L	
	Yellowtail or dusty dab	¾–2		Aug.–Jan.	44% to fillet	L	

	Pacific: Rex, petrale, sand-dab, Dover or English sole	½ to 2	Pacific	All year	about 40% to fillet form	L	
Grouper		5–12	Gulf	All year	43% to fillet	L	All forms
Haddock		1½–7	New England	All year	48% to fillet	L	Fillet, sticks
Hake	Boston, squirrel or white hake; red or mud hake	2 to 5	New England	All year	43% to fillet	L	Fillet
Halibut		5–75	Pacific or Atlantic	Apr.–Oct.	59% to fillet	L	All forms
Herring, sea		2–4 oz	Atlantic, Pacific	Nov.–Feb.	51% to fillet	F	Round
Herrkin, lake		⅓–1	Great Lakes	Oct.–Dec.	72% to dressed	F	Round, dressed, smoked
Mackerel, jack		½–2½	Atlantic	Apr.–Oct.	54% to fillet	F	Round, dressed, fillet
Mackerel, Spanish		1–4	South Atlantic, Gulf	Summer		F	Round, dressed
Mackerel, king	Cero, kingfish	5–20	North Atlantic	Jan.–Apr.	53% to fillet	F	All forms
Lingcod		5–20	North Pacific	All year	38% to fillet	L	Dressed, fillet
Mullet		½–3	South Atlantic, Gulf	Sept.–Dec.	53% to fillet	L	Round, dressed, fillet
Perch, white		⅓–¾	Great Lakes	All year	36% to fillet	L	Dressed, fillet
Perch, yellow		½–¾	Great Lakes	All year	38% to fillet	L	Dressed, fillet
Perch, ocean	Rosefish	½–1¼	New England	All year	31% to fillet	L	Fillet
Pickerel		1½–3½	North Lakes	Apr.–Oct.	51% to fillet	L	Dressed, fillet
Pike, blue		½–2	Great Lakes	Sept.–Nov.	44% to fillet	L	Round, fillet
Pike, sauger		½–1½	Great Lakes	Apr.–Oct.		L	Dressed, fillet
Pike, yellow		1–3½	and	Apr.–Oct.	57% to fillet	L	Dressed, fillet
Pike, northern		1–4	Canadian	Apr.–Oct.	39% to fillet	L	Dressed, fillet
Pike, wall-eyed		1–4	Lakes	Apr.–Oct.	41% to fillet	L	Dressed, fillet
Pollock		1½–12	New England	All year	45% to fillet	L	Fillet
Pompano		½–2½	South Atlantic Gulf	All year	52% to fillet	L	Dressed, round
Sablefish, black cod	1–15	North		Apr.–Nov.	68% to dressed	F	Dressed, steaks, smoked
Salmon, Atlantic		5–10	Atlantic	June–July	65% to fillet	F	Dressed, steaks
Salmon, chum		5–11	North Pacific	Aug.–Nov.	76% to drawn	F	Drawn, dressed, steaks, fillet
Salmon, king		5–30	North Pacific	Apr.–Aug.	73% to dressed	F	Drawn, dressed, steaks, fillet

At the present time, the following standards for grades have been established for frozen fish by the U.S. Bureau of Commercial Fisheries: (1) fried fish sticks, (2) raw breaded shrimp, (3) fish blocks, (4) haddock fillets, (5) halibut steaks, (6) cod fillets, (7) salmon steaks, (8) raw headless shrimp, (9) raw breaded fish portions, (10) ocean perch fillets, (11) fried scallops, (12) fried fish portions, (13) breaded fish steaks, and (14) flounder and sole fillets.

In 1963 over 215 million lb of fish and shellfish were inspected and certified. Skinless portions are classified as Style I and those with skin, Style II. Type I portions are uniformly shaped and Type II (specialty cut) are portions not covered in Type I. Grades are A and B with minimum scores of 85 and 70, respectively. Grades are established by scoring factors such as (1) flavor and odor, (2) packing, (3) imperfections of trim and cutting, (4) blemishes, (5) bones, (6) color, (7) dehydration, (8) skin on items from which it should be removed, (9) appearance, (10) uniformity of size, (11) texture, (12) mashed, broken or otherwise damaged pieces, (13) coating defects, if coated, (14) texture including tenderness and moistness, and (15) extraneous material.

Frozen halibut and salmon steaks, sole and flounder fillets, and raw, headless shrimp may be protected by a surface glaze of ice in addition to packaging materials. The maximum allowable glaze is 6%. Beyond this, it is considered excessive, and downgrading will result. Loose breading is considered a grade defect. Excessive breading is not allowed, and the relative amount of breading to flesh has been established for the following products: fish portions 75%, fish sticks 72%, fried fish portions 65%, fried fish sticks 60%, and shrimp 50%. This author considers these excessive.

Fish deteriorates rapidly after catching unless chilled. Most fish live in water from 40 to 50°F, and their enzymatic processes and defense mechanisms against bacteria operate best at lower than air temperatures. So, when the temperature rises about 50°F, fish deteriorate rapidly.

When caught, a fish is soft, but the flesh soon stiffens and firms. Fresh fish should be firm and elastic. The flesh should spring back when pressed and not easily pull from the bones. As fish stales, the flesh softens, becomes flabby, and an indentation of the finger remains in it. The color of the flesh should be bright and clear. White-meated fish should have a white and slightly translucent flesh, not pink or gray, especially around the backbone. Steaks and fillets (pronounced fǐl-lěts) should have no traces of brown at the edge. The odor should be fresh and mild, not stale, sour, strong, or sharp with ammonia. The eyes should be bright and clear, full and bulging, not dull, wrinkled, or sunken. The gills should be reddish pink, free from slime, and not dull brown or gray. As a fish stales, the gill color fades to a pink gray, then becomes greenish, and then brown. The scales should adhere tightly to the skin and be bright colored, with a sheen. The bloom should not be dull or slimy.

Shellfish should be purchased alive if in the shell, although some cooked shellfish in the shell may be marketed. Crustaceans turn red when cooked, which distinguishes them from the uncooked or green products. Some cooked crab may be creamy colored, flecked with red. Some purveyors, failing to sell their crustaceans alive, may cook them after they perish and market them in cooked form. A live lobster, crayfish, or shrimp has muscle tension. The tail curls up under the body, rather than hanging down limply. Crab shows slight movement, and the antennas and eyes of many crustaceans move. A live clam or oyster holds its shell firmly together when pressure is applied to open it. Dead mollusks usually can be detected by their open shells. Tension may remain with some even though the mollusk is dead. Sometimes live mollusks left in water can be seen to open and close their shells and clams may extend their necks. A slight jar causes the immediate withdrawal of the neck or closing of the shell. If the odor is strong, disagreeable, and sharp with a distinct odor of ammonia, the shellfish is not in good condition. A slippery, slimy surface indicates spoilage.

Upon delivery, live shellfish should be spread out, covered with moist seaweed, cloths, or sacks and held at around 45°F. Crustaceans may be placed in tanks; mollusks may be placed in pails of water. If fresh, live shellfish stay alive in cool salt water for approximately 5 days and somewhat longer if placed into tanks. Live hard-shell crabs do not ship well, but the soft-shell varieties packed in excelsior or seaweed do.

Shucked mollusks should be plump, have a clear color and sweet odor, and be free from pieces of shell, silt, and sand. The liquid should be clear. If the mollusks appear bloated or have more than 8% liquid on them, they have probably been watersoaked, which increases their weight considerably. Mollusks should have a pH around 6.0. As they age, they become more and more acid, a condition that can be detected by tasting the liquor. Fresh-picked shrimp, crab, or lobster meat, and fresh-shucked scallops, oysters, or clams should be held at 32°F but never frozen at the facility. Use should be within several days.

Select plump, full fish; fish with big heads are wasty. Order those sizes most plentiful if they yield proper size portions because off sizes are apt to be more expensive. The largest fish may not be the best quality. Locally caught fish are apt to be better than those shipped in and are better known and accepted by patrons. Buyers should consult reputable dealers to learn what is on the market and the best buys. Labor cost in preparation should be considered. Frequently, final cost is less if the fish is received ready for use rather than being prepared with much labor.

The federal specifications for either chilled (not previously frozen), Type I, or frozen, Type II, state that Form I is whole or round fish and Form II is the same but glazed. Form III are single fillets (a) skin on or (b) skinless or they may be specified butterfly (double) as (a) or (b). Fillets must weigh from 3 to 24 oz except yellowtail, blackback, or dab flounder or lemon, English, gray, Dover, or petrale sole can be a minimum of 2 oz; ocean (Pacific) perch, 1 oz minimum; single whiting $1^1/_3$ oz or butterfly $2^2/_3$ oz minimum; yellow perch, $1^1/_3$ oz minimum; white sea bass, yellowtail, cabrilla, or grouper, 16 oz minimum; and jewfish, 24 oz minimum. Form IV is steaks ⅝ to an inch thick; if frozen, they must be glazed. Steaks cannot weigh less than 3 oz and cannot come from napes (necks), including collarbones or longitudinal tail cuts. To make the weight, a steak may be cut in two. Form V, chunks, must be glazed, if frozen, and Form VI, portions, shall be weights of 2, 3, 4, or other ounces as specified and be solid pieces of fish flesh. Require the latter be boneless or nearly so.

Chilled fish must reach an internal temperature of 40°F or less immediately following processing and must be kept at this temperature until delivery. Frozen fish must be frozen within 2 hours of processing and reach an internal temperature of 0°F or less within 72 hours of processing. Glazing must be accomplished using potable water and placing the fish into 0°F or lower temperature. Fillets in processing may be washed with a sodium chloride solution no more than 15° salometer for not more than 2 minutes so that they will not soak up water and gain weight. The maximum frozen storage time is 180 days except halibut which can be stored for 270 days, but fillets of Pacific ocean perch and bocaccio must be no longer than 120 days, chilipepper, lobe-jawed rockfish, red rockfish, and channel rockfish 60 days maximum, and Atlantic ocean perch 120 days.

The federal specifications require that halibut come from chicken halibut dressed at 5 to 10 lb; cod from fish dressing at 2½ to 10 lb except fillets can come from fish weighing 1½ to 2½ lb; steaks cannot weigh more than 24 oz. Rockfish fillets (skinless) must come from the bocaccio, chilipepper, or rockfish varieties mentioned previously. Dressed salmon must weigh over 6 lb and steaks not more than 24 oz. If they come from the poke area (body cavity), untrimmed, they shall have not less than a ½-in.-thick abdominal wall.

Sole and flounder fillets should have the skin removed from both sides except petrale or English sole may have the skin remaining on the blind (ventral) side. The following species of sole or flounder are acceptable: yellowtail, blackback under 3½ lb, dab, English sole, lemon sole over 3½ lb, gray sole, petral sole, Dover sole, and starry flounder.

Haddock fillets must come from fish from 1½ lb up, and pollock fillets from fish 2½ lb over. Mackerel fillets shall come from fish weighing over a lb and cannot be washed in water that contains salt. Ocean or Pacific ocean perch fillets should be cut from fish over ½ lb. The maximum count per 10-lb fillets is 120 and 10 fillets per 10 lb can weigh less than an ounce. At certain times, when specified, the maximum count can be 130 per 10 lb with a tolerance of 15 fillets under an ounce.

Whiting fillets must come from fish ¾ lb up, and butterfly fillets must exclude the vent. White sea bass can come dressed from 6 to 50 lb, and steaks cannot weigh over 24 oz. Yellowtail must come dressed from 4 to 15 lb, and steaks cannot be more than 24 oz. Cabrilla must come dressed 5 to 20 lb, and dressed jewfish and grouper 10 to 100 lb. Barracuda must have a dressed weight 2½ lb up, and boneless fillets must be cut from fish over 4 lb; steaks from barracuda cannot be over 24 oz. Swordfish steaks cannot weigh more than 24 oz and, if cut from the poke, must have an abdominal wall at least ½-in. thick. Boneless swordfish fillets must come from fish weighing 10 to 50 lb. Acceptable smelt varieties are smelt (*Osmerus mordax*), surfsmelt, and eulachon. Red snapper steaks cannot weigh over 24 oz, and fillets must come from fish ¾ lb up.

Frozen fish should be solidly frozen, with no discoloration or brownish cast at the outer surfaces. There should be little or no odor. Wrappings on stored fish should be moisture-vapor proof. They should fit tightly around the flesh. Many large, whole or dressed fish are glazed with ice, and it is desirable that this glaze still remain upon delivery. Frozen fish may lack, after cooking, the abundant flavor and moistness of fresh fish, and there also is a flavor and quality loss in extended storage. Some types freeze better than others. Some crab meats, for instance, lose flavor and are dry and pulpy even after short freezing. Minimum drip loss is obtained when fish is thawed under 40°F. If possible, cook frozen fish unthawed, but where breading, filleting, or stuffing must occur this is not possible. Heavy losses in quality occur if fish is refrozen. Cooked crab and crab meat lose quality rapidly after freezing, and, as a rule, buyers should select fresh or canned crab rather than frozen. Shrimp, lobster, spiny lobster, shucked oysters, and clams freeze better than crab. Some oysters and clams are frozen in the shell without much loss in quality.

Many frozen fish items are available on the market and most come from the cod varieties. Fish sticks, either fried (1972) or raw breaded (1964), are on the market. Frozen raw breaded (1963) or fried breaded fish portions (1966) either Style I (skinless) or Style II (skin on) are available. Such portions must be 1½ oz or more and be ⅜ in. thick or more. Blocks of either

Style I or II fillets, about 25 lb each, can be obtained. All these frozen products can be graded either U.S. A or B under jurisdiction of the Department of Interior.

Quantity to Purchase

The quantity required to give a desirable portion may vary considerably depending upon the market form of purchase. Many fish in the round or drawn have a high waste in being brought to EP weight. Most shellfish in the shell have very low EP yields. Tables 8-3 and 8-4 indicate quantities usually required to serve given numbers. Buyers also should compile their own information. Dressed fish, usually from 8 to 12 lb each, will cut out to best advantage for steaks or baking.

TABLE 8-2
A Buyer's Guide for the Purchase of Shellfish

Shellfish	Other Names	Main U.S. Producing Area	Peak Production Month	Weight Information, EP Yields and Miscellaneous Information
Abalone		South Pacific	May	42% meat in shell
Clams, butter		North Pacific	All year	Shell—100 lb/sack; shucked—100–250/gal
Clams, hard*	Quahog, quahaug	North and Mid-Atlantic	All year	Bu—11 lb EP; 80 lb/sack; shucked 100–250/gal
Clams, littleneck		North and Mid-Atlantic or Pacific	All year	60 lb/bu
Clams, razor		North Pacific	Fall	80 lb/box; 16 EP/bu
Clams, soft*		North and Mid-Atlantic	All year	45 lb/bu; 200–700/gal shucked; 16 lb EP/bu
Clams, surf	Skimmer	North Atlantic	June	180–300/gal shucked
Conch				15 lb EP/bu
Crabs:				
Blue, hard shell		Mid-Atlantic	All year	10 to 18% meat; 5 lb EP/bu
Rock		New England		10 to 18% meat; 5 lb EP/bu
Blue, soft shell		Mid-Atlantic	May–June	used whole; 3 lb EP/doz
Dungeness		North Pacific	Apr.–June	22–26% meat
King		Alaska	June	legs only 14% meat

TABLE 8-2 (cont'd)
A Buyer's Guide for the Purchase of Shellfish

Shellfish	Other Names	Main U.S. Producing Area	Peak Production Month	Weight Information, EP Yields and Miscellaneous Information
Lobsters		New England	may-Dec.	25% meat
Lobsters, spiny	Rock or sea crayfish, laguna lobster	Pacific	Nov.	46% tails only; most of these are imported except the Laguna caught off the coast of California and Mexico
Mussels		New England	May–Dec.	45–55 lb/bu; 10 lb EP/bu; 29% meat
Oysters:†				
Eastern		Atlantic	Fall and winter	80 lb/bu; 150–200/gal shucked (Bluepoints)
Pacific	Japanese		Nov.–Jan.	80 lb/sack; 64–240/gal shucked
Olympia	Western		Dec.–Jan.	120 lb/sack; 1600–1700/gal
Scallops:				
Bay		Atlantic	Feb.–May	500 per gal shucked; few taken in Pacific
Sea		Atlantic	Jan.–Sept.	150 per gal shucked
Sea urchins	Sea eggs			5 lb EP/bu
Shrimp:‡				
Gulf		Gulf	All year	12 to 70 per lb
Alaska pink		North Pacific	Dec.–Jan.	150–250 shelled/lb
California		Mid-Pacific	Aug.–Sept.	125–250 shelled/lb
Squid		North Pacific	June–July	5 to 6 per lb round form
Snails		Atlantic	Winter	Most imported; 20% gross weight is meat
Terrapin	Diamondbacks	Gulf	All year	21% raw muscle
Turtles:				
Sea and fresh water			All year	24% raw muscle

*Long shell or surf clams 35% yeild; hard-shell clams (round shell) 17% yield drained meat average; hard-shelled clams by areas: New England 14–20%, Chesapeake 7–8%, Mid-Atlantic 10–12%, South Atlantic 6–8%, Pacific 24–28%, soft-shell yields: New England 23–33%, Mid-Atlantic 27–32%.

†Eastern oyster yield: New England and Mid-Atlantic 8–11%, Chesapeake 6–7%, South Atlantic 4–6%, Gulf 5–7%, Pacific (Japanese) 10–14%.

‡Yield from frozen headless shrimp in thawing, cooking, shellind and deveining—43% meat.

TABLE 8-3
A Buyer's Guide for Estimating Quantities of Fish

Fish	Preparation Information	Round	Drawn	Dressed	Fillet
		\multicolumn{4}{c}{Estimated Pounds AP Required for 100 Portions}		
Barracuda	5–6 oz steaks			31–38	
Bass, all types	5–6 oz steaks: 4–5 oz fillets		35–50	35	30
Bluefish	Half 1½ lb round fish	75		50	
Bullhead	½ 1-lb fish split			50*	
Butterfish	1 fish to the lb size		50		
Catfish	5 oz fillet	165			30
Chub	1 to 3 fish depending on size		38		
Cod	4 to 5 oz fillet	100			30
Cod	5–6 oz steak cut from 8 lb dressed fish			35–50	
Cod, scrod	Split 1¼-lb round scrod into two portions	68		50	
Cod, salt, dry	For fish cakes or creamed cod				10
Croaker	4 to 5 oz fillet	80			30
Cusk	4 to 5 oz fillet	64			30
Eels	Smoked 4 oz			25	
Flounder					
Blackback (winter)	†	76		50	30
Fluke (summer)	†	75		50	30
Dab	†	90		50	30
Gray sole	†	80		50	30
Lemon sole	†	80		50	30
Southern	†	58		50	30
Yellowtail	†	70		50	30
Pacific sole	†	82		50	30
California halibut	†	62		50	30
Grouper	5–6 oz steaks cut from 8 lb fish			35	
Haddock	5–6 oz steaks, 4–5 oz fillets	60		50	30
Hake	4–5 oz fillets	74			
Halibut	5–6 oz steaks, 4–5 oz fillets	60		35	30
Herring, sea or lake	Round 1-lb fish per portion	100			
Herring, salted	8 oz split pieces			50	
Herring, smoked	5–6 oz				38
Mackerel	¾-lb split	100	75		
Mackerel, king	4–5 oz fillets				30
Mackerel, Spanish	3 to lb average, split	75	50		
Ling cod	4–5 oz fillets	62	50		30
Mullet	4–5 oz fillets	60			30

TABLE 8-3 (cont'd)
A Buyer's Guide for Estimating Quantities of Fish

Fish	Preparation Information	Round	Drawn	Dressed	Fillet
		Estimated Pounds PA Required for 100 Portions			

Fish	Preparation Information	Round	Drawn	Dressed	Fillet
Perch, all types	2 fillets 2 to 2½ oz each				30
Pickerel	4–5 oz fillets				30
Pike, all types				35–50	30
Pollock	1½ to 2 lb each or 4–5 oz fillets			35–50	30
Pompano	Use ¾ to 1½ lb fish split or whole, depending on portion size desired.	75		50	30
Sablefish	5–6 oz steaks, smoked 5 oz pieces			35–50 35–50	
Salmon, baking size	Buy 5 to 12 lb dressed salmon			40	
Salmon	5–6 oz steaks, 4–5 oz fillets			35–50	30
Scup (Porgy)	Purchase dressed 5 to 8 oz each or split 1-lb dressed fish.			35–50	
Shad	Steaks 5–8 oz, fillets 4–5 oz			38	30
Smelt	3 to 5 fish dressed 12 to 16 to lb			35–33	
Snapper, red	5–6 oz steaks cut from 8–9 lb fish			35–50	
Snapper, red	4–5 fillets				30
Shad roe	Purchase *medium* roe averaging 8 to 10 oz per pair; portion size may vary considerably, depending on type operation.				15–30
Swordfish	Steaks 5–6 oz			35	
Tilefish	5–6 oz steaks	82	60	35–50	
Whitefish	Purchase around 4 lb dressed and cut into 5–6 oz portion; fillets 4–5 oz.			50	30
Whiting	Split 1½ lb rounds or purchase ½ lb dressed fish and use 1 per portion; 4–5 oz fillets.	75		50	30
Whiting, king	4–5 oz fillets				30
Wolffish	5–6 oz steaks cut from 6 lb drawn fish; 4–5 oz fillets.	90	60		30

*Skinned.
†Small sizes may be split, center bone removed; or select fillets about 3 to the lb or cut larger fillets into 4 to 5 oz portions.

TABLE 8-4
A Buyer's Guide for Estimating Quantities of Shellfish Required

Shellfish	Portion Size or Other Preparation Information	Form in Which Purchased AP	Quantity Required for 100 Portions
Abalone	4 oz	Steaks	25 lb
Clams, hard	On the shell: little necks 450 to 650 per bu or cherry stones 300 to 325 per bu; 4 per serving.	In shell	34 doz
Clams, shucked	Cocktails, approx. 1½ oz.	Shucked	1⅓ gal
Clams, chowder	Quahaugs, 150 per bu.	In shell	1⅓ to 1⅔ bu
Crab meat*	Backfin lump from Blue crab or solid meat from Dungeness	Solid meat	or 2 gal shucked
	1½ oz per cocktail		10 lb
	2 oz for small salads		12 lb
	4 oz for large salads.		24 lb
Crab meat*	Lump or flake for creamed, creole or extender dishes, use about 1⅓ to 1½ oz.	Solid meat	8–10 lb
Crabs, soft shell	1 each about 4 to 4½" in diameter.	Alive	100 crabs
Lobster	¾ to 1¼ lb chicken lobster	Alive	100 lobster
	or 1½–2 lb and split.	Alive	50 lobster
Lobster meat*	See crab meat.		
Oysters, blue points	Purchase 300–400 oysters per bu (approx. 75 lb per bu), 4 per serving.	In shell	34 doz
Oysters, olympia	For cocktails, 1¼ oz.	Shucked	1 gal
Oysters, fried or scalloped	Purchase *counts* 125/150 per gal or *selects* 175–200 per gal.	Shucked	2½–3 gal
Oysters, stew	Purchase *standards* 250 to 300 per gal.	Shucked	1½ gal
Scallops, sea	Medium size 175 approx. per gal for deep frying.		3½ to 4 gal
Shrimp, fried	Use Jumbo split or butterflied, about 20 per lb, using 4 to 5 per portion, or large split or round.		20 to 25 lb
Shrimp	Cocktails 1½ oz, small or Pacific.	Shelled	10 lb
Shrimp	Cocktails 5 Jumbo or Large.	Green, unshelled†	25–33 lb
Shrimp	Small salad, 2 oz shrimp, ½ c salad.	Green, unshelled†	12 lb EP, cooked
Shrimp	Large salad, 4 oz shrimp, 1 c salad.	Green, unshelled†	24 lb EP, cooked

*From 10 to 12 cans 14 oz net weight contents of crab or lobster meat are the equivalent of the quantities given here.
†Shrimp are headless AP.

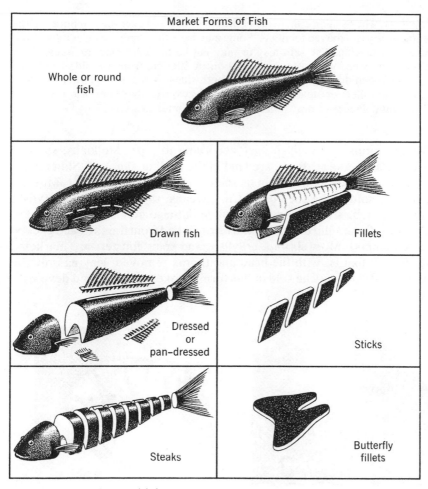

Fig. 8-2. Market forms of fish.

Specifications for fish should state market form which are:

1. *Whole or round:* As it comes from the water and perhaps scaled.
2. *Drawn:* Eviscerated and perhaps scaled.
3. *Dressed (pan-dressed):* Scaled and eviscerated; usually head, tail, and fins are removed. Some, like trout, smelt, and salmon, may not have these removed. Wide differences exist in markets on what is pan-dressed and dressed fish. Trout, because of their fine scales, are not scaled. Pan-dressing usually refers to dressed small fish with the head on.
4. *Steaks:* cross sections or slices of larger sizes of dressed fish. State portion size and variation allowed in portion size.

5. *Fillets:* The flesh on either side of the backbone and over the fish bones of the thoracic cavity is removed for fillets. Some may have tiny bones, such as fillets from mackerel or herring. The skin may or may not be on. For some, breaking up in cooking is lessened when the skin is left on. A fillet cut from one side is called a *single* and when double or coming from both sides, it is called a *butterfly* fillet.

6. *Sticks:* Fillets or steaks in lengthwise pieces, usually of uniform size.

7. *Chunks:* Pieces of drawn or dressed fish, sometimes scaled.

Market forms for shellfish vary according to type. Mollusks, such as oysters, clams, and scallops, are sold in the shell or shucked. Shucking is the removal of the mollusk from its shell, leaving only clear meat. Mussels are usually sold in the shell only. Crustaceans, such as lobster, crayfish, shrimp, or crab, are frequently sold alive but also may be sold cooked in the shell, as fresh solid meat (cooked meat picked from the shell and packed into containers). Most shrimp, crayfish, and spiny lobsters are marketed "headless"; that is, with the head and thorax removed, leaving only the tail. Some shrimp may be sold in this form, cooked, shelled, and deveined,

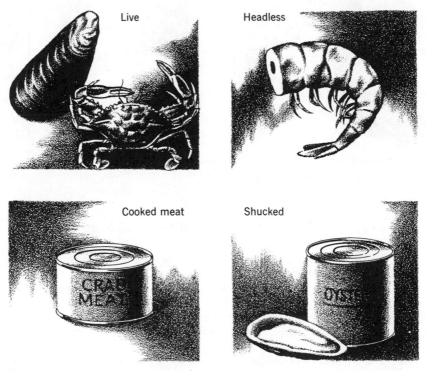

Fig. 8-3. Market forms of shellfish.

but most shrimp, lobster, and crayfish are marketed raw, called *green*.

Fish Cookery

Lean fish do not broil or bake well but they do steam poach, deep-fry (if breaded) or sauté well. Fat fish bakes, steams, broils, and boils well. Fish has little connective tissue and almost any method gives a tender product. High heat can toughen, however, and make the fish dry and pulpy. If shellfish are cooked too long or at too high a heat, it toughens and so we now recommend just poaching shrimp and simmering lobster. Clams and oysters should be cooked only to doneness and served. Most fish is rich in flavor; sometimes we mask or heighten flavor by serving tart, piquant, or flavorful sauces.

FRESH WATER AND SEA FISH

Bass

There are a wide number of bass, some of which are fresh water varieties not too important commercially. Atlantic bass are striped, sea, black, and white (common) bass; the Pacific coast produces striped and sea bass and rockfish, All are closely similar. Bass are rich in flavor, moderately high in fat, and the flesh flakes off in moist segments after cooking. It has a pleasant, rich taste. The cooked flesh is usually grayish-white and the flavor is slightly stronger than cod. It is available most of the year around as a fresh product. Best sizes and range of size are:

	Best Size	Range of Size
Striped bass	8 to 12 lb	1 to 40 lb
Sea bass	¾ to 2 lb	1 to 1¼ lb
Rockfish	3 to 4 lb	3 to 5 lb
White bass	cut portions	50 lb
Black bass	cut portions	50 to 600 lb

Bass has large scales and a large head. The large bass will be filleted or steaked. The Pacific areas and Chesapeake Bay produce striped bass throughout the year. The big bass catch comes in the fall and perhaps early summer from Long Island to northern Maine. Rockfish come largely from the Pacific Coast and is an excellent fish to smoke. Sea, black, and common bass are largely caught from Cape Cod to Florida. Catches are heaviest in May and June. Some market sizes are:

	Boston		New York	Seattle	
Jumbo	over 15 lb	Jumbo	15 lb and up	Rockfish	4 to 5 lb
Large	10 to 15 lb	Large	5 to 15 lb		
Medium	5 to 10 lb	Medium	2 to 5 lb		
Small	3 to 5 lb				

New York sizes sea bass as large, 1½ lb up; medium, ¾ to 1 lb; and small, under ½ lb.

Bluefish

The flesh of bluefish is excellent, with a distinctively sweet and savory flavor. Sizes run from with head on 1 to 8 lb with best sizes 3 to 8 lb. The average weight in Gulf markets is 4 lb, but they run from 10 to 20 lb. Baby blues weigh ¼ to 1¼ lb. New York classifies round or drawn bluefish as large, 2½ lb up; medium, 1½ to 2½ lb; small, ¾ to 1¼ lb and snapper, ¾ lb. Pollock may be called *Boston bluefish* and is not an acceptable substitute.

Butterfish

Butterfish also is called *harvest fish, dollar fish, shiner, sheepshead,*[2] and *pumpkin seed.* They are small, averaging about ½ lb each, and are 6 to 8 in. long. The Boston market classifies the round form as large, mixed, and small, respectively, ¾ lb or more, ¹/₅ lb and over, and under ¹/₅ lb. New York classifies them by number per 100 lb: jumbo—200 fish or under. large—200 to 300, medium—300 to 350, and small—350 or omer.

Cod

Atlantic cod (groundfish) are called *haddock, pollock, hake, cusk,* and *whiting.* Pacific cod are a slightly different species and are called *cod* or *lingcod.* Cod is on the market as fresh, frozen, and dried. Market forms of cod are round, dressed, steaks, skin on fillets, or skinless fillets. Most cod is marketed drawn, but pollock is usually dressed. Hake is often sold round. Most varieties average 10 to 12 lb, but the best size is 5 to 8 lb. Federal

[2]This is a different sheepshead sold on the Chicago fresh water market or the one caught in Gulf waters.

grades have been established for frozen cod fillets; grades are A and B. Specify fresh cod fillets from 1¼ to 2 lb. They are not a legitimate substitution for sole or flounder. The finer white, slightly drier flesh of sole is superior to the flaky, slightly gray, and moist flesh of cod. Cod is low in fat. Common market sizes and sizer terms are:

Boston		New York		Seattle	
Cod		Cod			
Whale	Over 25 lb	Whale	20 lb up	Cod	3 lb up
Market	2½ to 10 lb	Large	8 lb up	Lingcod	5 lb up
Scrod	1½ to 2½ lb	Market	2½ to 8 lb	(Cod fillets are avail-	
Snapper	under 1½ lb	Scrod	1½ to 2 lb	able in 25-lb cans).	
		Steak	5 lb up		
Cusk					
Cusk	over 3 lb	(Cusk fillets 2 to 3 lb are often called *Deepsea*			
Scros	1½ to 3 lb	*Whitefish* and are best purchased fresh.)			
Hake (red)	½ to 1½ lb	Hake (red)	½ to 2 lb		
Hake (white)					
Large	6 lb up				
Small	2½ to 6 lb				
Pollock		Pollock			
Large	4 lb and up	Steak	4 lb up		
Scrod	1½ to 4 lb	Market	4 lb up		
		Scrod	1 to 4 lb		

Flounder or Sole

The flounder family has many varieties; sole is flounder. The Atlantic produces 5 major varieties: winter sole, lemon sole, yellowtail (also Boston or dab), gray flounder, and sea dab. Two large flounders from this area are the fluke and southern. Pacific varieties are rex, petrale, sanddab, and Dover (English) sole. The last is of high quality, resembling the fine English or Dover sole of Europe. Seattle calls the larger sizes of this fish *Dover sole* and the smaller sizes *English sole*.

These fish usually come drawn with the head off; the best sizes are ¾ to 2 lb. Purchase fillets at from 2 to 6 oz. Many like the gray sole since it rolls or stuffs well and does not break up. On the New York market Boston sole fillets run ½ to 1 lb.

Flounder or sole is a flatfish with a dark and a white side. Both eyes rotate to the top, and the fish lives on the flat bottom and swims with an up-and-down motion. Halibut and some other fish belong to the same family. Sole and flounder are usually on the market all year.

Winter sole is a high-quality fish with thick, meaty, and delicately flavored white flesh. Lemon sole is its equal in quality and may be sold as Boston sole on the New York market. The yellowtail is marketed in considerable quantities but is not as high in quality as the first two. Gray sole has an excellent flavor and also may be called *fluke, craig, pole,* or *witch.* The true fluke is a large flounder. Gray sole may be 4 lb in round form. True Dover (English) sole may be imported fresh or frozen. Sizes are 1 to 1¼ lb, 1¼ to 1½ lb, and 1¾ to 2 lb. They usually come whole but sometimes may come drawn or ready-to-cook. Federal grades, A and B, exist for frozen sole and flounder fillets. Market classifications for flounder and sole are:

Boston Market		New York Market		Seattle Market	Gulf Market
Blackback		Blackback		Dover	All varieties
Large	¾ lb up	Large	1½ lb up	Large 24″ to 30″	Large 1 to 5 lb
Small	under ¾ lb	Medium	¾ to 1½ lb	Small 10″ to 23″	Small ½ to 1 lb
		Small	under ¾ lb		
Gray	1 to 4 lb	Gray		English	
		Jumbo	4 lb and up	Large 13″ to 15″	
		Large	2 to 4 lb	Small 11″ to 13″	
		Medium	1½ to 2 lb		
Dab	1 lb and up	Dab	1 lb and up	Petrale 16″ to 18″	

Haddock

Haddock belongs to the cod family but is caught in such quantity, it is considered a separate type. It averages 3 to 8 lb but may go as high as 16 lb. Fillets run 1 to 1¼ lb. The flesh is white and firm, with a mild, pleasing flavor. Haddock is salted and smoked. It also is marketed frozen in large quantity. When lightly salted and smoked, it is "finnan haddie." Some fillets of cod salted and smoked are called "*finnan haddie* but are not. True finnan haddie runs from 3 to 5 lb each. Boston markets the fresh fish drawn as large, over 2½ lb; scrod, 1½ to 2½ lb; and snapper, under 1½ lb. New York markets it drawn as large, 2 lb and up; scrod, 1 to 2 lb; and small scrod, under 1 lb. In some markets, the term "scrod" or "schrod" can mean almost any size haddock. Considerable haddock is marketed frozen as fillets. Federal grades, A and B, have been established for them (1959).

Halibut

The International Pacific Halibut Commission allows this country from early May to October to catch 65 to 70 million pounds a year in the Pacific halibut grounds. Small catches of Atlantic halibut also appear. The flesh freezes well. The eastern halibut comes with the head on and the western halibut with the head off. The best size is 10 to 20 lb. Chicken halibut run 8 to 10 lb.

Halibut is white, translucent, mild in flavor, and highly prized. It comes round, dressed, steaks, fillets, or chunks.

Federal standards exist for frozen halibut steaks. A steak is a piece of sliced halibut 2 oz or more packed at random or uniform weight. Uniform weight packs may be called *portion packs,* and all steaks in the lot must be within a specified weight range. A slice ½ to 1¼ in. thick is recommended. Grades are A and B.

Factors affecting grade are dehydration or freezer burn, amount of glaze remaining, uniformity of thickness and weight, and minimum bruises, foreign material, backbone, and collar bone remaining, cartilage and poor workmanship in cutting. Texture defects may be toughness, dryness, fibrousness, or wateriness. Color defects are discoloration of the drip liquor, light meat, dark meat, or nonuniformity of color. "Honeycombing," a distinct openness of grain or slight holes in the surface, is a defect. Halibut on the market is sold as follows:

Boston		New York		Seattle		Chicago	
		Eastern Halibut (Dressed)					
Drawn				(Both these markets have			
Whale	over 125 lb	Whale	over 80 lb	very little eastern			
Large	60 to 125 lb	Large	50 to 80 lb	halibut)			
Medium	12 to 60 lb	Medium	10 to 50 lb				
Chicken	7 to 12 lb	Chicken	5 to 10 lb				
Snapper	under 7 lb	Snapper	under 5 lb				
		Western Halibut (Dressed)†					
Whale	over 80 lb	Whale	over 80 lb	Whale	over 80 lb	Large and	
Large	60 to 80 lb	Large	60 to 80 lb	Large	60 to 80 lb	whale	over 60
Medium	10 to 60 lb	Medium*	10 to 60 lb	Medium*	10 to 60 lb	Medium*	10 to 60 lb
Chicken	5 to 10 lb	Chicken	5 to 10 lb	Chicken	5 to 10 lb	Chicken	5 to 10 lb

*Some markets differentiate Medium A, Medium B, Medium C halibut as running 10 to 20 lb, 20 to 40 lb, and 40 to 60 lb, respectively.
†Largely sold on the Seattle, Chicago and some other Pacific markets.

Mackerel

Jack (Boston) mackerel, 1 to 2 lb each, are caught in large numbers from Cape Cod to northern Maine in the spring and summer. Spanish mackerel 1½ to 3 lb (fillets 6 to 8 oz) is caught in the Atlantic in considerable quantities. The Pacific mackerel from California is a pilchard and canned as a large sardine.

Mackerel are fat with a rich, slightly strong flavor that is highly prized. The average mackerel is about a pound or less but King mackerel may go over 12 lb. It appears in quantity on the New York market. Market differentiation of varieties does not always occur. The Gulf market has Spanish mackerel, drawn, at 1 to 3 lb. Chicago has market sizes running from 1½ to 2 lb, and this is usually Spanish mackerel. Mackerel are marketed as follows:

Boston		New York	
Large	2¼ lb up	Large	1 lb up
Medium	1½ to 2½ lb	Medium	¾ to 1¼ lb
Small	1 to 1½ lb	Tinker	½ to ¾ lb
Tinker	½ to 1 lb	Small	under ½ lb
Tack or	Spanish is clas-sified:		
Spike	under ½ lb	Large	1½ lb up
		Small	under 1½ lb
Mackerel Shark*		King mackerel	
	25 to 200 lb	Jumbo	12 lb and up
		Large	8 to 12 lb
		Medium	5 to 8 lb
		Small	under 5 lb

Pompano

Pompano should come from Florida, Bermuda, or Gulf waters; do not accept Mexican pompano which is actually permit, an inferior fish. True pompano is rich and delicate in flavor and weighs 1 to 1½ lb. New York and Gulf markets classify round pompano: New York —large, 1½ to 2½ lb; medium, ¾ to 1¼ lb; and small, under ¾ lb; and Gulf—mixed sizes, ½ to 3½ lb.

Rosefish (Sea or Ocean Perch)

Large quantities of rosefish are caught in New England. It is much like a perch with the same texture and flavor. It is often frozen. The red under-belly distinguishes it. It is relatively low in cost. Federal grades, A and B, exist for frozen ocean perch fillets.

Red Snapper

Snapper has many imitations and substitutions. Do not accept "Jap Snapper" which is a grouper. True snapper has a flesh with large and moist segments. It is considered one of the finest fish to serve, with a rich, usually creamy pinkish-white flesh. It is caught in Florida and Gulf waters. Watch for substitutions.

Sablefish

Unlike other flatfish, sablefish are high in fat and are caught in substantial quantity in the North Pacific. It also is called *black cod* and is frequently smoked. Fresh forms are round and dressed. Seattle and Chicago use the same terminology: large, over 5 lb, and small, under 5 lb.

Salmon

A few Atlantic (Kennebec) salmon are marketed but most come from the Pacific, where, from Oregon to Alaska, large numbers are caught. Land-locked salmon, called *Kokanee* or *salmon trout,* are caught in lakes and are small, sometimes 6 to 8 oz, but the flesh is bright salmon and the flavor equals that of true salmon. They are not marketed in large quantity.

Atlantic (Kennebec) salmon averages 5 to 10 lb but may be 60 lb. The orange-colored flesh and delicate flavor make it a prized fish, and it is high in price. Federal grades, A and B, exist for frozen salmon steaks.

Pacific salmon is fresh, frozen, smoked (kippered), and canned. The redder the salmon the higher the cost, but the nutritional value is the same. The fat content drops as color declines. Red or Sockeye salmon runs 6½ to 12 lb and has the reddest flesh. Silver or medium red or Coho is about the same size as sockeye, averaging 9 lb with a rich orange flesh, slightly touched with red. Chinook (King) salmon is the largest, averaging 15 to 25 lb but may be 80 lb. It has a bright salmon-colored flesh. It appears from May to October as a fresh product. Pink or humpback is small running from 4 to 8 lb with a lighter flesh but an excellent flavor and of good baking size. Chum (keta or white) salmon is light colored and usually caught in rivers or bays, running from 8 to 16 lb. Chum salmon may be called *fall* or *silver bright*. The catch comes mostly in the fall. If river-caught, it is of lower quality. Some institutions do not accept chum salmon.

Markets classify salmon as follows:

New York Market		Seattle and Chicago Markets	
Atlantic	5 lb and up	Chinook	
		Large red	12 lb and over
Chinook		Small red	Not under 26 in. and up to 12 lb
Large	10 lb and up	White	26 in. and over
Medium	5 to 10 lb		
Chum	7 to 10 lb	Chum	5 to 11 lb
		Pink	4 to 6 lb
Silver			
Large	7 to 10 lb	Silver	6 to 12 lb
Medium	4 to 7 lb		

Shad

Shad, a member of the herring family, is caught in Atlantic waters mostly, but some is caught in the Pacific. The female averages 4½ lb and varies from 3 to 8 lb. Its roe is considered a delicacy and is broiled, baked, batter-fried or deep fried. The roe comes in pairs or strips of 2, each strip being about 5 to 6 in. in length, 2½ to 3 in. wide, and approximately an inch thick. Buyers should know that the roe of other fish is not equal in quality to shad roe. The male is called *jack* or *buck* shad and averages about 3 lb varying from 1½ to 6 lb. Its flesh is considered of slightly higher quality than that of roe shad. Shad may be obtained fresh, frozen, lightly smoked, or canned. The New York market classifies shad: roe shad (round), 3 lb up; buck shad (round), 1½ lb up; skip shad (round), ¾ to 1 lb; cut (drawn), 2 lb up. Roe is listed as jumbo, 14 oz up; large, 10 to 14 oz; medium, 8 to 10 oz; small, 8 oz and under. Shad fillets should be boneless, 8 oz to 1 lb.

Smelt

Smelt are marketed round, headed and drawn (dressed) or as boned fillets. The small smelt of the Pacific also may be called *Columbia River, silver,* or *surf.* There are several sea varieties. Market classifications are:

Boston	Boston	New York	Chicago	Seattle
Native	Canadian	New Brunswick	Great Lakes	Eulachon
Green medium	Extra	Jumbo	Jumbo	5 to 8 per lb
5½ to 7 in. or	over 7 in. or 8	7 in. and over	4 to 6 per lb	Silver
12 to 14 per lb	to 10 per lb	No. 1	No. 1	5 to 12 per lb
Green, small	No. 1	5¾ to 7 in.	7 to 10 per lb	
under 5½ in. or	5½ to 7 in.	Medium	Medium	
15 up per lb	or 12 to 14	4½ to 5¾ in.	over 10 per lb	
Sea	per lb	Small		
Large	Medium	under 4½ in.		
over 7 in. or 10 or	under 5½ in. or			
less per lb	15 up per lb			

Swordfish

Swordfish are large, averaging 200 to 300 lb each. The flesh is like halibut but is slightly more gray and has less fat, although it broils well. Specify fresh or frozen as center cuts with no nape (flake) or tail cuts permitted. American or Canadian products are higher in quality than the Japanese.

Trout

There are a wide variety of sea trout which are docked in substantial quantities. Many western trout farms produce a high-quality rainbow or brook trout averaging 8 to 10 oz drawn. Danish fresh-water trout are considered the equal in quality of the American western-water product, but the Japanese fresh water trout are not. Some large lake trout also are marketed. Market classifications are as follows:

New York Market		Chicago Market		Gulf Market	
Sea trout		Fresh-water trout (drawn)		Sea trout	
Gray (drawn or round)		Lake trout		Spotted (round or drawn)	
Large	3½ lb and up	Large	8 to 10 lb	Large	1 to 4 lb
Large-		Medium	4 to 10 lb	Medium	¾ to 1 lb
medium	1½ to 3½ lb	No. 1	2 to 4 lb	Small	½ to ¾ lb
Medium	1¼ to 1½ lb	Headless	over 8 lb	White trout	½ to 1½ lb
Small	¾ to 1¼ lb		(dressed)		
Pin	under ½ lb	Halfbreed			
Spotted (drawn or round)					
Large	over 3½ lb				
Medium	1½ to 3½ lb				
Small	under 1½ lb				
Fresh-water trout					
Brook trout (round)					
Thirds	⅓ lb				
Quarters	¼ lb				

Turbot

Turbot is imported usually frozen, although some may be obtained fresh. It runs from 30 to 40 lb in the round form and is a member of the flatfish family. Its flesh resembles halibut but is more delicate. Some markets may try to make illegitimate substitutions with sole, halibut, or flounder.

Tuna

Fresh or frozen tuna is used in limited quantity in institutions. Most tuna is canned. The following are legitimate tuna varieties: Bluefin, Southern bluefin, Oriental, Albacore, Big-eyed, Yellowfin, Northern bluefin, Skipjack, Little tunny, and Kawakawa varying in size from 10 to 1000 lb. Bonito is a related species but cannot be called tuna. Purchase smaller sizes or steaks, fillets or chunks from them. The Boston market has usually only large tuna but the New York market offers *little* tuna from 2 to 10 lb drawn. The Seattle market has tuna running from 10 to 15 lb.

Whitefish

Whitefish is prized for its white, delicate, flaky flesh that has a sweet, mellow flavor. Most comes from the Great Lakes and Canada and may be called *Lake Superior* whitefish. It averages about 4 lb, round form, and with the head on, dressed, 2 to 3 lb. Purchase fresh. The New York market classifies Jumbos as 3 lb up; No. 1, 1½ to 3 lb; medium, 1 to 1½ lb, or in dressed form as mixed sizes. The Chicago market classifies Jumbos as over 4 lb; medium-large, 3 to 4 lb; and No. 1, 1 to 3 lb.

Whiting (Silver Hake)

The whiting is a small fish caught in substantial quantities in the Atlantic. The *king whiting* also is called *kingfish* or *ground mullet*. Market classifications in Boston are: round, ½ to 4 lb; dressed, ½ to 4 lb; steak, ½ to 4 lb. New York classifies regular whiting as ¼ lb up with kings running large over a pound and small under a pound in round form. The minimum size for a fillet should be 2 oz. Gulf kings are found from 4 oz to 1 lb in round form. A form of cod also may be called *whiting* but should not be confused with true whiting, a smaller fish. U.S. Grades A and B (1966) are available for headless dressed whiting.

Miscellaneous Fish

There are many other fish on the market used locally. Canada ships in large quantities of pickerel, muskalong, pike, and so forth. Catfish farms are becoming more and more common in Louisiana and other southern states. Tables 8-5 and 8-6 indicate some of these other fish and their usual market sizes.

SHELLFISH[3]

Abalone

Abalone is a large snail found in Pacific waters from Southern California to Alaska. California prohibits shipment from the state so most abalone will come sliced and frozen from Mexico in 5- or 10-lb boxes 3 to 4 oz each. Unless properly tenderized, it can be a very tough product. Imported frozen and canned abalone is available from Japan.

---

[3] Specifications for shellfish should state that these products should come from approved areas under the conditions set forth in Parts I and II of the cooperative Program for the Certification of Interstate Shellfish Shippers of the U.S. Public Health Service Publication No. 33.

TABLE 8-5
Miscellaneous Salt-Water Fish

Boston Market		New York Market		Gulf Market	
Perch, ocean		Croaker*		Blue runner*	½ to 1 lb
(Rosefish)		Large	1½ lb up	Croaker*	¼ to 1 lb
Mixed	½ to 3 lb	Medium	¾ to 1½ lb	Grouper†	5 to 15 lb
Skate‡		Small	½ to ¾ lb	Drum‡	
Saddles	1 to 10 lb	Pins	under ½ lb	Black	
Wolffish (Ocean		Mullet*		Bulls	15 to 40 lb
Catfish)†		Large	1 lb up	Large	4 to 15 lb
——	2 to 30 lb	Medium	¾ to 1 lb	Medium	1 to 4 lb
		Small	under ¾ lb	Small	¼ to 1 lb
		Skate**		Red	
		Wings or		Bulls	15 to 40 lb
		Saddles	1 to 10 lb	Medium	3 to 15 lb
		Spot*		Rats	1½ to 3 lb
		Large	¾ lb up	Mullet*	½ to 2 lb
		Medium	½ to ¾ lb	Sheepshead†	¾ to 10 lb
		Small	under ½ lb		
		Swellfish††			
		——	all iszes		
		Tautog*			
		——	½ lb and up		
		Tilefish†			
		Large	7 lb up		
		Medium	4 to 7 lb		
		Kitten	under 4 lb		

*Round.
†Drawn.
‡Round or drawn.
**Dressed.
††Dressed and skinned.

Clams

Atlantic clams are usually the soft shell and surf varieties. Hardshell clams are found from Cape Cod to Texas and may be called *quahaugs, littleneck,* and *cherrystone* depending upon size. The latter sizes are usually served raw, whereas the large ones are used for chowder and may be called *chowder* clams. New Englanders call the soft-shell clam the *true, steamer,* or the *long-neck* clam. Purchase clams in the shell fresh and alive. A bushel should weigh 75 lb gross (72 lb net). Specify per bushel cherrystones as 320 to 360, littleneck 690 to 700, and chowder clams 150 to 200. Steamers will run 400 to 600 per bushel with a gross weight of 58 to 63 lb and yield net 55 to 60 lb. The Boston market has a shucked hard-shell clam that runs about 100 to 125 per gallon and is called *sharp*. Sometimes this market also calls quahogs as *sharps*. The New York market has shucked soft-shell clams running per gallon large, 200 to 300; medium, 350 to 400; and small, 600 to 700. The Boston market sizes them slightly differently but keeps the same names.

TABLE 8-6
Miscellaneous Fresh-Water Fish

New York Market		Gulf Market		Chicago Market	
Blue pike*		Buffalofish‡	3 to 20 lb	Blue pike*	½ lb
Jumbo	1½ lb up	Catfish†	1 to 40 lb	Pins	5 to 6 per lb
Regular	½ to 1½ lb	Sheepshead	(gaspergou)†	Buffalofish*	
Buffalofish*			1 to 5 lb	Jumbo	over 8 lb
Jumbo	over 7 lb			No. 1	4 to 8 lb
No. 1	4 to 7 lb			Medium	2 to 4 lb
Carp*				Bullheads††	
Jumbo	7 lb and up			Jumbo	over ¾ lb
No. 1	4 to 7 lb			Large	½ lb
Medium	under 4 lb			Carp*	
Lake herring*				Jumbo	over 8 lb
Large	3 per lb			No. 1	4 to 8 lb
Regular	4 per lb and up			Medium	2 to 4 lb
Sauger*	½ to 1½ lb			Chub†	
Sucker (mullet)*				Large	3 to 4 per lb
Mixed	1 to 3 lb			Medium	5 to 7 per lb
Yellow pike*				Small	over 7 per lb
Large	3½ lb and up			Lake herring†	
No. 1	1½ to 3 lb			Regular	4 to 7 per lb
No. 2	1 to 1½ lb			Bluefin	3 to 4 per lb
				(Minnesota)	
				Pickerel	
				Large**	over 3 lb
				Medium*	1½ to 3 lb
				Sauger*	
				Lake Erie	1 lb
				Winnipeg	½ to ¾ lb
				Manitoba	¾ to 1 lb
				Sheepshead*	
				Hard and soft meat:	
				Large	over 5 lb
				Medium	1½ to 5 lb
				Small	¾ to 1½ lb

TABLE 8-6 (cont'd)
Miscellaneous Fresh-Water Fish

New York Market	Gulf Market	Chicago Market	
		Lake Erie	1 to 5 lb
		Sucker	
		Jumbo†	4 to 6 lb
		Medium†	under 4 lb
		Mullet*	all iszes
		Yellow perch*	
		Native:	
		Jumbo	½ to ¾ lb
		Large	3 fish per lb
		Medium	4 fish per lb
		Small	over 4 fish per lb
		Canadian	
		Jumbo	¾ lb
		Large	2 per lb
		Yellow pike*	
		No. 1 hard	2½ to 3½ lb
		No. 2 hard	1 to 2½ lb

*Round.
†Drawn.
‡Round or drawn.
**Dressed.
††Dressed and skinned.

Pacific hard-shell clams are *butter* and *littleneck* clams found in the North Pacific; *pismo,* a large clam from California used for chowders; and the *razor* or *soft-shell* clam taken from the surfs in Washington. No size is specified for butter or littleneck clams except that they must be mature clams. They are marketed in the shell in mixed sizes in 100-lb bags or 80-lb boxes.

Shucked fresh (chilled) clams, called Type I, should be delivered iced or from 32 to 38°F within 72 hours of shucking. Frozen clams (Type II) should be stored at 0°F or less for not over 180 days. Classes of shucked clams are: Class 1, hard-shell, (a) hard, round, or quahog from the Atlantic or Florida, (b) ocean quahogs (Atlantic), (c) butter (Pacific), (d) littleneck (Pacific), and (e) cockle (Pacific); Class 2, soft-shell, which are soft-shells, sand clams, nanynose or maninose clams from either the Atlantic or Pacific and Class 3, surf or skimmer, from the Atlantic usually available minced. There are no size restrictions for these clams except:

Class I, a, Hard-shell			Class II, Soft-shell		
Type I/gal	Type II/6-l 6-lb Pack	Term for Size	Type I/gal	Type II/ 6-lb Pack	Term for Size
Up to 110	Up to 82	Chowders	Up to 300	Up to 225	Large
110 to 175	82 to 131	Mediums	300 to 500	225 to 375	Medium
175 to 250	131 to 188	Cherrystones	Over 500	375 up	Small
Over 250	188 up	Littlenecks			

Note: AA gallon runs 8 lb and a bushel of hard-shells weigh 80 lb.

Clams should come from sound, strictly fresh clams; dead clams (gapers) cannot be used. Potable water must be used in rinsing. The clams cannot be in water longer than 30 minutes with the time of blowing (rinsing or soaking in fresh water) not to exceed 5 minutes. Such blowing counts as 10 minutes of the total 30 minutes. They should be thoroughly drained and should not have more than 8% by weight of drainable liquor on them either before freezing or when delivered as chilled clams. Freezing to an internal temperature of 0°F or less should be accomplished within 24 hours of shucking. Frozen clams should show no evidence of being thawed and then being refrozen. No unapproved chemicals or other products can be used and the clams should be free of seaweed or algae, sand, or other foreign matter. Only 4 pieces of shell per quart should be allowed. There should be no more than 5 cut, torn, or broken clams per pint. The color, odor, and flavor should be good and the texture firm, not soft.

Crab

The Atlantic *blue* crab weighing ¼ to 1 lb is marketed in greatest quantity. New England *rock* crab averages 1 to ½ lb. Its flesh is slightly brown in color and not white like the blue crab. Florida *stone* crabs are considered a delicacy. Only the front claw is eaten. Soft-shell crabs are blue crabs just after they have molted or lost their shell. They are frequently marketed alive. *Dungeness* crab from the Pacific averages 1¾ to 3½ lb. It has a delicate, sweet, tender white meat. Claw meat brings a higher price than body meat. Only the legs and claws of the Alaska *king* crab are eaten. This crab may weigh from 6 to 20 lb and measure 6 ft from one leg tip to the tip of the opposite leg. It is usually available only frozen in the shell. Dungeness crab is available alive in the shell, cooked in the shell, claw meat only, claw and body meat, and body meat only. Sizes in the shell are Ocean, 24 lb per doz, and Puget Sound, 22 lb per dozen. Laws prohibit the sale of soft-shell Dungeness crab. California produces some *rock* crab, and a crab called the *tanner* is caught in Alaska waters. Both are consumed only on local markets.

Blue crabs are sized on the Gulf markets: hard-shell $^1/_3$ to $^2/_3$ lb each and soft-shell $^1/_8$ to $^1/_2$ lb each. New York classifies them as jumbo, 5½ in.; large prime, 5 to 5½ in.; prime, 4½ to 5 in.; hotel prime, 4 to 4½ in.; large medium, 3½ to 4 in.; and medium, under 3½ in. Culls are all sizes. Measurements are point to point as diameter across the back.

Purchase blue crab meat either fresh or pasteurized as lump, all body chunk meat; flake, small pieces of body meat or claw. Claw meat is brownish in color and lowest in price. New York distinguishes between large lump meat and smaller chunks, calling the former *jumbo* and the other *flake* or *special of the back fin. Mixed* must be over 50% lump, the remainder being flake. The best blue crab comes from around Maryland, but Virginia and Florida crab are almost its equal. Frozen crab meat loses quality rapidly after freezing.

Crayfish and Spiny Lobster

Crayfish are small crustaceans without 2 front claws. They are caught in inland streams and river inlets and average 6 to 25 per pound. We import some crayfish. *Spiny* or *rock* lobster is a large sea crayfish sold with the head and thorax removed. The *Laguna* or Pacific lobster is sold with the head on, frequently cooked in the shell. It weighs 10 oz to 2 lb. Imported spiny lobster tails come from Africa, Australia and New Zealand largely. They average 8 oz to a lb. The New York market grades them *jumbo,* 1 lb up; *large,* 12 to 16 oz; *medium,* 9 to 12 oz; *small,* 6 to 9 oz. Some picked, cooked spiny lobster meat is sold and it is difficult to tell it from true lobster meat.

Lobster

The *common* or *true* lobster has two large claws near the head. Most of our lobster comes from Maine and Massachusetts, but we may import some from Europe. Lobsters may be shipped alive up to 3000 miles. An uncooked lobster is a dark bluish-green or brownish-olive or blackish-brown color which changes to a bright red on cooking. They are purchased in the shell fresh alive or frozen and sometimes cooked. Picked meat also is available. The cost of lobster is extremely high because of its scarcity and a large demand. The meat of the male is said to be firmer and the color of the shell, after cooking, a brighter red than the female. Some prefer the female meat because it contains the roe or coral.

A lobster with one claw is called a *cull* and finds its way usually to picked, cooked meat. Boston grades live lobster: *jumbo,* 3 lb up; *select,* 1¼ to 3 lb; *chicken* 1 lb; and *weaks,* all sizes but of such low vitality they can live only a very short time. New York classifies them: *jumbo,* 3 lb up; *large,* 1½ to 2½ lb; *quarter,* 1¼ to 1½ lb; *chicken,* ¾ to 1 lb. A chicken lobster is considered an average portion. Lobsters cannot be caught during their breeding season. A lobster that has just molted (lost its shell) has very little meat. As they outgrow the shell, it splits away and a new one forms. A lobster may molt 14 to 17 times the first year and a lobster about 5 years old has molted about 25 times. Immature lobsters are protected by law.

Mussels

A mussel is a bivalve resembling an oyster but is razor shaped and about 2½ in. or more long. A bushel alive in the shell weighs from 45 to 55 lb and contains from 350 to 400 medium-sized ones. Most come from the North Atlantic but some fresh-water ones are sold on local markets.

Oysters

Oysters and other shellfish should come from beds certified for sanitation by the Public Health Service. Labels on containers should carry a certification number.

Atlantic oysters come from the Canadian Maritimes to Texas. Chesapeake Bluepoints are an excellent, white oyster. Long Island oysters run about 250 to 300 per bushel. Chincoteagues average 300 to 350 per bushel and Cape Cod oysters, the ones from around Chatham being preferred, run 200 to 250 per bushel. A bushel of oysters should weigh gross about 65 to 70 lb and net 62 to 67 lb with the lighter weights being more characteristic early in the season and the heavier ones later as the oysters mature.

The Pacific produces the Olympia and Japanese (Pacific) oyster. The Pacific came from Japanese seed and is a large, gray oyster often cooked rather than eaten raw. Pacifics are sold in the shell by the pound and shucked by the gallon. A gallon should weigh not less than 8 lb net.

The Olympia is also called the *western* oyster and is native to the Puget Sound area. They are prized for use raw in cocktails. A gallon contains about 1600 to 1700 shucked Olympias. A sack contains about 120 lb in the shell.

Oysters can absorb considerable water if shucked and left in a low salt water. They therefore should not be in contact with potable water more than 30 minutes. If the water contains less than 0.75% salt, all excess liquid must be drained away before packing. After draining 2 minutes, shucked oysters should not have more than 5% liquid draining from them. Federal standards for oysters give the following sizes per gallon (about 8 lb):

Eastern		Pacific or Japanese	
Extra large	160 or less	Large	64 or less
Large	160–210	Medium	65–96
Medium	210–300	Small	97 144
Small	300–500	Extra small	144 or over
Very small	over 500		

Market classifications are

Eastern Oysters					Pacific or Japanese Oysters
Boston Market		New York Market			Seattle Market
		Live in the shell			
Large	500 per bbl	Box	150 per bu		By the sack priced by
Medium	700–750	Medium	200		the pound; 80-lb per
Small	900–1050	Half shell	325*		sack; average 200 per
Extra small	1050–1200	Blue point	400		sack for smaller sizes.
		Shucked per gallon			
Count	135–160	Count	160 or less		Grade A	40–64
Select	180–230	Extra select	160–210		Grade B	65–80
Standard	300–350	Select	210–300		Grade C	81–96
					Grade C	97–120
					Grade E	121–144
					Grade F	over 144

*Also called *Long Island* and may be specified 250 to 300 per bu.

Some Pacific oysters are graded small, medium, and large. *Straights* are ungraded for size. Eastern oysters are sold in the shell alive by the dozen, peck, bushel, or crate and in gallons shucked, fresh, or frozen.

Scallops

A mollusk having a scalloped edge shell produces either bay or sea scallops. Sea scallops are also called *New Bedford* scallops and run 100 to 170 per gal. Bay scallops are considered better than sea scallops. Scallop meat is only the adductor muscle or "eye" that opens and closes the shell. It is about 10% of the flesh and 1½ bushels of scallops give 8½ to 9 lb of clear meat, just over a gallon. Scallops can be purchased in the shell but usually are sold as clear meat fresh or frozen. The color of bay scallop meat is creamy white, light tan or pinkish while sea scallops are more white. Genuine Cape Cod scallops are creamy white. They run 480 to 640 per gallon. Most scallops come from New England waters. Bay scallops come from shallower waters than sea scallops. Some scallops also come from the Pacific.

Frozen raw scallops are solid (Style I), glazed (substyle a), or not glazed (substyle b) or individually quick frozen (IQF) (Style II) so they can be separated without thawing. These IQF scallops may or may not be glazed. These are 2 types: (1) adductor muscle only and (2) adductor muscle with catch (gristle and sweet) portion removed. Federal grades are A (85) and B (70) and the scallops qualify for a grade after being evaluated for texture, extraneous material, color, uniformity of size, small or undesirable pieces, and, if frozen, dehydration. Federal grades for frozen fried scallops also exist. Style I is a random pack and Style II a uniform pack. Grades are A (85) and B (70).

Boston lists bay scallops as 480 to 850 per gal and sea scallops 110 to 170 per gal. New York classifies the former as *large* if ¾ in. or more in diameter; *medium,* ½ to ¾ in. in diameter; and *small,* ½ in. or less in diameter. It has no grade sizes for sea scallops. The New York market may call Long Island scallops *Cape* scallops. Scallops from Long Island or north are considered to be superior to scallops from the Carolinas or Florida.

Shrimp

We import about twice as much shrimp as we produce in our own waters. Most of our shrimp come from Gulf waters. White and pink varieties of shrimp are considered better than the browns and the deep water reds. The Pacific coast and north Atlantic produce a much smaller shrimp that is used locally and frequently canned.

To meet a three-fold increase in the demand for shrimp in the last 20 years, we now import considerable shrimp from Mexico, Panama, Japan, Ecuador, and India. Some shrimp are alive but most are sold fresh and headless or frozen with heads on or off. Some may be peeled, deveined, and quick frozen (PDQ). They still need cooking. Cooking loss is about 50% for these.

Federal shrimp grades are A (85) and B (70) for frozen, raw breaded shrimp, free of sand veins.* Types are I—fantail, split (butterfly) with tail fin on but free of all shell segments; II—round fantail, same as fantail but not split; III—split without tail fin and shell segments; and IV—round, same as II but unsplit. Breading may not be over 50% but a preferable standard would be 35%.

A federal specification exists also for chilled and frozen (raw and cooked) shrimp. It classifies shrimp as Type I, raw, class 1 (chilled) and class 2 (frozen either glazed or unglazed). Class 2 shrimp may be headless but not peeled (Style A) and peeled and deveined (Style B). Type II shrimp are cooked with class 1 being chilled, class 2 frozen either glazed or unglazed. Class 2 are only Style B which are peeled and deveined. These shrimp may be prepared from fresh (chilled) raw shrimp, headless raw shrimp stored at 0°F or below for 90 days or less, headless raw shrimp stored at 0°F for 150 days or less. Sizing is per pound and price is frequently related to size:

Commercial Name*	Type I, Raw, Chilled or Frozen Not Peeled Peeled, Deveined	Peeled, Deveined	Type II, Cooked, Chilled or Frozen Peeled, Deveined
Colossal	15 or less	19 or less	30 or less
Extra jumbo	16 to 20	20 to 25	31 to 40
Jumbo	21 to 25	26 to 31	41 to 60
Extra large	26 to 30	32 to 38	61 to 90
Large	31 to 35	39 to 44	91 to 125
Medium large	36 to 42	45 to 53	126 up
Medium	43 to 50	54 to 63	
Small	51 to 60	64 to 75	
Extra small	61 and over	76 and over	

*These commercial names apply to Type I only and not Type II. The market also classifies shrimp 10 or under per lb as Extra Colossal and over 70 per lb as Tiny.

The Gulf markets size shrimp with heads on: *large,* under 18 per lb; *medium,* 18 to 35 per lb; *small,* over 35 per lb. The New York and Chicago markets size per lb as follows:

*Breaded *Size 1* is 19 or less per lb; *Size 2* is 19 to 24 per lb; and *Size 3* is 23 to 28 per lb.

Chicago Market		New York Market
Extra jumbo	Less than 15	No grade terms are used; buyers
Jumbo	16 to 20	purchase by count per pound as under
Large	21 to 25	15, 15 to 20, 21 to 25, 26 to 30, 31–35,
Large-medium	26 to 30	36–40, 41–45, 46–50, 51–60 and
Medium	31 to 42	over 60.
Small	43 to 65	
Very small or bait	more than 66	

The equivalent size between headless shrimp in the shell and shelled are considered:

In the Shell	Shelled
15 to 20 per lb	21 to 25 per lb
21 to 25 per lb	26 to 30 per lb
26 to 30 per lb	31 to 35 per lb

These counts are somewhat different than those of the federal government above but only slightly so.

Miscellaneous Shellfish or Marine Products

Sea turtles run from 2 to 100 lb and may be purchased alive or dressed. Fresh water Diamondback terrapin are usually sold alive as *cows*, 1½ to 2 lb; *heifers*, 1 lb and *bulls*, ½ to 1 lb. Turtle meat may be purchased out of the shell, raw or cooked. Turtle meat is used for soup, steaks and other dishes.

Live frogs run from ½ to a lb each but most facilities purchase legs and saddles (lower part of the back) fresh or frozen. Sizes are per lb *extra large*, 2 to 3; *large*, 4 to 5; *medium*, 6 to 8; *small*, 9 to 12. The Japanese market a high quality frog leg equal to those coming from our southern states.

Eels come live, dressed and skinned or smoked and are available throughout the year although caught most heavily in the fall. Round form sizes are *large*, 2 to 5 lb; *medium*, 1 to 2 lb; and *small*, under 1 lb.

Conchs and snails are sold usually alive in the shell. Large snails run around 32 to the pound. Imports come from France. Cuttlefish (sepia) average in round form ½ to ¾ lb. Octopus are usually sold in round form; small ones run ¾ lb up. Squid run 5 to 6 to the pound in round form.

Canned Fish

More canned fish is consumed in this country than fresh or otherwise. Price is increasing and consumption is dropping as the popularity of fresh and frozen fish increases. The high cost of meat is causing a higher consumption of fish per capita. There are many kinds of canned fish.

Buyers should look for neatness of pack, unbroken fish and freedom from bruises, brown blood spots, cracks, blood, entrails, scales and other defects. The color of the flesh and liquid should be clear and typical. Unevenly colored flesh or that bearing pink or red streaks is undesirable. Flavor and odor should be pleasant, free from rancidity, acrid taste, spoilage or other off-flavors or odors. The texture should be firm but not fibrous.

The drained weight for dry vacuum pack fish should be nearly 100% of the can contents. The drained weight of items in juice or liquid such as oysters should be at least 59% of the weight of the water capacity of the can. For dry pack shrimp this is usually desirable at 60% or more and for wet pack 64%. Fish that pack heavily, such as sardines, tuna or salmon have higher drained weights.

TABLE 8-7
Purchase Quantities for Fish and Shellfish

Type	Weight AP	Yield % AS	Portion AS (oz) Cooked	Portions per Purchase Unit	Number Units per 100 Portions
Fish, Fresh or Frozen					
Fillets	lb	64	2 to 3	3.4 to 5.1	19¾ to 29½
Steaks	lb	58*	2 to 3	3.1 to 4.6	21¾ to 32½
Dressed	lb	45*	2 to 3	2.4 to 3.6	28 to 41¾
Drawn	lb	32*	2 to 3	1.7 to 2.6	39¼ to 58½
Whole (round)	lb	27*	2 to 3	1.4 to 2.2	46½ to 69½
Breaded, raw	lb	85	3 to 4	3.4 to 4.5	22 to 29¾
Breaded, fried	lb	95	3 to 4	3.8 to 5.1	19¾ to 26½
Shellfish, Live					
Clams, hard†	doz	14*	6 raw	2.0	50
Clams, soft†	doz	29*	12 raw	1.0	100
Crabs, blue	lb	14*	2 to 3	.7 to 1.1	89½ to 133½
Crabs, Dungeness	lb	24*	2 to 3	1.3 to 1.9	52¼ to 78¼
Oysters†	doz	12*	6 raw	2.0	50
Shellfish, Fresh or Frozen					
Clams, shucked	lb	48	2 to 3	2.6 to 3.8	26 to 39¼
Crabs, blue	lb	14*	2 to 3	.7 to 1.1	89½ to 133½
Crabs, Dungeness	lb	24*	2 to 3	1.3 to 1.9	52¼ to 78¼
Crabmeat	lb	97*	2 to 3	5.2 to 7.8	13 to 19½

TABLE 8-7 (cont'd)
Purchase Quantities for Fish and Shellfish

Type	Weight AP	Yield % AS	Portion AS (oz) Cooked	Portions per Purchase Unit	Number Units per 100 Portions
Lobster, in shell	lb	25*	16 to 20	about one	100 to 125
Lobster meat	lb	91	2 to 3	4.9 to 7.3	13¾ to 20¾
Oysters, shucked	lb	40	2 to 3	2.1 to 3.2	31¼ to 47
Scallops, shucked	lb	63	2 to 3	3.4 to 5.0	20 to 30
Shrimp, cooked‡	lb	100	2 to 3	5.3 to 8.0	12½ to 19
Shrimp, raw	lb	50	2 to 3	2.7 to 4.6	25 to 37½
Shrimp, raw‡	lb	62	2 to 3	3.3 to 5.0	20¼ to 30½
Clams, breaded, raw	lb	83	2 to 3	4.4 to 6.4	15¼ to 19¾
Clams, breaded, fried	lb	85	2 to 3	4.5 to 6.8	14¾ to 22¼
Crabcakes, fried	lb	95	2 to 3	5.1 to 7.6	13¼ to 19¾
Lobster tail	lb	51*	4 to 8	about 1 to 2	50 to 100
Oysters, breaded, raw	lb	88	2 to 3	4.7 to 7.0	14¼ to 21½
Scallops, breaded, fried	lb	93	2 to 3	5.0 to 7.4	13½ to 20¼
Scallops, breaded, raw	lb	81	2 to 3	4.3 to 6.5	15½ to 23¼
Shrimp, breaded, fried	lb	88	2 to 3	4.7 to 7.0	14½ to 21½
Shrimp, breaded, raw	lb	85	2 to 3	4.5 to 6.8	14¾ to 22¼
Canned Fish Products					
Mackerel	15 oz	83	2 to 3	4.2 to 6.3	16 to 24 cans
Salmon	16 oz	81	2 to 3	4.3 to 6.5	15½ to 23¼ cans
Salmon	64 oz	78	2 to 3	16.7 to 25.0	6 to 4 cans
Sardines, Maine	4 oz	90	2 to 3	1.2 to 1.8	55 to 83 cans
Sardines, Maine	12 oz	90	2 to 3	3.6 to 5.4	18¾ to 28 cans
Sardines, Pacific	15 oz	77**	2 to 3	3.8 to 5.8	17½ to 26¼ cans
Sardines, Pacific	15 oz	100**	2 to 3	5.0 to 7.5	13½ to 20 cans
Tuna	4 oz	93	2 to 3	1.8 to 1.2	55 to 84 cans
Tuna	6½ oz	93	2 to 3	2.0 to 3.0	50 to 33 cans
Tuna	60 oz	93	2 to 3	18.6 to 27.9	3.4 to 3.6 cans
Clam chowder, condensed	51 oz	200	8	12.5	8 cans
Clam juice	12 oz	100	3	4.0	25 cans
Clams, minced	7½ oz	100	2 to 3	2.5 to 3.7	26¾ to 40 cans
Clams, minced	51 oz	100	2 to 3	17.0 to 25.5	4 to 6 cans
Crabmeat	6½ oz	85	2 to 3	1.8 to 2.8	36½ to 54¾ cans
Oysters, whole	5 oz	100	2 to 3	1.7 to 2.5	40 to 60 cans
Oyster stew	10½ oz	100	8	1.3	76½ cans
Shrimp	4½ oz	100	2 to 3	1.5 to 2.3	44½ to 66¾ cans

*Edible portion.
†Served in the shell.
‡Peeled and the cooked are deveined.
**In brine while those that follow are in mustard or tomato sauce.

Canned Fish Products

Anchovies are a small fish caught largely in Mediterranean waters. They are filleted, given a high salt cure and canned in 1-lb or smaller cans. They are also sold rolled; some rolls may have special fillings in the center such as capers, nuts or small onions. Anchovy paste is also available.

Canned clams may be purchased whole or minced (chopped). Minced should be all meat from ¼ to 1 in. in size. Whole clams should not be in juice over 3% in salt and minced in juice not over 1¼%. Acceptable varieties of clams are butter, littleneck, hard (quahog), razor, soft, surf (skimmer) and pismo. Most clams for institutions are packed in No. 3 cylinder or No. 10 cans. The liquor on canned clams may be milky but otherwise clear. The meat can be creamy or white but not dark or gray. There should be little evidence of silt, dirt or shells on the can bottom or in the clams. The meat must be tender, flavorful and free from objectionable odors.

Canned codfish is used for the preparation of codfish balls or other codfish dishes. Canned codfish balls are also available.

Canned crab meat is acceptable from blue, Dungeness or king crab. The two latter varieties may also be sold mixed. Can sizes (net weight) are 3, 6½, 7½, 15, and 16 oz. The odor should be pleasant and sweet with no appearance of black on the flesh. King crab is bright red on the surface; dungeness is light pink to orange on the surface and blue crab claw meat is brown on the surface but the flesh is almost white. Some crab meat—and shrimp or lobster—is specified vacuum packed and wrapped in paper inside the can. The texture of the flesh should be free of shell and cartilage and somewhat firm but soft, not stringy or tough. Specialty crab pastes are available.

Some canned herring is available, sold packed similar to sardines in tomato sauce, liquid, oil or mustard sauce. Note evidence of viscera, poor

TABLE 8-8
Recommended Weights of Canned Clams in Ounces

Can Size	Net Contents	Drained Weight	Cans/Case
No. ½ flat	7.2	3.4	24
No. 1, picnic	10.0	4.5	24
No. 300	15.0	6.7	24
No. 2	19.9	10.0	24
No. 3 cylinder	49.0	22.0	12
No. 10	96.0	43.2	6

خاویار آستر درجه یك

قوطیهای فاقد پلمب و برچسب شرکت سهامی شیلات ایران

از درجه اعتبار ساقط است

Caviar grain Ossetra Premiere qualité

Les boîtes non plombées et sans l'étiqutte spéciale de
la Sociéte Sahami Chilate Iran. ne soet pas valables

Fig. 8-4. Some genuine Beluga (Iranian) caviar comes sealed with a metal tag as shown at the top. The label is both in Arabic and in French.

workmanship, etc. since these products move on the market at low prices and processors may attempt to cut corners.

Canned lobster meat comes in cans sized similarly as for crab. The meat may come from either common lobster or spiny lobster. Specialty lobster pastes are available for use in sandwiches, *hors d'oeuvres,* and so on.

Fish roe may be obtained in black or salmon-colored form. Only roe from the sturgeon may be labeled caviar. Most comes from either Russia or Iran (beluga). The best is a light tan color and as it darkens the quality and price drop. Imitation caviar comes from whitefish, shad, salmon or other fish.

Salmon is packed in 4, 8, 16, or 64 oz cans, net contents, but the most popular size is the 1-lb can. Price is frequently based on redness of color but all salmon is equally nutritious although the red types will have more oil on them. The best salmon comes from the large body pieces and in a ½ or lb can there should not be more than three pieces and a patch and in a 4-lb can not more than 12 pieces and a patch. Style I has skin and bones included and Style II has these removed. Dietetic packs should not have more than 60 mg of sodium per 100 grams of drained meat. The following summarizes the color of flesh and its texture as found in various salmon varieties:

Type Salmon	Flesh Color	Flesh Texture
King (Chinook)	Light red to almost white	Moderately firm to soft
Red (Sockeye or Blueback)	Deep red to deep orange	Very firm to soft
Silver (Coho)	Red to orange-red or light pink	Moderately firm to soft
Pink	Light pink with orange shading to yellow	Moderately firm to soft
Chum (Keta)	Pink to light yellow	Moderately firm to firm

Three types of sardines are available on our market. Imports are largely from Norway and come packed in 3¼-oz cans containing around 8 sardines. The fish is either Brisling or Silt, a small herring-type fish. Most of these imports are in oil. The second type available is the California pilchard, a large sardine that is usually packed in 15-oz net oval cans. Type of pack may be oil, mustard or tomato sauce. These sardines are coarser in texture than the small sardines and may be stronger in flavor. The Maine sardine is the third type and comprises about 70% of the total market. Most of the pack is in 3¼-oz cans in oil, but some packs are available in 12-oz cans. Most of the larger packs are in mustard or tomato sauce.

Maine sardines come from a small herring. The sizes range from 4 to 12 fish per 3¼-oz can, but the average will be found to be around 5 to 6 per can. The oil used is usually soybean oil. There are one hundred 3¼-oz cans per case.

Federal standards for grades exist for Maine sardines. In 1958 the Maine sardine industry asked the state legislature to pass a mandatory law requiring all oil-packed sardines processed in the state to be federally graded. There are four grades: Fancy, Extra Standard, Standard and Substandard. Substandard lots must be plainly marked "Substandard grade—good food—not high quality" and cannot be marketed as sardines. Factors considered in grading are defects that are largely based on workmanship, odor, taste and texture. Sardines with objectionable rancid, foreign, acrid, strong or unusual taste or odor are given zero scores and cannot be graded above substandard. Good character or texture is indicated if the sardine remains intact when lifted with a 4-tined fork (¾ in. wide) without breaking. The sardine should not be tough or fibrous. Mushy or gritty sardines are graded down.

Most of the canned shrimp are small. Some may be in brine while others may be vacuum dry pack. The product should be whole and contain no foreign material or loose or adhering appendages. The flavor and odor should be good. All varieties of shrimp are acceptable except the sea-bob variety. Can sizes and minimum counts of shrimp are as follows:

Type Pack	Can Size	Drained Weight	1	2	3	4	5	6	Maximum Weight of Defective Shrimp‡
Wet	307 × 201	5½ oz	15	22	31	56	106	†	½ oz
Wet	307 × 208	6¾ oz	19	26	38	68	129	†	⅝ oz
Dry	307 × 208	6¼ oz	19	26	38	68	129	†	⅝ oz
Wet	211 × 400	7 oz	19	27	39	71	133	†	⅝ oz
Dry	211 × 400	6½ oz	19	27	39	71	133	†	⅝ oz
Wet	307 × 400	11¼ oz	32	44	63	115	216	†	1⅛ oz
Dry	307 × 400	10½ oz	32	44	63	115	216	†	1 oz
Wet	307 × 409	13 oz	36	50	71	130	244	†	1¼ oz
Wet	401 × 411	19 oz	52	74	105	191	359	†	1⅞ oz
Wet	502 × 510	38 oz	105	148	210	382	718	†	3¾ oz

*Trade sizes would be 1, colossal; 2, jumbo; 3, large; 4, medium; 5, small; and 6, tiny or broken.
†There are no maximum or minimum number for tiny or broken.
‡Defective shrimp would be those broken, improperly deveined, etc.

Canned tuna must come from Bluefin, Southern bluefin, Oriental, Albacore, Big-eye, Yellowfin, Northern bluefin, Skipjack, Little tunny or Kawakawa varieties. Some high quality Italian *tonno* is available packed in olive oil. Packs are solid, chunks, flakes or grated. Solid (fancy) pack must come from the loins or large body muscles and is used for solid pieces where appearance is important. Chunk is a mixture of solid pieces. Around 50% may pass through a ½ in. screen. Flakes are small pieces but the muscular structure is retained. Grated tuna is almost granular but not pasty. Tuna comes as white or light meat, white being considered of higher quality. Albacore has the whitest meat. Japanese imported Grade A albacore is of high quality.

Tuna is packed in vegetable or olive, water and salt or just water. If the pack is dietetic (low sodium), the flesh cannot have more than 50 mg of sodium per 100 grams. Regular packs will run ½% to 2¼% salt. Drained weights are usually 63 to 64% of net can contents. Recommended net and drained weights in ounces are:

Can Size	Type	Net Contents	Drained Weight	Can Size	Type	Net Contents	Drained Weight
211 × 109	Solid	3.50	2.25	401 × 206	Solid	13.00	8.76
	Chunks	3.40	1.98		Chunks	12.50	7.68
	Flakes	3.40	1.98		Flakes	12.50	7.68
	Grated	3.45	2.00		Grated	11.75	7.76
307 × 113	Solid	7.00	4.47	603 × 408	Solid	64.00	43.20
	Chunks	6.50	3.92		Chunks	60.00	37.90
	Flakes	6.25	3.92		Flakes	60.00	37.90
	Grated	6.25	3.96		Grated	59.00	38.30

Cured Fish

There are many different kinds of smoked, salted or otherwise cured fish. Cod, halibut, trout, whitefish, chub, sablefish and others are smoked. Mackerel, herring, cod, ling cod, haddock are salted. Genuine finnan haddie is lightly smoked and salted haddock. It is split and comes with the skin and bones, averaging 3 to 5 lb. Boneless smoked cod fillets may be called finnan haddie so buyers should understand which product they are obtaining. Individual specifications must be written to secure the type of cured fish needed. It is best to specify "current pack" since some products deteriorate with age.

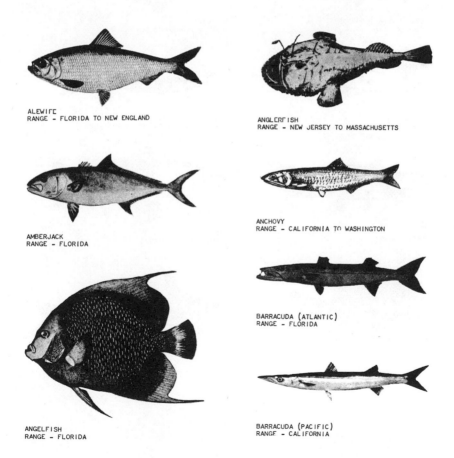

ALEWIFE
RANGE - FLORIDA TO NEW ENGLAND

ANGLERFISH
RANGE - NEW JERSEY TO MASSACHUSETTS

AMBERJACK
RANGE - FLORIDA

ANCHOVY
RANGE - CALIFORNIA TO WASHINGTON

BARRACUDA (ATLANTIC)
RANGE - FLORIDA

ANGELFISH
RANGE - FLORIDA

BARRACUDA (PACIFIC)
RANGE - CALIFORNIA

BLUEFISH
RANGE - GULF OF MEXICO TO NEW ENGLAND

BURBOT
RANGE - GREAT LAKES

BLUE RUNNER OR HARDTAIL
RANGE - GULF OF MEXICO

BUTTERFISH
RANGE - FLORIDA TO NEW ENGLAND

BONITO (ATLANTIC)
RANGE - NORTH CAROLINA TO MASSACHUSETTS

CABIO
RANGE - FLORIDA TO VIRGINIA

BOWFIN
RANGE - FRESH-WATER

CARP
RANGE - FRESH-WATER

BUFFALOFISH
RANGE - FRESH-WATER

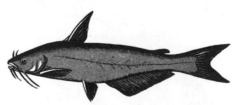

CATFISH
RANGE - FRESH-WATER

CHUB
RANGE - GREAT LAKES

CROAKER
RANGE - GULF OF MEXICO TO NEW YORK

CIGARFISH
RANGE - FLORIDA

CUNNER
RANGE - NEW ENGLAND

COD
RANGE - VIRGINIA TO MAINE, WASHINGTON,
          AND ALASKA

CUSK
RANGE - NEW ENGLAND

CRAPPIE
RANGE - FRESH-WATER LAKES

DOLLY VARDEN TROUT
RANGE - PACIFIC

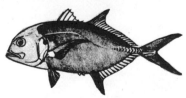

CREVALLE
RANGE - SOUTH ATLANTIC AND GULF STATES

DOLPHIN
RANGE - FLORIDA TO NORTH CAROLINA

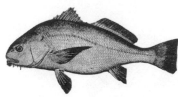

DRUM, BLACK
RANGE - TEXAS TO NORTH CAROLINA

LEMON SOLE
RANGE - NEW YORK TO MAINE

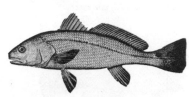

DRUM, RED
RANGE - TEXAS - MARYLAND

DAB
RANGE - MASSACHUSETTS TO NOVA SCOTIA

EEL, COMMON
RANGE - FLORIDA TO NEW ENGLAND AND IN
         MISSISSIPPI RIVER, LAKE ONTARIO

BLACKBACK OR WINTER FLOUNDER
RANGE - NORTH CAROLINA TO MAINE

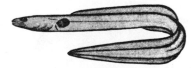

EEL, CONGER
RANGE - FLORIDA TO NEW ENGLAND

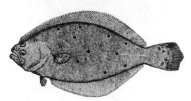

FLUKE
RANGE - TEXAS TO MASSACHUSETTS

GRAY SOLE
RANGE - MASSACHUSETTS TO MAINE

FLYING FISH
RANGE - PACIFIC AND ATLANTIC OCEANS

FRIGATE MACKEREL
RANGE - MIDDLE ATLANTIC

GARFISH
RANGE - FRESH-WATER

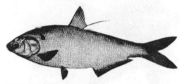

GIZZARD SHAD
RANGE - NORTH CAROLINA TO MARYLAND,
          GREAT LAKES

GOLDFISH
RANGE - LAKES AND RIVERS

GRAYFISH
RANGE - PACIFIC

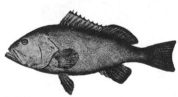

GROUPER
RANGE - TEXAS TO SOUTH CAROLINA

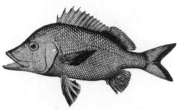

GRUNT
RANGE - FLORIDA

HADDOCK
RANGE - NEW ENGLAND STATES

HAKE, RED
RANGE - CHESAPEAKE BAY TO NEW ENGLAND

HAKE, WHITE
RANGE - CHESAPEAKE BAY TO NEW ENGLAND

HAKE (PACIFIC)
RANGE - PACIFIC

HALIBUT
RANGE - PACIFIC COAST - NEW ENGLAND

HARDHEAD
RANGE - CALIFORNIA

HARVESTFISH OR "STARFISH"
RANGE - NORTH CAROLINA TO CHESAPEAKE BAY

HERRING, LAKE
RANGE - GREAT LAKES

HERRING, SEA
RANGE - NEW JERSEY TO NEW ENGLAND, PACIFIC
        COAST STATES AND ALASKA

HICKORY SHAD
RANGE - FLORIDA TO RHODE ISLAND

HOGCHOKER
RANGE - CHESAPEAKE BAY

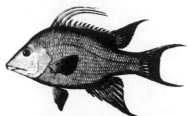

HOGFISH
RANGE - FLORIDA

JEWFISH
RANGE - FLORIDA

JOHN DORY
RANGE - MIDDLE ATLANTIC STATES

KING MACKEREL
RANGE - TEXAS TO NEW YORK

MACKEREL, ATLANTIC
RANGE - CHESAPEAKE BAY TO MAINE

KING WHITING
RANGE - TEXAS TO MASSACHUSETTS

MACKEREL, JACK
RANGE - CALIFORNIA

LAKE TROUT
RANGE - GREAT LAKES

MACKEREL, PACIFIC
RANGE - CALIFORNIA

LAMPREY
RANGE - FRESH-WATER

MENHADEN
RANGE - GULF OF MEXICO TO NEW ENGLAND

LAUNCE
RANGE - NEW ENGLAND

MOONEYE
RANGE - GREAT LAKES

LINGCOD
RANGE - CALIFORNIA TO ALASKA

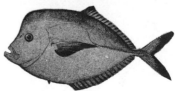

MOONFISH
RANGE - FLORIDA

MULLET
RANGE - TEXAS TO NEW JERSEY

SARDINE, PACIFIC (PILCHARD)
RANGE - CALIFORNIA TO WASHINGTON

OCEAN POUT
RANGE - NEW ENGLAND

PINFISH
RANGE - FLORIDA TO NORTH CAROLINA

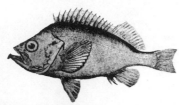

OCEAN PERCH (**ROSEFISH**)
RANGE - NEW ENGLAND

POLLOCK
RANGE - MIDDLE ATLANTIC AND NEW ENGLAND STATES

PADDLEFISH
RANGE - GULF OF MEXICO, MISSISSIPPI RIVER

POMPANO
RANGE - TEXAS TO NORTH CAROLINA

PIGFISH
RANGE - FLORIDA

PIKE OR PICKEREL
RANGE - FRESH-WATER

QUILLBACK
RANGE - FRESH-WATER

RATFISH
RANGE - WASHINGTON TO ALASKA

SALMON, CHINOOK OR KING
RANGE - CALIFORNIA TO ALASKA

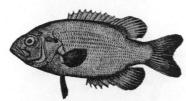

ROCK BASS
RANGE - GREAT LAKES

SALMON, CHUM OR KETA
RANGE - OREGON TO ALASKA

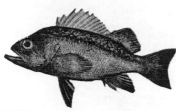

ROCKFISH
RANGE - CALIFORNIA TO ALASKA

SALMON, PINK
RANGE - WASHINGTON TO ALASKA

RUDDERFISH
RANGE - CALIFORNIA

SALMON, RED OR SOCKEYE
RANGE - OREGON TO ALASKA

SALMON, SILVER OR COHO
RANGE - CALIFORNIA TO ALASKA

SABLEFISH
RANGE - PACIFIC COAST STATES AND ALASKA

SAUGER
RANGE - GREAT LAKES

SCULPIN
RANGE - PACIFIC COAST STATES AND ALASKA

SEA TROUT OR WEAKFISH, GRAY
RANGE - FLORIDA TO MASSACHUSETTS

SCUP OR PORGY
RANGE - FLORIDA TO NEW ENGLAND

SEA TROUT OR WEAKFISH, SPOTTED
RANGE - MARYLAND TO TEXAS

SEA BASS
RANGE - FLORIDA TO NEW ENGLAND

SEA TROUT OR WEAKFISH, WHITE
RANGE - GULF OF MEXICO

SEA CATFISH
RANGE - TEXAS TO CHESAPEAKE BAY

SHAD
RANGE - FLORIDA TO NEW ENGLAND

SEA ROBIN
RANGE - CHESAPEAKE BAY TO NEW ENGLAND

SHARK
RANGE - ATLANTIC COAST, GULF, PACIFIC COAST STATES

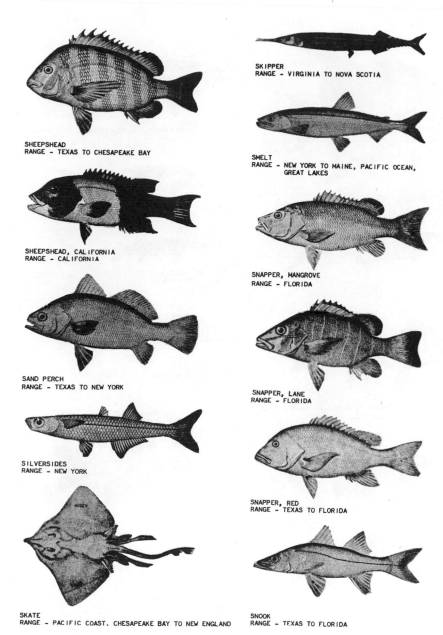

SHEEPSHEAD
RANGE - TEXAS TO CHESAPEAKE BAY

SHEEPSHEAD, CALIFORNIA
RANGE - CALIFORNIA

SAND PERCH
RANGE - TEXAS TO NEW YORK

SILVERSIDES
RANGE - NEW YORK

SKATE
RANGE - PACIFIC COAST. CHESAPEAKE BAY TO NEW ENGLAND

SKIPPER
RANGE - VIRGINIA TO NOVA SCOTIA

SMELT
RANGE - NEW YORK TO MAINE, PACIFIC OCEAN,
         GREAT LAKES

SNAPPER, MANGROVE
RANGE - FLORIDA

SNAPPER, LANE
RANGE - FLORIDA

SNAPPER, RED
RANGE - TEXAS TO FLORIDA

SNOOK
RANGE - TEXAS TO FLORIDA

SPADEFISH
RANGE - FLORIDA

SPANISH MACKEREL
RANGE - TEXAS TO VIRGINIA

SPOT
RANGE - GULF OF MEXICO TO MIDDLE ATLANTIC STATES

SQUAWFISH
RANGE - CALIFORNIA

STEELHEAD TROUT
RANGE - OREGON TO ALASKA

STRIPED BASS
RANGE - NORTH CAROLINA TO NEW ENGLAND, CALIFORNIA
          TO OREGON

STURGEON
RANGE - COASTAL AND RIVER AREAS

STURGEON, SHOVELNOSE
RANGE - FRESH-WATER

SUCKER
RANGE - FRESH-WATER

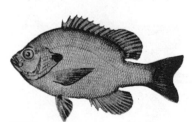

SUNFISH
RANGE - FRESH-WATER

SWELLFISH
RANGE - CHESAPEAKE BAY TO MIDDLE ATLANTIC

SWORDFISH
RANGE - NEW ENGLAND AND CALIFORNIA

TRIGGERFISH
RANGE - FLORIDA

TAUTOG
RANGE - CHESAPEAKE BAY TO NEW ENGLAND

TRIPLETAIL
RANGE - FLORIDA

TENPOUNDER
RANGE - FLORIDA

TUNA, ALBACORE
RANGE - PACIFIC COAST

THIMBLE-EYED MACKEREL
RANGE - CHESAPEAKE BAY TO NEW ENGLAND

TILEFISH
RANGE - MIDDLE ATLANTIC AND NEW ENGLAND STATES

TUNA, BLUEFIN
RANGE - CALIFORNIA, NEW JERSEY TO MAINE

TOMCOD
RANGE - PACIFIC COAST, MIDDLE ATLANTIC AND
       NEW ENGLAND STATES

TUNA, LITTLE
RANGE - MASSACHUSETTS TO TEXAS

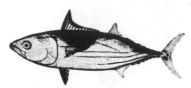

TUNA, SKIPJACK
RANGE - CALIFORNIA

TUNA, YELLOWFIN
RANGE - PACIFIC

WHITE BASS
RANGE - GREAT LAKES

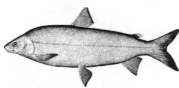

WHITEFISH, COMMON
RANGE - GREAT LAKES

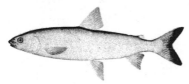

WHITEFISH, MENOMINEE
RANGE - ALASKA, GREAT LAKES

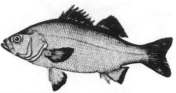

WHITE PERCH
RANGE - NORTH CAROLINA TO MAINE

WHITING
RANGE - VIRGINIA TO MAINE

WOLFFISH
RANGE - MASSACHUSETTS AND MAINE

YELLOW PERCH
RANGE - GREAT LAKES, OTHER LAKES

YELLOW PIKE
RANGE - GREAT LAKES

BLUE CRAB
RANGE - TEXAS TO RHODE ISLAND

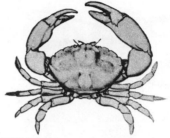

STONE CRAB
RANGE - FLORIDA

DUNGENESS CRAB
RANGE - PACIFIC COAST STATES AND ALASKA

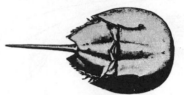

HORSESHOE CRAB
RANGE - MARYLAND TO NEW YORK

KING CRAB
RANGE - ALASKA

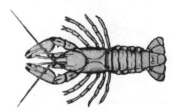

FRESH-WATER CRAWFISH
RANGE - RIVERS AND LAKES

ROCK CRAB
RANGE - NEW ENGLAND

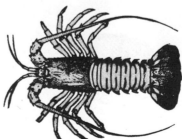

SPINY LOBSTER
RANGE - CALIFORNIA AND FLORIDA

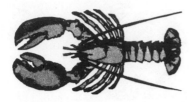

LOBSTER, NORTHERN
RANGE - VIRGINIA TO MAINE

HARD CLAM
RANGE - FLORIDA TO MAINE

SHRIMP
RANGE - TEXAS TO NORTH CAROLINA, MAINE,
        CALIFORNIA, WASHINGTON, AND ALASKA

RAZOR CLAM, PACIFIC
RANGE - OREGON, WASHINGTON AND ALASKA

BUTTER CLAM
RANGE - PACIFIC COAST

SOFT CLAM
RANGE - MIDDLE ATLANTIC TO NEW ENGLAND,
        PACIFIC COAST STATES

LITTLE NECK CLAM
RANGE - PACIFIC COAST

CONCH
RANGE - FLORIDA TO MAINE

LIMPET
RANGE - NEW YORK AND NEW ENGLAND

SEA SCALLOP
RANGE - NEW JERSEY TO MAINE

FRESH-WATER MUSSEL
RANGE - FRESH-WATER STREAMS

STARFISH
RANGE - ATLANTIC AND PACIFIC COAST

SEA MUSSEL
RANGE - NORTH CAROLINA TO MAINE

TERRAPIN
RANGE - TEXAS TO NEW JERSEY

OYSTER
RANGE - TEXAS TO MASSACHUSETTS, PACIFIC COAST

BAY SCALLOP
RANGE - FLORIDA TO MASSACHUSETTS, WASHINGTON

GREEN TURTLE
RANGE - FLORIDA

LOGGERHEAD TURTLE
RANGE - FLORIDA TO NEW JERSEY *

FROG
RANGE - FRESH-WATER, MARSHES, POND

HAWKSBILL TURTLE
RANGE - GULF OF MEXICO, AND ATLANTIC COAST
TO NEW YORK

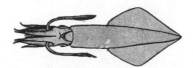

SQUID
RANGE - VIRGINIA TO MAINE, CALIFORNIA AND
WASHINGTON

SOFT-SHELL TURTLE
RANGE - LAKES AND RIVERS

SPONGE
RANGE - FLORIDA

IRISH MOSS
RANGE - NEW ENGLAND

BIBLIOGRAPHY

Brooker, J. R., "Five Years of Voluntary Fish Inspection," USDI, Fish and Wildlife Series, No. 693, Washington, D.C., 1963.

Brooker, J. R., "Weights and Measure Activities in the USDI Fishery Products Standards and Inspection Programs," USDI, Fish and Wildlife Series, No. 711, Washington, D.C., 1963.

Crowther, H. E. "Voluntary versus Mandatory Inspection in the Seafood Industry," USDI, Washington, D.C., 1967.

Jacobs, Morris B., Ed., *Chemistry and Technology of Food Products,* Vol. 1, 2nd ed., Wiley (Interscience), New York, 1951.

National Association of State Purchasing Officials, *Specifications,* No. 1, 2, 3, 4, 5, 6, and 7, USDI, Washington, D.C., various dates.

Tressler, Donald K., and James, Lemon, *Marine Products of Commerce,* 2nd ed., Reinhold, New York, 1951

U.S. Department of Interior, Fish and Wildlife Service, Washington, D.C.,
Distributing and Marketing of Frozen Fishery Products, Leaflet 431, 1956.
Fishery Statistics of the U.S., 1957, Statistical Digest No. 41.
Fresh and Frozen Fish Buying Manual, USDI Circular No. 20, 1954.
Handling Fresh Fish, Fishery Leaflet No. 428, 1956.
Instructions for Grading Fish Products, various dates.
Preparation, Freezing and Cold Storage of Fish, Shellfish and Precooked Fishery Products, Fishery Leaflet No. 430, 1956.
U.S. Standards for Grades of Fish, various dates.

U.S. Federal Supply Service, *Federal Standard Stock Catalog,* "Fishery Products," Washington, D.C., various dates.

9
Meats*

Meat is perhaps one of the most important foods purchased by a food service. It is usually the center of the meal, and its selection largely dictates the other foods served with it. About a third to half of the total food budget is spent for meat, fish, and poultry—and most goes for meat. The per capita consumption per year is about 150 lb, 50% of which is beef, 40% pork (including cured), 7% veal and lamb, and 3% mutton. We also consume over 47 lb of poultry and 12 lb of fish a year per person.

Considerable change has occurred within the last decade in the marketing and purchase of meat. Meat now is purchased in a more servable state than it used to be. The Institutional Meat Purchase Specifications also have been widely accepted by the institutional market, and buying is done almost entirely on the basis of these specifications. Cooked meat is used now much more than it was previously. Grading has changed considerably. New classifications have been added. For instance, in 1973 young bulls were allowed to be graded the same as steers and heifers. Meat shortages also have forced considerable market compromise. Thus if one learned to purchase meats 10 years ago and is still using the information available then, he is using outdated material and purchase methods and needs to learn a great deal to come up-to-date.

To purchase meat well, a buyer must define his needs precisely. Specific menu items require special cuts and kinds of meat of a proper quality. If this is not obtained, the right product is not obtained. Shoulder veal chops are good for braising but not broiling; lamb shoulder makes a better Irish stew than leg meat. Lower-grade cuts make a more suitable ground beef than the top grades. Buyers should know a lot about the cooking of meat to buy it. A

*The author is grateful to Robert F. Blasey, Meat Specialist, National Livestock and Meat Board, for his reading of this chapter. While he is not in any way responsible for the content of this chapter, that is solely the responsibility of the author, his comments have been extremely helpful in indicating proper terminology for many meat cuts on the market.

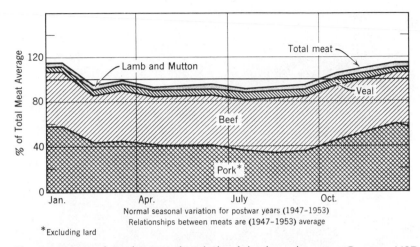

Normal seasonal variation for postwar years (1947–1953)
Relationships between meats are (1947–1953) average

*Excluding lard

Fig. 9-1. Seasonal production of pork, beef, lamb, and mutton. Courtesy USDA

good knowledge of meat and its preparation can do much to lower meat costs.

The price of meat is based largely on supply and demand. Within a grade, the cut also influences price. Prices also can be affected by market conditions. A drought in grazing lands may force growers of cattle and other meat animals to send more than normal numbers in to slaughter. A plentiful corn crop means lower corn prices, thus giving feeders an ample supply of product they can turn into higher prices in meat. Meat supply follows seasons. It is usually most plentiful during January through March, and prices are lowest at these times. (See Figure 9-1.) Buyers must be alert to other factors. In a Kosher area certain cuts are higher because of their desirability, whereas others are lower because the market does not buy them. In the summer quick-cooking meats are higher and in shorter supply because homemakers do not want to cook the longer-cooking meats.

The *real price* of meat is not its AP price but what it costs on the plate AS. Buyers need to know yields to calculate true costs, and frequent cutting and cooking tests should be made to keep data accurate on losses. Fat, bone, or trim losses can vary and throw off calculations. The fact that meat loses about 1% of its weight per day hanging in a refrigerator can mean a large dollar loss in a year if a large meat inventory is hung. Table 9-1 indicates the estimated percent of edible meat in some cuts. Table 9-2 lists the percent yield normally obtained from some wholesale cuts, but variations will occur depending upon grade, carcass size, fat, bone, and so forth. In Table 9-2 meat items on the far left in heavy print and starred are wholesale cuts from which the indented items underneath them are taken. Different yields may be indicated because of different cutting. For instance, from a No. 102 forequarter of beef one may get a No. 103 full rib, a

Fig. 9-2. The crossing of breeds such as the White-faced Hereford and the Brahman has been practiced in the South to produce an animal that grows better in warm climates. The cross has become less popular, however, as meat processors have found that some of the Brahman characteristics produce a wasty carcass. Courtesy USDA

No. 127 cross-cut chuck, and a No. 121 short plate with bone in. Or cutting differently gives a No. 113 square-cut chuck, a No. 117 foreshank and a No. 118 brisket.

Institutions today should give serious consideration as to whether they should operate their own meat-cutting departments. One institution today estimates it costs at least 12 cents a pound to cut its own meat. This can vary in different operations. A consistent policy must be established because it is not possible to operate a meat department one day and shut it down the next.

TABLE 9-1
Approximate Percent Edible Meat from
Beef, Lamb and Pork

	Grade		
Beef	Choice	Good	Standard
Carcass	85%‡	84%‡	82%‡
Wholesale cuts:			
Brisket	88	87	85
Chuck	86	85	83
Flank	100	100	100
Foreshank	58	58	56

TABLE 9-1
Approximate Percent Edible Meat from
Beef, Lamb and Pork

Beef		Grade	
	Choice	Good	Standard
Loin end (Sirloin)	89	88	86
Round with hindshank	85	84	82
Rump	87	86	84
Short loin	90	89	87
Standing Rib (7 ribs)	85	83	80
Short plate	90	89	86

Lamb		Grade	
	Choice	Good	Standard
Carcass	86%‡	83%‡	82%‡
Wholesale cuts:			
Breast and flank	89	86	86
Leg	87	85	84
Loin	90	87	86
Neck	79	75	75
Rib (9 ribs)	86	82	80
Shoulder (3 ribs)	87	85	84

Pork		Weight of Carcass	
	200 lb live, 158 lb dressed	225 lb live, 178 lb dressed	250 lb live, 197 lb dressed
Carcass	79%‡	80%‡	82%‡
Wholesale cuts:			
Bacon	92	93	94
Ham	85	85	86
Head, full cut	47	50	53
Loin	78	79	79
Shoulder, full cut (Picnic & Boston)	84	85	86
Shoulder, ribs	40	42	45
Spareribs	53	61	63

‡The remaining percentage in these columns consists of bone and skin.
Adapted from USDA Agr. Handbook 484.

TABLE 9-2
Percent Yields from Various Meat Cuts

Item No.	Yield	% Yield
Beef, forequarter, No. 102*		
103	Full rib	19
127	Cross-cut chuck	66
121	Short plate, b-in	15
113	Sq-cut chuck	75
117	Foreshank	10
118	Brisket	14
103	Full rib	20
113	Sq-cut chuck	50
117	Foreshank	6
118	Brisket	9
121	Short plate, b-in	15
103	Full rib	19
132	Triangle	81
Beef, hindquarter, No. 155*		
172	Full loin, trmd	35
158	Round, primal	47
193	Flank steak	1
	Trim meat	4
	Fat	13

Item No.	Yield	% Yield
	Shrink	2
	Trim meat	3
	Fat	1
	Bones	13
115	Sq-c chuck, clod in, bnls	77
	Trim meat	3
	Fat	2
	Bones	15
	Waste	3
	Shrink	1
119	Brisket, bnls, deckle on	69
	Bone	31
120	Brisket, bnls, deckle off	55
	Deckle	3
	Trim meat	3
	Fat	13
	Bones	25
Beef, primal round, No. 158*		
159	Round, R on, S off, 3-way bnls	82

Item No.	Yield	% Yield
	Bones	6
	Fat	1
165	Round, R and S off, bnls	55
	Rump butt, bnls	17
	Trim meat	9
	Fat	4
	Bones	14
	Waste	1
167	Knuckle	12
168	Inside (top) round	25
170	Gooseneck, bnls	34
	Shank	6
	Bones	16
	Fat	6
	Waste	1
172	N Y round	88
167	Knuckle	12
166	Round, R and S off, bnls	64
	Rump butt, bnls	3
	Shank	7

Beef, full rib, No. 103*

Code	Item	Value
104	OP rib, regular	81
123	Short ribs, trmd	4
	Stew and trim meat	6
	Fat	2
	Bones	8
107	OP rib, short-cut	72
123	Short ribs, trmd	11
	Fat	3
	Stew and trim meat	6
	Bone	8
109	Roast-ready rib	60
123	Short ribs, trmd	9
1100	Cube steaks	2
	Trim meat	13
	Bone	9
	Fat	8
109	Roast-ready rib	57
123	Short ribs, trmd	15
1100	Cube steaks	1
	Trim meat	11
	Bone	9
	Fat	8

Beef, sq-cut chuck, b-in, No. 113*

Code	Item	Value
114	Shoulder clod	20

Code	Item	Value
	Trim meat	2
	Fat	11
	Bone	5
160	Round, R on, S off, partially bnls	80
	Short shin	4
	Shank meat	3
	Trim meat	7
	Fat	5
	Bone	1
161	Round, R on, S off, bnls	78
	Short shin	3
	Trim meat	6
	Bone	6
	Fat	7
162	Round, R on, S off, BRT	70
	Stew and trim meat	7
	Fat	6
	Bones	17
163	Round, R on, S off, 3-way bnls	60
	Stew meat	8
	Trim meat	7
	Fat	8
	Bones	16
	Shank meat	1

Code	Item	Value
	Trim meat	4
	Fat	5
	Bones	17
167	Knuckle	12
168	Inside (top) round	25
169	Outside (bottom) round	23
	Rump butt, bnls	5
	Shank meat	11
	Trim meat	3
	Fat	5
	Bones	16

Beef, full loin, trmd. No. 172*

Code	Item	Value
173	Short loin	48
	Sirloin butt, bone in	52
184	Top sirloin butt, bnls	18
185	Bot sirloin butt, bnls	16
189	Tenderloin, full, reg	13
175	Strip loin, bnls, reg	21
	Flank end	4
	Trim meat	3
	Bone	17
	Waste	1
	Fat	7
184	Top sirloin butt, bnls	13
185	Bot sirloin butt, bnls	10
189	Tenderloin, full, reg	13
175	Strip loin, bnls, reg	20

TABLE 9-2

Percent Yields from Various Meat Cuts

Item No.	Yield	% Yield
116	Sq-c chuck, clodless, bnls	62
	Bones	18
	Fat	8
	Waste	1
174	Short loin, diamond-bone	52
	Sirloin butt, bone-in	48
182	Sirloin butt, bnls	34
189	Tenderloin, full, reg	13
176	Strip loin, reg, bnls	23
	Flank end	4
	Trim meat	3
	Bone	14
	Fat	7
	Waste	1
181	Sirloin (loin end)	52
173	Short loin, reg	48
175	Strip loin, bone-in	32
184	Top sirloin butt, bnls	18
185	Bot sirloin butt, bnls, reg	14

Item No.	Yield	% Yield
164	Round, R and S off	60
	Rump butt, bone-in	27
	Shank and trim meat	6
176	Strip loin, bnls	25
184	Top sirloin butt, bnls	19
185	Bot sirloin butt, bnls, reg	16
189	Tenderloin, full, reg	12
	Flank end	7
	Fat	6
	Bone	14
	Waste	2
Beef, strip loin, b-in, reg. No. 175*		
177	Strip loin, b-in, interm	84
	Trim meat	10
	Bone	1
	Fat	4
	Shrink	1
178	Strip loins, bnls, interm	79
	Trim meat	2
	Fat	6
	Bone	13

Item No.	Yield	% Yield
	Boneless butt	11
	Flank end	4
	Trim meat	3
Beef, sirloin butt, bnls, trmd, No. 183*		
184	Sirloin top butts, bnls	53
185	Sirloin bottom butt, bnls	47
Pork		
1400	Tenderloin cutlets from reg loin	10
	Tenderloin steaks from whole tenderloin	76
	Center-cut chops from light, lean 12/16 lb loins, b-in or	38
	Bnls	28
	Semi-center chops, b-in from light, lean 8/10 lb loins	68
	Fresh ham rest from b-in ham	76
	Bnls loin from b-in loin	57
	Center-cut ham steaks, b-in from hams	26

189 Tenderloin, full, reg — 13
Fat — 7
Bone — 9
Waste — 1
Flank end — 5

178 Strip loin, bnls — 23
182 Sirloin butt, bnls, reg — 34
189 Tenderloin, full, reg — 14
Trim meat — 17
Bone — 11
Shrink — 1

Beef, shortloin, reg. No. 173*
175 Strip loin, bone-in — 80
Tip tender — 10
Fat — 10

176 Strip loin, bnls — 82
Bone — 18

179 Strip loin, b-in, sh-cut — 76
Trim meat — 19
Fat — 5

Beef, strip loin, b-in, sh-cut, No. 179*
180 Strip loin, bnls, sh-cut — 82
Bone — 18

Beef, sirloin butt, b-in*
182 Sirloin butt, bnls — 72
191 Butt tender — 13
Trim meat — 8
Fat — 4
Bone — 4

Beef, sirloin butt, reg. bnls, No. 182*
183 Sirloin butt, trmd, bnls — 79
Trim meat — 9
Fat — 13

Center-cut ham steak, bnls from boned hams — 76
Ham ends, end cut from ham butts and shank ends — 33

Lamb
71 Leg, b-in from reg leg
65 Leg, bnls from reg leg
67 Shoulder, bnls from b-in shoulder

Veal
75 Leg, rst, b-in from b-in leg
68 Leg rst, bnls from b-in leg
60 Shoulder bnls from b-in shoulder

*The number is that of the Institutional Meat Purchase Specification for that cut.

THE MARKET

Meat production is widely scattered over the United States. The West and Texas produce vast quantities of range-fed cattle and sheep, but Virginia, Pennsylvania, and others also produce respectable quantities. The production of hogs is concentrated largely in the corn-growing states.

Meat animals are raised on farms or ranches and when ready for marketing are brought to auctions close by. Here representatives of feeders or meat packers bid and buy. Most shipment today is by large van trucks either to slaughter houses or to feeders. Slaughtering is no longer centralized, but slaughter houses now are strategically scattered over the country close to the growers and also the users. Chicago, at one time the big slaughtering area, now has no slaughter house. The closest is about 70 miles away. It takes meat about 7 to 10 days to reach the consumer after slaughter. Fresh meat should have an external and internal temperature of 40°F, and frozen meat should have these temperatures at 0°F or less.

Fig. 9-3. A common way of marketing cattle is to auction them in local areas and ship them by truck to feeders. This animal is being auctioned in this manner for shipment. Courtesy USDA

Fig. 9-4. A typical feeder lot in East Lake, Colorado. Courtesy USDA

THE MAKEUP OF MEAT

Meat is largely moisture, being about 59% moisture, 20% protein, 5% fat, and 16% bone. Lean flesh is made up of bundles of fibers held together by connective tissue. These fibers are extremely small in diameter but quite long. Young animals have fine fibers. As an animal ages the fibers become coarser. Connective tissue also increases, which increases toughness. Those muscles receiving the most exercise contain the most connective tissue.

Tender meat is cooked by dry-heat methods, whereas tougher meats are cooked by moist-heat methods. If meat is cooked at too high a temperature or for too long, it shrinks badly, and some tender cuts may be toughened because they dry out too much. Very tough meat may have to be ground, cubed, pounded, or otherwise mechanically treated to make it tender. Meat also can be treated with enzymes such as papain to digest connective tissue in cooking. Some animals may be injected with a papain solution before slaughter. This enzymatic solution is then pumped by the animal's heart throughout the tissues so that later after slaughter when the meat is cooked, distribution is even and thorough. Such meat may be known as "Proten" on the market.

Fat in meat is distributed throughout the tissues in small particles and may be called *marbling*. Fat also will cover the muscles and this is called *cover* or *finish*. A good fat cover is needed in aging to deter the growth of microorganisms on the surface. Much of this fat discolors in aging and must be trimmed away. Fat contributes moisture in meat; some fatty tissues may be 50% moisture. It also gives flavor.

AGING

Beef and some other meats are aged or ripened at 36°F at 75 to 80% humidity. The aging process is complex. A short time after death an animal's muscles stiffen, a condition known as *rigor mortis*. Such meat is called *green,* and cooking it at this time gives a very tough product. After a few days, enzymatic actions and increased acidity are thought to be factors that relax the muscles. The meat then continues to undergo further change that improves flavor and increases flavor and moistness. These benefits continue rapidly up to about 2 weeks, after which the aging process slows down; not much occurs after 6 weeks. Beef, game animals, and game birds are aged up to 28 days and sometimes more. Lamb or mutton may be aged about 7 to 10 days. Poultry and pork are usually not aged, and they develop very little rigor.

Aging can be hurried, but the danger of spoilage is greater. At 60°F, with the use of ultraviolet light to reduce surface deterioration, meat ages in 3 days as much as it does in 10 days at 36°F, and at 45°F as much in 7 or 8 days as in 11 to 15 days at 36°F. Surface deterioration can be slowed by rubbing the surface with a cloth dipped in vinegar. If the humidity is kept too low, there is an excessive loss of moisture and the meat dries out. Normal evaporative losses run about 8 to 10%.

Much trim and moisture loss in aging is avoided if meat is aged in a plastic wrap (Cryovac). In such a wrap, meat without a good fat cover and in small cuts can be successfully aged. A slightly musty odor is evident when this wrap is first opened, but this quickly dissipates. Although Cryovac meat loses less weight in aging, it usually loses more moisture in cooking than dry-aged meat. Aged meats cook to a done stage more quickly than unaged ones.

MARKET REGULATION

The Meat Act of 1908 was previously discussed in Chapter 1. Under this act and other regulations, the government inspects meat before and after slaughter for wholesomeness. Processed meat is included. Harmful dyes, preservatives, chemicals, and other unapproved ingredients may not be used. Plants must meet sanitary standards. In 1968 state plants also had to meet the federal provisions, and so most meat sold today is inspected. Poultry came under the act in 1958.

Meat and poultry passing inspection can bear a red or blue ink circle stamp reading "U S Insp'd & P'S'D" or "U S Inspected and Passed by the USDA" on each wholesale cut or bird. A number inside the stamp indicates the official number of the establishment where slaughter and inspection occurred. (Thus a buyer who wishes to know if he has obtained Kansas City beef as specified need only check the number inside the inspector's stamp against the federal list of numbers for establishments to see if this number is assigned to a Kansas City plant.) Animals or carcasses suspected of being unfit for human consumption may be labeled by an inspector "U S Suspect" and, if further inspection is required, he tags the carcass or animal "U S Retained." Unwholesome meat is labeled "U S Condemned." Some of this may be cooked or made into fertilizer and put on the market, but other condemned meat must be destroyed.

GRADING

The federal government has established quality grades for dressed beef, veal and calf, lamb and mutton, and hogs. Administration of grading is under the Meat and Livestock Division of the USDA. These grades are:

Heifer or Steer	Prime, Choice, Good, Standard, Commercial Utility, Cutter, Canner
Cow	Choice, Good, Standard, Commercial, Utility, Cutter, Canner
Bullock	Prime, Choice, Good, Standard, Utility
Bull or Stag	Choice, Good, Commercial, Utility, Cutter, Canner
Calf or Veal	Prime, Choice, Good, Standard, Utility, Cull
Lamb or Yearlings	Prime, Choice, Good, Utility, Cull
Mutton	Choice, Good, Utility, Cull
Pork	U.S. No. 1, 2, 3, 4, Utility

Beef also is graded as Top or Bottom of a grade, and buyers should specify which level is wanted. Some grade standards cover all factors for a kind, such as those for pork, but a number of different standards are required for cattle, as noted previously.

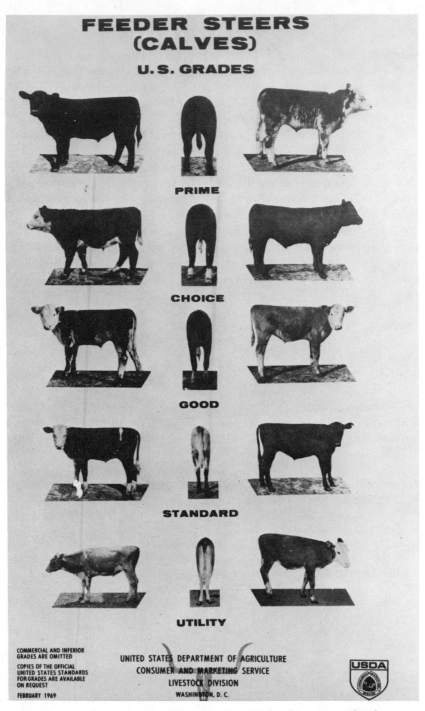

Fig. 9-5. Federal grades exist for live animals as well as for carcass. The characteristics of animals to meet certain live grades are shown here. Courtesy USDA

Fig. 9-6. A federal inspector inspects hog viscera. Note that the carcass moves along with its respective viscera until passed for wholesomeness. The carcass directly behind the inspector has been tagged "Retained" until closer examination can be given. Courtesy USDA

Fig. 9-7. The grade shield Choice plus the initials of the grader "BN" are placed on the carcass in a continuing strip from the neck to the rump. The U.S. Inspected and Passed stamp is put on only each wholesale cut. Courtesy USDA

Fig. 9-8. An inspector marking a carcass condemned. Courtesy USDA

Two factors make up grade: quality and conformation. Finish or the amount of fat cover on the carcass used to be a factor but is no longer. Changes in the grading criteria and the use of yield grades caused discontinuance of this factor. Quality considers factors such as texture and flesh color, bone condition, maturity, and so forth. Conformation considers flesh yield; bulky animals have better conformation than thin and lean ones.

Many buyers use packers' brands rather than federal grades. This is adequate if the buyer is experienced and knows what each grade term means. Thus a buyer should know that for a top grade he must specify "Premium" for Swift meats or "Star" for Armour meats.

Weight and Grade

Weight can influence grade. Since it is related to conformation, this is

Fig. 9-9. Stamps used to indicate a product has been inspected and passed for wholesomeness. The left stamp is used frequently on fresh meat; the stamp on the right appears on packaged meats; the bottom stamp usually appears on boxed meats. The number in the stamp is the number given the establishment where the inspection occurred, and it is called the "official establishment number." Courtesy USDA

understandable. A heavy beef carcass is more apt to be to be found in higher grades than in lower ones. Southern cattle do not grow as big as those raised in the North and so the federal standards in the South allow lighter animals to qualify than the same standards do in the North. Changes in breeding also is causing a lighter animal to come onto the market, and therefore lighter carcasses are qualifying for grades than in the past. Normally, a veal carcass under 60 lb is downgraded. Some spring lambs can be over 50 lb and be graded Choice. Hogs must range between certain weights to be able to make a grade. Table 9-3 indicates some of the more common carcass weights seen on the market.

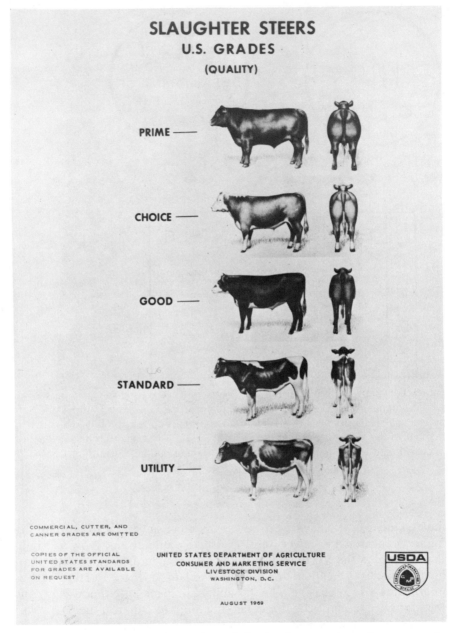

Fig. 9-10. Conformation usual in cattle ready for slaughter must be as shown to put the animal within the grades shown. Courtesy USDA

TABLE 9-3

Carcass	Light	Medium	Heavy
Veal	60 to 100 lb	100 to 140 lb	140 to 175 lb
Calf	125 to 175 lb	175 to 215 lb	215 to 260 lb
Milk-fed veal	up to 80 lb	80 to 110 lb	110 lb up
Grasser veal	up to 110 lb	110 to 165 lb	165 lb up
Beef	under 600 lb	600 to 850 lb	850 lb up
Lamb	30 to 45 lb	45 to 60 lb	60 to 75 lb
Mutton	55 to 80 lb	80 to 110 lb	110 to 130 lb
Pork, young	120 to 140 lb	140 to 175 lb	175 lb up
Pork, sows	under 300 lb	300 to 400 lb	over 400 lb

Note: Lamb also may be classed as Genuine (30 to 35 lb), Spring (40 to 50 lb), Yearling (50 to 60 lb), and Mutton (60 lb up).

Sex and Grade

Only steers, heifers, and bullocks (young bulls) can qualify for Prime grade; cows, bulls, and stags cannot grade above Choice, and few bulls and stags will ever grade Choice. Sows and boars are graded differently than gilts (young females) and barrows (young males). Sex differences in young lambs, veal, calves, or hogs are so minor that grade is not influenced by them until they become pronounced. When thick, heavy necks and shoulders of uncastrated males are evident, there can be a grade loss. Stags, males castrated after sexual maturity, may respond to a feeding program enough to offset sex differences.

Bullocks were allowed to be graded differently starting July 1, 1973. Research indicated that young bulls put on weight faster and more flesh and less fat than steers, and so the market was changed to allow young, uncastrated cattle to qualify under standards formerly not permitted. Bullock flesh is somewhat more variable than that of steers and heifers; therefore the quality grade stamp must always bear the word "bullock" for this meat. In addition, today old bulls are no longer given a quality grade but are only graded for yield of lean meat. Bull meat is used for purposes in which tenderness and flavor are not major factors, and so the grade assignment meant little.

Male carcasses can be identified by the pizzle eye, which is a white spot of gristle on the aitchbone. This appears when the pizzle muscle attached to the penis is removed. It is rather prominent in males that have matured

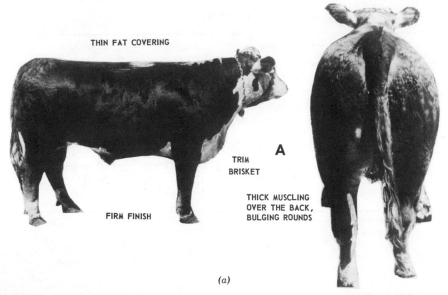

THIN FAT COVERING

TRIM
BRISKET

A

THICK MUSCLING
OVER THE BACK,
BULGING ROUNDS

FIRM FINISH

(a)

Fig. 9-11a. Steer A has thick muscling over the back, bulging rounds, and thin fat covering indicating a good meat yield, trim brisket, and a firm finish.

(b)

Fig. 9-11b. This steer is "over-finished." It will produce a high quality beef but yields less meat and more fat than the steer shown in (a). Courtesy USDA

sexually and less so in young males or those castrated when young; on a steer it is quite small. A bald spot on mature males usually also shows where fat is lacking between the end of the aitchbone and the rump fat covering. When the pizzle is removed, the fat above it falls down and divides the lean strip near the middle of the aitchbone. After the testicles are removed from a male, cod fat develops in the scrotum. This may be rough and pronounced, differing from the smooth udder of a heifer or cow. Older, uncastrated males may lack fat cover, and the flesh may be almost a purplish red. Some older bull flesh may have an iridescent sheen and open texture. A hump or a crest over the shoulders develops on males. Many sexually mature males may show a small round muscle adjacent the hip-bone called the *jump muscle*. This may be covered in quite fat animals.

Females after bearing young have barreled sides, a large pelvic cavity, flat, somewhat ossified ribs, and a nearly straight aitchbone. If not re-moved, the udder is evident. Young females will show a smaller, smoother udder, a smaller pelvic cavity, and a slightly curved aitchbone. Older females may have a coarser flesh and a somewhat yellowish fat.

Grade and Class

Animals also are divided for grading into classes by sex or maturity as follows:

Lamb, veal or calf	Very young animal, either sex, little or no sexual develop-ment
Barrow	Male hog castrated when young
Gilt	Young female hog having had no litter
Sow	Female hog having had one or more litters
Boar	Sexually mature male hog
Steer	Male cattle castrated when young
Heifer	Female cattle having had no calf
Heiferette	Young female having had a calf; not acceptable in lieu of a heifer
Cow	Female cattle having calved
Bullock	Young mature male cattle
Bull	Sexually mature male cattle
Wether	Young castrated male sheep; over a year classed as mutton
Ewe	Female sheep having had a lamb
Ram	Sexually mature male sheep
Mutton	Sheep of either sex over a year old
Yearling mutton	Sheep of either sex just about or over a year old
Stag	Male sheep, cattle, or hog desexed after sexual maturity
Doe	Female of the antlered animals
Stag	Sexually mature male of the antlered animals
Fawn	Young antlered animal of either sex.

Fig. 9-12. The yield stamp used to show the relative yield of the carcass. No. 1 indicates the highest yield. Courtesy USDA

Yield Grade

Yield grades have been introduced to indicate the amount of flesh in cattle. They are more suited to the retail market trade than to institutions since institutions can better control flesh yield in specifications by stating the depth of fat, distance of the loin flank end or rib end from the loin-eye or rib-eye muscle, and so forth. There are 5 yield grades, numbered 1 through 5. No. 1 indicates the highest yield, whereas No. 5 indicates the lowest.

Fig. 9-13a. A Black Angus bull, which will produce progeny with thick, firm, bulging, full muscles—more meat on the expensive cuts.

Fig. 9-13b. This Holstein bull will not produce calves that will develop a lot of meat in the rounds and over the loin, but progeny who will produce a high quantity of milk if females. Courtesy USDA

The yield grade results from an evaluation of 4 factors: (1) the amount of external fat, (2) the amount of inside fat, (3) the size of the rib-eye muscle, and (4) the carcass weight. Standards for these 4 factors are, briefly:

1. The thickness of external fat over the rib eye three-fourths of its length from the chine bone is measured. In addition, the fat at the brisket, plate, flank, cod or udder, inside round, and rump is checked; if it is excessive, the value for fat depth over the rib eye is increased, and if it is low, the value over the rib eye is decreased. The yield grade value is calculated as decreasing 25% for every $1/10$ in. of fat the rib-eye value is over the standard and increasing the same for every $1/10$ in. of fat the rib-eye value is below the standard.
2. As the quantity of interior fat around the heart, pelvic area, and kidney increases, the yield grade drops. A 1% change up or down in carcass weight from this factor can cause a 20% change up or down in the yield grade.

3. The size of the rib eye is measured by a grid calibrated in $^1/_{10}$-sq-in. spaces. A large rib eye indicates a high yield of meat. A change of a square inch up or down in the rib eye can change the yield grade up or down by 30%.
4. Carcass weight is determined while the carcass is warm. If it is cold, the weight is multiplied by 1.02 to compensate for the weight loss that occurs in cooling. A change of 100 lb in weight over a standard changes the yield grade 40%.

TABLE 9-4
Qualifying Yields for Lamb, Yearling or Mutton

| | Yield Grade | | | | |
Grade	1	2	3	4	5
Prime		X	X	X	
Choice		X	X	X	X
Good	X	X	X	X	X
Utility	X	X	X	X	X

Note: To qualify for a grade the animal must qualify for the yield grade indicated. Note that the grade based on quality and conformation is not correlated with the yield grade.

Mathematical calculations based on the score points given for the 4 yield factors indicate the final yield grade. If a carcass scores finally 3.9, it is left at No. 3 yield grade and cannot be lowered to No. 4. The requirements for a lower-weight carcass will be higher in some of these factors than for heavier ones. For instance, a 500-lb carcass must have no more than $^3/_{10}$ in. of fat over the rib eye, 11½ sq in. of rib eye, and not more than 2½% of its weight in inside fat to make Yield No. 1, whereas an 800-lb carcass can have $^4/_{10}$-in., 16-sq-in., and 2½%, respectively, in these factors and qualify for Yield No. 1. Carcasses at 500-lb and 800-lb to make No. 4 would need the following in these categories:

Carcass Weight	Depth of Rib-eye Fat	Rib-eye Size	% Inside Fat of Weight
500 lb	1.0 in.	9.0 sq in.	4½%
800 lb	1.1 in.	13.5 sq in.	5%

TABLE 9-4a
USDA Yield Grades for Beef

Quality Grades	Yield Grades* 1 2 3 4 5				
U.S. Prime			X	X	X
U.S. Choice		X	X	X	
U.S. Good	X	X	X		
U.S. Utility	X	X			
U.S. Cull	X	X			

*The yield grades reflect differences in yields of boneless, closely trimmed, retail cuts. As such, they also reflect differences in the overall fatness of carcasses and cuts. Yield grade 1 represents the highest yield of retail cuts and the least amount of fat trim. Yield grade 5 represents the lowest yield of retail cuts and the greatest amount of fat trim. (Note that some of the higher-grade carcasses in quality do not qualify for a higher yield grade. This is because the extra fat on the carcass adds to quality but detracts from yield.)

Conformation

Top conformation requires a high proportion of lean to bone and a high proportion of weight in the more desirable cuts. Good conformation is reflected by a very wide, thick carcass in relation to its length. It should have a very plump, full, and well-rounded appearance. In contrast, inferior conformation indicates a low proportion of edible meat to bone and a low proportion of carcass weight in the more desirable cuts. The carcass is very narrow in relation to length and has a very angular and thin, sunken (dished) appearance.

Today, external fat over what is considered normal on retail cuts is scored as poor in yield. Thus a good conformation developed by high fat cover does not aid the yield grade. Although fat texture and color are not grade factors, they influence grade opinions. A good fat is somewhat brittle in texture and creamy white in color. Soft, greasy fat or hard, flinty fat may indicate a lack of quality. A very yellow fat may indicate maturity or a grass-fed animal. Dairy cattle usually have more yellow in their fat than those raised for their meat.

Quality

Quality is decided by at least 5 factors that influence flesh quality. These are (1) texture, (2) flesh firmness, (3) marbling and fat characteristics, (4) flesh

Ideal and Poor Conformation on a Beef Carcass
(Side View)

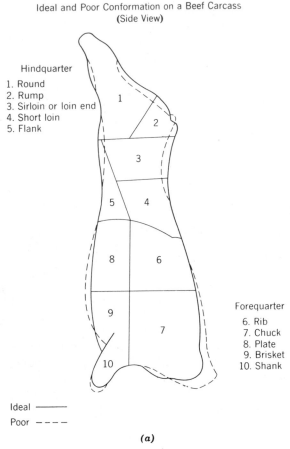

Hindquarter
1. Round
2. Rump
3. Sirloin or loin end
4. Short loin
5. Flank

Forequarter
6. Rib
7. Chuck
8. Plate
9. Brisket
10. Shank

Ideal ———
Poor — — — —

(a)

Fig. 9-14. Dotted lines indicate poor conformation and straight lines ideal conformation.
Fig. 9-14a. View is from side.

color, and (5) bone condition. Maturity is considered in evaluating these since they vary with maturity. Older animals are downgraded in quality since their meat is usually tougher and lacks the best eating quality. Quality is usually judged by looking at a cut surface, but if there is none, it can be inferred by (a) the quantity of fat intermingled with lean between the ribs, called *feathering,* (b) the streaking of fat within and upon this inside flank muscles, and (c) the firmness of fat and lean.

(1) A fine, smooth texture and a dry, firm flesh in the lean is desirable.

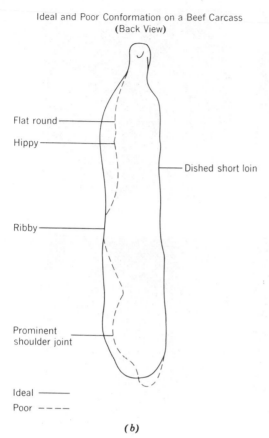

Ideal and Poor Conformation on a Beef Carcass
(Back View)

Flat round

Hippy

Dished short loin

Ribby

Prominent
shoulder joint

Ideal ————
Poor — — — —

(b)

Fig. 9-14b. View is from back. Courtesy National Livestock and Meat Board

Excess moistness or flabbiness or an open, coarse texture lowers quality. Young animals such as veal or lamb have a finer textured flesh than old animals. Old beef has a very coarse textured flesh. (2) Firmness also varies with age, and younger animals have a less firm flesh than older ones. An animal's physical condition can affect the texture, color, and firmness of the lean. (3) Marbling up to a certain point is desirable, but very young and very old animals usually lack it. Marbling in beef is classified as maximum, moderately abundant, slightly abundant, moderate, modest, small, slight, traces, and practically devoid. Cattle above maximum abundant marbling lose quality points because the meat is too fat. Marbling is usually judged by scanning the lean at the ribeye between the twelfth and thirteenth ribs. Some buyers also look for a protrusion of flesh and fat between the chine

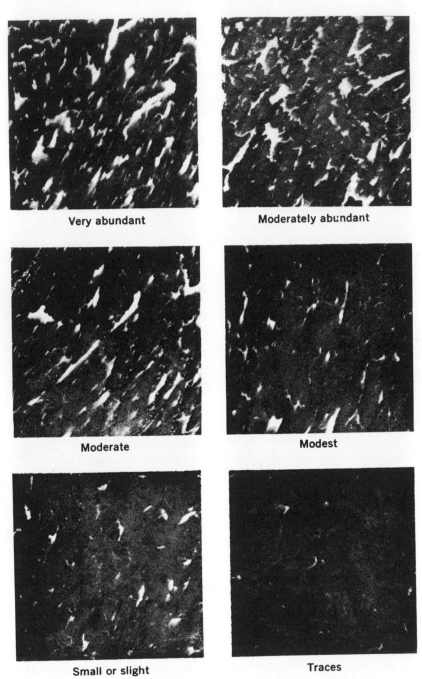

Very abundant

Moderately abundant

Moderate

Modest

Small or slight

Traces

Fig. 9-15. Marbling, an indicator of quality, may vary in muscles and in animals. Excessive marbling gives a fatty tasting meat, whereas not enough gives a dry meat.

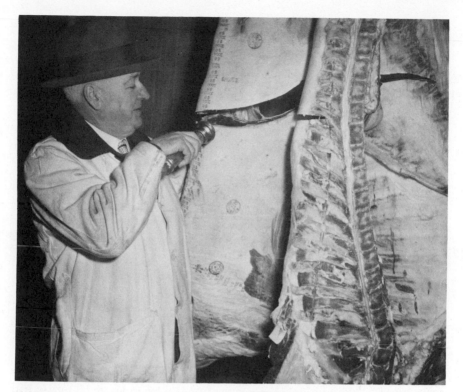

Fig. 9-16. An inspector checks the quality of the lean at the point where the carcass is ribbed between the 12th and 13th rib. Courtesy USDA

bones called *pop* because the flat and flesh is popped out at this point.

(4) Younger animals have lighter-colored flesh than older ones. Young veal is a grayish pink, calf somewhat red, and mature beef is quite red. Old beef sometimes has almost a purplish red color to it. The flesh colors of the various animals are described later under the discussion for each kind.

(5) Maturity is indicated by bone size, shape, and ossification. Cartilage is growing bone, and therefore younger animals show more of this than older ones do. Thus buyers look for "buttons" on the ends of the chine bone fingers which are white areas of cartilage indicating that the spine of the animal is still growing. Young animals also have red bone interiors. These become progressively harder, flintier, and whiter with age. Veal has very red small rib bones, whereas a calf has larger and whiter ones. Ossification or complete maturing of the bones begins in the lumbar area vertebrae and moves up into the thoracic area. A very young animal may have tail bones that are not ossified and are still flexible, but these soon

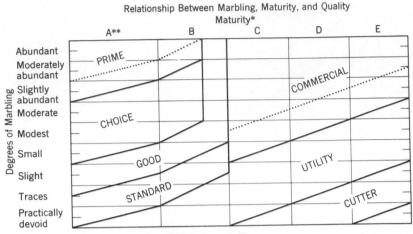

Relationship Between Marbling, Maturity, and Quality

*Maturity increases from left to right (A through E).
**The A maturity portion of the Figure is the only portion applicable to bullock carcasses.
.... Represents midpoint of Prime and Commercial grades.

Fig. 9-17. Maturity may run from perhaps about 8 months old through to about 5 or more years. Note that marbling must increase as age increases if a carcass is to stay within grade. Courtesy USDA

become firm. The size and shape of the bones is an index to maturity. Rib bones become wider and flatter as an animal ages. A cow has barreled out ribs because of calf carrying.

Only cattle are divided for grading purposes into classes of maturity. These divisions are A, B, C, D, and E. Only younger cattle are in the A or B group, whereas older cows, bulls, and others are in the D and E group.

Figure 9-17 shows how the federal government relates maturity, marbling, and quality in establishing grade. Note that bullock beef *must be* in the A age group to grade Prime. Note also that Standard is a grade reserved for young animals of somewhat low quality, whereas cows that have the same quality are put into Commercial grade. Any age animal can go into Utility or Cutter grades.

The Quality and Conformation Grade

The final grade based on quality and conformation is a composite score of these factors. In grading today a trade-off of values between quality and conformation is possible. This was not permitted at one time. Thus an extremely high quality in a carcass may offset a slight lack of conformation.

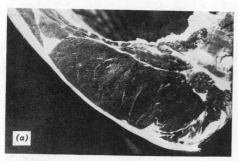
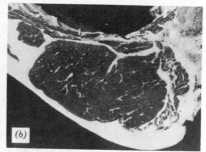

Fig. 9-18a. A U.S. Standard grade club steak compared with
Fig. 9-18b. a U.S. Choice club steak. Note the difference in fat finish on the outside and the quantity of marbling. Courtesy USDA

In a trade-off between quality and conformation, values must be equal. There are limits in trading off. For instance, a maximum degree of compensation in cattle is a third of a conformation grade for a third of a grade in quality either way or vice versa. And a superior development in conformation cannot be traded off for an inferior development of quality in the Prime, Choice, and Commercial grades of cattle. Some specific trade-offs for different animals are discussed later under their grading. Some trade-offs are not defined by the federal standards and are left up to the individual doing the grading.

The Grading of Cattle

Prime beef must have thick, full muscles in relation to length, with short necks and shanks. Maximum evidence of age can be slightly red and slightly soft chine bones, some evidence of ossification of the chine buttons, completely fused sacral vertebrae, and cartilage at the ends of the lumbar vertebrae nearly ossified. The rib bones can be slightly wide and flat and the ribeye lean, firm, fine in texture, and light red in color. As age increases, marbling must increase from a minimum of slightly abundant to the maximum slightly abundant. (See Figure 9-17.)

Choice grade must have muscling that is moderately thick in relation to length, plump rounds and necks, and moderately short shanks. Greater maturity is permitted as indicated by more ossification, which now can be evidenced in the thoracic vertebrae. The sacral vertebrae can be completely fused. Rib bones are perhaps wider and flatter. The degree marbling must increase with maturity. The ribeye color is moderately light red and fine in texture but can be slightly soft. A carcass must be minimum Choice quality to be Choice, regardless of the extent to which conformation exceeds the grade minimum. There can be no trade-off here.

Conformation in Good grade requires slightly thick muscling throughout. Muscles must display a tendency to be slightly wide and thick in relation to length, and necks and shanks a tendency to be slightly long and thin; rounds will be only slightly plump. Thoracic vertebrae will show evidence of ossification and sacral ones can be completely fused with little cartilage showing. The ribs are slightly wide and flat and the ribeye is slightly soft and slightly light red but still fine in texture. Quality superior to the minimum for the Good grade can be traded-off *without limit* for lack of conformation. Thus with a midpoint Good quality, a carcass may have conformation to the midpoint of Standard and remain Good, or a carcass with at least a third grade of conformation over the minimum for Good can trade this off for quality equivalent to the lower limit of the upper third of Standard grade. Compensation of superior conformation for inferior quality is limited to a third of the quality grade.

Standard and Commercial beef show progressively lower quality, greater maturity, and poorer conformation than do the higher grades. For instance, the loins in Commercial beef will be sunken with prominent hips, ribs slightly thick and full, chucks thin, and briskets wide and spready. Necks and shanks are long and thin. Utility, Cutter, and Canner beef is purchased only occasionally by institutions. Some institutions use these lower grades in boneless beef, for example, for mixing with the trimmings from higher quality beef for hamburger, and so forth.

Veal and Calf Grading

Veal is usually a calf under 3 months and a calf is usually from 3 to 8 months, but maturity is differentiated more on the color of the lean than on chronological age. Other factors such as character of fat, bones, general carcass contour, and size also will be considered. Veal and calf are graded on the basis of quality and conformation. Good veal flesh is a grayish pink, smooth and velvety in texture with a soft, somewhat pliable fat. Veal has narrow, very red rib bones.

Calf has a grayish red flesh, a flakier fat, and flatter, wider rib bones with less evidence of red. Even if a calf shows the maturity factors of veal, but the flesh color is darker than grayish pink, it must be classed as a calf. To be calf and not young beef, the flesh color must not be more than moderately red. The rib bones must show some redness and only a slight tendency to flatness. The cartilage on the button ends must be quite evident and all the spinal column vertebrae in the sacral area must show distinct separation. If a carcass has evidence of maturity in bones and so forth typical of calf but has a flesh lighter than midway for the darker half of veal flesh color, it can be classed as veal. And if a flesh color is within the lighter half of veal, a calf can be called veal providing the evidences of maturity are not greater than that associated with the demarcation between calf and young beef.

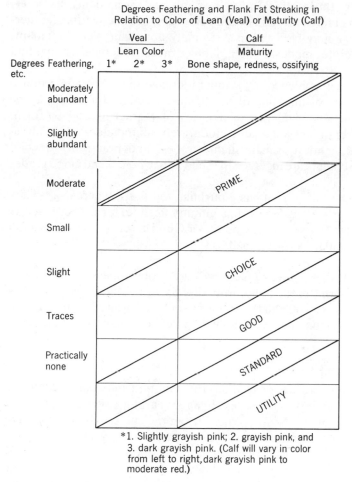

Degrees Feathering and Flank Fat Streaking in Relation to Color of Lean (Veal) or Maturity (Calf)

*1. Slightly grayish pink; 2. grayish pink, and 3. dark grayish pink. (Calf will vary in color from left to right, dark grayish pink to moderate red.)

Fig. 9-19. Veal and calf grades are usually assigned on the above basis for quality. Thus a veal can get a Choice grade if it has practically no feathering or streaking of fat on the flank and has only a slightly grayish pink lean. To grade Prime a calf carcass must show at least slight feathering, and so forth, a dark grayish pink lean, and limited ossification, fairly red bones, and so on. Trade-offs between conformation and quality can occur and modify the standards indicated here but only within prescribed limits. The double line at the top indicates the top level of prime. Courtesy USDA

Sex in veal and calf may be differentiated as steers, heifers, and bulls, but unless the carcass shows definite sex differences, grading is not affected.

Conformation is evaluated by the same factors as used in beef. Other factors are evaluated such as the firmness of the lean, the amount and character of fat and its feathering on the outside, the amount of fat over the diaphragm (skirt), the fat streaking on the flank, and the amount, character, and distribution of fat in the kidney and pelvic areas. Fat covering, feathering, or streakings may be listed as extremely abundant, very abundant, abundant, moderate, modest, small, slight, traces, practically none, and none.

As age increases, evidence of fat must increase to meet grade requirements. The degree of marbling of the flesh, especially for calf, may be judged to supplement evidence of degrees of feathering and so forth. Degrees of marbling are abundant, moderately abundant, slightly abundant, moderate, modest, small, slight, traces, and practically devoid. Marbling requirements are included in the Prime, Choice, and Good grades for calf.

"Dark cutting" calf or veal has a purplish red flesh, whereas a "black cutter" has a nearly black lean with a gummy flesh texture. These factors may reduce an otherwise Prime, Choice, or Good carcass as much as a full grade and a Standard down a half grade. In Utility, this factor is not considered.

Firmness of flesh is a grading factor. Degrees of firmness are extremely firm, very firm, firm, moderately firm, slightly firm, slightly soft, moderately soft, soft, very soft, and extremely soft. No grade credit is given, however, beyond maximum slightly firm in veal or maximum moderately firm in calf.

Lamb, Yearling, and Mutton Grading

Lamb and mutton grades are based on conformation and quality. Maturity also is a factor. Lamb is under a year in age, yearling mutton a year or so old, and mutton older than a year. Chronological age is not the real determinant of maturity, however. Flesh characteristics are heavily emphasized in judging age, plus the characteristics of bones and skeleton. To be classed lamb, the carcass can have only slight wide and moderately flat rib bones and a light red color and fine lean texture. It must show break joints on both front shanks. A break joint is a jagged ridged edge that results when the fetlock is snapped away from the foreshank. This break shows instead of a spool joint because the animal is so young that the cartilage at the fetlock joint breaks readily from the bone instead of leaving an ossified, smooth spool.

Fig. 9-20. A rough drawing indicating a spool joint found on yearling or older mutton (left) and the break joint (right) with its 8 points found on a young lamb.

Yearling mutton has a spool joint on both front shanks, moderately flat rib bones, and a slightly dark red flesh with a slightly coarse texture.

Mutton has wide, flat rib bones, a dark red color, and coarse textured lean. It always has spool joints. If a carcass has been modified so that it cannot be told whether a break or spool joint is on the carcass, the assumption is made that it is a spool joint.

Quality is evaluated on the basis of lean texture, firmness of the lean, and marbling, plus the apparent maturity. Lean texture is judged by the quantity of feathering intermingled within the lean of the ribs, fat streaking within and upon the inside flank muscles, and firmness of fat and lean. Lamb should have the least fat, yearling mutton next, and mutton the most.

Conformation is the result of weighing of the carcass's yield of meat. The best conformation is shown by thick, plump, full muscles on the more expensive cuts.

Lamb grades cover all levels of maturity, but Prime, Choice, and Good lamb carcasses have separate standards for conformation and quality based on maturity. The lower lamb grade standards for Utility and Cull and all grades for yearling and mutton consider only one level of development of quality. A more mature yearling mutton or mutton carcass must have a slightly greater development in quality than a younger carcass and, conversely, less mature animals, within limits, can receive higher grade points even though they may show some slight lack of quality for the grade. Sex may affect a grade when thick, heavy necks and shoulders of uncastrated rams are evident. The loss is less than a half grade for young lambs in which sex is barely noticeable to 2 full grades for a mature ram.

Limits have been established for trade-offs between conformation and quality. For instance, a lamb showing the midpoint of conformation in Choice grade can be raised to Prime, if it is at the midpoint or above Prime in quality. At times, interpolation of grade standards is necessary when a carcass falls between lamb and mutton or between yearling mutton and mutton.

Fig. 9-21. A federal grader runs the grade roller down a side of beef. In actual practice he rarely does this but instead identifies the grade with a single stamp on the carcass and later, under his supervision, the packing house applies the roller until a ribbon of grade names appears on every major part of the carcass. Courtesy USDA

The Grading of Pork

Pork is graded on the basis of sex or class, the quality of the lean, and the relative proportion of lean to fat and bones. Lean yields are based on an evaluation in barrows and gilts on the hams, loins, picnics (shoulders), and Boston butts.

Classes are barrow, gilt, sow, stag, and boar.

The quality of the lean is noted by the condition at the loineye muscle at the tenth rib. A buyer should expect a U.S. No. 1 carcass to yield in the hams, loins, picnics, and Boston butts a total of 53% or more lean meat,

Fig. 9-22. This young gilt shows desirable conformation characteristics. It has a long body to give a good bacon (belly), thick muscling with the hams longer than the width of the loin, the lower parts of the shoulder and ham trim and firm, feet wide apart because of the thick muscling, trim in the middle and rear flank, and jowls also trim and firm. Courtesy USDA

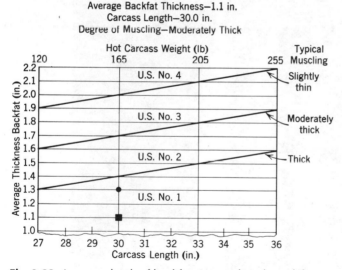

Fig. 9-23. Average depth of backfat, carcass length, and degree of muscling indicate the grade of a hot packer-style hog carcass. Thus a carcass 30 in. long weighing 165 lb with very thick or thick muscles and an average fat depth of 1.1 in. would grade where the square is placed in the chart, but when it trades 2 fat tenths of an inch for 2 degrees of muscling, it moves up to where the dot is shown. A carcass weighing about 150 lb, 29 in. in length, which has an average backfat thickness of 1.5 with thick muscling would grade U.S. No. 2. Courtesy USDA

No. 2 grade, 50 to 52.9%, No. 3 Grade, 47 to 49.9%, and No. 4 Grade, less than 47%.

The depth of backfat is important and is measured at 3 specific points. If the carcass appears leaner or fatter than the depth of backfat indicates, the grader may modify the measurements. Figure 9-23 is a chart used by graders to indicate grade according to average backfat thickness weighed against carcass weight hot and carcass length. The amount of fat to lean is judged by the amount of fat to muscle fullness.

There are 6 degrees of muscling: very thick, thick, moderately thick, slightly thin, thin, and very thin. A carcass with very thick or thick muscles

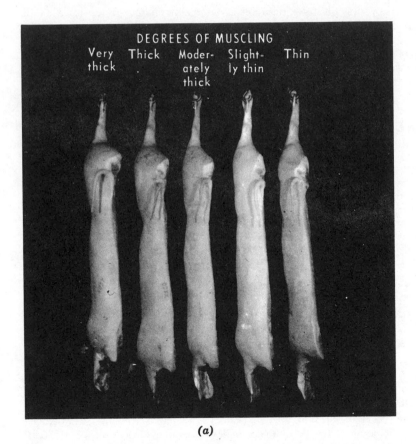

(a)

Fig. 9-24a. Illustrations of the degrees of muscling used in the grading of pork. Courtesy USDA

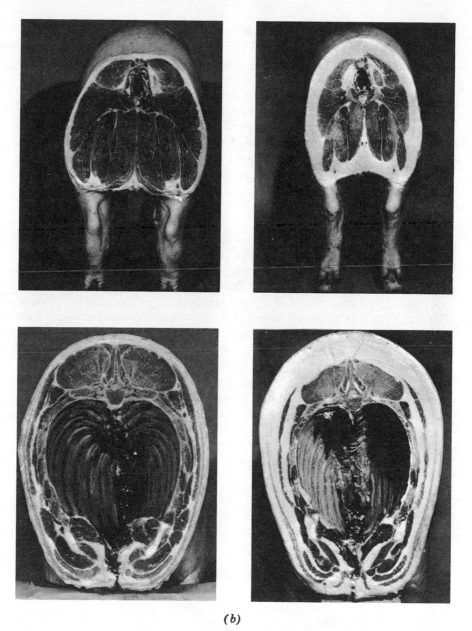

(b)

Fig. 9-24b. The yield of meat on hog carcasses is readily seen from these views. The hog on the left weighed 233 lb, whereas the hog on the right weighed 225 lb, only slightly less, and yet note how much more meat is obtained from the hog on the left. Courtesy Iowa State University

can grade U.S. No. 1, with moderately thick, U.S. No. 2, with slightly thin, U.S. No. 3, and with thin or very thin, U.S. No. 4.

A trade-off of average depth of backfat and degrees of muscling can occur. With certain limitations, $^1/_{10}$ in. of backfat can be traded off for a degree of muscling. Thus if a carcass is 30 in. long, 165 lb, with backfat 1.1 in., and moderately thick muscling, it is not No. 1 because it should have thick muscles or better. It still can be U.S. No. 1 because $^1/_{10}$ in. of backfat depth can be traded for 1 degree of muscling giving the carcass thick muscling, which is required. A carcass with less than moderately thick muscles cannot make No. 1 Grade regardless of trade-off fat depth values. Thus if a carcass had slightly thin muscling and an average fat depth of 1.0 in., it could not trade-off $^3/_{10}$ (3 values) of fat depth for 3 values of muscling to make U.S. No. 1 Grade. Graders have some discretion in adjusting the many variations that can occur in weight, length, and fat distribution.

The lean of U.S. No. 1 pork should be a grayish pink to moderately dark red, have a slight amount of feathering and marbling, and be slightly firm, with slightly firm fat. For U.S. No. 2, these factors are pink to moderately red color, slight marbling, and slightly firm lean with firm fat, respectively. For No. 3 the lean is slightly firm and grayish pink to moderately dark red, slightly firm fat, and a slight amount of feathering. No. 4 and Utility pork will not be purchased too frequently by food services.

TABLE 9-5
Percent Grade Distribution and Expected Yield in Pork*

Grade	Grade Distribution	Expected Four Lean Cut Yield on Chilled Carcass†
U.S. No. 1	8	53 up
U.S. No. 2	42	50 to 52.9
U.S. No. 3	36	47 to 49.9
U.S. No. 4	12	Less than 47
Utility	2	

*Barrows and gilts.
†The four cuts are: ham, loin, picnic shoulder, and Boston butts.

Grading Identification

When a carcass has been inspected and passed, it will be stamped with a circle stamp of wholesomeness. It then can be graded. The grade stamp is in the form of a shield inside of which is the grade. The stamp is a roller that can be pressed against the carcass at the neck and brought all along the shoulder and loin to the rump. If a buyer wishes to specify that a grade stamp not be removed from portion meats, he can indicate that every other, every tenth, or otherwise cut shall have the grade stamp remaining as a small raised portion. Federal inspectors can be asked to stamp packages with the grade of the meat when grade stamps are removed in making up portion cuts.

Identification of Cuts

The kind and cut of meat is identified by shape, size, color, fat, skin, bone, or muscle. Of these, bone and muscle are perhaps the most important, but in the case of pork, the skin would be an important factor in identifying kind. The bone shape indicates the cut. Practice in identifying bones and muscles can help in learning to know the different cuts. Some of the most important bones in meat animals are:

1. *Vertebrae or spine bones*
   Cervical   7 neck bones
   Thoracic   13 attached to rib bones
   Lumbar   6 in abdominal cavity
   Sacral   5 in loin end or hip portion
   Coccygeal   3 in rump or tail area (also called *caudal bones*)
2. *Bones of forequarter*
   Shoulder blade or scapula
   Arm bone or humerus
   Shank bones or radius and ulna
   Ribs—in the Chicago cut, 5 are in the chuck, 7 in the ribs, and 1 in the hindquarter. Seven are attached to the sternum or the breast bone.

   Chine bone—the spine bone sawed in two.

3. *Pelvis or aitchbone area*
   Forehalf or part parallel to sacral vertebrae is called the *hip* bone or *pin* bone. Sirloin steaks from this area with bone-in may be called *wedge* bone or *round* bone sirloin steaks. The latter bone should not be confused with the round bone (femur) in the hind leg.

   Rear half parallel to coccygeal vertebrae is called the *rump* bone. The socket joint to which the round bone of the hind leg (femur) is attached is about midway in the aitchbone.

4. *Hind leg area*
   Round bone or femur attached to pelvis.
   Knuckle is the kneecap bone, specifications should call for removal of this bone when bottom round is ordered.
   Tibia and fibula are bones in the hind leg attached to lower end of the femur.

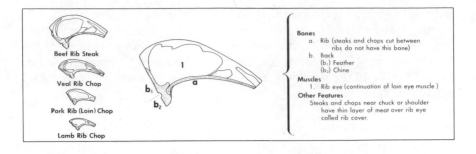

Bones
  a. Rib (steaks and chops cut between ribs do not have this bone)
  b. Back
    (b_1) Feather
    (b_2) Chine
Muscles
  1. Rib eye (continuation of loin eye muscle)
Other Features
  Steaks and chops near chuck or shoulder have thin layer of meat over rib eye called rib cover.

Beef Rib Steak
Veal Rib Chop
Pork Rib (Loin) Chop
Lamb Rib Chop

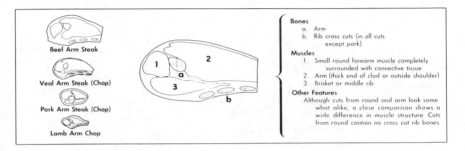

Bones
  a. Arm
  b. Rib cross cuts (in all cuts except pork)
Muscles
  1. Small round forearm muscle completely surrounded with connective tissue
  2. Arm (thick end of clod or outside shoulder)
  3. Brisket or middle rib
Other Features
  Although cuts from round and arm look somewhat alike, a close comparison shows a wide difference in muscle structure. Cuts from round contain no cross cut rib bones.

Beef Arm Steak
Veal Arm Steak (Chop)
Pork Arm Steak (Chop)
Lamb Arm Chop

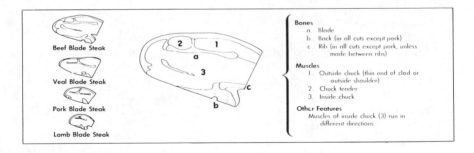

Bones
  a. Blade
  b. Back (in all cuts except pork)
  c. Rib (in all cuts except pork, unless made between ribs)
Muscles
  1. Outside chuck (thin end of clod or outside shoulder)
  2. Chuck tender
  3. Inside chuck
Other Features
  Muscles of inside chuck (3) run in different directions.

Beef Blade Steak
Veal Blade Steak
Pork Blade Steak
Lamb Blade Steak

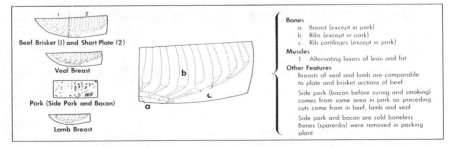

Bones
  a. Breast (except in pork)
  b. Ribs (except in pork)
  c. Rib cartilages (except in pork)
Muscles
  1. Alternating layers of lean and fat.
Other Features
  Breasts of veal and lamb are comparable to plate and brisket sections of beef.
  Side pork (bacon before curing and smoking) comes from same area in pork as preceding cuts come from in beef, lamb and veal.
  Side pork and bacon are sold boneless. Bones (spareribs) were removed in packing plant.

Beef Brisket (1) and Short Plate (2)
Veal Breast
Pork (Side Pork and Bacon)
Lamb Breast

Fig. 9-25. Main muscles and bone shapes of the forequarter. Courtesy National Livestock and Meat Board

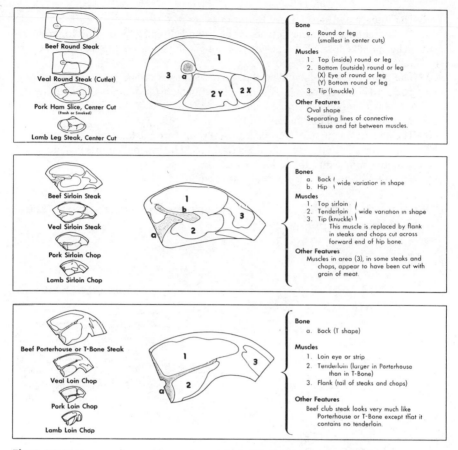

Fig. 9-26. Main muscles and bone shapes found in the hindquarter. Courtesy National Livestock and Meat Board

Some of the important muscles to learn to identify are:

1. The eye of the meat or rib-eye (longissimus dorsi), the long back muscle that runs from the neck to the rump. This is the largest muscle of the body and from it comes the highest priced cuts.

2. The tenderloin (psoas major), the muscle that lies beneath the lumbar vertebrae on the inside of the animal. It is the small muscle in the T-bone or porterhouse steak. The large muscle in these steaks is the longissimus dorsi.

3. The intercostal muscles are found between the ribs.

4. The complexus muscle lies adjacent to and directly below the longissimus dorsi. The spinalis dorsi also runs with the longissimis dorsi in the rib and is next to the backbone.

5. The diaphragm is also called the *skirt, butcher's steak,* or *hanging tender.*

6. The clod is the chuck's largest muscle lying over the scapula and is triangular in shape. Also known as arm muscle.

7. The gluteus medium major is a large sirloin muscle.

8. The inside and outside (top and bottom) round are the hind leg's rear muscles. The knuckle or sirloin tip is on the leg's forepart. The biceps femoris is a muscle of the knuckle running into the sirloin area.

9. The heel on the rear leg is the gastro cnemius muscle.

Figures 9-25, 9-26, and 9-27 show typical bone and muscle shapes. These can be used to identify meat cuts.

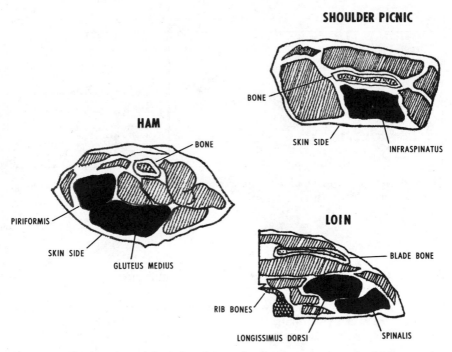

Fig. 9-27. The location of the infraspinatus, longissimus dorsi, and spinalis muscles and the blade (scapula) bone are shown in (a) and (b); the location of the leg (femur) bone plus the piriformis and gluteus muscles in the ham (round) are shown in (c). Courtesy USDA

MEAT SPECIFICATIONS

Well-written specifications stating exactly what is required are needed if the right meat is to be obtained at a favorable price. The development of the Institutional Meat Purchase Specifications (IMPS)[1] marked a progressive step in meat purchasing. Previous to their development, institutions wrote their own specifications, and wide variation existed in cutting methods, cut names, and so forth. The introduction of the IMPS brought a great deal of order and standardization to the market. The basis for cutting used in the IMPS was the Chicago method. Today the New York, Boston, and Philadelphia methods are used far less except for specialty needs.

Most institutions now use the IMPS, modifying them to suit special needs. For instance, one large international hotel chain uses the IMPS No. 103 specification for Primal Rib but wants it cut 9 in. instead of 10 in. on the inside of the sixth rib. Its specification also asks for removal of skirt and channel fat. A great deal of detail in the specifications for meat can be avoided if the IMPS meat cut numbers are used. Thus a food service wanting a fresh pork boneless shoulder butt need only write in a specification: "Fresh, No. 407, Shoulder Butt, Boneless, U.S. No. 2, 4 lb average, each unit not more nor less than 6 oz from specified weight." Or, if modification is desired, a specification for frenched rib lamb chops could read: "No. 1204A, Rib Chops, Frenched, Choice, 7 oz each, double with only one bone frenched and the other removed for the distance the frenched rib is exposed, plus all other factors included in IMPS."

The IMPS start with the largest meat pieces, and each cut taken from these must incorporate the specification factors mentioned. Thus if heart fat is specified as removed in the carcass, a rib roast taken from this carcass also must have the heart fat removed, and it is not necessary to state that it must be removed. This is understood because it has been a specification factor mentioned previously.

A food service's specifications should require that meats be federally or state inspected and have a federal or state grade stamp or packer's brand

[1]These IMPS, originally established in 1960 by Mr. Constantine of the USDA Livestock Division, now include Series 100, Fresh Beef; 200, Fresh Lamb and Mutton; 300, Fresh Veal and Calf; 400, Fresh Pork; 500, Cured, Cured and Smoked and Fully Cooked Pork Products; 600, Cured, Dried, and Smoked Beef Products; 700, Edible By-products; 800, Sausage Products; and 1000, Portion-cut Meat Products. Copies are available from the Superintendent of Documents, U.S. Government Printing Office, Washington, D.C. 20402 from 10 cents to 20 cents each. The National Association of Meat Purveyors, 252 W. Ina Road, Tucson, Ariz. 85704, also has published these IMPS illustrated in color.

indicating grade. The portion or cut weight should be specified. A weight range is given in the IMPS for larger cuts. They also indicate weights or thicknesses of portion cuts with allowed tolerances over and above these. A food service specification should indicate which should be followed if the IMPS give an allowed variation in these weights or thicknesses. Many IMPS list fat depths, but buyers should be alert to change these whenever it improves meat purchases. The labor cost of the product trimmed to meet fat requirements at the operation should be weighed against the increase in price the purveyor must charge for such trim. Fat on units can be measured quickly by inserting an aluminum needle that bends when it hits solid flesh. Depths of fat are listed for specified meat items in the IMPS, but institutions should carefully scan these to see that they meet requirements. Trim also may have to be specified differently than those mentioned in the IMPS.

The sex may have to be stated. Some want only steer beef and not heifer, although many state that while heifers are lighter muscled, their smaller bone size may bring the final meat yield close to equal.

The aging of the meat must be specified. General specifications should include type of packaging, method of shipment and delivery, billing, payment, number of copies of invoices to be mailed, and so forth. All packaging should be free from flavors and odors, clean and sanitary, and suited to the items. Carcass or wholesale cuts may be wrapped in crinkled brown paper, stockinettes, grease- and moisture-resistant paper, or other approved wrap. Smaller cuts usually are packed in boxes, plastic, and so forth. Buyers frequently specify that fabricated, boneless cuts or portion cuts must be packaged separately and closely packed in suitable grease- and moisture-resistant paper or suitable wrappers and placed in boxes. Normally, boxes shall not be filled with more than 25 lb of meat. Cured items such as frankfurters, sausages, and sliced bacon may be packaged in smaller lots. Frozen meats may need special packaging and dry ice. Packages should be strapped as specified if shipment is for some distance.

If boneless cuts are made from the forequarter or foresaddle for the purpose of pieces, dicing, or grinding, the bones, bone slivers, and cartilages plus the following should be removed:

a. The backstrap and all neck ligaments.
b. The prescapular lymph gland, located in the shoulder.
c. The exposed large arteries and veins in the neck.
d. Discolored meat and blood.
e. The white membrane (periosteum) remaining on the clod, chuck, and rib after removal of the shoulder blade (scapula).
f. The serous membrane (peritoneum) over the inside of the abdominal section of the navel.

g. The strip of heavy connective tissue along the lower edge of the navel and the brisket.
h. The tendon ends of the shank to a point at which the cross-section of the shank is at least 75% muscle.
i. The fibrous tissue (deckle) on the bone surface of the brisket.
j. All connective tissue and serous membranes from both sides of the skirt or diaphragm.

When boneless cuts for the same purpose are made from the hindquarter or hindsaddles, the bones, bone slivers, cartilages, and the following must be removed:

a. The backstrap in the loin section.
b. The white tissue on the gracilis muscle on the inside round.
c. The white, fibrous sheet on the boned surface of the sirloin butt and rump.
d. The heavy connective tissue on the edge of the outside round adjacent to the knuckle.
e. The popliteal and preformal lymph glands.
f. The fibrous tissue over the outside of the knuckle and the white tissue (periosteum) remaining on the knuckle where removed from the round bone (femur).
g. The kneecap (patella) and surrounding heavy connective tissue.
h. The serous membrane (peritoneum) over the inside of the flank.
i. The heavy sheet of connective tissue (abdominal tunic) between the muscles of the flank.
j. The strip of heavy connective tissue along the lower edge of the flank.
k. The tendon ends of the shank to a point at which the cross-section is at least 75% muscle.
l. All mammary tissue, udders, codfat, pizzle ends, kidneys, and kidney knobs.
m. Blood or discolored meat.
n. Blood vessels and heavy external and internal connective tissue in the hanging tenders.

Acceptance Service

The use of acceptance service for purchasing other foods has been mentioned. It also is available for meats. The service is provided for a fee, usually paid for by the purveyor. The specifications or requirements needed by the food service must be given to the federal inspectors. These should include the IMPS number, grade, weight or weight range, state of refrigeration, aging, and so forth needed to get the right item. Federal inspectors will use these when inspecting meats and will certify that they meet these specifications, if they do. The inspector stamps the food with a shield containing the words "USDA Accepted as Specified" with the inspector's initials included in the shield. The grade, inspected and passed, and the yield stamps also will be on the meat or packages. Slightly different methods are used under different conditions. The method of stamping, stamp location, and so forth are carefully prescribed. Buyers can ask that grading certificates accompany the shipment.

Fig. 9-28a. A grader measures a boneless strip loin to see if it meets the buyer's specifications for distance of the flank end to the eye of the meat.

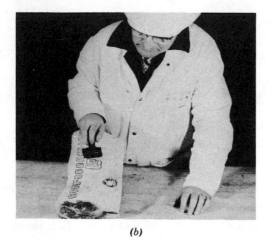

Fig. 9-28b. If the item meets the buyer's specifications, the grader puts the acceptance stamp on the item.

Fig. 9-29. The stamp on the left is a federal grade stamp that indicates a prime grade. The stamp on the right indicates that the item meets the specifications of the purchaser under acceptance purchasing. Courtesy USDA

CUTTING METHODS

Beef—Series 100 and 1000

Beef carcasses and units from them must come from sound, well-dressed meat handled in accordance with good commercial practices. The skirt and tendinous portion must be removed, exposing lean tissue. And the hanging tender, thymus gland, mediastinal tissue, heart fat, excess fat in the lower thorax or brisket and short plate must be removed as well as the kidney and kidney knob and bloody tissue. Only 2 tail (caudal) vertebrae should remain. Cuts excessively trimmed or cut long to meet specified weights or those that are substandard, because of any reason, should be rejected. The meat should be free from objectionable odors, blood clots, scores, mutilations (other than slight), discoloration, ragged edges, superficial appendages, blemishes, deterioration, damage, mishandling, bruises, evidence of freezing or defrosting (unless frozen), freezer burn, rancidity, or other detrimental factors and be in excellent condition at delivery.

Tables 9-6A and B cover beef cuts in Series 100 of the IMPS. Most commercial food services will specify units from weight ranges C or D, hospitals or other institutions may specify B or C. The maximum depth of fat at the thinnest point over the rib eye unless specified otherwise will be:

Weight Range	Prime	Choice	Good	Standard	Commercial
A or B	⅞ in.	⅝ in.	⅜ in.	¼ in.	⅝ in.
C, D, or E	1¼ in.	1 in.	¾ in.	⅜ in.	⅞ in.

TABLE 9-6A
Index of Products and Weight Range
Weight Range for Carcasses and Wholesale and Fabricated Forequarter Cuts, in Pounds

Item No.	Product	Range A	Range B	Range C	Range D	Range E
100	Carcass	500–600	600–700	700–800	800–900	900–up
101	Side	250–300	300–350	350–400	400–450	450–up
102	Forequarter	131–157	157–183	183–210	210–236	236–up
102A	Forequarter, Boneless	104–125	125–146	146–168	168–188	188–up
103	Rib, Primal	24–28	28–33	33–38	38–43	43–up
104	Rib, Oven-Prepared, Regular	19–22	22–26	26–30	30–34	34–up
105	Rib, Oven-Prepared, Regular (Bnls)	15–17	17–21	21–24	24–27	27–up
106	Rib, Oven-Prepared, Regular (Bnd, Rolled, Tied)	15–17	17–21	21–24	24–27	27–up
107	Rib, Oven-Prepared, Short Cut	17–19	19–23	23–26	26–30	30–up
108	Rib, Oven-Prepared, Short Cut (Bnd, Rolled, Tied)	13–16	16–19	19–22	22–25	25–up
109	Roast Ready Rib	14–16	16–19	19–22	22–25	25–up
110	Roast Ready Rib (Bnls)	11–13	13–16	16–19	19–22	22–up
111	Spencer Roll	10–12	12–15	15–17	17–20	20–up
112	Rib-Eye Roll	5–6	6–8	8–10	10–12	12–up
113	Square-Cut Chuck	66–79	79–93	93–106	106–120	120–up
114	Shoulder Clod	13–15	15–18	18–21	21–24	24–up
115	Square-Cut Chuck, Bnls (Clod In)	54–65	65–77	77–88	88–100	100–up
116	Square-Cut Chuck, Bnls (Clod Out)	40–48	48–57	57–65	65–75	75–up
116A	Chuck Roll (Bnd and Tied)	13–15	15–18	18–21	21–24	24–up
117	Foreshank	7–8	8–10	10–12	12–14	14–up
118	Brisket	12–14	14–17	17–20	20–23	23–up
119	Brisket, Bnls (Deckle On)	9–10	10–12	12–14	14–17	17–up

No.	Cut					
120	Brisket, Bnls (Deckle Off)	6–8	8–10	10–12	12–14	14–up
121	Short Plate	16–23	23–27	27–31	31–34	34–up
122	Full Plate, Bnls	21–27	27–29	29–32	32–35	35–up
123	Short Ribs, Trimmed	2–3	3–4	4–5	5–6	6–up
124	Corner Piece	1–2	2–3	3–4	4–5	5–up
125	Armbone Chuck	77–88	88–103	103–118	118–133	133–up
126	Armbone Chuck, Bnls (Clod In)	59–70	70–82	82–94	94–106	106–up
127	Cross-Cut Chuck	86–103	103–120	120–138	138–156	156–up
128	Cross-Cut Chuck, Bnls (Clod In)	68–81	81–95	95–109	109–123	123–up
129	Cross-Cut Chuck (Diced)	Amount As Specified				
130	Cross-Cut Chuck (Diced), Chili Beef	Amount As Specified				
131	Cross-Cut Chuck (Ground)	Amount As Specified				
132	Triangle	107–129	129–150	150–172	172–193	193–up
133	Triangle, Bnls (Clod In)	83–101	101–117	117–134	134–151	151–up
134	Beef Bones	Amount As Specified				
135	Diced Beef	Amount As Specified				
136	Ground Beef, Regular	Amount As Specified				
137	Ground Beef, Special	Amount As Specified				

Note: The weight ranges of the primal, fabricated, and boneless cuts as shown in the above table and on pages 520–521 do not necessarily reflect any relation to the carcass weight ranges. Studies have shown that all carcasses within a given weight range will not produce cuts that are uniform in weight. Therefore, in ordering cuts, purchasing officials should order the specific weight range(s) desired without regard to the carcass weights shown in the various ranges.

TABLE 9-6B

Index of Products and Weight Range

Weight Ranges for Carcasses and Wholesale and Fabricated Hindquarter Cuts

Item No.	Product	Range A	Range B	Range C	Range D	Range E
100	Carcass	500–600	600–700	700–800	800–900	900–up
155	Hindquarter	119–143	143–167	167–190	190–214	214–up
155A	Hindquarter, Boneless	90–108	108–126	126–143	143–162	162–up
156	Hindquarter, Trimmed	100–120	120–141	141–160	160–180	180–up
157	Sirloin Round, Trimmed	75–90	90–106	106–123	123–140	140–up
158	Round (Rump and Shank On) Primal	59–71	71–83	83–95	95–107	107–up
159	Round, Primal (Rump and Shank On) 3-Way Bnls	44–53	53–62	62–71	71–80	80–up
160	Round, (Rump On-Shank Off)	47–57	57–67	67–76	76–86	86–up
161	Round, (Rump On-Shank Off) Bnls	44–53	53–62	62–71	71–80	80–up
162	Round, (Rump On-Shank Off) Boned, Rolled, Tied	41–50	50–58	58–66	66–75	75–up
163	Round, (Rump On-Shank Off) 3-Way Bnls	41–50	50–58	58–66	66–75	75–up
164	Round, (Rump and Shank Off)	40–48	48–56	56–64	64–73	73–up
165	Round, (Rump and Shank Off) Bnls	35–43	43–50	50–57	57–65	65–up
166	Round, (Rump and Shank Off) Boned, Rolled, Tied	35–43	43–50	50–57	57–65	65–up
166A	Round (Rump Partially Removed-Shank Off)	44–52	52–61	61–70	70–79	79–up
166B	Round (Rump Partially Removed-Shank Off) Bnls	39–47	47–56	56–65	65–74	74–up
166C	Round (Rump Partially Removed-Shank Off) Bnd., Rolled, Tied	39–47	47–56	56–65	65–74	74–up
167	Knuckle	8–9	9–11	11–13	13–15	15–up
168	Inside Round	14–17	17–20	20–23	23–26	26–up
169	Outside Round	8–10	10–13	13–16	16–19	19–up
170	Gooseneck Round Bnls	18–21	21–25	25–29	29–33	33–up

No.	Item					
171	Round (New York Style)	51–61	61–72	72–82	82–92	92–up
172	Loin, Full-Trimmed	35–42	42–50	50–57	57–64	64–up
173	Short Loin Regular	17–21	21–25	25–28	28–32	32–up
174	Short Loin (Diamond Bone Cut)	18–22	22–26	26–30	30–34	34–up
175	Strip Loin, Bone-In (Regular)	11–13	13–16	16–19	19–21	21–up
176	Strip Loin, Bnls (Regular)	8–10	10–12	12–14	14–16	16–up
177	Strip Loin, Bone-In (Intermediate)	10–12	12–14	14–16	16–18	18–up
178	Strip Loin, Bnls (Intermediate)	8–9	9–11	11–13	13–15	15–up
179	Strip Loin, Bone-In (Short Cut)	8–10	10–12	12–14	14–16	16–up
180	Strip Loin, Bnls (Short Cut)	7–8	8–10	10–12	12–14	14–up
181	Sirloin (Loin End)	16–19	19–24	24–28	28–31	31–up
182	Sirloin Butt (Bnls) Regular	11–14	14–16	16–19	19–21	21–up
183	Sirloin Butt (Bnls) Trimmed	9–10	10–13	13–15	15–17	17–up
184	Top Sirloin Butt (Bnls)	6–7	7–9	9–11	11–13	13–up
185	Bottom Sirloin Butt (Bnls) Regular	4–5	5–6	6–7	7–8	8–up
186	Bottom Sirloin Butt (Bnls) Trimmed	2–3	3–4	4–5	5–6	6–up
187	Full Hip	49–59	59–69	69–79	79–89	89–up
188	Short Hip	15–18	18–21	21–24	24–27	27–up
189	Full Tenderloin, Regular	4–5	5–6	6–7	7–8	8–up
189A	Full Tenderloin, Defatted	3–4	4–5	5–6	6–7	7–up
190	Full Tenderloin, Special	2–3	3–4	4–up		
191	Sirloin (Butt) Tenderloin	1–2	2–3	3–4	4–5	5–up
192	Short (Tip) Tenderloin	2–3	3–4	4–up		
193	Flank Steak	under 1	1–2	2–up		

If the yield grade is not specified, wholesale or fabricated beef cuts in Series 100 may have a maximum average thickness of surface fat (not seam fat) with a maximum depth at any point specified as follows:

Max. Av. Depth	Max. Depth Any Point	Max. Av. Depth	Max. Depth Any Point
1 in.	1¼ in.	½ in.	¾ in.
¾ in.	1 in.	¼ in.	½ in.

Many IMPS state the quantity of fat that can remain on meat cuts. If a buyer wishes different fat depths, this must be specified. For portion meats in Series 1000, surface fat shall be the following (except for roasts) unless otherwise specified:

Steaks	Not over ½ in. average; not over ¾ in. at any point
Chops, cutlets, filets	Not over ¼ in. average; not over ⅜ in. at any point
Roasts	Specify either ¾ average (1 in. maximum at any point) or ½ in. average (¾ in. maximum at any point.)

Unless stated otherwise, portion cuts can have the following tolerances over or under the specified weight:

Portion Wt. Specified	Tolerance	Portion Wt. Specified	Tolerance
Less than 6 oz	¼ oz	12 oz to nearly 18 oz	¾ oz
6 to nearly 12 oz	½ oz	18 oz or more	1 oz

(Thus when 8-oz portions are specified, individual units can weigh 7½ to 8½ oz.)

When thickness tolerance is not specified, portion cuts can have the following tolerance over or under that specified for thickness of the cuts:

Thickness Specified	Tolerance
1 in. or less	³/₁₆ in.
More than 1 in.	¼ in.

(Thus when 1¼-in. units are specified, individual units measuring 1 to 1½ in. are acceptable.)

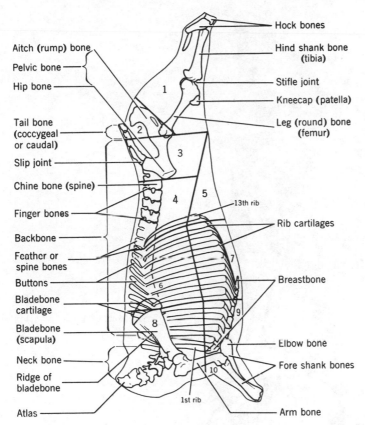

Fig. 9-30. The skeletal structure of beef with the wholesale cuts numbered as shown in Figure 9-31.

If a cut is specified as tied, individual loops of strong cotton twine should be uniformly spaced at 2-in. intervals girthwise, and it also may be desirable to specify lengthwise tieing. Some buyers permit approved netting to be used instead of tieing.

A beef carcass (100)[2] is broken down into sides (101) and then into quarters (102). Boneless quarters are No. 102A. A forequarter (102) contains the square-cut chuck, shank, brisket, short plate, and rib. (See Fig. 9-31.) To reduce handling and lifting, the forequarter may be divided into the full rib and short plate (see Fig. 9-32a and b), and chuck with the

[2]The numbers in parentheses are IMPS numbers. Other names used in the trade also are given, many of which are used incorrectly. It is best to use the terminology used in the IMPS.

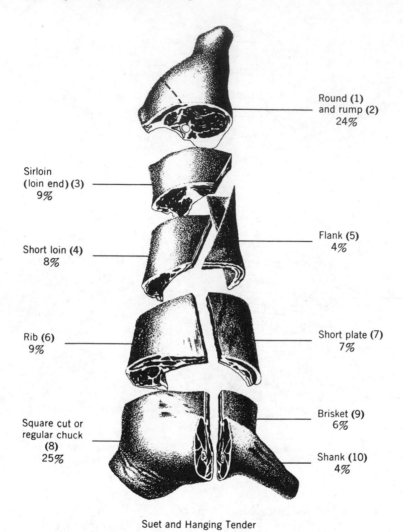

Round (1)
and rump (2)
24%

Sirloin
(loin end) (3)
9%

Flank (5)
4%

Short loin (4)
8%

Rib (6)
9%

Short plate (7)
7%

Square cut or
regular chuck
(8)
25%

Brisket (9)
6%

Shank (10)
4%

Suet and Hanging Tender

Fig. 9-31. Wholesale cuts from a side of beef. Rump may be specified as separated from the round. The shank (10) is frequently separated from the brisket (9). Percent of wholesale cut as a part of side also is given.

foreshank and brisket by cutting close to the fifth rib between the fifth and sixth ribs. The foreshank (117) (also called in the trade the *shin,* the *foreshin,* or just *shank*) is removed by cutting through the cartilage juncture of the first rib and the front end of the breast bone (sternum) cartilage by following the dividing or natural seam between the brisket and chuck, leaving the entire "lip" or web muscle on the brisket. The brisket (118), also called the *deckle, boneless brisket, bone-in brisket, fresh boneless brisket, beef breast, brisket pot-roast, "barbecue" beef brisket,* or *corned beef* by the trade is removed by cutting along a line that removes the portion between the second and fifth ribs along a straight line just below the clod. It

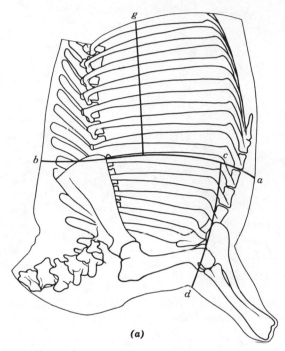

(a)

Fig. 9-32a. Cutting on line ab along the fifth rib separates the chuck from the wing. The wing is the rib and plate or rear half of the forequarter.

(b)

Fig. 9-32b. Dividing the wing into the rib and the plate.

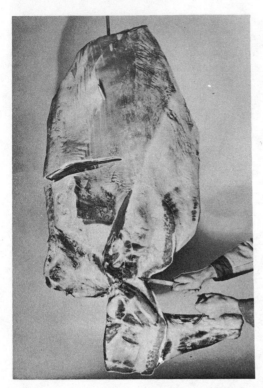

Fig. 9-33. The first cut usually made in a hanging forequarter is that which separates the shank. Courtesy National Livestock and Meat Board

can be specified boneless, deckle on (119) or boneless, deckle off (120). The deckle is a fat, spongy mass on the brisket front and should be removed when specified at the natural seam, exposing lean meat. Specify a maximum of ¾-in. fat cover on either Nos. 119 or 120. Removing the brisket and shank from the chuck after the wing is removed leaves the square-cut chuck (113). (A kosher chuck is everything *before* the sixth rib including the chuck, shank, and brisket.) The clod (114) is the large top muscle below the elbow joint. It sets over the blade bone. (See Fig. 9-34.) It is removed in one piece by removing the entire muscle, stripping it from the blade bone. The heavy tendons at the elbow end should be removed. It should not be less than an inch thick at any point.

The square-cut chuck can be specified boneless, clod in (115) or boneless, clod out (116). In No. 115, the clod can be separated from the chuck and individually wrapped. A chuck roll (116A) is made from No. 116

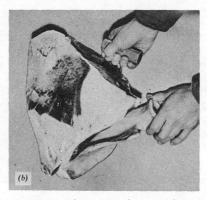

Fig. 9-34. (a) The triangular cut shown here removes the clod. The muscle sets over the shoulder blade or scapula. Note that the wing has been partially separated from the cross-cut or New York chuck by cutting between the fifth and sixth ribs. (b) The clod lifts off easily from the scapula blade.

(boneless chuck with clod out) after trimming to remove bloody tissue, veins, cartilage, and so forth. For this cut, the neck is removed and the lower portion of the chuck is separated at about 3 in. of the chuck-eye muscle (longissimus dorsi). This gives a rectangular piece of even thickness that rolls well. If desired in smaller rolls, it should be cut through at right angle to the length. If the wing (rib and plate) is removed on the forequarter, the cut is the cross-cut or New York chuck (127). This is made up of the square-cut chuck, the brisket, and foreshank. It may be made boneless, clod in (128). This must be a solid piece of meat, not heavily scored with cutting. The clod is usually separate and wrapped. An armbone chuck (125) is the cross-cut chuck without the brisket. It can be specified boneless with clod in (126). Workmanship should be that given No. 128. Two smaller roasts from the chuck are called the *armbone pot roast,* which includes a part of the shank bone, and the *blade pot roast,* which includes a part of the scapula. These are somewhat like the picnic and the Blade Boston on pork.

The cross-cut chuck is frequently diced (129) from No. 128. It should be well chilled and strictly fresh and be cut into 1- to 1½-in. cubes either by hand or by machine, grinding through a plate with holes 1 to 1½ in. in diameter. Specify size and whether by hand or machine. Surface or seam fat must not be over ½ in. deep. Diced chili beef (130) is made of ½-in. cubes either by hand or machine cut. Ground cross-chuck (131) is made by

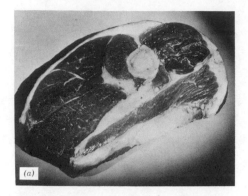

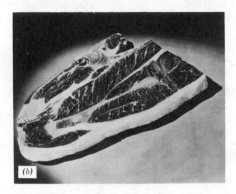

Fig. 9-35. (a) An armbone round steak taken from the foreshank. (b) A blade bone steak taken from the shoulder. Courtesy USDA

grinding through a plate first with ¾- to 1-in. holes and then through a plate with holes ⅛ to ³/₁₆ in. in diameter. Friction developed in grinding can make beef warm, so steps must be taken to keep it cool. Fat should be evenly distributed and not exceed 25% determined visually. (Federal insepctors can identify the amount fairly accurately. But this is only visual fat. The meat itself contains fatty substances that are not seen, and therefore the *total* fat is over 25%.)

If only a 7-rib (103) is removed from the forequarter, a triangle (132) is left, which is the square-cut chuck, brisket, plate, and shank. It can be boneless, clod in (133). It must conform in workmanship to a boneless cross-cut chuck (No. 128). The primal rib (103) is the sixth to twelfth ribs inclusive cutting close to the fifth rib. It is separated from the plate by cutting in a straight line through the intercostal muscles and ribs 10 in. down from the twelfth thoracic vertebrae (chine bone) on the loin side to not more than 10 in. down from the sixth thoracic vertebra. Some specify this to be 9 in. instead of 10 at the sixth rib. Maximum fat should be ¾ in. A number of cuts are made from the primal rib as follows:

IMPS No.	Name of Cut	Description
104	Rib, OP*, Regular	Cut 4 in. from the rib eye on the 12th rib and 8 in. from it on the 6th rib. Chine, feather, and scapula (blade) bones are removed.
105	No. 104, bnls*	All rib bones removed by scalping, which is removing all meat around the bones to leave a smooth surface on the rib side; backstrap and intercostal meat (meat fingers) also are removed.
106	No. 105, R&T*	Rolled and tied girthwise and lengthwise.
107	Rib, OP, Short-cut	Same as No. 104 except cut 3 in. from the rib eye on the 12th rib and 4 in. from it on the 6th rib.
108	Rib, OP, Short-cut R&T	No. 107 but boned, rolled and tied as for Nos. 105 and 106.
109	Roast-ready rib	Cut as for No. 107 with the chine bone vertebrae removed, completely exposing lean meat where they join the featherbones. The featherbones are left attached but the backstrap, the fat cover, and the lean muscle over the blade bone (scapula), the scapula, the small muscle under the scapula, and the cartilage are removed. The fat cover is then returned and the entire rib is tied lengthwise and girthwise.
110	Roast-ready rib, bnls	No. 109 but boneless.
111	Spencer roll	The boneless rib eye is removed by a cut measuring not more than 2 in. from the outer tip of the rib-eye muscle at the loin end to a point not more than an inch from the outer tip of the rib-eye muscle on the chuck end. Entirely boneless, and rib bones removed by scalping.
112	Rib-eye roll	Only the rib-eye muscle or the rib with the complexus muscle lying under it. Completely boneless; ribs removed by scalping.

*OP = oven prepared, bnls = boneless, R&T = rolled and tied, usually boneless.

Shortribs, trimmed (123) should be specified as 2½ to 3½ in. wide and come from the bottom of a primal rib or Items 104 through 109. They also can come from the short plate using only the sixth to tenth ribs one width only from the top of the plate where it joins the rib. Shortribs in the trade also may be called *middle ribs* or *English shortribs*. Ribs from the plate should not include the costal rib cartridges. Maximum surface fat depth is ¼ in.

A shortplate (121) is the lower rib bones and belly portion remaining after the rib is removed from the wing. A full plate (122) is No. 121 plus the brisket. Both No. 121 and No. 122 should come boneless unless specified otherwise. Specify also close trimming and defatting. The skirt (diaphragm), cartilage, intercostal meat (rib fingers), and serous membrane (peritoneum) from the abdominal area must be removed. A steak from the skirt (diaphragm) is called a *skirt steak* or *skirt steak filet*.

Beef bones (134) should not be over 6 in. long and should be cut to expose the marrow. They should be fresh, sound, and not show any evidence of rancidity, sourness, or deterioration. They should come from the round,

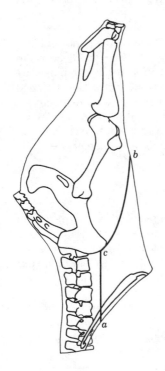

Fig. 9-36. A cut to remove the flank is made from the cod fat located at "b" to the end of the pelvic bone at "c." The cut then follows through the thirteenth rib at "a." This distance from the top of the chine bone is about 10 in. on this cut from "c" to "a." Courtesy National Livestock and Meat Board

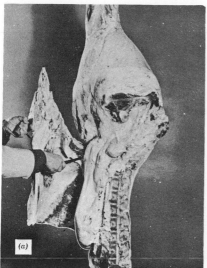 

Fig. 9-37. (a) Many times beef in the quarter may be best cut up from the hook. This illustration shows the first cut usually made in doing this on a hindquarter separating the flank from the round and loin. (b) The flank is stripped from its fatty tissue as shown here. Courtesy National Livestock and Meat Board

shank, femur, chuck, neck, or humerus. Diced beef (135) must come from natural proportions of carcass beef or, if from wholesale cuts, at least 50% from square-cut chucks, ribs, short loins, loin ends with tenderloins excluded, or rounds. The remainder can be from flanks, briskets, navels, or shanks. Many specifications exclude skirts, hanging tenders, necks, and rib fingers. These percentages are based on bone-in weights. Surface fat should not be over ½ in. "Special" ground meat (137) must be from No. 135 and be ground first through a 1-in.-diameter plate and then through a ⅛-diameter plate. Fat should not be over 25%, observed visually. Fat can be specified as less, however. Buyers also should specify that all ground or diced meat should not have a bacterial plate count over 100,000 per gram. Ground beef, regular (136) can be from beef trimmings normally obtained in commercial boning of beef, including meat from shanks, flanks, skirts, or hanging tenders. Meat from heads, gullets, tongues, hearts, glands, or added fat such as suet, cod, heart fat, and so forth is not to be included. Fat content is to be not over 25%, observed visually.

Break down the hindquarter by first removing the flank (193), cutting it from the cod fat just below the last fifth sacral vertebra to a point about 10 in. from the chine bone tip on the thirteenth rib. It is pulled from its fatty tissue and the serous membrane is then stripped from it, leaving only minute flakes of fat. The flank steak also may be called wrongly *London broil, cube steak, minute steak, flank steak filet*, or *Swiss steak*. (See Figure 9-36.)

The full loin (172) is separated from the rump and round by cutting through the last (fifth) sacral vertebra and the first tail (caudal) vertebra continuing to the flank area until the round is reached immediately in front of the femur bone where the socket ball is exposed. (See Figures 9-37 and 9-38.) No more than an inch of cod or udder fat should remain. The tip or rear innermost corner of the fifth sacral vertebra attached to the first tail bone remains.

Full loins under 50 lb and those over 50 lb are cut, respectively, in a straight line from the flank end 9 in. and 10 in. from the chine bone. A ½- to 1-in. fat trim should be specified. Fat should not be over 1 in. deep in the sacral (pelvic) area and be trimmed in the internal lumbar area showing the

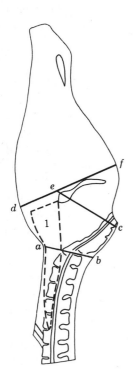

Fig. 9-38. The round and loin are frequently cut as shown. The short loin ends at line "ab"; the loin end or sirloin is found between lines "ab" and "dec." The rump forms the triangle made by lines "fce." The tenderloin is indicated by the dotted line and the rear part behind line "ab" marked "1" is the butt tender.

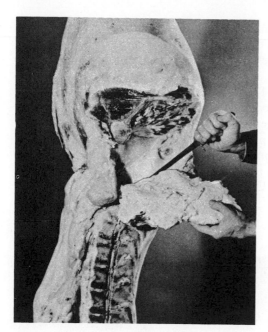

Fig. 9-39. Before the loin in the lower portion of this illustration is removed from the round, kidney fat, cod fat, and other tissue are removed. The hip bone is shown protruding from the round.

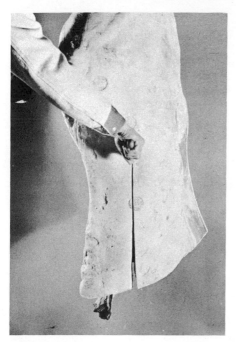

Fig. 9-40. Cutting this short into the loin gives a full loin with steaks which have a small tail or flank on them. Courtesy National Livestock and Meat Board

full loin. Fat extending above a flat plane parallel to the surface of a cutting bench that is level with the protruding edge of the chine bone should be removed; trim should be close elsewhere. This cut also may be called the *rough loin* and contain the flank. A full loin contains the short loin (173) and the sirloin or loin end (174). These two cuts are separated by cutting between the fifth and sixth lumbar vertebrae, through a point flush against the hipbone, taking no cartilage. (See line *ab* in Figure 9-38.)

A full hip (187) is the sirloin plus the knuckle, which runs down on the round and is often purchased boned and tied for a roast. The short hip (188) is the sirloin portion remaining after most of the bottom sirloin. A sirloin round, trimmed (157) is the hindquarter left after removing the short loin.

Fig. 9-41. When the hindquarter hangs, it is easy to separate the loin and flank from the round, as shown here. Courtesy USDA

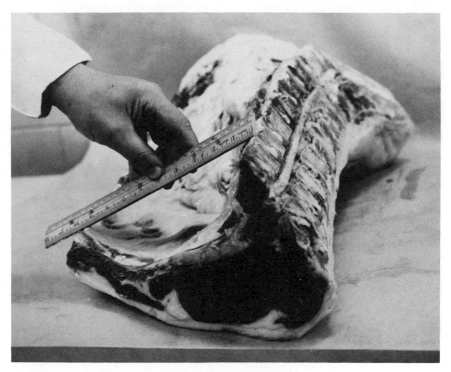

Fig. 9-42. Some specifications may call for a measurement, such as shown here, of 10 in. from the tip of the chine bone to the flank end of the loin.

Fig. 9-43. A square-cut sirloin, well trimmed; fat depth is not over ½ in.

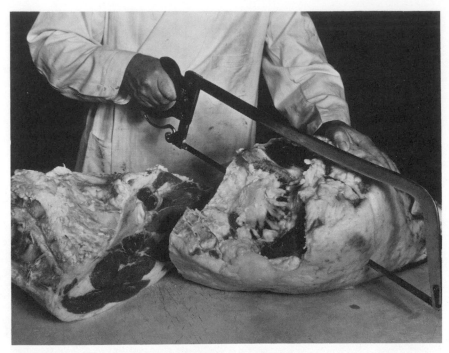

Fig. 9-44. The sirloin has been separated from the rump, and now the rump is being separated from the leg or round. Courtesy USDA

When a closely trimmed tenderloin is removed from a shortloin, a shell or striploin, bone in, regular (175) remains. This should be cut so the loineye muscle is not more than 6 in. from the flank edge at the rib end and not more than 4 in. at the butt end. Striploins may be cut as follows:

IMPS No.	Name of Cut	Description
176	Striploin, bnls, reg.	All bones and cartilage from No. 175 are removed; scalping is required.
177	Striploin, bone-in, intermediate	Same as No. 176 except the bone is in and the flank is not more than 4 in. on the loin end and 3 in. at the butt end from the extreme outer tip of the loineye muscle.
178	Striploin, bnls, intermediate	Same as No. 177 except all bones and cartilage are removed; scalping is required.

IMPS No.	Name of Cut	Description
179	Striploin, bone-in, short-cut	Same as No. 176 except the bone is in and the flank end is not more than 3 in. on the loin end and 2 in. on the butt end from the extreme tip of the loineye muscle.
180	Striploin, bnls, short-cut	Same as No. 179 but boneless; cartilage is removed; scalping is required.
181	Sirloin	Loin end or rear portion of the full loin; the sirloin remains after the shortloin is removed. Also called *hip, short hip, head loin, rumpl K-style butt, sirloin butt bone-in, sirloin butt, Sir butt, boneless sirloin butt,* and *family steak.*
182	Sirloin butt, bnls	All bones and the butt tenderloin removed from No. 181.
183	Sirloin butt, bnls, trimmed	Same as No. 182 except fat and flank muscle are removed exposing underlying gland and heavy white membrane (sacrosciatic ligament) near the sacral vertebrae is removed. When well trimmed, this may also be called the *square-cut sirloin butt.*
184	Top sirloin butt, bnls	Thick upper portion of No. 183 left after removing the bottom sirloin butt; the separation is made by cutting through at the natural (blue tissue) muscle seam.
185	Bottom sirloin butt, bnls, regular	The portion left from No. 183 after removing the top sirloin butt (184).
186	Bottom sirloin butt, bnls, trimmed	No. 185 except the flank and the underlying membrane on the bottom sirloin must be completely removed and the fat on the underside is trimmed to expose the underlying gland.
189	Full tenderloin, regular	The tenderloin is removed from the full loin by cutting it free in one piece; it includes the butt tenderloin. It should be trimmed so that fat is not greater than ¾ in. at the butt end where the large lymph gland is exposed and tapered down to the blue tissue not beyond ¾ of the length of the whole tenderloin. Scoring over ½ in. deep is not permitted.

IMPS No.	Name of Cut	Description
189A	Full tenderloin, defatted	No. 189 except all surface fat is removed but the side strip muscle and underlying fat are still firmly attached.
190	Full tenderloin, special	No. 189 except all surface fat and the attached side strip muscle and fat are removed and loose visible tissue. The principal membranous tissue over the tenderloin is left intact.
191	Butt tenderloin	The tenderloin in the sirloin with not over ¾-in.-thick fat at any point. May be called *filet mignon* as a steak.
192	Short tenderloin	The tenderloin in the short loin or diamond-bone short loin. Fat should not be over ½ in. deep and follow fat trim as for No. 189. The smallest part may be called the short *tip tender, tips, tenderloin tips,* or *tournedos.* Steaks from the short tenderloin may be called *petite filets.* They may be called as a whole piece the *tenderloin roast.*

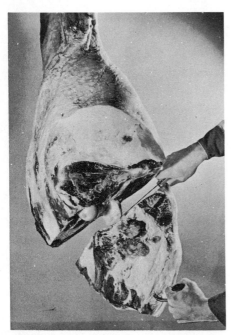

Fig. 9-45. Separating the rump from the round when the round is hanging. Courtesy National Livestock and Meat Board

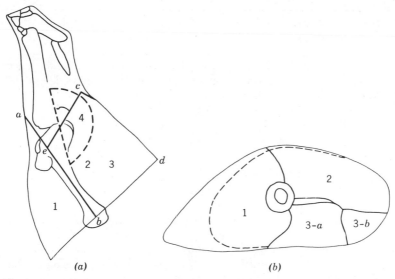

(a)   *(b)*

Fig. 9-46. (a) Remove the knuckle (1) by cutting through the meat to the leg bone from (a) to (b) on both sides. Remove the inside (top) round (2) by starting along line (e-c) and following seams from (c) to (d) and (e) to (b). Remove heel (4) by cutting around the shank and leg bones. (b) 1. Knuckle (tip); 2. inside (top) round; 3a and 3b. outside (bottom) round.

The round (158) includes the round, the rump, and shank. It remains on the hindquarter after the full loin and flank are removed. (See Figures 9-46 through 9-49.) The round may be incorrectly called *eye of the round, top* or *bottom round.* Correct trade name Beef Round. Full-cut round is frequently used. There are a number of ways of cutting the round.

IMPS No.	Name of Cut	Description
159	Round, 158, 3-way, bnls	No. 158 completely boneless divided into the inside, outside round with the heel, shank, rump attached and knuckle. All bones and cartilage must be removed especially around the kneecap.
160	Round, ROn-SOff,* partially bnls	The rump bone, tail bones, shank meat, and shank are removed, but the round bone (femur) is left in. All connective tissue is removed.

IMPS No.	Name of Cut	Description
161	Round, ROn-SOff, bnls	No. 160 with all bones removed and the thick and opaque gracilis membrane on the inside muscle is removed.
162	Round, ROn-SOff, boned, rolled and tied tied	No. 161 rolled and tied girthwise and lengthwise.
163	Round, ROn-SOff, 3-way, bnls	No. 159 made completely boneless with the shank removed from the outside round.
164	Round, R&SOff,	No. 158 with shank meat, shank bone, and rough rump removed. No part of the aitchbone is left and the ball joint of the femur is also removed with the rump. Sometimes No. 164 is called the *steamship round*.
165	Round, R&SOff, bnls	No. 164 made boneless. The kneecap and surrounding heavy tissue is removed at the stifle joint and the round bone is removed along with thick, opaque gracilis membrane inside the muscle.
166	Round, R&SOff, boned, rolled and tied	No. 165 rolled and tied with string girthwise and lengthwise.
166A	Round, R partially removed-SOff	No. 160 but the pelvic bone and tail bones are removed when the rump is taken by a straight cut beginning at the ball joint and cutting up perpendicular to the length of the round bone.
166B	Round, R partially off-SOff, bnls	166A made completely boneless. The kneecap and its connective tissue is removed at the stifle joint; the round bone is removed as described for Nos. 161 and 165.
166C	Round, No. 166B, boned, rolled and tied	No. 166B tied with string girthwise and lengthwise.

IMPS No.	Name of Cut	Description
167	Knuckle	The knuckle muscle with the kneecap and heavy connective tissue removed. A sirloin tip includes the knuckle and a part of the sirloin may also be called the *short sirloin, top sirloin* (incorrect), *sirloin butt* (incorrect), *crescent, veiny bell of knuckle, face, face rump, face round, boneless sirloin* (incorrect), *round tip, ball tip, loin tip, family steak,* and *sandwich steak.* If the knuckle and loin end are left in one piece, it may be called a full hip. A short hip is the same but has the bottom sirloin removed. The preferred name is "tip".
168	Inside (top) round	The interior muscle on the hind leg (round). In cutting the round, this muscle when the leg is on the block is on top. The gracilis membrane below the aitchbone must be removed. Maximum fat is 1 in. Specify also the opaque membrane be removed. This cut is boneless.
169	Outside (bottom) round	The outside leg muscle, which is usually on the bottom in cutting the round. The heel and rump are removed along with sinews, ligaments, heavy connective tissue and popliteal lymph gland. It is boneless. It may also be called the *silverside, gooseneck* (incorrect), *silver tip,* or *Swiss steak cut.*
170	Gooseneck round, bnls	Outside round and boneless rump in one piece. The knuckle, shank meat, heavy connective tissue, popliteal lymph gland, and all bones are removed.
171	The New York round	No. 158 with the knuckle and all heavy tissue removed. The rump and its bones (no more than 2 tail vertebrae), the round, and shank bone remain.

*ROn is "rump on", SOff is "shank off."

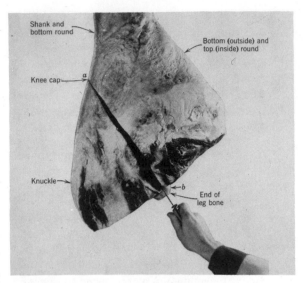

Fig. 9-47. Cutting from the knee cap at "a" to the end of the leg bone (femur) "b" removes the knuckle, leaving the bottom and top round with the shank. Courtesy National Livestock and Meat Board

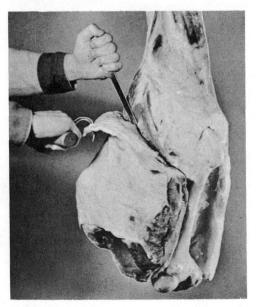

Fig. 9-48. The top or inside round is removed after the knuckle. Note that the knee cap bone has been removed with the knuckle. Specifications should state that this bone should not be delivered with the knuckle. Courtesy National Livestock and Meat Board

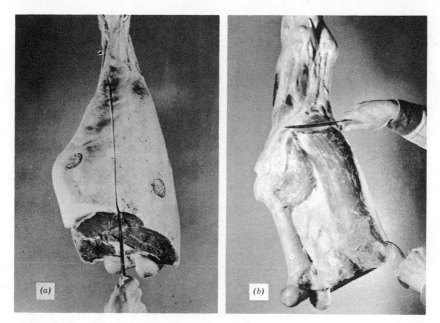

Fig. 9-49. (a) The bottom or top round may be divided as shown along the natural seams. (b) The top or inside round is first removed and then the bottom and outside, shown here, is removed, leaving shank meat. Courtesy National Livestock and Meat Board

The heel on the round is the shank meat with the bone removed. It may be called *Pike's Peak, diamond wedge, gooseneck* (incorrect), *horseshoe, upper round, lower round, Jew daube,* or the *Denver pot roast.** A cafe round is a display roast for carving in front of customers. It is the inside and outside round only, with the femur bone still in.

Low-grade cattle may be boned and utilized for cured beef, canned meat, or sausage. Boneless 8- to 14-lb loins, 2- to 8-lb tenderloins, 4- to 12-lb well trimmed rib eyes, 6- to 15-lb shoulder clods, and other cuts may be marketed from such cattle. Some low-grade cattle may be injected with an enzyme before slaughter to make the meat more tender. Or cuts may be treated with tenderizing enyzmes after slaughter.

Portion cuts from cattle are included in Series 1000. A roast-ready shoulder clod (1114R) is the clod (114) with all tendons, periosteum on the boned surface, and fat in excess of that specified removed. For small roasts, the thin end must be split lengthwise, the ends reversed, and the

*The National Livestock and Meat Board recommends this be called the Beef Round Heel of the Round.

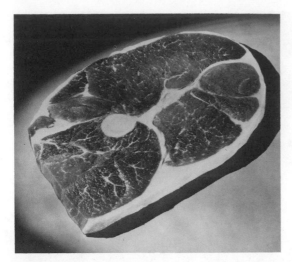

Fig. 9-50. This round steak shows a part of the knuckle remaining to the left of the round bone (femur). The bottom round is at the bottom right. (This is the gluteus medius muscle shown in Fig. 9-27.) The small muscle to the right of the gluteus medius is often called the *kernel*. The top round is shown at the top. Courtesy National Livestock and Meat Board

Fig. 9-51. A No. 1180 boneless strip loin with only an inch flank (short cut) is being processed here. The distance from the farthest edge of the steak on the chine bone side is 8 in.

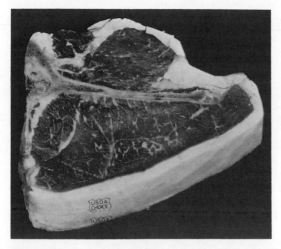

Fig. 9-52. A Porterhouse steak (No. 1173). A T-bone steak (No. 1173A) must have a much smaller tenderloin muscle (top muscle in this picture), but it must measure more than ½ in. in diameter. Courtesy USDA

boned surfaces put together to produce a uniformly thick roast. It should be tied.

A chuck roll, boneless and tied (1116R), is 116 with the chuck tender and chuck cover removed. The neck is removed from the chuck at the natural seam. The lower part of the chuck must be trimmed so the chuckeye (longisimuss dorsi) is not more than 3 in. from the edge of the cut. This gives a large rectangular piece of fairly clear muscle that can be rolled and tied. When smaller roasts are specified, the chuck roll is cut through at approximately right angle to the length.

The boneless knuckle (1167R), inside round (1168R), outside round (1169R), and gooseneck round (1170R) roasts from the leg are boneless and come, respectively, from Nos. 159, 168, 169, and 170, they must have a better trim, and exposed connective tissue, cartilage, gracilis membrane, and so forth, must be all removed. A short-cut boneless strip loin roast (1180R) from No. 180 must be cut so that the flank edge is not more than 3 in. from the loineye muscle on the rib end and not more than 2 in. on the butt end. A boneless top sirloin butt roast (1184R) comes from No. 184 with the flank muscle and underlying membrane completely removed. Individual roasts, if specified, may be held intact by tying parallel to the cut surface made by separating the loin from the round. A trimmed, boneless, bottom sirloin butt (1186R) is obtained from No. 186. Individual roasts may be similarly tied as stated for No. 1184R. A regular full tenderloin (1189R) is nothing but No. 189. A wide number of trade names are given steaks and

TABLE 9-7A

Index of Beef Steaks and Patties and Suggested Portion Sizes

Item No.	Item Names	Suggested Portion Sizes (see note below)												
		3 oz	4 oz	6 oz	8 oz	10 oz	12 oz	14 oz	16 oz	18 oz	20 oz	24 oz	28 oz	32 oz
1100	Cubed Steaks, Regular	X	X	X	X									
1101	Cubed Steaks, Special	X	X	X	X									
1102	Braising Steaks, Bnls (Swiss)		X	X	X									
1103	Rib Steaks (Bone In)				X	X	X	X	X					
1103A	Rib Steaks (Bnls)		X	X	X	X	X							
1112	Rib-Eye Roll Steaks		X	X	X	X	X							
1136	Ground Beef Patties, Regular	X	X	X	X									
1137	Ground Beef Patties, Special	X	X	X	X									
1167	Knuckle Steaks	X	X	X	X	X								
1168	Inside Round Steaks	X	X	X	X	X								
1169	Outside Round Steaks	X	X	X	X	X								
1173	Porterhouse Steaks						X	X	X	X	X	X	X	X
1173A	T-Bone Steaks				X	X	X	X	X	X	X	X	X	
1177	Strip Loin Steaks (Bone In) Intermediate				X	X	X	X	X	X	X	X	X	
1178	Strip Loin Steaks (Bnls) Intermediate				X	X	X	X	X	X	X	X		
1179	Strip Loin Steaks (Bone In) Short Cut				X	X	X	X	X	X	X	X		
1179A	Strip Loin Steaks (Bone In) Extra Short Cut				X	X	X	X	X	X	X	X		

No.	Description										
1179B	Strip Loin Steaks (Bone In) Special						X	X	X	X	X
1180	Strip Loin Steaks (Bnls) Short Cut					X	X	X	X	X	
1180A	Strip Loin Steaks (Bnls) Extra Short Cut					X	X	X	X	X	
1180B	Strip Loin Steaks (Bnls) Special				X	X	X	X	X		
1184	Top Sirloin Butt Steaks (Bnls)				X	X	X	X	X		
1184A	Top Sirloin Butt Steaks (Bnls) Semi-Center Cut				X	X	X	X		X	X
1184B	Top Sirloin Butt Steaks (Bnls) Center Cut				X	X	X	X			
1189	Tenderloin Steaks, Close Trim			X	X	X	X				
1190	Tenderloin Steaks, Special Trim	X		X	X	X	X				

Note: Because it is impractical to list all portion weights for steaks that purchasers may desire, those identified by the letter "X" in the index table are suggested only. Other portion weights may be ordered if desired.

TABLE 9-7B
Index of Beef Roasts and Stew and Suggested Weight Ranges

Item No.	Item Names	Suggested Weight Ranges (see note below)				
		lb	lb	lb	lb	lb
1107R	Rib, Bone-In, Short Cut	Under 20	20–23	23–26	26–30	30–up
1108R	Rib, Bnls, Tied, Short Cut	Under 17	17–19	19–22	22–25	25–up
1109R	Rib, Bone-In, Tied, Roast Ready	Under 17	17–19	19–22	22–25	25–up
1109AR	Rib, Bone-In, Tied, Roast Ready, Special	Under 17	17–19	19–22	22–25	25–up
1110R	Rib, Bnls, Tied, Roast Ready	Under 14	14–16	16–19	19–22	22–up
1112R	Rib Eye Roll	Under 7	7–8	8–10	10–12	12–up
1114R	Shoulder Clod, Roast Ready	Under 16	16–18	18–21	21–24	24–up
1116R	Chuck Roll, Bnls, Tied	Under 15	15–17	17–21	21–25	25–up
1167R	Knuckle, Bnls	Under 10	10–up			
1168R	Inside Round	Under 18	18–20	20–23	23–26	26–up
1169R	Outside Round	Under 11	11–13	13–16	16–19	19–up
1170R	Gooseneck Round	Under 18	18–20	20–23	23–26	26–up
1180R	Strip Loin, Bnls, Short Cut	Under 8	8–10	10–12	12–14	14–up
1184R	Top Sirloin Butt, Bnls	Under 8	8–10	10–13	13–up	
1186R	Bottom Sirloin Butt, Bnls Trimmed	Under 4	4–6	6–up		
1189R	Full Tenderloin, Regular	Under 5	5–7	7–9	9–up	
1195	Beef For Stewing	Amount Specified				
1196	Beef For Chop Suey	Amount Specified				

Note: Because it is impractical to list all weights for roasts that purchasers may desire, those included in the index table are suggested only. Other weight ranges may be ordered if desired.

cuts from the loin. Loin strip steaks (Nos. 1176 to 1189) are called *top loin* steak, *sirloin* steak, *boneless sirloin* steak, *New York* steak, *Kansas City* steak, *club* (incorrect) steak, *Delmonico* steak, *shell* steak, and *strip* steak. A porterhouse steak (1173) also is called *T-bone* steak (incorrect), *large T-bone* steak, *tenderloin* steak (incorrect), and *king* steak. A T-bone steak (1173A) also is called a *porterhouse* steak (incorrect), *small T-bone* steak, *club* steak (incorrect), or *tenderloin* steak (incorrect). A club steak that is one of first several steaks from the rib side of the loin may also be called a *sirloin* steak (incorrect), *Delmonico* steak, *market* steak, and *individual* steak. A boneless sirloin steak (1184) also is called the *top loin* steak, *hip* steak, *rump* steak (incorrect), *Top of Iowa* steak, *top sirloin butt* steak, or *bottom sirloin butt* steak.**

**The National Livestock and Meat Board recommends that a strip steak be called a Top Loin Steak, a club steak be called a Top Loin Steak and the boneless sirloin steak be called by the federal name Boneless Sirloin Steak. They also note that a porterhouse steak must have a tenderloin muscle greater than 1¼ in. in diameter and a T-bone must have the tenderloin no less than ¼ in. and no more than 1¼ in. in diameter.

Beef for stewing (1195) comes from the primal rib, cross-cut chuck, round with rump and shank on, or full trimmed loin. It msut be clear meat and the fat on any piece must not exceed ¼ in. in thickness. The fat content for the lot must not be over 20%. Beef for chop suey (1196) comes from the roast-ready shoulder clod, boneless chuck, boneless knuckle, or the inside or outside round. Cuts must be made along the natural seams, and practically all surface and seam fat must be excluded. No. 1196 is cut by putting it into a grinder with a sharp 3-blade knife and a plate with ¾ in.-diameter holes. It may be machine cut into pieces of comparable size. Buyers also can specify hand cutting.

Regular cubed steaks (1100) may come from any solid, boneless meat that is free from membranous tissue, tendons, or ligaments. They must be reasonably uniform in shape and can be knitted from 2 or more pieces or folded during cubing to hold them together. Buyers can specify that knitting not occur. Surface fat after cubing must not exceed ½ in. in width. Surface and seam fat cannot cover more than 15% of the total area on either side. The steak must not break when suspended from any point ½ in. from the outer edge. Special cubed steaks (1101) come from No. 1100 but must be taken from boneless muscles such as a round, loin, rib, square-cut chuck, and so forth. Knitting and folding are not permitted. Braised steaks (Swiss) (1102) must mcet the requirement for special cubed steaks and come from boneless cuts from the rib-eye roll (112), shoulder clod (114), knuckle (167), inside (168) or outside (169) round, boneless short-cut strip loin (180), boneless top sirloin butt (184), and trimmed bottom sirloin butt (186). If they come from the boneless gooseneck round (170), none of the heel meat can be used. Each steak must be trimmed practically free of fat on at least half of the circumference, and the other half cannot have more than an average of ½-in. exterior fat (¾ in. maximum at any point). Cubing may be specified, but knitting is not permitted.

The following describes rib and other steaks in portion cuts:

IMPS No.	Steak	Description
1103	Rib steak, bone in	From No. 107, but no more than 3 in. from the rib eye to the end of the rib bone is permitted. All fat, meat, and bone above the rib eye, feather bones, and backstrap must be removed.
1103A	Rib steak, bnls	No. 1103 with rib bones and rib fingers removed.
1112	Rib-eye roll steaks	Cut from No. 112; butterfly steaks are not permitted.

IMPS No.	Steak	Description
1167	Knuckle steaks	From No. 167 with the knuckle cover, flank meat and membranous tissue removed. Can be cut lengthwise to get the proper size steaks.
1168	Inside round steaks	From No. 168; can be cut lengthwise to get proper size steaks.
1169	Outside round steaks	From No. 169; can be cut lengthwise to get proper size steaks; if from the gooseneck round, no steaks can come from the heel.
1173	Porterhouse steaks	From No. 173; the flank edge should not be more than 3 in. from the loineye muscle and the tenderloin muscle must not be less than 1¼ in. in diameter.
1173A	T-bone steaks	From No. 173; the flank edge should not be more than 3 in. from the loineye muscle and the tenderloin muscle must not be less than ½ in. in diameter.
1177	Strip loin steaks, bone-in, intermediate	From No. 177; flank end shall not be more than 3 in. from the loineye muscle.
1178	Strip loin steak, bnls, intermediate	No. 1177 boneless.
1179	Strip loin steak, bone-in, short cut	From No. 179; flank end shall not be more than 2 in. from the loineye muscle.
1179A	Strip loin steak, bone-in, extra short cut	From No. 179; flank end shall not be more than 1 in. from the loineye muscle.
1179B	Strip loin steak, bone-in, special	From No. 179; all flank end must be removed from the loineye muscle following the muscle contour.
1180	Strip loin steak, bnls, short cut	From No. 180; 1 in. flank only.
1180A	Strip loin steak, bnls, special	From No. 1179B made boneless.

IMPS No.	Steak	Description
1184	Top sirloin butt steak, bnls	From No. 184; last steak of top sirloin butt with excessive ligaments and connective tissue cannot be excluded. Can be cut to give proper size steaks; butterfly steaks are not permitted.
1184A	Top sirloin butt steaks, bnls, semicenter cut	No. 1184, but only longissimus dorsi, gluteus medius, and biceps femoris muscles can be included.
1184B	Top sirloin butt steaks, bnls, center cut	No. 1184, but only the major sirloin muscle, the gluteus medius, is in the steak.
1189	Tenderloin steak, close trim	No. 189 or a tenderloin portion. No lean can be under 1 in. in diameter and butter-flying is not permitted. No fat can be more than ¼ in. deep on the average (½ in. at the deepest point). No steak from a butt tenderloin can be less than 1½ in. in diameter and from other areas not less than 1 in., but buyers should specify differently if this is too small.
1190	Tenderloin steak, special trim	No. 1189, but all fat and the silver skin must be removed.

A short cut, bone-in, rib roast (1170R) is nothing but 107, and Nos. 1108 and 1109, respectively, are the same thing as Nos. 108 and 109, but a 1109AR, roast-ready, bone-in, special rib roast has a limit of 3 in. from the rib-eye muscle at the twelfth rib and requires special beveling and trimming of the fat cover, which is tied back on. A boneless, roast-ready, tied rib (1109AR) also comes from No. 109. A rib-eye roll roast (1112R) includes the eye muscle (longissimus dorsi) and the spinalis dorsi and complexus muscles that run with the eye muscle in the rib area. All other muscles, cartilage, bone, backstrap, and exterior fat covering must be removed.

Lamb and Mutton—Series 200 and 1200

Lamb, yearling mutton, and mutton are covered by IMPS. As in beef, the carcass (200) must be in good condition. No pluck (heart, liver, or lungs), spleen (melt), caul fat, bloody tissue, or excessive fat cover must remain and most heart fat and perhaps the skirt (diaphragm) and hanging tender are removed. A fabricated carcass (201) is split and divided into fore and hind

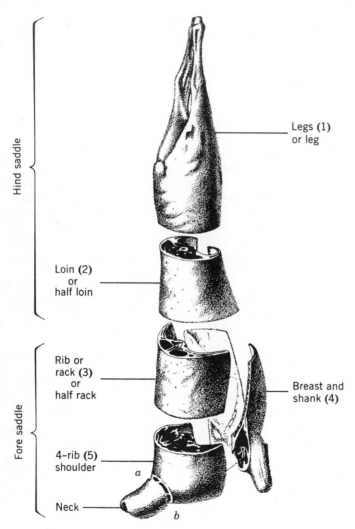

Fig. 9-53. The main wholesale cuts of lamb or mutton are shown. The neck may be separated from the shoulder (5) and the cut is usually along line ''ab'' as shown. Only 3½ ribs are left on the shoulder (5) leaving 8½ ribs in the rack (rib or bracelet) section (3). If division of the fore and hind saddle is after the thirteenth rib, the rack will have 9½ ribs. Courtesy National Livestock and Meat Board

quarters by cutting through the side between the twelfth and thirteenth ribs. The bones of the fore and hind shanks must be removed, but the meat must be left intact. No more than 2 tail vertebrae can remain. Whole baby lambs (dressed 30 to 35 lb) should be specified with the pelt on and whole spring lambs (50 to 55 lb) with the pelt off.

If the carcass is not split but divided between the twelfth and thirteenth ribs, a foresaddle (202) and hindsaddle (230) are obtained. A cut, long hindsaddle (237), regular, is the hind part of the carcass after the double chuck (206) is removed from the forepart. The double chuck is removed by cutting through between the fourth and fifth ribs on either side. The double chuck (206) contains the fifth to twelfth rib area, plus the neck, shoulders, briskets, and foreshanks. A trimmed long cut saddle results when the back is trimmed as for No. 236 which is described later.

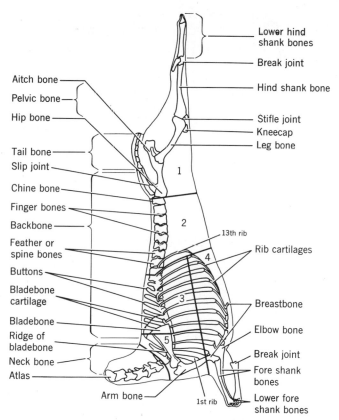

Fig. 9-54. The skeletal structure of the lamb or mutton is shown with the hind and fore saddle divisions as indicated in Fig. 9-53. Courtesy National Livestock and Meat Board

TABLE 9-8
Index of Products and Weight Range
Weight Range for Carcasses and Wholesale and Fabricated Cuts

Item No.	Product	Range 1 Lamb	Range 1 Mutton	Range 2 Lamb	Range 2 Mutton	Range 3 Lamb	Range 3 Mutton	Range 4 Lamb	Range 4 Mutton
200	Carcass	30–41	55–75	41–53	75–95	53–65	95–115	65–75	115–130
201	Carcass, Fabricated								
202	Foresaddle	15–21	28–38	21–27	38–48	27–33	48–58	33–38	58–65
203	Bracelet (Double)	5–6	8–11	6–8	11–14	8–10	14–17	10–12	17–19
204	Hotel Rack, Trimmed (Double)	3–5	6–8	5–6	8–10	6–7	10–13	7–8	13–14
205	Chucks and Plates (Double)	12–16	22–30	16–21	30–38	21–26	38–46	26–30	46–52
206	Chucks (Double)	11–14	19–26	14–19	26–33	19–23	33–40	23–27	40–46
207	Shoulders (Double)	8–10	14–19	10–13	19–24	13–16	24–29	16–19	29–33
208	Shoulders (Boned, Rolled, Tied)	3–4	6–8	4–6	8–10	6–7	10–12	7–8	12–26
209	Breast and Shank	4–6	8–11	6–7	11–13	7–9	13–16	9–11	16–18
230	Hindsaddle	15–21	28–38	21–27	38–48	27–33	48–58	33–38	58–65
231	Loin, Regular (Double)	5–6	8–11	6–8	11–14	8–10	14–17	10–11	17–20
232	Loin, Trimmed (Double)	3–4	6–8	4–5	8–10	5–7	10–12	7–8	12–15
233	Legs (Double)	11–14	19–26	14–19	26–33	19–23	33–40	23–27	40–46
234	Leg, Oven-Prepared	4–6	8–10	6–8	10–13	8–9	13–16	9–11	16–18
235	Back, Regular	9–12	17–23	12–16	23–29	16–20	29–35	20–23	35–39
236	Back, Trimmed	6–8	11–15	8–11	15–19	11–13	19–23	13–15	23–26
237	Hindsaddle, Long-Cut, Regular	20–27	36–49	27–34	49–62	34–42	62–75	42–49	75–85
238	Hindsaddle, Long-Cut, Trimmed	17–23	30–41	23–29	41–52	29–36	52–63	36–41	63–72

Note: When single fores, chucks, shoulders, hotel racks, hinds, loins, legs, backs, and so forth are specified, their respective weights must be one-half of that prescribed for double (i.e., in pairs) cuts.

Note: The weights of the various wholesale, fabricated, and boneless cuts as shown in each weight range group in this table are those usually produced from carcasses of the weights indicated in the corresponding weight range groups. It should not be expected that all carcasses whose weight is within one of the indicated weight ranges will always produce cuts within the weight ranges shown. Neither should it be expected that cuts of the weights shown in each weight range will always originate from carcasses in the indicated weight range. Therefore, in ordering cuts, purchasing officials should order the specific weight range(s) desired without regard to the carcass weights shown in the various ranges.

The foresaddle (202) yields a double bracelet (203) after the double chuck is removed. The bracelet contains the fifth through twelfth rib area, plus the plate below it. If the breasts are removed from No. 203 by cutting a straight line 4 in. from the extreme outer tip of the rib eye on the twelfth rib to 4 in. below the rib eye on the fifth rib, a double trimmed hotel rack (204) is obtained. Removing only the hotel rack from the forequarter leaves the chucks and plates (205). The double shoulder (207) is a double chuck after removing the foreshanks, briskets, and neck. The shank is severed from the brisket by cutting through the front part of the sternum cartilage (breast bone) continuing in a straight line through to the fourth rib. The neck is neatly removed, leaving no more than an inch of neck meat. A double lamb chuck (206) (also called a *lamb fore* or *forequarter*) is that portion remaining after the bracelet is removed and contains the neck, breast, shank, and shoulder. A boned, rolled and tied shoulder results when the double shoulder is split and boned, completely excluding all cartilage, backstrap, large exposed arteries and veins, dark, bloody, or discolored meat, and the prescapular lymph gland just in front of the shoulder joint. This clear meat is rolled and tied. The breast and shank (209) can vary from (1) a shank, breast, and flank, (2) a shank and breast, or (3) just a brisket and shank. Specifications should name which is desired. The first comes by cutting straight across through the cartilage of the breast bone to the lower portion of the bracelet, removing the breast. The cut is continued under the loin to the leg, removing the flank; the second is the same but does not contain the flank from the thirteenth rib on; the brisket and shank is that portion of the lower part of the chuck to the fourth rib—thus the plate is not included.

A regular double loin (231) (also called the *lamb pie* or *kidney tip*) is both loins after the hindsaddle has the double legs (233) removed by cutting through just in front of the hip bone, leaving all this bone in the leg portion. A trimmed loin (232) has the flank portions removed by cutting on the thirteenth rib to not more than 4 in. from the loineye muscle in a straight line to the leg not more than 4 in. from the loineye muscle there. The kidney knobs must be removed. Lumbar fat must be trimmed so it is not over ½ in. at the butt end. It is then tapered down to the lean surface at a point not beyond ¾ the length of the entire loin. A partially oven-prepared boneless leg (234) is severed from a double leg section by cutting through the spine and then removing the entire flank, all cod or udder fat, fat cover in excess of ½ in., and the pelvic, back, and tail bones. Only the femur bone remains. A regular back or Boston back (235) results when the double chuck and double legs are removed, leaving the bracelet and loin portions intact as a saddle. A trimmed back (236) is the back after its lower portion is cut away in a straight line starting on the fifth rib not more than 4 in. from the rib eye continuing to a point on the leg end not more than 4 in. from the loineye muscle. The kidney knobs and lumbar fat must be trimmed as described for a trimmed loin (232).

Buyers may find that heavy lambs or yearling mutton or mutton over 65 lb in a carcass may be cut differently than under the IMPS standards. Since these methods may vary, buyers should learn how this cutting is to be done from a specific purveyor. The Lamb Council also can be helpful.

Rib chops (1204) come from a rack with the rib-eye not more than 3 in. from where the breast is cut from the rack. The fell or crisp membranous skin on the outside must be removed. The chine must be completely removed by sawing at an approximate 45° angle, and chops from the blade bone area must be free of the rib cover (the bone, related cartilage, fat, and flesh above the bone). French chops (1204A) come from 1204 and must have the meat (fingers) around the rib bone completely removed to at least 1½ in. from the rib bone end. If the chop is thick enough to include 2 or more rib bones, the rib bone closest to the center must be frenched as indicated and the other bones removed for the distance the frenched bone is exposed. Shoulder chops (1207) come from No. 207 by taking armbone chops first. They should be cut reasonably parallel to the normal line of separation of the shank and shoulder up to but not including the shank knuckle. These must have the riblets (rib bones) and fat in excess of ¼ in. removed. Blade chops then must be cut closely parallel to the rib bones up to the juncture of the blade and knuckle bones. Loin chops (1232) have the fell removed and are cut from a loin that leaves no more than 3 in. from the loineye to the flank end of the chop. No. 1208, a boned, rolled and tied shoulder is Item 208. Item 1234R, a partially boneless leg, is Item 233, a boneless, rolled and tied leg with the femur bone, the kneecap, and the adjacent heavy tendons removed. It is tied girthwise and lengthwise. Lamb for stewing (1295) is cubed meat from lamb shoulders (207) after it is completely boned and all cartilage, backstrap, discolored meat, glands, and so forth, removed. Surface or seam fat on any piece cannot exceed ¼ in. Trimable fat for the lot must not exceed 20%.

Veal and Calf—Series 300 and 1300

The carcass of a veal or calf is cut much the same as beef. The carcass (300) may come with or without the hide. The hide may be left on because the carcass, having little fat cover, may dry out excessively in cooling down and develop a dry, hard surface. The trim and condition of the carcass follows that for beef. A fabricated carcass (301) is the same as for a lamb or mutton carcass (201). Calf or veal boned carcasses (302) must have all bones, bone slivers, kidney knobs, and cartilages removed. Fat must not exceed 10% on the carcass, determined visually. All cuts must be proportional to the carcass, and if any are excluded, they may not be replaced by others unless otherwise specified. Buyers can specify that tenderloins, flanks, navels, briskets, shanks, skirts, hanging tenders, necks, or rib fingers be excluded. Carcasses with a large quantity of good lean removed may not be included unless the removed lean comes from minor cuts and are not loins, ribs, rounds, or chucks.

A side (303) comes from a carcass split through the spinebone. If specified, it can be made into a hind and fore quarter by dividing between the twelfth and thirteenth ribs. A foresaddle (304) is the same as the lamb or mutton (204). Similarly, a double bracelet (305), double trimmed hotel rack (306), double chuck and plate (307), double regular chuck (308) are cut the same as are lamb and mutton Nos. 205, 206, 207, and 208, respectively. A double square-cut chuck (309) is a regular chuck (308) having the shank and brisket removed as for No. 209. Items 310, shoulder clod, and 311, square-cut chuck, boneless, clod out are the same as Nos. 114 and 116, respectively, for beef except that the clod cannot be less than ¾ in. at any

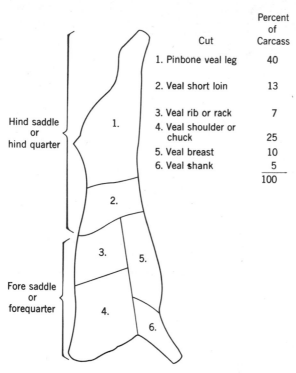

Cut	Percent of Carcass
1. Pinbone veal leg	40
2. Veal short loin	13
3. Veal rib or rack	7
4. Veal shoulder or chuck	25
5. Veal breast	10
6. Veal shank	5
	100

Fig. 9-55. The division of the fore and hind saddle of veal or calf on a side is shown. The percentage of carcass in each cut also is given. The veal shoulder or chuck (4) also may be called the *square cut*.

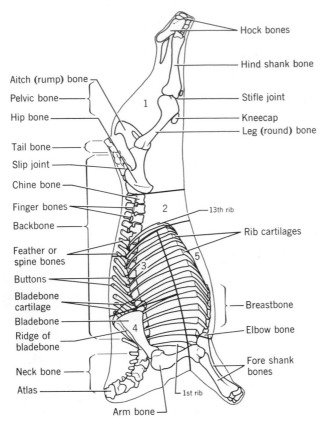

Hock bones

Hind shank bone

Aitch (rump) bone

Pelvic bone

Stifle joint

Hip bone

Kneecap

Leg (round) bone

Tail bone

Slip joint

Chine bone

Finger bones

Backbone

13th rib

Rib cartilages

Feather or
spine bones

Buttons

Bladebone
cartilage

Breastbone

Bladebone

Ridge of
bladebone

Elbow bone

Fore shank
bones

Neck bone

Atlas

1st rib

Arm bone

Fig. 9-56. The skeletal structure of veal with wholesale divisions shown in Figure 9-55. Note that division of the hind and fore saddles is between the twelfth and thirteenth ribs. Courtesy National Livestock and Meat Board

point in depth. Similarly, the foreshank (312) is processed in the same way the foreshank for beef (117) is. The breast (313) is obtained by removing the foreshank and then cutting through the cartilage of the sternum similar to the manner in which a brisket is obtained from beef.

The double hindsaddle (330), regular double loin (331), and double trimmed loin (332) are the same as Nos. 230, 231, and 232, respectively, for lamb and mutton. A single trimmed full loin (333) is taken from a half hindsaddle by first removing the flank and cutting at the juncture of the last (fifth) sacral vertebra and the first tail vertebra going down to a point immediately below the protuberance of the femur bone. This exposes the ball. The cut continues in a straight line, separating the leg. The flank is removed by cutting at the leg end so no more than a ½ in. of fat and muscle on the sirloin edge is included. Cutting continues in a straight line to the thirteenth rib so not more than 4 in. of flank exists from the rib-eye muscle. The kidney knob and the fat around it is removed by starting at the rear end of the kidney, slanting to the thirteenth rib to remove almost all lumbar fat. The hanging tender must be removed at the juncture of the first and second lumbar vertebrae. All cover fat must be well trimmed and pelivc fat must not exceed ¾ in. in depth.

Double legs (334) are prepared similarly to No. 233 on lamb and mutton. A single, boneless, oven-prepared leg (335) has the shank, pelvic, back, tail, round, and kneecap bones removed. All cartilage, tendons, and gambrel cord must be removed. The femur must be removed by cutting through the natural muscle seam. The leg should be in one piece and tied. A single, boneless leg with the shank off (336) is 335 with the shank meat and bone removed by cutting through at the natural seam between the heel and shank meat, following this to the stifle joint. A single leg with the rump and shank off (337) is 336 with the rump and sirloin end removed, leaving no part of the aitchbone. A single, boneless leg with rump and shank off is No. 338 but made boneless by the same method as No. 336 with the rump and sirloin removed as in No. 337. A short cut, single leg is half of a double leg with the flank portion trimmed as indicated for a single, trimmed, full loin (333). In these leg cuts, it is desirable that when the flank is removed, fat and cod or udder fat over ½ in. thick be removed.

A regular back (340) is the carcass after the regular chucks and the double legs are removed; a trimmed back (341) is No. 340 with the breasts and flanks removed but cutting from the sixth rib at a point not more than 4 in. from the rib eye to a point not more than 4 in. from the loineye muscle. The kidney knobs must be removed and lumbar fat trimmed so it is not over ½ in. deep. This then is tapered down to the lean at a point not beyond ¾ the length of the loin. A regular, long cut hindsaddle (342) is the carcass after the regular chucks are removed. A trimmed, long cut hindsaddle (343) includes the double legs (334) and the trimmed back (341).

Veal and calf regular cube steaks (1300) are prepared from cuts much the same as regular beef cube steaks are. The folding, knitting, steak shape and ability to not break when suspended from any point ½ in. from the outer edge also are the same. After cubing, surface fat should not be over ¼ in. wide at any point, and surface and seam fat should not be more than 15% of the total area on either side of the steak. Special cubed steaks (1301) must come from either square-cut chucks, trimmed hotel racks, trimmed loin, or legs. Knitting is not permitted. Otherwise, they must meet the same standards as for regular beef cube steaks.

Rib chops (1306) come from a single hotel rack (306), and the flank must

TABLE 9-9
Index of Products and Weight Range
Weight Range for Carcasses and Wholesale and Fabricated Cuts

Item No.	Product	Range 1 Veal	Range 1 Calf	Range 2 Veal	Range 2 Calf	Range 3 Veal	Range 3 Calf
		lb	lb	lb	lb	lb	lb
300	Carcass	60–100	125–175	100–140	175–225	140–175	225–275
301	Carcass, Fabricated	57–95	119–165	95–133	165–214	133–165	214–261
302	Carcass, Boneless	46–77	96–135	77–108	135–173	108–134	173–212
303	Side	30–50	63–88	50–70	8–133	70–88	113–138
304	Foresaddle	31–51	64–89	51–71	89–115	71–89	115–140
305	Bracelet (Double)	6–10	12–17	10–13	17–21	13–17	21–26
306	Hotel Rack, Trimmed (Double)	5–8	9–13	8–11	13–17	11–13	17–21
307	Chucks and Plates (Double)	26–43	54–75	43–61	75–97	61–75	97–118
308	Chucks, Regular (Double)	25–42	52–73	42–58	73–93	58–73	93–114
309	Square-Cut Chucks (Double)	14–24	29–42	24–33	42–53	33–42	53–65
310	Shoulder Clod	2–3½	4–6	3½–4½	6–7½	4½–6	7½–9
311	Square-Cut Chuck, Bnls (Clod Out)	10–19	23–33	19–26	33–41	26–33	41–51
312	Foreshank	1–2	2½–3½	2–3	3½–4½	3–3½	4½–5½
313	Breast	3½–6	7–9½	6–7½	9½–12	7½–9½	12½–15
330	Hindsaddle	29–49	61–86	49–69	86–110	69–86	110–135
331	Loin, Regular (Double)	5–9	11–16	9–13	16–19	13–16	19–25
332	Loin, Trimmed (Double)	4–7	9–12	7–10	12–16	10–12	16–19
333	Full Loin, Trimmed (Single)	6–9	11–15	9–12	15–19	12–15	19–24
334	Leg (Double)	24–40	50–70	40–56	70–90	56–70	90–110
335	Leg, Oven-Prepared, Bnls (Single)	9–15	18–26	15–21	26–33	21–26	33–40
336	Leg, Shank Off, Bnls. (Single)	7–11	13–19	11–15	19–24	15–19	24–29
337	Leg, Rump and Shank Off (Single)	4–8	9–13	8–10	13–17	10–13	17–20
338	Leg, Rump and Shank Off, Bnls (Single)	3½–7	7–12	7–9	12–15	9–12	15–18
339	Leg, Short-Cut (Single)	9–16	20–28	16–23	28–36	23–28	36–44
340	Back, Regular	11–19	22–30	19–26	30–42	26–41	42–51
341	Back, Trimmed	9–15	18–25	15–20	25–33	20–25	33–40

TABLE 9-9
Index of Products and Weight Range
Weight Range for Carcasses and Wholesale and Fabricated Cuts

Item No.	Product	Range 1		Range 2		Range 3	
		Veal	Calf	Veal	Calf	Veal	Calf
		lb	lb	lb	lb	lb	lb
342	Hindsaddle, Long-Cut, Regular	35–58	73–102	58–81	102–131	81–100	131–160
343	Hindsaddle, Long-Cut, Trimmed	33–55	69–96	55–77	96–124	77–96	124–151

Note: When single fores, hotel racks, chucks and plates, square-cut chucks, hinds, loins, backs, legs, and so forth are specified their respective weight shall be one-half of that prescribed for double (i.e., in pairs) cuts.

Note: The weights of the various wholesale, fabricated, and boneless cuts as shown in weight range group in the table are those usually produced from carcasses of the weights indicated in the corresponding weight range groups. It should not be expected that all carcasses whose weight is within one of the indicated weight ranges will always produce cuts within the weight ranges shown. Neither should it be expected that cuts of the weights shown in each weight range will always originate from carcasses in the indicated weight range. Therefore in ordering cuts purchasing officials should order the specific weight range(s) desired without regard to the carcass weights shown in the various ranges.

Note: Because it is impractical to list all weights that purchasers may desire, those identified in the index table are suggested only. Other weight ranges may be ordered if desired.

not be more than 3 in. from the rib eye. Thoracic vertebrae must be removed at a 45° angle. Chops from the blade bone area must be free of this bone, related cartilage, and all muscles and fat lying above the bone. Shoulder chops (1309) comes from the square-cut chuck (309) and are similar to those for lamb or mutton (1207) with rib bones (riblets) and underlying fat in excess of ¼ in. removed. Shoulder clod steaks (1310) come from the shoulder clod. They can be separated lengthwise and cut to give the desired sized steaks. Loin chops (1332) come from the trimmed loin except the flank is removed so not more than 3 in. of flank from the rib eye is at the thirteenth rib and not more than the same is from the loineye of the leg end. They must not contain any hip bone. A portion of the thirteenth rib can be in chops from this end. A regular cutlet (1336) must come from the boneless leg except the flank from the loin end and heel must be removed. Major leg muscles must be separated by cutting through natural seams and all fat and membranous tissue must be removed. Cutlets can be cubed but not more than twice. They may be folded during cubing unless specified differently. Knitting is permissible. Special cutlets (1336A) come from the boneless leg with shank off, except the flank from the sirloin end, heel, popliteal lymph gland, and heavy connective tissue must be removed. The surface fat must not exceed ¼ in. in thickness at any point—specify this also for No. 1336—and cubing is done twice, unless specified otherwise. Knitting of 2 or more pieces together is not permitted.

Other veal or calf cuts are on the market as follows:

IMPS No.	Name of Cut	Description
1309R	Bnls, tied, square-cut chuck	From No. 309; boned by scalping; all cartilages, backstrap, bloody meat, and so forth removed, and fat cannot be in excess of ½ in. Rolled and tied.
1310R	Roast-ready, shoulder clod	Is No. 310 with better trimming.
1311R	Bnls, tied, square-cut chuck, clod out	From No. 311; rolled and tied with the eye muscle lengthwise.
1335R	Roast-ready, bnls, rolled and tied leg	From No. 335; except entire flank, all cod or udder fat and exterior fat in excess of ½ in. are removed.

Veal for stewing (1395) can come from any boneless portion of the regular chuck, leg or breast. Shank meat, cartilage, periosteum, heavy connective tissue, major ligaments and tendons or tendinous ends must be removed. Specify size and how the dice is made. Surface or seam fat must not be over ¼ in. and the trimable fat for the lot must not be over 20% visually estimated.

Fresh Pork—Series 400 and 1400

Most institutions purchase little carcass or side pork but only fresh pork legs, pork loins, spareribs, pork shoulders, and perhaps ground fresh pork and fresh pork sausage. Some buyers may still use the old grade indicators. Selection No. 1 or No. 2—and this text also may because not all materials have been updated. These two old indicators are for pork which would come under the new grades of U.S. No. 1 and No. 2.

Pork carcass (400) should come from packer style hogs without heads, liver, heart, lungs, kidneys, and ham facings. Sides may be specified but

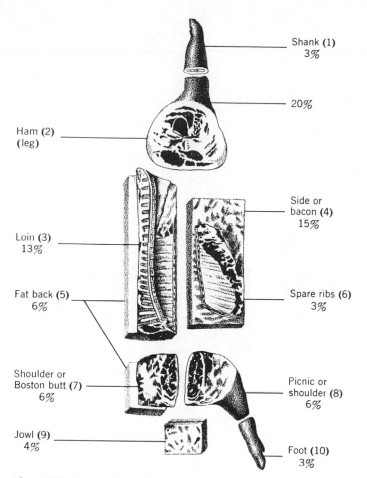

Shank (1)
3%

20%

Ham (2)
(leg)

Side or
bacon (4)
15%

Loin (3)
13%

Fat back (5)
6%

Spare ribs (6)
3%

Shoulder or
Boston butt (7)
6%

Picnic or
shoulder (8)
6%

Jowl (9)
4%

Foot (10)
3%

Fig. 9-57. The usual wholesale cuts of a pork side are shown. The fat back (5) is frequently removed in one piece before removal of the loin (3) and the Boston butt (7). The cut as a percent of side also is given.

have no IMPS number. Leaf and other fat should be closely trimmed and defective parts removed.

The regular short shank ham (401) is separated from the carcass by cutting between the sacral and tail vertebrae about 2¼ to 2¾ in. in front of the rear end of the aitchbone down through the pelvic bone center leaving the whole aitch and hip bone in the leg. The skin is on approximately half or

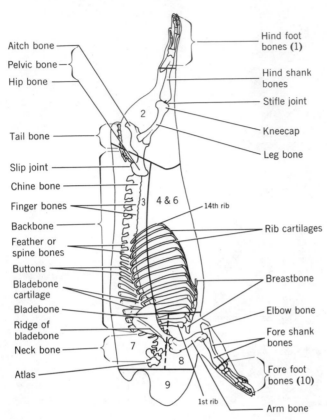

Aitch bone
Pelvic bone
Hip bone

Hind foot bones (1)

Hind shank bones

Stifle joint

2

Kneecap

Tail bone

Leg bone

Slip joint
Chine bone
Finger bones
Backbone
Feather or spine bones
Buttons
Bladebone cartilage
Bladebone
Ridge of bladebone
Neck bone
Atlas

3   4 & 6   14th rib

Rib cartilages

Breastbone

Elbow bone

Fore shank bones

7

8

9

1st rib

Fore foot bones (10)

Arm bone

Fig. 9-58. The skeletal structure of pork is shown. The numbers on the cuts correspond with those shown in Figure 9-57. Note that this pork has 14 ribs, whereas cattle and sheep always have 13. The number of ribs on pork may vary according to breed. Courtesy National Livestock and Meat Board

more of the shank, but not beyond the stifle joint. Tail bones and tail are removed. Pelvic (gut) fat and other loose fat must be removed. The other fat should be trimmed at edge of the butt as follows:

Ham Wt (lb)	Maximum Fat Depth No. 1*	No. 2*	Ham Wt (lb)	Maximum Fat Depth No. 1*	No. 2*
8 to 10	1 in.	1½ in.	14 to 16	1¾ in.	2¼ in.
10 to 12	1¼ in.	1¾ in.	16 to 18	2 in.	2½ in.
12 to 14	1½ in.	2 in.			

*For Selection No. 1 or No. 2 or U.S. No. 1 or No. 2.

Other fat should be well trimmed to give a smooth product. The ham must have a smooth, well-rounded skin collar on the face side extending not more than 2½ in. inward from the center of the stifle joint on a line from the bone on the butt end. A skinned short shank ham (402) is No. 401 partially skinned, leaving a well-rounded skin collar not exceeding 15% of the distance from the stifle joint to the edge of the butt. This collar should be shaped so that the line is at a slant of at least 15 to 18° toward the cushion side. This line should start at the flank side and leave a skin collar approximately an inch longer on the flank edge. The fat at the collr and butt ends must be smoothly trimmed and not measure at any point more than 1½ in. in depth.

A regular skin collar shoulder (403) is cut by separating the shoulder not more than an inch back of the elbow joint not exposing the joint. It then goes up between the second and third rib through the rear end of the scapula. The jowl, neck bones, ribs, related cartilages, breast bone, intercostal meat, breast flap, and any bloody discolorations must be removed. The "ear dip" should be on the jowl. Overhanging skin or fat must be neatly beveled. Fat depth should not be more than

Shoulder Wt (lb)	Maximum Fat Depth No. 1*	No. 2*	Shoulder Wt (lb)	Maximum Fat Depth No. 1*	No. 2*
8 to 10	1 in.	1½ in.	14 to 16	1¾ in.	2¼ in.
10 to 12	1¼ in.	1¾ in.	16 to 18	2 in.	2½ in.
12 to 14	1½ in.	2 in.			

*Selection No. 1 and No. 2 or U.S. No. 1 or No. 2.

Buyers may vary these fat depths in specifications. On these shoulders, the foot must be neatly removed above the upper joint. Unless specified otherwise, shoulders cut beyond the elbow joint are unacceptable. A skinned shoulder (404) is No. 403 with a well-rounded skin collar at the shank end that does not exceed 45% of the length of the entire back (skin-side) surface, measured lengthwise from the approximate center at the edge of the butt to the extreme outer tip of the shank end when the shank is removed at or near the upper knee joint or, for shoulders in which the foot is cut shorter, not more than 25% of the length measured centrally along the back of the shoulder on a straight line starting at the juncture of the elbow joint at the edge of the butt end. The shoulder picnic (405) is the forepart of the shoulder containing all the humerus bone and about 2 in. of the blade bone just above where the humerus joins the blade bone. It is cut

TABLE 9-10A
Index of Products and Weight Range
Weight Range for Carcasses and Wholesale and Fabricated Cuts

Item No.	Product	Pounds									
		120–165	165–209	4–6	6–8	8–10	10–12	12–14	14–16	16–18	18–20
400	Carcass	X	X								
401	Ham, Regular						X	X	X	X	X
402	Ham, Skinned							X	X	X	X
403	Shoulder, Regular					X	X	X	X	X	
404	Shoulder, Skinned			X		X	X	X	X		
405	Shoulder, Picnic			X	X	X	X				
406	Boston Butt				X	X	X	X			
407	Shoulder Butt (Bnls)			2–6							
408	Belly, Skin-On					X	X	X	X		
409	Belly, Skinless					X	X	X	X	X	
410	Loin, Regular					X	X	X	X		
411	Loin, Bladeless					X	X	X			
412	Loin, Center-Cut				X	X	X				
413	Loin (Completely Bnls)			X	X	X	X				
414	Canadian Back			X	X	X					
415	Tenderloin, Trimmed*	¼ to ½; ½ to ¾; ¾ to 1 lb									
416	Spareribs	3 lb or less; 3 to 5; 5 lb or more									
417	Hocks (shoulder)	½ to 1; 1 to 1½; 1½ to 2½ lb									

418	Pork Trimmings (90% Lean)	Amount As Specified
419	Pork Trimmings (80% Lean)	Amount As Specified
420	Feet (Front)	¾ to 1½ lb
421	Neck Bones	¾ to 1; 1½ to 2 lb

*If the weight range is not specified, commercially packaged tenderloins of mixed weights ranging from ¼ to 1 lb will be acceptable.

Note: Because it is impractical to list all weights that purchasers may desire, those included in the index table are suggested only. Other weight ranges may be ordered if desired.

TABLE 9-10B
Index of Pork Filets, Steaks, Chops and Roasts and Suggested Portion Sizes and Weight Ranges

Item No.	Item Names	Suggested Portion Sizes and Weight Ranges (see note below)									
		3 oz	4 oz	5 oz	6 oz	8 oz	10 oz	4–6 lb	6–8 lb	8–10 lb	10–12 lb
1400	Pork Filets	X	X	X	X						
1406	Boston Butt Steaks, Bone-In		X	X	X	X					
1407	Shoulder Butt Steaks, Bnls	X	X	X	X	X					
1410	Pork Chops, Regular	X	X	X	X						
1410A	Pork Chops, With Pocket			X	X	X					
1410B	Pork Rib Chops, With Pocket			X	X	X					
1411	Pork Chops, Bladeless	X	X	X	X	X					
1412	Pork Chops, Center Cut	X	X	X	X	X					
1412A	Pork Chops, Center Cut, Special	X	X	X	X	X					
1412B	Pork Chops, Center Cut, Bnls	X	X	X	X	X					
1413	Pork Chops, Bnls	X	X	X	X	X					
1402R	Fresh Ham, Bnls, Tied								X	X	X
1406R	Boston Butt, Bnls, Tied							X	X		
1413R	Pork Loin, Bnls, Tied								X	X	X
1496	Pork For Chop Suey	Amount Specified									

Note: Because it is impractical to list all portion-weights for chops and all weight ranges for roasts that purchasers may desire, the portion-weights and weight ranges identified by the letter "X" are suggested only. Other portion-weights and weight ranges may be ordered if desired.

No. 8 in Figures 9-57 and 9-58. The forefoot is removed just above where it joins the humerus. The shoulder must be neatly trimmed including the ''lip'' and breast flap. Fat depth at the skin edge of the bevel immediately below the scapular bone must not be greater than indicated previously for No. 403. The Boston butt (406) is the top portion of the shoulder after removing the picnic below. It contains almost all of the scapula bone. The skin and underlying fat in excess of ¼ in. over the butt must be smoothly and uniformly removed to expose the false lean or seam fat on the back or skin side. The cut must be neatly beveled. The boneless shoulder butt (407) is the intact, fleshy, lean portion of the Boston butt lying underneath the flat (interior) side of the blade bone. It must be closely trimmed by removing loose flesh and ragged edges. Fat depth should not exceed ¼ in. The belly with skin on (408) or skinless (409) are seldom purchased by institutions.

The regular, blade-in, loin (410) is much used. It contains 11 or more ribs. (See Fig. 9-58 for an indication that pork varies in the number of ribs it will have.) It should contain at least 3 sacral vertebrae. The cut separating it from the side or bacon must not be more than 1¾ in. from the junction of the foremost rib and the foremost thoracic vertebra to a point on the ham end which is immediately adjacent to the major tenderloin muscle. This muscle must be practically intact in the loin. The loin should be well trimmed and the outside muscle (false lean) over the blade must be exposed lengthwise on the loin for a distance of 4 or more inches. Loin fat must not exceed ¼ in. over the major loin muscle and fat at the ham end over the sacral region must be beveled to meet the lean. No excessive removal of lean should occur. Lumbar and pelvic fat over ¼ in. and bloody portions must be closely removed. The diaphragm and hanging tender must be removed from U.S. No. 1 loins and may be removed from U.S. No. 2. Any damaged loins should be excluded. A bladeless loin (411) has the blade and all related cartilage and overlying flesh removed. A center cut loin (412) has the portion including the blade bone and cartilage and the portion including the hip bone removed. The completely boneless loin (413) has the tenderloin with accompanying lumbar fat and tissue, skirt, hanging tender, and all bones and cartilages including intercostal meat (rib fingers) removed. The Canadian back (414) is the major loin muscle. It is more frequently seen as Canadian bacon after being cured and smoked. Trimmed tenderloin (415) is the tenderloin removed from the loin with its closely attached side strip muscle. It should be free from lumbar leaf, and any other fat exceeding ⅛ in. deep. All glandular parts, bloody tissue, or frayed ends must be removed. Weights are from ¾ to 1 lb. Spareribs (416) are the entire rib section neatly removed from the belly (bacon) portion of the pork carcass. They may or may not contain a portion of the split breast bone and skirt. Specify 3 lb or less. Shoulder hocks (417), front feet or pig's knuckles (420), and neck bones (421) are used for special needs. Specify pig's knuckles ¾ lb each. Pork trimmings, 90% lean, must come from fresh pork, not frozen, defrosted, or cured, from good firm, not oily or soft pork in good condition. The total visual fat content must not be over 10%. It cannot contain jowls, diaphragms, tongues, gullets, hearts, organs, or other trimmings not customarily used. Pork trimmings, 80% lean, are the same as 90% lean except for a more lenient fat content.

Cured and Smoked Pork Products—Series 500

Cured and/or smoked pork products should come from standard, well-trimmed items cut processed according to the best commercial practices. Curing salts should be a well-blended mixture of salt, sugar, or other sweetening agent; sodium nitrate, sodium nitrite, and potassium salts permitted by the government in any desired combination may be used to give a pleasantly flavored product. Cure may be with or without water and with or without pumping (spray or vascular) unless dry cure is specified. Cured or smoked products should not weigh more than they did when they went into processing. The product should have a characteristic flavor, aroma, texture, firmness, and appearance associated with well-smoked products of good quality. Smoked products shall be firm, dry, and of good condition and appearance. Encrusted surfaces of salt, extraneous matter, and smoke-house residue must be removed without washing. Color should be bright, stable, and natural. Stockinettes, strings, and other similar hanging devices should be removed prior to wrapping and packaging. Cures should be mild and thorough. Smoking should be done in dense natural smoke from burning hardwood or sawdust or both in an accepted conventional method in accordance with federal requirements. Smoking should impart a well-penetrated and fairly uniform smoke flavor and color. The appearance should be bright, uniform, and possess a smoked sheen. The items should be firm, dry, and in good condition. Cooking by dry heat for smoked meats should be accomplished during smoking, continuously conducted to give an appropriately dry product without undue rendering of fat, undercooking, overcooking, or other damage. Rendered surface fat and extraneous matter must be removed. If cooked with moist heat (hot water or hot water and steam), the product must be fully cooked. After cooking, it can be lightly showered to remove meat juices, jelly, or albumin and then trimmed lightly and smoothly to conform to specification requirements. The color of the lean must be fairly uniform and stable, characteristic of well-cured items without evidence of greening, streaking, or other discoloration, but a slightly two-toned or iridescent color is permissible. The lean must possess a fine, smooth texture, and be tender, cohesive, and firm. It can be slightly resilient but not unduly hard. The product must be fairly dry on the exterior and interior, including a well-sealed butt on hams not smoked in artificial casings, but not excessively dried or scorched. Hand pressure should not be able to force out drip or exuding moisture. Cooked products should be thoroughly cooked and practically free from air holes, pockets of moisture, rendered fat, gelatinous matter, ragged edges, surface strings—except those closely tied for stitching—and extraneous matter. They should be free from fermented or other off-odors or off-flavors foreign to the product, rancidity, mold, or other deterioration or damage. Cooked or smoked pork must be cooked to an internal temperature of 155°F to be sure all trichinae are destroyed.

Cured or smoked pork may be specified as Selection No. 1 or No. 2, No. 1 being the better quality. A cured regular short shank ham (500) is a fresh short shank ham (401) that has only been cured. If this is smoked, the IMPS number is No. 501. When No. 500 is partially skinned to leave a well-rounded skin collar not exceeding 15% of the distance from the stifle joint to the butt leaving a collar line with a slant of at least 15° toward the cushion side, making the skin collar about an inch longer at the flank edge, a partially skinned short shank cured ham results (502). Fat on this cannot be more than ½ in. measured at any point 1½ in. or more from the edge of the skin collar. It must be neatly beveled on the back to meet the lean at the butt end. It is smoked to produce a short shank, partially skinned, cured, and smoked ham (503) and, when completely skinned, the aitchbone with the overlying flesh and shank bones removed leaving only the femur bone, it becomes a partially boned, skinless cured and smoked ham (504). A good size for Nos. 503 and 504 is 12 to 14 lb. On this ham, exterior surface fat must not be over ⅜ in. It should be neatly beveled back for at least an inch at the outer area of the butt end from a point close to the lean meat edge of the butt. If the femur bone is removed, it becomes the boneless, skinless, cured, and smoked ham (505). Both No. 504 and No. 505 must be encased in an artificial casing to produce a smooth, plump, elongated, oval-shaped, skinless product. No. 505 also can be in stockinettes or similar units. The shank meat on No. 505 must be attached naturally and all tendons, connective tissue, and so forth must be removed. The shank meat, if used, must be folded back into the femur bone cavity as a plug and be preferably stitched in. If this ham is tied, it becomes No. 505A. Fully cooking No. 502 with dry heat gives No. 506, a fully cooked, dry heat, cured and smoked, partially skinned ham. If this ham is made completely boneless and skinless, it is No. 507. Cooking No. 505 in moist heat and making it into a rectangular, pear, or round shape makes it a fully cooked, moist heat, boneless, skinless, cured ham (508). It is not smoked. The encased ham must be practically free of gelatinous material, rendered fat, extraneous

TABLE 9-11

Index of Product and Weight Range for Cured and Smoked Pork Weight Range for Wholesale and Fabricated cuts (in lb)

Item No.	Product	4–6	6–8	8–10	10–12	12–14	14–16	16–18	18–20
500	Ham, Regular (Cured)				X	X	X	X	X
501	Ham, Regular (Cured and Smoked)				X	X	X	X	X
502	Ham, Skinned (Cured)				X	X	X	X	X
503	Ham, Skinned (Cured and Smoked)				X	X	X	X	X
504	Ham, Sknls (Cured and Smoked) Partially Boned			X	X	X	X	X	
505	Ham, Sknls (Cured and Smoked) Completely Boneless			X	X	X	X	X	
505A	Ham, Sknls, Boned, Rolled, and Tied (Cured and Smoked)			X	X	X	X	X	
506	Ham, Sknd (Cured and Smoked) Fully-Cooked, Dry Heat			X	X	X	X		
507	Ham, Bnls, Sknls (Cured and Smoked) Fully-Cooked, Dry Heat			X	X	X			
508	Ham, Bnls, Sknls (Cured) Pressed, Fully-Cooked, Moist Heat		X	X	X	X			
509	Ham, Bnls, Sknls (Cured and Smoked) Pressed, Fully Cooked Moist Heat		X	X	X	X			
515	Shoulder, Regular (Cured)			X	X	X	X	X	X
516	Shoulder, Regular (Cured and Smoked)			X	X	X	X	X	X
517	Shoulder, Skinned (Cured)			X	X	X	X	X	
518	Shoulder, Skinned (Cured and Smoked)			X	X	X	X	X	

No.	Product				Size / Container
525	Shoulder, Picnic (Cured)	X	X		
526	Shoulder, Picnic (Cured and Smoked)	X	X		
527	Shoulder, Picnic (Cured and Smoked) Boneless, Skinless, Rolled and Tied	X	X		
530	Shoulder Butt, Boneless (Cured and Smoked)	X			
535	Belly, Skin-On (Cured)	X			
536	Bacon, Slab (Cured and Smoked) Skin-On	X	X	X	X
537	Bacon, Slab (Cured and Smoked) Sknls	X	X	X	
539	Bacon, Sliced (Cured and Smoked) Sknls	X	X	X	
541	Bacon, Sliced (Cured and Smoked) End Pieces				Number of slices per lb (18–22; 22–26; 26–30; 28–32, or as specified)
545	Loin, Regular (Cured and Smoked)	X	X	X	3–5; 5–9 lb
546	Loin, Bladeless (Cured and Smoked)	X	X	X	
550	Canadian Style Bacon (Cured and Smoked)				5– and 10–lb containers, as specified
551	Canadian Style Bacon (Cured and Smoked) Sliced				5– and 10–lb containers, as specified
555	Jowl Butts, Cellar Trim (Cured)				1 to 2½; 2½ to 4 lb
556	Jowl Squares (Cured and Smoked)				¾ to 2; 2 to 3 lb
558	Spareribs (Cured)				3 lb or less; 3–5; 5 lb or more
559	Spareribs (Cured and Smoked)				3 lb or less; 3–5; 5 lb or more
560	Hocks, Shoulder (Cured)				½ to 1; 1 to 1½; 1½ to 2½ lb
561	Hocks, Shoulder (Cured and Smoked)				½ to 1; 1 to 1½; 1½ to 2½ lb
562	Fatback (Cured)	X			
563	Feet, Front (Cured)				¾ to 1½ lb

Fig. 9-59. A meat inspector examines hams in a smokehouse. Courtesy USDA

matter, appendages and strings, or mechanical fasteners. The end may be momentarily dipped into a clear gelatinous solution to facilitate stuffing into a casing. When No. 508 is smoked, it becomes a fully cooked, pressed, boneless, skinless, cured, and smoked ham (509). Nos. 505 through 508 hams are best purchased sized from 8 to 12 lb.

A regular cured shoulder (515) is a cured No. 403 fresh pork shoulder. When it is smoked, it becomes a regular, cured smoked shoulder (516). It can be partially skinned to give No. 517. Skinning should leave a well-rounded skin collar at the shank end not exceeding 45% of the length of the entire back (skin side) measured lengthwise from the approximate center at the edge of the butt to the extreme outer tip of the shank end when removed at or near the upper knee joint. If the foot is cut shorter than the upper knee joint but not beyond the elbow joint, the skin collar must not exceed 25% of the length measured centrally on the outside of the shoulder along a straight line extending from the elbow joint to the edge of the butt end. The collar line should slant from the elbow side ventrally toward the jowl side at least 15°. Fat must not be over the following depending upon the selection number and weight as indicated for fresh hams (403) on p. 568.

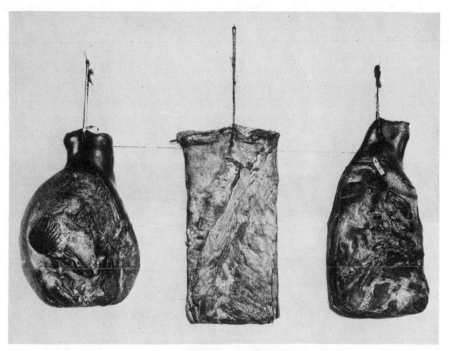

Fig. 9-60. A ham, bacon, and shoulder after curing and smoking. These 3 items are the most common of the cured and smoked items from pork. Courtesy USDA

If No. 517 is smoked, it becomes No. 518, a cured, smoked, skinned shoulder. A cured shoulder picnic is No. 405 cured (525). Fat depth on No. 525 should not exceed those listed on p. 568 for fresh pork hams (405). Picnic No. 525 may be obtained as No. 527 as a cured, smoked, boneless, skinless, rolled and tied shoulder picnic. All bones and skin must be removed without excessive scoring and leave a neat, compact unit. The shank meat, if left on intact with all tendons and practically all surface fat removed, must be folded back into the elbow bone cavity as a plug and preferably stitched. Exterior fat surface must not exceed ⅜ in. It must be rolled and tied by loops of strong twine girthwise and lengthwise to produce a firm, compact, rolled roast. The boneless, cured, and smoked shoulder butt (530) is the portion of the Boston butt on the flat or interior side of the blade bone removed intact and closely trimmed by removing loose flesh, ragged edges, and surface fat in excess of a fourth inch. The trimmed, boneless shoulder butt must be cured and stuffed into a close and smooth-fitting artificial casing subsequent to smoking. Grease and extraneous matter must be removed. A weight size of 2½ to 3 lb is usually preferred.

A cured belly with skin on (535) is not too often used, but it is the basis for a number of units that are. It must be completely boneless with the cartilages of the sternum and ribs removed closely and smoothly without deep scoring. Any embedded cartilage tips must be approximately level with or slightly lower than the surface lean. Any exposed cartilage must not be over ⅜ in. in diameter. Practically all leaf fat and other abdominal surface fat must be removed. The belly must be separated from the fat back on a straight line not more than ¾ in. beyond the outermost curvature of the scribe line, which must not exceed ¼ in. in depth. This surface where the fat back was removed must not be unduly scalped or "snowballed." The belly sides must be reasonably straight and parallel and at approximate right angles to the shoulder end. The ham end may be cut at a slant so the flank side is about an inch longer than the fat back side. No lean meat can be

Fig. 9-61. A federal inspector oversees the packaging of bacon to check quality and weight and the cleanliness of plant employees, packaging materials, and equipment used. Courtesy USDA

removed except that needed in necessary squaring and trimming and any enlarged soft, porous, or seedy mammary tissue and the pizzle recess on barrows must be removed. Severe or excessive trim to make specified weights, undue removal of lean meat, poor workmanship, damage, and so forth can be cause for rejection of the belly. Cured and smoked slab bacon with the skin on (536) is No. 535 well squared on all edges and having straight and parallel sides and ends to give a high yield of full cut slices. Institutions will find that bacon slabs weighing 8 to 10 lb from 8 to 10 in. wide give the best yield in slices. Bacon cut from wider and heavier slabs cannot be cut into slices 18 to 24 to the lb, desirable counts, because they are almost too thin for cooking. Bacon should be well streaked with lean and packaged in approximately the same order as cut, if specified this way. No. 536 can be completely skinned and pressed to give a well-shaped rectangular unit. Sliced bacon (539) should have no comb marks, product residue, punctured or mutilated sections, cracked slices due to hard or granular fat, cutting on an appreciable slant or bias, small or irregular pieces, or any other damage. A part slice can be used to make the exact weight of a package. Many institutions order sliced bacon preset so it can be placed onto a baking sheet or griddle without pulling the bacon apart and setting it out in individual slices. Precooked bacon also is available and many institutions specify this product. Sliced ends and pieces of bacon (541) may show frayed, shredded, broken, or otherwise damaged slices, small unsliced pieces, slices showing string or ganger marks, or slices from small or extreme sections and machine scrap pieces.

A cured and smoked regular loin (545) is No. 410 after curing and smoking. No. 546 similarly is the bladeless loin, No. 411, after curing and smoking. When the Canadian back, No. 414, is cured and smoked, No. 550 is obtained, which when sliced becomes No. 551. Slicing standards should follow those for bacon. Cellar trim, cured jowl butts, No. 555, are the cheeks of pork having a standard cellar trim with boot jack points and ragged ends smoothly removed. Some slightly irregular trimming is permissible. It must be free from excess moisture when hand-pressed. If specified, dry salted, some clear granulated salt can remain but not that that is loose or encrusted. It should be sound and in good condition and not show evidence of over- or under-curing or improper storage. When these are smoked, they become No. 556. They must be well trimmed and squared.

Spareribs, No. 416, may be cured to give No. 558 and when smoked after curing become No. 559. Similarly, No. 417 when cured become No. 560, cured shoulder hocks, and when cured and smoked become No. 561, cured and smoked shoulder hocks. The front feet No. 420 are sometimes cured to give No. 563. Clear fat back can be cured to produce No. 562. This is the thick, fatty portion obtained by removing the loin. They should be relatively short and thick and uniform throughout with square edges. They should be fairly dry and free from loose or encrusted salt.

Dry curing is a process in which only dry curing salts and seasonings are placed on the product. After a short time, these salts draw out meat juices sufficient to make a brine which cures or preserves the meat. In doing this, a dry product results which is very different from the regular brine-pumped or brine-soaked product. Many country-style hams are dry-cured and smoked. A Virginia ham is dry-cured for 7 weeks and then is rubbed with a mixture of molasses, brown sugar, black pepper, cayenne pepper, and saltpeter and cured 2 more weeks. It is often not smoked but dried up to 12 months before being marketed. A Smithfield ham must come from a specified area around Smithfield, Virginia, when the hogs are given a diet consisting largely of peanuts. This gives the product a special flavor. The fresh hams are rubbed with saltpeter and salt, shelf-cured for 3 to 5 days, and then given a dry cure for 2 weeks. They are then washed and rubbed with black pepper and smoked for 30 days. After this, they are dried for 10 to 12 months. Most dry-cured products must be freshened (soaked in cool water for a day or so) before cooking.

Imported hams are available. Danish ham is excellent and has a slightly greater cure and smoke than that given our regular hams. Westphalian hams from Germany are noted for their quality. They are dry-cured, then sweet-pickled and smoked with beechwood and juniper branches with their berries. They may be purchased boned. Proscuitto, Italy, in the Po valley produces the famous Proscuitto ham, which is given a highly seasoned cure and a heavy smoke. It is dried for a long period. It is usually sliced thin and used for appetizers, especially with melon. Capicolli is a cured, boneless pork butt, lightly smoked and dried. It comes from Italy. Scotch hams have a mild cure, are usually not smoked. They are usually marketed boneless, skinless, and defatted, packed in transparent film casing.

Cured, Dried, and Smoked Beef Products—Series 600

Selection No. 1 and No. 2 corned beef and cured and smoked tongues are the 2 graded products in the category of cured, dried, and smoked beef products. Selection No. 1 is better quality. The average fat thickness for these should not exceed ½ in. (maximum .8 in. at any one point). All dried beef products should be practically free of surface fat and have not more than a slight amount of intermuscular and intramuscular fat. Standards for curing, cooking, and smoking shall be the same as those listed for cured pork products.

TABLE 9-12
Index of Cured Beef Products

Item No.	Product	Weight Range 1	Weight Range 2	Weight Range 3
600	Spencer Roll, Corned	Under 15	15–22	22–up
601	Brisket, Boneless, Deckle off, Corned	Under 9	9–12	12–up
602	Knuckle, Corned	Under 8	8–15	15–up
603	Knuckle, Dried	Under 5	5–8	8–up
604	Inside Round, Corned	Under 14	14–20	20–up
605	Inside Round, Dried	Under 9	9–12	12–up
606	Outside Round, Corned	Under 11	11–18	18–up
607	Outside Round, Dried	Under 8	8–14	14–up
608	Gooseneck Round, Corned	Under 16	16–27	27–up
609	Rump Butt, Corned	Under 8	8–12	12–up
613	Tongue, Cured	3–5		
614	Tongue, Smoked	3–5		
617	Process Dried Beef	Under 8	8–14	14–up
618	Sliced Process Dried Beef			
619	Sliced Dried Beef			
620	Sliced Drief Beef, Ends and Pieces	¼-pound, ½-pound, 1-pound individual packages, or bulk or layer packed.		

Note: Style A is the product drained, and Style B is the product in pickled brine. States of refrigeration are A or chilled and B or frozen.

Because it is impractical to list all weight ranges for the above products that purchasers may desire, those included in the index table are suggested only. Other weight ranges may be ordered if desired.

Corned beef products come from beef cuts previously described for the most part. A corned spencer roll is from Item 111, a corned boneless, deckle off brisket from Item 120. Items 602 through 608 are cut approximately as described in Series 100. The following describes a number of cured products:

Item No.	Name	Description
602	Knuckle, corned	From No. 167, corned.
603	Knuckle, dried	No. 602, dried.
604	Inside round, corned	No. 168, corned.
605	Inside round, dried	No. 604, dried.
606	Outside round, corned	No. 169, corned.
607	Outside round, dried	No. 606, dried.
608	Gooseneck round, corned	No. 170, corned.
609	Rump butt, corned	The back top part of a gooseneck round made by a straight cut approximately perpendicular to the skin surface when preparing an outside round. It is free of cartilage and exposed ligaments.

Tongues must be well trimmed with the tongue root smoothly removed at the base (thick) end immediately behind the hyoid (U-shaped) bones. Practically all glandular tissue and all of the trachea (windpipe) must be removed along with major blood vessels. They must have a natural color. A cured tongue is No. 613; a smoked tongue, which comes from No. 613, is No. 614.

Processed dried beef (617) is a coarsely ground, cured, smoked, and fully cooked product stuffed into casings or mechanically formed. Sliced process dried beef is No. 617 uniformly sliced to be 24 or more slices to the inch; 60% or more of the slices must be fairly intact and the rest composed only of broken slices. No extremely frayed, shredded, small, or scrap pieces or residue should be included. No. 619 is sliced dried beef produced from dried knuckle beef (603), dried inside round (605), or dried outside round (607). Slices must be uniform and be over 40 to the inch. Not less than 75% of the slices can be intact, and the other factors cited for No. 617 apply. No. 620 is sliced dried beef ends and pieces obtained from regular dried beef but may consist of frayed, shredded, and broken slices, machine scrap sliced pieces, and slices showing string or hanger marks. There must be no product residue.

Edible By-Products—Series 700

Beef tongue and various animal livers are graded Selection No. 1 and 2, No. 1 representing the better quality. No. 1 livers should be compact, thick, short, plump, and practically free from blemishes. Scores should not be deeper than 1 in. They should be bright and uniform in color. Young animals have light reddish tan to tan livers and older ones light to dark

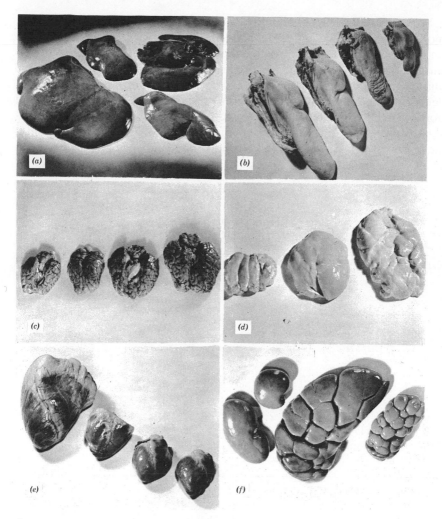

Fig. 9-62. Variety meats: (a) beef, pork, veal, and lamb livers; (b) tongues of beef, veal, pork, and lamb; (c) brains of lamb, pork, veal, and beef; (d) sweetbreads of lamb, veal, and beef; (e) hearts of beef, veal, pork, and lamb; and (f) kidneys of lamb, pork, beef, and veal.

brown. The No. 2 livers are moderately compact and not as plump and short as No. 1s. They may have scores up to 2 in. deep. Approximately a third of the liver can be cut away. Color should be bright and uniform. Reject bluish or black livers.

Selection No. 1 tongues should be moderately short in relation to width, moderately thick and not over ½ in. deep. Tongues with scores deeper than an inch or with the tip end removed are acceptable. Only 1 score is permitted. Selection No. 2 tongues are less short to width, slightly thick and plump, and moderately firm and resilient. Fat should not be over ½ in. deep, and there may be up to 3 scores but not over 1 in. deep. If a small portion of the tip end is removed, the tongue is still acceptable. All tongues should have the hyoid bones and epiglottis removed. Practically all glandular tissue and all trachea must be removed. Some specify that black tip tongues are not acceptable. Specify beef tongues from weights of 4 to 5 lb.

TABLE 9-13
**Index of Products and Weight Range
for Edible By-products**

Item No.	Product	Range 1 Pounds	Range 2 Pounds
701	Beef Liver	Under 13	13–16
702	Beef Liver, Sliced (Frozen)	Under 13	13–16
703	Beef Liver, Portion-Cut (Frozen)	5-to-the-pound	4-to-the-pound
704	Calf Liver	Under 6½	6½ –8½
705	Calf Liver, Sliced (Frozen)	Under 6½	6½–8½
707	Veal Liver	Under 3	3–5
708	Veal Liver, Sliced (Frozen)	Under 3	3–5
710	Pork Liver	Under 5	
713	Lamb Liver	Under 1½	
716	Beef Tongue	3–5	
720	Beef Heart	3–5	

Note: Because it is impractical to list all weight ranges for edible by-products that purchasers may desire, those included in this table are suggested only. Other weight ranges may be ordered if desired.

Tongues and livers should be fresh unless specified otherwise. Livers should be trimmed neatly, gall bladder evidence removed. All heavy connective tissue, large blood vessels, and ducts shall be removed if near the surface. Sliced liver shall not have any heavy connective tissue, large blood vessels, or ducts. Type B for calf or beef liver means that the outer skin (capsula fibrosa) must be removed except for small pieces on the edges and in the crease of the small (caudate) lobe. Veal livers are not skinned. Livers may be molded, frozen, tempered (but not thawed) for slicing. Pressing before slicing is acceptable. Broken slices are not acceptable. Look for sawdust. Sliced liver should come with slices in natural sequence and may be specified as being wrapped separately if frozen. Portion cut liver cannot have any of the small lobe or skin on them and must be layer packed. Table 9-13 summarizes the IMPS specifications for liver, tongue, and heart. Reject coarse or netted livers. Many institutions specify the thickness of slices as ⅜ to ½ in. thick. Beef liver runs from under 13 to 16 lb, calf liver 3 to 8½ lb, veal liver 2½ to 5 lb, pork liver 2 to 5 lb, and lamb liver under 1½ lb.

Beef hearts should be thick, firm, and trimmed free of fat with the gristly portion on top and the heart cap removed. They should have a bright appearance with fat color from creamy white to slightly yellow. They should be free from blood clots and have only slight scores, if any. They may be ordered chilled or frozen. Occasionally, calf, veal, and other hearts may be purchased on specifications like those used for beef hearts. Normal weight ranges for calf or veal hearts is ½ to 1 lb, pork ½ lb, beef 3 to 5 lb, and lamb about ¼ lb.

Kidney from beef, veal, lamb, and sometimes pork is used. Kidneys should be plump, firm, and only flecked with fat, bright in appearance, and free from scores. The weight is around 1 lb for beef, ¾ lb for veal or calf, ¼ lb for pork, and ⅛ lb for lamb. Sweetbreads are taken from beef, calf, veal, or lamb, but calf or veal sweetbreads are preferred. Throat (thymus) sweetbreads are superior to those taken near the heart. They should be of good, reddish cream color, firm and fresh. Normally, they are sold frozen in 5-lb pails. Veal and calf sweetbreads are from 2 to 4 oz each.

Only the brains from veal or calf are used. They should be somewhat firm but much softer than sweetbreads and almost the same color. They should not be bloody nor heavily veined. They are usually frozen in 5-lb pails and run about 6 oz. each.

Tripe is the first or second stomach of beef. Honeycomb tripe is considered superior to plain tripe. It comes fresh, pickled, salted, or frozen. Order the 1½ to 2 lb size. Specify ox tails as 1½ to 2 lb each.

TABLE 9-14
Normal Portions of Edible By-products

Item	AP/Portion	Item	AP/Portion
Liver	3 to 4 oz	Tongue	3 to 6 oz
Kidney	3 oz	Tripe	3 to 4 oz
Heart	3 to 4 oz	Sweetbreads	3 to 4 oz
Brains	3 to 4 oz		

Sausage Products—Series 800

Ground-meat products can vary considerably in quality and value. As ground products they can carry a high bacterial count and studies[3] have shown that 4 out of 8 samples of frankfurters on the market had bacterial counts higher than 5 million per gram, a very high count. A count of 100,000 or less should be maximum. There also is a chance that the product is made of inferior substances or does not contain the substances it should. Specifications should require that they be prepared from inspected and passed meats that are sound and good, not low quality trimmings, questionable meat, and so forth. The federal government allows 30% fat in most sausage products but does not take action against offenders until it is 31.7% or more. Recent tests show that the average frankfurter or weiner contains about 28% fat. A product such as these or boloney would be better if it had 20% or slightly less. Frankfurters and similar products must be 85% meat or more. They may contain up to 2% corn syrup solids, 3% other flavorings and curing substances, and 2% extender such as cereal, bean flour, or dry milk. Cooked or smoked sausage products can contain up to 10% added water and fresh sausage 3%. The total protein content of weiner and similar mixtures should be 20%, but recent tests indicate this runs closer to 12%. The federal government says that the water ratio should not be more than 4 times the protein ratio. Thus a sausage product with 11% protein should contain not more than 44% water, but the federal government will permit up to 54% in such a product before the word "imitation"—not "excessive water"—must be put on the label. High-quality sterilized spices should be specified.

The IMPS allow buyers to indicate major ingredients, style casings, color, state of refrigeration, and other factors for sausage products; A is chilled and B is frozen. Fresh sausage must be cooked before it is eaten and must be kept under refrigeration. It has a short shelf-life—about a week. Besides the quality of substances in it, the rind and proportion of substances in it is important. Total fat should not be over 40% for pork sausage (802) and less for breakfast sausage (810), the 2 fresh products listed in the IMPS. Grinding should be specified as first through a 1-in. plate and then through a $^3/_{16}$- or ¼-in. plate. Pork sausage must be all ground pork mixed with salt and spices. Breakfast sausage is predominantly pork with smaller amounts of beef and/or veal, all ground to moderate coarseness. Both may be packed in bulk or stuffed into artificial or hog casings (intestines). If in unlinked hog casings, no more than 1 piece can be less than 12 in. in length

[3]See *Consumer Reports,* pp. 73–74, February 1972.

in the group in a container. Differences in length between the shortest and longest link should not be more than ½ in. Only limited splits or ruptures in the casings should be evident, and none should be greater than 0.3 in. There should be no evidence of foreign material, foreign flavor, or off-odor, bone or other substances. Order links 12 to 14 per lb.

Frankfurters or weiners (800) and Bologna (801) are smoked and cooked. They may be made from very finely ground beef and pork or only beef. The interior cut surface must be smooth, fine-textured, light to moderately dark pink in background color, with fine mottling evenly distributed with light to dark flecks. Frankfurters and weiners should be from 5 to 6 in. in length; normally, franks run 7 to 8 per lb and weiners 8 to 10, but either may be specified in sizes of 6 to 12 per lb.

Bologna is a large sausage, about 1.3 to 5 in. in diameter; the 1 to 1½ lb should be ring style. Different mixtures may be specified: A—beef and pork in any combination, B—beef and pork with beef predominating, C—pork and beef with pork predominating; A_1 indicates nonfat dry milk is to be added; similarly, if subscript 1 is used with B or C, dry milk must be an added ingredient. Many institutions specify B or B_1 with 60% beef and 40% pork. A specification also should indicate whether the sausage should be A in color (natural) or B in color (artificial color can be used). Franks and weiners can come skinless (Style C), in sheep casings (Style B_3), or in collagen casings (Style C). Bolognas in artificial casings (Style A) run 1.3 to 1.5 in. in diameter (1 to 1½ lb), 2.5 to 3.5 in. diameter (4 to 7 lb), and 3.5 to 5.0 in. diameter (7 to 12 lb), and in natural casings 1.3 to 1.5 in. diameter (1 to 1½ lb). Because of the use of same letters in the IMPS, food services should in their specifications indicate what is wanted by wording rather than by letter to avoid confusion, specifying sizes, coloring, and style casing, and also if they should be chilled or frozen. Berliner is like Bologna but is not smoked. It also should be slightly drier. Lebanon Bologna (806) is smoked, uncooked, all beef finely ground and stuffed in artificial casings, which are from 3½ to 4½ in. in diameter and run 5 to 10 lb when filled. It has a characteristic sharp or fermented flavor. The cut surface is smooth, with a uniformly dark reddish-brown color with fine fat particles evenly distributed in it. Vienna sausages have a smaller diameter than weiners and are made about 20 in. long and then are cut into 2- to 2½-in. lengths. They are usually skinless and are frequently canned.

Liver (Braunschweiger) sausage (803) is cooked and has a slight smoke flavor. It is finely ground pork liver, pork with smoked jowls and/or bacon ends, or just pork liver and pork. Onion is a seasoning. Many specify it be made with 150-lb fresh hog livers, 110-lb pork jowls and/or bacon ends, and 40-lb fresh, lean pork. It is stuffed into artificial or natural casings (specify which) and cooked 1 or 2 hours at 155°F and then smoked 4 to 6

Fig. 9-63. A federal inspector checking samples of sausages. Courtesy USDA

hours at 80 to 90°F. The IMPS formula A is only pork livers and pork, whereas its formula B includes jowls and/or bacon ends with pork liver. A subscript 1 as in A_1 or B_1 indicates that dry milk is an added ingredient.

There are many kinds of dry or summer sausage types, many of which originated in Europe but are today made domestically in this country. There are a number of salamis in which the seasoning, grind, or proportion of ingredients make a great difference in kind or quality. Salami and other summer sausages are called *dry* types because the meat is diced and dried for 48 to 72 hours on a bench. After this it is ground, seasoned, and placed into casings. This drying and grinding are called *rocking*. Smoking is done at temperatures 70 to 80°C for 24 to 48 hours, depending upon the sausage size and desired degree of smoke. Italian types may not be smoked, whereas Scandinavian, German, and Austrian dry sausages are given a heavy smoke. Further drying occurs with this "green sausage" by hanging it in rooms at 60 to 70°F. In such drying, molds should not develop and no putrefaction should occur.

Regular cooked salami (804) is made of moderately coarse-cut pork and finely ground beef; finely ground beef heart may be included. Seasonings include garlic and peppercorns. It has a moderately coarse texture and a light to dark reddish-brown color. The casing is artificial. The sausage is about 3½ to 4½ in. in diameter and from 7 to 12 lb. Dry salami (808) comes in natural or artificial casings from 2 to 3 in. in diameter and weighs from 2 to 5 lb. It should be much firmer, harder, and drier than No. 804. Genoa-type salami may be wrapped with many loops and longitudinal strands of cord. Milano-type has 2 circular twins. Typical salamis from southern Italy are quite hot. Italian sausages have more garlic than those from other countries. Cervelat (809) is made from beef and pork with either predominating. It is firm, hard, and dry like dry salami and in about the same size casing.

Cervelats and the 2 popular German dried sausages much like it called *Farmer* and *Holsteiner* are not corded. Thuringer (807) is smoked but uncooked. It is made from coarse or moderately coarse beef. Beef heart may be added. It comes in artificial casings 2½ to 3½ in. in diameter and weighing from 4 to 8 lb. The texture is coarse, and the color is a uniform dark reddish-brown.

Miscellaneous Italian sausages or dried cured meat are Pepperoni, Frisses, and Mortadellas. Pepperoni has a smaller diameter than salami and is usually more sharply seasoned. Mortadella is made from select, finely ground lean pork with a little beef added. Small cubes of fat are added. It is delicately seasoned with cardamon, other spices and garlic, stuffed into hog bladders, and corded in basket shape. It is not smoked but is cooked and dried.

Polish sausage is a smoked, cooked link sausage made of moderately coarse-cut pork or moderately coarse-cut pork with finely ground beef. Garlic is a seasoning. It is stuffed in either hog or collagen casings which may be linked 3- to 5-in. lengths or 11- to 13-in. lengths. The following indicates IMPS formula standards for some sausages:

Formula	Cooked Salami	Dry Salami	Cervelat	Polish Sausage
A	Pork and beef*	Beef	Beef, pork†	Pork
B	Pork and beef* and beef hearts	Beef and beef hearts	Pork, beef†	Pork, beef†
C		Beef and pork*		
D		Beef and pork* with beef hearts		
E		Beef, pork†		
F		Beef, pork† with beef hearts		

*Any Combination.
†The first ingredient predominates in the mixture.

Buyers should indicate in specifications for sausage the type casing, if chilled or frozen, coloring, and the formula. Formula A Thuringer is all beef; B Thuringer is beef and beef heart. Dry sausages may be specified; A—chilled, B—frozen, or C—unrefrigerated.

A smoked sausage (811) is cooked and made into links running 6 to 8 and 8 to 10 per lb in hog casings. It may be all pork or pork and beef with beef tripe, beef and pork hearts and beef and pork tongues moderately coarse in texture. They may come skinless (style C) or in hog casings (style B). Formulas may be A—pork, B—pork, beef (pork predominating), C—beef, pork (beef predominating), and D—beef and pork, plus any one or any combination of beef tripe, beef heart meat, pork heart meat, beef tongue meat, or pork tongue meat. Specify also whether A—chilled or B—frozen. New England brand sausage (812) is smoked and cooked and made predominately from pork chunks in a small amount of finely ground beef. It comes in artificial (A) or hog (D) casings about 3½ to 4½ in. in diameter and weighing between 5 and 10 lb. From 70 to 80% of the cut surface should show pork chunks, with the remainder fine-textured.

Meat loaves (814) and meat food product loaves (815) are baked (A—dry heat) or cooked (B—moist heat) and should be specified A—smoked, B—unsmoked, or C—browned in hot oil or fat. Shapes must be specified as A—rectangular and B—rounded. They also can be specified A—chilled or B—frozen. Meat loaves are made from finely ground beef, pork and veal. Meat food product loaves are made from beef, pork, or veal used singly or in any combination with other ingredients such as meat by-products, pickles, pimientoes, cheese, nuts, and so forth. Lungs, spleens, tripe, udders, blood, skin, cracklings, brains, lips, ears, snouts, kidneys, tongue trimmings, and meat and meat by-products from lamb, yearling mutton, mutton and goats shall not be used. Nonfat dry milk may be an ingredient. All ingredients must be evenly distributed. They should be specified by name such as pickle loaf, ham and cheese loaf, and so forth. Institutions can specify mixtures other than those listed in the IMPS formulas. Meat loaves and meat food product loaves weigh from 4 to 8 lb and should come individually wrapped in grease- and moisture-resistant paper or plastic film. The cut surface should be smooth, fine-textured, and with typical color for the product. IMPS formulas for these 2 products are:

Formula*	Meat Loaves	Meat Food Product Loaves
A	Pork, veal†	Pimiento loaf
B	Pork, beef†	Pickle and pimiento loaf
C	Pork, beef, veal	Pickle loaf
D	Pork	Olive loaf
E	Veal	Pepper loaf

Formula*	Meat Loaves	Meat Food Product Loaves
F	Beef	Cheese loaf
G	Ham	Macaroni and cheese loaf
H		Liver loaf

*A subscript 1 means dry milk is added.
†Pork is predominant.

Headcheese is cooked pork head meats or predominantly pork head meats with pork, cured pork and/or other pork by-proudcts, except that ears, livers, and spleens cannot be used. The meat is coarse to fine cut. Onion is a seasoning. Some may have caraway added. Souse is a head-cheese with vinegar added. Both can have gelatin added. They are usually stuffed in artificial (A) or natural (B4—hog stomachs or B5—beef bungs) casings and weigh from 4 to 8 lb. The interior cut surface is resilient and very coarse textured with an even distribution of ingredients. Specify whether chilled (A) or frozen (B). Also indicate whether souse or head-cheese and if caraway should be an added ingredient.

Ready-to-Serve Meats

No greater change has occurred in the last 2 decades in the food market than in the type of meat product offered. A wide range of meat dishes now come prepared and need only slight reconditioning to make them ready for service. In fact, there are so many prepared meat dishes available that many food services need only restricted or no kitchens to prepare complete meals. Because these new meat dishcs havc only been on the market for a short time, few specifications exist for their purchase, and buyers are often at a loss to know how to secure the products they need.

A number of buyers just sample the market and then specify by brand the products they want. This involves the testing and evaluation of products offered and may be one of the best methods to use until more standards have been developed on these foods.

The federal government's standards for foods that are similar can be used to establish standards for these new foods. Buyers can study these standards and then adapt them to the new foods. Many of these establish the quantity of meat the product must contain, plus other foods and ingredients. For instance, a buyer wishing to purchase a frozen or chilled beef stew could ask for a minimum of 14% on a cooked or 25% raw basis of meat since these are the standards established by the federal government for canned beef stew. Or if one is purchasing a meat pie on this same standard, an 8-oz filling would be specified as needing 1½ oz of cooked meat or 2 oz of raw meat before cooking. The type and amount of vegetables and gravy or other products should be specified. Flavors should be true for the product, and the color natural. Broken, mushy, or otherwise unnatural pieces should not be evident. Tables 9-15 and 9-16 indicate some of the federal standards that have been established for canned or processed items. An asterisk indicates that the meat item is on a raw basis; all others are on a cooked basis.

Federal standards of identity exist for corned beef hash and chopped ham. Corned beef hash must contain at least 35% corned beef on a cooked basis, plus fresh, dehydrated, or frozen potatoes or a mixture of these. Optional ingredients are onions, garlic, seasonings, curing agents, beef broth, or beef fat. Maximum moisture content is 72%. Chopped ham must contain fresh, cured or smoked ham along with approved curing agents and seasonings. It also may contain certain optional ingredients in specified amounts, including finely chopped ham, shank meat, dehydrated onions, dehydrated garlic, corn syrup, other chemical substances permitted in the federal standards and not more than 3% water to dissolve the curing agents.

The provisions previously cited relative to frankfurters and similar products also apply in many instances to these new processed foods.

The Veterans Administration, General Services of the United States, the Armed Forces, state agencies, and other large buying groups have specifications for these new meat products that can be helpful in establishing specifications for other operations. Purveyors also can be helpful in setting up specifications for these products. These purveyors often know objective, technical or other factors which, when added to a specification, assure one which better meets the operation's needs.

Another method by which a specification for these new meat products can be established is to take a recipe which gives a desirable product and use this as a model for the specification. For instance, a recipe yielding 50 5-oz (²/₃ c) portions of chicken a la king (16¾ lb) contains cubed cooked chicken 4 lb, mushrooms 1½ lb, green pepper 1 lb, pimientos 1 lb, flour 12 oz, margarine 10 oz, chicken stock 2½ qt (5 lb), milk 1 qt (2 lb), and evaporated milk 1 pt (1 lb) can be converted to percentage of ingredients. Thus, of the 16¾-lb yield chicken is 24%, mushrooms 9%, green pepper 6%, pimiento 6%, flour 4%, margarine 3¾%, stock 30%, milk 12%, and evaporated milk 6%. From this a specification could be written as follows: "The cooked chicken shall be in natural proportions in approximately ½-in. cubes and be 25% of the total weight; no chicken skin shall be added

TABLE 9-15
Minimum Quantities of Meat in Some Food Products

Product	Minimum Quantity	Product	Minimum Quantity
Beans with bacon in sauce	12% bacon*	Beans with frankfurters in sauce	20% franks*
Beans with ham in sauce	12% ham	Beef with barbecue sauce	50% beef
Beef withh gravy	50% beef	Gravy with beef	35% beef
Beef Stroganoff	30% beef**	Chili con carne	40% meat*
Chili sauce with meat	6% meat*	Chop suey vegetables with meat	12% meat*
Chow mein	12% meat*	Egg foo yung with meat	12% meat*
Deviled ham	no more than 35% fat	Egg rolls with meat	10% meat*
		Frozen breakfast	15% meat
Enchiladas with meat	15% meat*	Ham chowder	10% ham
Ham and cheese spread	25% ham	Hash	35% meat
Ham spread	50% ham*	Lima beans with ham or bacon in sauce	12% ham or bacon*
Lasagna with meat and sauce	12% meat*	Macaroni and cheese with ham	12% ham
Liver, paste, pudding, etc.	30% liver*		
Macaroni and beef in tomato sauce	12% beef*	Meat casseroles	18% meat, 25%*
		Meat pies	25% meat*, 18%
Meat salad	35% meat	Meat tacos	15% meat*
Meat turnovers	25% meat*	Omelet with bacon	12% bacon
Omelet with ham	18% ham	Pizza with meat	15% meat*
Pork with barbecue sauce	50% pork	Pizza with sausage	12% or 10% dry sausage
Sauerkraut with weiners and juice	20% weiners*	Scallopine	35% meat
Scrapple	40% meat***	Spaghetti with meat and sauce	12% meat*
Spaghetti with meat balls	12% meat*		
Spaghetti sauce with meat	6% meat*	Spanish rice with beef	20% beef
Stews	25% meat*	Sukiyaki	30% meat*
Sweet and sour pork or beef	25%* or 16% meat	Swiss steak with gravy	50% meat
		Tamales	25% meat
Tamales with sauce or gravy	20% meat*	Veal birds	60% veal*, 40% dressing
Veal Cordon Bleu	60% veal* 5% ham* plus cheese	Veal fricassee	40% meat*

*Raw basis

**Plus not less than 10% sour cream.

***Or meat by-products.

TABLE 9-16
Miscellaneous Specifications and Standards for Some Cooked Meats

Item	Purchase Description
Roast beef, frzn	Precooked rounds from choice grade steer or heifer, deli-style, 7 to 12 lb each. Individually wrapped in moisture- and grease-resistant paper; can be ordered sliced and tied also; bnls.
Roast beef, frzn	Precooked top round from choice grade steer or heifer, 6½ lb average, not varying more than ½ lb in individual pieces; bnls.
Roast beef, frzn	Precooked cross-rib, from choice steer or heifer, 12 to 15 lb each, bnls.
Barbecued ground beef, frzn	51½% ground coarse beef, 48½% tomato gravy, cooked basis.
Barbecued meat	The weight of meat when barbecued cannot exceed 70% of the fresh uncooked meat; must have a barbecued (crusted) appearance.
Beef, sliced with gravy, frzn	Meat to be not less than 55% on a cooked basis.
Beef, Burgundy, frzn	45% choice cubed beef, 53% Burgundy wine sauce, 2½% garnish of onions and mushrooms.
Beef casserole, Italian style, frzn	Not more than 50% cooked macaroni; at least 25% cooked beef.
Beef patty, charbroiled, frzn	Cooked, 3% textured vegetable protein may be added; 95% beef, 2% flavoring and spices; 3 oz patties, layer packed.
Beef rolls, frzn	Ground beef in pastry roll with sauce; shall be at least 2 oz ground beef on a cooked basis; 4¾-oz portions.
Beef stew, frzn	25% beef, not more than 20% peas, carrots, green beans, small onions, and celery on a proportional basis.
Beef and pork fritters	Chop shape 3-oz patties, 53 per cs (10 lb), layer packed; 65% lean pork, 30% beef, 3% coating, 2% seasonings.
Cabbage rolls, frzn	8-oz portions, 4 oz of filling with remainder cabbage and sauce; filling should be 50% meat.
Cannelloni with meat sauce, frzn	20% meat filling.
Meat balls in sour cream, frzn	55% veal or beef on cooked basis from choice grade meat, 45% sauce; ½ oz meat balls; no extender permitted.
Sirloin tips in mushroom gravy, frzn	From choice top sirloin in ½-oz cubes after cooking, broiled and then added to a gravy. Shall be 41.875% meat on cooked basis, 55% mushroom gravy and 3.125% mushrooms.
Stuffed peppers in sauce, frzn	60% filling and peppers; 40% sauce; filling shall be 50% meat on a cooked basis with corn, rice and seasonings plus moisture 50%.

TABLE 9-16 (Continued)
Miscellaneous Specifications and Standards for Some Cooked Meats

Item	Purchase Description
Liver, beef, frzn	Raw, 4/lb, Style A, Selection 1, skinned, sliced, IMPS 702SL.
Veal cutlets	Shall come from the large muscle of the shoulder or leg. Should be clear slices and not knitted or cubed. Each cutlet to be 4 oz not over or under ¼ oz. Maximum breading 20%, 80% meat.
Veal drumsticks, frzn	Finely ground meal containing not over 1% salt, 2% cereal, 3½% dry milk (nonfat). Added moisture shall not exceed 7½%. Breading shall be first by dipping into wheat (white) flour and then a mixture of 50% eggs and 50% milk and then into fine crumbs or prepared breading mix. Breading shall not be more than 25% of total weight. Shall be 2 or 4 oz each as specified. Shall be layer packed separated by moisture-grease-resistant paper.
Pork, breakfast patties, cooked, frzn	Fresh pork sausage. Rounds should not be less than 2 in. in diameter and ³/₁₆ inch thick.

as a part of the chicken nor as an additional ingredient. Other ingredients shall be mushrooms 8%, green peppers 5%, pimientoes 4%, and sauce 58%. The total milk solids shall be 1.8% of the sauce weight. Fat shall be from 6 to 7% of the sauce weight. Flour or other starch thickeners should be approximately 4% of the total weight and give a medium thick sauce that is smooth, not pasty, and of acceptable, delicate flavor." Today some operations have recipes that manufacturers use to make specific products for them. The volume must be fairly large when this is done.

Any specification should require that the manufacturing plants and products meet all sanitary and other requirements of the Food, Drug and Cosmetic Act plus other regulations that support the wholesomeness of products. Imports should satisfy all requirements for entry into the U.S. and be wholesome. The products should be free from foreign or objectionable material and insect infestation. If necessary, the cooking and other procedures can be defined. (See also poultry.) Require that all meat and poultry in these foods[4] be inspected and passed in a plant under continuous

---

[4]Federal regulations are that foods containing more than 2% meat or poultry must have the meat or poultry inspected and passed for wholesomeness.

inspection by the USDA. Indicate also what seasonings, emulsifiers, preservatives, and other additives can be used and how much. Require that chilled products on their exterior and interior be below 40°F upon delivery and frozen items at delivery be 0°F. Specify freezing at −20°F or lower with carbon dioxide, liquid nitrogen, dioxide nitrogen, or blast chamber methods. Many products can be specified quick frozen individual (IQF). Time for freezing may be specified. For instance, small individual cubes may be required to be frozen within 10 minutes.

Bacterial limits should be established. Most products per gram or cubic centimeter should not exceed the following: total count, 100,000; coliform, 100; fecal (E. coli), 10, pathogens, 0; staphylococcus, 100; coagulase positive, 0; yeast, 100; and mold, 100. The State of Texas requires that the following factors be filled out by manufacturers and this be submitted with invoices:

A. Total Plate Count _____   C. Staphylococcus   _____
B. Coliform   _____   1. Coagulase Positive _____
    1. Fecal   _____   D. Pathogens   _____
    2. Salmonella   _____   E. Yeast   _____
                                                    F. Mold   _____

Products can be required to meet a maximum for moisture or fat. Since fat in sauces or gravies can quickly go rancid, a specific peroxide number can be required—some specify either a Hanus or iodine number; for instance, a peroxide value over 4MM/peroxide/kg fat is sometimes set as a maximum value.

Frozen products should show no evidence of thawing and refreezing, freezer burn, or exhibit any off-colors or odors. After thawing, the product should be tender with a characteristic cooked flavor and aroma, be free of rancidity and other objectionable off-odors and off-flavors, and be free of or contain only approved other ingredients.

Packaging should be specified, but it is extremely difficult to establish standards for this since the practices of different manufacturers vary. Most frozen products should be sealed in polyethylene bags and placed in a strong fiberboard container to protect them. Items should be delivered in good shape, with good appearance, and without encrusted materials or other substances adhering to them. Roasted, broiled, or fried products should possess a good brown sheen. A tenderness factor may be specified according to standards established using a Bratzler tester.[5]

Type and amount of trim and fat on the surface or as seam fat also can be

[5]Mr. Bratzler, Professor at Michigan State, developed a device which indicates the pressure required to cut through cooked particles of meat and indicate relative toughness or tenderness.

specified. Sliced or cut items can be specified as to thickness, weight, or size. Indicate weight variations allowed. Many items may need to be specified as to packaging. Most cooked units are specified as layer-packed between layers of grease- and moisture-resistant paper. Breading should be specified and the percent of meat. Indicate also the products to be used for thickening and also quantities. Amounts of fat in gravies and sauces need definition.

Nutritional values may be important and can be specified. The federal government has proposed that labels on frozen dinners indicate whether they meet or do not meet federal nutritional quality guidelines for the product. If the product fails to meet them, the label should state why. A minimum of 340 calories is a part of the proposal which would yield the following nutrients per 340 calories: protein 15 gm (4.6 gm/100 calories), vitamin A 510 I U (150/100 calories), thiamine 0.17 (0.05/100 calories), riboflavin 0.21 (0.06 mg/100 calories), niacin 3.3 mg (0.99 mg/100 calories), and iron 2.1 mg (0.72 mg/100 calories). Iodine should be present in the same quantity as it would be if iodized salt were used. Other proposals have indicated that the minimum nutrients per dinner should be 15% of the required daily allowance (RDA). No minimums have been established for calcium or phosphorus, but they should be present in a 1:1 ratio. Minimums for other nutrients may be proposed later.

Buyers can use acceptance inspection for these prepared meat items to assure that these foods comply with the specifications. Each container or master container should bear the acceptance inspection stamp imprint and a legible date of inspection. Each shipment may be required to have with it all necessary papers certifying sanitary standards, acceptance inspection, and so forth.

Textured Vegetable Protein Products

The use of simulated meat products made from soy protein has increased, and as meat prices continue to climb, this substitute which meets all the requirements for essential amino acids will find increasing use. Textured vegetable protein products sales doubled in the world in 1973. In that same year the USDA School Feeding Program allowed the use of it with ground meats at about a 1:2 ratio. Hospitals are using it to lower food costs and for diets that must be low in animal fats. Homemakers are purchasing it largely as a "hamburger stretcher." Many things can be done to soy as a textured product. It can be made into a product that looks and tastes very much like ground beef, ground ham, ground turkey, or ground veal. It also can be made to look and taste like cubes of chicken, beef, veal, ham, and so forth. The popular "Baco-bits," which very much resemble crisply diced bacon, are made from soy. Undoubtedly, the institutional market in the future will see an extending use of the product.

Fig. 9-64. The use of soy products to simulate meat is becoming more and more common. Many of the hamburger, tuna or other extenders, such as the TVP (textured vegetable protein) egg noodles stroganoff, seen above are being widely used by the homemaker. Institutions are also using significant quantities and will be used more to reduce food cost, supply extra protein and reduce high cholesterol fats. The savory "burga-style" mix shown above is used with ground meat products in a ratio of about 1:2 to 1:3. Courtesy General Mills and the British Arkady Co., Ltd.

Soy cannot only be used to make analogs which are excellent substitutes for meat, but it also can be used to make milk and other dairy substitutes. And soy is used to make imitation nuts that are remarkably like the real thing in both appearance and taste. Soy protein also is being used to enrich items such as macaroni, which may lack a complete protein. The protein from soy is not the only high protein product containing all the essential amino acids in adequate amounts that can be used. The protein from rape seed, cottonseed, and other seeds or nuts is almost as adequate nutrition- ally, and investigations are being made into the possibility of using these.

As yet, few purchase standards have been established for these new analogs. The USDA's School Lunch Program has established certain criteria that institutions could use to set up specifications. At the present time, as with other experimental products, it is perhaps best to test the items offered on the market until a suitable one is found, and then purchase it. Perhaps as use becomes more common, we will then be able to set up standards by which a specification for a product of this type could be offered for bid.

Canned Meats

If fresh meat supplies are difficult to obtain or if refrigeration is not availa- ble to hold them, a food service may depend upon considerable amounts of canned meats. Most purchase some. As noted previously, canned meat products must conform to federal regulations for wholesomeness, and plants and workmen must meet standards for sanitation, and so forth. Additives must be approved. Usually the poorer grades of meat and excess market quantities are processed.

It is much more difficult to preserve meat by canning than fruits or vegetables. The solid mass and its resistance to heat penetration make it difficult to sterilize in the can. Because of this, some meat products may not be completely sterilized and may have to be held under refrigeration, such as canned hams. Storage of other smaller canned meat products is usually adequate at 40 to 70°F. Above 70°F, thermophilic bacteria can cause deterioration. Canned meats should not be kept over a year. Freezing may cause a loss of quality, but the edibility and nutritional value are not harmed. Freezing, however, may swell and break the can, causing spoil- age. Lacquered cans are used to prevent the meat from reacting with the metal in can linings.

The use of the 18 psi method of canning which allows the addition of thick meat products such as stews, macaroni and meat, hash, and so forth hot at sterilizing temperatures into cans has made it possible to avoid heating them for long periods in retorts to obtain sterilization and has made possible a more palatable product.

Canned slab bacon comes in 14-lb rectangular cans with 3 to 4 pieces making the weight. Sliced canned bacon is usually sliced 5/32 in. thick and the lot is wrapped in oiled or parchment paper in the can. There is a gradual deterioration even though there is little oxidation; therefore the product should not be kept over 6 months. Sliced bacon is usually sold in cans holding 5, 5½, 7½, and 16 lb net weight. Canadian style bacon also is canned.

Boned chicken or turkey usually comes in 46-oz cans or smaller cans. The amount of added broth without notation on the label is limited to 10%. (See poultry.) Corned beef may contain 3 to 4% meat jelly and is usually sold in 12-oz, 1-lb, 1½-lb, 5-lb, or 6-lb cans. Cornbeef hash is a combination of ground corned beef with 40 to 50% potatoes and onions. It is sold in No. 10 or No. 2 cans.

Roast beef is cut into strips or pieces about 1½ to 2 in. wide, with most of the fat trimmed. It is roasted and then placed into cans with gravy, sauce, or broth. It comes in 12-oz, 1½-lb, and 6-lb cans. There must be 50% meat on a raw basis. Various stews and other products are made from beef and are canned. Some may be beef and vegetables, beef in gravy, meat balls, meat loaf, and so forth.

Canned luncheon meat may be all pork or a beef-pork mixture. It is finely chopped, seasoned, pressed into loaves, and cooked in the cans. Pork sausage meat and pork sausage links are canned, the former in loaf form. Vienna sausage contains 40 to 70% beef and 30 to 60% pork. Canned frankfurters are similar mixtures. Chili con carne is a mixture of beans and meat with 50% beef, 25% beans, and the remainder vegetables and moisture. Many other meat products which are mixtures also are canned. Frequently, the federal government sets as the minimum quantity of meat on a raw basis that can be in the product as 25%.

Cooked hams may be oval, round, or pullman shape. They vary from 6 to 16 lb each. An 8- to 10-lb canned ham is usually best for institutional use. Some institutions find that the Danish imported canned hams are excellent products. If a canned ham contains more than 10% moisture, it must be labeled "imitation."

TABLE 9-17*
A Guide to Number of Pounds of Beef to Buy for Roasting to Serve 100†

Cut	Style	Weight of Cooked Serving	Approximate Amount to Purchase‡
		Ounces	*Pounds*
Rib	Seven-rib standing	2.5	44
		3.0	50
		4.0	67
		5.0	88
		6.0	100
		8.0	134
Round	Rump and shank off	2.1	39
		3.0	55
		4.0	74
		5.0	91
		6.0	110
Sirloin butt	Boneless	2.1	26
		3.0	32
		4.0	50
		5.0	63
		6.0	75
Ground beef	Meat loaf (all meat)	2.1	24
		3.0	35
		4.0	46
		5.0	58
		6.0	69
Ground beef	Meat loaf (with cereal filler)	2.6	18
		3.0	21
		4.0	28
		5.0	35
		6.0	42

*Courtesy National Livestock and Meat Board.
†University of Texas, 1942.
‡If the roasting temperature is increased above 300°F. the number of pounds of meat purchased to provide any certain weight of cooked servings will necessarily have to be increased.

TABLE 9-17 (Continued)
A Guide to Number of Pounds of Lamb to Buy for Roasting to Serve 100

Leg	Bone-in	2.2	34
		3.0	46
		4.0	62
Shoulder	Bone-in	2.7	29
		3.0	32
		4.0	42
Shoulder	Boneless	2.7	27
		3.0	30
		4.0	40

A Guide to Number of Pounds of Pork to Buy for Roasting to Serve 100

Cut	Style	Weight of Cooked Serving	Approximate Amount to Purchase
		Ounces	*Pounds*
Loin	Bone-in	2.5	37
		3.0	44
		4.0	59
		5.0	74
Loin	Boneless	2.0	31
		3.0	47
		4.0	62
		5.0	78
Shoulder	Cushion	2.8	38
		3.0	41
		4.0	54
		5.0	68
Fresh ham (leg)	Bone-in	2.5	38
		3.0	46
		4.0	61
		5.0	76
Smoked or pickled ham	Bone-in	1.9	35
		2.0	37
		3.0	55
Canadian style bacon		2.7	21
		3.0	23

TABLE 9-17 (Continued)
A Guide to Number of Pounds of Veal to Buy for Roasting to Serve 100

Leg	Bone-in	2.7	34
		3.0	38
		4.0	50
Shoulder	Cushion	2.4	22
		3.0	28
		4.0	37
Shoulder	Rolled	2.6	27
		3.0	31
		4.0	41
Round	Rump and shank off	2.0	27
		3.0	41
		4.0	54

A Guide to Number of Pounds of Beef Steak to Buy to Serve 100

Cut	Style	Weight of Cooked Serving	Approximate Amount to Purchase
		Ounces	*Pounds*
Round	Cubed steak	3.0	26
		4.0	36
		5.0	45
		6.0	54
Round	Steak (Swiss)	3.6	31
		4.0	35
		5.0	44
		6.0	52
Loin	Steak	3.8	33
		4.0	35
		5.0	42
		6.0	53
Flank	Steak	2.7	24
		3.0	26
		4.0	35
		5.0	43
		6.0	61

TABLE 9-17 (Continued)

A Guide to Number of Pounds of Beef to Buy for Braising and for Simmering to Serve 100

Sirloin butts	Boneless	1.9	13
		2.0	14
		3.0	20
		4.0	27
		5.0	34
		6.0	40
Chuck	Boneless	2.4	25
		3.0	30
		4.0	41
		5.0	51
		6.0	61
Plate or short ribs		4.6	38
		5.0	42
		6.0	50
		7.0	58
		8.0	66
Brisket	Corned	2.1	25
		3.0	29
		4.0	40
		5.0	50
		6.0	60

A Guide to Number of Pounds of Lamb to Buy for Chops and Riblets to Serve 100

Cut	Style	Weight of Cooked Serving	Approximate Amount to Purchase
		Ounces	*Pounds*
Loin or rib	Chops	2.8	36
		3.0	38
		4.0	51
Breast	Riblets	3.2	30
		4.0	38

TABLE 9-17 (Continued)

**A Guide to Number of Pounds of Pork Chops, Pork Cutlets,
Pork Sausage, and Bacon to Buy to Serve 100**

Loin	Pork chops	4.0	40
		5.0	50
Pork Cutlets		2.4	13
		3.0	16
		4.0	22
		5.0	27
Sausage	Bulk	1.3	15
		2.0	23
		3.0	34
Bacon	Sliced	0.5	9
		1.0	18
		1.5	27

**A Guide to Number of Pounds of Veal to Buy for Steaks,
Chops and Cutlets to Serve 100**

Tenderloin	Steaks	2.6	24
		3.0	30
		4.0	37
Loin	T-bone chops or steaks	4.1	38
		5.0	46
		6.0	56
Rib	Chops	4.9	40
		5.0	41
		6.0	48
Round	Cutlets	2.6	24
		3.0	30
		4.0	37

BIBLIOGRAPHY

American Meat Institute, *Science of Meat and Meat Production,* W. H. Freeman, San Francisco, Calif., 1960.

Bull, S., *Meat for the Table,* 6th ed., McGraw Hill, New York, 1951.

Levi, Albert, *Meat Handbook,* 2nd ed., Avi Press, Westport, Conn., 1967.

National Livestock and Meat Board, *Meat Manual,* 4th ed., Chicago, 1950.

National Livestock and Meat Board, *Ten Lessons in Meat Cookery,* 7th ed., Chicago, 1950.

Rivers, Frank, *The Hotel Butcher, Garde Manger and Carver,* Hotel Monthly Press, Chicago, Ill., 1935.

Swift and Co., *Boning and Cutting Veal for Profit, Facts You Should Know about Beef, How to Buy Meat, Cuts of Meat and How You Can Identify Them,* Chicago, n. d.

U.S. Department of Agriculture, *"Official United States Standards for Grades of Carcass Beef, Official United States Standards for Grades of Veal and Calf, Official United States Standards for Lamb, Yearling Mutton and Mutton, Official Grades for Pork Carcasses,* Agricultural Marketing Service, Washington, D.C.

U.S.D.A., *Institutional Meat Purchase Specifications:* Fresh Beef (Series 100); Fresh Lamb and Mutton (Series 200); Fresh Veal and Calf (Series 300); Fresh Pork (Series 400); Cured, Cured and Smoked and Fully-cooked Pork Products (Series 500); Cured, Dried and Smoked Beef Products (Series 600); Edible By-products (Series 700); Sausage Products (Series 800); and Portion-Cut Meat Products (Series 1000). U.S. Government Printing Office, Washington, D.C. 20402, 1973.

Ziegler, P. T., *Meat We Eat,* 4th ed., Interstate Printers and Publishers, Danville, Ill., 1954.

Author's note: As this book was going to press the Meat Division of the USDA announced new grading standards for beef. Although complete information is lacking the change broadened the Choice grade even more than it presently is and reduced standards for marbling with some grades. This will make it possible for the Charlo and other breeds of cattle to qualify for some grades they had difficulty in qualifying for previously. It will also allow some grass fed cattle to qualify for some grades they previously could not. Buyers should be sure to indicate now whether beef should be the top or bottom of the grade and perhaps in the Choice grade should now indicate top, middle or bottom. The bottom grade of Choice will, under the new grading, be the upper part of the top in Good grade.

10
Alcoholic Beverages

Good purchasing of alcoholic beverages is difficult. Quality is dependent on factors difficult to detect and evaluate, which frequently can be differentiated only by the expert. Furthermore, quality may not be important because in a patron's mind a specific brand may be preferred over an unknown product of higher quality. Price also is not an indicator of quality. Buyers will find few bargains in alcoholic beverages.

Purchasers must be well coordinated with the operation's merchandising and sales plans. Maintaining an adequate inventory, while at the same time holding stock levels as low as possible to avoid tying up too many dollars in inventory, is essential. If wines are stocked the value of the inventory may turn over 4 to 5 times a year, but if beers and spirits are heavily sold the turnover ratio will be higher. Unless buyers are sure they can move products, they should not stock them. Off-brand buying is best done only by the expert and by a company that can merchandise the products well.

TYPES OF ALCOHOLIC BEVERAGES

Alcoholic beverages are classified as wine, beer, and distilled spirits. The last includes alcohol, whiskey, brandy, rum, vodka, gin, cordials, and liqueurs. Most are produced in plants operating under federal licenses unless imported. Wine and beer manufacturing must also conform to federal regulations. Regulation usually does not establish formulas or methods of manufacture but, rather, outlines general conditions under which producers operate.

Standards of identity and methods of labeling and advertising have been established for items moving in interstate commerce, and most states have additional requirements that must be observed. Buyers should know these

607

regulations and follow them. Monopoly states purchase and sell all alcoholic beverages, usually through their own state-owned and state-operated stores. "Local option" areas are those where a community, county, or other part of a governmental unit decides to have or not have alcoholic beverages dispensed.

Distilled Spirits

Quality and cost of distilled spirits are determined largely by the materials from which they are made, the manufacturing process, and the aging. Advertising can be a significant cost factor.

Ethyl alcohol results when yeast feeds on carbohydrates such as starch in grain or sugar in malt or grapes. Two percent carbohydrate makes 1% alcohol. The chemical change is $C_6H_{12}O_6 \rightarrow 2C_2H_5OH + 2CO_2 \uparrow \Delta$ (heat). Yeast cannot work in a solution over 14% alcohol (15½% in some special cases). Thus, if grape juice contains 34% sugar, 28% will produce a wine of 14% alcohol (2% carbohydrate = 1% alcohol), leaving 6% sugar; this makes a sweet wine. If the juice were 20% sugar, a dry wine (no sugar) of 10% alcoholic content might result.

The alcohol in spirits comes from various fermented solutions such as grains, sugar cane, or fruits. The type of product used gives the spirit its distinctive flavor and quality partially because of the flavor esters and other components in the product and brew that distill off with the alcohol. A rye whiskey has a distinct rye flavor different from a bourbon made from corn. Each varies considerably in flavor from vodka, which has very little flavor or aroma. The pears used to make pear brandy or the grapes used to make Cognac greatly influence their flavor. Dark rums are richer in flavor and heavier in body than light ones because they come from different products.

The quantity of alcohol in a spirit is indicated by its proof. In this country proof is twice the percent of alcohol by volume. Thus, an 86-proof whiskey is 43% alcohol by volume. Federal regulations require that whiskeys not be higher than 110 or lower than 80 proof. At one time, proof was tested crudely by taking a spirit and dampening it with gunpowder. If the spirit at 60°F burned vigorously, it was 42.9% or more alcohol by weight or 57.1% or more by volume. If it was below this percent, the mixture would not burn at all. The British, who invented this sensitive test, said that when such a gunpowder mixture burned vigorously, it was *proof* of its alcoholic content—thus the origination of the word "proof." The British set their standard of 57% by volume as 100 proof, which made pure (100%) alcohol 175.25 proof; this was reckoned as 175 proof because of the small quantity of water remaining in pure alcohol.

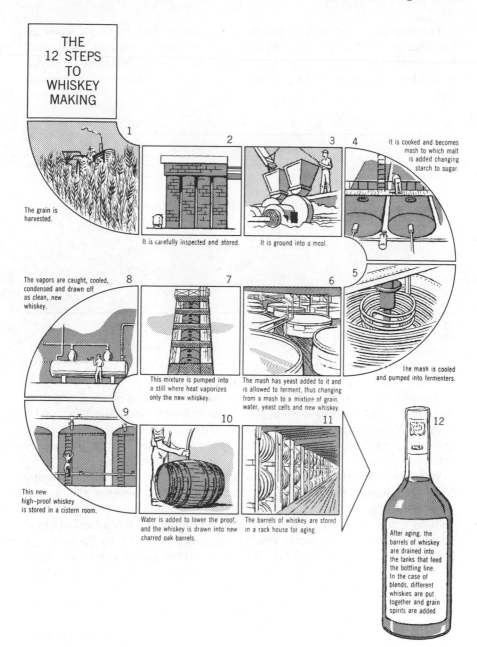

Fig. 10-1. The 12 steps in making whiskey. Courtesy Licensed Beverage Industries, Inc., New York

The Europeans use a different proof system, called the Gay-Lussac or Continental Metric System. This lists proof as exactly the percent alcohol by volume in the spirit. Thus, an 80-proof American spirit is about 70 proof in Britain and 40 proof Gay-Lussac. These three systems compare as follows:

	British	American	Metric
Pure alcohol	175	200	100
	100	114	57
	88	100*	50
	85	98	49
	80	90	45
	75	86†	43
	70‡	80**	40
	65	74	37
Pure water	0	0	0

*U.S. bonded whiskey.
†The proof of most U.S. blends.
‡The proof of most British whiskeys.
**Lowest proof allowed in U.S. whiskeys.

American beers, ales, and so forth are stated in percent alcoholic content by *weight,* which makes them appear to have less alcohol than if stated by volume. Most European products are stated by volume, which makes them appear higher in alcoholic content than American ones. Wines are usually stated as percent by volume and spirits always by volume.

Whiskey is aged in charred oak barrels, the reddish-brown color coming from the charred oak. The longer the aging, the smoother the flavor. Whiskey is made from selected grain, finely ground into meal and then cooked with water into a mash or pastelike product. Malt is added to assist in fermentation, and special yeasts are used. After 72 to 96 hours of fermentation under carefully controlled conditions, the product is distilled, producing new whiskey (about 190 proof). The alcoholic content is then reduced to that desired.

Bonded whiskey is required to be aged (stored) 4 years in a government warehouse, must be the product of a single distillery during a single season, and must be 100 proof. The government's green stamp certifies it as bonded. Bonding should not be misunderstood as a guarantee of quality, but usually the better spirits are bonded. The Bureau of Internal Revenue controls the whiskey during the time it is in the warehouse and keeps records of entries and withdrawals. No spirits can be withdrawn without governmental permission, and individuals can enter the premises only when accompanied by a federal official. Bonded products must be bottled under federal supervision.

A straight whiskey is nothing but whiskey diluted with water to the desired proof and aged for not less than 24 months. A blend is 100-proof straight whiskey blended with other whiskey or neutral spirits not under 80 proof. The minimum ratio of 100-proof straight whiskey to 80-proof neutral spirits or other whiskey is 20:80. Before being marketed, blends are aged a short time—a period called "marrying." The flavor and quality of a blend is very much affected by the quality of straight whiskey used in it, a good blend being made from a very fine straight whiskey. A reddish-pink stamp from the federal government indicates a spirit made from nonbonded spirits.

Sour-mash whiskey is made by using part of a previous day's mash to start and assist the fermentation of a new batch. This is much the same as the use of a "starter" for sour-dough hotcakes or bread. Such spirits will have a distinctive sour flavor. Bourbon is made from a mash containing 51% or more of corn with the balance any other grain, usually rye grain or barley malt. Corn whiskey must come from a mash 80% or more of corn. It need not be stored in charred wooden containers, but may be stored in plain wooden ones and therefore lack color. Rye whiskey must be distilled from a mash of 51% or more of rye. Canadian whiskey (the English and Canadians spell it "whisky") is made from a mash largely rye, but it may contain some corn; it is at least 2 years old. Most Canadian whiskeys exported to this country are blends blended either before or after the aging period. No limitations with respect to proof or distillation are placed on this product by the Canadian government, but imports must conform to our regulations. Often, if a customer in this country asks for a rye whiskey, he will be served a Canadian whiskey.

Scotch is a distinctive whiskey of Scotland, the base of which is a mash of smoked barley for the heavy-bodied types and smoked corn for the lighter-bodied ones. Many are distilled by the pot method. Aging is at least 3 years in uncharred oak barrels or used sherry casks. Most Scotch is a blend of malt and grain whiskeys. No Scotch may enter this country under 4 years old unless so labeled. Most Scotch is aged 5 years or more before blending.

Irish whiskey is made from malted barley plus other grains. Occasionally, it may be a blend with other grain spirits. It may or may not be smoked with peat. Many Irish whiskeys are pot-made, which means that a single batch of mash is distilled until the alcohol is extracted. The mash is then discarded and a new batch distilled. Most whiskeys are distilled by a continuous process, a method whereby new mash is constantly introduced while old mash is withdrawn after the alcohol is distilled from it.

Rum is distilled from fermented molasses or other products from sugar cane and must be not more than 190 proof or less than 80 proof. New England rum is a full-bodied, straight rum, distilled at less than 160 proof. A product just labeled "rum" is generally a blend of rums. The label on a rum must show the geographical area where it is made. There are 3 main areas: (1) Cuba, Puerto Rico, Haiti, and the Dominican Republic, which produce a light-bodied or "dry" rum, (2) full-bodied or "rich" rum from Jamaica, Barbados, Trinidad, Virgin Islands, Demerara, or Martinique, and (3) the aromatic or Batavia Arak rum from Java.

A neutral spirit is alcohol distilled from a mash that gives a colorless, flavorless, and odorless product at 190 proof. A grain-neutral spirit is made from grain. Gin is flavored neutral spirits made by passing distillation vapors through flavoring herbs held in a "gin head." The herbs will be juniper berries with perhaps cassia bark, coriander seed, orange peel, cardamom, and angelica. Gin can also be made by steeping it in these products and then straining them out. This may also be called "bathtub" gin. London gin is dry, lacking sweetness. It has no grain taste or odor left from the mash. Holland gin is also called schnapps or Geneva or Schiedam gin; it is made in Holland from a low-proof, malt spirit base to which juniper and other seasonings have been added. It has a rather heavy body and usually carries a taste and odor from its mash. Old Tom gin is a sweetened gin; simple syrup is usually used as the sweetener. Sloe gin is a cordial flavored with sloeberry, a berry from the blackthorn bush.

Vodka is neutral spirits distilled at or above 190 proof and reduced to 80 to 110 proof. It is then filtered through charcoal so it has no distinctive character, aroma, or taste. Most vodka is made from grains, not potatoes.

Brandy is distilled from fermented fruit or fruit juices and cannot be less than 80 proof. If labeled brandy only, it must come from grapes. If it comes from another product, it must bear the name of the product, such as pear brandy, cherry brandy, blackberry brandy, or whatever. Cognac comes from grapes grown in the Charente area in France, where the city of Cognac is located. The closer the production area to Cognac, the finer the quality usually. Armagnac brandy comes from grapes grown in the Department of Gers, southeast of Bordeaux, France. Napoleon brandy must be aged a specified number of years. Brandy is usually aged in oak barrels from 3 to 8 years. A label need not state the age unless it is under 2 years old. Some American brandies are bottled in bond. These must be straight brandy, 4 years or older and 100 proof. Specific terms, symbols, or letters on a brandy label indicate age, quality, and so on. But since there is no consistency among brandy producers in their use, buyers should learn what they mean on the various labels.

Buyers to differentiate all the necessary quality characteristics of a spirit and to evaluate them requires painstaking training and a critical taste. Quality is indicated by body, character, clarity, color, and proof. A heavy body is distinguished by a full flavor and aroma, while a light one has less of these characteristics.

Good flavor is indicated by a smoothness and a lack of strong, raw, harsh, or off-flavors. The aroma should be full, characteristic, and true. A good spirit should have a good taste while in the mouth and for a short time after; there should be no oily, lingering aftertaste.

Buyers should learn to be able to identify the true aroma and flavor of the grain, fruit, or other product used in the mash. Some rums will have a heavy body and full flavor from molasses while others will have a more delicate one from cane juice. The flavor of Scotch depends on the grain used and the amount of smoking given it. Character refers to the sensory qualities that distinguish the spirit. Most spirits should be sparkling clear. Spirits vary in color and its intensity depending on how they are made. A spirit aged in a noncharred cask is lighter than one aged in a charred one. A darker Scotch is made from barley instead of corn.

Price is not always an indicator of quality. Buyers should be sure, when comparing prices, that they are doing so not only on the basis of quality but also on the basis of proof. Thus, an 86-proof whiskey costing 20.2 cents per ounce compares in price with a 100-proof whiskey at 23.5 cents per ounce (20.2¢ + .86 = 23.5¢).

Table 10-1 gives the federal taxes on alcoholic beverages; besides these, most states also tax them. A U.S. gallon or wine gallon is 231 cu in. A proof gallon is a U.S. gallon of spirit at 60°F of 50% ethyl alcohol by volume (100 proof). A British- or Canadian-proof gallon is the Imperial gallon of 277.4 cu in. containing 57.1% (100 proof) ethyl alcohol by volume. A barrel as applied to beer represents 31 wine gal or U.S. gallons. A hogshead is two barrels. Note that rectified distilled spirits, wine cordials, and liqueurs in Table 10-1 have a tax over and above that of spirits over 24% alcohol. ("Rectification" is a term used to indicate the blending of distilled spirits, such as the blending of a straight 100-proof whiskey with grain neutral spirits to make a blended whiskey at 86 proof.)

Cordials and liqueurs are distilled spirits flavored with fruits, aromatic herbs, flowers, juices, or other essences containing at least 2½% sugar by weight. Many of the formulas are secret (such as Benedictine, Cointreau, and Chartreuse), and some have been made for centruies by monastic orders. Neutral spirits, with the aid of flavoring essences and other materials, are rectified into cordials or liqueurs. Whenever imitation flavorings are used, the label must indicate this.

Wine

Wine is the product of partial or complete fermentation of the juice of fruit or berries. Fermented apple juice is called cider, and even though made in a bonded wine cellar is sold as cider and not wine. Cider is not taxed nor does it come under federal regulations or permit requirements. To bear only the name "wine," the product must come from grapes; if made from other fruit, the fruit name must be before the term "wine" (such as "blackberry wine"). Labels must also state the fact that a wine is made from raisins or dried fruits, if that is the case.

TABLE 10-1
Federal Taxes on Alcoholic Beverages

Item	Tax Base*	Current Tax Rate
Artificially carbonated wine	Wine gallon	$2.40
Beer	Barrel	9.00
Champagne	Wine gallon	3.40
Distilled spirits	Tax gallon	10.50
Rectified products:		
Distilled spirits	Proof gallon	†.30
Wine cordials and liqueurs	Wine gallon	†1.92
Still wines:		
Not more than 14% alcohol	Wine gallon	0.17
More than 14% and not exceeding 21% alcohol	Wine gallon	0.67
More than 21% and not exceeding 24% alcohol	Wine gallon	2.25
More than 24% alcohol	Same as distilled spirits	

*Gallon: A gallon or wine gallon is a U.S. gallon of liquid measure equivalent to the volume of 231 cu in. A proof gallon is the alcoholic equivalent of a U.S. gallon at 60°F, containing 50% of ethyl alcohol by volume. A tax gallon for spirits of 100 proof or over is equivalent to the proof gallon. For spirits of less than 100 proof, the tax gallon is equivalent to the wine gallon.
Barrel: As applied to beer, a barrel represents 31 wine gallons.
Proof: Proof is the ethyl alcohol content of a liquid at 60°F, stated as twice the per percent of ethyl alcohol by volume.
(A British or Canadian proof gallon is an Imperial gallon of 277.4 cu in. containing 57.1% of ethyl alcohol by volume.)
†This tax is in addition to the basic distilled spirits and wine tax.
Source: Table from *What You Should Know About the Alcohol and Tobacco Tax Division,* Publication No. 425 (11–58), Internal Revenue Service, U.S. Treasury Department.

Wine-Making

Wine quality is affected by the kind of fruit used, the geographical area where grown, the climatic conditions of growing, the care the fruit gets during growth and its selection, the making of the wine, and the care it gets after it is made. Aging is also a factor. Most wine is made from grapes.

There are two wine grapes: European (*Vitis vinifera*) and American (chiefly *Vitis lubrusca*), often called "the fox grape" because of its wild or foxy flavor. Grapes grown for table use, raisins, juice, jellies, or brandy usually make poor wine, although some vintners are beginning to make better wine from some table grapes than previously possible.

Most wine grapes grow on the roots of an American grape, since its roots are resistant to attack from the Phelgra, a small aphis or plant louse that once destroyed most of Europe's vineyards. This insect was unknown to the European vineyards but when some American grapes were imported to England infested with them they quickly spread over Europe. The European grape being non-resistant to their attack in a few years was almost wiped out. It was then discovered that by grafting European vines onto American grape roots, the European grape could also resist the attack of the Phlox and so today most European grapes grow on the roots of the American grape.

Specific grapes must be used to make specific wines. A Pinot Noir grape must be used for Burgundy, a Semillon for a Graves or Sauterne, a Palomino for sherry, a Johannisberger for a Rhine, and 70% Sangiovese at least for a Chianti. The blending of juice or wines is common in the United States. In this country, if the name of the grape is used on a label, the wine must be made from 51% or more of that grape. Thus, a buyer selecting an American wine would be more likely to get a wine resembling a French Burgundy if the label read "Pinot Noir" than if it read "Burgundy," which may or may not be like the French wine. And, a wine would be more apt to resemble a French claret or red Bordeaux if the label read "Cabernet Sauvignon," the grape used for that wine.

Distinctive American wines are being made from grapes developed here, such as the Zinfandel and Emerald Dry. American vintners claim that blending makes it possible to have a more consistent quality each year and to adjust for variations in sweetness, acid, alcoholic content, flavor, and so on. If an old wine is blended with a small amount of a young one, a freshness of flavor or fruitiness of flavor results. Some wine merchants in Bordeaux are so skilled at blending clarets that they sometimes produce a wine superior to many estate-bottled ones. The French allow champagne to be blended because it is difficult to get a good wine using the juice of only one type of grape. Sherry is a blended wine usually made by the "solera" method, which is a process in which sun-baked sherries of different ages

Zinfandel (black), for
Claret and Port

White (Johannisberger)
Riesling (greenish-yellow),
popular for Rhine Wine

Pinot Blanc (yellowish-green),
noted for Chablis types

Palomino (straw-colored),
famous Sherry grape

Pinot Noir (black), noted
Burgundy grape

Semillon (greenish-yellow),
famous Sauterne grape

Cabernet Sauvignon (jet black)
makes red dinner wine

Muscat of Alexandria
(golden) makes Muscatel

Grenache (reddish-black),
popular Rosé wine grape

Fig. 10-2. Nine of the main grapes used for making wine in California. All are European-type grapes, but the Zinfandel was originated in California from European stock.

are blended together. Blending must be done in this country under federal supervision, and filtering and bottling must take place in a tax-paid wine bottling house.

Some countries permit the addition of sugar to the fruit juice to either develop sweetness or make more alcohol. Wines below 10½% do not ship well. Thus, Rhine wines and champagne may be from sugared juice if the grapes of one year's grapes lack sugar.

A dry wine is not necessarily tart or acid but is dry because it lacks sugar. A juice of 28% sugar can make a 14% alcohol wine, which is dry; but if a juice contains 32% sugar the wine will be sweet because, after a wine reaches 14% alcohol, fermentation usually stops leaving the excess sugar for sweetness. Wines higher than 14% alcohol are fortified by adding brandy or rectified spirits.

Good wine grapes result from vines that are properly cared for and pruned. Producing an excess of grapes can lead to a poor wine. The weather has much to do with grape quality. There must be enough rain, sun, and other factors to produce a good grape with sufficient sugar. Since sugar develops late in the season, vintners hope for good sun and warmth at that time. Pickers must also use care in selecting the fruit, avoiding green or other poor grapes. Full and juicy grapes make a good wine. To develop maximum sugar, some grapes must be left on the vines until they mold or almost become raisins. The famous sweet German Trockenbeeren Auslese (dry berry, special selection) requires grapes that are left on the vine until they become almost dry. The sweet Sauternes come from Semillon grapes left on the vine until they crack and develop a mold called *botrytis cinerea* or *pourriture noble* (noble mold), which helps to concentrate sugar and flavor. This mold is called *edefäule* on German grapes.

Grapes are stemmed, washed, and crushed at the vinery. Crushing stems and seeds may produce a bitter wine, so it must be done carefully. Crushing with the feet gives about the right pressure. Some very fine wines may be made from juice allowed to run freely from the grapes after crushing. Most wines are made from juice pressed from the grapes after crushing.

Fermentation must be controlled to prevent the development of undesirable aldehydes or acids. The action of yeast can be stopped by sulfur fumes. So, some wines, especially white ones, may have their fermentation stopped by sulfur; but an excess of sulfur may produce an off-flavor in a wine. Sulfur is also used to destroy yeasts in casks and vats.

Red grapes produce red wine, the color coming from the skins. Some bitterness or astringency also comes from the skins. A rosé, or pink, wine, called the wine of the night (vin du nuit), results when the skins are fermented only a short time, usually overnight. A white wine results from white grapes or red grapes with the skins removed after pressing. Some wines may be colored: Port's deep red color comes partially from elderberries added to the must; sweet white wines may have a deep-tan-to-brownish color, the depth of which is usually an indicator of the degree of sweetness of the wine.

After fermentation, the wine is run from vats into casks to age. The fermentation residue, called pomace, may be used for distilling into brandies or to make tartrates, ethyl alcohol, wine vinegar, or other products.

Aging in the cask may be from a few weeks to several years. It is said that wine ages in the cask and matures in the bottle. Bottling largely stops aging. During aging, wine clarifies and increases in brilliance. Flavor also develops partly because of some slight oxidation. Flavors also blend and smooth out in aging, a process called "marrying." Chemical changes may give smoothness and flavor; glycerine develops, which gives smoothness. Aging and maturing can improve wine up to a certain period, after which it declines in quality. Some red Bordeaux (clarets) improve in quality for 20 or even 50 years. A wine still improving in the cask or bottle is said to be "going uphill."

Age does not necessarily indicate wine quality. Some wines are best consumed young, while others are best only after long aging. Normally, white wines last up to 6 or 7 years and should be consumed when 3 to 4 years old. Many red wines are good only after they are 6 or more years old.

Most wines are in the cask during the winter and are bottled in the spring, when a good indication of quality can be gained. Many wine merchants buy in the spring, frequently before the wine is bottled, and may ship in the cask. Some wines are aged best in cellars or rooms at 55°F, while sherry is cooked or aged best in the sun at temperatures from 100 to 140°F. During aging, wines are run off from one cask to another, leaving deposits of lees, tartrates, and so on. Casks are usually kept well filled to prevent undue oxidation and development of wine vinegar. Most European and other countries clarify wine by decanting, but American wines are frequently filtered to produce a high clarity; this filtering is called "finishing." Overaging may give an excessively woody flavor.

Wine Storage

Dry wines in bottles should be stored on their side so the corks do not dry out. Sweet and sparkling wines can be stored standing up. Elevated temperatures, light, dampness, and movement (such as the shaking of the storeroom area from the passage of subway trains or transporting the wine) may harm wine. Inventories should be carefully controlled and excess stocks avoided. The best storage temperature is about 50°F.

Vintages

Many wines carry a date on the label. This usually indicates the year the grapes were grown, the must fermented, and the wine casked. Because growing conditions and other factors can make a difference in wine quality, the date may be important.

A year in which wines are above average in quality may be called a vintage year. Table 10-2 indicates vintage evaluations on some European wines. Because California has a very consistent climate and also blends wines, its wines vary less than those of some other areas of the world. Vintage years will therefore be less common, although the use of a vintage date on the label is increasing.

Types of Wines

There are four types of wines: (1) appetizers, (2) dinner or table wines, red or white, (3) sweet dessert wines, red and white, and (4) sparkling wines. Many kinds exist in each type. Confusion occurs in wine identification because the same wine can be called by different names. Table 10-3 summarizes the common names of wines used in this country. Italicized names after a wine indicate a similar foreign wine or a similar American wine. Wines are named from their geographic origin, from the fruit from which they come, or for some other descriptive reason such as Lacryma Christi (Tears of Christ) or Liebfraumilch (milk of the Beloved Mother) or Egri Bikaver (blood of the ox).

France strictly controls the names of its wines and indicates this on the label with *appellation contrôlée* (name controlled). If a label states *mise du château* or *mis en bouteille au château* the wine must be produced from grapes grown *only* at an estate (vineyard) and the wine must be bottled there. If a label carries a vineyard or town name, the wine must come only from grapes grown there; it must not be blended. If a vintage is claimed, the wine must be of that year. In France the *Institut National des Appellations d'Origine* and the *Service des Fraudes* are bodies empowered to see that the French regulations are observed.

German labels must identify wine by the vintage date, the area where the grapes are grown, and the name of the shipper. Its wine may be estate bottled or bottled on the estate by the shipper, come from a general district

TABLE 10-2
Vintage Chart

	Alsace	Bordeaux Red	Bordeaux White	Burgundy Red	Burgundy White	Champagne	German
1947	****	****	****	****	****	****	***
1948	***	**	**	***	***	**	****
1949	****	****	****	***	**	****	****
1950	***	***	***	***	***	**	***
1951	**	**	**	**	**	**	**
1952	***	****	***	****	****	****	***
1953	***	****	***	****	***	****	****
1954	****	**	**	**	**	**	**
1955	***	****	****	****	***	****	***
1956	**	**	**	**	**	**	**
1957	****	***	***	****	***	**	***
1958	***	***	***	****	****	***	***
1959	****	****	****	****	****	****	****
1960	***	***	***	**	****	**	**
1961	****	****	****	****	****	****	***
1962	****	***	***	****	****	***	***
1963	**	*	*	***	***	**	***
1964	****	****	***	****	****	****	****
1965	—	**	***	*	**	**	**
1966	****	****	****	****	****	****	***
1967	****	****	****	***	***	*	***
1968	*	**	*	*	**	*	***
1969	****	****	****	****	****	****	****
1970	****	****	****	****	****	****	***
1971	****	****	****	****	****	***	****

—Poor
*Fair
**Good
***Very Good
****Excellent
Courtesy Julius Wile Sons & Co.

or township or bear the shipper's label (as some Bordeaux wines do). If a label uses the following terms, they mean:

Auslese (select picking)　　　　*Eigengewächs* (own growth)
Beerenauslese (select grapes)　　*Fass* or *Fuder Nr.* (cask number)
Bestes Fass or *Fuder* (best cask)　*Feine* or *Feinste* (fine or finest)

Gewächs (place of origin)
Hochfeine (of the best)
Kabinett Wein (special wine)
Kellerabfullung (cellar filling)
Kellerabzug (cellar bottling)
Korbrand (brand of the estate)
Kreszenz (growth of)
Nurrein (natural wine, unsugared)

Naturwein (natural wine, unsugared)
Original Abfullung (original filling)
Original Abzug (original bottling)
Slossabzug (chateau or castle bottling)
Spatlese (late picking)
Trockenbeeren (dry berry)
Ungezuckerter wein (natural wine)
Wachstum (place where grown)

The Germans have laws for controlling wine production and allow their wines to be blended and also sugared.

Many other countries do not control their wine industry as do France and Germany, and buyers should purchase wines from those countries with care. They should test purchases before buying and know the reputations of individual shippers or producers. Buyers must also keep up on market conditions, vintages, exchange rates, and price trends.

Sparkling Wines

Sparkling wines result from carbon dioxide gas developed during natural fermentation or from carbonization, the former considered the most desirable method. A still wine, one that lacks bubbles, can be made effervescent by adding carbon dioxide to it under pressure during bottling. To make champagne, a bit of syrup is added to a still wine. The bottle is sealed and inverted, neck down, in a rack to ferment. Each day it is given a good shake. The man who does this wears a mask and gloves because some bottles blow up from the fermenting pressures. This shaking brings sediment down into the neck of the bottle.

During fermentation the added sugar develops alcohol and carbon dioxide gas, which dissolve in the wine. At a desired time the sediment is frozen in the neck of the bottle and removed as a plug. After this, the wine is quickly bottled to retain the gas so that when the bottle is opened and pressure released, carbon dioxide bubbles appear. Some German and other wines may show tiny bubbles in the glass. This is called "spritz," and although it is much less than the effervescence in champagne, it does give a zest to the wine. There are many sparkling wines, and buyers should watch quality carefully. Fine bubbles and continued effervescence indicate a good wine but flavor, clarity, and so on must also be considered.

Judging a Wine

Louis Forest, a famous Parisian gourmet, said, "The tasting of wine begins, like love, with the eyes." Thus, to test a wine, pour some into a clear, white glass and hold it before a white napkin in a well-lighted room. It should be clear, not murky, and have no sediment in it. The color should be true. White wines may be almost colorless, a pale greenish-gold, or almost

TABLE 10-3
A Common Classification of American Wine Types

Appetizer Wines

Sherry (dry to sweet) *(Sherry, Sack, Maderia, Marsala)*
Vermouth (dry to sweet) *(Vermouth)*

Red Dinner Wines

Burgundy	Claret (dry)	Rosé or Grenache (pink, dry
Barbear *(Barbera)*	Cabernet *(Red Bordeaux)*	to sweet) *(Tavel)*
Charbono	Grignolino *(Grignolino)*	Vino Rosso (semisweet)
Gamay *(Beaujolais)*	Zinfandel	Chianti (dry) *(Chianti)*
Pinot Noir *(Burgundy)*		
Red Pinot		

Others: Concord (sweet)

White Dinner Wines

Chablis (dry)	Rhine Wine (dry)	Sauternes (dry to sweet)
Chardonnay *(White*	Riesling *(Rhine)*	Sauvignon Blanc *(Graves)*
Burgundy)	Sylvaner *(Rhine or Alsace)*	(dry to sweet)
Folle Blanche	Traminer *(Alsace)*	Semillon (dry to sweet)
Pino Blanc *(White*		*(Graves)*
Burgundy)		Haut or Chateau
White Pinot *(Loire)*		Sauternes
(White Pinot may also		(sweet) *(Barsacs,*
be labeled Chenin or		*Chateau Y'Chem)*
Pineau)		

Others: White Chianti (dry); Muscat (dry to sweet), Catawba (dry to semisweet), Delaware (dry)
Elvira or Eastern Riesling (not a true Riesling)

Sweet Dessert Wines

Port (red, white, tawny)	Muscatel (red, gold or black)	Tokay
(Port)	Muscat *Frontignon*	Angelica

Sparkling Wines

Champagne (gold or pink)	Sparkling Burgundy (semisweet to sweet)
(brut or extra dry, sec or	
semidry and doux or	
sweet)	

Others: Sparkling Muscat (sweet), Sparkling Rosé (dry to semisweet)

---

a tan; red wines may be pink (rosés) to a light or bright red to almost a purple. Others may be brown, such as a very sweet Marsala, and some may even be somewhat black touched with brown. The color should be typical for the wine.

Next, swirl the wine in the glass to increase the aroma—the wine should be at the proper serving temperature—and then sniff it. It should have a pleasing smell and no off-odor or excessive fermentation smell. The bouquet (aroma) should also be typical of the wine. Now, swish a bit into the mouth. It can be either sweet or dry but should not have an excessively tart or unpleasant taste. Swallow it. It should leave an agreeable taste. The feel of the wine in the mouth, plus inspection in the glass, should indicate the body of the wine. Some wines should be light, such as a white dry Rhine, while a Burgundy should have considerable body. "Finish" relates to the clarity of the wine and its sparkle and brilliance.

Some old red and even some young wines may drop sediment called *lees* into the bottle bottom. Many bottles have a concave bottom to help catch and hold the lees. Decant such a wine before tasting by pouring it *very carefully* into a clean, empty bottle until just a trace of sediment appears in the neck. Do this over a light or a burning candle to see easily into the neck when the lees start to come off.

Some wines must rest after shipment or being moved and may not be tasted for several months. Store dry wines on their sides and when they are moved, move with care.

Rating Chart for Wine Tasting

Type Wine	Color	Bouquet	Aroma	Taste	Body	Finish	Bubbles	Overall	Total	Remarks

Standard form used by many wine societies to evaluate wine.

Foreign Wines

French Wines

France produces a great amount of high-quality wine, which it ships to many other countries. It imports more than it ships, however, but this is a wine of lesser distinction commonly consumed by the French, called *vin ordinaire*.

Fig. 10-3. This worker wears a wire mask when "riddling" Champagne to protect him from glass fragments when an occasional bottle explodes. The riddling process consists of slightly turning and shaking each bottle every day for 6 months. Courtesy Wine Institute of America

Champagne District Wines. The Champagne district is northwest of Paris and south of Reims. The small city of Epernay is in its center. Champagne probably resulted by chance when a monk, Dom Pérignon, bottled a wine that had stopped fermenting probably because it had become chilled, as is common in this northern area of France. However, with the coming of spring, the wine (which still had sugar in it) began to work in the bottle, creating carbon dioxide—which was absorbed as carbonic acid in the wine. When he opened the wine, it showed bubbles that gave the wine wonderful sparkle and zest, prompting him to remark, "I am drinking stars!" Even today it is not unusual for champagne to stop working in the fall and then begin to ferment again in the spring before it is bottled.

Champagne is usually a blend of Chardonnay (white Pinot) and Pinot Noir grapes. A *blanc de blanc* champagne is made only from Chardonnay grapes and has a more delicate flavor and a pale, greenish-gold color. Only the *cuvee* and the *première taille* (first and second pressings) are usually used for champagne. The third and fourth (*duxième taille* and *rebèche*), pressings are used for other wines. After fermentation, the wines are blended in the spring to give the proper qualities and then are bottled. Sugar is added to promote additional fermentation. At the time sediment is disgorged as a frozen plug, additional sugar and perhaps brandy, if the alcoholic content is not sufficient, will be added. This sugar, called *le dosage* or *liqueur d'expédition* (shipping sugar), gives the champagne its sweetness. Labels indicate this sweetness as:

Brut (Nature)*	very dry	½ to 1½% sugar
Extra Sec or Dry	fairly dry	1½ to 3% sugar
Sec or Dry	medium sweet	3 to 5% sugar
Demi Sec	fairly sweet	5 to 7% sugar
Doux	quite sweet	7% or more sugar

Nature on the label should mean that no sugar has been added, but it might not.

No vineyard or estate name appears on a label of champagne unless certain small producers or vineyards decide to produce a small amount from grapes grown only from a limited area. Instead, the company labeling the champagne or shipper is identified on the label. Some of these are known the world over as shippers of the highest quality product. Some will not make champagne in a year when the grapes are poor; others may reserve their wine for blending in years when the grapes are better. In good years nonvintage champagne is made. In very good years vintage champagnes may be made, carrying a date on the label. When the skins on red grapes are left to ferment a short time, a pink, or rosé, champagne is made.

The 10 largest champagne shippers in order of amounts shipped are Moet et Chandon, Mercier, Pommery-Grano, Mumm, Veuve Cliquot, Heidsieck Monopole, Charles Heidsieck, Lanson, Ayala-Montebello Duminy, and Piper-Heidsieck. This omits many shippers of high-quality champagne such as Bollinger, Taittinger, Perrie-Jouet, and Roederer among others.

Some very good French sparkling white wines made by the champagne process cannot be called champagne because they are not produced in the Champagne district, but they are often very good.

The Burgundy District. The French *Côte d'Or* (Golden Slope) district has two distinct areas, the Côte des Nuits and the Côte du Beaune. The Côte des Nuits is famous for its red, rich-bodied wines made from Pinot Noir grapes; it is just south of the Champagne district. It contains many small vineyards that make famous wines such as the Chambertins or the wines of the Clos Vogeout, so prized that one of Napoleon's generals instructed his soldiers to salute when they marched by its vineyards.

Not all red Burgundies are good, and buyers should learn the various vintners and the quality of their product. Some shippers market some mediocre Burgundies. Some wines of the area are named after the commune or parish where they are grown. Some may be not labeled with a vineyard name but just "Côte d'Or" or "bourgogne rouge." In either case, purchase after testing is recommended for these.

The great Chablis wines and others called white Burgundy come from several areas near the Côte d' Or and in the Côte de Beaune. They produce excellent white Chardonnay or white Pinot grapes. The great greenish-gold or yellow wine from these grapes, with a rich body, is world famous. The vineyards les Clos, Pommard, Meursault, Valmur, Montrachet, Aloxe-Corton and others produce high-quality wines most years. Buyers should keep up-to-date, however, on the quality of wine produced each year if they wish to make the best buys.

In addition to these Chablis, the area from Chalon to Lyons produces the famous Maconnais and Beaujolais, dry red wines with less body than Burgundy. They are produced from the famous Gamay grape. These wines do not keep well, but last slightly longer than dry white wines. Few red wines from here are estate bottled since many are blends. The term *supérieur* frequently indicates a wine of better than average quality from the area.

The Rhone District. Just south of the *Côte de Beaune* lies the Rhone River area called the *Côtes du Rhone*. The vineyards of the *Chateauneuf-du-Pape* are in this area. They got the name "new castle of the Pope" because, while the Popes were held prisoners by the French from 1305 to 1377 in nearby Avignon, this vineyard furnished much of the wine consumed at the new Vatican chateau.

The *Côtes du Rhone* produce excellent red and white dinner wines. The Cinsant and Syrrah grapes grow well here and, because of the warmth of the climate, the red wines from them will be deep red with a heavy body and richness of flavor just escaping harshness. Many of the reds throw a heavy sediment, as do the reds from close-by Piedmont in Italy.

The Heritage vineyards of the area are well known for their good reds and whites, especially the reds. The Granache grape grows well around the town of Tavel, which gives its name to the famous pink or rosé wine from the area. Tavels do not hold long and should be used when about 5 years old or less.

The Bordeaux District. The Bordeaux, or Gironde, area is France's most important wine-growing district. It produces the famous red Bordeaux (clarets), the dry, austere Graves, the luscious, golden sweet Sauternes and their close brethren, the Barsacs. Vintage years are common. The red wines of the area come mainly from the Cabernet Sauvignon grapes, sometimes with mixtures of others. The sweet and dry whites both come mainly from the Semillon, the Sauvignon Blanc, and the Muscadelle grapes

Over 4,000 vineyards of the area bottle clarets as *château* (estate) wines. However, many sell their production to Bordeaux merchants who blend and ship under their own labels. Most château-bottled wine has a cork branded with the château name and the year. If it is from a particular château but not bottled there, such as might happen if bottled by a wine merchant, the cork brand will still be used but the words *mise en bouteilles au château* will not be on the label.

A *monopole* brand is a private brand of a shipper, often one upon which he stakes his reputation. Some wines may be labeled only with the name of the district, such as Médoc, Pomerol or St. Emilion. Names that cannot be used unless the wine is from the area named will bear the term *appellation contrôlée* on the label. A wine bearing the name of a district and not a vineyard may be blended from wines from the area. Buyers should learn to know the best shippers and vineyards.

In 1855 many wines from the Gironde were ranked by experts, who put the clarets of 61 vineyards into 5 main classes (or *crus*) and 21 sauternes into two classes. The famous sweet sauternes from the *Château Y'Chem* were put into a class by themselves because they were considered so superior. In some years there may be little difference between the wines of the Gironde vineyards, or they may change relative positions, but they still hold to some degree their 1855 ranks, and buyers can still use this ranking to ascertain the probable quality of the wine. Certainly, clarets from the vineyards of either the first or second class would be almost sure to be good any year.

Miscellaneous French Wine Districts. Another important wine district of France is the Loire, which produces the famous Anjou rosé and some good white wines. Other good reds, rosés, and whites come from around Anjou, such as Vauvray, Touraine, Pouilly, Sancers and Nantais.

Both the Berne and Roussillon areas near the Pyrenees produce some good reds and whites. The Savoy, or Jura, area near Switzerland produces good reds and whites that resemble very much the Italian wines of nearby Lombardy. A Jura white wine called *Château Chalons* is allowed to ferment and age from 7 to 8 years before bottling. It is high in alcohol and lives in the bottle almost as long as the red Bordeaux.

Alsace, near Germany, produces wines much like the German ones and they are put into the tall, slim, light green bottles similar to those of the Moselle area. Many good wines are produced, and the wines of the grape varieties Sylvaner, Riesling, Traminer, Gewuerz-Traminer, and Edelzwicker are considered very good.

Just because a wine comes from France does not mean it is good or even acceptable. Many poor wines come from here but, of course, many of the world's best do too. It is up to buyers to learn how to select the right ones, and knowing a lot about French wines and the year helps.

Fig. 10-4. Wine aging in 1000-gallon oak casks. Courtesy Wine Institute of America

German Wines

Moselle Wines. Excellent wines come from the Moselle area in Germany. They are marketed in tall, slim, green bottles. The best wines come from the middle Moselle, such as Piesporters, Bernkastel Doctor, Zeltingers, and Erdener Treppchen. Their alcoholic content is light, about 8 to 9%, and they keep well for about 6 years. They are fragrant, light, crisp, and dry. As with many other wines a famous name can increase the price, probably over the true value, whereas a wine of equal or almost equal quality produced nearby may sell for much less. Buyers who can locate such lesser-known wines and merchandise them successfully may be able to make better margins.

Rheingau Wines. The Rheingau wine area is northwest of the Rhine river bend as it moves to Coblenz. It includes the adjoining west bank of the Main River, where it flows into the Rhine. Like nearly all German wines, Rheingaus are presented in tall, slim, brown bottles. (Colored glass is often used for dry white wines because light can destroy their quality.) Rheingaus are delicate with a light body and flavor, a fragrant bouquet, and a brilliant sparkle, but are apt to be somewhat austere and hard. They are light in alcohol and may vary in quality from year to year. The label on wines from this area has the name of the township or the word *Schloss* (castle) before the vineyard's name, such as Johannisberger Hölle or Schloss Johannisberg.

Hessian Wines. Another important area is the Rheinhessen, or Hessia, which is on the other side of the bend of the Rhine from Mainz to Worms. The wines are like those of the Rheingau but somewhat softer and richer, and they are apt to have a slightly higher alcoholic content and a heavier bouquet and flavor. *Liebfraumilch* (Milk of the Blessed Mother) is a Hessen wine. When good it is soft, slightly sweet. Most Liebfraumilchs are blends, and poor ones may be heavily sulfured. The wine is apt to be good if it comes from Nierstein, Nackenheim, or Oppenheim under good shippers' labels or if the label indicates grapes from late picking (*spätlese*) or special picking (*auslese*). Many poor wines called Liebfraumilch are marketed in the United States. The true Liebfraumilch comes from vineyards around the Church of Our Beloved Lady (Liebfrauenkirche) in the City of Worms; they will not be labeled Liebfraumilch, but will carry the names of the vineyards, Liebfrauen Stiftswein or Kirchenstük. Niersteiner Domtal is another German-blended wine that can vary considerably in quality.

The best wines of the Hessian area come from near the Rhine or alongside it and should be made from the Sylvaner or Reisling grape. Buyers should learn the town and *lagename* (vineyard name) from which the best wines come and purchase them.

Palatinate Wines. The Rheinpfalz, or Palatinate, area is to the east of the Rhine, south of Hessia, and next to Alsace-Lorraine on the south and west. The Mittel-Hardt area between Neustadt and Bad Dürkheim produces the best wine, especially around Wachenheim, Forst, Deidesheim, Ruppertsberg, Bad Dürkheim, Kallstadt, Leistadt, and Königsbach. The area can ship out poor as well as good wines, however. The best wines have a delicate flavor, rich fruitiness, soft bouquet, and great delicacy. They are less crisp and harsh than the Rheingaus. The famous sweet wines, Beerenausleses, are produced here during years when the grapes become high in sugar and the climate allows them to dry on the vines. These wines are extremely high in price but usually worth it. The poorest wines from this area are coarse, lack flavor, and may taste heavily from the soil (described by the term *bodengeschmack*).

Miscellaneous Wines. Three other German wines deserve mention. Steinwein (stein wine), Moselblümchen (little Moselle flower), and Hock. The first is a Sylvaner or Reisling white wine produced near Würzburg and marketed in the flat, flasklike Bocksbeutel; some Chilean Sylvaner or Reisling imitations may be marketed in a similar bottle. It should more truly be called a Frankenweine, which is light, dry, delicate, and well-balanced, with a more substantial body than most German wines.

Moselbümchen is a generic wine, blended usually from poor Moselles. It is usually sugared and has the heavy aftertaste found in sugared wines.

Hock is the word *Hockheimer,* which the English shortened and today may mean almost any German wine. (Some American wines that resemble the German ones today may also be called Hock.) This wine is a good, substantial, delicate German wine and should not be confused with the wines from the Hock vineyards in Bodenheim in Hessia. Sparkling Hock and sparkling Moselle are Sekts *(Schaumweins);* for their quality, they sell at a low price compared with champagnes. Some have a heavy aftertaste and a sweet flavor that results from liberal sugaring.

Italian Wines.

Italy produces a number of good wines, but the Italians have never been as fussy as the French and Germans about vintages, bottling requirements, wine identification, and so on. Buyers, therefore, will not be able to depend on a general set of standards established to assure quality in the Italian wines, as they can for French and German wines. They must instead depend more on the reputation of a specific wine and its quality, determined after a careful check of the wine itself. Certain wines have developed international reputations, but frequently these can vary from year to year. For instance, Chianti has such a reputation; but *all* Chiantis are not good and one must know the shipper and what he produced in a specific year. Buyers will usually find the wines from northern Italy more dependable than those from the south. This is because the grapes in the south develop considerable sugar and flavor from the warmth and sun. This makes them produce a heady wine with considerable bouquet, aroma, and flavor and one usually high in alcohol. The colors are apt to be intense, deep in the reds and straw-colored in the whites.

Northern Wines. The most famous wine of the Piedmont area in northern Italy is the Barolo, a wine of ruby-red color, full body, and a soft, velvety, rich flavor that is said to have the taste of a rosé and the aroma of a violet. It is bottled in a Burgundy-type bottle and lives for a long time; but like many of the Italian reds from the area it is apt to develop considerable lees, requiring that it be decanted before using. This in no way detracts from its quality. The Barbaresco is a lighter red wine resembling a claret but slightly richer. It is marketed in a Bordeaux wine bottle. The Barbera is not as good as the Barolo and although deep-colored, full-flavored, and full-bodied, it is somewhat astringent and harsh. It does not hold up well and should be consumed when young. The Freisa is a lighter red wine that has a raspberry bouquet—hence its name, which translates "raspberry." It is slightly sweet and may possess some effervescence or frizzance. Cortese Bianco, or Gavi, is a white, pale, light wine with a fresh flavor and delicate bouquet. It should be consumed when young.

The Italian champagne, which is sweet, is called *Spumante* (meaning "foaming"). Asti Spumante is a sweet sparkling wine with the rich flavor of the Muscat grape. It is one of the finest of Italian wines. A Gran Spumante is less sweet, and it also is bottle-fermented.

TABLE 10-4
Sizes of Wine Containers

Tank cars (1 to 6 compartments)	6,000 to 10,000 gal
Puncheon	84 to 160 gal
Pipe	117 to 140 gal
Butt	100 to 140 gal
Barrel (average)	50 gal
Half-barrel (average)	25 gal
Kegs	15, 10, 5, 3, 2, and 1 gal
Demijohns	4.9, 3, and 2 gal
Gallon jug	128 fluid oz
Half-gallon jug or bottle	64 fluid oz
Magnum	52 fluid oz
Quart	32 fluid oz
Vermouth bottle	30 fluid oz
Chianti bottle	30 fluid oz
Four-fifths quart ("fifth")	25.6 fluid oz
Three-fourths quart	24 fluid oz
Champagne bottle	24 to 26 fluid oz
Champagne half-bottle	12 to 13 fluid oz
Pint	16 fluid oz
Four-fifths pint (half-bottle or "tenth")	12.8 fluid oz
Three-fourths pint (half-bottle)	12 fluid oz
Dinner wine splits	6 and 6.4 fluid oz
Chianti split	8 fluid oz
Champagne splits	6.2 and 8 fluid oz
Miniatures	2, 3, and 4 fluid oz

The area north of Milan at the Swiss border, called Valtellina, produces some good red wines. They may be called by this name or by the names of Sassella, Grumello, Inferno, Grigioni, or Fracia, which are the best vineyards in the area (near the town of Sondrio). Their red color has a blackish cast. They are well-developed wines and usually improve slowly in the bottle.

The area around Venice and Verona produces the fine, dry, suave, straw-colored Soave, wine that is marketed in light green, slim bottles

Wine ... CROWNING TOUCH TO YOUR DINING PLEASURE

Food and wine are the perfect marriage — even a sandwich takes on special magic when wine accompanies it. Here are the wine-and-food combinations we believe you'll enjoy. But there are no rules. Try any wine, and see how much pleasure it adds to your favorite dish!

APPETIZER WINES

BEFORE YOUR MEAL: *As a cocktail, or with appetizers or soup*

Order No.			Glass
1	Sherry, Brand Name	(Calif.)	$.00
2	Dry Sherry, Brand Name	(Calif.)	.00
3	Dry Sherry, Brand Name	(Spain)	.00
4	Vermouth-on-the-Rocks, Brand Name	(Calif.)	.00

RED DINNER WINES

WITH HEARTY DISHES: *Such as steak, roast beef, chops or Italian dishes*

Order No.			½ Bottle for 2	Bottle for 4
10	Burgundy, Brand Name	(Calif.)	$.00	$0.00
11	Pinot Noir (Burgundy), Brand Name	(Calif.)	.00	0.00
12	Claret, Brand Name	(Calif.)	.00	0.00
13	Cabernet (Claret), Brand Name	(Calif.)	.00	0.00
14	Zinfandel, Brand Name	(Calif.)	.00	0.00
15	Chianti, Brand Name	(Calif.)	.00	0.00

WHITE DINNER WINES

WITH LIGHTER DISHES: *Such as fish, chicken, sweetbreads or omelets*

Order No.			½ Bottle for 2	Bottle for 4
20	Chablis, Brand Name	(Calif.)	$.00	$0.00
21	Pinot Blanc (Chablis), Brand Name	(Calif.)	.00	0.00
22	Riesling, Brand Name	(Calif.)	.00	0.00
23	Sylvaner, Brand Name	(Calif.)	.00	0.00
24	Sauterne, Brand Name	(Calif.)	.00	0.00
25	Semillon (Sauterne), Brand Name	(Calif.)	.00	0.00

ROSÉ (Pink) WINES

WITH ALL FOODS: *Luncheon or Dinner*

Order No.			½ Bottle for 2	Bottle for 4
30	Rosé, Brand Name	(Calif.)	$.00	$0.00
31	Rosé, Brand Name	(Calif.)	.00	0.00
32	Vin Rosé, Brand Name	(Calif.)	.00	0.00

SPARKLING WINES

PERFECT ANYTIME: *To make any meal a festive occasion*

Order No.			½ Bottle for 2	Bottle for 4
40	Champagne Brut (Dry), Brand Name	(Calif.)	$0.00	$0.00
41	Champagne Sec (Medium), Brand Name	(Calif.)	0.00	0.00
42	Champagne, Brand Name	(France)	0.00	0.00
43	Pink Champagne, Brand Name	(Calif.)	0.00	0.00
44	Sparkling Burgundy, Brand Name	(Calif.)	0.00	0.00

DESSERT WINES

AFTER DINNER: *With cheese or coffee*

Order No.			Glass
50	Port, Brand Name	(Calif.)	$.00
51	Muscatel, Brand Name	(Calif.)	.00

Fig. 10-5. The format for a wine list recommended by the Wine Advisory Board for the use of those who do not know wine selection. Courtesy Wine Institute of America

similar to those used for Alsace wines and the velvety, fruity, delicate-bodied, subtle red wine called Valpolicella. Both should be consumed fairly young. A Lambrusco is produced near Bologna. It is a subtle, red, sparkling wine.

Five communes in Tuscany are controlled by an association that enforces certain wine standards and produces Chianti Classico, identified by the black-and-gold seal with the black cock inside; Classico is usually reliable. Another group, using as an identification mark a white Della Robbia angel *(putto)*, produces a chianti usually above average in quality. Also, Chiantis from the Brolio vineyard or from the Rufina, Montalbano, Colli Fiorentini, and Colli Pisani areas are usually good. The best chiantis are not marketed in the straw-covered flasks, but in bottles shaped like the Bordeaux wine bottle. Buyers should select chiantis carefully because there are many poor ones marketed in attractive straw-covered flasks. Chianti is not a subtle wine and is somewhat fiery, harsh, and rough with a rich, full body and somewhat tart flavor. A white chianti is also produced. The Tuscany area also produces a light, dry wine called Vernaccia di San Gimignano of delicate freshness. The rich, sweet Vin Santo also comes from there.

The wine Est Est Est got its name when a bishop sent his valet ahead to taste the wines of the area just north of Rome. When he tasted it, he exclaimed "Est! Est! Est!" ("It is! It is! It is!"). Evidently, the bishop also found it so because tradition has it that upon arriving he consumed so much he died. It is a golden wine with a rich, delightful bouquet and a pleasing flavor. The sweet Est Est Est is considered superior to the dry one.

Southern Wines. Lacryma Christi (Tears of Christ) comes from the Vesuvius area near Naples and is a soft, slightly sweet, pale gold, aromatic wine. A red, rather inferior, wine with the same name is also made. Most wines produced from south of Naples are rather ordinary. But Sicily has several famous wines. For example, the Corvino from the white grapes grown on the slopes of Mt. Etna is a fine, dry, white wine with a somewhat fiery character. Sicily also produces some good wines from the muscat grape, especially the great Marsala, which has a character somewhat like cream sherry or Madiera.

Spanish Wines

Sherry comes from around Jerez, Spain, usually from Palomino grapes. It is a blend of aged and lesser-aged wines. Three casks of sherry are usually placed one on the other, called the Solera. The bottom one contains aged sherry; the middle cask, sherry of a lesser age; and the top cask, young sherry. Aging in the casks is in the sun, which makes the wine warm and ripens it. After withdrawing from a third to half of the bottom cask's contents for bottling, wine from the second cask is drawn down into the bottom one and the second is filled from the top one. A period of sun-ripening again occurs. When the top cask is empty, another one filled with young wine is placed there.

All sherries are dry, but are made sweet and deeper in color by adding a desirable amount of grape juice reduced to a heavy syrup by boiling. The blending of sherries takes great skill. Brandy is added to bring 13 to 14% sherries to 17 to 20% alcoholic content. Sherries are classified by their color and degree of sweetness. This classification is:

Manzanilla*	Pale and light bodied	Very dry
Fino	Very pale with more body	Very dry
Amontillado	Golden with some body, nutty	Dry
Amoroso	Golden to light amber, some body	Medium dry
Oloroso†	Deep golden to tan, full body	Sweet
Cream	Deep tan to brown, full body	Very sweet

*Some aged Manzanillas become dark and quite high in alcoholic content.
†This may also be called "cream sherry."

Spain also produces some excellent dry white wines and some very good dry reds, but buyers should know what they are buying before purchasing them. Most of these come from north Spain near the Gironde area of Bordeaux and are called *Riojas*, from the district where produced, regardless of whether they are red or white.

Portuguese Wines

Portugal's most famous wine is Port, which is a sweet, fortified wine. In certain years a vintage port is produced. Ruby and tawny ports are aged in wood. Tawny port changes color and flavor during aging, becoming less sweet and a brownish-purple less intense color. A crusted port is an aged port of a single year. Most ports are blends. A white port is produced from white grapes.

Only wines produced in the upper Douro River region can be called Port. Some other red sweet wines of quality and nature similar to Port are called "Lisbon wines." Portugal is also marketing a fairly large quantity of sparkling rosés, such as Mateus or Lancer's. A delicate, fragrant, slightly tart white wine called Vinho Verde, which should be consumed young, is also well liked.

Hungarian Wines

Hungary produces the famous sweet wine called Tokaj Azu often called the "wine of emperors." It is made from dry sweet grapes much the same as the German trockenbeerenauslese grapes. They also mold, so the wine has somewhat the flavor of a Sauterne. There are two other dessert Tokays, but they are not as sweet. Hungary produces some excellent dry whites and reds. A dry red wine having a splendid bouquet, rich flavor, and full body is Egri Bikaver (bull's blood). Many Hungarian dry whites resemble those of the Rhine but are slightly richer in flavor and have more body.

Other Wines

Switzerland, Chile, Argentina, Austria, Czechoslovakia, Greece, the Balkans, Israel, the Middle East countries, Africa, Australia, Madeira, and others produce some good wines. Buyers who know wines and how to couple them with a good merchandising program can build a profitable offering of such wines and at the same time please customers. For the quality presented, they are usually much lower in cost than some of the better-known wines of the world.

American Wines

California. Within a 50-mile radius from San Francisco, some of the finest wines in the world are produced. For the most part they come from European grape varieties, and they resemble the wines of Europe. California has an even climate, so its grapes are much the same each year. For this reason vintage years are not as common as in Europe, but some vintners are beginning to date wines in better-than-average years. Because of the continued growing demand for wine in this country, California and other American wines have increased greatly in price. Plantings are also much, much heavier.

Buyers would be advised to purchase California and other American wines on their own characteristics rather than try to find wines that duplicate imports. Also, buyers should purchase domestic wines differently than they do imports. A wine listed as "Pinot Noir" in this country is apt to be a better one than one listed "Burgundy": When the name of the grape is on the label 51% or more must come from that grape, whereas using a generic name means the wine may only be an imitation of a Burgundy—and a poor one at that.

The Napa Valley, north of San Francisco, produces some red wines resembling Bordeaux. The Sonoma Valley, just north and west of San Francisco, produces some heavy-bodied reds; they are excellent Burgundy-like wines if they come from Pinot Noir grapes. The white dinner wines from these areas are also good, as are some of the champagnes. The Livermore area, just east of San Francisco, produces some excellent dry white wines as well as reds. The dessert wines are also of good quality. Just south of San Francisco around Santa Clara, San Benito, and Santa Cruz, some good reds and whites plus dessert wines and champagne are produced. Because of the greater warmth and sunshine, the best wines of the central and southern California areas are dessert wines, but some acceptable dry whites and reds and some champagnes are produced.

California produces some sherries from Palomino grapes using the *solera* process. However, most California sherries are not sun-baked, but are heated during aging to temperatures as high as 140°F. This gives them their nutty flavor and deepened color. California also produces some good brandies.

Buyers should note whether an American champagne they are considering for purchase is made by the natural process (bottle-fermented) or is artificially carbonized by adding gas to it. The former is considered much better.

Eastern Wines. The Finger Lake region, the area along the Hudson River, and the high country in Sullivan County of New York produce excellent wines. New York champagnes from the Finger Lake region compete in quality with the French product, although they may have a slight foxy flavor from the American grape used. In the United States any sparkling wine can be called champagne, even red, if it is bottle-fermented for sparkle and bears on the label its place of origin (e.g., "New York State Champagne").

In Ohio, along Lake Erie from Sandusky to Cleveland, another good wine-producing region exists. The wines from this area are light, well-balanced, and pleasant. Both red and white wines are produced, dry and sweet, but perhaps the whites are slightly superior. A few islands in Lake Erie produce a very high quality of wine that is considered some of the best in this country.

Michigan produces a considerable quantity of wine, but only a few of its wines are of sufficient quality to compete with some of the better American or European wines. Missouri, Virginia, Delaware, Tennessee, and the southern Atlantic states also produce some wine; Virginia and Delaware produce some very good semisweet wines. Some good champagnes produced around St. Louis are a blend of American grapes of the region and European grapes from California or wine from California.

The American grape is used substantially for all wines, outside of California, and so the flavor is that of the *labrusca,* with some foxiness because of it. Many people do not object to this, however. It is also true that the middle and eastern wine-growing areas import each year a considerable quantity of California grapes (which are of the European variety) or California wines and thus reduce some of the foxy flavor in their own wines.

Wine Merchandising

Much wine is shipped in barrels, railroad tank cars, or tank trucks to distant bottling points. It is also becoming more common to ship imports in casks or other large quantities and then bottle them after shipment. This shipment saves costs and avoids precipitation of sediment in the bottle that sometimes occurs in shipping. Some states prohibit the sale of wines from bulk sales, while some may allow a food service to dispense it in bulk or in carafes or bottles. Wine is sold in food services as follows:

Glass 2 to 6 oz	Magnum 52 oz	Rehoboam 156 oz
Fifth ¹/₅ wine gal	Double Magnum	Methusaleh 208 oz
Tenth ¹/₁₀ wine gal	(Jeroboam) 104 oz	Salmanazar 312 oz
	Tappit-hen 128 oz	Balthazar 416 oz
		Nebuchadnezzar 520 oz

The larger bottles of wine are used only for special occasions. Occasionally an operation may dispense wine in a pitcher or other such container. Carafes are usually in ¼, ½, or 1 or more liters. The fine line at the top indicates the level to which the wine must be poured. Italian carafes must also bear the official imprint of the Italian government, the metal stamp encased in the glass. The imprint indicates the quantity the container holds.

Wine Storage

Wine should be stored at around 55°F. A storage area 5 ft high and 7 ft long holds about 40 cases of wine. Shelves should be 18 to 24 in. deep and divided into bins so wines can be located and identified quickly. The Wine Advisory Board, 717 Market Street, San Francisco 94103, will assist buyers in setting up standards for stock and stockrooms, as well as give valuable information on merchandising and selling wines.

BIBLIOGRAPHY

Adams, Leon D., *The Commonsense Book of Wine,* David McKay Co., New York, 1958.

Allen, H. Warner, *Sherry and Port,* Constable, London, 1952.

Allen, H. Warner, *White Wines and Cognac,* Constable, London, 1952.

Allen, H. Warner, *Natural Red Wines,* Constable, London, 1952.

Allen, H. Warner, *A Contemplation of Wine,* Michael Joseph, London, 1951.

Amerine, M. A. and W. V. Cruess, *The Technology of Wine Making*, Avi Publishing Co., Westport, Conn., 1960.

Berry, Charles Walter, *In Search of Wine*, Constable, London, 1935.

Bode, Charles G., *Wines of Italy*, McBride Co., New York, 1956.

Campbell, Ian Maxwell, *Reminiscences of a Vintner*, Chapman & Hall, London, 1950.

Churchill, Creighton, *A Notebook for the Wines of France*, Alfred A. Knopf, New York, 1961.

Consumers Union, *Report on Wines and Spirits*, Mt. Vernon, N.Y., 1962.

Fisher, M. F. K., *The Story of Wine in California*, University of California Press, Berkeley.

Grossman, Harold J., *Grossman's Guide to Wines, Spirits and Beers*, Charles Scribner's Sons, New York, 1955.

Grossman, Harold J., *Practical Bar Management*, Ahrens, New York, 1959.

Hyams Edward, *The Wine Country of France*, J. B. Lippincott, Philadelphia, 1960.

Jacquelin, L. and R. Poulain, *The Wines and Vineyards of France*, G. P. Putnam & Sons, New York, 1962.

Layton, T. A., *Choose Your Wine*, Gerald Duckworth & Co., New York, 1949.

Lichine, Alexis, *Wines of France*, 3rd ed., Alfred A. Knopf, New York, 1960.

Massee, William Edman, *Massee's Wine Handbook*, Doubleday, Garden City, N.Y., 1961.

Nelville, John, *Guide to California Wines*, Doubleday, Garden City, N.Y., 1955.

Postgate, Raymond, *The Plainman's Guide to Wine*, Dolphin Books, Garden City, N.Y., 1961.

Saintsbury, George, *Notes on a Cellar-book*, 3rd ed., Macmillan, New York, 1963.

Schoonmaker, Frank, *Encyclopedia of Wine*, Hastings House, New York, 1964.

Shand, P. Morton, *A Book of French Wines*, 2nd Rev. ed., Alfred A. Knopf, New York, 1960.

Shepherd, C. W., *Wines, Spirits and Liqueurs*, Abelard, Schuman Ltd., New York, 1959.

Simon, Andre L., *The History of Champagne*, Ebury Press, London, 1962.

Simon, Andre L., *The Noble Grapes and the Great Wines of France*, McGraw-Hill, New York, 1961.

Simon, Andre L., *Guide to Good Food and Wines*, Colins, London, 1960.

Simon, Andre L., *A Dictionary of Wines, Spirits and Liqueurs*, Herbert Jenkins, London, 1958.

Storm, John, *An Invitation to Wines*, Simon and Schuster, New York, 1955.

Street, Julian, *Wines*, Rev. ed., Alfred A. Knopf, New York, 1948.

Todd, William J., *Handbook of Wine*, Jonathan Cape, London, 1922.

Vizetelly, Henry, *Facts About Champagne*, Ward, Lock and Co., London, 1879.

Wagner, Philip M., *American Wines and Wine-Making,* Alfred A. Knopf, New York, 1956.

Waugh, Alec, *In Praise of Wine,* Wm. Sloane Assoc., New York, 1959.

Wine Advisory Board, *Wine Advisory Board Handbooks,* San Francisco, Calif., various dates.

Winkler, A. J., *General Viticulture,* University of California Press, Berkeley, 1962.

11
Nonfood Supplies

A food service requires many things other than food if it is to operate adequately, and a substantial amount of money must be spent for them. Equipment is needed to produce the food; the proper tableware, napery, furniture, and other items must be purchased if the food is to be attractively presented. A facility must assure those who eat the food that it is not only safe to eat, but clean, and that the facility itself is kept in a clean sanitary condition. Supplies are needed to do this properly. Workers must also be neat and clean and wear attractive apparel. Flooring and walls, as well as furniture, should be carefully selected and well maintained. Many other items needing purchase are included in the nonfood category.

It takes a knowledge of what is required and how to select the best of such supplies to obtain maximum performance. As in buying food, there is much to know and one must be able to search the market and evaluate offerings. This chapter, therefore, presents a broad summary of some of the information needed for a buyer to do an adequate job of purchasing nonfood items.

CLEANING AND SANITIZING

"Clean" and "sanitary" are not quite the same. Normally, when we say something is clean we imply it is sanitary, but we may sometimes call something clean when it is not sanitary. An eating utensil, for instance, might appear quite clean and yet harbor harmful, unseen bacteria. A plate might not appear clean because it shows egg left from breakfast after it is washed; but it might be completely sanitary and safe to eat from because, in the final rinse in the dishwasher, the temperature was sufficient to destroy any bacteria. Therefore, in deciding on which cleaning compounds to purchase, a buyer must know the cleaning and sanitary requirements. It is important that dishwashing compounds do a good job of cleaning, but they should also aid in sanitizing. A food facility might not need to purchase a cleaning compound that will sanitize a floor completely, but a hospital will have to have one that not only does a good job of cleaning the floor but sanitizes it as well.

Soil on items is removed not by one but by a number of factors working together. If soil can be moistened it softens and is more easily removed, or the water dissolves the soil so it can be washed away. Therefore, many cleaning compounds contain substances that help water enter into soil more quickly. Fats and oils resist water so solvents that dissolve them, such as carbon tetrachloride, naphtha, benzene, or other organic solvents may be used. Special substances may be added to increase the ability of a cleaner to remove soil more easily, such as a special compound in a detergent that removes wax from a floor while cleaning it.

Some solvents work more quickly if they are warm, but a buyer must be sure that he does not purchase something which, when warmed, could be dangerous. Thus, warming benzene or alcohol over a burner could result in a dangerous fire. It is best to eliminate such items and use others. Carbon tetrachloride is nonflammable and an excellent solvent for fats and oils, for instance.

Many individuals think that suds indicate a good cleaning solution. This is not true. In some cases suds can reduce the cleaning impact, the sudsy solution not soaking items nearly as well as one that has no suds at all. Technically, soil is moistened quickly if the surface tension or the resistance soil has to the penetration of water or other cleaning substances can be broken down. This is often an important factor to look for in a cleaning compound.

Certain chemical reactions can also remove soil. For instance lye or other alkaline substances saponify fats and oils, that is, they join with them to make soap. Too much saponification, however, can create so many suds in a dishwasher that effectiveness of sprays and pumps is reduced. Other substances will emulsify fats and oils. This means they will assist in dividing them into small particles so they remain suspended in water. Other substances, such as egg protein or other proteins, peptize soil; that is, the substance partially digests or changes the chemical structure so the item is much more easily put into solution as a colloid. Other compounds ionize soil; ionization is a process in which the soil is given an electrical charge that makes it attracted to other substances so it can be pulled away from the item to be cleaned.

Many cleaning substances contain compounds that keep soil away from an item once soil is removed from it. Thus, we may remove soil from dishes and then have in the cleaning compound a substance that grabs onto the soil and does not let it get back on the dishes. Such compounds are called chelating or sequestering compounds. (A "chela" is the pincher claw of a lobster or crab, and "sequester" means to hide away.)

However, after we do everything we can to make a cleaning compound as effective as possible, one more factor is required: physical force to remove the soil. Actually, in cleaning dishes in a dishwasher, about 30% of the work is done by the cleaning agent and 70% by the physical force exerted by water forced through sprays. Water and the cleaning agent can help prepare the soil for removal, but mechanical force must then remove it.

Water in Cleaning

While water is an excellent solvent, it must be properly conditioned if it is to be most effective in cleaning. If a water is hard, that is, if it contains a large number of alkaline salts, it will lack effectiveness as a cleaning agent because many of the mineral salts in the water combine chemically with the cleaning compound, destroying its soil-removing properties. (Water is hard if it contains 10 grains of hard-water salts per gallon; if it contains 17 grains per gallon, it is quite hard. Or, water is hard if it contains 171 parts per million (ppm) of hard-water salts.) Hard water can also leave a film or spots on cleaned items that make the items appear soiled. This is what has happened when dishes, glasses, or silverware are spotted after having been cleaned.

Hard water can also deposit many of its mineral salts on equipment or in pipes. This reduces the effectiveness of the equipment and eventually plugs up the pipes. Such deposits are called "scale." They are a whitish substance seen inside a dishwasher or on a pan in which hard water was heated. Such scale must be removed.

Extremely soft water is called "metal hungry," which means that it can eat up some metals. It is necessary to treat some water frequently so it will not be too hard or too soft. We use phosphate, sodium-exchange, resin, or other types of water-softening compounds to make water soft. Or, we may have to treat extra-soft water so it will not attack metals. When scale becomes a problem in equipment, we may use descaling compounds that dissolve and remove these hard-water salts.

Cleaning Substances

A soap is a chemical mixture of a fat and an alkali. Soaps are used much less today than previously because there are many chemical compounds that do a better and more specialized job of cleaning. These compounds are called *detergents,* and they usually contain substances that are either soil removers or water softeners or both. The most commonly used substances in detergents are the following:

Soil Removers

1. Silicates
   a. sodium metasilicate
   b. sodium sesquisilicate
   c. sodium orthosilicate

2. Carbonates
   a. sodium carbonate (soda ash or washing soda)
   b. sodium bicarbonate (baking soda)

3. Phosphates
   a. trisodium phosphate (TSP)
   b. chlorinated trisodium phosphate*

4. Caustics
   a. sodium hydroxide (lye or caustic)

Water Conditioners

1. Sodium hexametaphosphate
2. Sodium tripolyphosphate
3. Tetrasodium pyrophosphate

4. Sodium tetraphosphate
5. Tetrasodium salt of ethylene-diamine-tetra-acetic acid

*The chlorine, around 2% of total ingredients, acts as a sanitizer in the washing process; this, coupled with sanitizing in the rinsing, assures a better bacterial kill.

Most soaps and detergents are alkaline, and frequently they will contain a sufficient amount of these to give a rather strong alkaline reaction. Some dish-washing detergents may have a pH of 11 or more, and these can be dangerous if they get on the body or into the eyes. Because they are highly corrosive to brass, bronze, and aluminum, much milder agents must be used on these.

Some cleaning agents are buffered to reduce their corrosive action. An agent used for the hand-washing of pots and pans should not have a pH of over 9 or 10. Dangerous products must be labeled with the amount of active ingredients they contain and worded so that users will understand they are using a product that might be harmful. Some pot and pan and other detergents have a color reactor that changes when the cleaning properties of the detergent are exhausted.

The cost of dish-washing has been said to be 7% detergent, 8% hot water, 19% breakage, 16% equipment, and 50% labor. Automatic dispensers may be advisable on some cleaning equipment to give a steady, even flow of detergent. They may also reduce costs by preventing excessive doses and may improve job efficiency.

Liquid, powder, or other types of cleaners are used for special cleaning jobs. Abrasive powders should contain inert scouring substances that do not scratch (or do so only lightly) a glass plate when rubbed vigorously on it. They should have a pH of 5 (slightly acid) to 11.5 and should rinse easily after use.

Various floorings require specific types of cleaners, and buyers should ascertain the proper type. For instance, some asphalt and rubber may be attacked by some types of solvents.[1] Any cleaner used should clean well, dilute easily, mix readily with water, and rinse easily leaving no residue or film. Most should have low-foaming properties, and sanitizing substances may be desirable in some of them. A wax stripper should be easily diluted and applied, possess low-foaming characteristics, rinse well, and leave no residue that interferes with cleaning or repolishing. Oils or other substances used on dusting or floor mops should not leave a slippery film or other undesirable residue. Floor polishes should have nonslip properties and be self-polishing or need buffing. A solid floor polish should contain not less than 16% solids and a liquid type, not less than 12%. Polishes should protect floors against abrasion and water spotting; give a high, durable luster that stands up under heavy traffic; and be resistant to heel-marking and soil. They should not powder or pile up under traffic.

Vinyl floors usually do not need waxing because they have a soft luster that is little improved with additional waxing. Select a mild liquid or other shampoo for cleaning rugs and furniture. It should clean soil away quickly and easily and not injure the fabric, backing, or colors. It is desirable for a rug cleaner to give antisoiling properties and a longer-lasting luster to a fabric. In most institutions, shampoos used with a rotary electric brush can be labor saving. Some good powder or flake cleaners are efficient in removing inert soil.

Furniture polishes should impart a soft luster and be resistant to the action of water or alcohol. They should not be oily or greasy nor attract or hold dust; they should have a pleasant odor and be antistatic and nonflammable—giving a good, long-lasting luster to the wood.

Laundry Cleaners

Some facilities may operate laundries. It has even been found economical to install a small home-type washer and dryer in a foodservice to wash dishcloths, towels, and other light items. In larger units, a larger laundry may be operated and highly specialized substances will be required. Pur-

---

[1]The Rubber Manufacturers' Association and the Asphalt and Vinyl Asbestos Tile Institute will advise on proper types of detergents to use. The Institutional Research Council (221 West 57 Street, New York City 10019) can also be very helpful in giving advice on cleaning agents and in indicating what good specifications for them should contain.

veyors who sell laundry supplies can be helpful in indicating the most desirable items for solving specialized problems.

Some common stain-removal agents are sodium hydrosulfite or sodium-sulfoxalate-formaldehyde. Detergents are usually tallow or low-titer (mild) soaps that work well in softened water. They should not be harmful to polyester or other natural or chemical fibers. Soak fabrics in them to test them. Other detergents needed to give a more vigorous cleaning action may contain sodium metasilicate, sodium sesquisilicate, sodium orthosilicate, and TSP either together or singly. For milder needs, an anionic detergent containing allyarylsulfonates or sulfonated alcohols will be used. If the items to be washed are greasy, a carboxylated methyl-cellulose (CMC) will be used; when the fabric will not be harmed, caustic soda or bentonite clays are used. Most laundries use a sodium hypochlorite bleach or a high-test powdered hypochlorite with about 70% available chlorine. For white cottons, a bleach containing dichloro-di-methyl-hyantoin and trichloro-isocyanine acid is good. To remove alkaline substances remaining after rinsing, an acid compound called a "sourer" will be used; these are either sodium-, ammonium-, or zinc-fluorosilicate or ammonium fluoride. Some types of fabrics are harmed if they are allowed to have any alkaline substance left in them after washing.

TABLEWARE

The "top of the table" presented by an establishment makes an important contribution to its general decor and merchandising effort. Food that is attractively presented with bright, sparkling, clean glassware, silverware, and dishes of suitable design and color is much more appealing than food which is not as suitably placed before a consumer. Intense colors such as green, yellow, brown, or orange may decrease appeal, while soft colors or white can enhance it.

The quantity of tableware needed depends on a number of factors. An operation having a fast turnover will need more dishes than a club where leisurely dining occurs. The speed at which items are washed and returned to service may be another factor. If needs are calculated on the number of seats and if the dining area is never fully filled, a higher-than-necessary inventory might be carried. A reserve must be carried, and its size usually depends on how long it takes to get replacements after they are ordered and also whether or not management is willing to tie up the capital required to carry it.

The number and type of menu items served and how frequently they are selected are also influential factors in deciding what and how much is needed. For example, it is not necessary to have an oyster fork for every seat in the house if only a few orders are sold at a time.

Many operations try to use one type of item for as many purposes as possible. Thus, a bar may eliminate stem cocktail glasses and serve most of its drinks in footless, old-fashioned glasses or roly-poly glasses. A common dinner fork can be used for salads and desserts as well. An 8-oz grapefruit bowl can be used for fruit, dessert, salad and even small servings of soup; a 6¼-in. plate can be used for salads, bread and butter, and desserts.

Other factors may be important. For instance, one cafeteria system found that it could reduce breakage by nearly 25% if it carried enough tableware to carry it through a whole meal without washing any dishes.

Dishes

Various ceramics are used for table services. Some facilities trying to create a certain atmosphere may use earthenware or pottery, but most will use china or porcelain. Earthenware (terra cotta, brick, or flower-pot ware) is clay-baked to around 1000°F into an unvitrified, soft, porous, and coarse product. It shatters easily and is usually made of low-grade clay. Pottery is the same thing, but is baked to a higher temperature. Stoneware is baked to around 2200°F, which vitrifies it or makes it into a solid, completely fused product like porcelain. It is usually used for small casseroles, storage crocks, mixing bowls, and so on.

China is porcelain, a high-grade refined clay, baked to around 2500°F. It is completely fused or vitrified. It must be resilient and withstand sharp shocks and raps. It should be able to be heated to 347°F in a dry oven, removed, and plunged into 68°F water immediately and not shatter. The ratio of water to china in this test should be 8:1. No crazing, cracks, or other defects should appear after this test. A broken piece of porcelain at least 2½ in. square should not absorb more than 0.03% of its weight in water when boiled in water 5 hrs and soaked in cold water 20 hrs more. Federal standards for taking a blow or rap of a specified intensity in foot-pounds on the body or edge are indicated in the following table:

Type Dish	Body Impact Ft-Lb	Type Dish	Body Impact Ft-Lb	Edge Impact Ft-Lb
Bowls	0.30	Mugs	0.30	
Fruit dishes	0.24	Platters, saucers, plates		
Cups to 8 oz	0.06	with plain edges	0.18	0.10
Cups over 8 oz	0.10	Platters, saucers, plates		
		with rolled edges	0.20	0.15

The strength of a ceramic depends upon the quality of its clay and how it is processed. Bubbles, impurities, or poor mixing or blending can produce weak spots. A good china clay should be 40% kaolin, 6% ball clay (for plasticity), 18% flint or ground quartz (for strenth), 15% feldspar (to give good fusing or vitrifying), and 1% whiting. If aluminum oxide replaces the flint or quartz, strength is increased 1½ times; lightweight china used in institutions is often made of this blend. Adding ground bone or calcium phosphate gives a more translucent and slightly stronger china called *bone* or *English* china.

Other factors affecting strength are the thickness of the china and "fashioning," such as putting on a rolled edge or an extra rim bead underneath—(a scalloped edge is stronger than a plain one). Compactness of shape also strengthens. Putting extra clay in the well or center bottom of the dish helps to strengthen it and reduces star-cracking.

Clay products are made by first forming the clay into the desired shape; this is called a *bisque*. It is then baked, and it emerges from the kiln as a dull, rough but hard unit. A glaze, or miffle, is then put on it and it is baked so the glaze bakes into the dish, producing a hard, bright, durable glaze that resists wear and improves appearance. A thin, tough glaze gives good wear. If the glaze is good, a unit should be serviceable for 5 years.

Decoration is a big factor in cost. If dishes are undecorated they are usually lowest in cost. Plain-colored or white china with a thin-line band is next in cost, and very simply decorated ware or plain ware with a scalloped edge next. China with a sprayed-on design, print decorated, decal decorated, and hand decorated follow in that order in cost. If the unit can be machine printed, the cost is lower. All decorating is done before the glaze is put on except for gold and silver, which must be put on afterward and usually by hand. Thus, gold and silver designs may not wear as well as others because they have no glaze to protect them.

Dishes are usually quoted per place setting, which includes five pieces: cup, saucer, plate, sauce dish, and bread-and-butter plate. A light-weight service costs about 25% more than heavy because of the extra loss in breakage during manufacture. The finest china can run as high as 55 to 80 dollars per setting. Sizes vary among manufacturers. Cups, creamers, pitchers, bowls, and other similar items are sold by the number of ounces they hold; plates, platters, saucers, and the like are sold by their actual or overall diameter size or by their trade size, which is the distance between the edge of the well to the opposite outside edge. It is recommended that actual measures be used in specifications, giving the width of the rim desired, if necessary.

Dishes should have good proportion and balance and stack well. Handles and other attachments should be firmly attached and permit easy handling.

Deep cups or mugs are not comfortable to drink from because of the distance the head has to move back to empty them, shallow ones cool items too quickly. Heavy wear holds heat longer than lighter ware. Dishes should also be uniform in shape, weight, and thickness and be properly stressed to take shock and wear. A buyer should check the glaze for pitting, depth, and so on. He should also state, in specifications, the name of the dish, size, weight, pattern, shape, order number, and perhaps price. Open stock is a pattern held by manufacturers or dealers for immediate delivery—usually within 30 days. Custom-designed china costs more and orders take 4 to 6 months, replacements usually 2 or more months.

The five grades of china from best to poorest are (1) selects, (2) firsts (nearly perfect), (3) seconds (minor defects), (4) thirds (obvious defects but usable), and (5) culls or lumps (badly warped, chipped, or surface-scarred. Run-of-the-kiln is the two best grades plus the best of the seconds. Rejects are those not qualifying for any grade.

Plastic dishware is being used in many operations. It has a soft beauty and does not break; but it stains and abraids, although new methods of surface hardening have lessened these defects. It is also fairly resistant to the action of acids, alkalis, and other substances used in food production. It is light in weight, low in cost, and cleans well. However, it has a tendency to hold water on its surface and does not hold a great deal of heat, so drying is a problem.

Plasticware should be resistant to cracking when heated for 8 hrs at 170°F. Buyers should use the federal government's commercial standards CS 173-50 for establishing specifications for these items. Melamine and vinyl are the most frequently used plastics; although others are used —some being disposable.

Common glass is made from silica, soda, lime, and cullet (old broken glass). Crystal or rock crystal is common glass with lead oxide and potassium silicate added. If boric oxide replaces lime, the product can be used for cooking, as Pyrex is. Corning glass can also be heated, and because it contains metals and other substances to give it strength and durability it is stronger. Pyroceran is a new type of glass originally developed for use in the nose of rockets that had to reenter the atmosphere. It is fused clay, silica, and some rare metals.

Common glass is the least expensive and increases in cost as other substances are added to it. Decoration can also increase cost. Corning ware is less expensive than decorated china and Pyroceran is about twice as expensive as china. Cut glass is crystal that has been cut so the cut surfaces give a special brilliance to it. It is quite expensive.

Glass can be decorated by giving it various colors or by etching with fluorine or sand-blasting. Or, it can be decorated by placing enamel on it by decal or silk screen; the enamel is then fused to the glass by heat. Companies usually require that a gross of an item be ordered before they will put a special decorative design or a logo on glassware.

The least expensive glass is shaped by machine molding or pressing. Glass can also be blown by machine, which reduces its cost over blowing by mouth. A faintly raised line indicates glass made by machine molding. If a mold is lined with wet clay paste a smoother, brighter surface is obtained, giving what is called line-paste molded glass. Mouth-blown glass is also called custom-made. Some glassware may have the edges hand-beveled or ground down. This increases the cost.

Buyers should check glassware to see that parts fused to it are strong and secure. Glass can be hardened by reheating it so as to reorient the molecular structure on the surface; this is called annealing. While this gives added durability, if the item is chipped or cracked it is apt to shatter from the heavy force or pull exerted on the item. Corning ware does this. A rolled bead, added thickness of glass, giving a barrel or bell shape, plus other things can be done to strengthen glass. Flared and stemmed glassware is weak. If the flare is returned to a smaller area, the glass is strengthened and if a thick, short, fluted stem is used instead of a long stem breakage will be less. Air bubbles, specks, muddiness, uneven surface, poor balance and proportion, and untrue, rough edges are considered defects. Bottom weight helps reduce top heaviness, and glassware should be tested to see that it does not tip over easily.

Metalware

Flatware

Metal eating utensils such as spoons, forks, and knives are often referred to as flatware. It may be made of silver, silver plate, or stainless steel.

Very few operations use pure silver flatware because of the cost and its softness. Instead silver plate, which is much more durable and less expensive, is used. The interior of plated flatware is a blank or metal alloy, frequently nickel and silver. Some blanks today are an alloy of 60 to 67% copper, 17% nickel (to give hardness), and not more than 0.35% iron, 0.5% manganese, 0.05% sulfur, and 0.25% other impurities; the remainder is about 15% zinc. Such blanks are called nickel brass or erroneously, nickel silver. Sometimes, areas of greatest wear may be specified as having 18% nickel to give extra hardness. Britannia, or white metal, used for blanks is a tin alloy containing not less than 80% tin. If a blank contains much iron, it will rust.

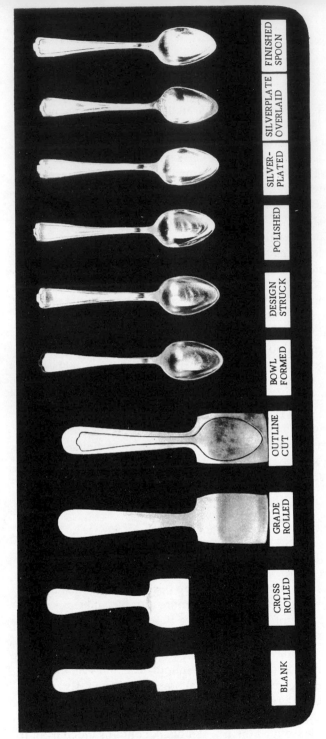

Fig. 11-1. Flatware is first made from a blank that is cross and grade rolled and then outline cut to give the desired shape. The bowl then is formed by machine, and any desired designs are made. It then is polished and silverplated. If specified, an overlay will be put on and final polishing will occur. Courtesy Edward Don & Co.

Silver is put onto the blanks by a process called electrolysis. The amount of depth of the silver is based against a standard of the quantity of silver deposited on a gross of standard-size teaspoons, and all other units will have an equal depth. Thus, 8 oz of silver on a gross of teaspoons is called heavy hotel plate or quadruple plate; 6 oz, triple; 5 oz, standard or A-1; banquet, 4 oz; half-standard, 2½ oz. Some standards for a rather light blank but good silver coverage frequently used in setting up specifications for silverplate flatware are the following:

Item	Blank weight, Avoir. oz/doz*	Silver, Troy oz/gross*
Forks, dessert	18	15
Forks, dinner	24	20
Knives, dessert, hollow handle		15
Knives, dinner, hollow handle		20
Knives, dinner, hollow handle only		10
Knives, dinner, solid handle only		8
Spoons, coffee	13	6
Spoons, dessert	18	15
Spoons, soup	18	15
Spoons, table	24	20
Spoons, tea	11	9

*Blanks are usually stated in avoirdupois ounces and silver in troy ounces.

Sometimes a finished weight is listed in the specification, and the following are frequently used as standards for fairly heavy plateware in ounces per dozen:

Forks, oyster	10.67	Spoons, dessert	24.33	Knives, dinner*	40.67
Forks, dessert	24.67	Spoons, table	32.00	Knives, dessert*	34.67
Forks, salad	22.67	Spoons, tea	16.33	Knives, tea*	20.00
Forks, dinner	29.33	Spoons, iced tea	16.00	Knives, meat or	
Spoons, coffee	6.40	Spoons, bouillon	16.67	viand*	32.00

*Hollow handle only.

Often, a specification will indicate the standard weight the blanks must be by stating the weight of a gross of teaspoons, and then all the other blanks must conform to this standard. The heaviest blank weight specified for a gross of teaspoons is 11 lb; 10½ lb is next, and the lightest is 9 lb. The weight of the silver plate is also specified in troy ounces or as "extra heavy hotel," "triple," and so on.[2] A tolerance of 15% under the specified weight is permitted on individual units, and 5% of the average of three or more units is permitted in the same shipment.

Wear will occur more at points of use or contact, such as the tips of fork tines, backs of the bowls of spoons, or tips of handles where the object rests on a surface. Specifications may require that such spots be "inlaid" with extra silver, which is brushed, sprayed, or dipped on at these points before silverplating.[3] Usually the specification states that the minimum depth on the middle line of the bearing surface at this inlaid point shall not be less than 0.0018 in. deep after silver-plating. An inlaid spoon will have about 60% of its silver on the back and 40% on the front.

The quantity of silver plate on flatware is checked by soaking a teaspoon in 19 parts sulfuric acid to 1 of nitric acid warmed to 180°F until the silver disappears. Banquet-weight teaspoons should lose about 0.8 gr, a triple plate 1.2 gr, and extra heavy hotel 1.6 gr. Inlays are checked by allowing the acid to remove the silver only until the inlay is exposed as bright spots or as lines on the bearing point of the blank.

The composition of the blank is not the only factor that gives good durability to silver plate. Fashioning is also important. Blanks are stamped out and then may receive further shaping, sometimes called grade-rolling, which hardens the blank and also increases thickness where stress occurs and thins the item where less stress occurs. Good grade-rolling also gives the item better balance lines and proportion. A buyer may check strength by:

1. Placing a fork tine on a hard edge and putting pressure on it to bend it.
2. Bending a spoon where the bowl joins the handle.
3. Noting junctures of stainless-steel blades into handles, noting whether the blade is cemented or soldered in or is solid with the handle (cemented blades loosen easily).
4. Trying to dent a spoon bowl by striking it a hard blow with a hard, sharp object.
5. Checking junctures to see if they are secure, well plated, and well burnished; tacking should not be permitted.

---

[2]Instead of this, the actual depth will be stated, such as a depth of 20 microns of silver (extra heavy hotel) or a depth of 0.00125 in. of silver plate (triple), which is about a troy ounce per square foot of surface covered.

[3]Inlays are sometimes put on after silver-plating and are burnished to remove evidence of the addition. This works as well as putting it under the silver plate. When this is done, the added silver is called an "overlay."

Ware should be checked to see that it has a smooth, even coating of silver and proper placement of inlays or overlays. Knife blades should be good stainless steel and usually serrated. The ware should have good balance in the hand and a good grip. Designs should be deep and neatly done. There should be no pitting or other defects. (Silver plate that is highly decorated or has considerable design shows scratches less easily.) Designs are usually stamped by machine.

An institution may use silver-plated items other than flatware, such as pitchers, platters, creamers and sugars, and the like. Edges should be turned in to give extra strength and reduce chances for denting. Seams should clean easily. Handles should be separated from the unit by insulation if the container is to hold hot items. Require that the insulation be guaranteed against loosening. Points of juncture should be well soldered with silver or hard solder that has a melting point of 1300 to 1600°F and not the soft solder sometimes used on home ware. The gauge should be heavy enough to take the heavy wear given such units. Frequently, the blank is copper, but it may be a blend. Points of extra wear may be specified as having an extra inlay of silver. Spouts on pitchers and other units from which liquids are poured should be of the nondrip type. Lids should open to at least 150 to 180° and rest against the handle so the item can be washed and then inverted for good draining.

Stainless-steel flatware is being used more and more, and very fine quality items that are quite attractive are now available. It is a strong, durable metal that is difficult to dent, stain, or scratch. It does not need burnishing, is rust free, and is easy to clean. Unlike silver plate, it does not need replating and resists tarnishing. It requires little care.

Specifications for stainless-steel flatware should require either 18-8 or 17-7 chrome-nickel steel (18 or 17% chromium, 8 or 7% nickel and 74 or 76% steel), or a higher chrome alloy called 301, 302, or 410 can be specified. The federal government standard RR-F 450a specifies 410 for knives and 301 or 302 for spoons and forks. A cheaper ware is made using 430-type chrome-steel. Chrome is used to give a soft luster, and nickel and steel are used for hardness and strength. Lower grades of stainless steel show a blue, metallic color that may also be uneven. If too much chrome is present, the alloy corrodes more easily. Stainless steel pits if it comes into too much contact with soft metals such as aluminum or brass. Pitchers, platters, dishes, and other stainless-steel ware should be specified as 18-8 16 gauge or better. The heaviest gauge used is No. 10, about 9/64 or 0.1345 in. thick. Flatware should be from 0.087 to 0.105 in. (about 12 to 13 gauge) thick.

The best flatware is fashioned or grade-rolled to vary the thickness and give the item better proportion, lines, and balance; it will also be strengthened by this fashioning. Lower-quality ware may be stamped out and have the same thickness throughout. It will also show rough edges where the cutting stamp cut the piece from the stainless-steel sheet. All fork edges should be round and smooth, and the back of handles should be slightly concave. Tines should be smoothly tapered, with their insides ground or coined so all edges are well rounded. All edges should be rounded and smooth and show no roughness. The items should be free of rough grinding marks, pits, scales, burns, or other imperfections. Usually mirror finish is specified for the inside of spoon bowls and No. 7 finish, called satin, for the other parts.

Knives are best serrated, with serrating at least 1¾ in. from the tip along the blade. The cutting edges of knives should be canneled, and the blade should taper uniformly from the tip to a point not more than ¾ in. from the handle. Hollow handles should be securely welded to the blade and not soldered. Solid handles should be integral with the blade.

Since stainless steel is a poor heat conductor, it is seldom used for cooking utensils. If it is, the cooking is done over steam or with steam so a more uniform heat is obtained. Frying pans and other cooking units will either be double bonded with an iron core inside, which spreads the heat around uniformly, or will have a copper bottom to distribute the heat uniformly into the stainless steel. Since stainless steel is durable and does not react with many food alkalis or acids, it is very suitable for use for many pots and pans when cooking is not done in them.

Specification Sizes for Stainless Steel Flatware

Item	Approx. Length in. in.	Av. Min. Handle Thickness in in.	Av. Min. lb per gross
Spoon, tea	6	0.085	8¾
Spoon, dessert (oval)	7⅛	0.095	14
Spoon, bouillon	6	0.085	8½
Spoon, iced tea	7⅝	0.090	9¼
Spoon, table or serving	8¼	0.095	17½
Fork, table (utility)	7⅜	0.090	12
Fork, salad	6⅝	0.065	8
Knife, solid handle	8½		22

Specifications for flatware should indicate the weights, qualities, sizes, material from which made, polish or finish, quality of workmanship, and wrapping; it is usually wrapped to insure against scratching and boxed according to good commercial practices (not more than 3 doz per box), and shipping instructions. The specification may require the submission of samples prior to acceptance of the bid and be withheld to see if the shipment conforms to the samples.

TEXTILES

A food service will use many different textiles. A good seated-service restaurant will want good tablecloths and napkins and workers who appear neat and attractive in their uniforms. Washcloths, towels, and other textile items are needed. Fabrics will cover furniture, draperies will be made from them, and rugs or carpeting will be made of textile fibers. For best service, attractiveness, quality, and lowest cost, a buyer has to know a lot about textiles—how to select and care for them. Gaining applicable knowledge is complicated by the fact that there is constant change. For instance, within a period of a year, almost the entire carpet industry changed from traditional methods of manufacture to a process by which yarns are set into plastic or rubberized backings. And, in a short time knits began to be widely used for uniforms. New manufactured fibers may suddenly appear on the market, causing rapid change in fabrics offered on the market and their subsequent care. Wrinkle-proof, waterproof, wash-and-dry, and many other treatments have considerably changed fabric selection.

Fibers

Natural fibers much used for textiles are cotton, linen, wool, and silk. Others used less often are hemp, ramie, and jute. Cotton, linen, hemp, ramie, and jute are called *cellulose fibers*. They are related to substances such as wood, grass, and other plant tissues. Wool and silk are animal or protein fibers.

Cotton is one of the least expensive and most used fibers. It is attacked by acids but not by moderate alkalis. It is durable and comfortable at warm temperatures because it absorbs moisture well and makes nice-appearing fabrics that drape well. Creasing and wrinkling are problems unless the cotton is made resistant to them. It is stronger wet than dry, which gives it a long laundering life. Cotton seams hold well and show little slippage in uniforms and other fabrics. Cotton launders well and washes rather easily; it shrinks about 5%, but can be made shrink-proof. Good cottons can be woven into very fine yarns, but can also be made into heavy ones for making canvas and the like.

Fig. 11-2. Cotton has long been one of the most used fibers for clothing and other textiles. It is one of the lowest in cost and also has perhaps more utility than any other fiber. Because of competition from other man-made fibers, the use of cotton has declined, but it still is the fiber used more than any other. Courtesy USDA

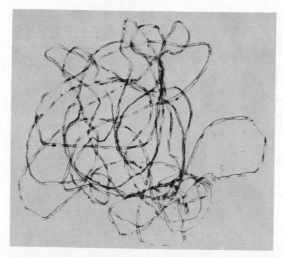

Fig. 11-3. Each fiber has special characteristics that make it more or less suitable for uses in textiles. A single cotton fiber looks like this under a microscope. The actual length is 1¼ in., nearly 200 times its width. Courtesy USDA

Linen is a bast fiber, the inner portion of flax. It absorbs moisture well and therefore is excellent for toweling. It does not retain its strength as well as cotton in laundering and is attacked by alkalis and bleaches more easily. It is expensive but because it has a soft gloss and a crisp texture, it is especially suitable for table napery. It sheds dirt easily but wrinkles and creases more easily than cotton.

Ramie, also a bast fiber, comes from the stalks of China grass. It is strong, has good flexibility, and makes crisp fabrics that have even better luster than linen. It is therefore used in napery but is more expensive than linen. Jute and hemp are low-cost fibers used for burlap sacks, rope, rug backings, nets, and so forth.

Wool is the fleece of sheep or other animals, such as camels, llamas, vicunas, guanacos, alpacas, angora rabbits, angora goats (mohair), Kashmir goats (cashmere), and reindeer; even some animal furs are included. Most are expensive. Some wools, like cashmere, abraid easily. This causes pilling, which is a rolling up of the fibers into tiny balls on the fabric. Mohair has excellent tensile strength and durability and for this reason is used as a furniture covering. If wool is coarse, it is an excellent fiber for making carpeting.

Wool is attacked by alkalis but not by mild acids. It has excellent resiliency and does not wrinkle easily. It springs back into shape after being pressed. It is weaker wet than dry and shrinks badly. It will also felt or pack. It takes dyes fairly well but not as well as some of the competitive man-made fibers such as Acrilan. It will nap well and therefore is a warm fiber because it holds air. Wool has good moisture absorption and feels warm even when damp. To test the strength of the nap of a blanket or other napped item, stick a pin into it and lift up. The pin should not break out; pinching and lifting is about as good a test. When ironed wool creases well and holds shape. Because it does not burn easily, it is desirable for blankets and rugs, where cigarettes might be dropped.

Silk comes from the cocoon of a silkworm. Wild silk (*tussah* or *tussore*) comes from undomesticated silkworms that live outside; it is stronger and coarser. Silk is a poor conductor of heat and is therefore warm. It builds up static electricity. Dyes hold well in it. It is strong but abraids and has less strength when wet. The fabric water-spots easily. It is expensive but is used for some finer draperies, uniforms, and furniture coverings. Silk rug fibers are strong and beautiful. Silk can be weighted, which gives it added weight; but can make it lose strength. Acids, especially strong ones, attack silk—as do some caustics.

Many man-made fibers are produced today. Rayon and acetate are cellulose-base fibers, and rayon was at one time next to cotton in use. Both are low in cost.

Rayon lacks resiliency and strength but absorbs moisture well and launders or cleans well. It stretches when damp and shrinks when dry but has good moisture absorbency, especially in toweling. Rayon is highly flammable and should not be used for napped items such as bath mats or for draperies, bedspreads, and the like unless treated to be nonflammable. Modified rayon, such as Fortisan, is good for curtains and draperies because it has low moisture absorption and does not expand or contract. Cross-linked rayons, such as Zantrel, and blends of cotton and rayon are very suitable for some uniforms. Rayon can be treated to have wash-and-wear and other minimum-care properties.

Acetates are used largely for draperies or curtains because of their soft, luxurious luster. They hold dyes well but may fade from atmospheric gas attack. They launder and bleach well but must be ironed at low temperatures. Some acetates are easily attacked by alkalis found in mild soaps and detergents so may not be as suitable for use as some other types of fibers.

There are a number of man-made acrylic fibers. They are light in weight, wash and dry easily, shrink little, and dye well. They are strong and wear well, but some pill easily. They are excellent for carpeting and blankets. Acrilan blankets are much lighter than wool ones and almost as warm.

Some, like the modacrylics, are highly resistant to chemicals. Orlon is an excellent acrylic fiber for use on outdoor furniture coverings, awnings, and draperies because it is light resistant and quite durable. It is flammable unless treated. Because of the number of acrylics and the fact that they may not be suitable for some purposes, buyers should check their specific properties before purchasing.

Nylon is one of the strongest fibers made. It has a soft, fine luster that gives it silklike qualities. It is fairly resistant to chemicals and other factors that attack fabrics and has low moisture abosrbency, drying quickly. It is static, but can be treated for this, and it yellows in time. Nylon is excellent for carpeting but quite static when so used. It may be used for uniforms but is hot because it holds heat in. It makes beautiful draperies and upholstering fabrics but may tend to slip in the latter.

Saran is a very durable fiber, excellent for use in outdoor furniture and for carpeting, where stains are a problem. For this reason it is often used for carpeting dining or kitchen areas. However, it is rather harsh and lacks flexibility when used in carpeting.

Olefins are light fibers that equal wool in warmth. They do not wrinkle easily and have good elasticity and washability. They also are fairly resistant to alkalis and acids. Unlike some other woollike man-made fibers, olefins do not pill and have a low static buildup. However, they take dyes poorly and crock easily (crocking is a defect where the dye tends to transfer from the fabric to the body or to other items contacting it). Mineral and food oils can stain them, and they are not strong and have poor abrasion qualities. But, because of their other qualities they are often used for blankets and so on.

Polyester fibers such as Dacron, Fortrel, Kodel, and Vycron are widely used today for drip-dry clothing, curtains, washable rugs, and other items. For tablecloths and napkins, Dacron may be combined 50–50 with cotton. Polyester fibers resist wrinkling and some may pill. They are not easily attacked by mildews, acids or alkalis, or insects.

Glass is mostly used for curtaining materials. It has a beautiful sheen and drapes well; but it can absorb soil, which is difficult to remove. If the fabric gets too much movement, it shatters or abraids. Cleaning is a problem because rough handling can shatter it. Also, it takes dyes poorly.

Yarns

Fibers are spun into yarns and these are woven into fabrics. Spinning can have much to do with the appearance, wear, and utility of the fabric. Fibers must be long enough to bind together. Some fibers bind together better than others, and this makes a stronger yarn. Short fibers make heavy, bulky yarns and long ones make the finer yarns used in thinner fabrics. Long wool yarns are called *worsted,* while short ones are called *woolen yarns.* Silk fibers are usually long enough to spin into fine yarns. Staple cotton is long and makes a fine yarn. Combed or carded yarns are short and are made into heavier yarns.

Yarns may be single-ply two-ply, or corded ply. If made from the same yarn, two-ply or corded ply yarns are stronger than single yarns. The tightness and direction of the twist given the yarn also affect its strength and utility. Tight twisting gives a strong yarn, but too tight a twist can weaken some yarns. A low twist would be 2 to 3 twists per inch (tpi), while a loose blanket yarn for napping might have 12 tpi in the warp and 6 to 8 in the fill. A hard twist might run as high as 40 tpi. By varying the twist we get different fabrics. A duck fabric and a stretch ("strex") fabric are much the same except for a difference in the twist of their yarns. A *Z* twist (the twist goes in the direction of the slant of the *Z* or left to right) usually gives a looser twist than an *S* twist. Yarn sizes for cotton, wool, or linen are stated in hanks, while silk and other filament yarns are stated in denier sizes.

Weaving

When yarns are interlaced together in weaving a fabric is made. Yarns running lengthwise in the fabric are called *warp* and are usually of a higher twist and better quality than fill yarns that run across the fabric. If a yarn crosses two or more yarns in weaving, it might be called a *float yarn.*

The strength of the fabric is decided by the type of fiber in the yarn, the way the yarn is spun and its size, and the manner in which the fabric is woven. A loose weave may produce a weak fabric that is called *sleezy* because the yarns move in it. The number of the yarns per inch in the warp and fill also has much to do with the strength of the fabric. Thread count is usually stated in number of warp and fill yarns per square inch. Thus, a utility percale used for sheets with a thread count of 90 and 90 (a balanced count) will be called Type 180. A fabric with a high count usually shrinks less and has less tendency to ravel.

Most woven goods have selvages, which are the two edges that are usually woven of stronger warp yarns and are much tighter than the rest of the fabric so it has stability and will not ravel. Different types of selvages are used, but a plain selvage is usually on sheets, towels, and so forth.

The basic weaves are plain, twill, and satin; plain is frequently used for sheets, pillowcases, uniform fabrics, and the like. A basket weave is one with two or more yarns in the warp and fill, which give the fabric a basket appearance effect. It is used in monk's cloth, which is suitable for draperies. A rib weave is one in which filling yarns are heavier or are

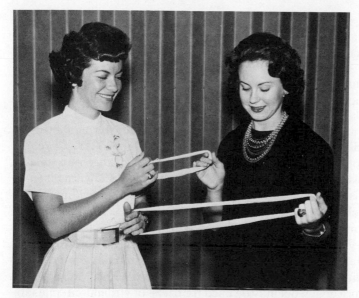

Fig. 11-4. An all-cotton stretch yarn is the result of research established to develop this quality in cotton so that it can be used for the new high-stretch fabrics used in dresses, sweaters, and so forth. Courtesy USDA

bunched together to give a raised or rib effect to the fabric. A twill weave uses floats to give a different effect to the fabric, which may be serge, flannel, surah, drill, denim, or gabardine; a herringbone is a twill weave. Twill weaves are usually quite strong, and soil shows less on them than many others. They also wrinkle less, have good softness and draping qualities, and look well usually after considerable wear. For this reason they may be used for such things as suiting materials.

Satin is a weave produced by using floats; it may snag easily for this reason. Sateen is a fabric with a slightly different weave than satin and is usually less expensive. A Jacquard weave is one made by a machine and is usually quite intricate and elaborate. Until Jacquard invented the machine to do this, such designs had to be woven by hand, which made them very expensive. Jacquard is used in designs for draperies and furniture coverings. Brocades are produced by a Jacquard loom but they can also be made by hand, which today makes them prohibitively costly. A damask is woven on a Jacquard loom and is used for linen, cotton, or other tablecloth materials. It has the same design on each side of the fabric. A huck, or huckaback, weave is used for hand towels. This is a weave in which yarns are raised by using two or more and floating them over other yarns, which raises them up and gives them a loose surface so they absorb water better. Many linen hand towels are woven with this weave, which may look like small diamond shapes in the fabric. Since linen itself is an excellent absorber of moisture, when woven with a huck weave it makes an excellent drying towel. Some dish towels may be made of part cotton and part linen and be given this weave.

Pile weaves are used in toweling, carpeting, or upholstering fabrics. A pile has three dimensions—the warp, the fill, and a loop. Terry toweling, Axminster carpets, or velvet or velour are examples of this loop (pile or "hairy caterpillar") weave. Chenille is a pile fabric, but the yarn also has extra fiber across it, which actually gives it four and not three dimensions. This is why a chenille rug is so durable and is often used in institutions where there is much wear but a good-appearing product is still desired. A frieze is a pile yarn, tightly twisted, with a stuffer (extra) yarn in it; that makes it popular for furniture fabrics because it has good wearing qualities and the ability to keep a good appearance over hard wear. Mohair yarns made from angora goat wool may be used for frieze or straight-cut pile fabrics to give extra wear because this fiber is very strong and still has good resilience. Pile in a fabric used in an institution should be heavy and dense to give good durability and, in terry toweling, good drying. Dense pile in carpeting and upholstery material prevents shedding pullout and makes the pile stand more erect. A pile that flattens is unattractive in many upholstering or carpet materials. A pile fabric's quality is affected by the number of threads per square inch, the type of fiber and yarn, and the weaving. Check a pile fabric by getting hold of the pile or loop and pulling to see if it comes out.

Treatments and Finishes

Fabrics are dyed, and some take dyes well while others do not. Crocking (dye that rubs off) is a problem in some and should be checked. Rub a piece of dyed fabric on the hand when it is slightly moistened and see if any of the dye rubs off. Also, some dyes are not fast, that is, they will bleed or leach in washing. As a result, the colors fade, run together, and produce a very unsuitable fabric.

Some patterns in fabrics result from the use of different colored yarns, such as in plaid or brocade. In others, the fabric itself is dyed. Some materials are designed by roller printers, and these are good and low in cost. Screen dyeing can be expensive if done by hand, but machine screen

Fig. 11-5. Wash-and-wear fabrics are fast gaining popularity in uniforms for workers. Some, however, of these products have not been entirely satisfactory because they have not held a press and they show wrinkling (note the coat on the right). The coat on the left has been treated with a special resin that, after wear and washing, leaves a neat-appearing product. Buyers should be careful in the purchase of these items to see that they obtain products that will show such appearance and will not lose this factor over a period of use. Courtesy USDA

dyeing is possible and its cost is much less. Block printing is a hand method and expensive.

Fabrics are finished today to give them a high gloss or glaze, many of which are only temporary and may be lost in the first washing. Most fabrics are filled with some starch to give them extra weight and stiffness; this washes out easily. Buyers should check fabrics by washing them to note the amount of fill and shrink, the fastness of the dye, and other qualities. Frequently specifications state the amount of fill that a fabric can have.

Other finishes common in fabrics are the following:

Wash-and-wear	The result either of the fiber and yarn used or treatment of the cloth.
Singeing	Freeing a fabric of lint.
Napping	Plucking wool or other yarns in a fabric to free fibers so they hold air and create warmth. Blankets, flannels, and other fuzzy fabrics are treated this way.
Calendaring	Filling with resins and then glazing with hot rollers.
Mercerizing	Treating cotton fabrics with a strong caustic to give them more sheen and strength.

A permanent press can be given by adding certain resins. Some fabrics are treated to be fire resistant; new regulations require that such fabrics be used in institutions. Other treatments are given to reduce the chance of attack from chemicals, insects, mildew or rot, and atmospheric attack.

Laws and Standards

Specific laws have been passed to protect buyers and give better organization to the market. Woolen-fabric labels must state the quantity and type wool, if the fabric contains more than 5% wool. If the label states the wool is "virgin wool," it must be that; reused wool must be named. Laws also prohibit false or deceptive statements in labels on fabrics. Stuffing in furniture must be identified. The type of fiber or the blends in a fabric must be stated. If a label says a product is shrink-proof, it cannot shrink more than 5%. No label can say a fabric is colorfast because all fabrics fade some. Buyers should learn to read labels. Certain colors on labels indicate the type of washing the fabric can receive:

Purple	Washing at 160°F with bleach
Green	Washing at 160°F without bleach
Blue	Washing at 120°F without bleach
Yellow	Washing at 105°F without bleach
Red	Dry cleaning only.

In most hotels, motels, and other institutions open to the public, fabrics must now be treated to be nonflammable.

The textile industry has established a number of self-regulating standards. The American Standards Association developed the *American Standard Performance Requirements for Textile Fabrics*, L-22-1960, and the *Minimum Performance Requirements for Institutional Textiles*, L-24. These establish standards helpful to buyers and have given a base upon which to write specifications. Many of the trade magazines and other publications in the industry also help to maintain standards.

Specifications

A specification for a textile product and the use to be made of it in the institution must be specifically written for that product. A variety of conditions may underlie the requirements; these must be considered and the specification must be written to cover them. Specifications can be written in considerable detail, naming many of the following factors:

Breaking strength of the fabric, warp, and fill, either wet or dry
Resistance against yarn shifting or slippage
Colorfastness to many different factors
Maximum shrink
Resistance against abrasion, pilling, moths, mildew, atmospheric, or other attack
Washing or dry cleaning qualities
Water repellency or ability to resist soil or other factors
Nonflammability or other treatment, such as wrinkling or crease resistance

Sheets and Pillowcases

Sheets and pillowcases should be specified by type of fabric, which is usually based on a good yarn from staple cotton or a blend of cotton and polyester fiber, if nonpress. A thread count of 70 × 70 is about the heaviest yarn used and is called Type 140. The yarn is called *carded cotton muslin* and should have a minimum tear strength of 70 lb, wet or dry; have 4% maximum sizing and 6% maximum shrink; and weigh 4.6 lb per sq yd. Type 180 (90 × 90 thread count) is called *utility percale* and has a carded or combed cotton thread. Wet or dry strength, fill, shrink, and weight-per-square-yard standards should be 60 lb, 2%, 5%, and 3.6 respectively. Luxury or supercale, type 200 (100 × 100), should have 60 lb, 1%, 4%, and 3.6 lb respectively. Some specifications state that a sheet of torn-length-size of 108 in. should not shrink more than 5 in. in 5 washings. Sheets and cases should be specified as non-bleach-retentive. If they are colored, the specification should state a colorfastness of 40 hrs under a Fadeometer light. Also, these products should be colorfast to high temperatures and bleach.

Sheets are specified in torn size, after hemming and washing; a 108-in. torn-size sheet will be about 98 in. This permits a 6–7-in. tuck at the head and foot. Some buyers specify sheets at 113 in. torn size, while others find 99 in. long enough. A 6–7-in. tuck is usually desired on either side. Fitted sheets should be carefully specified, and not more than 1½% shrink should be allowed.

Buyers should specify pillowcases from tubular rather than flat material since it gives a better-fitting pillow. They should also be specified to be sized after hemming and to have shrinkage 2 in. longer and 4–8 in. wider than the pillow.

Sheets and pillowcases are usually given a 2–3-in. hem. Hems should be stitched with a No. 60/3-ply thread not less than 12 stitches per in. Hem ends should be back stitched and thread ends tacked to give extra strength and prevent raveling. Bar tacking may be recommended. Selvages should be strong, even, and not over ⅜ in. wide. The tensile-strength loss of the fabric should not be over 10% after 20 washings.

Towels

Terry toweling should be specified to weigh a minimum of 11.9 oz per square yard and to have double thread, loose twist, and ⅛ in. loops on both sides. The fabric should also have a tight, close weave. Maximum shrink should be 10% for the warp and 4% for the fill. Breaking strength of warp should be 50 lb and, for the fill, 40 lb.

Honeycomb or huckaback (huck) towels are usually made of carded cotton, rayon, or union (a combination of linen and cotton). Specify the minimum weight per square yard as 6.2 oz with maximum sizing 5%, maximum shrink 14% for warp and 5% for fill, and minimum breaking strengths of 58 lb (warp) and 48 lb (fill). (Note that in textile specifications, standards for warp always come first and fill last). Colors in toweling should be fast to 40 hr under a Fadeometer light. Seams should be from ¼ to ⅜ in. wide with a minimum of 10 stitches per in. Corners should be backstitched or bar tacked at least ¼ in. back, and raw edges should be turned in for the same distance. Dacron-reinforced selvages wear longer than plain cotton. Hemmed towels are not as durable as those with selvage ends. Specify uniform shrinkage of all materials.

Dish or glass towels are made from cotton, rayon, linen, or their combinations. Minimum thread counts should be 54 in. (warp) and 38 in. (fill), and breaking strength for both should be 50 lb; maximum shrink is 14 and 5%. The towels should be fully bleached and lint-free.

Napery

Napery (tablecloths and napkins) may be made from linen, cotton, rayon, or other fibers. Linen gives a high luster and a crisp, durable fabric that is quite lint-free. Rayon is lower in cost and has good sheen but is weak when wet. Mercerized cotton has good sheen, is not expensive, and wears well. All napery should be non-chlorine-retentive (chlorine weakens the fabric) and be able to be washed at 160°F with bleach. A blend of 50:50 cotton and

Dacron is often used for nonpress napery. Calendered fabrics have a higher sheen, and singed ones have less lint.

Napery is usually specified as double damask, which is heavy and wears better than single. Good double damask should not have more than 7 float yarns in the fill and not less than 195 threads per sq in. and a maximum shrink of 8%. Single damask should not have more than 4 fill floats and not less than 140 threads per sq in. Weights should be, respectively, not less than 8 to 10 oz and 5½ oz per sq yd. Specify single damask with a minimum breaking strength of 75 lb and a maximum shrink of 6%. Yarn shift should not be more than 05. on a 2-lb pull.

Indian head, crash, broadcloth, and other tight, solid weaves are used in napery. These are inexpensive compared to damask and give good wear. They should usually weigh from 4 to 5 oz per sq yd. If used, the following standards are frequently written into specifications: Indian head (suiting), minimum thread count 66 × 76; carded-yarn broadcloths, 116 × 56 thread count and minimum breaking strength of 55 and 25 lb; and combed-yarn broadcloth, 148 × 74 threads per sq in. with a breaking strength of 74 and 28 lb. Momie cloth (monk's cloth) of mercerized cotton should have a minimum breaking strength for warp and fill of 90 lb, maximum shrinks of 6 and 5% respectively, and a minimum count of 62 × 56 using yarns sized from 13s to 15s. For low-cost napery, 128-count carded cotton sheeting is used. An 8–11-in. hang over the table side is recommended after complete shrinkage has occurred. Check seams for strength and workmanship. Good damask should have a minimum tear-out seam strength of 64 lb. All napery should be able to be washed in 160°F water with bleach.

Blankets

Wool, Acrilan, and Orlon make good warm blankets. Wool is quite durable and resilient, but Orlon and Acrilan retain nap better. Naps should be strong enough to permit lifting the blanket by the nap. Acrilan is as expensive as wool but lighter. All heavy blankets should have a wet or dry strength of 30 and 25 lb. Warps may be specified as being blended with strong combed cotton and made from 2-ply 12½-tip yarns. Fillings should have a 7 tpi and a Z-twist for looseness for warmth and napping. The basic weave should be tight, and holding the blanket to the light should permit the buyer to see a tight weave. Light blankets about 0.12 in. thick should weigh not less than 8 oz per sq yd, and the heaviest 0.24 in. should weigh 15 oz per sq yd.

A twill weave of double fill, and a 1 up and 3 down wale makes the best cotton blanket. Weight should be 1⅓ lb per sq yd with counts of 36 × 30 or more and a breaking strength of not less than 30 and 25 lb. Shrinkage should be a minimum of 11 and 6%. Maximum sizing should be 5%.

Curtains and Drapes

Curtains for glass windows should be quite sheer and permit a large quantity of light to go through them. A good Dacron curtain with a leno weave should have a count of approximately 76 × 64, and quality improves as the count goes up. A ninon weave gives a very sheer curtain and should run 144 threads per sq in. Batiste weaves of combed cotton should be 168 threads per sq in., but if Dacron is the fiber the count can be nearer 150. Specify twice-stitching on the inner and outer edges of seams. Check draping qualities, washability and ironing, and so on. Drip-dry curtaining materials are good for institutional use. Curtaining fabrics can deteriorate from sunlight; least affected to most are, respectively: Dacron, Orlon, Saran, Fiberglas, Fortisan, nylon, Chromespun, Celasperm, acetates, rayon, Arnel, and cotton. Orlon and Dacron make soft, lustrous curtains that drip-dry and hang well. Fiberglas has great beauty and good draping qualities and will hold its shape well without sag; but it abraids easily unless it is Beta Fiberglas. Rayon is lustrous and low in cost but holds its shape poorly.

Many different drapery fabrics are suitable for institutional use. Silk has great beauty and excellent wear but is very expensive. Nylon and some of the other polyesters drape well and have good beauty, but some may suffer from sunlight attack. Rayon is low in cost and has good appearance but must be treated against flammability and does not retain dimensional length too well in humid climates. Specify most drapery materials with a dry-breaking-strength minimum of 35 lb. Momie should be made of heavy yarn and have a 16 × 72 count. Crash or other heavy cotton draperies should have a count of 68 × 76 or more, and Jacquard weaves should be 100 × 30 or over. Check seams and hems. Corners should be mitered.

TABLE 11-1
Upholstery Fabrics

Weave	Count		Oz/54 in. yd	Material
	Warp	Fill		
			Flat Weaves	
Brocatelle	85	85	16	Can be cotton, linen, rayon, nylon, silk, or
Damask	120	50	12	polyester; mixtures with nylon or polyesters
Matellassee	95	75	22	should not be over 50% of these fibers.
Tapestry	72	60	20	
Crash	32	32	15*	100% cotton, vat dyed, 2-ply twisted yarns.

TABLE 11-1
Upholstery Fabrics

Flat Weaves

Weave	Count Warp	Fill	Oz/54 in. yd	Material
Duck	50	40	12*	100% cotton, 2-ply cotton or more, vat dyed. If for outdoors, specify mildew- and water-resistant.
Cretonne	60	50	10*	100% cotton, vat dyed, not too durable.

Pile Weaves

Weave	Count per sq in. Warp Pile	Stuffer	Ground	Filling	Loops	Oz/54 in. yd Pile	Total	Material
Plain-rib friezé	36	72	18	29	522	12½	29	Face-warp all mohair; back warp and filling all cotton.
Plain friezé	9	72	18	23	103	17	33	50% or more wool or mohair face; backing 100% cotton or rayon or their mixture.
Pattern friezé	26			24	312			Pattern may leave bare spots, so 50% or more should be covered with loops; material should be same as for plain friezé.
Mohair velvet, 0.13 in. thick	28	28	28	48	385	·15	25	100% mohair, cut pile.
Mohair velvet, 0.14 in. thick	27		54	30	405	12	19	100% mohair, cut pile.
Velour, .085 in. thick	40		40	36	560	16¼	22	100% cotton

*48. in wide; heavy materials should have a minimum 80-lb dry breaking strength, and lightest ones should have a minimum 50-lb dry breaking strength.

Carpets and Rugs

Today most carpets and rugs are made by setting yarns into a rubberized or plastic backing. Cut or uncut piles are common, and Jacquard-type designs or a variation in pile height, called *sculptured,* can be made to give a design in the rug without colors. Tight, short piles of wool, Acrilan, nylon, or their blends are usually best for institutional use. A square yard of good wool carpeting should weigh around 5¼ lb, acrylics 5 lb, and nylon 4½ lb. Man-made fibers must be spun to 12–15-denier thickness to equal thick, heavy, wool yarns. Rayon or cotton is not usually good in institutional carpeting. Acrilan 41, Creslan, Zefran, and Verel are other acrylic fibers used. They usually outwear wool but not nylon.

The yarn in many carpets develops a plus electrical charge, while individuals walking over them develop a minus charge. When the relative humidity is below 40%, such charges build up rapidly; 3 kilovolts (kV) can build up quickly, which gives a fairly strong shock when someone touches a ground such as a door knob. Carpets can be made to drain off electrical charges by using metallic yarn and grounding the carpet. Where employees get shocks, special nonconductive shoes can be worn; but this is not usually possible for guests. Wool will build up the highest amount of electricity, 12.6 kV being possible; nylon, 10 kV; and acrylic or modacrylic, 9 kV. With metallic conductors the voltage usually drops down to 2½ kV. Antistatic sprays can be used; these are usually humectants that absorb moisture. Manufacturers are also busily engaged in supporting research to develop antistatic fibers.

Tight, nubby, twisted piles from strong fiber yarns show footprints less easily and wear better than longer yarns. Long-yarn carpeting, unless made from good, resilient fibers such as wool or Acrilan 41, flatten and do not appear attractive. They also soil more easily. Nylon shows footprints easily but a mixture of 50% nylon, 40% acrylics, and 10% rayon or cotton gives good service. Saran resists oil and grease stain, so may be used in dining areas or food-service areas. It has a rather harsh texture, however.

Uniforms

Uniforms must be attractive, fit well, drape well, wear well, and resist soil. They should clean easily and hold a press. Comfort and safety are also factors to consider. Nylon is durable, extremely attractive, and has many other favorable qualities; but it is warm, builds up static, yellows in use if white, and will absorb body stains.

The fiber, yarn, and weave are important in giving wear. Hard, tight fabrics wear best but may develop shine. Weaves suitable for work uniforms are twills, denim, plain, or others. Suitings that wear well are whipcord, gabardine, serge, tight twills, and sharkskin. Tweeds and flannels bag and hold a press poorly. They may also be too casual. A number of uniforms are now being made of knit fabrics. These have excellent drape, good appearance, and can be treated to hold a press and will drip-dry.

Dacron or Orlon in a tight yarn woven into a good fabric gives excellent wear and looks good. Dacron and Orlon are often blended with cotton up to about 50% of the material, which gives a good drip-dry fabric that is cool, wears well, is not too expensive, and washes well.

Uniforms should be specified preshrunk and should not shrink over 1½%. They should have treatment for static qualities, press fastness, antipilling, and nonflammability. Dye fastness, anticrocking features, and fading should be mentioned. Thread counts, tearing strengths, and minimum weight per square yard for the fabric should also be mentioned. Seams should be well sewn and linings should be specified—rayon makes a good lining. Check pockets for sewing, lining, and strength. Note buttonholes. The L-24 standards of the American Standards Association (10 East 40th Street, New York City) can be helpful in selecting good uniforms and other textile products. Styling is extremely important to employee satisfaction.

The sizes of manufacturers can vary, so buyers should check to see that the size specified is proper. It is not unusual to specify chest measurements, sleeve length, armhole circumference, cuff circumference, coat length, hem length, back length, and the like. The following shows the general sizes of tight-fitting waiters' and loose-fitting cooks' coats:

	Extra Small	Small	Medium	Large	Extra Large
Waiter	30 in.	34 in.	38 in.	42 in.	46 in.
Cook	34 in.	38 in.	42 in.	46 in.	52 in.

Women's uniforms are usually specified as size 10, 12, and so on. Caps come sized small, 6¾ (21¼-in. circumference); medium, 7⅛ (22⅜ in.); or large 7½ (23½ in.). All sizes will have a variation, and the tolerance for caps is plus or minus ⅜ in.

Mops

Mops must be durable, hold a large quantity of water, rinse well, and dry adequately. Check yarn strengths. They must be twisted loosely to give good water absorbency which may weaken them. They should have yarns spun from long staple cotton, possibly blended with some polyester or other fiber. Linen gives good absorbency, durability, and resistance against abrasion, but it increases expense. Specifications can cover the following:

Pounds per dozen	9	12	15	18	20	24
Minimum yarns/mop	105	120	135	145	165	190
Width at center (in.)	6	6	6¼	6¼	6¼	6¼
Length (in.)	28	32½	36	40	41	42

BIBLIOGRAPHY

American Standards Association, *American Standard Performance Requirements for Textile Fabrics*, L-22-1960, and *American Standard Minimum Performance Requirements for Textile Fabrics*, L-24, 10 E. 40th St., New York.

Berkeley, Bernard, "The Selection and Maintenance of the Commercial Carpet," *Cornell Quarterly*, School of Hotel Administration, Cornell University, Ithaca, N.Y., 1967.

China Council, lecture by William Christopher, 1850 Los Tunas Drive, Santa Barbara, California 93103, 1973.

Grimshaw, Rex W., *The Chemistry and Physics of Clays and Allied Materials*, 4th ed., Wiley (Interscience), New York, 1971.

Hollen, Norma, and Jane Saddler, *Textiles*, McGraw-Hill, New York, 1970.

Institutional Research Co., *Cleaning Agent Standards*, 221 W. 57th St., New York 10019.

Kornreich, E., *Introduction to Fibers and Fabrics*, 2nd ed., Elsevier Publishing, New York, 1966.

Kotschevar, Lendal H., and Margaret Terrell, *Food Service Planning*, Wiley, New York, 1961.

Mark, H. F., S. M. Altas, and E. Cernia, *Man-made Fibers*, Wiley (Interscience), New York, 1967.

Maryon, H., *Metalwork and Enameling*, 5th ed., Dover Publishing, New York, 1971.

Nelson, Glenn C., *Ceramics*, Holt, Rinehart & Winston, New York, 1960.

Norton, F., *Fine Ceramics*, McGraw-Hill, New York, 1970.

Oneida, Ltd., Brochures on silver and flatware manufacture, no dates, Oneida, N.Y.

Taylor, G., *Silver Through the Ages*, Barnes & Noble, New York, 1964.

U.S. Supply Services, *Standard Stock Catalog*, GSA, Washington, D.C., various dates for standards for textiles, flatware, china, and so forth.

Appendix

The use of well-prepared specifications in purchasing is increasing among some large corporations and multiple units. On the whole these are well-written, concise, and clearly define the purchase needs of the companies. The following is an example of what are some of the best specifications this author has seen. They are those of the Canteen Corporation, which has permitted their printing in this text with the hope they will be a contribution to better purchasing in our industry. No establishment should copy these because a specification should be developed for the specific needs of the operation; those of others often do not fit these needs. Instead, they can be used as a model.

CANTEEN CORPORATION, EXECUTIVE OFFICES

This invitation to bid issued by Canteen Corporation is for services and products described in the enclosed bid sheets. Bids must be signed by an authorized person or agent of your Company. Unsigned and/or bids submitted on another form will be disqualified. It is not required, but you may include as a supplement to your bid, all items you stock and sell.

Bids should be marked, "Personal & Confidential," and addressed as follows:

Canteen Corporation_____

_____

_____

_____

Attention:_____

_____
(title)

Bids are to be received no later than noon_____

(month)   (day)   (year)

Sincerely,

Liter   — Basic unit of measure; is 1000 milliliters and equal to 1000 grams of water; slightly more than our quart.

Gram — Basic unit of mass; 1000 grams is equal to a liter of water; equivalent of about 2.2 pounds.

Meter— Basic unit of length; slightly longer than our yard.

Deca — Means 10 times; thus a decameter is 10 meters.

Hecto— Means 100 times; thus a hectoliter is 100 liters.

Kilo   — Means 1,000 times; thus a kilogram is 1,000 grams.

Mega — Means 1,000,000 times; thus a megacycle is a million cycles.

Giga   — Means a billion times; thus a gigameter is a billion meters.

Tera   — Means a trillion times; thus a teragram is a trillion grams.

Deci   — Means 1/10 of; such as a decimeter.

Centi — Means 1/100 of; such as a centigram.

Milli   — Means 1/1000 of; such as a milliliter.

Micro— Means a millionth of; such as a micrometer.

Nano — Means a billionth of; such as a nanoliter.

Pico   — Means a trillionth of; such as a picometer.

Index